In memory of Raman Selden and Raymond Williams

A Practical Reader in Contemporary Literary Theory

Edited by
Peter Brooker and
Peter Widdowson

Prentice Hall/Harvester Wheatsheaf
London   New York   Toronto   Sydney   Tokyo   Singapore
Madrid   Mexico City   Munich

First published 1996 by
Prentice Hall/Harvester Wheatsheaf
Campus 400, Maylands Avenue
Hemel Hempstead
Hertfordshire, HP2 7EZ
A division of
Simon & Schuster International Group

Library of Congress Cataloging-in-Publication Data

This information is available from the publisher

British Library Cataloguing in Publication Data

A catalogue record for this book is available from the British Library

ISBN 01344 25677 (pbk)

1 2 3 4 5 00 99 98 97 96

Contents

A Note on the Text

Cuts in the essays that follow are indicated by [...]. Where appropriate, summarizing editorial statements are given for omitted passages. Where cross-references are made to Raman Selden and Peter Widdowson, *A Reader's Guide to Contemporary Literary Theory* (Prentice Hall/ Harvester Wheatsheaf, 3rd edition, 1993), this is shown throughout as *A Reader's Guide* 3/e.

Introduction: Theory and Criticism at the Present Time

In its title and design, as readers will see, this volume parallels *A Reader's Guide to Contemporary Literary Theory*. What new emphasis this *Practical* Reader brings to theory and literary study we seek to explain below. Both books, first of all, reflect developments in the recent history of criticism and theory in higher education. 'A generation ago', says Fredric Jameson, writing in the early 1980s, 'there was still a technical discourse of professional philosophy ... alongside which one could still distinguish that quite different discourse of the other academic disciplines – of political science, for example, or sociology or literary criticism. Today,' he continues, 'increasingly, we have a kind of writing simply called "theory" which is all or none of these things at once.' This 'theoretical discourse' has marked 'the end of philosophy as such' and is 'to be numbered among the manifestations of postmodernism' – that eclectic and self-reflexive mode which for Jameson and others, friend and foe alike, has come to signal a new phase in the correlation between cultural forms and social and economic life.[1]

Where, a decade on, has this development brought us? To the point, it might seem, where the transgression of boundaries between academic disciplines has been institutionalized, and 'theoretical discourse', in self-generating fashion, requires ever more guides, handbooks and Readers to help us through its unfamiliar and expanding terrain. The empire of 'English' – the key site of many of these changes – has been effectively decolonized, transformed by its continuing 'crisis' to the point, it sometimes seems, of complete metamorphosis, to emerge, in fact, if not always in name, as versions of textual or discourse analysis or of cultural studies.[2] After the originary theoretical texts of the late 1960s and 1970s of the kind Jameson has in mind – from Barthes, Derrida, Foucault, Lacan, Althusser, Kristeva, for example – and after the Readers, Guides and Introductions of the 1980s which effectively put 'Theory' on the syllabus – publishing and teaching are now launched upon the quest for a second-generation textbook which will join theory with practice. Hence, K. M. Newton's *Theory into Practice* (1992), Steven Lynn's *Texts and Contexts* (1994), Le Bihan and Green's *Critical Theory and Practice* (1995), two new series in 'Theory and Practice' from the Open University and Routledge and, obviously enough, the present volume.

Two other significant and contrary developments have occurred in the last decade, however. One has seen the capitalized and singular 'Theory' of Jameson's description devolved into 'theories': often overlapping and in fruitful dialogue, but also contesting – even within a seemingly given and homogenous field, such as Marxism or feminism or psychoanalysis. At the same time this impact has been retroactive; that is to say, where 'Theory' had seemed the new thing, it has become clear that it was always already the old thing too. Criticism, we realized, had always been theoretical, always dependent on general, informing ideas about the literary and about literary value and critical practice, always grounded in aesthetic and cultural ideologies.

In the contrary development, following a continuing mood of anxiety and outright hostility to 'Theory's' self-importance, its hermeticism, or uncontrolled pluralism, there has been a turn, most recently, to a more traditional stability and set of priorities. The verdict from this quarter is that 'Theory Has Failed'.[3] This is not, as might be expected, the triumphant cry of an older generation of English men of letters, nor even of former radicals turned liberal-conservatives in a familiar story of co-option and incorporation. Increasingly, some younger academics (who one suspects have 'done theory' or had theory done to them as undergraduates) have heard enough of postmodernism's endless end of things and are set to challenge the dominance of theoretical discourse over the discourses of literature itself. The literary text, the experience of literature, a common(sense) way of talking and making personal judgements about it, need, from this point of view, to be defended and freshly mobilized. No less than the identity of English, Literature and Criticism, so it seems once more, are at stake.[4]

Paradoxically, the second generation of textbooks share some of this concern, if in somewhat different terms. What they signal is less an obeisance to 'Theory' than a need to show theories at work. K. M. Newton, for example, presents his volume *Theory into Practice* (1992) as a 'supplement' to his own earlier *Twentieth-Century Literary Theory: A Reader* (1988). The second book is a response, he says, to students who find that the high level of abstraction of much theory makes it difficult to grasp and deploy, and who constantly ask 'where they can find theory being applied to practice' (p.1). The preface to the Open University series talks in a similar vein of the editors'. wish 'to help bridge the divide between the understanding of theory and the interpretation of individual texts'.[5]

Still others, it is clear at the same time, see textbooks of this kind as more of the old poison than a cure. Readers and textbooks are said to simplify and so distort difficult theory, to collapse the proper distinction between philosophy and criticism in the interests of 'applying' their own edited selections, or to obscure the literary text behind a wall of 'readings'. In other words, they hinder rather than help, substituting themselves for the real thing. It is time, it is then said, that this tendency was reversed.[6]

The central issue here, of course, is the relation between theory and criticism. What, after all, is 'theory', let alone 'Theory? And if we truly live and think in a world of theories in the plural, what is the common, distinctively 'theoretical' activity which marks out and identifies this work? And how then does the kind of thinking designated as theory impinge on more empirically based or 'practical' textual analysis? What does theory do, or what should it do? In our view, the function of *literary* theory is to explain and generalize both literary discourse and critical practice, making strange what has become naturalized and taken for granted. Theoretical discussion reveals and debates the assumptions of literary form and identity, the interleaved criteria of aesthetic, moral and social value on which critical modes depend and which their procedures enact and confirm. As a consequence, it may come to transform critical practice. This is not to imply, however, that theory has a privileged role in a hierarchy of conceptual, critical and creative work, since the proper relation between theory and practice is a dialectical one in which they test and transform each other. Nor is it to say that theory in any sense exists outside of the kinds of assumptions and ideologies it discloses. As Terry Eagleton has commented, 'just as all social life is theoretical, so all theory is a real social practice'.[7] Theory, or the concepts and questions different theories produce, might suddenly illuminate a literary text or critical essay, like an anglepoise turned their way, but theoretical work is nevertheless still part, as the last three decades have shown, of contemporary cultural history and the intellectual and social narratives inscribed there.

To talk of the 'failure' of theory therefore is seriously misleading – as if we had been brought to the stark choice at a crossroads that offers us one way, a (false) route along the high road of autonomous theory, and another along the (good) low road of an accessible language of criticism and a direct encounter with the literary text. As it turns out, the first path is named 'metaphysics' and the second 'new criticism' and we have been there before. In reality, there is no such fork or crossroads; theory shadows criticism as a questioning and interiorized companion and the conversation between them goes on, whatever their apparent separation. No justification should be needed, therefore, for an attempt to encourage this conversation further, to make criticism's theoretical assumptions explicit, to assess one theory by another, to ask how a theoretical framework influences the interpretation of literary texts.

The more interesting and important judgement is not that theory, as such, has failed, but that the radical, politicizing theory of the post-1960s years has failed to produce a criticism to match its radicalizing intentions. Instead of a theoretically aware, interventionist and socially purposive criticism, the age of theoretical discourse has produced works of wayward or leaden abstraction, or self-promoting dogma, books like sledge-hammers to crack textual nuts. So, at least, it sometimes seems, and not only to theory's opponents. Yet the answer, as above, to bad theory and criticism lies in neither a separated realm of 'pure' theory nor a return to a 'theory-free' Romantic or New Criticism, for all their familiarity and practical, pedagogic convenience. As the authors of *A Reader's Guide to Contemporary Literary Theory* put it, 'even the apparently "spontaneous" discussion of literary texts is dependent on the *de facto* (if less self-conscious) theorizing of older generations ... full of dead theory which is sanctified by time and has become part of the language of common sense'.[8] Equally, the kinds of radical theory and political criticism which have sought to expose, transform or overturn this common sense have themselves adapted and changed through a series of set-backs and new initiatives over the last two or three decades. The work of a figure such as Raymond Williams, who has been a major example and influence upon the developments sketched above, should tell us that this intellectual and cultural narrative cannot be read as a simple story of 'failure', if it is this at all.

Our own emphasis in the present volume is upon criticism rather than theory; more precisely, on exhibiting the way theory works upon and within criticism. The claims of any critical mode or model can be assessed in theoretical terms, of course, or – as here – in a comparative study with another different approach to an author or specific literary text. But to stress the importance of critical activity or textual analysis this way does not mean that we seek to return to some earlier, less complicated, less poststructuralist or less postmodern moment; nor to an assumption of the integrity of the isolated, autonomous text. Contemporary theory, following as ever its different agendas, has taught us too much about the importance of ideology and language, about intertextuality, about the formation and reformation of the subject in contemporary culture, and about literary study's own situatedness for a new formalism to be possible or desirable. Rather, criticism must discover its working practices, its interpretative strategies and purpose, its conception of its object of study, its academic and cultural role, by way of such theory. These strategies and intentions will be focused in the work of literary criticism; at best in the consciously theoretical and necessarily dialogic analysis of literary texts. The task we assign to the present *Reader* is therefore, in one way, a traditional one: an aid to the study of literature and the function of criticism, recast in and beyond the era of Jameson's postmodernism. His all-consuming 'Theory' is alarmingly nothing or everything. We would prefer literary study to draw upon, and do, *some*thing. This book is one way of encouraging this; of instilling ways of reading and thinking about literary texts which are open to theoretical debate and consciously involved in the world of literary and cultural values. In short, we hope it will be a contribution to the making of an engaged, theoretically informed criticism for the present time.[9]

In higher education – during a period in which debates about theory have had to take their place in line with day-by-day discussions of the pressing, material issues of interdisciplinarity, modularization, expanding student numbers, cuts in core funding and student pauperization – two factors, at least, have impeded rather than assisted the kind of goal we have in mind. First, students have been introduced to theory via theoretical essays which are conceptually and often stylistically far removed from their own experience of reading and writing about literature and which, in their unfamiliarity, difficulty and variety, have been perplexing and intimidating. As a result, the teaching and learning of theory have become acutely problematical: can students engage in a meaningful seminar discussion of complex, often abstruse theoretical texts when they have little or no experience of theory or theoretical discussion, a limited acquaintance with the debates that literary theory addresses, and little knowledge perhaps of the literary texts to which theory often does no more than allude? Do teachers respond by simply lecturing on theory? But to what end? In fact, the choice is never quite this simple because students, like theory, are not all the same and different theoretical positions are accessible, stimulating and useful, or impossible, at different stages – not only to students but to teachers and critics. Nevertheless, when the singular 'it' of theory is pluralized and the student body simultaneously multiplied, existing structural and pedagogic problems can simply be compounded. A second problem is that the teaching of theory has often proceeded independently of courses on the familiar literary genres and the assessment of these, a formal separation of areas of study which effectively boxes theory into a ghetto, especially in modular schemes. The worst result of this misplaced autonomy, however, has been the kind of easy-going pluralism which assumes all approaches are equal and that you can shop around as the fancy takes you, or the cynical pragmatism which apes what is taken to be the module tutor's fancy.

We have tried, in this volume, to redress some of these effects by supplying what we believe has been lacking, and by attempting strategically to meet the difficulties other Readers and textbooks have encountered. The result is a *practical* Reader intended to serve both as a working introduction and a textbook for undergraduates and for more advanced study. Our first aim is to present students with examples of contemporary theoretical positions and to do this by grouping essays in criticism by renowned theorists, chapter by chapter, around widely used literary texts and well-known authors. In conception and content, therefore, this volume differs from earlier Readers organized around edited blocks of theory, and from those, now numerous, collections of essays which 'represent' different theoretical or critical approaches, or which – like Raman Selden's *Practising Theory and Reading Criticism* (1989) – offer illuminating but pastiched readings of literary texts 'in the style of' theory or criticism X or Y.

Where possible, then, we have wanted to present critical essays by leading theorists. Hence our use of essays by Lacan and Derrida rather than by a Lacanian or Deconstructionist critic; our use of essays by Wolfgang Iser, Edward Said, Gayatri Spivak and influential Marxist or feminist critics and cultural materialists rather than by those who work within these traditions or in a debate with these figures. In this way, we hope to answer one obvious kind of question – how would Derrida actually read a literary text? – and to provide an authoritative example of the assumptions and procedures associated with a particular approach. This does not mean, however, that these essays comprise perfect or definitive models, to be replicated or parodied along an assembly-line or supermarket shelf of critical styles. Rather, they are grouped in sets of different possible and often antagonistic readings of a given literary text in what we want to be understood and used as 'exercises' which facilitate the exploration of these differences. Theoretical questions can, of course, be pursued at an abstract and generalized level, but literary theories need, in our view, to be demonstrated and tested in relation to literary texts. We want, once more, to encourage and enable the development of a theoretically informed criticism, to promote the teaching and study of theoretical, critical and literary texts in dialogue together. No one textbook, as other editors will have realized, can do all that this requires. But we believe the practical orientation of the following exercises means that they can provide a forum and a base to return to from the further reading which it is a serious part of our purpose also to encourage. As such, the individual essays we have included are open to elaboration and interrogation in their immediate relations to a particular text and its accompanying set of essays; but they are open too, beyond this textbook, to the challenge of other theory and criticism as well as the literary texts which students will encounter elsewhere.

Clearly, the literary texts which provide a focus for these exercises are not randomly selected. This is a further co-ordinate such a collection has to consider. We realize that a list of ten texts will be seen as either too long or too short, and that some might see *this* list of ten as reinforcing a canon of largely British or Anglo-American authors and texts; as tokenist in its representation of women, issues of colour and sexuality; as buttressing the hegemony of modernism and of prose fiction. So, why these texts? Certainly, we believe these ten texts are interesting and worthy of study; but this is not to say that in our view they comprise a perfect literary curriculum, or even a suitcase of desert-island books. Several factors have, in fact, governed our selection, and not all of them were of our own making. First, this book is intended for a student readership in Great Britain, the United States and the English-speaking world. We could not assume those students would, for example, know or come to read Rabelais and therefore be in a confident position to read Bakhtin on Rabelais. Second, we wanted to include texts or authors representing different periods and genres, and to include examples which addressed questions of gender, sexuality and ethnicity. Third, and fast approaching a point of gridlock, we wanted ideally, as we say, to present critical essays on these texts or authors by leading theorists. Aside from the determinate financial restraints which make the inclusion of work by some authors impossible, we were guided here by three considerations: the contents of *A Reader's Guide to Contemporary Literary Theory*, which we wanted this book to support and complement; the need to represent earlier seminal positions (in Eliot, Leavis, Woolf and New Criticism, for example); and to include, of course, examples of the major schools and movements in later theory and criticism by theorists/critics who could be fairly thought to exemplify this new diversity of positions.

At the same time, these factors were overdetermined all along by another incontrovertible and revealing fact. Georg Lukács did not write on George Eliot; Barthes did not write on Oscar Wilde; Stephen Greenblatt has not written on *Beloved*; Foucault, Lyotard and Baudrillard barely refer to individual literary texts. And so on. Otherwise, major theorists, critics and schools or movements have gravitated towards the mainstream texts and authors in their own national literatures, or to those who, as a result of this critical attention, come to represent a high profile counter-canon. Thus, of course, are canons sustained and reconstituted. Superficially at least, our choice of texts follows this process, seeming to help maintain a dominant literary taste. But it also, and more importantly, questions this: by enlisting innovative and challenging perspectives upon mainstream texts and upon those writers who have extended or reconfigured the canon – Oscar Wilde, Toni Morrison and Salman Rushdie, for example – together with the new theoretical and cultural agendas associated with their work.

The result is a textbook which groups essays representing key theoretical debates around canonic or new, but well-known and much-taught, texts and authors. 'Literature', said Roland Barthes, is 'what gets taught'. Here, by implication, not only literature, but theory and criticism too are what get taught. Which returns us finally to the main purpose of this collection. Beyond decisions on the contents, the problem facing editors of Readers is a pedagogic one: how to introduce new and difficult ideas or new approaches where guidance and commentary are deemed necessary and useful, but to present this in such a way as to encourage independent critical thought. Our solution – in the contextual information of the 'General Introduction' to each exercise and the following Headnotes to individual essays – is to steer a course between the *à la carte* and *table d'hôte* menus of direct teaching and student-centred learning. In the latter we invite students to tease out a difficulty or contradiction, trace a keyword, extrapolate an implied theoretical position, compare essays or sketch an alternative approach. In using the book, teachers may or may not themselves choose to follow precisely these questions, but they provide enough guidance, we think, for students to use the book independently, inside or outside the classroom or in relation to other courses: to use it, indeed, as a 'workbook' in the best sense of the now often dubiously rationalized doctrine of 'independent learning'.

A last word on our position. All criticism, we believe, is dependent on theory, and this in turn we see as comprising notions of literary and social form and value, ideas of order and power, subjectivity and sexuality. These are the vital knowledges of a literary education, learned and unlearned in reading, discussion and written criticism. The problem with presenting a range of perspectives and positions in a Reader of this kind is that it may reinforce the undifferentiated pluralism it is meant to counter. But critical approaches and theories of literature and criticism are not all compatible or equal for the student or for the professional academic critic. Criticism is about 'choosing'; about taking and developing positions in the fullest sense. And this is neither a matter of indifference in the end for students, nor in the beginning for the teacher or editor.

The contents of the Reader, and what we have said above, imply an attitude, first of all, towards mainstream traditions in literature and theory. Quite simply, in our view, these are neither to be rejected nor revered but critically examined (read and re-read) from a perspective located, inevitably, both inside and outside an available and changing culture. This double life characterizes the position or, better, the attitude of 'critique'; a mode and mentality derived in the main, in our own case, from traditions in Marxism and political criticism, coupled at once with the mixed influence of tendencies in poststructuralism, postmodernism, social semiotics and dialogics, and a persistent belief in the virtues of textual analysis. The result is eclectic yet committed. It is the *attitude* of critique, however, not the details of a personal formation, that we wish to inscribe and foster in this book. We spoke earlier of the function of criticism at the present time, alluding half jokingly to Arnold's famous essay of that title. But the kind of criticism we are invoking – self-conscious, theoretically aware, textually focused, sceptical of established opinion, alive to the part that literature and a critical mentality can play in positive cultural change – would indeed, we think, be a criticism worth taking seriously at the present time.

The *Practical Reader* will, we hope, be a modest contribution to this high aim. We ask many questions in the course of it, at moments indeed seeming to spin out an almost comical surfeit. Not all of these questions need be answered. Students will select their own from those we have put and ask others, and so come in their turn to question the critics – and the editors. We too, after all, are open to question. That, in so many words, is our position.

Notes

1. Fredric Jameson, 'Postmodernism and Consumer Society', in Peter Brooker, ed., *Modernism/ Postmodernism* (Longman, 1992), p. 165.
2. See Peter Brooker, 'Why Brecht, or is there English After Cultural Studies', in Michael Green, ed., *Broadening the Context* (John Murray, 1987), and Antony Easthope, *Literary into Cultural Studies* (Routledge, 1991). One of the major influences on this self-consciousness in conceptions of 'English' and 'Literature' has been Raymond Williams. See essays in his *Marxism and Literature* (Oxford University Press, 1977) and *Writing in Society* (Verso, 1984).
3. See Patrick Parrinder, *The Failure of Theory. Essays on Criticism and Contemporary Fiction* (Harvester, 1987); Bernard Bergonzi, *Exploding English* (Clarendon Press, 1991); Peter Washington, *Fraud. Literary Theory and the End of English* (Fontana, 1989).
4. On this development, see Steven Earnshaw, *The Direction of Literary Theory* (Macmillan, 1996), and Simon Dentith, 'Teaching and "Theory" Again', *English*, 44, 178, Spring 1995, pp. 71–8. Both writers are thoroughly alert to the radicalizing claims, at least, of theory, and Dentith concedes it has an informing influence upon literary study. Nevertheless, he wishes to assert that 'the primary purpose of an English course is to get students to engage with "literature" and not with theory'. Theory, he says, must be 'subservient' to this engagement and to 'a process of self-discovery' (pp. 73, 77).
5. Tony Davies and Nigel Wood, eds, *The Waste Land* (Open University Press, 1994), p. ix.
6. This is the view of Catherine Burgass, 'Theory and Practice', from unpublished PhD thesis, University of Leicester, 1995.
7. Terry Eagleton, *The Significance of Theory* (Basil Blackwell, 1990), p. 24.
8. Raman Selden and Peter Widdowson, *A Reader's Guide to Contemporary Literary Theory* (Prentice Hall/Harvester Wheatsheaf, 1993), p. 3.
9. We would enlist collections such as A. Easthope and J. O. Thompson, eds, *Contemporary Poetry Meets Modern Theory* (Prentice Hall/Harvester, 1991); and J. Collins, H. Radner and A. Preacher Collins, eds, *Film Theory Goes to the Movies* (Routledge, 1993) in this aim, though they do not put things in these exact terms. In the second volume the editors talk of the need for 'critical readings', 'textual analysis' and the 'engaged interventionist analysis' of popular film texts. This formulation echoes an earlier moment of film study, but they do not advocate 'a simple return to the good old days of film theory in the 1970s ... grounded in semiotics, Marxism and psychoanalysis'. This cannot be, they say, since the altered 'cultural terrain' of film and film study has also changed the nature of cultural analysis (pp. 3–4). An analogous development has occurred in literary studies.

Chapter I

William Shakespeare
Hamlet

GENERAL INTRODUCTION

Hamlet (1601) is one of Shakespeare's four major tragedies (the others are *King Lear*, *Othello* and *Macbeth*), all of which were written in the period 1600–5.

In recent years Shakespeare has been a special object of attention for 'new historicist' and 'cultural materialist' critics – numbering, amongst others, Stephen Greenblatt and Jean E. Howard in the United States; and John Drakakis, Catherine Belsey, Jonathan Dollimore, Alan Sinfield, Graham Holderness and Terence Hawkes in the United Kingdom. Often these two tendencies have been associated with different critical methods and aims in the two countries; thus American 'new historicism' has been seen as more textualist and oriented towards the past, and British 'cultural materialism' as more directly contemporary and political. (See the editors' General Introduction and Headnotes to Chs 2 and 5, and the commentary in *A Reader's Guide* 3/e, pp. 161–9. See also Barker *et al.* and Kamps, in Further Reading below, for some engagement with the different conceptions of history these approaches involve.)

In *Meaning by Shakespeare* (Routledge, 1992), Terence Hawkes presents the case for cultural materialism by way of *Hamlet* and Hamlet's use of the play 'The Murder of Gonzago' (the play within the play). After its performance, Ophelia asks Hamlet what the play meant ('What means this, my lord?'), as if she assumes, Hawkes says, it has an inherent, agreed and paraphrasable meaning. Hamlet's reply, 'Marry, this is *miching malicho*. It means mischief', shifts the ground to a more pragmatic concept of meaning; one more in keeping with the anti-essentialist and historicist assumptions of Hawkes and other cultural materialists. Like Hamlet, readers in different generations and societies give the play *Hamlet* meaning – they mean something 'by' it, in the terms of Hawkes' title. As he argues:

> A text is surely better served if it is perceived not as the embodiment of some frozen, definitive significance, but as a kind of intersection or confluence which is continually traversed, a no-man's land, an arena, in which different and opposed readings, urged from different and opposed political positions, compete in history for ideological power: the power, that is, to determine cultural meaning – to say what the world is and should be like. We try to make Hamlet mean for our purposes now: others will try to make it mean differently for their purposes then (or now). (p. 8)

Alan Sinfield's study *Faultlines* (1992) is a provocative recent example of making Shakespeare mean differently now. He argues that Shakespeare presents us with an ambiguous or polymorphous sexuality and that readings of the plays in these terms can help critique homophobic and dominant heterosexual norms in contemporary society. However, Hawkes' statement is quite clearly meant to apply, beyond the example of Shakespeare, to all literary and cultural texts. Cultural materialism invites a plurality of meanings or readings and has logically to assume that its own readings will be contested – by more traditional readings, for example. The implication is that all readings, whether radical or traditional, of all kinds of texts, are at some point ideologically motivated and constructed in the interests of a specific literary and cultural agenda. We represent an example of a cultural materialist or historicist reading of Hamlet, below, in the essay by Lisa Jardine, though this debates some of the implications of a 'textualization' of history associated with new historicism. In her essay, as in the essays by Showalter and Rose which share some of the assumptions of cultural materialism, this approach is informed by an explicitly feminist project. These not only give both textual and historical study a new tone and direction, they should – if we are to follow through the logic of this position – bring us to ask questions about the aesthetic and ideological assumptions of the other essays, by Eliot and Lacan, included here. Students should have this in mind when examining these essays.

Further Reading

The critical discussion of Shakespeare is, of course, extensive. The following are recent studies which contain some discussion of critical debate and of the play *Hamlet*.

Francis Barker *et al.*, *Uses of History, Marxism, Postmodernism and the Renaissance* (Manchester University Press, 1991).

Jonathan Dollimore and Alan Sinfield, *Political Shakespeare* (Manchester University Press, 1985).

John Drakakis, ed., *Alternative Shakespeares* (Methuen, 1985).

John Drakakis, ed., *Shakespearean Tragedy* (Longman, 1992).

Terry Eagleton, *William Shakespeare* (Basil Blackwell, 1986).

Graham Holderness, ed., *The Shakespeare Myth* (Manchester University Press, 1988).

Jean Howard and Marion F. O'Connor, eds, *Shakespeare Reproduced. The Text in History and Ideology* (Methuen, 1987).

Ivo Kamps, ed., *Shakespeare Left and Right* (Routledge, 1991).

Patricia Parker and Geoffrey Hartman, eds, *Shakespeare and the Question of Theory* (Methuen, 1987).

Kiernan Ryan, *Shakespeare*, 2nd edn (Prentice Hall, 1995).

Students may consult earlier discussions of *Hamlet*, from the eighteenth century to the early 1960s, in John Jump, ed., *Hamlet. A Casebook* (Macmillan, 1968). This contains the comments and essays on the play by Freud and Ernest Jones referred to in the following essays. Full references to these are given in Rose below, pp. 42–53. A further volume of interest is Martin Coyle, ed, *Shakespeare: Hamlet: A Selection of Contemporary Criticism* (Macmillan 'New Casebooks', 1992).

1.1   T. S. ELIOT: 'HAMLET' (1919)

T. S. Eliot (1888–1965) was born in St Louis, Missouri, USA, and came to Europe and then England in 1915. His first volume of poetry was published in 1917, but it was his critical essays, published as *The Sacred Wood* (1920) and *The Waste Land* (1922), that decisively established his reputation. Thenceforth Eliot combined his career as poet and critic with the editorship of *The Criterion*. In 1925 he became a director of Faber & Faber and in 1927 he joined the Church of England and also became a naturalized British subject.

Eliot's essay on *Hamlet* performed a dual function, as both an essay on the play and a way of developing an aesthetic which was to guide Eliot's own poetry. These purposes come together in the idea of the 'objective correlative' which he introduces here. Eliot used this term to describe the way poetic imagery gives an internal emotion or state of mind artistic expression through the presentation of an equivalent set of external objects. This formed part of his own theory of the necessary impersonality of modern poetry, and helped provide one of the key concepts of literary modernism. At the same time he employs this concept in his reading and judgement upon Shakespeare's play. Thus, in Eliot's view, Hamlet's emotions of disgust exceed their ostensible object in the figure of his mother. Hamlet, that is to say, cannot find an adequate object for his emotions. This situation in the play Eliot sees as a prolongation of Shakespeare's own inability to find an artistic 'objective correlative'. The play is consequently an artistic failure.

Eliot's judgement has prompted many replies, and readers are bound to respond to it in assessing his essay. Just as interesting and relevant, however, is his idea of artistic success (he cites the play *Coriolanus*). What emerges is not simply an individual judgement on an individual play but a notion of the work of art and the task of the critic. How would you describe Eliot's views on these more general questions, and how do you think they compare with the position taken by later critics? Compare, for example, Eliot's opening paragraphs with Hawkes' 'historicist' view (see above, p. 9) that there is no fixed or inherent meaning in Shakespeare.

Eliot's closing remarks are also of interest. In his view, Shakespeare 'tackled a problem which proved too much for him'. This would seem to lead criticism into speculations on the playwright's personal life and psychology – though this at the same time presents 'an insoluble puzzle', Eliot says. Is this interest consistent, do you think, with his earlier arguments in the essay about art and criticism?

The essay 'Hamlet' is taken from *Selected Prose*, ed. John Hayward (Faber, 1953), pp. 104–9.

Hamlet

Few critics have ever admitted that *Hamlet* the play is the primary problem, and Hamlet the character only secondary. And Hamlet the character has had an especial temptation for that most dangerous type of critic: the critic with a mind which is naturally of the creative order, but which through some weakness in creative power exercises itself in criticism instead. These minds often find in Hamlet a vicarious existence for their own artistic realization. Such a mind had Goethe, who made of

Hamlet a Werther; and such had Coleridge, who made of Hamlet a Coleridge; and probably neither of these men in writing about Hamlet remembered that his first business was to study a work of art. The kind of criticism that Goethe and Coleridge produced, in writing of Hamlet, is the most misleading kind possible. For they both possessed unquestionable critical insight, and both make their critical aberrations the more plausible by the substitution – of their own Hamlet for Shakespeare's – which their creative gift effects. We should be thankful that Walter Pater did not fix his attention on this play.

Two writers of our time, J. M. Robertson and Professor Stoll, have issued small books which can be praised for moving in the other direction. Mr Stoll performs a service in recalling to our attention the labours of the critics of the seventeenth and eighteenth centuries,[*] observing that:

> They knew less about psychology than more recent Hamlet critics, but they were nearer in spirit to Shakespeare's art; and as they insisted on the importance of the effect of the whole rather than on the importance of the leading character, they were nearer, in their old-fashioned way, to the secret of dramatic art in general.

Qua work of art, the work of art cannot be interpreted; there is nothing to interpret; we can only criticize it according to standards, in comparison to other works of art; and for 'interpretation' the chief task is the presentation of relevant historical facts which the reader is not assumed to know. Mr Robertson points out, very pertinently, how critics have failed in their 'interpretation' of *Hamlet* by ignoring what ought to be very obvious: that *Hamlet* is a stratification, that it represents the efforts of a series of men, each making what he could out of the work of his predecessors. The *Hamlet* of Shakespeare will appear to us very differently if, instead of treating the whole action of the play as due to Shakespeare's design, we perceive his *Hamlet* to be superposed upon much cruder material which persists even in the final form.

We know that there was an older play by Thomas Kyd, that extraordinary dramatic (if not poetic) genius who was in all probability the author of two plays so dissimilar as *The Spanish Tragedy* and *Arden of Feversham*; and what this play was like we can guess from three clues: from *The Spanish Tragedy* itself, from the tale of Belleforest upon which Kyd's *Hamlet* must have been based, and from a version acted in Germany in Shakespeare's lifetime which bears strong evidence of having been adapted from the earlier, not from the later, play. From these three sources it is clear that in the earlier play the motive was a revenge motive simply; that the action or delay is caused, as in *The Spanish Tragedy*, solely by the difficulty of assassinating a monarch surrounded by guards; and that the 'madness' of Hamlet was feigned in order to escape suspicion, and successfully. In the final play of Shakespeare, on the other hand, there is a motive which is more important than that of revenge, and which explicitly 'blunts' the latter; the delay in revenge is unexplained on grounds of necessity or expediency; and the effect of the 'madness' is not to lull but to arouse

---

[*] I have never, by the way, seen a cogent refutation of Thomas Rymers' objections to *Othello*. [*Author's note*]

the king's suspicion. The alteration is not complete enough, however, to be convincing. Furthermore, there are verbal parallels so close to *The Spanish Tragedy* as to leave no doubt that in places Shakespeare was merely *revising* the text of Kyd. And finally there are unexplained scenes – the Polonius-Laertes and the Polonius-Reynaldo scenes – for which there is little excuse; these scenes are not in the verse style of Kyd, and not beyond doubt in the style of Shakespeare. These Mr Robertson believes to be scenes in the original play of Kyd reworked by a third hand, perhaps Chapman, before Shakespeare touched the play. And he concludes, with very strong show of reason, that the original play of Kyd was, like certain other revenge plays, in two parts of five acts each. The upshot of Mr Robertson's examination is, we believe, irrefragable: that Shakespeare's *Hamlet*, so far as it is Shakespeare's, is a play dealing with the effect of a mother's guilt upon her son, and that Shakespeare was unable to impose this motive successfully upon the 'intractable' material of the old play.

Of the intractability there can be no doubt. So far from being Shakespeare's masterpiece, the play is most certainly an artistic failure. In several ways the play is puzzling, and disquieting as is none of the others. Of all the plays it is the longest and is possibly the one on which Shakespeare spent most pains; and yet he has left in it superfluous and inconsistent scenes which even hasty revision should have noticed. The versification is variable. Lines like

But look, the morn, in russet mantle clad,
Walks o'er the dew of yon high eastern hill,

are of the Shakespeare of *Romeo and Juliet*. The lines in Act V. Sc. ii,

Sir, in my heart there was a kind of fighting
That would not let me sleep ...
Up from my cabin,
My sea-gown scarf'd about me, in the dark
Grop'd I to find out them: had my desire;
Finger'd their packet ...

are of his quite mature. Both workmanship and thought are in an unstable position. We are surely justified in attributing the play, with that other profoundly interesting play of 'intractable' material and astonishing versification, *Measure for Measure*, to a period of crisis, after which follow the tragic successes which culminate in *Coriolanus*. *Coriolanus* may be not as 'interesting' as *Hamlet* but it is, with *Antony and Cleopatra*, Shakespeare's most assured artistic success. And probably more people have thought *Hamlet* a work of art because they found it interesting, than have found it interesting because it is a work of art. It is the 'Mona Lisa' of literature.

The grounds of *Hamlet's* failure are not immediately obvious. Mr Robertson is undoubtedly correct in concluding that the essential emotion of the play is the feeling of a son towards a guilty mother:

'[Hamlet's] tone is that of one who has suffered tortures on the score of his mother's degradation. ... The guilt of a mother is an almost intolerable motive for drama, but it had to be maintained and emphasized to supply a psychological solution, or rather a hint of one.'

This, however, is by no means the whole story. It is not merely the 'guilt of a mother' that cannot be handled as Shakespeare handled the suspicion of Othello, the infatuation of Antony, or the pride of Coriolanus. The subject might conceivably have expanded into a tragedy like these, intelligible, self-complete, in the sunlight. *Hamlet*, like the sonnets, is full of some stuff that the writer could not drag to light, contemplate, or manipulate into art. And when we search for this feeling, we find it, as in the sonnets, very difficult to localize. You cannot point to it in the speeches; indeed, if you examine the two famous soliloquies you see the versification of Shakespeare, but a content which might be claimed by another, perhaps by the author of *The Revenge of Bussy d' Ambois*, Act V. Sc. i. We find Shakespeare's *Hamlet* not in the action, not in any quotations that we might select, so much as in an unmistakable tone which is unmistakably not in the earlier play.

The only way of expressing emotion in the form of art is by finding an 'objective correlative'; in other words, a set of objects, a situation, a chain of events which shall be the formula of that *particular* emotion; such that when the external facts, which must terminate in sensory experience, are given, the emotion is immediately evoked. If you examine any of Shakespeare's more successful tragedies, you will find this exact equivalence; you will find that the state of mind of Lady Macbeth walking in her sleep has been communicated to you by a skilful accumulation of imagined sensory impressions; the words of Macbeth on hearing of his wife's death strike us as if, given the sequence of events, these words were automatically released by the last event in the series. The artistic 'inevitability' lies in this complete adequacy of the external to the emotion; and this is precisely what is deficient in *Hamlet*. Hamlet (the man) is dominated by an emotion which is inexpressible, because it is in *excess* of the facts as they appear. And the supposed identity of Hamlet with his author is genuine to this point: that Hamlet's bafflement at the absence of objective equivalent to his feelings is a prolongation of the bafflement of his creator in the face of his artistic problem. Hamlet is up against the difficulty that his disgust is occasioned by his mother, but that his mother is not an adequate equivalent for it; his disgust envelops and exceeds her. It is thus a feeling which he cannot understand; he cannot objectify it, and it therefore remains to poison life and obstruct action. None of the possible actions can satisfy it; and nothing that Shakespeare can do with the plot can express Hamlet for him. And it must be noticed that the very nature of the *données* of the problem precludes objective equivalence. To have heightened the criminality of Gertrude would have been to provide the formula for a totally different emotion in Hamlet; it is just *because* her character is so negative and insignificant that she arouses in Hamlet the feeling which she is incapable of representing.

The 'madness' of Hamlet lay to Shakespeare's hand; in the earlier play a simple ruse, and to the end, we may presume, understood as a ruse by the audience. For Shakespeare it is less than madness and more than feigned. The levity of Hamlet, his repetition of phrase, his puns, are not part of a deliberate plan of dissimulation, but a form of emotional relief. In the character Hamlet it is the buffoonery of an emotion which can find no outlet in action; in the dramatist it is the buffoonery of an emotion which he cannot express in art. The intense feeling, ecstatic or terrible, without an object or exceeding its object, is something which every person of sensibility has known; it is doubtless a subject of study for pathologists. It often occurs in adolescence: the ordinary person puts these feelings to sleep, or trims down his feelings to fit the business world; the artist keeps them alive by his ability to intensify the world to his emotions. The Hamlet of Laforgue is an adolescent; the Hamlet of Shakespeare is not, he has not that explanation and excuse. We must simply admit that here Shakespeare tackled a problem which proved too much for him. Why he attempted it at all is an insoluble puzzle; under compulsion of what experience he attempted to express the inexpressibly horrible, we cannot ever know. We need a great many facts in his biography; and we should like to know whether, and when, and after or at the same time as what personal experience, he read Montaigne, II. xii, *Apologie de Raimond Sebond*. We should have, finally, to know something which is by hypothesis unknowable, for we assume it to be an experience which, in the manner indicated, exceeded the facts. We should have to understand things which Shakespeare did not understand himself.

1.2   JACQUES LACAN: FROM 'DESIRE AND THE INTERPRETATION OF DESIRE IN *HAMLET*' (1959, 1982)

Jacques Lacan (1901–81) was a radical post-Freudian psychoanalyst often associated with the general movement of poststructuralism. His critique of orthodox psychoanalytic theory and practice led to his expulsion from the International Psychoanalytic Association in 1959 and to his setting up of the Ecole Freudienne in Paris in 1964. His work is known chiefly in translation through *The Four Fundamental Concepts of Psychoanalysis* (Penguin, 1979) and the 'seminars' conducted at the school, a selection of which appeared as *Ecrits* (Tavistock, 1977).

Traditional psychoanalytic criticism has been chiefly indebted to Freud and has tended to use literature to interpret the psychology of an author or character. Lacan's semiotic reading of Freud and his general emphasis on language called this approach into question. The unconscious, in Lacan's view, is structured like and produced by language at the point of the subject's entry into the 'Symbolic Order'. This realm is governed by the 'Law of the Father' and is thought to subordinate or repress the pre-symbolic realm of the 'Imaginary', associated with desire and the figure of the Mother.

In general terms the influence of this theory upon literary studies, in common with other poststructuralist theory, has been to confirm the idea of the divided or split subject and the textual construction of subjectivity. In more detailed terms, the significance of Lacan's writings has been debated within contemporary feminism and in gay, or queer, theory in relation particularly to the politics of transgressive sexuality (see the editorial commentary and the essays on Oscar Wilde, Ch. 5, below).

In Freud's discussion of *Hamlet*, a repressed and unnamed impulse struggles into expression and action (see Sigmund Freud, *Art and Literature*, Penguin, 1986, pp. 126–7). Hamlet cannot fulfil the task of revenge because, in usurping the place of the King, his uncle Claudius has enacted Hamlet's own repressed sexual desire for his mother. The disgust which ought to motivate his revenge is therefore turned upon himself in expressions of guilt and reproach. Lacan reads *Hamlet* as a tragedy of desire and sees Hamlet as a type of the 'obsessional neurotic'. Confronted by the ideal image of his father and the degraded person of Claudius, Hamlet cannot act; or, until the play's denouement cannot act in his own terms or own time, as Lacan puts it, but only 'at the hour of the Other'. In the body of the play, Lacan argues, Hamlet's desire for and loathing of his mother are transferred to Ophelia. As the object of his deflected emotions, she 'takes the place ... of what the subject [Hamlet] is – symbolically – deprived of': she is the symbolic representation, that is to say, of the phallus, 'exteriorized and rejected' by Hamlet.

Few would deny that *Hamlet* can be seen as a reworking of the Oedipal narrative. Ophelia's role in the text of this Oedipal drama would therefore appear to be of central interest (that this is less obvious than it might seem is made plain by the other essays selected here). Are you persuaded, however, by Lacan's argument and by the role he assigns Ophelia? What further or different construction might be put upon this character in the text of the play – or is her real significance to be found, as Showalter's essay would seem to suggest, outside the confines of the text?

Lacan also concentrates on the theme of mourning in the play. Invariably, as he points out, this ritual is abrupt or improperly conducted. Why is this, and what relation does Lacan's reading suggest it has with the other major theme of desire? Lacan asks us not only to consider Ophelia once more in this connection, but also Hamlet's father; Polonius, whom Hamlet kills; and Claudius, whom he cannot bring himself to kill in the Chapel scene. What is specific to Hamlet, Lacan says earlier, is that he 'just doesn't know what he wants'. In the Chapel scene he is said to realize that neither Polonius nor Claudius was quite what he was after. What then does this scene reveal of Hamlet's unspoken wishes or desires? Does the association of phallus, ghost, king and father, which Lacan points to, provide an explanation for the delay, inaction and incompleteness commonly thought to lie at the heart of the play?

Lacan's direct discussion of literature includes reflections on Joyce and on Edgar Allen Poe's 'The Purloined Letter' as well as the essay on *Hamlet*. The essay on Poe's story appeared in translation in *Yale French Studies*, no. 48 (1973), p. 38–72, and should be consulted alongside Derrida's essay in reply ('The Purveyor of Truth', *Yale French Studies*, no. 52 (1975), pp. 31–113).

The essay on *Hamlet* from which extracts are presented below was given as a series of three talks or seminars, titled 'The Object Ophelia', 'Desire and Mourning' and 'Phallophany', delivered on 15, 22 and 29 April 1959 respectively. The essay originally appeared in translation in *Yale French Studies*, nos. 55/6 (1977, 1980) and subsequently in the reprint of this double volume in Shoshana Felman, ed., *Literature and Psychoanalysis. The Question of Reading: Otherwise* (Johns Hopkins University Press, 1982), pp. 11–54. The following has been taken from this volume. A number of minor cuts have been made in the text so as to give the student the main line of Lacan's argument. More substantive cuts are indicated by a summarizing statement in the text.

Further Reading
Terry Eagleton, *Literary Theory. An Introduction*, Ch. 5 (Basil Blackwell, 1983).
Richard Feldstein and Henry Sussman, eds, *Psychoanalysis and ...* (Routledge, 1990).
Elizabeth Grosz, *Jacques Lacan: A Feminist Introduction* (Routledge, 1990).
Barbara Johnson, 'The Frame of Reference: Poe, Lacan, Derrida', in Robert Young, ed., *Untying the Text: A Post-Structuralist Reader* (Routledge, 1981).
David Lacey, *Lacan's Contexts* (Verso, 1988). A combative study which contests Lacan's association with poststructuralism and his contribution to feminism.
Madan Sarup, *Jacques Lacan* (Harvester, 1992). Contains a chapter on 'Lacan and Literature'.

Desire and the Interpretation of Desire in *Hamlet*

The Object Ophelia
As a sort of come-on, I announced that I would speak today about that piece of bait named Ophelia, and I'll be as good as my word.

Our purpose, as you remember, is to show the tragedy of desire as it appears in *Hamlet*, human desire, that is, such as we are concerned with in psychoanalysis.

[...]

Shakespeare's play contains one shift in the plot that distinguishes it from previous treatments of the story, including both the narratives of Saxo Grammaticus and Belleforest and the other plays of which we possess fragments. This shift involves the character Ophelia.

[...]

she thus becomes one of the innermost elements in Hamlet's drama, the drama of Hamlet as the man who has lost the way of his desire. She provides an essential pivot in the hero's progress toward his mortal rendezvous with his act – an act that he carries out, in some sense, in spite of himself

[...]

The principal subject of the play is beyond all doubt Prince Hamlet. The play is the drama of an individual subjectivity, and the hero is always present on stage, more than in any other play. How is the desire of the Other manifested in the very perspective of this subject, Prince Hamlet? This desire, of the mother, is essentially manifested in the fact that, confronted on one hand with an eminent, idealized, exalted object – his father – and on the other with the degraded, despicable object Claudius, the criminal and adulterous brother, Hamlet does not choose.

His mother does not choose because of something present inside her, like an instinctive voracity. The sacrosanct genital object that we recently added to our technical vocabulary appears to her as an object to be enjoyed [*objet d'une jouissance*] in what is truly the direct satisfaction of a need, and nothing else. This is the aspect that makes Hamlet waver in his abjuration of his mother. Even when he transmits to her – in the crudest, cruellest terms – the essential message with which the ghost, his father, has entrusted him, he still first appeals to her to abstain. Then, a moment later, his appeal fails, and he sends her to Claudius' bed, into the arms of the man who once again will not fail to make her yield.

This fall, this abandon, gives us a model that enables us to conceive how it is that Hamlet's desire – his zeal with respect to an act that he so longs to carry out that the whole world becomes for him a living reproach for his perpetual inadequacy to his own will – how this zeal always flags. The dependence of his desire on the Other subject forms the permanent dimension of Hamlet's drama.

[...]

Lacan goes on to present a psychoanalytic commentary, supported by illustration, on the topology of the subject's relation to the Other. The object of the subject's desire (Gertrude-Ophelia in the play) takes the place of what that subject is symbolically deprived of: namely the phallus. He also adds a distinction between perversity and neurosis; the fantasy of the first is nameable and out of time, that of the second occurs in (delayed) time.

[...]

hysteria is characterized by the function of an unsatisfied desire and obsession by the function of an impossible desire. But beyond these two terms the two cases are distinguished by inverse relationships with time: the obsessive neurotic always repeats the initial germ of his trauma, i.e., a certain precipitancy, a fundamental lack of maturation.

This is at the base of neurotic behavior, in its most general form: the subject tries to find his sense of time [*lire son heure*] in his object, and it is even in the object that he will learn to tell time [*lire l'heure*]. This is where we get back to our friend Hamlet, to whom everyone can attribute at will all the forms of neurotic behavior, as far as you want to go, i.e., up to character neurosis. The first factor that I indicated to you in Hamlet's structure was his situation of dependence with respect to the desire of the Other, the desire of his mother. Here now is the second factor that I ask you to recognize: Hamlet is constantly suspended in the time of the Other, throughout the entire story until the very end.

Do you remember one of the first turning-points we focussed on when we were beginning to decipher the text of *Hamlet*? During the play scene the king becomes unsettled and visibly reveals his own guilt, incapable of viewing the dramatization of his own crime. Hamlet relishes his triumph and mocks the king. But on the way to the meeting he has already arranged with his mother, he comes upon his stepfather in prayer: Claudius is shaken to the depths of his being by the scene that has just shown him the very countenance and program of his deed. Hamlet stands before this Claudius, who by every indication is not only in no state to defend himself but also does not even see the threat that hangs over his head. And Hamlet stops, because it's not time. It's not the hour of the Other: not time for the Other to render his 'audit' to heaven. That would be too kind, from one point of view, or too cruel, from another. That might not avenge his father properly, because prayer, being a gesture of repentance, might open up the way to salvation for Claudius. In any case, one thing is sure: Hamlet, who has just managed to 'catch the conscience of the king' as planned – stops. Not for a moment does he think that his time has come. Whatever may happen later, this is not the hour of the Other, and he suspends his action. Whatever Hamlet may do, he will do it only at the hour of the Other.

Hamlet accepts everything. Let's not forget that at the beginning, in the state of disgust he was already in (even before his meeting with the ghost) because of his mother's remarriage, he thought only of leaving for Wittenberg. A recent commentary on a certain practicality that is becoming more and more typical of present-day life, used this as an illustration, noting that Hamlet was the best example of the fact that many dramatic crises can be avoided by the prompt issuance of passports. If Hamlet had been given his papers to travel to Wittenberg, there would have been no drama.

When he stays on, it is the hour of his parents. When he suspends his crime, it is the hour of the others. When he leaves for England, it is the hour of his stepfather. It's the hour of Rosencrantz and Guildenstern when he sends them on ahead to death – with a casualness that amazed Freud – by means of a bit of hocus-pocus that he brings off not half badly. And it is the hour of Ophelia, the hour of her suicide, when the tragedy will run its course, in a moment when Hamlet has just realized that it's not hard to kill a man, the time to say 'one' ... he won't know what hit him.

He receives word of an event that in no way seems to promise an opportunity to kill Claudius: a tournament, the rules of which have been worked out to the last detail. They tempt him with the stakes – all precious objects, swords, fittings, and other things that have value only as luxuries; this should be followed in the text, for these are the nuances of the world of the collector. Hamlet's sense of rivalry and honor is aroused by the assumption that Laertes is the more skillful swordsman and by the handicap thus granted to Hamlet in the terms of the wager. This complicated ceremony is a trap for him to fall into, laid by his stepfather and his friend Laertes: we know this, but Hamlet does not.

[…]

Thus he rushes into the trap laid by the Other. All that's changed is the energy and fire with which he rushes into it. Until the last term, until the final hour, Hamlet's hour, in which he is mortally wounded before he wounds his enemy, the tragedy follows its course and attains completion at the hour of Other: this is the absolutely essential framework for our conception of what is involved here.

This is the sense in which Hamlet's drama has the precise metaphysical resonance of the question of the modern hero. Indeed, something has changed since classical antiquity in the relationship of the hero to his fate.

As I have said, the thing that distinguishes Hamlet from Oedipus is that Hamlet *knows*. This characteristic explains, for example, Hamlet's madness. In the tragedies of antiquity, there are mad heroes, but, to the best of my knowledge, there are no heroes – in tragedy, I say, not in legends – no heroes who feign madness. Hamlet, however, does.

I am not saying that everything in his madness comes down to feigning, but I do underscore the fact that the essential characteristic in the original legend, i.e., in the versions of Saxo Grammaticus and Belleforest, is that the hero feigns madness because he knows that he is in a position of weakness. And from that moment on, everything hinges on the question of what's going on in his mind.

[…]

Thus we arrive at the point at which Ophelia must fulfill her role. If the structure of the play is really as complex as I have just portrayed it as being, you may be wondering, what is the point of the character Ophelia? Ophelia is obviously essential. She is linked forever, for centuries, to the figure of Hamlet.

[…]

We first encounter Ophelia – and this makes her quite a remarkable figure already – in the context of a clinical observation. She indeed has the good fortune to be the first person Hamlet runs into after his unsettling encounter with the ghost, and she reports his behavior in terms that are worth noting.

My lord, as I was sewing in my closet,
Lord Hamlet, with his doublet all unbraced,
No hat upon his head, his stockings fouled,
Ungartered, and down-gyvèd to his ankle,
Pale as his shirt, his knees knocking each other,
And with a look so piteous in purport
As if he had been loosèd out of hell
To speak of horrors – he comes before me.
… … … … … … … … … … … … … …
He took me by the wrist and held me hard.

Then goes he to the length of all his arm,
And with his other hand thus o'er his brow
He falls to such perusal of my face
As 'a would draw it. Long stayed he so.
At last, a little shaking of mine arm
And thrice his head thus waving up and down,
He raised a sigh so piteous and profound
As it did seem to shatter all his bulk
And end his being. That done, he lets me go,
And with his head over his shoulder turned
He seemed to find his way without his eyes,
For out o' doors he went without their helps
And to the last bended their light on me.

(Act II, Sc. I)

And Polonius cries out: This is love!

This distance from the object that Hamlet takes in order to move on to whatever new and henceforth difficult identification, his vacillation in the presence of what has been until now the object of supreme exaltation, gives us the first stage, which is, to use the English word, one of 'estrangement.'

That's all we can say. Nevertheless, I don't believe that it's excessive to designate this moment as pathological, related to those periods of irruption, of subjective disorganization which occur when something in the fantasy wavers and makes the components of the fantasy appear. This experience, called depersonalization, in the course of which the imaginary limits between subject and object change, leads us to what is called in the strict sense the fantastic dimension [*le fantastique*].

[...]

In the case of Hamlet, Ophelia is after this episode completely null and dissolved as a love object. 'I did love you once,' Hamlet says. Henceforth his relations with Ophelia will be carried on in that sarcastic style of cruel aggression which makes these scenes – and particularly the scene that occupies the middle of the play – the strangest in all of classical literature.

In this attitude we find a trace of what I mentioned a moment ago, the perverse imbalance of the fantasmatic relationship, when the fantasy is tipped toward the object. Hamlet no longer treats Ophelia like a woman at all. She becomes in his eyes the childbearer to every sin, a future 'breeder of sinners,' destined to succumb to every calumny. She is no longer the reference-point for a life that Hamlet condemns in its essence. In short, what is taking place here is the destruction and loss of the object. For the subject the object appears, if I may put it this way, on the outside. The subject is no longer the object: he rejects it with all the force of his being and will not find it again until he sacrifices himself. It is in this sense that the object is here the equivalent of, assumes the place of, indeed is – the phallus.

This is the second stage in the relationship of the subject to the object. Ophelia is at this point the phallus, exteriorized and rejected by the subject as a symbol signifying life.

What is the indication of this? There's no need to resort to the etymology of 'Ophelia.' Hamlet speaks constantly of one thing: child-bearing. 'Conception is a blessing,' he tells Polonius, but keep an eye on your daughter. And all of his dialogue with Ophelia is directed at woman conceived as the bearer of that vital swelling that he curses and wishes dried up forever. The use of the word 'nunnery' in Shakespeare's time indicates that it can also refer to a brothel. And isn't the relationship of the phallus and the object of desire also indicated in Hamlet's attitude during the play scene? In Ophelia's presence he says of her to his mother, 'Here's metal more attractive,' and wants to place his head between the girl's legs: 'Lady, shall I lie in your lap'?

Considering the great interest of iconographers in the subject, I don't think it excessive to note that the list of flowers in the midst of which Ophelia drowns herself, explicitly includes 'dead men's fingers.' The plant in question is the *Orchis mascula*, which is related to the mandrake and hence to the phallic element.

[...]

The third stage, [...] is the graveyard scene, in the course of which Hamlet is finally presented with the possibility of winding things up, of rushing to his fate. The whole scene is directed toward that furious battle at the bottom of the tomb, which I have stressed repeatedly, and which is entirely of Shakespeare's own invention. Here we see something like a reintegration of the object [...] won back here at the price of mourning and death.

[...]

Desire and Mourning

[...]

For Hamlet there is no hour but his own. Moreover, there is only one hour, the hour of his destruction. The entire tragedy of *Hamlet* is constituted in the way it shows us the unrelenting movement of the subject toward that hour.

Yet the subject's appointment with the hour of his destruction is the common lot of everyone, meaningful in the destiny of every individual. Without some distinguishing sign, Hamlet's fate would not be of such great importance to us. That's the next question: what is the specificity of Hamlet's fate? What makes it so extraordinarily problematic?

What does Hamlet lack? Can we, on the basis of the plan of the tragedy, as composed by Shakespeare, pin down and spell out this lack?

[...]

Let's start with an approximation. You can say in simple, everyday terms what Hamlet lacks: he's never set a goal for himself, an object – a choice that always has something 'arbitrary' about it.

To put it in commonsensical terms, Hamlet just doesn't know what he wants. This aspect is brought out in the speech that Shakespeare has him pronounce at one of the turning-points in the drama, the moment when he drops out of sight, the brief interval when he goes away on this nautical excursion from which he will return most rapidly. He has no sooner left for England, still obediant, in compliance with the king's orders, than he encounters the troops of Fortinbras, who has been present from the beginning in the background of the tragedy and who at the end will come to gather the dead, to tidy up, to restore order. In this scene our friend Hamlet is struck by the sight of these courageous troops going off to conquer a few acres of Polish soil for the sake of some more or less pointless military pretext. This gives Hamlet pause to consider his own behavior.

> How all occasions do inform against me
> And spur my dull revenge! What is a man,
> If his chief good and market of his time
> Be but to sleep and feed? A beast, no more.
> Sure he that made us with such large discourse,

– the expression that is glossed 'reason' is 'large discourse,' fundamental discourse, what I have referred to in other seminars as 'concrete discourse' –

> ... such large discourse,
> Looking before and after...

– now here's where the word 'reason' comes in –

> ... gave us not
> That capability and godlike reason
> To fust in us unused. Now, whether it be
> Bestial oblivion...

– 'bestial oblivion,' one of the key-words by which to measure Hamlet's existence in the tragedy –

> ... or some craven scruple
> Of thinking too precisely on th' event –
> A thought which, quartered, hath but one part wisdom
> And ever three parts coward – I do not know
> Why yet I live to say, 'This thing's to do,'
> Sith I have cause, and will, and strength, and means
> To do't. Examples gross as earth exhort me.
> Witness this army of such mass and charge,
> Led by a delicate and tender prince,
> Whose spirit, with divine ambition puffed,
> Makes mouths at the invisible event,
> Exposing what is mortal and unsure
> To all that fortune, death, and danger dare,
> Even for an eggshell. Rightly to be great
> Is not to stir without great argument,
> But greatly to find quarrel in a straw
> When honor's at the stake. How stand I then,
> That have a father killed, a mother stained,

> Excitements of my reason and my blood,
> And let all sleep, while to my shame I see
> The imminent death of twenty thousand men
> That for a fantasy and trick of fame
> Go to their graves like beds, fight for a plot
> Whereon the numbers cannot try the cause,
> Which is not tomb enough and continent
> To hide the slain? O, from this time forth,
> My thoughts be bloody, or be nothing worth!

(Act IV, Sc. IV)

Such is Hamlet's meditation on the object of human action. This object leaves the door wide open to us for all of what I shall call the particularizations that we shall consider. That is true dedication – shedding one's blood for a noble cause, for honor. Honor, too, is portrayed correctly: being totally committed by one's word. As for the gift, we as analysts cannot overlook this concrete determination, cannot help being struck by its weight, be it in flesh or in commitment.

What I'm trying to show you here is not merely the common form of all this, the least common denominator: it's not a question of formalism. When I write the formula $\$\Diamond a$ at the end of the question that the subject, in search of his last word, asks in the Other, this is not something that is actually open to investigation, except in that special experience. which we call psychoanalytic experience and which makes possible the exploration of the unconscious circuit running along the upper track of the graph.

What we're concerned with is the short circuit in the imaginary register between desire and that which is across from it, i.e., the fantasy. I express the general structure of the fantasy by $\$\Diamond a$, where $\$$ is a certain relationship of the subject to the signifier – it is the subject as irreducibly affected by the signifier – and where $\Diamond$ indicates the subject's relationship to an essentially imaginary juncture [*conjoncture*], designated by a, not the object of desire but the object *in* desire.

Let's try to get some notion of this function of the object in desire. The drama of Hamlet makes it possible for us to arrive at an exemplary articulation of this function, and this is why we have such a persistent interest in the structure of Shakespeare's play.

This is our starting point: through his relationship to the signifier, the subject is deprived of something of himself, of his very life, which has assumed the value of that which binds him to the signifier. The phallus is our term for the signifier of his alienation in signification. When the subject is deprived of this signifier, a particular object becomes for him an object of desire. This is the meaning of $\$\Diamond a$.

[…]

Lacan glosses this relationship further and returns in Part 2 of this section to the tournament in the final act. In this scene Laertes and Hamlet are in a 'mirror relationship'. In particular, Hamlet is Laertes' 'foil': a pun that makes him Laertes' double as well as the sword that kills him, and implies 'ultimately an identification with the mortal phallus'.

[...]

What is the connection between mourning and the constitution of the object in desire? Let's go at the question by way of what is most obvious to us, which will perhaps seem the most remote from the center of what we're seeking here.

Hamlet has acted scornfully and cruelly toward Ophelia, and then some. I have already stressed the demeaning aggression and the humiliation that he constantly imposes on her, once she has become for him the very symbol of the rejection of his desire. Then, suddenly, the object regains its immediacy and its worth for him:

> I loved Ophelia. Forty thousand brothers
> Could not with all their quantity of love
> Make up my sum. What wilt thou do for her?

(Act V, Sc. I)

These are the terms in which he begins his challenge to Laertes. Here, too, is a characteristic that presents Hamlet's structure in a different form and completes it: only insofar as the object of Hamlet's desire has become an impossible object can it become once more the object of his desire.

In the desires of obsessional neurotics we have already encountered the impossible as object of desire. But let's not be too easily satisfied with these overly obvious appearances. The very structure at the basis of desire always lends a note of impossibility to the object of human desire. What characterizes the obsessional neurotic in particular is that he emphasizes the confrontation with this impossibility. In other words, he sets everything up so that the object of his desire becomes the signifier of this impossibility.

But something even deeper demands our attention.

[...]

The object of mourning derives its importance for us from a certain identification relationship that Freud attempted to define most precisely with the term 'incorporation.' Let's see if we can rearticulate the identification that takes place in mourning, in the vocabulary that we've learned to use in our work so far.

If we pursue this route, armed with our symbolical apparatus, we will gain perspectives on the function of mourning that I believe to be new and eminently suggestive.

[...]

Let's stay with the most obvious aspects of the experience of mourning. The subject who descends into the maelstrom of sorrow finds himself in a certain relationship to the object which is illustrated most clearly in the graveyard scene: Laertes leaps into the grave and embraces the object whose loss is the cause of his desire, an object that has attained an existence that is all the more absolute because it no longer corresponds to anything in reality. The one unbearable dimension of possible human experience is not the experience of one's own death, which no one has, but the experience of the death of another.

Where is the gap, the hole that results from this loss and that calls forth mourning on the part of the subject? It is a hole in the real, by means of which the subject enters into a relationship that is the inverse of what I have set forth in earlier seminars under the name of *Verwerfung* [repudiation, foreclosure].

Just as what is rejected from the symbolic register reappears in the real, in the same way the hole in the real that results from loss, sets the signifier in motion. This hole provides the place for the projection of the missing signifier, which is essential to the structure of the Other. This is the signifier whose absence leaves the Other incapable of responding to your question, the signifier that can be purchased only with your own flesh and your own blood, the signifier that is essentially the veiled phallus.

It is there that this signifier finds its place. Yet at the same time it cannot find it, for it can be articulated only at the level of the Other. It is at this point that, as in psychosis – this is where mourning and psychosis are related – that swarms of images, from which the phenomena of mourning arise, assume the place of the phallus: not only the phenomena in which each individual instance of madness manifests itself, but also those which attest to one or another of the most remarkable collective madnesses of the community of men, one example of which is brought to the fore in *Hamlet*, i.e., the ghost, that image which can catch the soul of one and all unawares when someone's departure from this life has not been accompanied by the rites that it calls for.

What are these rites, really, by which we fulfill our obligation to what is called the memory of the dead – if not the total mass intervention, from the heights of heaven to the depths of hell, of the entire play of the symbolic register. [...]

Indeed, there is nothing of significance that can fill that hole in the real, except the totality of the signifier.

[...]

Here we see a new dimension in the tragedy of *Hamlet*: it is a tragedy of the underworld. The ghost arises from an inexpiable offense. From this perspective, Ophelia appears as a victim offered in expiation of that primordial offense. The same holds for the murder of Polonius and the ridiculous dragging around of his body by the feet.

Hamlet then suddenly cuts loose and mocks everyone, proposing a series of riddles in particularly bad taste which culminates in the expression 'Hide fox, and all after,' a reference to a sort of game of hide-and-seek. Hamlet's hiding of this body in defiance of the concerned feelings of everyone around him, is here just another mockery of that which is of central importance: insufficient mourning.

[...]

Phallophany

[...]

The introduction and Parts 1 and 2 of this section are concerned with the theme of 'insufficient mourning' (the rites of mourning in the play having been cut short or performed in secret) and the implications beneath this of the crime – the killing of the father – which makes *Hamlet* an Oedipal drama. An account of differences between the play texts of *Oedipus* and *Hamlet* and of Freud's theory of the Oedipus complex leads Lacan to conclude that the Oedipus complex finds its resolution or 'goes into its decline in so far as the subject must mourn the phallus'. This he seeks to explore further in the play.

[...]

The ghost of Hamlet's father has an inexpiable grievance. He was, he says, eternally wronged, having been taken unawares – and this is not one of the lesser mysteries as to the meaning of this tragedy – 'in the blossoms of [his] sin.' He had no time before his death to summon up the composure or whatever that would have prepared him to go before the throne of judgment.

[...]

the 'something rotten' with which poor Hamlet is confronted is most closely connected with the position of the subject with regard to the phallus. And the phallus is everywhere present in the disorder in which we find Hamlet each time he approaches one of the crucial moments of his action.

There's something very strange in the way Hamlet speaks about his dead father, an exaltation and idealization of his dead father which comes down to something like this: Hamlet has no voice with which to say whatever he may have to say about him. He actually chokes up and finally concludes by saying – in a particular form of the signifier that is called 'pregnant' in English, referring to something that has a meaning beyond its meaning – that he can find nothing to say about his father except that he was like anyone else. What he means is very obviously the opposite. This is the first indication, the first trace, of what I want to talk about here.

Another trace is that the rejection, deprecation, contempt that he casts on Claudius has every appearance of *dénégation*. [Lacan's translation of Freud's term *Verneinung*, usually translated in English as 'negation.' Its use here suggests that Hamlet's hostile references to Claudius can be interpreted as indications of repressed admiration. *Translator's note*] The torrent of insults that he unleashes on Claudius – in the presence of his mother, namely – culminates in the phrase 'a king of shreds and patches.' We surely cannot fail to relate this to the fact that, in the tragedy of Hamlet, unlike that of Oedipus, after the murder of the father, the phallus is still there. It's there indeed, and it is precisely Claudius who is called upon to embody it.

Claudius' real phallus is always somewhere in the picture. What does Hamlet have to reproach his mother for, after all, if not for having filled herself with it? And with dejected arm and speech he sends her back to that fatal, fateful object, here real indeed, around which the play revolves.

For this woman – who doesn't seem to us so very different from other women, and who shows considerable human feelings – there must be something very strong that attaches her to her partner. And doesn't it seem that that is the point around which Hamlet's action turns and lingers? His astounded spirit, so to speak, trembles before something that is utterly unexpected: the phallus is located here in a position that is entirely out of place in terms of its position in the Oedipus complex. Here, the phallus to be struck at is real indeed. And Hamlet always stops. The very source of what makes Hamlet's arm waver at every moment, is the narcissistic connection that Freud tells us about in his text on the decline of the Oedipus complex: one cannot strike the phallus, because the phallus, even the real phallus, is a *ghost*.

[...]

The question at hand is the enigmatic manifestation of the signifier of power, of potency: the Oedipal situation, when it appears in the particularly striking form in the real that we have in *Hamlet*, with the criminal, the usurper, in place and functioning as usurper. What stays Hamlet's arm? It's not fear – he has nothing but contempt for the guy – it's because he knows that he must strike something other than what's there. Indeed, two minutes later, when he arrives at his mother's chamber and is beginning to give her all holy hell, he hears a noise behind the curtain, and he lunges out without looking first.

I don't recall now what astute commentator pointed out that Hamlet cannot possibly believe that it's Claudius, because he's just left him in the next room. Nevertheless, when he has disemboweled poor Polonius, he remarks: 'Thou wretched, rash, intruding fool..../ I took thee for thy better.' Everyone thinks that he meant to kill the king, but in the presence of Claudius, the real king and the usurper as well, he did after all hold back: he wanted something or someone better, wanted to cut him off, too, in the blossoms of his sin. Claudius, as he knelt there before him, wasn't quite what Hamlet was after – he wasn't the right one.

It's a question of the phallus, and that's why he will never be able to strike it, until the moment when he has made the complete sacrifice – without wanting to, moreover – of all narcissistic attachments, i.e., when he is mortally wounded and knows it. The thing is strange and obvious, recorded in all sorts of little riddles in Hamlet's style.

Polonius for him is merely a 'calf,' one that he has in some sense sacrificed to the spirit of his father. When he's stashed him under the stairs and everyone asks him what's going on, he goes into a few of his jokes, which are always so disconcerting for his adversaries. Everyone wonders whether what he says is really what he means, because what he says gets them all where they're the touchiest. But for him to say it, he must know so much that they can't believe it, and so on and so forth.

This is a position that must be quite familiar to us from the phenomenon of the avowal made by the subject. He speaks these words which up till now have remained as good as sealed to the commentators: 'The body is with the king' – he doesn't use the word 'corpse,' please notice – 'but the king is not with the body.' Replace the word 'king' with the word 'phallus,' and you'll see that that's exactly the point – the body is bound up [*engagé*] in this matter of the phallus – and how – but the phallus, on the contrary, is bound to nothing: it always slips through your fingers. [....]

> Hamlet: The king is a thing –
> Guildenstern: A thing, my lord?
> Hamlet: Of nothing.

1.3 ELAINE SHOWALTER: FROM 'REPRESENTING OPHELIA: WOMEN, MADNESS AND THE RESPONSIBILITIES OF FEMINIST CRITICISM' (1985)

Elaine Showalter is currently Professor of English at Princeton University. Her theory of 'gynocriticism', or women-centred writing, first announced in *A Literature of Their Own. British Women Novelists from Charlotte Brontë to Doris Lessing* (Virago, 1978, rev. edn, 1982) exerted a formative influence on Anglo-American feminist literary study. In this text, Showalter reveals and reappraises 'the lost continent of the female tradition' which she divides into 'feminine', 'feminist' and 'female' historical phases. Her campaigning interest is in the direct expression of female experience in female writing, an emphasis which is at odds with the poststructuralist and textualist orientation of French feminist theory (see *A Reader's Guide* 3/e, especially pp. 218–21). Showalter is the author of, amongst other works, *The Female Malady. Women, Madness and English Culture, 1830–1980* (1987) and *Sexual Anarchy. Gender and Culture at the Fin de Siècle* (1992), and the editor of *The New Feminist Criticism* (1986).

In her essay 'Representing Ophelia', Showalter takes issue at the outset with Lacan's treatment of the play, or, more precisely, with what she sees as his subordinating treatment of Ophelia as the exteriorized figuration of the phallus. For the most part, says Showalter, Ophelia has been neglected in criticism. At the same time her character has been used in popular and general culture to represent the figure of woman, or to imply an identification of woman with madness. She turns her attention therefore to this cultural history, presenting her account as an example of a 'responsible' feminist criticism. How does her approach relate to the main traditions of contemporary feminist theory and criticism (see *A Reader's Guide*, 3/e, Ch. 8, and Ch. 3, above) and how far does her discussion bear out her declared aims?

   This leads to a further question. Showalter writes that the representations of Ophelia 'have overflowed the text'. What does this mean for our reading of Ophelia the character in the play, and for our interpretations of the text of *Hamlet*? Does her discussion of the cultural representations of Ophelia pose an effective challenge, for example, to Lacan's interpretation of the character's symbolic role in the play (since it appears that Showalter means particularly to counter his interpretation)? Or is the implication of her essay that a new interpretation of the character *in the text* is not possible or not a priority for a responsible feminist criticism? Would you agree with this?

The following essay is taken from Patricia Parker and Geoffrey H. Hartman, eds, *Shakespeare and the Question of Theory* (Routledge, 1985), pp. 72–94.

Representing Ophelia: Women, Madness, and the Responsibilities of Feminist Criticism

'As a sort of a come-on, I announced that I would speak today about that piece of bait named Ophelia, and I'll be as good as my word.' These are the words which begin the psychoanalytic seminar on *Hamlet* presented in Paris in 1959 by Jacques Lacan. But despite his promising come-on, Lacan was *not* as good as his word. He goes on for some forty-one pages to speak about Hamlet, and when he does mention Ophelia, she is merely what Lacan calls 'the object Ophelia' – that is, the object of Hamlet's male desire. The etymology of Ophelia, Lacan asserts, is 'O-phallus,' and her role in the drama can only be to function as the exteriorised figuration of what Lacan predictably and, in view of his own early work with psychotic women, disappointingly suggests is the phallus as transcendental signifier.[1] To play such a part obviously makes Ophelia 'essential', as Lacan admits; but only because, in his words, 'she is linked forever, for centuries, to the figure of Hamlet'.

The bait-and-switch game that Lacan plays with Ophelia is a cynical but not unusual instance of her deployment in psychiatric and critical texts. For most critics of Shakespeare, Ophelia has been an insignificant minor character in the play, touching in her weakness and madness but chiefly interesting, of course, in what she tells us about Hamlet. And while female readers of Shakespeare have often attempted to champion Ophelia, even feminist critics have done so with a certain embarrassment. As Annette Kolodny ruefully admits: 'it is after all, an imposition of high order to ask the viewer to attend to Ophelia's sufferings in a scene where, before, he's always so comfortably kept his eye fixed on Hamlet.'[2]

Yet when feminist criticism allows Ophelia to upstage Hamlet, it also brings to the foreground the issues in an ongoing theoretical debate about the cultural links between femininity, female sexuality, insanity, and representation. Though she is neglected in criticism, Ophelia is probably the most frequently illustrated and cited of Shakespeare's heroines. Her visibility as a subject in literature, popular culture, and painting, from Redon who paints her drowning, to Bob Dylan, who places her on Desolation Row, to Cannon Mills, which has named a flowery sheet pattern after her, is in inverse relation to her invisibility in Shakespearean critical texts. Why has she been such a potent and obsessive figure in our cultural mythology? Insofar as Hamlet names Ophelia as 'woman' and 'frailty', substituting an ideological view of femininity for a personal one, is she indeed representative of Woman, and does her madness stand for the oppression of women in society as well as in tragedy? Furthermore, since Laertes calls Ophelia a 'document in madness', does she represent the textual archetype of woman *as* madness or madness *as* woman? And finally, how should feminist criticism represent Ophelia in its own discourse? What is our responsibility towards her as character and as woman?

Feminist critics have offered a variety of responses to these questions. Some have maintained that we should represent Ophelia as a lawyer represents a client, that we should become her Horatia, in this harsh world reporting her and her cause aright to the unsatisfied. Carol Neely, for example, describes advocacy – speaking *for* Ophelia – as our proper role: 'As a feminist critic,' she writes, 'I must "tell" Ophelia's story.'[3] But what can we mean by Ophelia's story? The story of her life? The story of her betrayal at the hands of her father, brother, lover, court, society? The story of her rejection and marginalisation by male critics of Shakespeare? Shakespeare gives us very little information from which to imagine a past for Ophelia. She appears in only five of the play's twenty scenes; the pre-play course of her love story with Hamlet is known only by a few ambiguous flashbacks. Her tragedy is subordinated in the play; unlike Hamlet, she does not struggle with moral choices or alternatives. Thus another feminist critic, Lee Edwards, concludes that it is impossible to reconstruct Ophelia's biography from the text: 'We can imagine Hamlet's story without Ophelia, but Ophelia literally has no story without Hamlet.'[4]

If we turn from American to French feminist theory, Ophelia might confirm the impossibility of representing the feminine in patriarchal discourse as other than madness, incoherence, fluidity, or silence. In French theoretical patriarchal language and symbolism, it remains on the side of negativity, absence, and lack. In comparison to Hamlet, Ophelia is certainly a creature of lack. 'I think nothing, my lord,' she tells him in the Mousetrap scene, and he cruelly twists her words:

Hamlet: That's a fair thought to lie between maids' legs.
Ophelia: What is, my lord?
Hamlet: Nothing.

(III.ii.117–19)

In Elizabethan slang, 'nothing' was a term for the female genitalia, as in *Much Ado About Nothing*. To Hamlet, then, 'nothing' is what lies between maids' legs, for, in the male visual system of representation and desire, women's sexual organs, in the words of the French psychoanalyst Luce Irigaray, 'represent the horror of having nothing to see'.[5] When Ophelia is mad, Gertrude says that 'Her speech is nothing', mere 'unshaped use'. Ophelia's speech thus represents the horror of having nothing to say in the public terms defined by the court. Deprived of thought, sexuality, language, Ophelia's story becomes the Story of O – the zero, the empty circle or mystery of feminine difference, the cipher of female sexuality to be deciphered by feminist interpretation.[6]

A third approach would be to read Ophelia's story as the female subtext of the tragedy, the repressed story of Hamlet. In this reading, Ophelia represents the strong emotions that the Elizabethans as well as the Freudians thought womanish and unmanly. When Laertes weeps for his dead sister he says of his tears that 'When these are gone,/The woman will be out' – that is to say, that the feminine and shameful part of his nature will be purged. According to David Leverenz, in an important essay called 'The Woman in *Hamlet*', Hamlet's disgust at the feminine passivity in himself is translated into violent revulsion against women, and into his brutal behaviour towards Ophelia. Ophelia's suicide, Leverenz argues, then becomes 'a microcosm of the male world's banishment of the female, because "woman" represents everything denied by reasonable men'.[7]

It is perhaps because Hamlet's emotional vulnerability can so readily be conceptualised as feminine that this is the only heroic male role in Shakespeare which has been regularly acted by women, in a tradition from Sarah Bernhardt to, most recently, Diane Venora, in a production directed by Joseph Papp. Leopold Bloom speculates on this tradition in *Ulysses*, musing on the Hamlet of the actress Mrs Bandman Palmer: 'Male impersonator. Perhaps he was a woman? Why Ophelia committed suicide?'[8]

While all of these approaches have much to recommend them, each also presents critical problems. To liberate Ophelia from the text, or to make her its tragic centre, is to re-appropriate her for our own ends; to dissolve her into a female symbolism of absence is to endorse our own marginality; to make her Hamlet's anima is to reduce her to a metaphor of male experience. I would like to propose instead that Ophelia *does* have a story of her own that feminist criticism can tell; it is neither her life story, nor her love story, nor Lacan's story, but rather the *history* of her representation. This essay tries to bring together some of the categories of French feminist thought about the 'feminine' with the empirical energies of American historical and critical research: to yoke French theory and Yankee knowhow.

Tracing the iconography of Ophelia in English and French painting, photography, psychiatry, and literature, as well as in theatrical production, I will be showing first of all the representational bonds between female insanity and female sexuality. Secondly, I want to demonstrate the two-way transaction between psychiatric theory and cultural representation. As one medical historian has observed, we could provide a manual of female insanity by chronicling the illustrations of Ophelia; this is so because the illustrations of Ophelia have played a major role in the theoretical construction of female insanity.[9] Finally, I want to suggest that the feminist revision of Ophelia comes as much from the actress's freedom as from the critic's interpretation.[10] When Shakespeare's heroines began to be played by women instead of boys, the presence of the female body and female voice, quite apart from details of interpretation, created new meanings and subversive tensions in these roles, and perhaps most importantly with Ophelia. Looking at Ophelia's history on and off the stage, I will point out the contest between male and female representations of Ophelia, cycles of critical repression and feminist reclamation of which contemporary feminist criticism is only the most recent phase. By beginning with these data from cultural history, instead of moving from the grid of literary theory, I hope to conclude with a fuller sense of the responsibilities of feminist criticism, as well as a new perspective on Ophelia.

'Of all the characters in *Hamlet*,' Bridget Lyons has pointed out, 'Ophelia is most persistently presented in terms of symbolic meanings.'[11] Her behaviour, her appearance, her gestures, her costume, her props, are freighted with emblematic significance, and for many generations of Shakespearean critics her part in the play has seemed to be primarily iconographic. Ophelia's symbolic meanings, moreover, are specifically feminine. Whereas for Hamlet madness is metaphysical, linked with culture, for Ophelia it is a product of the female body and female nature, perhaps that nature's purest form. On the Elizabethan stage, the conventions of female insanity were sharply defined. Ophelia dresses in white, decks herself with 'fantastical garlands' of wild flowers, and enters, according to the stage directions of the 'Bad' Quarto, 'distracted' playing on a lute with her 'hair down singing'. Her speeches are marked by extravagant metaphors, lyrical free associations, and 'explosive sexual imagery'.[12] She sings wistful and bawdy ballads, and ends her life by drowning.

All of these conventions carry specific messages about femininity and sexuality. Ophelia's virginal and vacant white is contrasted with Hamlet's scholar's garb, his 'suits of solemn black'. Her flowers suggest the discordant double images of female sexuality as both innocent blossoming and whorish contamination; she is the 'green girl' of pastoral, the virginal 'Rose of May' and the sexually explicit madwoman who, in giving away her wild flowers and herbs, is symbolically deflowering herself. The 'weedy trophies' and phallic 'long purples' which she wears to her death intimate an improper and discordant sexuality that Gertrude's lovely elegy cannot quite obscure.[13] In Elizabethan and Jacobean drama, the stage direction that a woman enters with dishevelled hair indicates that she might either be mad or the victim of a rape; the disordered hair, her offence against decorum, suggests sensuality in each case.[14] The mad Ophelia's bawdy songs and verbal licence, while they give her access to 'an entirely different range of experience' from what she is allowed as the dutiful daughter, seem to be her one sanctioned form of self-assertion as a woman, quickly followed, as if in retribution, by her death.[15]

Drowning too was associated with the feminine, with female fluidity as opposed to masculine aridity. In his discussion of the 'Ophelia complex', the phenomenologist Gaston Bachelard traces the symbolic connections between women, water, and death. Drowning, he suggests, becomes the truly feminine death in the dramas of literature and life, one which is a beautiful immersion and submersion in the female element. Water is the profound and organic symbol of the liquid woman whose eyes are so easily drowned in tears, as her body is the repository of blood, amniotic fluid, and milk. A man contemplating this feminine suicide understands it by reaching for what is feminine in himself, like Laertes, by a temporary surrender to his own fluidity – that is, his tears; and he becomes a man again in becoming once more dry – when his tears are stopped.[16]

Clinically speaking, Ophelia's behaviour and appearance are characteristic of the malady the Elizabethans would have diagnosed as female love-melancholy, or erotomania. From about 1580, melancholy had become a fashionable disease among young men, especially in London, and Hamlet himself is a prototype of the melancholy hero. Yet the epidemic of melancholy associated with intellectual and imaginative genius 'curiously bypassed women'. Women's melancholy was seen instead as biological, and emotional in origins.[17]

On the stage, Ophelia's madness was presented as the predictable outcome of erotomania. From 1660, when women first appeared on the public stage, to the beginnings of the eighteenth century, the most celebrated of the actresses who played Ophelia were those whom rumour credited with disappointments in love. The greatest triumph was reserved for Susan Mountfort, a former actress at Lincoln's Inn Fields who had gone mad after her lover's betrayal. One night in 1720 she escaped from her keeper, rushed to the theatre, and just as the Ophelia of the evening was to enter for her mad scene, 'sprang forward in her place ... with wild eyes and wavering motion'.[18] As a contemporary reported, 'she was in truth *Ophelia herself*, to the amazement of the performers as well as of the audience—nature having made this last effort, her vital powers failed her and she died soon after'.[19] These theatrical legends reinforced the belief of the age that female madness was a part of female nature, less to be intimidated by an actress than demonstrated by a deranged woman in a performance of her emotions.

The subversive or violent possibilities of the mad scene were nearly eliminated, however, on the eighteenth-century stage. Late Augustan stereotypes of female love-melancholy were sentimentalised versions which minimised the force of female sexuality, and made female insanity a pretty stimulant to male sensibility. Actresses such as Mrs Lessingham in 1772, and Mary Bolton in 1811, played Ophelia in this decorous style, relying on the familiar images of the white dress, loose hair, and wild flowers to convey a polite feminine distraction, highly suitable for pictorial reproduction, and appropriate for Samuel Johnson's description of Ophelia as young, beautiful, harmless, and pious. Even Mrs Siddons in 1785 played the mad scene with stately and classical dignity. For much of the period, in fact, Augustan objections to the levity and indecency of Ophelia's language and behaviour led to censorship of the part. Her lines were frequently cut, and the role was often assigned to a singer instead of an actress, making the mode of representation musical rather than visual or verbal.

But whereas the Augustan response to madness was a denial, the romantic response was an embrace.[20] The figure of the madwoman permeates romantic literature, from the gothic novelists to Wordsworth and Scott in such texts as 'The Thorn' and *The Heart of Midlothian*, where she stands for sexual victimisation, bereavement, and thrilling emotional extremity. Romantic artists such as Thomas Barker and George Shepheard painted pathetically abandoned Crazy Kates and Crazy Anns, while Henry Fuseli's 'Mad Kate' is almost demonically possessed, an orphan of the romantic storm.

In the Shakespearean theatre, Ophelia's romantic revival began in France rather than England. When Charles Kemble made his Paris debut as Hamlet with an English troupe in 1827, his Ophelia was a young Irish ingénue named Harriet Smithson. Smithson used 'her extensive command of mime to depict in precise gesture the state of Ophelia's confused mind'.[21] In the mad scene, she entered in a long black veil, suggesting the standard imagery of female sexual mystery in the gothic novel, with scattered bedlamish wisps of straw in her hair. Spreading the veil on the ground as she sang, she spread flowers upon it in the shape of a cross, as if to make her father's grave, and mimed a burial, a piece of stage business which remained in vogue for the rest of the century.

The French audiences were stunned. Dumas recalled that 'it was the first time I saw in the theatre real passions, giving life to men and women of flesh and blood'.[22] The twenty-three-year-old Hector Berlioz, who was in the audience on the first night, fell madly in love, and eventually married Harriet Smithson despite his family's frantic opposition. Her image as the mad Ophelia was represented in popular lithographs and exhibited in bookshop and printshop windows. Her costume was imitated by the fashionable, and a coiffure 'à la folle', consisting of a 'black veil with wisps of straw tastefully interwoven' in the hair, was widely copied by the Parisian beau monde, always on the lookout for something new.[23]

[...]

Showalter comments on the influence of the 'romantic Ophelia' upon acting styles and as an image to be *looked* at.

[...]

Smithson's performance is best recaptured in a series of pictures done by Delacroix from 1830 to 1850, which show a strong romantic interest in the relation or female sexuality and insanity.[24] The most innovative and influential of De-lacroix's lithographs is *La Mort d'Ophélie* of 1843, the first of three studies. Its sensual languor, with Ophelia half-suspended in the stream as her dress slips from her body, anticipated the fascination with the erotic trance of the hysteric as it would be studied by Jean-Martin Charcot and his students, including Janet and Freud. Delacroix's interest in the drowning Ophelia is also reproduced to the point of obsession in later nineteenth-century painting. The English Pre-Raphaelites painted her again and again, choosing the drowning which is only described in the play, and where no actress's image had preceded them or interfered with their imaginative supremacy.

In the Royal Academy show of 1852, Arthur Hughes's entry shows a tiny waif-like creature – a sort of Tinker Bell Ophelia – in a filmy white gown, perched on a tree trunk by the stream. The overall effect is softened, sexless, and hazy, although the straw in her hair resembles a crown of thorns. Hughes's juxtaposition of childlike femininity and Christian martyrdom was overpowered, however, by John Everett Millais's great painting of Ophelia in the same show. While Millais's Ophelia is sensuous siren as well as victim, the artist rather than the subject dominates the scene. The division of space between Ophelia and the natural details Millais had so painstakingly pursued reduces her to one more visual object; and the painting had such a hard surface, strangely flattened perspective, and brilliant light that it seems cruelly indifferent to the woman's death.

These Pre-Raphaelite images were part of a new and intricate traffic between images of women and madness in late nineteenth-century literature, psychiatry, drama, and art. First of all, superintendents of Victorian lunatic asylums were also enthusiasts of Shakespeare, who turned to his dramas for models of mental aberration that could be applied to their clinical practice. The case study of Ophelia was one that seemed particularly useful as an account of hysteria or mental breakdown in adolescence, a period of sexual instability which the Victorians regarded as risky for women's mental health. As Dr John Charles Bucknill, president of the Medico-Psychological Association, remarked in 1859, 'Ophelia is the very type of a class of cases by no means uncommon. Every mental physician of moderately extensive experience must have seen many Ophelias. It is a copy from nature, after the fashion of the Pre-Raphaelite school'.[25]

[...]

In following passages Showalter finds supporting evidence of the above in medical textbooks, the *Study of Hamlet* (1863) by John Conolly, superintendent of the Hanwell Asylum, the photographs of female asylum patients by Dr Hugh Welch Diamond and Jean-Martin Charcot.

[...]

the iconography of the romantic Ophelia had begun to infiltrate reality, to define a style for mad young women seeking to express and communicate their distress. [...]

But if the Victorian madwoman looks mutely out from men's pictures, and acts a part men had staged and directed, she is very differently represented in the feminist revision of Ophelia initiated by newly powerful and respectable Victorian actresses, and by women critics of Shakespeare. In their efforts to defend Ophelia they invent a story for her drawn from their own experiences, grievances, and desires.

[...]

Showalter instances the 'feminist revision' of the Ophelia story as told in Mary Cowden Clarke's fictitious *The Girlhood of Shakespeare's Heroines* (1852).

[...]

On the Victorian stage, it was Ellen Terry, daring and unconventional in her own life, who led the way in acting Ophelia in feminist terms as a consistent psychological study in sexual intimidation, a girl terrified of her father, of her lover, and of life itself. Terry's debut as Ophelia in Henry Irving's production in 1878 was a landmark. According to one reviewer, her Ophelia was 'the terrible spectacle of a normal girl becoming hopelessly imbecile as the result of overwhelming mental agony. Hers was an insanity without wrath or rage, without exaltation or paroxysms'.[26] Her 'poetic and intellectual performance' also inspired other actresses to rebel against the conventions of invisibility and negation associated with the part.

Terry was the first to challenge the tradition of Ophelia's dressing in emblematic white. For the French poets, such as Rimbaud, Hugo, Musset, Mallarmé and Laforgue, whiteness was part of Ophelia's essential feminine symbolism; they call her '*blanche Ophélia*' and compare her to a lily, a cloud, or snow. Yet whiteness also made her a transparency, an absence that took on the colours of Hamlet's moods, and that, for the symbolists like Mallarmé, made her a blank page to be written over or on by the male imagination. Although Irving was able to prevent Terry from wearing black in the mad scene, exclaiming, 'My God, Madam, there must be only *one* black figure in this play, and that's Hamlet!' (Irving, of course, was playing Hamlet), nonetheless actresses such as Gertrude Eliot, Helen Maude, Nora de Silva, and in Russia Vera Komisarjevskaya, gradually won the right to intensify Ophelia's presence by clothing her in Hamlet's black.[27]

By the turn of the century, there was both a male and a female discourse on Ophelia. A. C. Bradley spoke for the Victorian male tradition when he noted in *Shakespearean Tragedy* (1906) that 'a large number of readers feel a kind of personal irritation against Ophelia; they seem unable to forgive her for not having been a heroine'.[28] The feminist counterview was represented by actresses in works such as Helena Faucit's study of Shakespeare's female characters, and *The True Ophelia*, written by an anonymous actress in 1914, which protested against the 'insipid little creature' of criticism, and advocated a strong and intelligent woman destroyed by the heartlessness of men.[29] In women's paintings of the *fin de siècle* as well, Ophelia is depicted as an inspiring, even sanctified emblem of righteousness.[30]

While the widely read and influential essays of Mary Cowden Clarke are now mocked as the epitome of naive criticism, these Victorian studies of the girlhood of Shakespeare's heroines are of course alive and well as psychoanalytic criticism, which has imagined its own prehistories of oedipal conflict and neurotic fixation; and I say this not to mock psychoanalytic criticism, but to suggest that Clarke's musings on Ophelia are a pre-Freudian speculation on the traumatic sources of a female sexual identity. The Freudian interpretation of *Hamlet* concentrated on the hero, but also had much to do with the re-sexualisation of Ophelia. As early as 1900, Freud had traced Hamlet's irresolution to an Oedipus complex, and Ernest Jones, his leading British disciple, developed this view, influencing the performances of John Gielgud and Alec Guinness in the 1930s. In his final version of the study, *Hamlet and Oedipus*, published in 1949, Jones argued that 'Ophelia should be unmistakably sensual, as she seldom is on stage. She may be "innocent" and docile, but she is very aware of her body'.[31]

In the theatre and in criticism, this Freudian edict has produced such extreme readings as that Shakespeare intends us to see Ophelia as a loose woman, and that she has been sleeping with Hamlet.

[...]

The most extreme Freudian interpretation reads *Hamlet* as two parallel male and female psychodramas, the counterpointed stories of the incestuous attachments of Hamlet and Ophelia. As Theodor Lidz presents this view, while Hamlet is neurotically attached to his mother, Ophelia has an unresolved oedipal attachment to her father. She has fantasies of a lover who will abduct her from or even kill her father, and when this actually happens, her reason is destroyed by guilt as well as by lingering incestuous feelings. According to Lidz, Ophelia breaks down because she fails in the female developmental task of shifting her sexual attachment from her father 'to a man who can bring her fulfillment as a woman'.[32] We see the effects of this Freudian Ophelia on stage productions since the 1950s, where directors have hinted at an incestuous link between Ophelia and Laertes. Trevor Nunn's production with Helen Mirren in 1970, for example, made Ophelia and Laertes flirtatious doubles, almost twins in their matching fur-trimmed doublets, playing duets on the lute with Polonius looking on, like Peter, Paul, and Mary. In other productions of the same period, Marianne Faithfull was a haggard Ophelia equally attracted to Hamlet and Laertes, and, in one of the few performances directed by a woman, Yvonne Nicholson sat on Laertes' lap in the advice scene, and played the part with 'rough sexual bravado'.[33]

Since the 1960s, the Freudian representation of Ophelia has been supplemented by an antipsychiatry that represents Ophelia's madness in more contemporary terms. In contrast to the psychoanalytic representation of Ophelia's sexual unconscious that connected her essential femininity to Freud's essays on female sexuality and hysteria, her madness is now seen in medical and biochemical terms, as schizophrenia. This is so in part because the schizophrenic woman has become the cultural icon of dualistic femininity in the mid-twentieth century as the erotomaniac was in the seventeenth and the hysteric in the nineteenth. It might also be traced to the work of R. D. Laing on female schizophrenia in the 1960s. Laing argued that schizophrenia was an intelligible response to the experience of invalidation within the family network, especially to the conflicting emotional messages and mystifying double binds experienced by daughters. Ophelia, he noted in *The Divided Self*, is an empty space. 'In her madness there is no one there. ... There is no integral selfhood expressed through her actions or utterances. Incomprehensible statements are said by nothing. She has already died. There is now only a vacuum where there was once a person.'[34]

Despite his sympathy for Ophelia, Laing's readings silence her, equate her with 'nothing', more completely than any since the Augustans; and they have been translated into performances which only make Ophelia a graphic study of mental pathology. The sickest Ophelias on the contemporary stage have been those in the productions of the pathologist-director Jonathan Miller. In 1974 at the Greenwich Theatre his Ophelia sucked her thumb; by 1981, at the Warehouse in London, she was played by an actress much taller and heavier than the Hamlet (perhaps punningly cast as the young actor Anton Lesser). She began the play with a set of nervous tics and tuggings of hair which by the mad scene had become a full set of schizophrenic routines – head banging, twitching, wincing, grimacing, and drooling.[35]

But since the 1970s too we have had a feminist discourse which has offered a new perspective on Ophelia's madness as protest and rebellion. For many feminist theorists, the madwoman is a heroine, a powerful figure who rebels against the family and the social order; and the hysteric who refuses to speak the language of the patriarchal order, who speaks otherwise, is a sister.[36] In terms of effect on the theatre, the most radical application of these ideas was probably realised in Melissa Murray's agitprop play *Ophelia*, written in 1979 for the English women's theatre group 'Hormone Imbalance'. In this blank verse retelling of the Hamlet story, Ophelia becomes a lesbian and runs off with a woman servant to join a guerrilla commune.[37]

While I've always regretted that I missed this production, I can't proclaim that this defiant ideological gesture, however effective politically or theatrically, is all that feminist criticism desires, or all to which it should aspire. When feminist criticism chooses to deal with representation, rather than with women's writing, it must aim for a maximum interdisciplinary contextualism, in which the complexity of attitudes towards the feminine can be analysed in their fullest cultural and historical frame. The alternation of strong and weak Ophelias on the stage, virginal and seductive Ophelias in art, inadequate or oppressed Ophelias in criticism, tells us how the representations have overflowed the text, and how they have reflected the ideological character of their times, erupting as debates between dominant and feminist views in periods of gender crisis and redefinition. The representation of Ophelia changes independently of theories of the meaning of the play or the Prince, for it depends on attitudes towards women and madness. The decorous and pious Ophelia of the Augustan age and the postmodern schizophrenic heroine who might have stepped from the pages of Laing can be derived from the same figure; they are both contradictory and complementary images of female sexuality in which madness seems to act as the 'switching-point, the concept which allows the co-existence of both sides of the representation'.[38] There is no 'true' Ophelia for whom feminist criticism must unambiguously speak, but perhaps only a Cubist Ophelia of multiple perspectives, more than the sum of all her parts.

But in exposing the ideology of representation, feminist critics have also the responsibility to acknowledge and to examine the boundaries of our own ideological positions as products of our gender and our time. A degree of humility in an age of critical hubris can be our greatest strength, for it is by occupying this position of historical self-consciousness in both feminism and criticism that we maintain our credibility in representing Ophelia, and that, unlike Lacan, when we promise to speak about her, we make good our word.

Notes (cut and renumbered)

1. Jacques Lacan, 'Desire and the interpretation of desire in *Hamlet*', in *Literature and Psychoanalysis: The Question of Reading: Otherwise*, ed. Shoshana Felman (Baltimore, 1982), pp. 11, 20, 23. Lacan is also wrong about the etymology of Ophelia, which probably derives from the Greek for 'help' or 'succour'. Charlotte M. Yonge suggested a derivation from 'ophis', 'serpent'. See her *History of Christian Names* (1884, republished Chicago, 1966), pp. 346–7. I am indebted to Walter Jackson Bate for this reference.
2. Annette Kolodny, 'Dancing through the minefield: some observations on the theory, practice, and politics of feminist literary criticism' (*Feminist Studies*, 6, (1980)), p. 7.
3. Carol Neely, 'Feminist modes of Shakespearean criticism' (*Women's Studies*, 9 (1981)), p. 11.
4. Lee Edwards, 'The labors of Psyche' (*Critical Inquiry*, 6 (1979)), p. 36.
5. Luce Irigaray: see *New French Feminisms*, ed. Elaine Marks and Isabelle de Courtivron (New York, 1982), p. 101. The quotation above, from III. ii, is taken from the Arden Shakespeare, *Hamlet*, ed. Harold Jenkins (London and New York, 1982), p. 295. All quotations from *Hamlet* are from this text.
6. On images of negation and feminine enclosure, see David Wilbern, 'Shakespeare's "nothing"', in *Representing Shakespeare: New Psychoanalytic Essays*, ed. Murray M. Schwartz and Coppélia Kahn (Baltimore, 1981).
7. David Leverenz, 'The woman in *Hamlet*: an interpersonal view' (*Signs*, 4 (1978)), p. 303.
8. James Joyce, *Ulysses* (New York, 1961) p. 76.
9. Sander L. Gilman, *Seeing the Insane* (New York, 1981), p. 126.
10. See Michael Goldman, *The Actor's Freedom: Toward a Theory of Drama* (New York, 1975), for a stimulating discussion of the interpretative interaction between actor and audience.
11. Bridget Lyons, 'The iconography of Ophelia' (*English Literary History*, 44 (1977)), p. 61.
12. See Maurice and Hanna Charney, 'The language of Shakespeare's madwomen' (*Signs*, 3 (1977)), pp. 451, 457; and Carroll Camden, 'On Ophelia's madness' (*Shakespeare Quarterly* (1964)), p. 254.
13. See Margery Garber, *Coming of Age in Shakespeare* (London, 1981), 155–7; and Lyons, op. cit. pp. 65, 70–2.
14. On dishevelled hair as a signifier of madness or rape, see Charney and Charney, op. cit., pp. 452–3, 457; and Allan Dessen, *Elizabethan Stage Conventions and Modern Interpreters* (Cambridge, 1984), pp. 36–8. Thanks to Allan Dessen for letting me see advance proofs of his book.
15. Charney and Charney, op. cit., p. 456.
16. Gaston Bachelard, *L'Eau et les rêves* (Paris, 1942) pp. 109–25. See also Brigitte Peucker, 'Dröste-Hulshof's Ophelia and the recovery of voice' (*The Journal of English and Germanic Philology* (1983)), pp. 374–91.
17. Vieda Skultans, *English Madness: Ideas on Insanity 1580–1890* (London 1977), pp. 79–81. On historical cases of love-melancholy, see Michael MacDonald, *Mystical Bedlam* (Cambridge, 1982).
18. C. E. L. Wingate, *Shakespeare's Heroines on the Stage* (New York, 1895), pp. 283–4, 288–9.
19. Charles Hiatt, *Ellen Terry* (London, 1898), p. 11.

20. Max Byrd, *Visits to Bedlam: Madness and Literature in the Eighteenth Century* (Columbia, 1974), p. xiv.
21. Peter Raby, *Fair-Ophelia: Harriet Smithson Berlioz* (Cambridge, 1982), p. 63.
22. Ibid., p. 68.
23. Ibid., pp. 72, 75.
24. Ibid., p. 182.
25. J. C. Bucknill, *The Psychology of Shakespeare* (London, 1859, reprinted New York, 1970) p. 110. For more extensive discussions of Victorian psychiatry and Ophelia figures, see Elaine Showalter, *The Female Malady: Women, Madness and English Culture* (New York, 1985).
26. Hiatt, op. cit., p. 114. See also Wingate, op. cit. pp. 304–5.
27. Terry, op cit., pp. 155–6.
28. Andrew C. Bradley, *Shakespearean Tragedy* (London, 1906), p. 160.
29. Helena Faucit Martin, *On Some of Shakespeare's Female Characters* (Edinburgh and London, 1891), pp. 4, 18; and *The True Ophelia* (New York, 1914), p. 15.
30. Among these paintings are the Ophelias of Henrietta Rae and Mrs F. Littler. Sarah Bernhardt sculpted a bas relief of Ophelia for the Women's Pavilion at the Chicago World's Fair in 1893.
31. Ernest Jones, *Hamlet and Oedipus* (New York, 1949), p. 139.
32. Theodor Lidz, *Hamlet's Enemy: Madness and Myth in Hamlet* (New York, 1975), pp. 88, 113.
33. Richard David, *Shakespeare in the Theatre* (Cambridge, 1978), p. 75. This was the production directed by Buzz Goodbody, a brilliant young feminist radical who killed herself that year. See Colin Chambers, *Other Spaces: New Theatre and the RSC* (London, 1980), especially pp. 63–7.
34. R. D. Laing, *The Divided Self* (Harmondsworth, 1965), p. 195n.
35. David, op. cit. pp. 82–3; thanks to Marianne DeKoven, Rutgers University, for the description of the 1981 Warehouse production.
36. See, for example, Hélène Cixous and Catherine Clément, *La Jeune Née* (Paris, 1975).
37. For an account of this production, see Micheline Wandor, *Understudies: Theatre and Sexual Politics* (London, 1981), p. 47.
38. I am indebted for this formulation to a critique of my earlier draft of this paper by Carl Friedman, at the Wesleyan Center for the Humanities, April 1984.

1.4 JACQUELINE ROSE: FROM 'HAMLET – THE "MONA LISA" OF LITERATURE' (1986)

Jacqueline Rose is Professor of English at Queen Mary and Westfield College, University of London. She is the author of, amongst other works, *The Case of Peter Pan, or The Impossibility of Children's Fiction* (1984), *Sexuality in the Field of Vision* (1986) and *The Haunting of Sylvia Plath* (1991), and editor with Juliet Mitchell of *Feminine Sexuality. Jacques Lacan and the Ecole Freudienne* (1982).

In her essay, Rose points to the unnoticed issue of femininity in T. S. Eliot's discussion of Hamlet's emotions and in the play itself (which Eliot terms revealingly 'the "Mona Lisa" of literature'). She links this with the focus upon women in psychoanalytic criticism generally and in criticism of this play in particular, notably in the interpretation by Ernest Jones.

Eliot had argued that Shakespeare had tackled a problem which was too much for him, but concluded that the reasons for his failure were inexpressible or unknowable. Rose suggests this 'unknowable' (if imperfect) cause is the repressed feminine; or, more precisely, female sexuality, represented by the figure of the mother who engenders both desire and violence. The enigmatic and unacknowledged feminine returns, she argues, to trouble the 'literary super-ego': the cultural order represented by the tradition, or canon, in which Eliot and *Hamlet* have an otherwise secure place.

Rose's essay poses some very interesting questions both in relation to Eliot's (and Ernest Jones') view of the play and the other essays presented in this selection. Here we raise just two points. First, 'femininity' is represented in Rose's essay by the figure of the mother. Does her argument extend, however, to the figure of Ophelia (whom Rose does not mention); and do the essays by Lacan and Showalter suggest, in their different ways, how Ophelia can be related to this theme? Second, Rose suggests that Eliot ties 'the enigma of femininity to the problem of interpretation itself' (p. 45, below). Clearly 'femininity' and 'interpretation' are closely linked in Rose's own reading, but what interpretation or judgement of the play emerges from her essay? Does she agree with Eliot that it is a 'failure', though an example too, in her view, of the repressive order of the tradition? Or does her reading suggest that Eliot's judgement can be turned around and the play seen as unsettling that tradition, as a drama whose 'fascination … even strength', in her words, brings us to reflect differently on the relation between 'aesthetic form and sexual difference'? What value, in other words, does she ascribe to the play?

The following discussion is taken from *Sexuality in the Field of Vision* (Verso, 1986), pp. 123–40.

Hamlet – the 'Mona Lisa' of Literature

It does not seem to have been pointed out that T. S. Eliot's famous concept of the 'objective correlative', which has been so influential in the assessment of literature and its values, was originally put forward in 1919 in the form of a reproach against the character of a woman. The woman in question is Gertrude in Shakespeare's *Hamlet*, and the reproach Eliot makes is that she is not good enough aesthetically, that is, *bad* enough psychologically, which means that in relationship to the affect which she generates by her behaviour in the chief character of the drama – Hamlet himself – Gertrude is not deemed a sufficient *cause*.

The question of femininity clearly underpins this central, if not indeed *the* central, concept of Eliot's aesthetic theory, and this is confirmed by the fact that Eliot again uses an image of femininity – and by no means one of the most straightforward in its own representation or in the responses it has produced – to give us the measure of the consequent failure of the play. *Hamlet* the play, Eliot writes, is 'the Mona Lisa of literature',[1] offering up in its essentially enigmatic and indecipherable nature something of that maimed or imperfect quality of appeal which characterises Leonardo's famous painting. The aesthetic inadequacy of the play is caused by the figure of a woman, and the image of a woman most aptly embodies the consequences of that failure. Femininity thus becomes the stake, not only of the internal, but also of the critical drama generated by the play.

Equally important, however, is the fact that femininity has been at the heart of the psychoanalytic approach to *Hamlet*, from Ernest Jones onwards – a fact which has again been overlooked by those who have arrested their attention at the famous Oedipal saga for which his reading of the play is best known. 'Hamlet was a woman'[2] is just one of the statements about *Hamlet* which Jones quotes as indicating the place of the 'feminine' in a drama which has paradoxically been celebrated as the birth of the modern, post-Renaissance, conception of man. In this essay, I will try to focus what I see as the centrality of this question of femininity to an aesthetic theory which has crucially influenced a whole tradition of how we conceptualise literary writing, and to the psychoanalytic theory which was being elaborated at exactly the same time, at the point where they converge on the same object – Shakespeare's *Hamlet* – described by Freud as an emblem of 'the secular advance of repression in the emotional life of mankind'.[3]

I

To start with T. S. Eliot's critique of Hamlet. T. S. Eliot in fact sees his reading of the play as a move away from psychological approaches to *Hamlet* which concentrate too much on the characters to the exclusion of the play itself: '*Hamlet* the play is the primary problem, and Hamlet the character only secondary'.[4] Eliot therefore makes it clear that what he has to say exceeds the fact of the dramatis personae and strikes at the heart of aesthetic form itself. The problem with *Hamlet* is that there is something in the play which is formally or aesthetically unmanageable: 'like the *Sonnets*' (another work by Shakespeare in which a question of sexual ambivalence has always been recognised) '*Hamlet* is full of some stuff that the writer could not drag to light, contemplate, or manipulate into art'.[5] Eliot then describes the conditions, as he sees it, of that in which *Hamlet* fails – the successful manipulation of matter into artistic form. It is here that he produces the concept of the 'objective correlative' for the first time: 'The only way of expressing emotion in the form of art is by finding an "objective correlative"; in other words, a set of objects, a situation, a chain of events which shall be the formula of that *particular* emotion; such that when the external facts … are given, the emotion is immediately evoked …. The artistic "inevitability" lies in this complete adequacy of the external to the emotion'.[6]

Emotion, or affect, is therefore only admissable in art if it is given an external object to which it can be seen, clearly and automatically, to correspond. There must be nothing in that emotion which spills over or exceeds the objective, visible (one could say conscious) facts, no residue or trace of the primitive 'stuff' which may have been the original stimulus for the work of art. This is where *Hamlet* fails: Hamlet the man is dominated by an emotion which is inexpressible, because it is in *excess* of the facts as they appear. And that excess is occasioned by Gertrude who precipitates Hamlet into despondency by her 'o'er hasty' marriage to his dead father's brother and successor, who turns out also to have been the agent of the former king's death. For Eliot, Gertrude is not an adequate equivalent for the disgust which she evokes in Hamlet, which 'envelopes and exceeds her'[7] and which, because she cannot adequately contain it, runs right across the fabric of the play. Gertrude is therefore disgusting, but not quite disgusting *enough*. Eliot is, however, clear that he is not asking for a stronger woman character on the stage, since he recognises that it is in the nature of the problem dealt with in this play – a son's feelings towards a guilty mother – that they should be in excess of their objective cause. On this count, Gertrude's inadequacy turns around and becomes wholly appropriate: 'it is just *because* her character is so negative and insignificant that she arouses in Hamlet the feeling which she is incapable of representing'.[8]

What is at stake behind this failing of the woman, what she fails to represent, therefore, is precisely unrepresentable – a set of unconscious emotions which, *by definition*, can have no objective outlet and which are therefore incapable of submitting to the formal constraints of art. What we get in *Hamlet* instead is 'buffoonery' – in Hamlet himself the 'buffoonery of an emotion which can find no outlet in action', for the dramatist the 'buffoonery of an emotion which he cannot express in art'.[9] Such 'intense', 'ecstatic' (Gertrude uses the word 'ecstasy' to describe Hamlet's madness in the bedchamber scene of the play) and 'terrible' feeling is for Eliot 'doubtless a subject of study for the pathologist' and why Shakespeare attempted to express the 'inexpressibly horrible' we cannot ever know, since we should have finally 'to know something which is by hypothesis unknowable and to understand things which Shakespeare did not understand himself'.[10]

Today we can only be struck by the extraordinary resonance of the terms which figure so negatively in Eliot's critique – buffoonery, ecstasy, the excessive and unknowable – all terms in which we have learnt to recognise (since Freud at least) something necessarily present in any act of writing (*Hamlet* included) which only suppresses them – orders them precisely into form – at a cost. Eliot's criticism of *Hamlet* can therefore be turned around. What he sees as the play's weakness becomes its source of fascination or even strength.

In this context, the fact that it is a woman who is seen as cause of the excess and deficiency in the play and again a woman who symbolises its aesthetic failure starts to look like a repetition. Firstly, of the play itself – Hamlet and his dead father united in the reproach they make of Gertrude for her sexual failing ('O Hamlet what a falling off was there'), and *horror* as the exact response to the crime which precedes the play and precipitates its drama ('O horrible! O horrible! most horrible!').[11] Secondly, a repetition of a more fundamental drama of psychic experience itself as described by Freud, the drama of sexual difference in which the woman is seen as the cause of just such a failure in representation, as something deficient, lacking or threatening to the system and identities which are the precondition not only of integrated artistic form but also of so-called normal adult psychic and sexual life. Located by Freud at the point where the woman is first seen to be different,[12] this moment can then have its effects in that familiar mystification or fetishisation of femininity which makes of the woman something both perfect and dangerous or obscene (obscene if *not* perfect). And perhaps no image has evoked this process more clearly than that of the 'Mona Lisa' itself, which at almost exactly this historical moment (the time of Freud and Eliot alike) started to be taken as the emblem of an inscrutable femininity, cause and destination of the whole of human mystery and its desires: 'The lady smiled in regal calm: her instincts of conquest, of ferocity, all the heredity of the species, the will to seduce and to ensnare, the charm of deceit, the kindness that conceals a cruel purpose – all this appeared and disappeared by turns behind the laughing veil and buried itself in the poem of her smile. Good and wicked, cruel and compassionate, graceful and feline she laughed.'[13]

By choosing an image of a woman to embody the inexpressible and inscrutable context which he identified in Shakespeare's play, Eliot ties the enigma of femininity to the problem of interpretation itself: 'No one has solved the riddle of her smile, no one has read the meaning of her thoughts', 'a presence ... expressive of what in the way of a thousand years men had come to desire'.[14] Freud himself picks up the tone in one of his more problematic observations about femininity when he allows that critics have recognised in the picture 'the most perfect representation of the contrasts which dominate the erotic life of women; the contrast between reserve and seduction, and between the most devoted tenderness and a sensuality that is ruthlessly demanding – consuming men as if they were alien beings'.[15]

What other representation, we might ask, has so clearly produced a set of emotions without 'objective correlative', that is in excess of the facts as they appear? T. S. Eliot's reading of *Hamlet* would therefore seem to suggest that what is in fact felt as inscrutable, unmanageable or even horrible (ecstatic in both senses of the term) for an aesthetic theory which will only allow into its definition what can be controlled or managed by art is nothing other than femininity itself.

At the end of Eliot's essay, he refers to Montaigne's 'Apologie of Raymond Sebond' as a possible source for the malaise of the play. Its discourse on the contradictory, unstable and ephemeral nature of man has often been seen as the origin of Hamlet's suicide soliloquy; it also contains an extraordinary passage anticipating Freud where Montaigne asks whether we do not live in dreaming, dream when we think and work, and whether our waking merely be a form of sleep.[16] In relation to the woman, however, another smaller essay by Montaigne – 'Of Three Good Women' – is equally striking for the exact reversal which these three women, models of female virtue, represent vis-à-vis Gertrude herself in Shakespeare's play, each one choosing self-imposed death at the point where her husband is to die.[17] The image is close to the protestations of the Player Queen in the Mousetrap scene of *Hamlet* who vows her undying love to her husband; whereupon Gertrude, recognising perhaps in the Player Queen's claims a rebuke or foil to her own sexual laxness, comments 'The lady doth protest too much'[18] (a familiar cliché now for the sexual 'inconstancy' of females). So what happens, indeed, to the sexuality of the woman, when the husband dies, who is there to hold its potentially dangerous excess within the bounds of a fully social constraint? This could be seen as one of the questions asked by *Hamlet* the play and generative of its terrible effect.

Before going on to discuss psychoanalytic interpretations of *Hamlet*, it is worth stressing the extent to which Eliot's theory is shot through with sexuality in this way and its implications for recent literary debate. Taking their cue from psychoanalysis, writers like Roland Barthes and Julia Kristeva have seen the very stability of the sign as index and pre-condition for that myth of linguistic cohesion and sexual identity which we must live by but under whose regimen we suffer.[19] Literature then becomes one of the chief arenas in which this struggle is played out. Literary writing which proclaims its integrity, and literary theory which demands that integrity (objectivity/ correlation) of writing, merely repeat that moment of repression when language and sexuality were first ordered into place, putting down the unconscious processes which threaten the resolution of the Oedipal drama and of narrative form alike. In this context, Eliot's critical writing, with its stress on the ethical task of writer and critic, becomes nothing less than the most accomplished (and influential) case for the interdependency and centrality of language and sexuality to the proper ordering of literary form. Much recent literary theory can be seen as an attempt to undo the ferocious effects of this particularly harsh type of literary super-ego – one whose political repressiveness in the case of Eliot became more and more explicit in his later allegiance to Empire, Church and State.

Eliot himself was aware of the areas of psychic danger against which he constantly brushed. He was clear that he was touching on 'perilous' issues which risk 'violating the frontier of consciousness' and when he talks of writing as something 'pleasurable', 'exhausting', 'agitating', as a sudden 'breakdown of strong habitual barriers', the sexuality of the writing process which he seeks to order spills over into the text.[20] And Eliot's conception of that order, what he sees as proper literary form, is finally an Oedipal drama in itself. In his other famous essay 'Tradition and the Individual Talent', which was written in the same year as the '*Hamlet*' essay, Eliot states that the way the artist can avoid his own disordered subjectivity and transmute it into form is by giving himself up to something outside himself and surrendering to the tradition that precedes and surrounds him. Only by capitulating to the world of dead poets can the artist escape his oppressive individuality and enter into historical time: 'Set [the artist] for contrast and comparison among the dead' for 'the most individual parts of his work are those in which the dead poets, his ancestors, assert their immortality most vigourously'.[21] Thus, just as in the psychoanalytic account, the son pays his debt to the dead father, symbol of the law, in order fully to enter his history, so in Eliot's reading the artist pays his debt to the dead poets and can only become a poet by that fact. Eliot's conception of literary tradition and form could therefore be described as a plea for appropriate mourning and for the respecting of literary rites – that mourning whose shameful inadequacy, as Jacques Lacan points out in his essay on *Hamlet*,[22] is the trigger and then constant refrain of the play: the old Hamlet cut off in the 'blossom' of his sin; Polonius interred 'hugger mugger'; Ophelia buried wrongly – because of her suicide – in consecrated ground.

In Eliot's reading of *Hamlet*, therefore, the sexuality of the woman seems to become the scapegoat and cause of the dearth or breakdown of Oedipal resolution which the play ceaselessly enacts, not only at the level of its theme, but also in the disjunctions and difficulties of its aesthetic form. Much has been made of course of the aesthetic problem of *Hamlet* by critics other than Eliot, who have pondered on its lack of integration or single-purposiveness, its apparent inability to resolve itself or come to term (it is the longest of Shakespeare's plays), much as they have pondered on all these factors in the character of Hamlet himself.

Hamlet poses a problem for Eliot, therefore, at the level of both matter and form. Femininity is the image of that problem; it seems in fact to be the only image through which the problem can be conceptualised or thought. The principal danger, femininity thus becomes the focus for a partly theorised recognition of the psychic and literary disintegration which can erupt at any moment into literary form.

[...]

Rose cites the lines – used by Eliot – from Tourneur's *The Revenger's Tragedy* as further evidence that the representation of the feminine harbours a 'horror of sexuality and death'.

[...]

[I]n *Hamlet*, these two themes – of death and sexuality – run their course through the play, both as something which can be assimilated to social constraint and as a threat to constraint and to the social altogether For *Hamlet* can be seen as a play which turns on mourning and marriage – the former the means whereby death is given its symbolic form and enters back into social life, the latter the means whereby sexuality is brought into the orbit of the law. When *Hamlet* opens, however, what we are given is *too much* of each (perhaps this is the excess) – too much mourning (Hamlet wears black, stands apart, and mourns beyond the natural term) and too much marriage (Gertrude passes from one husband to another too fast). As if these two regulators of the furthest edges of social and civil life, if they become overstated, if there is too much of them, tip over into their opposite and start to look like what they are designed to hold off. Eliot's essay on *Hamlet*, and his writing on literature in general, gives us a sense of how these matters, which he recognises in the play, underpin the space of aesthetic representation itself and how femininity figures crucially in that conceptualisation.

II

If Eliot's aesthetic theories move across into the arena of sexuality, Ernest Jones's psychoanalytic interpretation of *Hamlet* turns out also to be part of an aesthetic concern. His intention is to use psychoanalysis to establish the integrity of the literary text, that is, to uncover factors, hidden motives and desires, which will give back to rational understanding what would otherwise pass the limits of literary understanding and appreciation itself: 'The perfect work of art is one where the traits and reactions of the character prove to be harmonious, consistent and intelligible when examined in the different layers of the mind'.[23] Jones's reading, therefore, belongs to that psychoanalytic project which restores to rationality or brings to light, placing what was formerly unconscious or unmanageable under the ego's mastery or control. It is a project which has been read directly out of Freud's much contested statement '*Wo Es war, soll Ich werden*', translated by Strachey 'Where id was, there ego shall be'.[24] Lacan, for whom the notion of such conscious mastery is only ever a fantasy (the fantasy of the ego itself) retranslates or reverses the statement: 'There where it was, so I must come to be'.[25]

For Jones, as for Eliot, therefore, there must be no aesthetic excess, nothing which goes beyond the reaches of what can ultimately be deciphered and known. In this context, psychoanalysis acts as a key which can solve the enigma of the text, take away its surplus by offering us as readers that fully rational understanding which Shakespeare's play – Jones recognises like Eliot – places at risk. The chapter of Jones's book which gives the Oedipal reading of *Hamlet*, the one which tends to be included in the anthologies of Shakespeare criticism, is accordingly entitled 'The psychoanalytic solution'.[26] Taking his reference from Freud's comments in *The Interpretation of Dreams*,[27] Jones sees Hamlet as a little Oedipus who cannot bring himself to kill Claudius because he stands in the place of his own desire, having murdered Hamlet's father and married his mother. The difference between Oedipus and Hamlet is that Oedipus unknowingly acts out this fantasy, whereas for Hamlet it is repressed into the unconscious revealing itself in the form of that inhibition or inability to act which has baffled so many critics of the play. It is this repression of the Oedipal drama beneath the surface of the text which leads Freud to say of *Hamlet*, comparing it with Sophocles's drama, that it demonstrates the 'secular advance of repression in the emotional life of mankind'.[28]

[...]

Rose refers to the limits of Ernest Jones' type of psycholoanalytic criticism which speculates on Shakespeare's own life and gives Hamlet the character 'the status of a truth'.

[...]

For Freud [...] Hamlet is not just Oedipus, but also melancholic and hysteric, and both these readings, problematic as they are as diagnoses of literary characters, become interesting because of the way they bring us up against the limits of interpretation and sexual identity alike. The interpretative distinction between rationality and excess, between normality and abnormality, for example, starts to crumble when the melancholic is defined as a madman who also speaks the truth. Freud uses *Hamlet* with this meaning in 'Mourning and Melancholia' written in 1915: 'We only wonder why a man has to be ill before he can be accessible to a truth of this kind. For there can be no doubt that if anyone holds an opinion of himself such as this (an opinion which Hamlet holds of himself and of everyone else) he is ill, whether or not he is speaking the truth or whether he is being more or less unfair to himself.'[29]

Taken in this direction, *Hamlet* illustrates not so much a failure of identity as the precarious distinction on which this notion of identity rests. In 'Psychopathic Characters on the Stage', Freud includes *Hamlet* in that group of plays which rely for their effect on the neurotic in the spectator, inducing in her or him the neurosis watched on stage, crossing over the boundaries between onstage and offstage and breaking down the habitual barriers of the mind.[30] A particular *type* of drama, this form is nonetheless effective only through its capacity to implicate us *all*: 'A person who does not lose his reason under certain conditions can have no reason to lose'.[31]

[...]

Jones, says Rose, makes a similar point.

[...]

T. S. Eliot also gave a version of this, but from the other side, when he described poetry in 'Tradition and the Individual Talent' as an escape from emotion and personality, and then added 'but, of course, only those who have personality and emotion can know what it means to want to escape from these things'.[32] So instead of safely diagnosing Hamlet, his Oedipal drama, his disturbance, and subjecting them to its mastery and control, the psychoanalytic interpretation turns back onto spectator and critic, implicating the observer in those forms of irrationality and excess which Jones and Eliot in their different ways seek to order into place.

Calling Hamlet a hysteric, which both Freud and Jones also do,[33] has the same effect in terms of the question of sexual difference, since it immediately raises the question of femininity and upsets the too tidy Oedipal reading of the play. Freud had originally seen the boy's Oedipal drama as a straightforward desire for the mother and rivalry with the father, just as he first considered the little girl's Oedipal trajectory to be its simple reverse. The discovery of the girl's pre-Oedipal attachment to the mother led him to modify this too easy picture in which unconscious sexual desires in infancy are simply the precursors in miniature of the boy's and the girl's later appropriate sexual and social place.[34] We could say that psychoanalysis can become of interest to feminism at the point where the little girl's desire for the father can no longer be safely assumed. But equally important is the effect that this upset of the original schema has on how we consider the psychic life of the boy. In a section called 'Matricide' normally omitted from the anthologies, Jones talks of Hamlet's desire to kill, not the father, but the mother.[35] He takes this from Hamlet's soliloquy before he goes to his mother's bedchamber in Act III, scene ii of the play:

> Let not ever
> The soul of Nero enter this firm bosom;
> Let me be cruel, not unnatural.
> I will speak daggers to her, but use none.[36]

and also from Gertrude's own lines 'What wilt thou do? Thou wilt not murder me? Help! Ho!'[37] (the murder of Polonius is the immediate consequence of this). Thus desire spills over into its opposite and the woman becomes guilty for the affect which she provokes.

This is still an Oedipal reading of the play since the violence towards the mother is the effect of the desire for her (a simple passage between the two forms of excess). But the problem of desire starts to trouble the category of identification, involving Jones in a discussion of the femininity in man (not just desire *for* the woman but identification *with* her), a femininity which has been recognised by more than one critic of the play.[38] Thus on either side of the psychoanalytic 'solution', we find something which makes of it no solution at all. And Hamlet, 'as patient as the female dove',[39] becomes Renaissance man only to the extent that he reveals a femininity which undermines that fiction. Femininity turns out to be lying behind the Oedipal drama, indicating its impasse or impossibility of resolution, even though Freud did himself talk of its dissolution, as if it suddenly went out of existence altogether. But this observation contradicts the basic analytic premise of the persistence of unconscious desire.

The point being not whether Hamlet suffers from an excess *of* femininity, but the way that femininity itself functions *as* excess – the excess of this particular interpretative schema (hence presumably its exclusion from the summaries and extracts from Jones), and as the vanishing-point of the difficulties of the play. And in this, Ernest Jones outbids T . S. Eliot vis-à-vis the woman: 'The central mystery [of Hamlet] has well been called the Sphinx of modern literature'.[40] The femininity of Hamlet is perhaps finally less important than this image of the feminine which Jones blithely projects onto the troubled and troubling aesthetic boundaries of the play.

III

If the bad or dangerous woman is aesthetic trouble, then it should come as no surprise that the opposite of this disturbance – an achieved aesthetic or even creativity itself – then finds its most appropriate image again in femininity, but this time its reverse: the good enough mother herself. As if completing the circuit, André Green turns to D. W. Winnicott's concept of the maternal function as the basis for his recent book on *Hamlet*. Femininity now appears as the very principle of the aesthetic process. Shakespeare's Hamlet forecloses the femininity in himself, but by projecting onto the stage the degraded and violent image of a femininity repudiated by his character, Shakespeare manages to preserve in himself that other femininity which is the source of his creative art: 'Writing *Hamlet* had been an act of exorcism which enabled its author to give his hero's femininity – cause of his anxieties, self-reproaches and accusations – an acceptable form through the process of aesthetic creation .... By creating *Hamlet*, by giving it representation, Shakespeare, unlike his hero, managed to lift the dissociation between his masculine and feminine elements and to reconcile himself with the femininity in himself.'[41]

[...]

Rose cites the source of Green's reflections in D.W. Winnicott's paper, 'Creativity and its Origins': 'Creativity *per se* … arises for Winnicott out of a femininity which is that primordial space of being which is created by the mother alone' – a state of being before or outside of representation. Like Eliot, Green and Winnicott – says Rose – reproduce the contradictorily degraded and idealized image of woman.

[…]

Winnicott's definition, like Green's, and like that of Eliot before them, once again starts to look like a repetition (one might ask what other form of analysis can there be?) which reproduces or repeats the fundamental drama of *Hamlet*, cleaving the image of femininity in two, splitting it between a degradation and an idealisation which, far from keeping each other under control (as Green suggests), set each other off, being the reverse sides of one and the same mystification. And like Eliot, Green also gets caught in the other face of the idealisation, the inevitable accusation of Gertrude: 'Is the marriage of Gertrude consequence or cause of the murder of Hamlet's father? I incline towards the cause (*Je pencherai pour la cause*)'.[42] And at the end of his book he takes off on a truly wild speculation which makes Gertrude the stake in the battle between the old Fortinbras and the old Hamlet before the start of the play.

But the fact that Hamlet constantly unleashes an anxiety which returns to the question of femininity tells us above all something about the relationship of aesthetic form and sexual difference, about the fantasies they share – fantasies of coherence and identity in which the woman appears repeatedly as both wager and threat. 'Fantasy in its very perversity' is the object of psychoanalytic interpretation,[43] but this does not mean that psychoanalysis might not also repeat within its own discourse the fantasies, or even perversions, which it uncovers in other forms of speech.

In Lacan's own essay on *Hamlet*, he puts himself resolutely on the side of the symbolic, reading the play in terms of its dearth of proper mourning and the impossibility for Hamlet of responding to the too literal summons of the dead father who would otherwise represent for the hero the point of entry into his appropriate symbolic place (the proximity between this essay and Eliot's 'Tradition and the Individual Talent' is truly striking). Lacan therefore places the problem of the play in the symbolic, on the side of the father we might say; Green in the 'before' of representation where the mother simply *is*. The difference between them is also another repetition, for it is the difference between the law of the father and the body of the mother, between symbol and affect (one of Green's best known books in France was an account of the concept of 'affect' in Freud and a critique of Lacan's central premise that psychic life is regulated by the exigencies of representation and the linguistic sign).[44] But it is a difference with more far-reaching implications, which reconnect with the question of the fantasy of the woman and her guilt with which this essay began. For the concentration on the mother, on her adequacies and inadequacies, was the development in psychoanalytic theory itself which Lacan wanted to redress, precisely because, like *Hamlet*, it makes the mother cause of all good and evil, and her failings responsible for a malaise in all human subjects, that is in men *and* in women, which stems from their position in the symbolic order of culture itself. The problem of the regulation of subjectivity, of the Oedipal drama and the ordering of language and literary form – the necessity of that regulation and its constant difficulty or failing – is not, to put it at its most simple, the woman's fault.

Finally, therefore, a question remains, one which can be put to André Green when he says that Shakespeare saved his sanity by projecting this crazed repudiation of the feminine onto the stage, using his art to give it 'an acceptable form'.[45] To whom is this acceptable? Or rather what does it mean to us that one of the most elevated and generally esteemed works of our Western literary tradition should enact such a negative representation of femininity, or even such a violent repudiation of the femininity in man? I say 'esteemed' because it is of course the case that Eliot's critique has inflated rather than reduced *Hamlet*'s status. In 'Tradition and the Individual Talent', Eliot says the poet must 'know' the mind of Europe;[46] *Hamlet* has more than once been taken as the model for that mind. Western tradition, the mind of Europe, Hamlet himself – each one the symbol of a cultural order in which the woman is given too much and too little of a place. But it is perhaps not finally inappropriate that those who celebrate or seek to uphold that order, with no regard to the image of the woman it encodes, constantly find themselves up against a problem which they call femininity – a reminder of the precarious nature of the certainties on which that order rests.

Notes (cut and renumbered)

1. '*Hamlet*' in *Selected Prose of T. S. Eliot*, ed. Frank Kermode, London 1975, p. 47. Further references include page numbers to this essay in the present volume.
2. Ernest Jones, *Hamlet and Oedipus* (1949), New York 1954, p. 88.
3. Freud, *The Interpretation of Dreams*, *The Standard Edition of the Complete Psychological Works* (hereafter S.E.), 4–5, p. 264; *Pelican Freud* (hereafter P.F.), 4, p. 366.
4. '*Hamlet*', p. 45; p. 3 above.
5. Ibid., p. 48; p. 6 above.
6. Ibid.
7. Ibid.
8. Ibid., pp. 48–49; p. 6 above.
9. Ibid., p. 49; p. 6 above.
10. Ibid.
11. William Shakespeare, *Hamlet*, 1, v, 47 and 1, v, 80. All references to the Arden Shakespeare unless otherwise specified.
12. Freud, 'The Dissolution of the Oedipus Complex'; 'Some Psychical Consequences of the Anatomical Distinction Between the Sexes', S.E., 14, pp. 173–9 and pp. 243–58; P.F., 7, pp. 313–22 and pp. 323–43.
13. Angelo Conti, cit. Freud, 'Leonardo da Vinci and a Memory of his Childhood' (1910), S.E. 11, p. 109; P.F. 14, p. 201.
14. Muther and Walter Pater, cit. in ibid., pp. 108, 110; pp. 200, 202.
15. Ibid., p. 108; p. 200.
16. John Florio, tr., *The Essays of Michael, Lord of Montaigne* (1603), London and New York 1885, pp. 219–310.
17. Ibid., pp. 378–382.

18. *Hamlet*, III, ii, 225.
19. See, in particular, Roland Barthes, 'La mythologie aujourd'hui', *Esprit* 1971 (tr. Stephen Heath, 'Change the Object itself', *Image, Music, Text*, London 1977) and *S/Z*, Paris 1970 (tr. Richard Miller, *S/Z*, London and New York 1974); Julia Kristeva, *La révolution du langage poétique*, Paris 1974 (excerpts from Part I of this book have been translated in *The Kristeva Reader*, ed. Toril Moi, Oxford 1986).
20. T. S. Eliot, 'The Use of Poetry and the Use of Criticism' (1933), in *Selected Prose*, pp. 92, 89.
21. T. S. Eliot, 'Tradition and the Individual Talent' (1919), in ibid., p. 38.
22. Lacan, 'Desire and the interpretation of desire in *Hamlet*' in Felman, ed., *Literature and Psychoanalysis*.
23. Jones, p. 49.
24. Freud, 'The Dissection of the Psychical Personality', *New Introductory Lectures* (1932), S.E. 22, p. 80; P.F. 2, p. 112.
25. Lacan, 'The Agency of the Letter in the Unconscious', *Ecrits: A Selection* (1977) p. 171 (translation modified).
26. See, for example, Laurence Lerner, ed., *Shakespeare's Tragedies, An Anthology of Modern Criticism*, Harmondsworth 1963.
27. *The Interpretation of Dreams*, pp. 264–266; pp. 364–368.
28. Ibid., p. 264, p. 366.
29. Freud, 'Mourning and Melancholia' (1915), S.E. 14. pp. 246–247; P.F. 11, p. 255.
30. Freud, 'Psychopathic Characters on the Stage' (1905 or 1906), S.E. 7.
31. Lessing, cit. in ibid., p. 30n.
32. *Selected Prose*, p. 43.
33. Freud, *The Origins of Psychoanalysis*, letters to Wilhelm Fliess, Drafts and Notes, 1987–1902, ed. Marie Bonaparte, Anna Freud and Ernst Kris, London 1954, p. 224; Jones, p. 59.
34. Freud, 'Female Sexuality', S.E., 21, pp. 224–43; P.F., 7, pp. 367–92.
35. Jones, chapter 5, pp. 105–114.
36. *Hamlet*, III, ii, 384–387.
37. Ibid., III, iv, 20–21.
38. Jones, pp. 88, 106. The concept of femininity in relation to Hamlet's character appears again in Marilyn French, *Shakespeare's Division of Experience*, London 1982, p. 149 and in David Leverenz, 'The Woman in *Hamlet*: an interpersonal view', in *Representing Shakespeare, New Psychoanalytic Essays*, eds. Murray M. Schwarz and Coppélia Kahn, Baltimore and London 1980.
39. *Hamlet*, V, i, 281. The image of the female dove was objected to by Knight as a typographical error in the Variorum edition of the play, ed. H. H. Furness, 15th ed., Philadelphia 1877, Part 1, p. 410n.
40. Jones, pp. 25–26.
41. André Green, *Hamlet et HAMLET*, Paris, 1982, p. 256.
42. *Hamlet et HAMLET*, p. 61.
43. Lacan, 'Desire and the interpretation of desire in *Hamlet*', p. 14.
44. Green, *Le discours vivant, le concept psychanalytique de l'affect*. Paris 1973.
45. *Hamlet et HAMLET*, p. 256.
46. 'Tradition and the Individual Talent', p. 39.

1.5   LISA JARDINE: FROM '"NO OFFENCE I' TH' WORLD": *HAMLET* AND UNLAWFUL MARRIAGE' (1991)

Lisa Jardine is Professor of English at Queen Mary and Westfield College, University of London, and known chiefly for her work in Shakespeare criticism. Her writings include *Still Harping on Daughters. Woman and Drama in the Age of Shakespeare* (1983) and, with Julia Swindells, *What's Left. Women and Culture in the Labour Movement* (1990). The essay on *Hamlet* is announced as part of the groundwork for a larger forthcoming project titled *Reading Shakespeare Historically*.

In an opening statement, omitted here, which presents her essay as work in progress, Jardine writes of wishing to initiate a dialogue on the assumptions of 'historically based text-critical practice'. This careful description directs us to the main theoretical and methodological interest of her study. As her discussion makes clear, not all forms of cultural history or cultural materialism share the same assumptions. In what terms, therefore, does she distinguish her position from, say, the 'new historicism' of Stephen Greenblatt, from social history, text criticism, and psychoanalytic conceptions of the human subject or subjectivity? What are the key terms of her approach and what gives it its direction as an explicitly political and specifically feminist project?

This suggests some points of comparison not only with historians and text critics but with the approaches taken by Jacqueline Rose and Elaine Showalter in the present set of essays. The main point of interest in relation to the play *Hamlet*, however, concerns Jardine's treatment of the question of incest, introduced by T. S. Eliot's early essay. What new reading does Jardine give to this theme; what part does 'history' play in it; and to what extent does this, in her own terms, restore agency to the figure of Gertrude?

The essays by Lacan and Showalter, above, are concerned less with Gertrude than with Ophelia. Does the kind of historical-textual reading Jardine is seeking to develop suggest a different way of situating and understanding this character too? Would her approach differ, in particular, from Showalter's?

Students might usefully consult the examples and discussion of new historicism and cultural materialism, referred to above, in Chs 2 (especially pp. 69–70, 91) and 5 .

The following essay is taken from Francis Barker, Peter Hulme and Margaret Iverson, eds, *Uses of History. Marxism, Postmodernism and the Renaissance* (The Essex Symposia, Manchester University Press, 1991), pp. 123–39.

'No Offence i'th' World': *Hamlet* and Unlawful Marriage

Ham.   Madam, how like you this play?
Queen. The lady doth protest too much, methinks.
Ham.   O but she'll keep her word.
King.   Have you heard the argument? Is there no offence in't?
Ham.   No, no, they do but jest – poison in jest. No offence i' th' world.[1]

[...] the remarks which follow are prompted by my reading of a helpful article by David Simpson, entitled 'Literary criticism and the return to "history"' (in double inverted commas).[2] It is that 'return to', and then "history" in double inverted commas, in his title, which immediately takes my attention. And indeed, Simpson sets out to show that

> the status of historical inquiry has become so eroded that its reactive renaissance, in whatever form, threatens to remain merely gestural and generic. 'History' promises thus to function as legitimating any reference to a context beyond literature exclusively conceived, whether it be one of discourse, biography, political or material circumstances.[3]

In other words, he believes that many so-called historicist critics are using the catchword 'history' to mask a quite conventional (and conservative) commitment to a set of unscrutinised, idealised premises about a past already modelled to the ideological requirements of the present.[4] The implication of that idea of 'return', then, is that there is something retrograde, and above all something *positivistic*, about the undertaking – that is, that in invoking history we are privileging something called 'facts' or 'real-life events', whereas in truth we are all now supposed to know that there are only texts, that our access to facts and to history is only and inevitably textual.[5]

I start my own argument by making it clear that I do not regard the present endeavour as either a turn or a *return*. I do not think that we should let the marketing tag, 'new' (targeted at eager academic consumers, after the latest product), suggest fashionable change, any more than we should allow 'historicist' to suggest retroactive, backward-looking positivism (once historicism always historicism). What we should be looking at, I suggest, is the converging practices of social historians, intellectual and cultural historians, text critics and social anthropologists, as they move together towards a more sensitive integration of past and present cultural products. It is to this generally progressive trend or development that I consider my own work belongs.[6]

Both historians and text critics have learnt a lot from recent literary theory. We do, indeed, now begin from that position of understanding that our access to the past is through those 'textual remains' in which the traces of the past are to be found – traces which it will require our ingenuity to make sense of. Nevertheless, it is by no means the case that this inevitably leaves us in a position of radical indeterminacy. In fact, I begin to believe that it only appears to lead us in such a direction if we are committed (wittingly or unwittingly) to the view that what textual remains yield, in the way of an account of the past, is evidence of *individual subjectivity*. In this case, indeterminacy is apparently doubly inevitable. For what we recognise as individual subjectivity is the fragmented, partial, uncertain, vacillating trace of first-person self-expression. And if we take on board Stephen Greenblatt's suggestive idea of *self-fashioning* – an aspiration on the part of the individual, embedded in past time, towards a coherence of self, which is inevitably endlessly deferred, and historically incomplete – it can be argued that what the cultural historian can retrieve and reconstruct of the past will of necessity be correspondingly incomplete and indeterminate. Here, Greenblatt's primary model is an anthropological one, his methodology that of the social anthropologist (and with it some of his assumptions about the strangeness of other selves).[7]

But those of us who are committed to social and political change may consider that we have another agenda altogether, the focus of which is *group* consciousness (and intersubjectivity).[8] In my recent work, I have emphasised that the specified ground for my own textual and cultural interpretations is a strongly felt need to provide a historical account which *restores agency to groups hitherto marginalised or left out of what counts as historical explanation* – non-élite men and all women. And since that means the focus of my critical attention is social relations within a community, the shaping of events in telling the tale is part of the given of the kind of excavation of the past I am engaged in.[9] In other words, I find that I am able to accommodate competing accounts of a set of textually transmitted events (competing versions of what makes collections of incidents in past time culturally meaningful), without discarding as illusory the lost incidents in past time which gave rise to them. That is a methodological matter to be negotiated, the very fabric out of which perceived social relations are constructed, not a break-down or paradox within the community as such. Texts may be *generated* by individual, gendered selves, but we may nevertheless choose to give our attention to the way in which in any period, membership of a community is determined by a shared ability to give meaning to the shifting unpredictability of everyday life. This is the group consciousness on which social practice depends, and which provides the boundary conditions for individual self-affirmation and action.

'Restoring agency' is, for me, a matter of countering the apparent passivity of non-élite groups within the historical account. But this needs a little further glossing. The counter-position to passivity (by implication, powerlessness), is *active participation*, but not (without falsifying the account) *power*. In my recent exploration of the defamation of Desdemona in *Othello*, I was not able to give back to Desdemona *power* to accompany her activity – but I was able to reposition our attention in relation to the events which take place on the stage, so that representation no longer overwhelmed the interpersonal dynamics of an early modern community to which the text gives expression.[10] In so far as I was successful, this retrieval of agency for Desdemona was achieved by my treating the individual subject in the drama as a 'cultural artefact':[11] the play gives us a tale of Desdemona's actions in the (then) recognisably shared terms of the early modern community. We can retrieve that recognition, I argued, by juxtaposing the tales told in contemporary court depositions (where the recognition of the *infringing* of shared codes of behaviour is the essence of the story) with the dramatic text – both being 'performances' before 'audiences' in that same community. Our access to something like 'who Desdemona is' is given by learning to 'read' in the social relations dramatised, those situations which were meaningful – which established or expressed Desdemona's relationship to her community in ways acknowledged as socially significant. Those 'events' (as I choose to call such socially meaningful sets of relationships) are the expressed form of Desdemona's 'lived experience', and I mean that, since in my view it will not make a significant difference whether the 'person' who is presented via this shaped version of experience is real or fictional.[12]

What distinguishes this kind of retrospective critical activity from that of the social historian, I think, is that we want to position ourselves so as to *give meaning* to early modern agency, not simply to record it, to show that it was there. As Geertz says:

> We are seeking, in the widened sense of the term in which it encompasses much more than talk, to converse with [our 'native' informants], a matter a great deal more difficult, and not only with strangers, than is commonly recognized. 'If speaking *for* someone else seems to be a mysterious process,' Stanley Caveli has remarked, 'that may be because speaking *to* someone does not seem mysterious enough.'[13]

Or as Greenblatt puts it – consciously alluding to the Geertz, as he specifies his own methodological starting point:

> I began with the desire to speak with the dead.
>
> This desire is a familiar, if unvoiced, motive in literary studies, a motive organized, professionalized, buried beneath thick layers of bureaucratic decorum: literature professors are salaried, middle-class shamans. If I never believed that the dead could hear me, and if I knew that the dead could not speak, I was nonetheless certain that I could re-create a conversation with them.[14]

What distinguishes the kind of analysis I am after, in the new 'inter-discipline' I see my work as moving towards, from much literary criticism, and from much recent text criticism, is that it seeks to engage with the *external manifestations* of selfhood. It does not treat the 'lived experience' of the individual, as something with which the modern critical self can engage, and which it can make meaningful in its own terms. Nor does it posit an unchanging human nature immune to local circumstances, which it is the critic's task to retrieve.[15]

This brings me to a crucial distinction which in the consideration I shall be giving to *Hamlet* I shall particularly need to sustain, between the version of the term 'subject' which my own approach addresses, and the one which I introduced earlier – individual internalised selfhood (of which the related term 'subjectivity' is symptomatic).

The form that the pursuit of the 'lived experience' or untramelled universal selfhood in textual criticism currently takes is grounded in psychoanalytical theory. It is the pursuit of a gendered first-person, authentic utterance – a discourse which inscribes the individual's unique experience of reality. The *subject*, in this sort of textual study, *is* that first-person discourse – which is the only access we have to individual selfhood.[16] And this discourse, which inscribes the individual's experience and determines her selfhood, is a discourse of desire and sexuality. And since this symbolic construction of the subject depends on a sign system which the receiver of the discourse shares with the discourser, subjectivity, in so far as it is grasped and understood is transhistorical.

In Greenblatt's pioneering work, this pursuit of the psychoanalytical subject via psychoanalytic theory coexists with the methodology of social anthropology.[17] The individual critic acknowledges the distance which separates him from the discoursing subject in past time; he (*sic*) attempts to 'speak with the dead'. It follows that the *terms* of the dialogue he establishes are those which he can 'hear' as the textual trace of selfhood, within his own discursive formation: desire and sexuality. By reaching back into texts which preserve desirous discourse in the early modern period, the new historicist critic retrieves those sign systems which he (from his own position in time and culture) can recognise; it is those shared discursive strategies which are, for him, all we can know of selfhood in past time.

The drawback in such an approach for the feminist critic is that sexuality is explicitly assumed to code 'power' in ways which lead to the *subjection* of women (no longer *qua* women, but ostensibly as *standing for something else*) – even (ironically, and anachronistically) the subjection of Elizabeth I to her desirous male subjects.[18] But the main point to note is that, on this account of subjectivity, the 'actual' is coextensive with what two discourses *share* – a matter of intertextual identity. This is, in my view, a fundamental difficulty for such a theory, and its methodology of power relations and subjectivity construction, when we are trying to deal with an inaccessible historical past, and particularly when we are trying to recover female agency from the cultural traces of the past.[19]

Which brings me finally to the problem of 'feeling', and our access to it, in *Hamlet*. Hamlet's feelings towards his mother Gertrude were already described in recognisable terms of incestuous desire in the classic 1919 article on the play by T. S. Eliot:[20]

> The essential emotion of the play is the feeling of a son towards a guilty mother ... Hamlet (the man) is dominated by an emotion which is inexpressible, because it is in *excess* of the facts as they appear. ... Hamlet is up against the difficulty that his disgust is occasioned by his mother, but that his mother is not an adequate equivalent for it; his disgust envelopes and exceeds her.[21]

This is an appropriate starting point, both because this idea of excess has been a feature of all *Hamlet* criticism since Eliot, and because it already makes clear that an account of Hamlet's 'excessive' feelings in terms of *desire* (inexpressible emotion), immediately makes concrete and specific his *mother* as focus of attention for her *guilt* – she is pronounced guilty not as a judgement on her actions, but as a condition of her presence in the play in relation to Hamlet (thus textual rather than historical in my sense). If Hamlet's feeling is excessive it is because his sense of his mother's guilt exceeds what could possibly fit the facts of the plot: the guilt of a mother who has stimulated sexual desire in her son. Here 'desire' is taken in the psychoanalytic and deconstructive sense, and is not an event but (according to Lacanian theory (and then Derrida)) a permanent condition of language, with regard to which Hamlet adopts a particular (problematic) orientation, one which produces mothers as guilty of arousing excessive desire in their sons.[22]

If desire is taken to be 'a permanent condition of language', then the analysis of the subject, and the interpretation of the text (in our case, the text of *Hamlet*) tend increasingly towards one another. In a recent article entitled 'Sexuality in the reading of Shakespeare', Jacqueline Rose writes:

> The psychoanalytic concept of resistance ... assumes that meaning is never simply present in the subject, but is something which disguises itself, is overwhelming or escapes. Freud

came to recognize that its very intractability was not a simple fault to be corrected or a history to be filled. It did not conceal a simple truth which psychoanalysis should aim to restore. Instead this deviation or vicissitude of meaning was the 'truth' of a subject caught in the division between conscious and unconscious which will always function at one level as a split. Paradoxically, interpretation can only advance when resistance is seen not as obstacle but as process. This simultaneously deprives interpretation of its own control and mastery over its object since, as an act of language, it will necessarily be implicated in the same dynamic.

In both *Hamlet* and *Measure for Measure*, the play itself presents this deviant and overpowering quality of meaning which appears in turn as something which escapes or overwhelms the spectator.[23]

And if we add the increasing interest of some critics in social anthropology, and in kinship systems as reflected in social forms, including language, the collapse of (specifically) 'incest' from a specified, forbidden sexual union into a universal tendency towards non-conforming, problematic forms of desirous social relationships (manifested above all *in language*) is complete.

[…]

Jardine offers a supporting quotation from Marc Shell's *The End of Kinship* (1988).

[…]

I am not pretending, here, to cover this issue adequately. But I use this abbreviated discussion as a way of distinguishing 'subjectivity' approaches from my own approach, focused as it is on *agency* and *event*, in terms I outlined at the beginning of this [essay]. In my terms, what is striking in the play *Hamlet* is that Hamlet does not sleep with Gertrude; there is no incestuous 'event' in the play, between mother and son, to match the excessive emotion on his side, and the excessive guilt on hers.[24] *Claudius* sleeps with (marries) Gertrude, and it is in fact on her sexual relations with *him* that Hamlet's excessive emotion concerning Gertrude is focused. And the point about Claudius's marriage to Gertrude historically (as event) is (a) that it is 'unlawful' and (b) that it deprives Hamlet of his lawful succession. So I first turn my attention to what constituted unlawful marriage in the early modern period, and then show how the social relations of the play are altered if we put back the Gertrude/Claudius marriage in history – reinstate it as event – and look at the *offence* that it causes to Hamlet.

'Unlawful marriage', in early modern England, was a matter for the Ecclesiastical Courts. It is a key feature of the church canons (the legislation in canon law) that someone is *offended* by incest/unlawful marriage. As the 1603 canons put it:

> If any offend their Brethren, either by Adultery, Whoredome, Incest, or Drunkennesse, or by Swearing, Ribaldry, Usury, or any other uncleannesse and wickednesse of life, the Church-wardens … shall faithfully present all, and every of the said offenders, to the intent that they may be punished by the severity of the Lawes, according to their deserts, and such notorious offenders shall not be admitted to the holy Communion till they be reformed.[25]

And the crucial passage on incest itself in these canons runs:

> No person shall marry within the degrees prohibited by the lawe of god, and expressed in a table set forth by authority in the year of our lord 1563; and all marriages so made and contracted shall be adjudged incestuous and unlawful, and consequently shall be dissolved as void from the beginning, and the parties so married shall by course of law be separated. And the aforesaid table shall be in every church publickly set up, at the charge of the parish.[26]

Two depositions from the Durham Ecclesiastical Court Records, concerning an 'unlawful marriage' (around 1560) show clearly how this idea of 'offence caused' has a bearing on individual cases brought to the notice of the church courts:

> EDWARD WARD of Langton near Gainford husbandman, aged 40 years.
>
> He saith that ther is dyvers writing hanginge upon the pillers of ther church of Gainford, but what they ar, or to what effect, he cannott deposse; saing that he and other parishioners doith gyve ther dewties to be taught such matters as he is examined upon, and is nott instruct of any such.
>
> He saith, that he was married with the said Agnes in Gainford church by the curat S[r] Nicholas, about 14 daies next after Christenmas last past, but not contrary to the lawes of God, as he and she thought. And for the resydew of the article he thinks nowe to be trewe, but not then. Examined whither that he, this deponent dyd knowe at and before the tyme of their mariadg, that she the said Agnes was, and had bein, his uncle Christofore Ward's wyfe, ye or no, he saith that he knew that to be trew, for she had, and haith yet, fyve children of his the said Christofer's. Examoned upon the danger of their soules, and evyll example, he saith that both he and mayny honest men in that parish thinks that it were a good deid that thei two meght still lyve to gyther as they doo, and be no further trobled. + AGNES WARD, ALIAS SAMPTON, aged 40 years.
>
> – all the Lordship and paroch of Gainford knew howe nighe hir first husband and last husband was of kyn, and yet never found fault with their mariadg, neither when thei were asked in the church 3 sondry sonday nor sence – they haith bein likned [linked?] to gither more and 2 yere, and yett never man nor woman found fault – but rather thinks good ther of, bicause she was his own uncle wyf. +[27]

The purposive narrative of these depositions is not difficult to unravel: Edward Ward's marriage to his uncle Christopher Ward's widow, Agnes, is incest under ecclesiastical law, but 'mayny honest men in that Parish thinks that it were a good deid that thei two meight still lyve to gyther as they doo, and be no further trobled', and, as Agnes testified, everyone in the parish knew 'howe nighe hir first husband and last husband was of kyn', 'and yett never man nor woman found fault'. Not only did no one find fault; they 'rather thinks good ther of, bicause she was his own unclc wyf'.

Church law holds the marriage unlawful; Christian charity suggests that no one is harmed by the marriage, and widow and children are appropriately cared for. The 'dyvers writing hanginge upon the pillers of ther church' that Edward Ward refers to are the 'table [to] to be in every church publickly set up, at the charge of the parish', specified in the 1603 canons quoted above the tables of consanguinity and affinity which specified who might legally marry whom (as Edward Ward clearly deposes, he himself is illiterate, and unable to read the tables). And we may, I think, extend the idea of 'offence caused' one stage further. *Someone* had to draw the marriage to the attention of the courts; that person had to be someone to whom the 'unlawfulness' of the marriage gave some (material) offence.[28] This charge laid by another is what is referred to (but permanently uninterpretable without information now lost to us) in the sentence in Edward Ward's deposition: 'And for the resydew of the article he thinks nowe to be trewe, but not then'.[29]

If we look at the Levitical degrees, the tables of consanguinity and affinity, we see how these already incorporate the idea of 'offence caused'. 'Consanguinity' conforms broadly with what we might expect: a man may not marry his mother, his father's sister, or his mother's sister, his sister, his daughter, or the daughter of his own son or daughter.[30] The table of consanguinity prohibits marriages with close blood ties, in the generations in which it might plausibly occur (parent, sibling, offspring, grandchild). The table of affinity, by contrast, reflects unions which might produce conflicting inheritance claims.[31] A man might not marry his father's wife, his uncle's wife, his father's wife's daughter, his brother's wife, or his wife's sister, his son's wife, or his wife's daughter, nor the daughter of his wife's son or daughter. None of these are blood ties, but each creates complications over the *line*. In particular, the marriage of a widow to her dead husband's brother threatens the son's inheritance claim. The son is first in line, his father's brother second; the marriage of the dowager widow to the second in line threatens to overwhelm the claim of the legitimate heir.

Notoriously, Henry VIII's marriage to his dead brother Arthur's widow, Catherine of Aragon, was incestuous under the Levitican tables of affinity.[32] Since Claudius's marriage to Gertrude is, like Henry VIII's, a marriage to a dead brother's widow, there is no doubt in the play of the incest, and Hamlet states the case directly:

Let me not think on't – Frailty thy name is woman –
A little month, or ere those shoes were old
With which she follow'd my poor father's body
Like Niobe, all tears – why, she –
O God, a beast that wants discourse of reason
Would have mourn'd longer – married with my uncle,
My father's brother – but no more like my father
Than I to Hercules. Within a month
Ere yet the salt of most unrighteous tears
Had left the flushing in her galled eyes,
She married – O most wicked speed! To post
With such dexterity to incestuous sheets![33]

The ghost of Hamlet senior puts the case more forcefully still, but unlike Hamlet, gives the active part in the incest entirely to Claudius:

Ay, that incestuous, that adulterate beast,
With witchcraft of his wit, with traitorous gifts –
O wicked wit, and gifts that have the power
So to seduce! – won to his shameful lust

> The will of my most seeming-virtuous queen. ...
> O horrible! O horrible! most horrible!
> If thou has nature in thee, bear it not,
> Let not the royal bed of Denmark be
> A couch for luxury and dammed incest.[34]

An offence – incest – but (as in the case from the court records), some anxiety as to *who* has been materially offended. In kinship terms there is an offence. It goes unrecognised until someone claims it as such.

Kinship and inheritance are remarkably strong themes in the play from its opening moments.[35] Young Hamlet is heir to Old Hamlet, just as young Fortinbras is heir to Old Fortinbras: *he* comes at the head of an army to reclaim his inheritance.[36] Claudius's first entrance as King, with Hamlet as not-King (dressed in mourning black), immediately emphasises the alienation of the Hamlet line. Indeed, what is striking about this first entrance is that it is entirely *unexpected* in revealing to the audience *Claudius* as King (referred to throughout the play simply as 'King' – here only as 'Claudius King of Denmark'), sumptuously, with Hamlet in mourning black. Everything in the earlier scenes has prepared the audience for *Hamlet's* appearance as King. The prolonged mourning (an interesting topic itself in early modern history) insistently keeps the direct line, Old Hamlet/Young Hamlet present. And Claudius's opening words fix for the audience the *usurpation*:

> Though yet of Hamlet our dear brother's death
> The memory be green, and that it us befitted
> To bear our hearts in grief, and our whole kingdom
> To be contracted in one brow of woe,
> Yet so far hath discretion fought with nature
> That we with wisest sorrow think on him
> Together with remembrance of ourselves.
> Therefore our sometimes sister, now our queen,
> Th'imperial jointress to this warlike state,
> Have we ...
> Taken to wife.[37]

The first exchange of words between Claudius and Hamlet (somewhat late in the scene – it follows the 'fatherly' exchange with Laertes) underlines the fact that the 'unlawful' marriage has strengthened the line in Claudius's favour, and to Hamlet's detriment:

> *King.* But now, my cousin Hamlet, and my son –
> *Ham.* A little more than kin, and less than kind
> *King.* How is it that the clouds still hang on you?
> *Ham.* Not so, my lord, I am too much in the sun.[38]

If Hamlet is Claudius's cousin, Hamlet should be king; if Hamlet is Claudius's son, then he is confirmed as line-dependent on Claudius, who sits legitimately on the throne. I suggest that Act I in its entirety dwells deliberately on *incest* as a material offence committed against Hamlet.[39]

Claudius's unlawful marriage to Hamlet's mother, Gertrude, cuts Hamlet out of the line.[40] The offence is against Hamlet. But for a mother to connive in wronging her own blood-son (even if passively) makes her an *emotional* focus for the blame – not simply the unlawful marriage, but the unnatural treatment of a son.[41] She has indeed committed a sinful and unlawful act, on which Hamlet obsessively dwells. He does so as one to whom that act has caused harm, disturbing the conventional relationship between blood-bond and line-bonds so that his filial duty towards his mother is now at odds with his obligations towards his father and himself (the legitimate line). The act is sexual (as Hamlet insistently reminds us). Its consequences are *material* for the line, and Hamlet is equally insistent about that:

Ham.	Now mother, what's the matter?
Queen.	Hamlet, thou hast thy father much offended.[42]
Ham.	Mother, you have my father much offended...[43]
Queen.	Have you forgot me?
Ham.	No, by the rood, not so.
	You are the Queen, your husband's brother's wife,
	And, would it were not so, you are my mother. ...[44]
Queen.	What have I done, that thou dar'st wag thy tongue
	In noise so rude against me?
Ham.	Such an act
	That blurs the grace and blush of modesty.[45]

Offence against Old Hamlet ('my father'); offensive behaviour towards Claudius ('thy father', because Gertrude is '[her] husband's brother's wife', and thus he her son's father). Hamlet is caught between the knowledge of an unlawful marriage, a crime committed (and perhaps two), to which the community turns a blind eye,[46] and a sense of personal outrage at a wrong perpetrated against himself, by his close kin, when to rectify that outrage would be to commit petty treason.[47]

Here, I suggest, we have an alternative account of '(the man) ... dominated by an emotion which is inexpressible, because it is in *excess* of the facts as they appear' – one in which we can see quite clearly that in so far as Gertrude is supposed to have behaved monstrously and unnaturally towards her first husband *and* her son, her guilt – in direct contrast to Claudius's – is culturally constructed so as to represent her as responsible without allowing her agency.[48] In my version, the intensity of feeling, the sense of outrage on Hamlet's behalf is still there, but it is produced as a consequence of offences recognised within the early modern community (in which Gertrude is much more straightforwardly and specifically implicated). In *this* account, Gertrude has participated in the remarriage – has (literally) *alienated* her son, and Old Hamlet's name (and does not apparently accept Hamlet's urging to leave Claudius's bed, because that argument (his) does not affect *her*).

We have not, then, exonerated Gertrude, but we have recovered the guilt surrounding her as a condition of her oppression: she is required by the kinship rules of her community to remain faithful to her deceased husband; that same community deprives her of any but the proxy influence her *re*marriage gives her, over her son's future. Yet she is the emotional focus in the play's cultural construction of the guilt which taints the State of Denmark.

Let me end by reminding you of something I said at the start: that there are grave reasons why I have found myself pushed to look for evidence of such agency in history – this is by no means simply an urge to identify my own critical position as an end in itself. It is above all the consequences for women of thus shifting the focus from text and discourse to history and agency, which, for me, currently, 'motivates the turn to history'.[49] As a Shakespeare critic, I have become tired of having to listen to offensive critical discourses, for which the author need apparently take no responsibility, which excavate desire in discourse so as to 'objectivate' the female subject – object of desire, object of blame, permanently victim.[50] After my initial reaction, which was one of anger [...] it occurred to me that there must be something *wrong* with such accounts in relation to women, whether or not such critical enterprises were valuable in relation to men and patriarchy. For in history, women are not permanently in the object position, they are subjects. To be always object and victim is not the material reality of woman's existence, nor is it her lived experience. If we look at event, at agency in history, the inevitability of these accounts disappears. And we find that we are once again entitled to ask (as I have done in the case of Gertrude): Who, after all, has been wronged, and by whom?

Notes (cut and renumbered)
See the supplementary references below (pp. 67–8).

1. *Hamlet*, III.ii.224–30. All references are to the Arden edition, ed. Harold Jenkins (London, 1982).
2. Simpson 1987–8.
3. *Ibid.*, 724–5. For another powerful argument which meshes with Simpson's doubts about the authenticity of discourse theorists' commitment to 'history' see Montrose 1986.
4. 'In particular, given the current popularity of discourse analysis, it seems likely that for many practitioners the historical method will remain founded in covertly idealist reconstructions' (*ibid.*).
5. Catherine Belsey, in 'Making histories then and now: Shakespeare from *Richard II* to *Henry V*', gives an elegant account of the ideological motivation for the privileging of a master-narrative version of history in criticism of Shakespeare's 'history' plays (for a similarly astute account of the ideology of Hamlet criticism, see Terence Hawkes, 'Telmah', in Hawkes 1986). Unlike Simpson, however, she sees the possibility of a post-modernist deconstruction which 'uncovers the differences *within* rationality, and thus writes of it *otherwise*', and which will thereby 'activate the differences and promote political intervention'. She proposes this as an alternative to both 'the master-narrative of inexorable and teleological development' and 'a (dis)continuous and fragmentary present, a world of infinite differences which are ultimately undifferentiated because they are all confined to the signifying surface of things'.
6. For a challenging account of these developments in cultural history see Chartier 1988.
7. See, for instance, Geertz 1984; M. Rosaldo 1984; Shweder and Bourne 1984; Bruner 1986.
8. For a clear account of the way in which political commitment sharpens the focus of feminist historical work, see Jean Howard. 'Towards a postmodern, politically committed, historical practice.'
9. See most eloquently Davis 1987.
10. See Jardine 1990.
11. See first of all Geertz 1973, p. 51; then Greenblatt 1980, p. 3.
12. See Geertz 1973, pp. 15–16.
13. Geertz 1973, p. 13.

14. Greenblatt 1988, p. 1. I am grateful to Bill Sherman for making this helpful connection for me, and for his continued support for my efforts to get to grips with recent writings in social anthropology.

15. See Geertz 1973, p. 35: 'The image of a constant human nature independent of time, place, and circumstance, of studies and professions, transient fashions and temporary opinions, may be an illusion, that what man is may be so entangled with where he is, who he is, and what he believes that it is inseparable from them. It is precisely the consideration of such a possibility that led to the rise of the concept of culture and the decline of the uniformitarian view of man. Whatever else modern anthropology asserts – and it seems to have asserted almost everything at one time or another – it is firm in the conviction that men unmodified by the customs of particular places do not in fact exist, have never existed, and most important, could not in the very nature of the case exist. There is, there can be, no backstage where we can catch a glimpse of Mascou's actors as "real persons" lounging about in street clothes, disengaged from their profession, displaying with artless candor their spontaneous desires and unprompted passions.'

16. I leave aside here the issue of the disadvantaging of women *per se* in Lacanian theory, see Jardine 1989.

17. This coexistence is made easier by the fact that social anthropologists like Geertz have thoroughly absorbed psychoanalytical theory, and tend to assume the Freudian subject as the starting point for their discussions of the cultural construction of selfhood. See Geertz 1973; Rosaldo 1984.

18. See Neely 1988, pp. 5–18.

19. In our Symposium discussions it became clear, I think, that in this respect (and this respect *only*) feminist critics are currently at an advantage in the critical debate being conducted around historicist and deconstructive critical approaches to text. Since they have a declared political objective, they are entitled to discard methodologies which fail to contribute constructively to it.

20. I concede, after many discussions on the subject, that taking Eliot as starting-point is in some sense a rhetorical device. But I find it striking that Eliot is fully aware of Freud, and thus that psychoanalytical reading of the play is established before psychoanalytical theory is explicitly introduced into literary studies.

21. Eliot 1932, pp. 144–5.

22. For a clear account of the consistent allocation of blame to the woman in psychoanalytical readings of *Hamlet* and *Measure for Measure* see Rose 1985.

23. *ibid.*, pp. 116–7. See also her very clear rehearsal of a series of psychoanalytical readings of *Hamlet* prompted by Eliot's essay.

24. The same kind of account can be given of Ferdinand's 'incestuous desire' for his sister, in *The Duchess of Malfi*. See Jardine 1983b.

25. Gibson 1730; Burn 1763.

26. Gibson 1730; Burn 1763.

27. Surtees Society 1845, p. 59. The 'marks' made by both dependents indicates that they were illiterate (a fact which is confirmed within Edward Ward's deposition).

28. See Davis 1983 for a clear case in which an unlawful relationship goes unreported in the community until a charge is brought by an individual who regards the 'marriage' as depriving him of something (land) due to him: 'The new Martin was not only a husband, but also an heir, a nephew, and an important peasant proprietor in Artigat. It was in these roles that the trouble finally began' (p. 51).

29. In fact, the canons of 1603 were drawn up hastily upon Elizabeth's death, since at her death it was suddenly realised that there now was no body of valid ecclesiastical law (her own legislation having been specified as for the duration of her reign). Owing to an oversight, the 1603 canons did not go through Parliament until some three years later, when it was realised that the clergy was probably operating outside statute law, and the situation was rectified. Patrick Collinson has recently suggested to me that these canons in fact *never* went on to the statute book – that in fact the Tudor and Stuart governments left church law in a kind of deliberate limbo. All of this is really to suggest that (*a*) it was extraordinarily difficult to operate the various competing demands of common law, statute, and canon law, and (*b*) 'moral' and 'legal' demands might readily be perceived to be in opposition, the legal contrary to custom, or the moral dubious within the technical law.

30. There are exactly comparable tables of consanguinity and affinity for the woman.
31. Indeed, this is how theological dictionaries traditionally describe the rules of affinity – as concerning *property*.
32. So was Henry's marriage to Ann Boleyn, since he had already had a relationship with her sister (Catholic propaganda, interestingly, claimed more obvious incest: that Ann was in fact Henry's daughter).
33. *Hamlet* I.ii 146–57. And see the Book of Common Prayer, cit. Jenkins, *Hamlet*, 319, n. 14. For another example of explicit affinity incest in the drama see Spurio's relationship with his stepmother in Tourneur's *The Revenger's Tragedy*. There, as here, the unlawfulness of the relationship is emphasised by the repeated formula from the tables of affinity: '*Spurio*. I would 'twere love, but 't 'as a fouler name / Than lust; you are my father's wife, your Grace may guess now / What I call it' (1.ii.129–31). In *Cymbeline* Cymbeline tries both to force Imogen to divorce her true husband, Posthumous, and to enter into an incestuous marriage with her stepbrother, Cloten.
34. I.v.42–6; 80–3.
35. For extended discussion of the 'elective' monarchy in Denmark, see Harold Jenkins's discussion in the recent Arden edition. I point out for brevity that Scotland was an elective monarchy: the eldest son of the reigning monarch was removed at birth to the care of the Earl of Marr. In due course the clans were assembled, and he was 'elected' heir to his father.
36. 'Now sir, young Fortinbras, ... [comes] to recover from us by strong hand ... those foresaid lands / So by his father lost.' I.i.98–107.
37. I.ii. 1–14.
38. I.ii. 64–7, and then see 107–12: 'You are the most immediate to our throne,/ And with no less nobility of love / Than that which dearest father bears his son / Do I impart toward you.'
39. The offence is committed against Hamlet senior *and* Hamlet junior. See Greenblatt 1986, p. 219: 'The ghost of Old Hamlet – "of life, of crown, of queen at once dispatched" – returns to his land to demand that his son take the life of the imposter who has seized his identity.' There seems to be a useful notion here of 'Hamlet' as an identity, a nexus of relations that Hamlet junior *ought* to occupy. See Girard 1986, 285–6: 'This significance of twins and brothers ... must be present ... if we are to interpret correctly the scene in which Hamlet, holding in his hands the two portraits of his father and his uncle ... tries to convince his mother that an enormous difference exists between the two. There would be no Hamlet "problem" if the hero really believed what he says. It is also himself, therefore, that he is trying to convince.'
40. Had Hamlet an heir himself his position would be strengthened (the play stresses Gertrude's maturity). I have come to think that *this* is the emphasis which so insistently produces Ophelia as fallen woman – were she pregnant she would threaten the (new) line in Denmark.
41. The intensity of the blame this occasions stands comparison with the blame which drives Ophelia insane – the murder of a father by the daughter's 'husband' (an act of petty treason, carried out by a king's son). Early modern inheritance law consistently reflects anxiety as to whether mothers can be expected to act reliably on their male offspring's behalf, in the absence of a male head of household. See Jardine 1987, p. 9.
42. That is, 'been offensive to'.
43. That is, 'committed an offence against'.
44. See Bullinger: 'A woman maye not mary husbandes brother' (fol. xvir).
45. III.iv.7–41.
46. On this account the possible *murder* of the king is a secondary issue.
47. On murder by wife or child as petty treason see Sharpe.
48. It is because this particular cultural construction of female guilt is still current that it remains plausibly 'real' to critics.
49. The phrase comes from Howard 1986, p. 13, and is a question addressed to all those whose work has been called 'New Historicist' – 'What motivates the turn to history?' (p. 14).
50. 'Objectivate' is Chartier's term. See, for instance, Chartier 1988: 'To combat [the] reduction of thoughts to objects or to "objectivations" ... a definition of history primarily sensitive to inequalities in the appropriation of common materials or practices has come into being' (p. 102). 'Foucault has a

lot to say about the way 'public' discussion of sex constitutes the chief way in which public institutions manipulate the consciousness and intimate experiences of great masses of people' (Sintow, Stansell and Thompson 1983, p. 9).

The following references supplement the notes to Jardine's essay.

2. Simpson 1987–8: David Simpson, 'Literary Criticism and the Return to "History"', *Critical Inquiry*, 14, pp. 721–47.

3. Montrose 1986: Louis A. Montrose, 'Renaissance Literary Studies and the Subject of History', *English Literary Renaissance*, 16, 1, pp. 5–12.

5. Catherine Belsey, in 'Making ... *Henry V*': in Francis Barker *et al.*, eds, *Uses of History. Marxism, Postmodernism and the Renaissance* (Manchester, 1991), pp. 24–46.
Hawkes 1986: Terence Hawkes, *That Shakespeherian Rag: Essays on a Critical Process* (London and New York, 1986).

6. Chartier 1988: R. Chartier, *Cultural History: Between Practices and Representations*, trans. L. G. Cochrane (Cambridge, 1988).

7. Geertz 1984: Clifford Geertz, '"From the Native's Point of View": On the Nature of Anthropological Understanding', in R. A. Shweder and R. A. LeVine, eds, *Cultural Theory: Essays on Mind, Self and Emotion* (Cambridge, 1984), pp. 123–36.
M. Rosaldo 1984: M. Z. Rosaldo, 'Towards an Anthropology of Self and Feeling', in Shweder and LeVine, *op cit.*, pp. 137–57.
Shweder and Bourne 1984: R. A. Shweder and E. J. Bourne, 'Does the Concept of the Person Vary Cross-Culturally?', in Shweder and LeVine, *op cit.*, pp. 158–99.
Bruner 1986: E. M. Bruner, 'Experience and its Expressions', in V. Turner and E. M. Bruner, eds, *The Anthropology of Experience* (Urbana, Ill. and Chicago, 1986).

8. Jean Howard, 'Towards a ... practice', in Barker, *op cit.*, pp. 101–22.

9. Davis 1987: N. Z. Davis, *Fiction in the Archives: Pardon Tales and Their Tellers in Sixteenth-Century France* (Stanford, Cal. and Cambridge, 1987).

10. Jardine 1990: '"Why Should He Call Her Whore?": Defamation and Desdemona's Case', in M. Warner and M. Tudeau-Clayton, eds, *Strategies of Interpretation: Essays in Honour of Frank Kermode* (London, 1990).

11. Geertz 1973: Clifford Geertz, *The Interpretation of Cultures* (New York, 1973).
Greenblatt 1980: Stephen Greenblatt, *Renaissance Self-Fashioning: From More to Shakespeare* (Chicago, 1920).

14. Greenblatt 1988: Stephen Greenblatt, *Shakespearean Negotiations: The Circulation of Social Energy in Renaissance England* (Oxford, 1988).

16. Jardine 1989: Lisa Jardine, 'The Politics of Impenetrability', in T. Brennan, ed., *New Directions in Psychoanalysis and Feminism* (London, 1989).

18. Neely 1988: Carol Thomas Neely, 'Constructing the Subject: Feminist Practice and the New Renaissance Discourses', *English Literary Renaissance*, 18, pp. 5–18.

21. Eliot 1932: T. S. Eliot, *Selected Essays* (London, 1932).

22. Rose 1985: 'Sexuality in the Reading of Shakespeare', in John Drakakis, ed., *Alternative Shakespeares* (London, 1986).

24. Jardine 1983b: '*The Duchess of Malfi*: A Case Study in the Literary Representation of Women', in S. Kappeler and N. Bryson, eds, *Teaching the Text* (London, 1983).

25. Gibson 1730: Edmund Gibson, *Codex Iuris Ecclesiasticae Anglicanae* (1730).
Burn 1763: R. Burn, *Ecclesiastical Law* (1763).

27. Surtees Society 1845: *Depositions and Other Ecclesiastical Proceedings from the Courts of Durham, Extending from 1311 to the Reign of Elizabeth* (London, 1845).

28. Davis 1983: N. Z. Davis, *The Return of Martin Guerre* (Cambridge, Mass., 1983).

39. Greenblatt 1986: Stephen Greenblatt, 'Psychoanalysis and Renaissance Culture', in P. Parker and D. Quint, eds, *Literary Theory/Renaissance Texts* (Baltimore and London, 1986), pp. 210–24.
Girard 1986: Rene Girard, 'Hamlet's Dull Revenge', in Parker and Quint, *op cit.*, pp. 280–302.

41. Jardine 1987: 'Cultural Confusion and Shakespeare's Learned Heroines: "These Are Old Paradoxes"', *Shakespeare Quarterly*, 38 (1987), pp. 1–18.
49. Howard 1986: Jean Howard, 'The New Historicism in Renaissance Studies', *English Literary Renaissance*, 16, 1 (1986), pp. 13–43.
50. Chartier 1988: Chartier, *op. cit.*
    Sintow, Stansell and Thompson 1983: A. Sintow, C. Stanstell and S. Thompson, *Powers of Desire: The Politics of Sexuality* (New York, 1983).
    No details are given in the original essay for note 44, 'Bullinger', or note 47, 'Sharpe'.

Chapter 2

William Wordsworth:
'Ode – Intimations of Immortality from
Recollections of Early Childhood'

GENERAL INTRODUCTION

Written between 27 March 1802 and March 1804 – and first published simply as 'Ode' – the final poem in the two-volume *Poems* of 1807, Wordsworth's 'Immortality Ode' has long been regarded as one of the great poems in his poetical *oeuvre* and indeed as a key text of Romanticism in general. Though hugely admired, however, the poem has always puzzled critics, who have, therefore, also tended to find it not completely 'successful' (Cleanth Brooks's judgement, p. 72, below). The poem has been the focus for numerous critics of all persuasions whose principal concern is poetry or Romantic poetry in particular. But in the second half of this century, as the present exercise demonstrates, Romanticism, Wordsworth and the 'Ode' specifically have been one of the principal sites for three critical movements of considerable force and influence (especially in the US): 'new criticism', (American) deconstruction and 'new historicism'. The first of these, which dominated American literary academia from the 1940s to the 1960s, has strong affinities with British 'practical criticism' and with aspects of F. R. Leavis's work (q.v.; see also *A Reader's Guide* 3/e, Ch. 1). 'New criticism' by and large abjured biography, history, intellectual history and other 'contexts' of literature; and, in its close reading of 'the text itself', tended to favour the shorter poem as its principal object of study. A well-known essay by W. K. Wimsatt and Monroe C. Beardsley, 'The Intentional Fallacy' (1946), offers one of the few explicitly theoretical statements of the 'new critical' position, but Cleanth Brooks's essay here exemplifies its practice exactly. American deconstruction, especially as developed by the Yale school of critics under the influence, in particular, of Derrida (amongst them Geoffrey Hartman, see pp. 80–90, below, and J. Hillis Miller, see Ch. 4, pp. 167–75 below), has focused extensively on Romantic literature, and especially on Wordsworth, for its displays of the complex unpicking of contradictory and unstable textual discourses. Harold Bloom, Paul de Man and Hillis Miller, for example, have also written on Wordsworth, but Hartman's essay on the 'Ode' here is a small *tour de force* of deconstructive reading. During the 1980s, the domination of American intellectual life by deconstruction was challenged by the newer movement of 'new historicism' (see *A Reader's Guide* 3/e, pp. 161–9; also Ch. 1 on *Hamlet*, above, and Marjorie Levinson, Headnote and essay, pp. 91–106, below). Focused principally on the English Renaissance and Romantic periods, 'new historicism' attempts to re-situate literary texts in the complex discursive frame of their originating period. This requires, not the older crude juxtaposition of text and historical context, but a detailed allusive reading of the text's own discourses in their intertextual relation to the political, cultural, 'popular' and other discourses of their period. This 're-historicizing' of texts often reveals what they could not know about themselves, and thus places 'new historicism' within the broad frame of poststructuralism.

Compare and contrast the theoretical premises and reading practices in Brooks' and Hartman's essays as examples, respectively, of 'new criticism' and deconstruction. In what ways does Levinson's essay challenge both of them? All three extracts could be seen as focusing on the poem's 'not-said'; try to identify this and differentiate between its implications in each case; compare with other examples which make more direct use of this concept in other chapters (e.g. Ch. 3 on *Jane Eyre*). In so far as they all retain the 'Ode's' canonic status as a 'great' poem, consider the notion of 'literary value' which underlies each of the essays. How would you extrapolate the 'politics' (or cultural ideology) implicit in their positions and practices?

Further Reading
Earlier essays on the 'Ode' may be found in the Penguin critical anthology on Wordsworth edited by Graham McMaster (1972) and in Alan R. Jones, ed., *Wordsworth: The 1807 Poems* (Macmillan 'Casebook', 1990), including an influential essay by Lionel Trilling (1941). Major 'deconstructive' works include Harold Bloom and Geoffrey Hartman, eds, *Deconstruction and Criticism* (Routledge, 1979); Paul de Man, *The Rhetoric of Romanticism* (Columbia University Press, 1984); and J. Hillis Miller, *The Linguistic Moment: From Wordsworth to Stevens* (Princeton University Press, 1985). 'Left' or 'historicist' criticism may be found in John Barrell, *The Dark Side of the Landscape* (Cambridge University Press, 1980); David Simpson, *Wordsworth's Historical Imagination* (Methuen, 1987); Jerome McGann, *The Romantic Ideology: A Critical Investigation* (Chicago University Press, 1983); and Antony Easthope, *Wordsworth Now and Then: Romanticism and Contemporary Culture* (Open University Press, 1993). Feminist criticism of Wordsworth appears in Ann K. Mellor, ed., *Romanticism and Feminism* (Indiana University Press, 1988); Mary Jacobus, *Romanticism and Sexual Difference: Essays on 'The Prelude'* (Clarendon Press, 1989) and Gayatri Spivak's pioneering essay, 'Sex and History in "The Prelude"' (1981), reprinted in *In Other Worlds* (Routledge, 1987). This essay and a section from Jacobus' book also appear in John Williams, ed., *Wordsworth* (Macmillan 'New Casebook', 1993). Note that much of the work cited above, however, does not deal specifically with the 'Ode'.

2.1   CLEANTH BROOKS: FROM 'WORDSWORTH AND THE PARADOX OF THE IMAGINATION' (1947)

Cleanth Brooks (1906–94) was Professor of English at Louisiana State University, then Gray Professor of Rhetoric at Yale (he was also the American cultural attaché in London, 1964–6). One of the conservative Southern Agrarians or 'Fugitives' in the US between the wars – a number of whom were to be influential in creating the 'new criticism' – Brooks was editor of the *Southern Review* (with Robert Penn Warren), 1935–42. His and Warren's textbook anthologies, *Understanding Poetry* (1938) and *Understanding Fiction* (1943), were central to the spreading of 'new critical' doctrine and practice throughout the American education system in the 1940s and 1950s. Other works include *Modern Poetry and the Tradition* (1939/1965) and (with W. K. Wimsatt) *Literary Criticism: A Short History* (1957). For a useful further account, see Rick Rylance, 'The New Criticism', in M. Coyle *et al.*, eds, *Encyclopaedia of Literature and Criticism* (Routledge, 1990).

Like Leavis (q.v.), Brooks did not go in for theoretical writing *per se* (although the introductory essay to *The Well-Wrought Urn*, 'The Language of Paradox', is a kind of extrinsic statement of intent), but the informing 'theory' of 'new criticism' is everywhere apparent in his practice. What, then, on the evidence of Brooks' essay, would you identify as the reading strategies and leading assumptions of 'new criticism'? What is it that makes the poem not entirely 'successful' for Brooks, and what are the implications of this in his general evaluative system? What would be the constituent elements of this scheme, and why does Brooks hold the importance of 'great' poetry in such high regard? It has been claimed that the 'politics' of this kind of 'new criticism' were entirely appropriate to the war-time and Cold War periods in the American experience. Is this convincing? How could the present essay be seen to be 'political'? As with Leavis' work, 'new criticism' became the bogeyman of the radical critical movements in the 1960s and beyond. Which aspects of it would explain this? Do you see any continuities or significant differences in approach between this and the two later essays in the present chapter?

The following extracts are from Ch. 7 (title as above) of *The Well-Wrought Urn: Studies in the Structure of Poetry* (1947), Methuen edition, 1968, pp. 101–23, *passim*.

Wordsworth and the Paradox of the Imagination

Wordsworth's great 'Intimations' ode has been for so long intimately connected with Wordsworth's own autobiography, and indeed, Wordsworth's poems in general have been so consistently interpreted as documents pertaining to that autobiography, that to consider one of his larger poems as an object in itself may actually seem impertinent. Yet to do so for once at least is not to condemn the usual mode of procedure and it may, in fact, have positive advantages.

Wordsworth's spiritual history is admittedly important: it is just possible that it is ultimately the important thing about Wordsworth. And yet the poems are structures in their own right; and, finally, I suppose, Wordsworth's spiritual biography has come to have the importance which it has for us because he is a poet.

At any rate, it may be interesting to see what happens when one considers the 'Ode' as a poem, as an independent poetic structure, even to the point of forfeiting the light which his letters, his notes, and his other poems throw on difficult points.

(That forfeiture, one may hasten to advise the cautious reader, need not, of course, be permanent.) But to enforce it for the moment will certainly avoid confusion between what the poem 'says' and what Wordsworth in general may have meant; and it may actually surprise some readers to see how much the poem, strictly considered in its own right, manages to say, as well as precisely what it says.

If we consider the 'Ode' in these terms, several observations emerge. For one thing, the poem will be seen to make more use of paradox than is commonly supposed. Of some of these paradoxes, Wordsworth himself must obviously have been aware; but he was probably not aware, the reader will conjecture, of the extent to which he was employing paradox.

The poem, furthermore, displays a rather consistent symbolism. This may be thought hardly astonishing. What may be more surprising is the fact that the symbols reveal so many ambiguities. In a few cases, this ambiguity, of which Wordsworth, again, was apparently only partially aware, breaks down into outright confusion. Yet much of the ambiguity is 'rich' and meaningful in an Empsonian sense, and it is in terms of this ambiguity that many of the finest effects of the poem are achieved.

There are to be found in the 'Ode' several varieties of irony; and some of the themes which Wordsworth treats in the poem are to be successfully related only through irony. Yet the principal defect of the 'Ode' results from the fact that Wordsworth will not always accept the full consequences of some of his ironical passages.

Lastly, as may be surmised from what has already been remarked, the 'Ode' for all its fine passages, is not entirely successful as a poem. Yet, we shall be able to make our best defence of it in proportion as we recognize and value its use of ambiguous symbol and paradoxical statement. Indeed, it might be maintained that, failing to do this, we shall miss much of its power as poetry and even some of its accuracy of statement.

It is tempting to interpret these propositions as proof of the fact that Wordsworth wrote the 'Ode' with the 'dark' side of his mind – that the poem welled up from his unconscious and that his conscious tinkering with it which was calculated to blunt and coarsen some of the finest effects was, in this case, held to a minimum. But it hardly becomes a critic who has just proposed to treat the poem strictly as a poem, apart from its reflections of Wordsworth's biography, to rush back into biographical speculation. It is far more important to see whether the generalizations proposed about the nature of the poem are really borne out by the poem itself. This is all the more true when one reflects that to propose to find in the poem ambiguities, ironies, and paradoxes will seem to many a reader an attempt to fit the poem to a Procrustean bed – in fine, the bed in which John Donne slept comfortably enough but in which a Romantic poet can hardly be supposed to find any ease.

In reading the poem, I shall emphasize the imagery primarily, and the success or relative failure with which Wordsworth meets in trying to make his images carry and develop his thought. It is only fair to myself to say that I am also interested in many other things, the metrical pattern, for example, though I shall necessarily have to omit detailed consideration of this and many other matters.

In the 'Ode' the poet begins by saying that he has lost something. What is it precisely that he has lost? What does the poem itself say? It says that things uncelestial, the earth and every common sight, once seemed apparelled in celestial light. The word 'apparelled' seems to me important. The light was like a garment. It could be taken off. It was not natural to the earth; it *has* been taken off. And if the celestial light is a garment, the earth must have been clad with the garment by someone (the garment motif, by the way, is to appear later with regard to the child: 'trailing clouds of glory do we come').

The earth, which has had to be apparelled in the garment of light, is counter-balanced by the celestial bodies like the sun, moon, and stars of the next stanza. These are lightbearers capable of trailing clouds of glory themselves, and they clothe the earth in light of various sorts. One is tempted here to say that the poles of the basic comparison are already revealed in these first two stanzas: the common earth on which the glory has to be conferred, and the sun or moon, which confers glory. We can even anticipate the crux of the poem in these terms: has the child been clothed with light? Or does he himself clothe the world about him in light? But more of this later.

This celestial apparel, the garment of light, had, the speaker says, the glory and the freshness of a dream. A dream has an extraordinary kind of vividness often associated with strong emotional colouring. It frequently represents familiar objects, even homely ones, but with the familiarity gone and the objects endowed with strangeness. But the dream is elusive, it cannot be dissected and analysed. (Even if Wordsworth could have been confronted with Dr Freud, he would, we may surmise, have hardly missed seeing that Freud's brilliant accounts of dreams resemble science less than they do poems – 'Odes on the Intimations of all too human humanity from unconscious recollections of early childhood.') Moreover, the phrase, taken as a whole, suggests that the glory has the unsubstantial quality of a dream. Perhaps this is to overload an otherwise innocent phrase. But I should like to point out as some warrant for this suggestion of unsubstantiality that 'dream' is rhymed emphatically with 'To me did *seem*', and that it is immediately followed by 'It is not now as it hath been of yore'. The dream quality, it seems to me, is linked definitely with the transience of the experience. Later in the poem, the dream is to be connected with 'visionary gleam', is to be qualified by the adjective 'fugitive', and finally is to be associated with 'Those shadowy recollections'.

[...]

Seven pages are omitted here. They relate to Brooks' basic 'laying-in' of the patterns of imagery, symbolism and paradox in Stanzas I–V of the 'Ode'.

[...]

I have already discussed the manner in which the first two stanzas of the 'Ode' charge the imagery of the famous fifth stanza. I should like to take a moment to glance at another aspect of this stanza. The poet, in 'explaining' the loss of vision, says,

Our birth is but a sleep and a forgetting...

The connection with

The glory and the freshness of a dream

of Stanza I is obvious, but I think few have noticed that the expected relation between the two is neatly reversed. Our life's star is rising: it is dawn. We expect the poet to say that the child, in being born, is waking up, deserting sleep and the realm of dream. But instead, our birth, he says, is a sleep and a forgetting. Reality and unreality, learning and forgetting, ironically change places.

Parallel ambiguities are involved in the use of 'earth'. In general, earth is made to serve as a foil for the celestial light. For example, when the poet writes,

> ... when meadow, grove, and stream,
> The earth and every common sight,

it is almost as if he had said 'even the earth', and this is the implication of 'While earth *herself* is adorning', in Stanza IV. Yet, logically and grammatically, we can look back and connect 'earth' with 'meadow, grove, and stream' – all of which are aspects of earth – just as properly as we can look forward to connect 'earth' with 'every common sight'. The poet himself is willing at times in the poem to treat the earth as the aggregate of all the special aspects of nature, at least of terrestrial nature. This surely is the sense of such a line as

> ... there hath passed away a glory from the earth

where the emphasis suggests some such statement as: the whole world has lost its glory.

But these somewhat contradictory aspects of the word 'earth' overlay a far more fundamental paradox: in general, we think of this poem as a celebration of the influence of nature on the developing mind, and surely, to a large degree, this is true. The poem is filled with references to valleys, mountains, streams, cataracts, meadows, the sea. Yet, though these aspects are so thoroughly interwoven with the spontaneous joy of the child which the poet has himself lost, it is the earth which is responsible for the loss. Stanza VI is concerned with this paradox:

> Earth fills her lap with pleasures of her own. ...

What are these pleasures? They would seem to be suspiciously like the pleasures which engage the children on this May morning and in which the speaker of the poem regrets that he cannot fully indulge. It is true that the next stanza of the 'Ode' does emphasize the fact that the world of human affairs, as the stanza makes clear, is seized upon by the child with joy, and that this is a process which is eminently 'natural':

> Fretted by sallies of his mother's kisses,
> With light upon him from his father's eyes!

Earth, 'even with something of a Mother's mind', 'fills her lap with pleasures'.

> Yearnings she hath in her own natural kind.

What are these yearnings but yearnings to involve the child with herself? We can translate 'in her own natural kind' as 'pertaining to her', 'proper to the earth'; yet there is more than a hint that 'natural' means 'pertaining to nature', and are not the yearnings proper to the earth, *natural* in this sense, anyway?

In trying to make the child forget the unearthly or supernatural glory, the Earth is acting out of kindness. The poet cannot find it in him to blame her. She wants the child to be at home. Here we come close upon a Wordsworthian pun, though doubtless an unpremeditated pun. In calling the Earth 'the homely Nurse' there seems a flicker of this suggestion: that Earth wants the child to be at home. Yet 'homely' must surely mean also 'unattractive, plain'.* She is the drudging common earth after all, homely, perhaps a little stupid, but sympathetic, and kind. Yet it is precisely this Earth which was once glorious to the poet, 'Apparelled in celestial light.'

This stanza, though not one of the celebrated stanzas of the poem, is one of the most finely ironical. Its structural significance too is of first importance, and has perhaps in the past been given too little weight. Two of its implications I should like to emphasize. First, the stanza definitely insists that the human soul is not merely natural. We do not of course, as Wordsworth himself suggested, have to take literally the doctrine about pre-existence; but the stanza makes it quite clear, I think, that man's soul brings an alien element into nature, a supernatural element. The child is of royal birth – 'that imperial palace whence he came' – the Earth, for all her motherly affection, is only his foster-mother after all. The submerged metaphor at work here is really that of the foundling prince reared by the peasants, though the phrase, 'her Inmate Man', suggests an even more sinister relation: 'Inmate' can only mean inmate of the prison-house of the preceding stanza.

The second implication is this: since the Earth is really homely, the stanza underlines what has been hinted at earlier: namely, that it is the child himself who confers the radiance on the morning world upon which he looks with delight. The irony is that if the child looks long enough at that world, becomes deeply enough involved in its beauties, the celestial radiance itself disappears.

In some respects, it is a pity that Wordsworth was not content to rely upon this imagery to make his point and that he felt it necessary to include the weak Stanza VII. Presumably, he thought the reader required a more explicit account. Moreover, Wordsworth is obviously trying to establish his own attitude towards the child's insight. In the earlier stanzas, he has attempted to define the quality of the visionary gleam, and to account for its inevitable loss. Now he attempts to establish more definitely his attitude towards the whole experience. One finds him here, as a consequence, no longer trying to recapture the childhood joy or lamenting its loss, but withdrawing to a more objective and neutral position. The function of establishing this attitude is assigned to Stanza VII. The poet's treatment of the child here is tender, but with a hint of amused patronage in the tenderness. There is even a rather timid attempt at humour. But even if we grant Wordsworth's intention, the stanza must still be accounted very weak, and some of the lines are very flat indeed.

---

* It has been objected that 'homely' in British English does not have this sense. Perhaps it does not today, but see Milton's *Comus*:

It is for homely features to keep home,
They had their name thence.…

Moreover, the amused tenderness is pretty thoroughly overbalanced by the great stanza that follows. I am not sure that the poem would not be improved if Stanza VII were omitted.

If Stanza VII patronizes the child, Stanza VIII apparently exalts him. What is the poet's attitude here? Our decision as to what it is – that is, our decision as to what the poem is actually saying here – is crucial for our interpretation of the poem as a whole.

[...]

Two pages, 'going back over ... ground already traversed', by way of Coleridge and I. A. Richards on Wordsworth's paradoxes, are omitted.

[...]

Whatever Coleridge was to say later, there can be little doubt as to what Wordsworth's poem says. The lambs and birds are undoubtedly included, along with the children, in the apostrophe, 'Ye blessed Creatures.' It will be difficult, furthermore, to argue that the poet means to exclude the moon, the stars, and the sun. (If Wordsworth would have excluded the bee and the dog, the exclusion, we may be sure, would have been made on other grounds – not philosophical but poetic.) The matter of importance for the development of the poem is, of course, that the child is father to the man, to the man Wordsworth, for example, as the birds, the lamb, and the moon are not. But it is also a point of first importance for the poem that the child, whatever he is to develop into later, possesses the harmony and apparent joy of all these blessed creatures. It may not be amiss here to remind ourselves of Coleridge's definition of joy with which Wordsworth himself must have been familiar: '... a consciousness of entire and therefore well being, when the emotional and intellectual faculties are in equipoise.'

Consider, in this general connection, one further item from the poem itself, the last lines from the famous recovery stanza, Stanza IX:

> *Nor all that is at enmity with joy,*
> *Can utterly abolish or destroy!*
>
> *Hence in a season of calm weather*
>   *Though inland far we be,*
> *Our Souls have sight of that immortal sea*
>   *Which brought us hither,*
>   *Can in a moment travel thither,*
> *And see the Children sport upon the shore,*
> *And hear the mighty waters rolling evermore.*

Wordsworth has said that the child as the best philosopher 'read'st the eternal deep', and here for the first time in the poem we have the children brought into explicit juxtaposition with the deep. And how, according to the poem, are these best philosophers reading it? By sporting on the shore. They are playing with their little spades and sand-buckets along the beach on which the waves break. This is the only explicit exhibit of their 'reading' which the poem gives. [...]

In writing this, I am not trying to provoke a smile at Wordsworth's expense. Far from it. The lines are great poetry. They are great poetry because, although the sea is the sea of eternity, and the mighty waters are rolling evermore, the children are not terrified – are at home – are filled with innocent joy. The children exemplify the attitude towards eternity which the other philosopher, the mature philosopher, wins to with difficulty, if he wins to it at all. For the children are those

> *On whom these truths do rest,*
> *Which we are toiling all our lives to find.*

The passage carries with it an ironic shock – the associations of innocence and joy contrasted with the associations of grandeur and terror – but it is the kind of shock which, one is tempted to say, is almost normal in the greatest poetry.

I asked a few moments ago how the child was an 'Eye among the blind'. The poem seems to imply two different, and perhaps hostile, answers: because the child is from God and still is close to the source of supernal light; *and*, because the child is still close to, and like, the harmonious aspects of nature, just as are the lamb or the bee or the dog. According to the first view, the child is an eye among the blind because his soul is filled with the divine; according to the second, because he is utterly natural. Can these two views be reconciled? And are they reconciled in the poem?

Obviously, the question of whether 'divine' and 'natural' can be reconciled in the child depends on the senses in which we apply them to the child. What the poem is saying, I take it, is that the child, because he is close to the divine, is utterly natural – natural in the sense that he has the harmony of being, the innocence, and the joy which we associate with the harmonious forms of nature. Undoubtedly Wordsworth found a symbol of divinity in such 'beauteous forms' of nature; but the poem rests on something wider than the general context of Wordsworth's poetry: throughout the entire Christian tradition, the lamb, the lilies of the field, etc., have been used as such symbols.

But we may protest further and say that such a reading of 'nature' represents a selection, and a loaded selection at that, one which has been made by Wordsworth himself – that there are other accounts of nature which will yield 'naturalism' which is hostile to the claims of the divine. It is profitable to raise this question, because an attempt to answer it may provide the most fundamental explanation of all for the ambiguities and paradoxes which fill the 'Ode'.

[...]

Two pages – mainly of long quotations from Richards on the two doctrines ('realist' and 'projective') of the Imagination available to Wordsworth – are cut here.

[...]

We can argue for the reconciliation of these doctrines only if we can find where these doctrines impinge upon each other. Where do they meet? That is to say, where is the real centre of the poem? What is the poem essentially about?

The poem is about the human heart – its growth, its nature, its development. The poem finds its centre in what Richards has called the 'fact of imagination'. Theology, ethics, education are touched upon. But the emphasis is not upon these: Wordsworth's rather awkward note in which he repudiates any notion of trying to inculcate a belief in pre-existence would support this view. The greatness of the 'Ode' lies in the fact that Wordsworth is about the poet's business here, and is not trying to inculcate anything. Instead, he is trying to dramatize the changing interrelations which determine the major imagery. And it is with this theme that the poem closes. Thanks are given, not to God – at least in this poem, not to God – but to

> ... the human heart by which we live,
> Thanks to its tenderness, its joys, and fears. ...

It is because of the nature of the human heart that the meanest flower can give, if not the joy of the celestial light, something which the poet says is not sorrow and which he implies is deeper than joy: 'Thoughts that do often lie too deep for tears.'

If the poem is about the synthesizing imagination, that faculty by which, as a later poet puts it,

> Man makes a superhuman
> Mirror-resembling dream

the reason for the major ambiguities is revealed. These basic ambiguities, by the way, assert themselves as the poem ends. Just before he renders thanks to the human heart, you will remember, the poet says that the clouds do not give *to*, but take *from*, the eye their sober colouring. But in the last two lines of the stanza, the flower does not take *from*, but gives *to*, the heart. We can have it either way. Indeed, the poem implies that we must have it *both* ways. And we are dealing with more than optics. What the clouds take from the eye is more than a sober colouring – the soberness is from the mind and heart. By the same token, the flower, though it gives a colour – gives more, it gives thought and emotion.

It has not been my purpose to present this statement of the theme as a discovery; it is anything but that. Rather, I have tried to show how the imagery of the poem is functionally related to a theme – not vaguely and loosely related to it – and how it therefore renders that theme powerfully, and even exactly, defining and refining it. But I can make no such claim for such precision in Wordsworth's treatment of the 'resolution', the recovery. In a general sense we know what Wordsworth is doing here: the chilhood vision is only one aspect of the 'primal sympathy'; this vision has been lost – is, as the earlier stanzas show, inevitably lost – but the primal sympathy remains. It is the faculty by which we live. The continuity between child and man is actually unbroken.

But I must confess that I feel the solution is asserted rather than dramatized. Undoubtedly, we can reconstruct from Wordsworth's other writings the relationship between the primal sympathy and the joy, the 'High instincts' and the 'soothing thoughts', but the relationship is hardly digested into poetry in the 'Ode'. And some of the difficulties with which we meet in the last stanzas appear to be not enriching ambiguities but distracting confusions: e.g., the years bring the philosophical mind, but the child over which the years are to pass is already the best philosopher. There is 'something' that remains alive in our embers, but it is difficult for the reader to define it in relation to what has been lost. If we make a desperate effort to extend the implied metaphor – if we say that the celestial light is the flame which is beautiful but which must inevitably burn itself out – the primal sympathy is the still-glowing coal – we are forced to realize that such extension is overingenious. The metaphor was not meant to bear so much weight.

[…]

A few lines are cut here in which Brooks proposes comparisons of the 'Ode' with poems by Henry Vaughan and W. B. Yeats, which would illuminate Wordsworth's 'difficulties' and the 'Ode's' 'defects'.

[…]

Yet, in closing this account of the 'Ode', I want to repudiate a possible misapprehension. I do not mean to say that the general drift of the poem does not come through. It does. I do not mean that there is not much greatness in the poem. There is. But there is some vagueness – which is not the same thing as the rich multiplicity of the greatest poetry; and there are some loose ends, and there is at least one rather woeful anticlimax.

But if the type of analysis to which we have subjected the 'Ode' is calculated to indicate such deficiencies by demanding a great deal of the imagery, it is only fair to remind the reader that it focuses attention on the brilliance and power of the imagery, a power which is sustained almost throughout the poem, and with which Wordsworth has hardly been sufficiently credited in the past. Even the insistence on paradox does not create the defects in the 'Ode' – the defects have been pointed out before – but it may help account for them. Indeed, one can argue that we can perhaps best understand the virtues and the weaknesses of the 'Ode' if we see that what Wordsworth wanted to say demanded his use of paradox, that it could only be said powerfully through paradox, and if we remember in what suspicion Wordsworth held this kind of poetic strategy.

2.2   GEOFFREY H. HARTMAN: '"TIMELY UTTERANCE" ONCE MORE' (1987)

Geoffrey Hartman is Karl Young Professor of English and Comparative Literature at Yale University. Himself emerging from the 'new critical' ethos in the early 1960s (the title of a later book, *Beyond Formalism*, 1970, registers this move), Hartman's first, influential and highly regarded work on Wordsworth, *Wordsworth's Poetry 1787–1814* (1964), displays at once an affinity with (later) deconstructive thinking and his retention of a high regard for the literary. Its approach considered criticism to be 'inside' rather than 'outside' literature, and therefore minimized historical contextualization while foregrounding the complex, highly wrought analysis of the text's lexis and syntax. Hartman's more general project was to reveal how the presence of the poet in the text, and especially his 'imagination' or 'consciousness', 'humanizes' the poetry, and what his method exposes are the tensions and uncertainties traversing Wordsworth's poetry in the process of its coming to consciousness – a consciousness of which it could not itself be self-conscious. Indeed, critical reading, in Hartman's view, should aim not to produce consistent meaning, but to bring out contradictions and equivocations in order to make the text 'interpretable by making it less readable'. In the introduction to his later book, *The Unremarkable Wordsworth*, in answer to the question 'Where would I like the study of Wordsworth to go?', Hartman responds: 'Toward an understanding of the radicalism that shapes even his evasions or euphemisms' (p. xxvii). It is in pursuit of such understanding that his own distinctive textual play – at once deconstructive and 'creative' – is fashioned. Other works include: *The Unmediated Vision: An Interpretation of Wordsworth, Hopkins, Rilke and Valéry* (1954); ed., *New Perspectives on Coleridge and Wordsworth* (1972); *The Fate of Reading* (1975); *Criticism in the Wilderness* (1980); and *Easy Pieces* (1985).

In the light of the above, identify in the essay Hartman's characteristic 'turns' and tactics of reading. On p. 87, below, he says he has 'offered a mildly deconstructive reading'. How does he gloss this in the sentences that follow, and what does it generally imply? Does he explain what the phrase 'a timely utterance' might mean? How far can the critical charges be levelled at Hartman that he 'becomes one' with Wordsworth and, in a sense, substitutes his own text for the poem; or that his textual playfulness deconstructs his own criticism to the point where *it* becomes as incoherent and 'unreadable' as he believes criticism should render poetry? Would 'rehistoricizing' the poem significantly alter Hartman's reading; would it be possible in his terms? What would be the claim, always supposing there is one, that Hartman would make on behalf of Wordsworth or of poetry more generally? How would it differ from Brooks'?

The following essay is Ch. 10 of *The Unremarkable Wordsworth*, Methuen, 1987, pp. 152–62.

'Timely Utterance' Once More

I

'It would be not only interesting but also useful to know what the "timely utterance" was,' Lionel Trilling wrote in 1941. He eventually does 'hazard a guess.'[1] Time has not diminished our fascination with the phrase: the guessing continues, while Trilling's interpretation has become part of the poem's aura and entered the consciousness of many readers. Just as we find a ring of cosmic junk around planets, so it is with interpretive solutions stabilized by the gravitational field of a well-known poem. Moreover, Trilling's critical style is itself of interest. To 'hazard a guess' indicates a modest attitude (he does not speak as a specialist, rather as an educated, reflective reader) but also, perhaps, a subdued sense of venture. For Wordsworth's diction is a riddle as well as a puzzle, and we answer it at the risk of appearing foolish, of exposing our superficial views on language and life.[2]

'Timely utterance,' of course, is not the only crux in Wordsworth's Ode, nor the only mystery-phrase singled out by readers. There is the bombast (Coleridge's term) of stanza 8, addressed to the Child as Prophet and Philosopher; there is the delicate vatic vagueness of 'fields of sleep'; there is, at the end, 'thoughts that do often lie too deep for tears.'

These cruxes – and there are others – all share a problem of reference: we do not know what the 'timely utterance' was: 'fields of sleep' is a periphrasis that should yield a proper name, perhaps of a place as mythic as the Elysian fields ('fields of light,' cf. *Aeneid* VI, 640); the sublime words that describe the infant seem really to describe some other, more fitting, subject; and who knows what the deep thoughts are about.

Let me clarify, in a preliminary way, this problem of reference. Those deep thoughts: their occasion is clear (the simplest thing, the meanest flower), and their emotional impact also is clear. But where precisely do they lie, where is 'too deep for tears'? Is it, to quote a moving sonnet in which Wordsworth mourns the loss of his daughter Catherine, that 'spot which no vicissitude can find'?[3] Or is the obverse suggested, that they are *not* thoughts of loss, mortality or the grave, but arise from a still deeper level, from under or beyond the grave? But what can *that* mean? Or is Wordsworth adjuring himself not to cry, not to give in to a pathos permitted even to Aeneas ('Sunt lacrymae rerum...' *Aeneid* 1, 468), as he forbids mourning despite nature's valedictory intimations:

And O, ye Fountains, Meadows, Hills and Groves
Forbode not any severing of our loves!

I multiply questions because I suspect that a simple solution, or stabilizing specificity, cannot be found. Yet the nonspecific quality of such verses does not harm them. It acts somewhat like formal perspective, in which an abstract reference-point allows the imaginative construction of naturalistic space. For, with the partial exception of stanza 8 on the sublime Child, we remain very much in a familiar world. Wordsworth extends, it is true, the boundary of natural events, yet never crosses it decisively into another region. Plato's doctrine of anamnesis or pre-existence is made to support ordinary feelings, to give them a memorable frame, not to justify fantastic speculation. The Ode's closing sentiment even limits the kind of thoughtful brooding (the 'philosophic mind') that is its very concern: there is neither analytic nor visionary excess.

The more we press toward reference, the more a Wordsworthian thought-limit or boundary appears. One is tempted to ask, and without constraining an answer: are the thoughts secretly apocalyptic? Or so gravely sentimental that they border on a crazy sort of concreteness, as mind passes from the 'meanest' sign to the sublimest natural laws via an elided corpse? (For one could imagine the poet thinking: This flower at my feet may be nourished by the putrefaction of the dead, who are remembered unto life in this way.[4])

> The cloud of mortal destiny,
> Others will front it fearlessly –
> But who, like him, will put it by?

Wordsworth's poetry has the strength to absorb thoughts that might unbalance the mind. 'Dim sadness, and blind thoughts,' he calls them in 'Resolution and Independence,' 'I knew not, nor could name.' The 'burthen of the mystery' is acknowledged and lightened. Alas, the 'burthen of the mystery' is another one of those strange phrases, strong yet vague. I turn now to what occasioned these preliminary reflections: 'timely utterance.'

II

The context is not as much help as it might be.

> To me alone there came a thought of grief:
> A timely utterance gave that thought relief...

The thought is almost as unspecific as what gives it relief. Perhaps it does not have to be specific, since the stanza's first verses suggest that what mattered was the contrast of thought and season. To me alone, among all beings, there came this untoward thought, like an untimely echo. Hence, after it is dispelled, Wordsworth vows: 'No more shall grief of mine the season wrong.' Only 'seasonable sweets' (Keats) from now on. One possibility for interpretation, therefore, is that he was interested in expressing a relation, or a broken then restored relation, rather than the precise detail of this single experience. The broken relation between his heart and the 'heart of May' is always to be repaired. There may even be a repetition of that relational structure:

> The cataracts blow their trumpets from the steep;
> No more shall grief of mine the season wrong;
> I hear the Echoes through the mountains throng;
> The Winds come to me from the fields of sleep...

Two types of utterance are presented in asyndetic sequence: one comes from nature, and seems to heighten, like a punctuation from above, the timely utterance (indeed, there is a possibility that it was the timely utterance); and one comes from within the poet, as if to answer or echo nature (relation having been restored) and so to confirm, even structurally, that the disturbing fancy has passed. This echo-structure is made literal by the next line. 'I hear the Echoes from the mountain throng.' Together with 'The Winds come to me from the fields of sleep,' it suggests an extension of sensibility, some inner horizon opening up, as the poet hears into the distance. What is heard is not just waterfall or winds (whatever their message) but the principle of echo itself. Hence the echoes 'throng'; they are suddenly every-where; as thick as sheep at folding time. The stanza as a whole evokes a *correspondence* of breezes, sounds, feelings, one that has absorbed discordant elements (cf. 1850 *Prelude* 1, 85, 96ff., 340–50). Its culmination is the hallooing of 'Shout round me, let me hear thy shouts, thou happy Shepherd-boy!'

The movement of empathy here is so strong that we almost feel the apostrophe as a self-address, as if the poet were that 'Child of Joy.' His flock, as in Shelley's 'Adonais,' is composed of 'quick Dreams, / The passion-winged Ministers of thought.' Though we are moving toward the opposite of a pastoral elegy, the double form or echo-aspect of this provisional climax ('Shout . . . shout') may be modifying as well as intensifying. Is not the cry optative rather than indicative in mood, an utterance that *projects* an utterance, so that it is hard to tell the spontaneous from the forced joy? The 'let me hear' repeats as a variant the 'shout round me,' yet it also points inward: it seems to appeal for a sound so strong that the poet cannot but hear ('I hear, I hear...with joy I hear' is delayed to the next stanza, and is immediately counterpointed: 'But there's a Tree, of many, one...') An inward and meeting echo, a reciprocal response, is not assured even now.

III

Broken column, broken tower, broken ... response. The theme of lost Hellenic grace or harmony is not relevant except as it is also more than Hellenic and recalls the 'echo' formula of a poetry at once pastoral and elegiac:

> All as the sheepe, such was the shepeheards looke

Spenser writes in 'January,' the first eclogue of the *Shepheardes Calender*. And

> 'Thou barrein ground, whom winters wrath hath wasted,
> Art made a myrrhour to behold my plight...'

This correspondence of season with mood, or of nature with human feelings, is the simplest form of the echo-principle in pastoral verse. Echo is something more than a figure of speech:

> Now lay those sorrowful complaints aside,
> And having all your heads with girland crownd,
> Helpe me mine owne loves prayses to resound;
> Ne let the same of any be envide:
> So Orpheus did for his owne bride:
> So I unto my selfe alone wil sing;
> The woods shall to me answer, and my eccho ring.

Spenser gives himself away in an *Epithalamion* of his own making: his poetry participates in the marriage, it weds the world, the word, to his desire, or more exactly to the *timing* which builds his rime, and which can call for silence ('And cease till then our tymely joyes to sing: / The woods no more us answer, nor our eccho ring') as well as responsive sound. In this sense poetry is itself the 'timely utterance' – not Spenser's *Epithalamion* as such, nor 'Resolution and Independence' (or a part of it, as Trilling and Barzun suggest[5]), or any other specific set of verses.

Yet what is meant by *poetry* cannot be formalized, as I have seemed to suggest, in terms of generic features. I might like to claim that 'timely utterance' opens every poetic form to the incursion of pastoral;[6] and Wordsworth himself gives some purchases on such a view:

> The Poets, in their elegies and songs
> Lamenting the departed, call the groves,
> They call upon the hills and streams to mourn,
> And senseless rocks; nor idly; for they speak,
> In these their invocations, with a voice
> Obedient to the strong creative power
> Of human passion.

> (*The Excursion* I, 475–81)

Yet what matters is neither the pastoral setting nor the overt, figurative expression of sympathy ('Sympathies there are,' Wordsworth continues, 'More tranquil, yet perhaps of kindred birth, / That steal upon the meditative mind, / And grow with thought'). What matters is the sense of a *bond* between mind and nature, of a responsiveness that overcomes the difference of speech and muteness, or articulate and inarticulate utterance.

> Far and wide the clouds were touched,
> And in their silent faces could he read
> Unutterable love.
>   ......
> ... In the mountains did he *feel* his faith.
> All things, responsive to the writing, there
> Breathed immortality, revolving life,
> And greatness still revolving; infinite

> (*The Excursion* I, 203–5, 226–29)

The capacity for 'timely utterance' in this timeless, mute, or unutterable situation maintains the bond, and justifies the poetry. 'The strong creative power / Of human passion' is equivalent to poetry in this respect. 'Passion' often has, for Wordsworth, the sense of passionate speech that identifies with 'mute, insensate things.' 'My heart leaps up' – an 'extempore' lyric whose final lines come to serve as an epigraph to the Intimations Ode, and which has been nominated by some scholars as the 'timely utterance' – is about this bond. The poem is remarkable as an utterance, as a speech act that falls somewhere between vow and passionate wish:

> My heart leaps up when I behold
>   A rainbow in the sky:
> So was it when my life began;
> So is it now I am a man:
> So be it when I shall grow old,
>   Or let me die!

That 'Or let me die!' is a true 'fit of passion,' one of those Wordsworthian moments where feeling seems to overflow and be in excess of its occasion. It is, one might say, untimely.

Yet we feel its emotional truth, and it becomes timely again once we recall another utterance, that of God when he makes the rainbow a sign of His bond:

> I have set My bow in the cloud, and it shall be a token of a covenant between Me and the earth. And it shall come to pass, when I bring clouds over the earth, and the bow is seen in the cloud, that I will remember My covenant, which is between Me and you and every living creature of all flesh; and the waters shall no more become a flood to destroy all flesh.

(Genesis 9:13–16)

If Wordsworth's vow recalls that primal vow, it is a response that says: This is *my* bond, *my* way of binding each day to each and continuing in time. Cut the link of nature to human feelings and the bond is broken. Once dead to nature, I might as well die. Poetry is a marriage-covenant with nature, a 'spousal verse' even more demanding of 'dew' response than Spenser's *Epithalamion*.

IV

To utter things in a timely way is the ideal situation, of course; yet Wordsworth usually represents the ideal in its wishful or miscarried form. The words *tempus* and *tempest* are related; and the *Prelude*'s opening episode already suggests a problem. The 'correspondent breeze' is said to have become 'A tempest, a redundant energy / Vexing its own creation' (I, 37ff). There is a disproportion or discord between the 'gentle breeze' of the poem's first verse and this tempestuous, self-forcing power. The *untimely* is never far away (cf. I, 94–105).

But our own solution may have been untimely, that is, premature. Even should 'timely utterance' be an inspired periphrasis for poetry, and exclude the promoting of a particular poem or passage, we continue to think of poetry as a *manifold* of utterances that is *one* only if the idea of vocation is adduced: if poetry is also 'poesy.' The utterances are not only qualified by being timely (either vis-à-vis others or oneself); they are unified by being timely. That is their essential quality, or the predicate pointing to a predicament. A reader alerted by the Vergilian motto of the Ode ('paulo majora canamus') would recognize the question of poetic growth and maturation: of the *career* of the poet. Is there a future for Wordsworth as poet, or for poetry itself? Has the time for poetry, as 'timely utterance,' passed?

Moreover, the Ode's vacillating strain, its blend of humble and prophetic tones, recalls Milton's stylized hesitation in *Lycidas*: poetry is conceived of as a precarious venture, that may be prematurely launched, untimely tried by 'forc'd fingers rude.' It is Milton who linked poetry's timeliness explicitly to a vocation that was imperious, prophetic, dangerous. If not now, when?

The 'Now' that begins stanza 3 of Wordsworth's Ode may therefore be more than a pivoting or idle word. Its place in time, as well as its syntactical position, is not easily fixed. It is like the anchor of hope. Its prepositional and propositional components fuse into an absolute construction. The word stands outside the events it qualifies: like a symbol in mathematics it could refer to every phrase that follows. The sequence of tenses in stanza 3 shifts from present to past to present, as everything tends toward that 'Now.' Coming to it, after two reflective and chiefly elegiac stanzas, it is as if a person were to draw a deep breath, then to exhale it, signaling a new start. The present, or this very utterance, cancels what has been. 'Now' is in its virtuality the temporal word *par excellence*.

To make so ordinary a word extraordinary may be self-defeating in terms of the diction of poetry. Yet poetic language, it could be argued, is ordinary language in its always residual or always future promise. 'Now,' as common as herded sheep, is also remarkable as the index for 'A Presence which is not to be put by' (*Intimations Ode*, 120). A passage-word, it intimates the possibility – not the fact – of a decisive turning point, something about to be, or about to be ... uttered. Within the flow of language it is an open-vowelled *nunc stans*, a fleeting epiphanic sound. And the transition from 'thought of grief' to 'relief,' which it introduces, and then, in the next stanza, to 'blessing,' comes through drinking in a surround of sounds: the utterance itself, the cataracts, echoes, winds, and the first clear vocative of the poem, 'Shout round me. ...' It is as if Wordsworth had been released into voice as well as blessing, into a voice that is a blessing.

> Ye blessed Creatures, I have heard the call
>   Ye to each other make...

(St. IV)

It is a moment remarkably similar to the removal of the curse from the Ancient Mariner in Coleridge's poem; there is the same feeling of relief, the creatures (*res creatae*) are acknowledged and blessed. Coleridge, however, separates blessing and utterance, as if timely utterance were not, or not yet, possible.

> O happy living things! no tongue
> Their beauty might declare:
> A spring of love gushed from my heart,
> And I blessed them unaware.

Yet in Wordsworth too there may be a hesitation of the tongue, some impediment to the coincidence of voice and blessing. It emerges when we ask whether the action of stanza 4 takes place in real or fantasied time. 'Ye blessed Creatures, I have heard the call / Ye to each other make; I see / The heavens laugh with you....' need not be a descriptive statement about what is happening then and there. It could be an anticipatory and envisioning response to 'Shout round me, let me hear thy shouts....' A wish-fulfillment, then, a proleptic extension of the poet's own vocative, his pausal 'Now.' The 'I have heard' may refer to the past ('There was a time') or it may have come so close to the moment of speaking that it is a confirmatory 'Roger.' Wordsworth does not actually say that *he* is laughing with the creatures; but as he looks round once more, repeating the 'turning' described in the opening stanzas, he sees and hears the things he said he could no more.

The reader, of course, no less wishful than the poet, would like to assume that the thought of grief has passed and that the birds and beasts did in fact sing and bound, and that only the discordant heart of the poet had to be tuned. But the 'Now' remains slightly apart, hyper-referential, or just plain *hyper*. It is a wishing-word. The music of Wordsworth's Ode is so elaborate that it untunes the timely-happy connection between heaven and nature, as between heart and nature, a connection the poet is always reestablishing. His poem is the most complex Music Ode in English, conveying and absorbing the difference between voice and blessing, words and wishes, being and being-in-time.

V

All things, responsive to the writing
        Wordsworth

I have offered a mildly deconstuctive reading: one that discloses in words 'a "spirit" peculiar to their nature as words' (Kenneth Burke). Such a reading refuses to substitute ideas for words, especially since in the empiricist tradition after Locke ideas are taken to be a faint replica of images, which are themselves directly referable to sense-experience. One way of bringing out the spirit peculiar to words, and so, paradoxically, making them material – emphasizing the letter in the spirit – is to evoke their intertexual echoes. Ideas may be simple, but words are always complex. Yet the construction of an intertextual field is disconcerting as well as enriching because intertexual concordance produces a reality-discord, an overlay or distancing of the referential function of speech, of the word-thing, word-experience relation. Even though the *fact* of correspondence between language and experience is not in question (there is a complex answerability of the one to the other), the *theory* of correspondence remains a problem. I want to conclude my remarks by suggesting that intertextual awareness follows from the character of words, and that it does not divorce us from dearly beloved experience, or Wordsworth's 'the world, which is the world of all of us.'

'There was a time' (l. 1) immediately introduces the motif of time in a colloquial and inconspicuous way. Yet as the poem proceeds, the expression begins to border on myth. It becomes reminiscent of the *illo tempore*, the 'in those days,' of mythical thought. Wordsworth locates that mythical epoch at the barely scrutable edge of everyone's memory of childhood. During this numinous time, a 'celestial light' invests natural objects, although later we learn also about darker moments, 'Blank misgivings of a Creature/Moving about in worlds not realized' (Ode, 144–45). The darkness and the light are intervolved, as in a Grasmere storm. But the metaphor of light predominates, and the poet's loss is described in terms of it.

The third stanza deepens as well as qualifies that sense of loss. The 'to me alone' of line 22 points to an event closer to augury than subjective feeling; it singles the poet out. He haruspicates himself. His inability to respond fully to nature, what does it mean? Was the vanished natural light perhaps an inner and now failing light, not given from outside but rather *bestowed* from within by imagination?

That gleam, moreover, whatever its source, seems preternatural. It suggests that the bond between nature and imagination is precarious from the outset, with imagination seeking to wed itself to nature, in order to become poetry rather than prophecy. That is certainly how it seemed to Blake when he read the Ode. He was deeply moved by it, but denounced the 'natural man' in Wordsworth always rising up, as he put it, against the imaginative man.

Those acquainted with Wordsworth know that a simple turn of thought can trigger a radical turning about of his mind and release a near-apocalyptic sense of isolation. Blake is right in the sense that even when the final mood-swing or '*envoi*' of the Ode ends ominously,

> And O, ye Fountains, Meadows, Hills, and Groves,
> Forebode not any severing of our loves!

> (187–88)

Wordsworth pretends that the portent comes from nature rather than from himself. He will not acknowledge that the bond with nature – more psychic than epistemic – is broken. 'I could wish my days to be/Bound each to each by natural piety.'

'I *could* wish'? How strangely tentative that sounds! The wish hesitates, I suspect, because its very success, its potential fulfillment, might go against nature by confirming the omnipotence of wishful thought. A similar scruple may hover over stanza 3 and the 'timely utterance' that allows the ode to turn upward instead of spiraling downward or breaking off. The very discretion of the phrase protects it from being construed as a wish, or any sort of direct – imperative – speech-act.

'Timely utterance,' then, does not pose only a problem of reference. The indirect phrasing involves signifier as well as signified: the poet's attitude toward a higher mode of speech, whether wishful or prophetic. Wordsworth's expression is guarded: he does actually wish; rather, he 'could wish' that the bond with nature should continue, and that the mutability suggested by 'There was a time' should not bode an end to time itself, a discontinuity between *illo tempore* and his present or future state. The 'timely utterance' meets that anxiety about time; and as 'utterance' it suggests that someone else has made a wish for the poet and so relieved him of the responsibility. It is as if a thought had been taken out of his heart and uttered. The structure is similar to that of the famous dedication scene in *The Prelude*, which makes him aware of his calling as poet. 'I made no vows, but vows/Were then made for me; bond unknown to me/Was given...' (V, 534–36).[7] In the Ode, too, we do not know who utters what. Even if the utterance took place within the poet, it was not his but some other voice. A 'discours de l'Autre' (Jacques Lacan) takes away the burden of wishful or visionary speech. There exists, in fact, one such Discourse of the Other that is *timely* and *bonding*, and even joins the theme of speaking to that of giving light:

> And God said, Let there be light: and God divided the light from the darkness. And God called the light Day, and the darkness he called Night. And there was evening and there was morning, one day.

These are 'timely' words indeed: they create time, they establish it beyond all misgiving. What is founded, moreover, bonds a reponsive nature (or what is to be nature) to an utterance, and God to his own work, for he acknowledges by direct acts of naming and blessing what has been called into being.

I am tempted, at last, to make an assertion and identify the 'timely utterance.' 'Let there be light: and there was light' utters itself in the poet's mind as a proof-text, that is, not only as a deeply subjective wish for the return of the light whose loss was lamented in the first two stanzas, but also as that wish in the form of God's first words, His 'Let there be.'

I have taken one phrase as my starting point and made many angels dance on it. These revels would be in vain if Wordsworth's Ode were not involved in the question of voice as well as light: in what connection there still might be between poetry and prophecy. 'A Voice to Light gave Being,' Wordsworth writes in a later Great Ode, alluding to fiat or logos. Yet there is a fear lest poetic voice, in its very power, may call on darkness, and become decreative rather than creative and so a 'counter-spirit' or parody of the 'divine I AM.' Then the prophetic or poetic voice could serve, however involuntarily, the cause of cursing, not of blessing, and wish for an end, a dissolution of work and world. The utterance that surprised Wordsworth is, from one perspective, an archetypal instance of wish-fulfillment or omnipotence of thoughts. Yet from another perspective it is an exemplary instance of poetry as a creative speech-act that leads to natural piety rather than to apocalyptic solipsism or transcendence.

Wordsworth's most felicitous poetry merges wishing, responding, and blessing: merges, in fact, a first timely utterance, the fiat, and a second timely utterance, the covenant. If, in stanza 3 of his Ode, the sounding cataracts and the 'timely utterance' are echo-aspects of each other, it is because what was founded must be founded a second time, on the flood; just as the light that was has to be lit again, now. The Covenant is a second creation confirming the first; while the rainbow as a timely sign recalls an utterance that could make the poet's heart leap up. The Intimations Ode is the third of this series. It is the poet's response, his covenant-sign, his own 'timely utterance,' incorporating mutely – as silent light – the divine *davar*, that is, the text on which my own intertextual leaping comes to rest.

Notes

1. 'The Immortality Ode,' reprinted in *The Liberal Imagination* (1948).
2. That we are reluctant to develop the resonances of a critic's prose, even a critic as deliberate as Trilling, does not mean they are not felt. Ironically, Trilling's answer, when it does come (in the fourth section of his essay) is one that leads to a displacement from one phrase or word-complex to another, and so enlightens without disburdening the poem.
3. 'Surprised by joy, – impatient as the wind,' (1815).
4. Cf. in the second stanza of 'A slumber did my spirit seal' the verse 'Rolled round in earth's diurnal course.' An image of *gravitation* elides or displaces that of the *grave*; and the tacit verbal pun is reenforced by the fact that 'di*ur*nal' is followed by 'course,' a word that sounds like the archaic poetic pronunciation of 'corpse.' (I owe 'course-corpse' to Jay Farness.) Could one show, in Wordsworth, a convergence of nature's eliding (subliming) of the corpse, and poetry's eliding (subliming) of the referent?

5. See Trilling, *The Liberal Imagination* (New York, 1953), p. 130.
6. I agree with Paul de Man ('The Dead-End of Formalist Criticism,' *Blindness and Insight*, 2nd ed., 1983) in his understanding of pastoral as much more than convention or genre. 'There is no doubt that the pastoral theme is, in fact, the only poetic theme, that it is poetry itself.' De Man's insight comes by way of a critique of Empson and the doctrine of 'reconciliation,' a critique that limits the rigorous and principled criticism initiated by Richards.
7. The placement of 'unknown' causes an ambiguity. It could refer to the bond or to its character vis-à-vis the receiver. 'An unknown bond was given – to me, who was unaware (unknowing) of it at the time.' The 'unknown' points to what is knowable yet difficult to locate as conscious knowledge at a single spot in time. Its place in the verse-line is self-displacing.

2.3   MARJORIE LEVINSON: 'THE INTIMATIONS ODE: A TIMELY UTTERANCE' (1986)

Marjorie Levinson is F. L. Huetwell Professor of English at the University of Michigan. She has been a central figure in the development of 'new historicism' within Romantic studies, and the book from which the present essay is taken, *Wordsworth's Great Period Poems*, is regarded as one of its founding texts. Although it appeared a year before Hartman's essay, above, we have positioned it last in this chapter because, as Levinson's introduction to the book makes clear, it is a direct challenge to the dominance of Yale deconstruction and represents the direction Romantic studies were to take over the next ten years. This introduction itself offers a concise sketch of the situation in which 'the new historicist criticism' (p. 13) is emerging, and – while acknowledging the importance of the 'idealising interpretative model' of Bloom, de Man and Hartman on the one hand, and the 'historical', but not *'historicist'*, scholarship of David Erdman, Carl Woodring and E.P. Thompson on the other (p. 1) – proposes a project which will go beyond both. Drawing on the theoretical work of Althusser, Macherey, Jameson and Eagleton, and other critics she sees as 'at once materialist and deconstructive', the 'new historicism' would deploy the 'historical imagination' to restore to a work manifold 'contemporary meanings, originally associated with or systematically informing the poet's representations' (p. 11). Levinson's object, then, is to explain the 'constrained manner in which Wordsworth sought figurally, mythically, or formally to resolve those conflicts which were his *idées fixes*, so to speak, his ideological knowledges' (p. 3). She will do this, by way of 'a theory of negative allegory', in a criticism which will 'take possession of these trouble spots, or take up a position within but not *of* the ideology it seeks to articulate' (pp. 8–10). In this way, the 'new historicist' criticism acquires 'the capacity to know a work as neither it, nor its original readers, nor its author could know it' (p. 12). A later work to which Levinson contributes a further important introduction and essay is M. Levinson, Marilyn Butler, Jerome McGann and Paul Hamilton, *Rethinking Historicism* (Blackwell, 1989). A useful critique of the impact of the 'new historicism' on Romantic studies is Philip W. Martin's 'Romanticism, History, Historicisms', in Kelvin Everest, ed., *Revolution in Writing: British Literary Responses to the French Revolution* (Open University Press, 1991); see also the brief critique of Levinson's project in Easthope, *Wordsworth Now and Then, op. cit.*, pp. 131–2.

In light of the above, how would you relate Levinson's specific reading strategies on the 'Ode' to her general project? How does she interrelate deconstruction and materialist history? What is the exact nature of the 'negative allegory' deployed here: what, in her terms, is the 'Ode' made to say which it could not itself 'know'? Given that Hartman's essay also uses the same phrase from the 'Ode' – 'timely utterance' – in its title, consider what different meanings it is given in the two essays. Use this as a starting-point for an analysis of the kinds of deconstruction these critics employ. In her book's title, Levinson uses the word 'great' to describe Wordsworth's poems. How is this judgement arrived at or justified? What notions of 'literary value' does it suggest underlie her criticism? Finally, compare her understanding of 'new historicism' with the 'cultural materialism' practised by other critics in other exercises (e.g. Jardine in Ch. 1, pp. 54–68; Sinfield in Ch. 5, pp. 225–31). What different conceptions of history inform them? Does 'new historicism', as some have charged, lock literature away in its own past, so 'depoliticizing' it and effacing the interpretative role and perspective of the critic who reads in the present?

The following essay is Ch. 3 of *Wordsworth's Great Period Poems: Four Essays*, Cambridge University Press, 1986, pp. 80–104, *passim*.

The Intimations Ode: A Timely Utterance

The essay opens, by way of M. H. Abrams' work, with a discussion of the 'Ode's' essentially Romantic repudiation of politics, history and the Revolutionary concept of Nature.

[...]

In Wordsworth's poem, history acquires its meaning through its bearing on one man's life. The failure of the French Revolution is represented as exclusively the poet's loss, and as a strictly emotional, epistemological loss: 'To me alone there came a thought of grief.' The meaning of this representation resides in its originary function: to transfer ideologically *possessed* material from public to private domain.

[...]

One-and-a-half pages are omitted here which cite Hazlitt as contemporary evidence that the 'Ode' was seen as 'a commentary on the French Revolution and its metamorphoses'.

[...]

To suggest that Wordsworth's general theme – the terrors and *longueurs* of Experience – gets focused through a topical issue is not to trivialize or in any way depreciate that high theme. The Ode *is* about the inevitable loss of that celestial light which makes of everyone's childhood a 'visible scene / On which the sun is shining.' I propose only that the archetypically radiant state of Innocence remembered and recreated in stanzas 1–4 – a touchstone for the Ode's emotional and intellectual argument – was embodied for Wordsworth and his readers in the memory of a briefly enlightened epoch in human history. When the odal narrator observes, 'There was a time,' a reader such as Hazlitt may have recalled the opening phrase of Coleridge's 'Religious Musings' – 'This is the time' – itself an echo of Milton's 'This is the month.' In Coleridge's ode (1794), the phrase designates the millennium once glimpsed in the French Revolution. To read Wordsworth's general elegiac lament against Coleridge's (and Milton's) fiercely specific proclamation is to identify the occasion of that lament as the passage of a *particular* time, say, 1790–93.

The poet's nostalgia, then, for a vivid experience of Nature, must be the reflex and expression of his nostalgia for the particular idea of Nature which informed the Revolution and its philosophic discourse. The Nature addressed as a *dea abscondita* in stanzas 1–4 (and demystified in 5–8) is the concept personified in eighteenth-century libertarian art: fierce goddess of the Revolution, incarnation of freedom, ground of sociality, and guarantor of the meaning of mundane experience.[1] It is, moreover, and as I argue below, the Nature conceived by Holbach and the philosophic school he exemplified. The Child Wordsworth addresses in the strophe as a lost power – the power to feel Nature's meanings – is a displacement of the poet's own young manhood with its unconflicted attachments to Nature and mankind. And the child he celebrates in stanza 8, 'best philosopher,' is a negation of the ratiocinative methods and analytic values so famously associated with the French *philosophe* – implicitly, 'worst philosopher.'

Mary Moorman has remarked Wordsworth's habit of 'telescoping' incidents which occurred at different times, and her metaphor aptly describes the method of the Ode.[2] There, in a single field of vision, Wordsworth interweaves his and his generation's political and philosophic disillusion with his private memory of a season of 'glad animal spirits.' These two themes – the one derived from a recent, specific, and social experience, the other an eternal, existential fact – meet in Wordsworth's awareness that by negating the structure of ideas which had formed his young manhood, he renounced as well the vital self which he had experienced through that conceptual structure and in the era of its social hegemony.

By reconstructing the occasion, private and public, of this awareness and its expression, I hope to elucidate the function of the vision elaborated in stanzas 5–8, a vision sharply inconsistent with Wordsworth's canonical statement, as the poet himself acknowledged in 1843.

The first extrinsic factor to address is the immediate compositional situation. The odal strophe (stanzas 1–4) was written on a day of national significance, March 27, 1802, the day which concluded the negotiations for the Peace of Amiens. Wordsworth could not have known *on* the twenty-seventh that the peace with Napoleon was achieved that day, but the press had been full of the business for months. On March 15, the dispatches from Amiens arrived by special courier and the cabinet council hastily convened to examine them. The papers were returned for signing as reported in *The Times* of March 17, and on the thirtieth, the arrival of the definitive treaty was proclaimed.[3] Wordsworth, an avid reader of *The Times*, could not have been ignorant of the imminent conclusion to the negotations. The perfect coincidence of national events with Wordsworth's poetical calendar is sheer serendipity. But the fact that the Ode was conceived in mid to late March 1802, the season of the final talks, strongly urges a causal explanation. The ode is, of course, the traditional formal choice for a poem on the occasion of a major national event.

The treaty officially marked the end of the season of conflict for Wordsworth, the season which began in 1793, when he could hope only for a divorce between 'him who had been' and 'the man to come.'[4] With the end of hostility between his two early allegiances, Wordsworth could begin to reintegrate his experience. The treaty, which vastly favored France's imperialistic regime, underlined the perfidy of the Revolution and the faultiness of its guiding principles. (Sheridan called the treaty 'a thing of which every man must be glad but no man can be proud.') Thus while the Peace brought to Wordsworth a welcome end to his divided loyalties, it also impressed on him once and for all the error of his 'first affections.'

Moreover, spring 1802 was the season of Wordsworth's projected marriage to Mary Hutchinson and of his visit to and emotional divorce from Annette Vallon.[5] Wordsworth had, of course, given up Annette long before 1802; he had also emerged from his Jacobin enthusiasm at least two years before he began writing the Ode. But it is one thing to 'pass insensibly,' as it were, from one position to its 'contrary,' feeling all the while that 'things revolve upon each other.'[6] It is quite another to find that not altogether perspicuous decisions and/or circumstance have enjoined upon one a position sharply antithetical to a former structure of belief. Wordsworth's engagement to Mary not only cast the involvement with Annette as a digression from what had come to seem his domestic destiny, it officially marked the period of the romantic phase of the affair.[7] In the same way, the Peace of Amiens, by formalizing France's role as imperialist aggressor, had to figure a major breach in the poet's carefully integrative self-chronicle. The closures thus defined for Wordsworth by the peace and by his betrothal could well have compelled him to revise more deliberately than he had yet done his sense of the past.

By 1802, Wordsworth was well established in the country of his boyhood and in the domain of a remembered Nature associated with eternally recurrent revolutions, as opposed to violent, political, and singular Revolution. He had engaged to marry an old family friend, a countrywoman. At such a time, the gap between Wordsworth's childhood and his present maturity would have seemed especially wide. The closing of that gap – which is to say, the reinterpretation of those 'noisy years' of political passion – is a major objective of the Ode, as its headnote implies:

> The Child is Father of the Man;
> And I could wish my days to be
> Bound each to each by natural piety.[8]

Hence, I suggest, the indirection of Wordsworth's ideological revisions, by which he avoids the discontinuity of a recantation in the style of Coleridge's 'France: An Ode' (1798; reprinted October 1802).[9]

The poems written in closest proximity to the Ode – 'To the Cuckoo,' 'The Rainbow,' and the Sonnets Dedicated to Liberty – betray Wordsworth's preoccupation with what seemed to him the fragmented condition of his life, a condition foregrounded by personal and political developments.

[...]

A few lines on the first two lyrics are cut here.

[...]

The Sonnets to Liberty, most of which were written in 1802–3, many of them based on Wordsworth's 1802 visit to France, articulate in full voice some of the themes which are rendered *sotto voce* in the Ode. Whereas 'To the Cuckoo' and 'The Rainbow' treat abstractly of existential discontinuities, the sonnets anchor these sensations to the dispiriting view of Napoleonic France. In that several of the sonnets contrast England's moral decline to the glorious era of *her* Revolution, readers have associated the republican rhetoric of the series with a lofty Miltonic eloquence. This rhetoric had, however, become the stylistic exponent of the Jacobin position, and, in terms of referential priority, the French Revolution clearly took precedence over the Puritan. Moreover, the preponderance in both the sonnets and the Ode of certain key words and verbal effects evoking the classical naturalism of Enlightenment rhetoric strongly imputes to the Ode the political themes developed in the sonnets.[10] When one reads in Sonnet 11, 'Inland, within a hollow vale, I stood; / And saw, while sea was calm and air was clear, / The Coast of France ...' – prelude to a depressing political reverie – it is difficult not to think of the *meta*-physical prospect seized by the narrator toward the end of the Ode:

> Hence in a season of calm weather
> Though inland far we be,
> Our Souls have sight of that immortal sea
> Which brought us hither,
> Can in a moment travel thither,
> And see the children sport upon the shore,
> And hear the mighty waters rolling evermore.

To attend that echo means historicizing the Ode's ideal and imagined scene by associating the narrator's indefinite *accidie* with the spiritlessness infecting all those children of the Revolution who lost their Innocence and their Eden when France lost her virtue.

The third sonnet of the series, with its extended depiction of France's political springtime, presents some suggestive parallels to the pastoral festivities represented in the Ode. Wordsworth describes the French countryside, 1790, as 'like the May / With festivals of new-born Liberty' (1837 revision). 'The antiquated earth / Beat like the heart of Man,' and the narrator recalls the joyous expressions of this new rhythm: 'songs, garlands, mirth, / Banners, and happy faces.' Then, reductively and in rueful retrospect, he acknowledges the irrecoverability of 'these things.' Here, as in *The Prelude* (Books 6 and 10) and the Ode (stanzas 1–4), Wordsworth elegizes that perfect harmony of man with Nature, singular with social existence, which defined for the poet and through his experience of 'the gorgeous festival era of the Revolution' the meaning of that tremendous event.[11]

Wordsworth's style ultimately tells us more about his referential universe than do his representations per se.

[...]

A paragraph on critics' observation of the 'stylized, static, and ideal' manner of the poem follows here.

[...]

The simplicity of the Ode is, then, quite unlike the experiential and idiomatic inflection of 'Tintern Abbey,' despite the initial tonal and thematic resemblances. The Intimations Ode develops an austere, monumental, and self-conscious simplicity – a *philosophic* simplicity denoting the purity of a language and iconography purged of the topical, the local, the particular, the adventitious.[12]

Consider, with reference to the history of styles and their ideological meanings, Wordsworth's portentous isolation of common – and commonplace – nouns

(Rainbow, Rose, Moon, etc.); the pointedly archaic, hieratic pronominalization (thy, ye, thou) and phrasing (and cometh from afar, behold the Child); the oratorical expressions of pathos (stanzas 1 and 2); the conspicuous use of parallelism; the idealized simplification of Nature.[13] In his work on the art of the Revolution, D. L. Dowd has described the character of David's painting as follows:

> The form ... was 'classical' ... [or] characterized by all emphasis upon line rather than color, upon static composition rather than movement, and upon the imitation of Greek and Roman sculpture. On the other hand, the treatment of his subject matter was highly 'realistic' in its imitation of nature. Finally, the content of his art was essentially romantic, if by 'romantic' we mean ... an admiration of an enviable and idealized past, and an emphasis upon an emotional message.[14]

To read these comments in the light of the Ode is to recognize in the opening movement of that poem the look of a particular painterly school. It is to materialize the *meaning* of Wordsworth's style: the pictorial but highly abstract representation of an ideologically charged object (the organic community) focused through emblematic tableaux (babe leaps up, children culling flowers) and suffused with nostalgia for an enviable and idealized past.

Wordsworth not only organizes his imagery in an ideologically specific fashion, he draws his denotative and iconic materials from the dictionary of eighteenth-century libertarian discourse. Rather than gloss these materials individually, let me bring out the relevant correspondences by sketching the argument developed allegorically in the Ode.

There was a time when Nature, conceived as goddess of the Revolution, was instinct with providential omens signifying human fulfillment in time. During this season and by virtue of a certain widely held belief structure, the common was sublime and quotidian life a recurrent sacrament. The individual felt himself to be a member of a vast human family: then, 'joy of one / [was] joy for tens of millions.' The pastoral community so poignantly portrayed in stanzas 3 and 4 gives us the displaced representation of that defunct ideal. Those 'things' (line 9) – the dreams of a particular time, place, and culture – have vanished. The narration *does* imply that man's power to perceive existing realities has also fallen off, but it presents that cognitive debility as the result, not the cause, of a more primary and a political disillusion. The syntax of the first two stanzas is clear, even insistent, about this: 'The things which I have seen'; 'There hath past away a glory from the earth.' The lines unambiguously denote an external depletion.[15] Nature, the product of a historical moment and its modes of perception, no longer houses the glorious meanings which had endeared physical and social reality. The narrator faithfully records the presence, even in an unhallowed Experience, of illuminations, most of them secondary or reflective sources: rainbow, moon, glittering waters, stars. The conceptual and therefore organizing effulgence, however – the light of Reason and Nature as kindled by the Enlightenment, that 'master-light' – has faded, rendering all other sources of light dubious, unreliable, or simply insufficient.

The word glory, so hardworking a noun in the Ode, seems to have been something of a code word during the Revolutionary era. Hazlitt [...] employs the word, and, in the idiom of the day, glory apparently signified something like the classical and Renaissance *virtù*. Brissot, leader of the Girondins, the party which briefly won Wordsworth's loyalty, proudly exclaimed, 'j'ai prodigieusement aimé la gloire.' Marat, describing the ancient Greek republics, asserts that 'glory, that fruitful source of whatever men have done that is great or beautiful, was the object of every reward.'[16] In 'France: An Ode,' Coleridge adorns his personification of Revolutionary France with 'clustering wreathes of glory,' and, in his *Lectures on Politics and Religion*, he refers repeatedly to that 'small but glorious band' of 'thinking and disinterested Patriots,' a theoretically defined Jacobin group.[17] In a substantial passage of *The Prelude* treating of Wordsworth's involvement with the Revolution, that interval is designated 'a glorious time, / A happy time' (Bk. 6, lines 754–55), and in two major passages, from *The Excursion* and *The Prelude*, the one somewhat sincere in its remembered political enthusiasm, the other openly derisive, the narrator recurs to the word glory.[18] Finally, Wordsworth's decision to render his phrase, 'great and glorious birth' – a phrase describing France's upsurge of Revolutionary energy – as 'lovely birth' in his revision of 'Descriptive Sketches' argues his sensitivity to the political nuance of the word.[19] When the narrator of the Ode recalls, then, 'the glory and the freshness of a dream,' he remembers that vision of individual, social, and natural harmony which was the ideological center of the Revolution. ('Dream,' here, is used in its high-Romantic, realized character.) When he laments, 'there hath past away a glory from the earth,' he observes Nature's lack of personal meaning to him now that its public and ideological meaning has been discredited.[20]

The explanation of Wordsworth's original epigraph – 'paulo majora canamus' – seems to reside here, in the poet's memory of a golden age in its dawning. The quotation is the first line of Virgil's Fourth Eclogue. The eclogue is generally assumed to have been composed 'to announce the Peace [of Brundisium and] to anticipate the natural and desired consequences of the wedding of Antonius and Octavia.' The Peace of Amiens, and Wordsworth's recent betrothal to Mary Hutchinson, might seem to present a debased or parodic occasional analogy (or a particularly egotistical sublime), but the resonance is not implausible. In the Fourth Eclogue, Virgil ushers in a new era, a golden age, 'to be fulfilled or at least inaugurated by a child soon to be born,' the child of an actual Roman father and matron. Or, Virgil's 'child of destiny' images a spiritual regeneration effected through the political actions of a temporal leader.[21]

By transforming the 'golden hours' of the Revolution (*Prelude*, Bk. 6, line 340) into a psychic and metaphysical postulate, Wordsworth adapts to his purposes the pre- and trans-figurative logic so often applied to Virgil's celebrated eclogue, but he suppresses the militant, apocalyptic thrust of that traditionary reading. (The dynamic which the Ode dramatizes is Abrams's 'paradox of spiritual quietism.') Moreover, the Virgilian allusion situates the whole business of temporal and spiritual renovation in the discourses of poetry. The French Revolution and the Roman wars both begin to look like leitmotifs. Thus the Ode's epigraph supports its transcendental and interiorizing themes and, at the same time, identifies the factual original of those themes, in this, operating in much the same way as the poem's other images and allusions.[22]

The fiction of stanzas 1–4 is that the narrator's own inevitably evocative utterance reminds him how concrete a thing his loss is. His attempted escapes into poetic pastoral ('Now, while the birds thus sing ...') repeatedly fail, and he is compelled to confront the form and meaning of his despair. 'To me alone there came a thought of grief.' That grievous thought, so emphatically particularized, announces the narrator's recognition of the occasion of his *Angst*: his memory of a vision of earthly delight, a vision which was political in both the widest and the narrowest sense of that word.

The strangely specific allusion to a 'timely utterance' is usually glossed as a reference to one of the two lyrics written on March 26, 'To the Cuckoo' and 'The Rainbow' ('My heart leaps up'). The narrator's cryptic reassurance of recovery from his thought of grief – as I have suggested, a political memory – implies a political antidote. The narrator confesses that the conception of Nature developed in 'To the Cuckoo' and 'The Rainbow' – healer of existential breaches and eternally available mnemonic system – 'solves' the historical problem: the invalidation of the Enlightenment idea of Nature. Yet as the narrator strives to consolidate experientially this ahistorical notion, symbols of that other, ideological Nature intrude, giving us a peculiarly Wordsworthian *et in Arcadia ego*.

'But there's a Tree, of many, one, / A single Field which I have looked upon, / Both of them speak of something that is gone.' Of all the symbols generated by the Revolution, none was more prominent than the Tree of Liberty. Wordsworth was, of course, familiar with this commonplace symbol; in the passage from *The Excursion* cited above, the Solitary paraphrases the 'prophetic harps' as follows: 'Bring garlands, bring forth choicest flowers, to deck / The tree of liberty!' Wordsworth spent the summer of 1790 enjoying the Federation, a month of celebration to be encountered throughout France.[23] 'C'est probablement vers les premiers jours de l'année 1790 que l'on commença dans les campagnes à planter des maïs que l'on appela arbres de la liberté.' Wordsworth was back in France, in residence, during the great Federation Feast, July 1792. Carlyle, in *The French Revolution*, describes the feast: 'There are tents pitched in the Champ-de-Mars; ... There are Eighty-three symbolic Departmental Trees-of-Liberty; trees and *maïs* enough.' He describes the great *mai* in the 1790 celebration: 'All lamplit, allegorically decorated; a Tree of Liberty sixty feet high; and Phrigion Cap on it.'[24]

By associating Wordsworth's Tree and Field (Champ de Mars) with the emblems and events of a glorious and irrecoverable era, one is in a better position to explain the abrupt intrusion of these images and the disproportionate emotion which the narrator brings to them, as well as their extreme specificity. The narrator thus indicates that his attempt to liberate the fond, pastoral memory from its original, political context ('There was a [that is, *some, any*] time...') has failed. The historicity of the imagery is as a return of the repressed.

In the Revolutionary context, Tree and Field had signified an apocalyptic idea and its imminent fulfillment. In the Ode, these natural objects assume, for a moment, their former and symbolic character; they remind the narrator of something that is gone. With that loss, all those natural objects which had been raised into social symbols through the corporate conviction that Nature meant Liberty and a culture redeemed, lapse back into the unhallowed commonplace.[25] Wordsworth's blazon, stanzas 1 and 2, is a cold pastoral, enumeration of signs denoting vacancy where once there was meaning. The Pansy that had risen to prominence by virtue of an 'analogically meaningful' notion of Nature becomes in stanza 10 'the flower.' The subsequent designation, 'meanest flower,' a negative valorization, suggests the christological and otherworldly tendency of 'the philosophic mind.' The narrator protests that *nature* yet lives for him and by his redemptive acts, but he also confesses that *Nature* – the historical idea which had endeared the Creation by binding mankind's happiness to her tutelage – is dead and cannot be resurrected.[26]

What emerges from the elegiac strophe is the narrator's reluctance to yield up the mental categories of the Enlightenment along with their content. The project which the Ode takes up in its antistrophe (composed in 1804) is that of emptying those structures – Nature and Reason – of their inherited, perfidious meanings. By endowing them with a new content, Wordsworth could heal the breach defined for him by the events of March 1802.[27] Stanzas 5–8 bespeak the poet's unequivocal interest in devaluing historical experience. These stanzas have always been read across an ideology: Platonic and Stoic. It is important, however, to identify the immediate object of Wordsworth's critique and thus the stanzas' primary ideological commitment. By representing life in time as irremediably and radically circum-scribed, inimical to man's happiness, and spiritually degenerative, Wordsworth exposes the Enlightenment as a misconstruction of the very order of things.

[...]

A paragraph adducing Holbach's materialist critique of Enlightenment ideas as influencing Wordsworth in the 'Ode' is omitted here.

[...]

Tenet by tenet, phrase by phrase, image by image, Wordsworth deconstructs the Enlightenment's 'vision splendid.'[28] To each of the *philosophes'* idols – freedom, individuality, joy, progress, Reason, illumination, Nature – Wordsworth opposes a bleak other: imprisonment, uniformity, sadness, accommodation, degeneration, memory, darkness, mind.[29] To suggest that our greatest power, clearest amplitude, was in a past we can barely recall, much less recover, is to set a regressive ideal for mankind. Politically, the Ode advances a radical conservatism; ethically, a doctrine of consolation and compromise; intellectually, a curriculum grounded in memory. When, in the epode, the narrator gives thanks for those 'obstinate questionings / Of sense and outward things,' he celebrates his inability to see those 'things' of stanza I, a reference to the material expressions of the Revolution and to his own believing endowment. This is to say, Wordsworth constructs his counterfaith from the very materials of Enlightenment thought.

A serviceable formulation of the negated position might go as follows. We are born into the light of Nature, a light we perceive by our inner light, Reason, which participates in that visible light; our earthly experience can be a progressive exercise in self-enlightenment rewarded by enhanced vitality and worldly control. Against this program, Wordsworth develops a vision of mankind not just as Nature's 'foster' (rather than 'natural') children, but as Inmates of her indomitable 'prison-house,' a phrase which, eighteen lines preceding a reference to 'that imperial palace,' must bring to mind the Bastille. The prison, we learn, is life itself; Nature, which had meant Liberty in the context of the Enlightenment, is represented in the Ode as the supreme jailer. In characterizing mankind's native dimension (its being's heart and home) as an imperial palace, Wordsworth not only appoints the protective enclosure over imaginative expansion (so-called Romantic Nature), he adopts the language of the Royalist position. Although he undercuts the elitism of the phrase by representing this mansion as a universal source, universally inaccessible, the allusion identifies Wordsworth's vision as a critique of the Revolution's millennial thrust. Likewise the epithet 'Nature's priest' at once inscribes and negates the Revolutionary program.

As we know, a great deal of Wordsworth's poetry and that of his contemporaries develops its Edenic, Experiential, and Paradisal visions with reference to the Child, symbolically and naturalistically invoked. This is not to rule out, however, more typical uses and derivations of the image in particular poems. In the Intimations Ode – as we can now see, a very timely utterance – the representation of childhood draws its meaning from several contrastive relationships. In the context of 1807, apostrophes to a Child could not but conjure Rousseau, he who *made* the child father of the man. The Rousseauvian child, empowered by his ignorance of the coercive categories of social life and by his undefended instinctual life, was, of course, a political as well as a psychic postulate. The construct of a former (but historical) sublimity serves in Rousseau as sanction of a future, and a historical, renaissance.

It is under this politicized aspect that Wordsworth presents his *Lyrical Ballads* 'wise child,' an essentialist, Enlightenment figure. In the ballads, this figure typically converts a complacent (read, 'conservative') narrator to a perception of a universe instinct with apocalyptic energy. The *Lyrical Ballads* child seizes the authority traditionally (paternalistically) accorded to age; his unclouded intellect grasps the simple, subversive truths which we are toiling all our lives not to find.

The wisdom with which the odal Child (a far more sublime and generalized representation) is credited is that of the removed seer. He is the passive possessor of a vision 'into the life of things'; his metaphysical penetration is incommunicable and, but for the pleasure and memories it yields him, without effect. Whereas the *Lyrical Ballads* child, something of an *enfant terrible*, performs a monitory (and minatory) function, the odal Child develops a critique of pure reason which amounts to a lesson in 'wise passiveness.' There is a devilish irony in all this. The French *philosophe* had invented the child as a symbol of unfettered Reason, powerful to see and to act on its clear visions. Wordsworth not only restricts this power to a period of physical and political impotence, he enlists it in the service of Enlightenment critique.

> Childhood is the cornerstone of the philosophy of [Wordsworth's] great Ode. The child's joyous acquiescence in the free spirit of life and his indomitable instinct for the unseen and eternal make him humanity's best philosopher.[30]

This observation by Helen Darbishire may sound dated, but its substance would not be rejected by most modern Romanticists. Once we appreciate, however, the extent to which the Ode is informed by political associations and anxieties writ large elsewhere in Wordsworth's canon and illuminated by the discourses of the day, we perceive the developmental and psychological themes as a device for (dis)figuring a specifically treacherous vision.

The dark determinism of the mythic stanzas is reinforced by the suggestion that active resistance to Nature's deadening influence only hastens the inevitable enslavement. Since self-affirmation implies acquiescence in the categories, hence the reality of natural life, even Prometheanism ultimately constitutes a self-betrayal: betrayal of the eternal by the earthly self. The Enlightenment commitment to exertion in the service of personal, intellectual, and social liberty is opposed in the Ode to the spiritual freedom passively realized by the Child in his possession by the immortal Mind, which is to him 'a Master o'er a Slave.'

The Ode associates 'delight and liberty' – the 'simple creed' of the Revolution – with the nonreflective condition of childhood. According to the Ode, adult wisdom, such as it is, begins in the memory of an Edenic infancy, proceeds by inference (intimation) to the hypostasis of a more blessed, prenatal state, and concludes in the certainty that 'natural life is the history of the acceptance of loss.'[31] This is an epistemology based upon normatively contrastive acts; present perception and historical memory live, move, and have their being through shadowy recollection of a noumenal world.

This scheme is what is meant by 'thoughts that do often lie too deep for tears.' The phrase divests 'philosophic thought' (rational, inductive problem solving: a communicable process and product) of the supreme value it had acquired during the Enlightenment. Such thought – Reason in its most, or least, exalted mood – had failed Wordsworth dramatically. In the Ode, he develops a context wherein to redefine Reason, thereby preserving a shade from his past. The canceled passage (lines 121–24) where the narrator postulates an intellectual life in death was more clearly in the service of this de- and re-valuation – a salvaging action.

Those grand and pitiful concluding lines ('To me the meanest flower that blows can give / Thoughts that do often lie too deep for tears') are not nearly so devoid of polemic as they seem. With this announcement, Wordsworth denies a correspondence essential to the whole structure of Enlightenment rationalism: a consensus correspondence between objects of thought (meanest flower) and the conceptual object (thought). Wordsworth clearly intends this denial; the expected phrase is 'feelings' too deep for tears. The narrator's affirmation brings out his independence of Nature, any indifferent piece of which 'means' insofar as it awakens a private memory of a consecrating past. Moreover, a thought that lies too deep for tears is also too deep for words. One might observe that a thought which cannot be formulated cannot be disconfirmed and, further, that such thought is the stuff of ideology. With the final line of the Ode, Wordsworth installs a definition of thought not just independent of Reason and Nature but inimical to them. We can, at this point, look back to 'Tintern Abbey' and its epistemological workings, and glimpse in that grammar yet another historical imperative.

In sum, Wordsworth's myth of the soul, a pragmatic narrative never assimilated into his thinking, situates his grief over the failure of the Revolution and the invalidation of its ideology within a vision so vast and impersonal as to 'disappear' that pain. Those 'noisy' or politically passionate and 'restless' years are contextualized by the sobered narrator as but 'moments in the being / Of the eternal Silence.'[32] The 'truths' to which mankind should cling are those, we learn, 'that wake, / To perish never,' decidedly *not* those which were born of historical immediacies and which maintain their relation to those lived truths. Wordsworth celebrates the sort of truths that no amount of 'listlessness, nor mad endeavour' – one might say, no attempts at implementation – can destroy. History is exposed in the Ode as an unworthy object of human interest and involvement, its challenges nugatory. 'Another race hath been, and other palms are won'; there are victories, the narrator's Pauline allusion suggests, far greater than those once anticipated from the French Revolution. Rather than grieve over those mundane losses, the reader is exhorted to set his sights on those other and spiritual palms. The heroism that Wordsworth ultimately defines is the capacity to live in the absence of a 'consecrating dream,' a 'dream of human life' – by the end of the poem exposed as a belle dame sans merci.

In place of that treacherous dream or 'gleam,' the narrator recommends the 'soothing thoughts that spring / Out of human suffering.' By this substitutive reemphasis, Wordsworth rejects the hectic, hopeful fellowship promoted by the Revolution. He derives the authentic human community from a common pathos, which is to say, from a shared knowledge of irremediable human defect and deficiency. The object of Wordsworth's Ode is, like Gray's, to 'teach [us we] are men.'

Let me ask once again the question framed at the outset: why would a writer concerned to empty out history structure his statement by way of political allegory? I have argued that a dominant motive of the Ode is to expose the fallacy of those analogical assumptions which had governed Enlightenment thought and Revolutionary action. By his allegorical efforts to bridge the abyss separating Nature from Mind ('clouds' from 'colour,' 'meanest flower' from 'thoughts'), Wordsworth at once defines that abyss and identifies Mind as the source and stuff of Nature's meaning.

In that the Ode develops a metaphysics of absence punctuated by individual projective acts:

Not for these I raise
The song of thanks and praise;
But for those obstinate questionings

Of sense and outward things,
Fallings from us, vanishings;
Blank misgivings of a Creature
Moving about in worlds not realized,

it behooves us to notice the tension between the poet's 'act of mind and the material acted upon.'[33] Of course, the narrator's triumph in the Ode is his concluding, symbolic act: his vision of a 'paysage consacré,' its meanings ineffable and consubstantial with its appearances. Since, however, the value of this achievement is predicated on its factitiousness – on the special motives and acts that produce it – we read most sympathetically by refusing the symbolic, the Romantic option.

This is one reason why I have elaborated here a '"knowledge" of the text' – what Terry Eagleton has defined as a reconstruction of 'the conflicts and dispositions of its specific historical codes...'[34] I agree with Eagleton that this is not always and necessarily the most important thing to do. But with a poem like the Ode – one which has been so securely seized as 'literary,' which has been 'detached by a certain hermeneutic practice from its pragmatic context and subjected to a generalizing reinscription' – it does seem to me most important right now and for the politics of Romantic scholarship to nudge the work toward a less literary register.[35]

Notes (cut, renumbered and abbreviated)

1. I refer to such artists as Peyron, Barthélémy, Jeaurat de Bertry – painters of allegorical works wherein topical and ideological argument is developed by a specifically charged classical style. For an apt literary representation of Liberty in the 1790s, see 'Invocation to Liberty,' anonymous, in *The Watchman*, March 25, 1796, in *Collected Works of Samuel Taylor Coleridge*, ed. Lewis Patton and Peter Mann, *The Watchman*, vol. 2 (London and Princeton: Routledge and Kegan Paul and Princeton University Press, 1970), p. 130.
2. Mary Moorman, *William Wordsworth: A Biography. The Early Years 1770–1803* (London: Oxford Univ. Press, 1957; rpt., 1968).
3. This research executed by Rick Halpern, Department of History, University of Pennsylvania.
4. Moorman, *Early Years*, p. 223.
5. Wordsworth became engaged to Mary Hutchinson probably during mid-November 1802; they planned a spring wedding (Moorman, *Early Years*, p. 518). Toward the end of March, however, two or three days after composing the strophe of the Ode, Wordsworth decided to take advantage of the peace and visit Annette at Calais. [...] Further discussion of the visit follows.
6. William Wordsworth, 'Essay upon Epitaphs' in *The Prose Works of William Wordsworth*, ed. W. J. B. Owen and Jane Smyser, vol. 2 (Oxford: Clarendon Press, 1974), p. 53.
7. Wordsworth maintained a correspondence with Annette until the war interrupted it again. Upon the marriage of his and Annette's illegitimate daughter, Caroline, Wordsworth settled £30 a year upon her until 1834, when he gave her the sum of £400 (Moorman, *Early Years*, p. 565). The closure I discern in Wordsworth's relationship with Annette (as prompted by his marriage to Mary) refers to an internal, intellectual and emotional shift rather than to an active expression of detachment.
8. The headnote was added in 1815, and it replaced the Virgilian epigraph. The new extract, with its existential generalities, obviously discourages the sort of pointed, politically sensitive reception invited by the original epigraph. The substitution suggests Wordsworth's interest in deemphasizing, even obscuring, the Ode's topical and allegorical dimension. The emergence of this interest, or its gradual ascendancy, is consistent with what we know of Wordsworth's political and social development.

9. Spoken by the Solitary: 'Such recantation had for me no charm, / Nor would I bend to it.' Like the Solitary, Wordsworth would not declare, with others, '"Liberty, / I worshipped thee, and find thee but a Shade!"' or 'dream.' (*The Excursion*, Book III, 11. 776–79). He did, however, say just that in the Ode, but through a subtler language than, say, Coleridge's.

10. 'Star,' 'splendour,' 'glory,' 'Man,' 'hope,' 'master-spirit.' Of course, the most elaborate metaphor in the Ode is that of light, and the political resonance of this word and image would have been obvious to Wordsworth's early readers. [...] Evidence of the contemporary currency of the metaphor is given.

11. 'Wordsworth, it is well known to all who know anything of his history, felt himself so fascinated by the gorgeous festival era of the Revolution ... that he went over to Paris and spent about one entire year between that city, Orleans, and Blois.' De Quincy, quoted in Leslie Chard, *Dissenting Republican: Wordsworth's Early Life and Thought in Their Political Context* (The Hague: Mouton, 1972), p. 70.

12. 'But if I am to tell the very truth, I find ... the great Ode not wholly free from something declamatory.' Thus does Arnold distinguish the Ode from Wordsworth's best and most characteristic poems, those which 'have no style.' Matthew Arnold, 'Wordsworth,' 1879.

13. These also define the Pindaric ode. The Intimations Ode is, however, predominantly Horatian in its private, contemplative, and tranquil character. One could think of the poem as representing an attempt to marry the two traditions, but this is to treat the work as an academic exercise, or to situate it in a rather narrow aesthetic space. I have been trying to ascertain the meaning of particular styles and formal decisions during a particular interval.

14. David Lloyd Dowd, *Pageant-Master of the Republic: Jacques-Louis David and the French Revolution* (Lincoln, Neb.: *University of Nebraska Studies*, no. 3, June 1948), p. 22.

15. The received readings of this stanza indicate, more than any other single fact, the idealist character of so much Romantic criticism. The lines which conclude the first and second stanzas of the Ode – 'The things which I have seen I now can see no more' and 'There hath past away a glory from the earth' – are typically taken as statements of spiritual exhaustion, perceptual debility, and decrease in personal power to consecrate the objective contents of vision. The literal meaning of these lines – the expression of an external and imposed impoverishment – is consistently overlooked.

    The language of several critics, however, seems to expose unacknowledged associations and assumptions of the sort I have isolated above. [...] The note continues by adducing such in work by Mary Moorman, Clifford Siskin and George Watson.

16. Harold Parker, *The Cult of Antiquity and the French Revolution* (N.Y.: Octagon Books, 1965), pp. 47, 48.

17. Samuel Taylor Coleridge, 'A Moral and Political Lecture' and 'Conciones ad Populum,' in *The Collected Works of Samuel Taylor Coleridge. Lectures 1795 on Politics and Religion*, ed. Lewis Patton and Peter Mann (Princeton and London: Princeton University Press and Routledge and Kegan Paul, 1971), pp. 12, 40.

18. The note quotes *The Excursion*, Book 3, 11. 711–26, and *The Prelude*, Book 11, 11. 236 ff., and then discusses the possible influence of a 'Burkean polemic' on the attitudes and figures in the 'Ode.'

19. A cross-reference to M. H. Abrams' essay, 'English Romanticism: The Spirit of the Age'.

20. Nature's fall into historicity is explicitly represented in the Sonnets Dedicated to Liberty as the result of a historical treason: the failure of the French Revolution. The Ode's representation of an abruptly profane experience of Nature can be illuminated with reference to that theme in the sonnets (see Sonnet 19).

21. Peter Manning, 'Wordsworth's Intimations Ode and Its Epigraphs,' *Journal of English and Germanic Philology* 82, no. 4 (October 1983): 526–40. And see Sir Ronald Syme, *The Roman Revolution* (Oxford: Oxford University Press, 1939), pp. 218, 219 (on the Peace of Brundisium and Virgil's Fourth Eclogue). Manning takes an interesting psychoanalytic approach. I thank Mac Pigman, California Institute of Technology, for identifying the classical, political meanings embedded in Wordsworth's allusion.

22. As I noted above, Wordsworth's 1815 decision to replace the Virgilian epigraph with a headnote quotation from 'The Rainbow' suggests his wish to suppress the originally political burden of the

Ode, and to emphasize the priority of what has been treated here as instrumental: the metaphysical, psychological argument. In the absence of the new headnote, stanzas 1 and 2 need not be construed as a reference to childhood. Although the indeterminacy of the phrase 'there was a time' conjures a mythical past, the line could have been read as a reference to the Revolutionary era; the new headnote makes such a construction more problematic.

23. Alan Liu, 'Wordsworth: The History in Imagination,' *ELH* 51, no. 3 (Fall 1984): 505–48.

24. Thomas Carlyle, *The French Revolution* (London: Dent, 1906), 2 vols; II, (p. 102), 1, (p. 285). See Abbé Henri Grégoire, *Essai historique et patriotique sur les arbres de la liberté*, 1794. Wordsworth's phrasing echoes St. Augustine's [...] in *Confessions*, **X**, **8**, quoted. [...] To hear this echo is not, of course, to yield up one's sense of the Ode's topical gestures, but to appreciate the ambivalence of those gestures. Such two-toned statements underline for us the difference between a 'consumption of the text and a revelation of a text through a deliberated distance.' (John Goode, *George Gissing, Ideology in Fiction* {New York: Barnes and Noble, 1979}, p. 32). Or, it is to actualize historically the Derridean postulate of writing as *pharmakon*: poison and remedy, a 'complicity of contrary values,' (Jacques Derrida, 'Plato's Pharmacy,' in *Dissemination*, trans. Barbara Johnson, Chicago: Univ. of Chicago Press, 1981), p. 125. Finally, it is to recognize in the Intimations Ode the project defined through 'Tintern Abbey' and more critically, to glimpse the internal limits of that project – a problematic.

25. Nature meant Liberty and accordingly, when Liberty in its historical incarnation proved itself a false god, Nature too was emptied out. The clearest expression of the symbology which married Nature and Freedom is Coleridge's 'France: An Ode.' The poem, prompted by France's invasion of Switzerland, 1798, was published in that year and later reprinted in the *Morning Post*, October 14, 1802, with the addition of a note and Argument. [...] The note goes on to outline the thought in Coleridge's poem.

26. The note reflects on the different inflections of the word 'dream' in the poem, and on 'flower', as symptomatic of Wordsworth's deep despair at 'the failure of the Enlightenment dream'.

27. A consideration of Coleridge's influence on Wordsworth in respect of the 'Ode's' exploration of a historically determinate 'cultural depression' (about France), and its offsetting by 'philosophic vision'.

28. Two years intervened between the composition of the strophe and that of the antistrophe. One might conjecture that in 1802, Wordsworth's emotional commitment to 'the vision splendid' and to his quondam involvement in it was still too intense to permit the thoroughgoing repudiation enacted in stanzas 5–8. The admission of loss was candor enough. By 1804, Wordsworth was more firmly consolidated in every way; whereas 1802 found him on the verge of marriage, by 1804 he had been established with Mary for two years. Moreover, Wordsworth's return to France on 'Buonaparte's natal day' in 1802 and the bitterly ironic pall cast over that lengthy visit, as well as the resumption of the war soon after, had to destroy any lingering attachment to France, or it had to sever once and for all in Wordsworth's mind the France of 1789–92 from Napoleon's France. [...] More follows to the effect that Wordsworth's growing 'distance' from his experiences in France was 'the chief factor in [his] decision to resume work on the Ode'.

29. Although I lacked the opportunity to read Ronald Paulson's recent study, *Representations of Revolution, 1789–1820* (New Haven: Yale University Press, 1983), before or during the composition of this essay, I would like to note here its consonance with my line of argument, and its confirmation of some local matters (see pp. 22, 24, 27, 46, 47, 149–50, 190, 192, and 206).

30. Helen Darbishire, ed., *Wordsworth: Poems in Two Volumes, 1807* (Oxford: Clarendon Press, 1952), p. xlvii.

31. Kenneth Eisold, *Loneliness and Communion: A Study of Wordsworth's Thought and Experience, Salzburg Studies in English Literature, Romantic Reassessment*, ed. Hogg (Salzburg, 1973), p. 130.

32. Truths 'do rest' upon the child, whereas the man vainly 'is toiling all [his] life' to recover those early wisdoms. He is restless in pursuing them and the more desperate his pursuit, the more he estranges himself from its object. 'Restlessness,' in the context of Wordsworth's canon, denotes political anxiety, the condition which came to a head in Wordsworth's London experience, 1793.

33. Simpson, *Figurings of the Real*, p. 113.
34. Terry Eagleton, *Walter Benjamin or Towards a Revolutionary Criticism* (London: Verso and NLB, 1981), pp. 122, 123. And see pp. 6–10, 22, 117.
35. Eagleton, *Walter Benjamin*, p. 123.

Chapter 3

Charlotte Brontë:
Jane Eyre

GENERAL INTRODUCTION

First published in 1847 under the male *nom-de-plume* Currer Bell, *Jane Eyre* immediately established that a new fictional talent had emerged, and the novel has remained a widely read 'classic' ever since. It was followed by *Shirley* (1849), *Villette* (1853) and *The Professor* (the last was Brontë's first-written novel but it was not published until 1857, after her death), which also have central female protagonists. For much of its literary history, *Jane Eyre* has been regarded as a fictional by-blow of Romanticism, or as a 'romantic' story of the relationship between the masterful Rochester and the demure but finally triumphant Jane; the last chapter opens: 'Reader, I married him.' More recently, as this exercise clearly demonstrates, the novel has gained a new and very differently inflected kind of canonic status. For feminist critics in the 1970s and 1980s especially, it became a key text in the analysis of earlier women's writing, of how a woman's 'voice' and psyche are articulated both in the conscious and the repressed discourses of the fiction. Indeed, what the text cannot 'speak' – about sexuality, about gender relations, about patriarchy – became more important than its authorized discourse, and the novel significantly gave the title to a well-known and influential volume of feminist criticism, *The Madwoman in the Attic*, by Sandra Gilbert and Susan Gubar (from which an excerpt is reprinted below), a title-phrase which retains its currency in discussions about women within patriarchy. It is worth noting that Virginia Woolf – herself a formative influence on modern feminist literary criticism – should have found the 'sudden' coming upon of Grace Poole oddly 'upsetting' (see below, p. 110); and that the whole sub-text of the novel was given sharp redefinition in Jean Rhys' 'revisionary' novel *Wide Sargasso Sea* (1966), which tells Bertha Mason's 'story' from a very different perspective to that implicit in *Jane Eyre*. Gayatri Spivak, later in the essay reproduced below, discusses Rhys' novel in her own context of 'revising' Anglo-American feminist criticism's construction of *Jane Eyre* as a 'cult text' while being blind to its reproduction of imperialist ideology.

All the excerpts included here are by female and feminist critics. Is it possible to identify a line of development from Virginia Woolf's early brief comments on the social and sexual determinants of the 'woman writer' to the later, more self-consciously theorized approaches? Try to define the *kinds* of feminism which inform each of the essays: do they have elements in common (the notion of Charlotte Brontë's repressed 'anger', for example, or of the 'not-said' as the novel's most significant discourse), or are they markedly different? What makes the Marxist-Feminist Literature Collective's piece 'Marxist', do you think? (They refer to Terry Eagleton's book *Myths of Power* – another Marxist reading with which theirs should be compared.) What are the characteristics of Gilbert and Gubar's project to recuperate *Jane Eyre* as a text speaking for oppressed women? (Is Elaine Showalter's term 'gynocriticism' – see Ch. 1, p. 30 – a relevant one in this context?) Are the first three excerpts usefully described as representing 'Anglo-American' feminist criticism, and how would a 'French feminist' approach differ? (See *A Reader's Guide* 3/e, pp. 212–13, 218–30; also, Moi and M. Eagleton in Further Reading below.) Are the insights and initiatives of psychoanalysis to be perceived in any of the essays? In what respects may Spivak's essay reveal the limitations of Western feminism? What, finally, are the *textual* strategies involved in the critical reading of *Jane Eyre* which flow from and articulate the theoretical premises of each of the essays?

Further Reading

A good collection of earlier critical responses to *Jane Eyre* (and *Villette*) is the Macmillan 'Casebook' edited by Miriam Allott (1973). Terry Eagleton's *Myths of Power* (Macmillan, 1975) is an extended (Althusserian) Marxist reading of the Brontë sisters' novels. For a formative text in Anglo-American feminist criticism (and 'gynocriticism'), see Elaine Showalter's *A Literature of Their Own* (Princeton University Press, 1977). More general books on feminist literary theory and criticism (especially on the Anglo-American/French feminisms debate) include Toril Moi, *Sexual/Textual Politics* (Methuen, 1985); Maggie Humm, *Feminist Criticism* (Harvester, 1986) and *A Reader's Guide to Contemporary Feminist Literary Criticism* (Harvester Wheatsheaf, 1994); and Mary Eagleton, ed., *Feminist Literary Criticism* (Longman, 1991).

3.1   VIRGINIA WOOLF: FROM *A ROOM OF ONE'S OWN* (1928)

Virginia Woolf (1882–1941) is best known for her modernist fiction (e.g. *Mrs. Dalloway*, 1925; *To the Lighthouse*, 1927; *Orlando*, 1928; *The Waves*, 1931; and *Between the Acts*, 1941), but she also produced many critical essays ('The Common Reader' series) and two texts which are now seen as seminal to feminist theory (although she rejected the description of herself as a feminist): *A Room of One's Own* and *Three Guineas* (1938). The latter explores the relation of militarism, fascism and legal injustice to patriarchy; while the former famously outlines women's material disadvantages throughout history in comparison to men, and the determining effects upon women writers' production of not having education, money, freedom and privacy. Woolf is now generally regarded as among the 'founding mothers' of contemporary feminism, who 'announces' many of the issues it addresses, and is herself wrestled over in the Anglo-American/French debate as either the quintessential woman writer writing about women's experience for women, or a heteroglossic linguistic 'voice' which subverts and displaces notions of fixed gender identities.

In the chapter from which the present excerpt comes, Woolf offers a brief historical overview, down to the nineteenth century, of the problems besetting the woman writer – lack of resources and privacy, discouragement and censure, little experience of the world, and no female 'tradition' behind her to emulate and be sustained by. In the extract itself, she identifies Brontë's 'anger' as informing her text and, indeed, as constituting the 'flaw in the centre' of it (p. 111, below). How would later feminist critics regard this anger, this condition of being 'at war with her lot' (p. 110)? Do you regard *Jane Eyre* as 'flawed' ('deformed and twisted', p. 110) because of it? What notions of literary value underpin Woolf's ability to make this judgement? She also comments that it is Brontë's 'ignorance' which makes Rochester's portrait seem 'drawn in the dark' (p. 111). Consider this, and the lines which immediately follow it, in the context of more recent feminist criticism, and suggest how contemporary critics might 'read' Rochester's character.

The following extract is from Ch. 4 of the Penguin edition, 1967, pp. 68–75, *passim*.

A Room of One's Own

If Jane Austen suffered in any way from her circumstances it was in the narrowness of life that was imposed upon her. It was impossible for a woman to go about alone. She never travelled; she never drove through London in an omnibus or had luncheon in a shop by herself. But perhaps it was the nature of Jane Austen not to want what she had not. Her gift and her circumstances matched each other completely. But I doubt whether that was true of Charlotte Brontë, I said, opening *Jane Eyre* and laying it beside *Pride and Prejudice*.

I opened it at Chapter Twelve and my eye was caught by the phrase 'Anybody may blame me who likes'. What were they blaming Charlotte Brontë for? I wondered. And I read how Jane Eyre used to go up on to the roof when Mrs Fairfax was making jellies and looked over the fields at the distant view. And then she longed – and it was for this that they blamed her – that

> then I longed for a power of vision which might overpass that limit; which might reach the
> busy world, towns, regions full of life I had heard of but never seen: that then I desired

more of practical experience than I possessed; more of intercourse with my kind, of acquaintance with variety of character than was here within my reach. I valued what was good in Mrs Fairfax, and what was good in Adèle; but I believed in the existence of other and more vivid kinds of goodness, and what I believed in I wished to behold.

Who blames me? Many, no doubt, and I shall be called discontented. I could not help it: the restlessness was in my nature; it agitated me to pain sometimes. ...

It is vain to say human beings ought to be satisfied with tranquillity: they must have action; and they will make it if they cannot find it. Millions are condemned to a stiller doom than mine, and millions are in silent revolt against their lot. Nobody knows how many rebellions ferment in the masses of life which people earth. Women are supposed to be very calm generally: but women feel just as men feel; they need exercise for their faculties and a field for their efforts as much as their brothers do; they suffer from too rigid a restraint, too absolute a stagnation, precisely as men would suffer: and it is narrow-minded in their more privileged fellow-creatures to say that they ought to confine themselves to making puddings and knitting stockings, to playing on the piano and embroidering bags. It is thoughtless to condemn them, or laugh at them, if they seek to do more or learn more than custom has pronounced necessary for their sex.

When thus alone I not unfrequently heard Grace Poole's laugh. ...

That is an awkward break, I thought. It is upsetting to come upon Grace Poole all of a sudden. The continuity is disturbed. One might say, I continued, laying the book down beside *Pride and Prejudice*, that the woman who wrote those pages had more genius in her than Jane Austen; but if one reads them over and marks that jerk in them, that indignation, one sees that she will never get her genius expressed whole and entire. Her books will be deformed and twisted. She will write in a rage where she should write calmly. She will write foolishly where she should write wisely. She will write of herself where she should write of her characters. She is at war with her lot. How could she help but die young, cramped and thwarted?

One could not but play for a moment with the thought of what might have happened if Charlotte Brontë had possessed say three hundred a year – but the foolish woman sold the copyright of her novels outright for fifteen hundred pounds; had somehow possessed more knowledge of the busy world and towns and regions full of life; more practical experience, and intercourse with her kind and acquaintance with a variety of character. In those words she puts her finger exactly not only upon her own defects as a novelist but upon those of her sex at that time. She knew, no one better, how enormously her genius would have profited if it had not spent itself in solitary visions over distant fields; if experience and intercourse and travel had been granted her. But they were not granted; they were withheld.

[...]

Here follow two-and-a-half pages of more general reflection on women writers' lack of experience of 'the world', and, via *War and Peace*, on the structural 'integrity' of novels – the sense of 'conviction ... that this is the truth' – failing which 'they come to grief somewhere'.

[...]

for the most part, of course, novels do come to grief somewhere. The imagination falters under the enormous strain. The insight is confused; it can no longer distinguish between the true and false; it has no longer the strength to go on with the vast labour that calls at every moment for the use of so many different faculties. But how would all this be affected by the sex of the novelist, I wondered, looking at *Jane Eyre* and the others. Would the fact of her sex in any way interfere with the integrity of a woman novelist – that integrity which I take to be the backbone of the writer? Now, in the passages I have quoted from *Jane Eyre,* it is clear that anger was tampering with the integrity of Charlotte Brontë the novelist. She left her story, to which her entire devotion was due, to attend to some personal grievance. She remembered that she had been starved of her proper due of experience – she had been made to stagnate in a parsonage mending stockings when she wanted to wander free over the world. Her imagination swerved from indignation and we feel it swerve. But there were many more influences than anger tugging at her imagination and deflecting it from its path. Ignorance, for instance. The portrait of Rochester is drawn in the dark. We feel the influence of fear in it; just as we constantly feel an acidity which is the result of oppression, a buried suffering smouldering beneath her passion, a rancour which contracts those books, splendid as they are, with a spasm of pain.

And since a novel has this correspondence to real life, its values are to some extent those of real life. But it is obvious that the values of women differ very often from the values which have been made by the other sex; naturally, this is so. Yet it is the masculine values that prevail. Speaking crudely, football and sport are 'important'; the worship of fashion, the buying of clothes 'trivial'. And these values are inevitably transferred from life to fiction. This is an important book, the critic assumes, because it deals with war. This is an insignificant book because it deals with the feelings of women in a drawing-room. A scene in a battlefield is more important than a scene in a shop – everywhere and much more subtly the difference of value persists. The whole structure, therefore, of the early nineteenth-century novel was raised, if one was a woman, by a mind which was slightly pulled from the straight, and made to alter its clear vision in deference to external authority. One has only to skim those old forgotten novels and listen to the tone of voice in which they are written to divine that the writer was meeting criticism; she was saying this by way of aggression, or that by way of conciliation. She was admitting that she was 'only a woman', or protesting that she was 'as good as a man'. She met that criticism as her temperament dictated, with docility and diffidence, or with anger and emphasis. It does not matter which it was; she was thinking of something other than the thing itself. Down comes her book upon our heads. There was a flaw in the centre of it. And I thought of all the women's novels that lie scattered, like small pock-marked apples in an orchard, about the second-hand book shops of London. It was the flaw in the centre that had rotted them. She had altered her values in deference to the opinion of others.

3.2   THE MARXIST-FEMINIST LITERATURE COLLECTIVE: FROM 'WOMEN'S WRITING: *JANE EYRE*' (1978)

The provenance of this essay, and the membership of the Collective, are noted in the opening section below. The group disbanded a short time after the paper was written, which remains its only published production. All the members of the Collective now hold senior professional posts broadly within the fields of literature and women's studies. The essay's full title (and content) was 'Women's writing: *Jane Eyre, Shirley, Villette, Aurora Leigh*' (the last is by Elizabeth Barrett Browning). Other works by members of the Collective which represent a socialist or Marxist feminist criticism are Cora Kaplan's essay 'Radical Feminism and Literature: Rethinking Millett's *Sexual Politics*' (1979; reprinted in M. Eagleton, ed., *op. cit.*); her book, *Sea Changes: Culture and Feminism* (Verso, 1986); and Michelle Barrett's *Women's Oppression Today: Problems in Marxist Feminist Analysis* (Verso, 1980). See also Judith Newton and Deborah Rosenfelt, *Feminist Criticism and Social Change: Sex, Class and Race in Literature* (Methuen, 1985) and *A Reader's Guide* 3/e, Ch. 8 on feminist theories.

The Collective's project is signalled very clearly in its title, and spelt out in the 'Theoretical introduction' included here. The date is important, as this paper was an intervention into a situation, bequeathed by the later 1960s, comprised of radical feminist criticism, deriving mainly from the work of Kate Millett; a new Marxist criticism, principally driven by Althusser and Pierre Macherey; and the neo-Freudian psychoanalytic theories of Lacan and Kristeva. The Collective attempts to negotiate a position which can draw fruitfully on all three sources – at once leavening a class-dominated strand of Marxism with the insights about gender offered by feminism and psychoanalytic theory, and resisting a radical feminism's tendency to be 'separatist' and 'formalist' in its minimizing of the social and economic realities shaping women's oppression and women's writing. 'Patriarchy' and 'literature' needed to be reinserted into their specific material conditions of domination and production.

In what ways are the tributary elements brought together in the essay? Do you see any consonance between it and the 'liberal' account of material determinants on women writers given by Woolf? Does the essay, in a sense, 'correct' what has (later) been criticized as the narrow literariness of Gilbert and Gubar's approach in the following extract? Compare and contrast the (Machereyan) notion of the text's 'not-said' (pp. 117, 119, 120, below; what does the essay reveal it to be?) with the reading of Bertha Mason as Jane's 'truest and darkest double' (p. 126, below) in Gilbert and Gubar. For all its radicalism of intent and purpose, is it legitimate to criticize the essay for its (characteristically Anglo-American) tendency to re-tell the story of women's oppression, thus locking women into a realm of inescapable victimization, passivity and powerlessness? What model of a reading practice can you extrapolate from the paper in order to apply it to a different text – say, Emily Brontë's *Wuthering Heights*?

The essay from which the following extract is taken was first published in the (now defunct) journal, *Ideology and Consciousness*, 3, Spring 1978, pp. 27–48; pp. 27–34 are reprinted here (the remainder of the essay focuses on the other novels listed in its full title).

Women's Writing: *Jane Eyre*

Who Are We?

This paper arises from the work of a group which has been meeting in London for one and a half years (though some of its members joined more recently). It was presented at the Essex Literature Conference in July 1977, by the whole Collective, whose members at the time were Cheris Kramer, Cora Kaplan, Helen Taylor, Jean Radford, Jennifer Joseph, Margaret Williamson, Maud Ellmann, Mary Jacobus, Michèle Barrett and Rebecca O'Rourke.

The cumbersome title – Marxist-Feminist Literature Collective – covers (or perhaps conceals), on one side of the hyphen – in the adjective 'Marxist – a diversity of positions in relation to Marxism. On the other side of the hyphen, the adjective 'feminist' points, among other things, to an important aspect of our practice. A major contribution of the women's movement has been the organis-ational principle of collective work; for all of us, the method of work within the group has been a departure from and a challenge to the isolated, individualistic ways in which we operate in academic spheres. Our paper, in its polylogic structure and presentation, draws on the continuing play of ideas and debate from within which we speak, and challenges the monologic discourse of patriarchal literary criticism.

Theoretical Introduction

A Marxist-feminist critical practice proposes to account for the inadequacies of a standard Marxist approach to literature and ultimately to transform this approach. In this paper we discuss the articulation of class and gender in terms both of the historical conjuncture of 1848 and of the problems of a Marxist-feminist method in theorising literature. Literary texts are assumed to be ideological in the sense that they cannot give us a knowledge of the social formation; but they do give us something of equal importance in analysing culture, an imaginary representation of real relations.

A Marxist-feminist approach, by focussing on gender as a crucial determinant of literary production, can provide a better understanding of literature as a gender differentiated signifying practice. This is not to privilege gender over class, but to challenge the tradition in which women's writing has often been hived off from the mainstream of male writing and criticism.

Both Marxism and Feminism have rightly taken considerable interest recently in the possibility of an integration between Marxist and psycho-analytic thought. Both Marxism and psychoanalysis propose their methods as exhaustive; but we argue that it is only through a synthesis of these two, problematic though that is, that we can unfold the crucial interdependence between class structure and patriarchy.

Lukàcs argued that coherent literary works could only be produced by a unified, ascending social class, and in this context he stressed 1848 as the date at which the bourgeoisie as a class and realism as a literary form began to decline. The limitations of this approach are notorious, and too numerous to list here. What we shall do is not only, using the ideas of Jacques Lacan, Pierre Macherey and others (1), analyse the incoherences and contradictions in the texts we discuss, but also relate these precisely to the marginal position of female literary practice in this period.

Central to our analysis of these texts is a recognition of the marginality of their authors to the public discourse of mid-nineteenth century society. The partial exclusion of women from the public literary world is one aspect of the general marginality of women in this period, as instanced by their exclusion from the exercise of political power and their separation from production. This congruence between the marginality of women writers and the general position of women in society is represented in the situation of many female characters in the texts.

The period of protest which culminated in the political events of the 1840s marked the transition from a manufacturing economy to the industrial capitalist mode of production – developments which had serious consequences for women and the family. Working-class women were drafted into production as a source of cheap labour; bourgeois women remained in the home and were separated from production. In both cases women were excluded from ownership of the means of production, distribution and exchange.

However, the inadequacy of a solely economic mode of analysis is shown by Engels' optimistic claim in 1884 that, because of working-class women's entry into the industrial labour process, '… the last remnants of male domination in the proletarian home have lost all foundation' (2). It is clearly necessary also to analyse the contemporary ideological formation in terms of the hegemony of patriarchal attitudes. Such attitudes are represented for example in the double standard of sexual morality, whereby women were either madonnas or whores, and middle-class women in particular were subject to the constraints of the ideology of domesticity and the angel in the house. The ideology of romantic love, while masking the economic basis of bourgeois marriage in this period as the exchange of women, shows by its persistence that it exists autonomously, independent of its specific economic functions in a given historical conjuncture.

The four texts under consideration foreground these questions. *Jane Eyre* (1847), *Shirley* (1849), *Villette* (1853), and *Aurora Leigh* (1857), can be read as a discussion of gender definition, kinship structures, and to some extent the relation between these and social class. The texts of Charlotte Brontë and Elizabeth Barrett Browning refuse to reproduce contemporary economic and ideological determinations; instead they represent a systematic evasion or interrogation of the Law of these determinations. Althusser has stressed its inescapability: 'The Law cannot be "ignored" by anyone, least of all by those ignorant of it, but may be evaded or violated by everyone…..' (3).

We argue that this 'evasion' of the law occurs in the texts in the interrelated areas of social class, kinship and Oedipal socialisation. The necessary connections between these three areas are represented in the texts' presentation of two key points of articulation – the institution of marriage and the role of the *pater familias*.

All the major female characters of the texts have an extremely marginal and unstable class position, and all display an obvious discrepancy between their class position and their alleged rightful status; their status is bourgeois, but they are all orphans and most of them are without financial independence. Comparing these texts with those of Jane Austen, the lack of determinacy of class background is striking.

The bourgeois kinship structure of the period, predicated on the exchange of women, is similarly evaded. None of the heroines have fathers present to give them away in marriage. More importantly, we can analyse marriage itself as the crucial point of articulation between class and kinship structures. This can be seen in two ways: on one hand, the only women in the texts who are free to exercise choice in marrying – Jane Eyre, Aurora Leigh, Shirley and Polly de Bassompierre – have, or miraculously acquire, some degree of financial independence.

On the other hand, the example of Caroline Helstone demonstrates with great force the law which Charlotte Brontë otherwise evades, in that her marriage to Robert Moore can only take place when the repeal of the Orders in Council has enabled him to be a successful capitalist. Without this repeal, he would have emigrated to Canada and she would have been an Old Maid!

The evasion of Oedipal determination, so crucial to gender definition in this period, will be discussed in more detail in its most striking manifestation, in *Aurora Leigh*. But in all these texts the devised absence of the father represents a triple evasion of all the areas we have so far mentioned – class structure, kinship structure and Oedipal socialisation. Its consequences are that there is no father from whom the bourgeois woman can inherit property, no father to exchange her in marriage, and no father to create the conditions for typical Oedipal socialisation.

The subversiveness of this evasion was recognised by contemporary reviewers, for in 1848 Lady Eastlake wrote in the *Quarterly Review*:

> We do not hesitate to say that the tone of mind and thought which has overthrown authority and violated every code human and divine abroad, and fostered chartism and rebellion at home, is the same which has also written *Jane Eyre*. (4)

In discussing literary texts, it is important to look at the way women's access to language is ideologically determined. One of the effects of the lack of access to education of which women writers complain is to exclude them from the discourses of institutions such as universities, law, politics and finance which structure their oppression. Women, who are speaking subjects but partially excluded from culture, find modes of expression which the hegemonic discourse cannot integrate. Whereas the eruptive word cannot make the culturally inaccessible accessible, it can surely speak its absence. Kristeva has classified these modes of expression as 'semiotic' as opposed to 'symbolic'.

Inevitably, the work of Kristeva has been considered for its obvious bearing on our analysis. Her notion of the semiotic comprised the repressed, pre-linguistic elements which are located in the tonal, rhythmic, expressive and gestural qualities of poetic discourse. In our view, her association of these qualities with the feminine is fallacious; she has used a cultural ascription of femininity to describe pre-linguistic elements which are in fact universal, and she thus risks privileging and feminising the irrational. But as we all know, intuition is still the shortchange given women by the patriarchy. Not only are there limitations from a feminist perspective, but by calling the feminine, or the semiotic, subversive, she formulates an anarchic revolutionary poetics which is politically unsatisfactory. Her argument, seductive as it is, idealises and romanticises the discursive ruptures of the avant-garde. Her failure to locate these notions historically also tends to eternalise the social exaggeration of biological difference. Nevertheless, her suggestive writings have polyphonic resonances in our work, which alludes to, sometimes even dwells on, the explosive and temporarily liberating dissonance within the texts.

Introduction to the Texts: Gender and Genre
In 1859, Charlotte Brontë made a final, impatient plea to Lewes:

> I wish you did not think me a woman. I wish all reviewers believed 'Currer Bell' to be a man; they would be more just to him ..... I cannot, when I write, think always of myself and what you consider elegant and charming in femininity .... (5)

Criticism of women writers is in general divided between the extremes of gender-disavowal and gender-obsession. The second tendency, which Brontë struggles against in Lewes, patronises women writers as outsiders to literary history, without justifying this apartheid. The Brontës are considered important 'women novelists', not simply novelists. This kind of 'gender criticism' subsumes the text into the sexually-defined personality of its author, and thereby obliterates its literarity. To pass over the ideology of gender, on the other hand, ignores the fact that the conditions of literary production and consumption are articulated, in the Victorian period, in crucially different ways for women and men. Any rigorous Machereyan analysis must account for the ideology of gender as it is written into or out of texts by either sex. Women writers, moreover, in response to their cultural exclusion, have developed a relatively autonomous, clandestine tradition of their own.

Gender and genre come from the same root, and their connection in literary history is almost as intimate as their etymology. The tradition into which the woman novelist entered in the mid-19th century could be polarised as at once that of Mary Wollstonecraft and of Jane Austen, with the attendant polarisation of politics – between revolutionary feminism and conservatism – and of genre – between romanticism and social realism. Wollstonecraft and Austen between them pose the central question of access to male education and discourse on the one hand, on the other the annexing of women's writing to a special sphere, domestic and emotional.

Austen's refusal to write about anything she didn't know is as undermining to the patriarchal hegemony as Wollstonecraft's demand for a widening of women's choices: the very 'narrowness' of her novels gave them a subversive dimension of which she herself was unaware, and which has been registered in critics' bewilderment at what status to accord them.

Bourgeois criticism should be read symptomatically: most of its so-called 'evaluation' is a reinforcement of ideological barriers. Wollstonecraft's, and later Brontë's, ambivalent relation to Romanticism, usually described as clumsy Gothicism, is bound up with their feminism. Romanticism becomes a problem for women writers because of its assumptions about the 'nature of femininity'. The tidal rhythms of menstruation, the outrageous visibility of pregnancy, lead, by a non-sequitur common to all sexual analogy, to the notion that women exist in a state of unreflective bios, the victims of instincts, intuitions, and the mysterious pulsations of the natural world. Intuition is held to be a prelapsarian form of knowledge, associated especially with angels, children, idiots, 'rustics' and women. These excluded, or fabulous, groups act for the patriarchy as a mirror onto which it nostalgically projects the exclusions of its discourse. As a glorified, but pre-linguistic communion with nature, intuition lowers women's status while appearing to raise it.

While Wollstonecraft and Brontë are attracted to Romanticism because reluctant to sacrifice, as women writers, their privileged access to feeling, both are aware that full participation in society requires suppression of this attraction. The drive to female emancipation, while fuelled by the revolutionary energy at the origins of Romanticism, has an ultimately conservative aim – successful integration into existing social structures. Romanticism, after the disappointments of the French Revolution, was gradually depoliticised, and it is only in the mid-nineteenth century, in a period of renewed revolutionary conflict, that it once again becomes a nexus of ideological tension where gender, genre, politics and feminism converge.

Jane Eyre: Her Hand in Marriage

Charlotte Brontë's second preface to *Jane Eyre* states her authorial project as to 'scrutinise and expose' what she calls 'narrow human doctrines' of religion and morality (6). Our reading of *Jane Eyre* identifies Charlotte Brontë's interrogation of the dominant ideology of love and marriage; but also suggests the Machereyan 'not-said' of the novel – what it is not possible for her to 'scrutinise and expose', woman as a desiring subject, a sexual subject seeking personal fulfilment within the existing structures of class and kinship, i.e. in a patriarchal capitalist society. *Jane Eyre* is *about* kinship, *about* the fact that the social position of a woman, whether rich or poor, pretty or plain, is mediated through the family – to which she may or may not belong.

The text of *Jane Eyre* speaks that desire in the interstices of the debate on woman's social role, between the romance/realism divide, the conflict between Reason and Imagination in her heroine's consciousness. It speaks of women's sexuality in Victorian England, opening the locked room of a tabooed subject – just as that part of the text which concerns Bertha Mason/Rochester disrupts the realistic narrative of Jane's search for an adequate kinship system, i.e. an opening into the family structure from which she is excluded. Charlotte Brontë's general fictional strategy is to place her heroines in varying degrees of marginality to the normative kinship patterns. Frances Henri, Crimsworth (a female surrogate), Jane, Shirley, Caroline Helstone and Lucy Snowe, all have a deviant socialisation, all confront the problem of a marriage not negotiated by a *pater familias*.

Why? By excluding them from a conventional family situation in which their socialisation and their exchange in marriage cannot follow the practice of Victorian middle-class women, Charlotte Brontë's fiction explores the constraints of the dominant ideology as they bear on female sexual and social identity.

'At the centre of Charlotte Brontë's novels is a figure who either lacks or deliberately cuts the bonds of kinship' (Eagleton, *Myths of Power*). But Eagleton, although stressing this structural characteristic, discusses it primarily in terms of class-mobility. This treatment of Jane Eyre herself as an asexual representative of the upwardly-mobile bourgeoisie leads to a reductionist reading of the text. It neglects gender as a determinant, by subsuming gender under class. The meritocratic vision of 'individual self-reliance', as Eagleton puts its, *cannot* be enacted by a woman character in the same way as it can be by a male. For a woman to become a member of the 'master-class' depends on her taking a sexual master whereby her submission brings her access to the dominant culture.

The social and judicial legitimacy of this relationship – its encoding within the law – is of primary importance; hence Jane's rejection of the role of Rochester's mistress. She would not merely *not* acquire access – she would forfeit the possibility of ever doing so. The structure of the novel, Jane's development through childhood and adolescence into womanhood does not simply represent an economic and social progression from penniless orphan to member of the landed gentry class; it represents a woman's struggle for access to her own sexual and reproductive potential – in other words, her attempts to install herself as a full subject within a male-dominated culture.

For example, the structure of the five locales of the novel is customarily seen as the articulation of the heroine's progress – a progress described in liberal criticism as the moral growth of the individual, in vulgar sociological terms as 'upward social mobility'. To foreground kinship provides a radically different reading.

Jane's progress is from a dependent orphan to the acquisition of the family necessary for her full integration into mid-nineteenth century culture as a woman. Her cousins, the Rivers, and the Madeira uncle who intervenes twice – once via his agent, Bertha's brother, to save her from becoming a 'fallen woman' as Rochester's bigamous wife, and again at the end of the novel with a legacy which is in effect a dowry – provide Jane with the necessary basis for her exchange into marriage.

Each of the five houses through which the heroine passes traces the variety and instability of a kinship structure at a transitional historical period, and the ideological space this offers to women.

At Gateshead, as the excluded intruder into the Reed family and at Thornfield as the sexually tabooed and socially ambiguous governess, Jane's lack of familial status renders her particularly vulnerable to oppression and exploitation. At Lowood, she acquires a surrogate sister and mother in Helen Burns and Miss Temple – only to lose them through death and marriage. The instability of kinship relations is imaged in the patterns of gain and loss, acceptance and denial, enacted at each 'home' – most dramatically in the loss of a lawful wedded husband, spiritually and sexually akin but socially tabooed. The subsequent flight from Thornfield reduces her to a homeless vagrant lacking both past and identity. Throughout the text, the symmetrical arrangement of Reed and Rivers cousins, the Reed and Eyre uncles, the patterns of metaphors about kinship, affinity and identification articulate the proposition that a woman's social identity is constituted within familial relationships. Without the kinship reading, the Rivers' transformation into long-lost, bona-fide blood-relations at Moor End appears a gross and unmotivated coincidence. This apparently absurd plot manipulation is in fact dictated by the logic of the not-said.

Like such violations of probability, the Gothic elements in the novel are neither clumsy interventions to resolve the narrative problems nor simply the residues of the author's earlier modes of discourse, the childhood fantasies of Angria. Their main function is to evade the censorship of female sexuality within the signifying practice of mid-Victorian realism. For the rights and wrongs of women in social and political terms, there existed a rationalist language, a political rhetoric, inherited from Mary Wollstonecraft. But for the 'unspeakable' sexual desires of women, Charlotte Brontë returned on the one hand to Gothic and Romantic modes, on the other to a metonymic discourse of the human body – hands and eyes for penises, 'vitals' or 'vital organs' for women's genitalia – often to comic effect:

> I am substantial enough – touch me.' ....
> He held out his hand, laughing. 'Is that a dream?' said he, placing it close to my eyes. He had a rounded, muscular, and vigorous hand, as well as a long, strong arm. (7).

The tale told of women's sexual possibilities is a halting, fragmented and ambivalent one. The libidinal fire of Jane Eyre's 'vital organs' is not denied, not totally repressed, as the refusal of St John Rivers suggests:

> At his side, always and always restrained, always checked – forced to keep the fire of my nature continually low, to compel it to burn inwardly, and never utter a cry, though the imprisoned flame consume vital after vital. (8).

The marriage proposed here, significantly, is an inter-familial one which denies the heroine's sexuality. If women's sexuality is to be integrated, reconciled with male patriarchal Law, a compromise must be achieved with the individual Law-bearer, in this case through a return to Edward Rochester.

The alternative to either repression or integration is examined through that part of the text concerned with Bertha Mason/Rochester. Her initial intervention, the uncanny laughter after Jane surveys from the battlements of Thornfield the wider world denied her as a woman, signifies the return of the repressed, the anarchic and unacted desires of women. Bertha's appearances constitute a punctuating device or notation of the not-said – the Pandora's box of unleashed female libido. Bertha's tearing of the veil on the eve of Jane's wedding, for example, is a triumphant trope for the projected loss of Jane's virginity unsanctioned by legitimate marriage. Thus while other spectres were haunting Europe, the spectre haunting Jane Eyre, if not Victorian England, was the insurgence of women's sexuality into the signifying practice of literature.

The myth of unbridled male sexuality is treated through Rochester, whose name evokes that of the predatory Restoration rake, here modified by Byronic sensibility. In the vocabulary of Lacanian psychoanalysis, his maiming by the author is not so much a punitive castration, but represents his successful passage through the castration complex. Like all human subjects he must enter the symbolic order through a necessary acceptance of the loss of an early incestuous love object, a process he initially tries to circumvent through bigamy. His decision to make Jane his bigamous wife attempts to implicate the arch-patriarch, God himself ('I know my maker sanctions what I do'). The supernatural lightning which this presumption provokes is less a re-establishing of bourgeois morality than an expression of disapproval by the transcendental phallic signifier of Rochester's Oedipal rivalry. It is God at the end of the novel who refuses to sanction Jane's marriage to St John Rivers when invoked in its support, and who sends Rochester's supernatural cry to call Jane to him; and it is God's judgement which Rochester, in his maimed condition, finally accepts with filial meekness.

By accepting the Law, he accepts his place in the signifying chain and enters the Symbolic order, as bearer rather than maker of the Law. Sexuality in a reduced and regulated form is integrated – legitimised – within the dominant kinship structure of patriarchy and within the marriage which he (by Bertha's death-by-fire), and Jane (by her acquisition of a family) are now in a position to contract. *Jane Eyre* does not attempt to rupture the dominant kinship structures. The ending of the novel ('Reader, I married him') affirms those very structures. The feminism of the text resides in its 'not-said', its attempt to inscribe women as sexual subjects within this system.

Notes

1. Relevant works by Lacan, Macherey and others are listed in the bibliography below.
2. Engels, F. *The Origins of the Family, Private Property and the State*, Pathfinder, New York, 1972, p. 80.
3. Althusser, L. 'Freud and Lacan' in *Lenin and Philosophy and Other Essays*, New Left Books, London, 1975, p. 195.
4. Lady Eastlake, review of *Jane Eyre*, *Quarterly Review*, Vol LXXXIV December 1848, p. 174. (Quoted in Stern, J. 'Women and the Novel' in *Women's Liberation Review*, No. 1, October 1972.)
5. Wise, T. J. and Symington, J. A. (eds). *The Brontës: Their Lives, Friendships and Correspondence*, 4 Vols, Shakespeare Head, London, 1932. Vol iii, p. 31.
6. Currer Bell, Preface to the Second Edition of *Jane Eyre*, Smith, Elder & Co., London, 1847.
7. *Jane Eyre*, Penguin, Harmondsworth, 1966, pp. 306–7.
8. ibid. p. 433.

Additional reading

Charlotte Brontë's *Jane Eyre*, *Shirley* and *Villette* are widely available in paperback.
Aurora Leigh and Other Poems by Elizabeth Barrett Browning, with an Introduction by Cora Kaplan, The Women's Press, London, 1978.
ALTHUSSER, L. (1971) 'Ideology and Ideological State apparatuses' in *Lenin and Philosophy and Other Essays*, London: New Left Books.
EAGLETON, T. (1975), *Myths of Power: a Marxist Study of the Brontës*, London: Macmillan.
KRISTEVA, J. (1976), *La Révolution du Langage Poétique*, Collections Tel Quel, Paris: Seuil.
KRISTEVA, J. (1976), 'Signifying Practice and Mode of Production' translated and introduced by G. Nowell-Smith, *Edinburgh Film Festival Magazine*, 1.
LACAN, J. (1977) *Ecrits*, translated by Alan Sheridan, London: Tavistock.
MACHEREY, P. (1970) *Pour une Théorie de la Production Littéraire* Paris: Maspéro.
MACHEREY, P. (1977) Interview translated and introduced by Jean Radford and Colin Mercer, *Red Letters*, 5.

3.3   SANDRA M. GILBERT AND SUSAN GUBAR: FROM 'A DIALOGUE OF SELF AND SOUL: PLAIN JANE'S PROGRESS' (1979)

Sandra M. Gilbert is Professor of English at the University of California, Davis; and Susan Gubar is Professor of English at the University of Indiana, Bloomington. Their other works together include *Shakespeare's Sisters: Feminist Essays on Women Poets* (1979); *The Norton Anthology of Literature by Women* (1985); and *No Man's Land: The Place of the Woman Writer in the Twentieth Century* (1988).

This extract is taken from a longer chapter with the above title. Much of what has been omitted is a further detailed textual account of the stages in Jane's 'pilgrimage' towards maturity, which the authors see as constituting the whole novel. Included here are the introductory section; passages which focus most specifically on Jane's relationship with Rochester; and those on the nature and function of the 'madwoman in the attic' herself, Bertha Mason. The book as a whole proposes a feminist poetics for identifying a 'distinctively female literary tradition' in the nineteenth century (p. xi of its preface and long introductory section). Dominated by patriarchal ideology in general, and in the literary domain in particular, women writers had to find their own voice: 'achieving true female literary authority by simultaneously conforming to and subverting patriarchal literary standards' (p. 73). The 'madwoman' of their title (exemplified by Bertha in *Jane Eyre*) is, then, the central figure in Gilbert and Gubar's thesis: the 'mad' double of the author expressing her anxiety and 'rage'. This is the 'true' female literary voice within patriarchy: 'parodic, duplicitous, extraordinarily sophisticated, all this female writing is both revisionary and revolutionary, even when it is produced by writers we usually think of as models of angelic resignation' (p. 80).

   In some respects, Gilbert and Gubar's essay is not dissimilar to those of the New Critics (see Cleanth Brooks' essay in Ch. 2, pp. 71–9) and their heirs in the 1960s and 1970s who performed close reading of texts, tracing patterns of imagery and symbolism, to reveal the text's own logic of signification. What, if anything, makes the present essay more than a close 'formalist' reading; what is *different* about it? How does it relate to the book's feminist theoretical project as outlined above, and what is the authors' specific project in their reading of *Jane Eyre*? In this context, try to decode the implications of the chapter's title. Both this essay and the previous one in a sense have trouble with the novel's ending (the balanced and 'egalitarian' marriage of the re-fashioned Rochester and the mature Jane). Do they solve this problem in accceptably feminist terms? Mary Jacobus, in a review of *The Madwoman in the Attic (Signs*, 6, 3, 1981, pp. 517–23), and then Toril Moi in *Sexual/Textual Politics* (*op. cit.*), have offered incisive critiques of the book and its theoretical stance. *Inter alia*, they point to the problematics of emphasizing women writers' debilitating 'anxiety of authorship' within patriarchy; the book's insistence on the identity of author and character – hence on the presence of a 'real' woman beneath the patriarchal textual façade – and its belief in a true 'female' (rather than 'feminine') authorial voice speaking the 'real truth' through the sub-text of women's writing. The implication, as they see it, of releasing the heroic 'madwoman' from all women's texts would be to repeat endlessly – with no prospect of breaking free of it – the fundamental story of women's oppression by (a monolithic) patriarchy. Is the present excerpt open to these criticisms? Are they valid?

The following extract is from Ch. 10 of *The Madwoman in the Attic: The Woman Writer and the Nineteenth-Century Literary Imagination*, Yale University Press, 1979, pp. 336–71, *passim.*

A Dialogue of Self and Soul: Plain Jane's Progress

Three quotations – from Virginia Woolf, Jean Rhys and Emily Dickinson – appear as epigraphs to the chapter.

If *The Professor* is a somewhat blurred trance-statement of themes and conflicts that dominated Charlotte Brontë's thought far more than she herself may have realized, *Jane Eyre* is a work permeated by angry, *Angrian* fantasies of escape-into-wholeness. Borrowing the mythic quest-plot – but not the devout substance – of Bunyan's male *Pilgrim's Progress*, the young novelist seems here definitively to have opened her eyes to female realities within her and around her: confinement, orphanhood, starvation, rage even to madness. Where the fiery image of Lucia, that energetic woman who probably 'once wore chains and broke them,' is miniaturized in *The Professor*, in *Jane Eyre* (1847) this figure becomes almost larger than life, the emblem of a passionate, barely disguised rebelliousness.

Victorian critics, no doubt instinctively perceiving the subliminal intensity of Brontë's passion, seem to have understood this point very well. Her 'mind contains nothing but hunger, rebellion, and rage,' Matthew Arnold wrote of Charlotte Brontë in 1853.[1] He was referring to *Villette*, which he elsewhere described as a 'hideous, undelightful, convulsed, constricted novel,'[2] but he might as well have been speaking of *Jane Eyre*, for his response to Brontë was typical of the outrage generated in some quarters by her first published novel.[3] 'Jane Eyre is throughout the personification of an unregenerate and undisciplined spirit,' wrote Elizabeth Rigby in *The Quarterly Review* in 1848, and her 'autobiography ... is preeminently an anti-Christian composition.... The tone of mind and thought which has fostered Chartism and rebellion is the same which has also written *Jane Eyre*.'[4] Anne Mozley, in 1853, recalled for *The Christian Remembrancer* that 'Currer Bell' had seemed on her first appearance as an author 'soured, coarse, and grumbling; an alien ... from society and amenable to none of its laws.'[5] And Mrs. Oliphant related in 1855 that 'Ten years ago we professed an orthodox system of novel-making. Our lovers were humble and devoted ... and the only true love worth having was that ... chivalrous true love which consecrated all womankind ... when suddenly, without warning, *Jane Eyre* stole upon the scene, and the most alarming revolution of modern times has followed the invasion of *Jane Eyre*.'[6]

We tend today to think of *Jane Eyre* as moral gothic, 'myth domesticated,' *Pamela*'s daughter and *Rebecca*'s aunt, the archetypal scenario for all those mildly thrilling romantic encounters between a scowling Byronic hero (who owns a gloomy mansion) and a trembling heroine (who can't quite figure out the mansion's floor plan). Or, if we're more sophisticated, we give Charlotte Brontë her due, concede her strategic as well as her mythic abilities, study the patterns of her imagery, and count the number of times she addresses the reader. But still we overlook the 'alarming revolution' – even Mrs. Oliphant's terminology is suggestive – which 'followed the invasion of *Jane Eyre*.' 'Well, obviously *Jane Eyre* is a feminist tract, an argument for the social betterment of governesses and equal rights for women,'

Richard Chase somewhat grudgingly admitted in 1948. But like most other modern critics, he believed that the novel's power arose from its mythologizing of Jane's confrontation with masculine sexuality.[7]

Yet, curiously enough, it seems not to have been primarily the coarseness and sexuality of *Jane Eyre* which shocked Victorian reviewers (though they disliked those elements in the book), but, as we have seen, its 'anti-Christian' refusal to accept the forms, customs, and standards of society – in short, its rebellious feminism. They were disturbed not so much by the proud Byronic sexual energy of Rochester as by the Byronic pride and passion of Jane herself, not so much by the asocial sexual vibrations between hero and heroine as by the heroine's refusal to submit to her social destiny: 'She has inherited in fullest measure the worst sin of our fallen nature – the sin of pride,' declared Miss Rigby.

> Jane Eyre is proud, and therefore she is ungrateful, too. It pleased God to make her an orphan, friendless, and penniless – yet she thanks nobody, and least of all Him, for the food and raiment, the friends, companions, and instructors of her helpless youth.... On the contrary, she looks upon all that has been done for her not only as her undoubted right, but as falling far short of it.[8]

In other words, what horrified the Victorians was Jane's anger. And perhaps they, rather than more recent critics, were correct in their response to the book. For while the mythologizing of repressed rage may parallel the mythologizing of repressed sexuality, it is far more dangerous to the order of society. The occasional woman who has a weakness for black-browed Byronic heroes can be accommodated in novels and even in some drawing rooms; the woman who yearns to escape entirely from drawing rooms and patriarchal mansions obviously cannot. And Jane Eyre, as Matthew Arnold, Miss Rigby, Mrs. Mozley, and Mrs. Oliphant suspected, was such a woman.

Her story, providing a pattern for countless others, is – far more obviously and dramatically than *The Professor* – a story of enclosure and escape, a distinctively female *Bildungsroman* in which the problems encountered by the protagonist as she struggles from the imprisonment of her childhood toward an almost unthinkable goal of mature freedom are symptomatic of difficulties Everywoman in a patriarchal society must meet and overcome: oppression (at Gateshead), starvation (at Lowood), madness (at Thornfield), and coldness (at Marsh End). Most important, her confrontation, not with Rochester but with Rochester's mad wife Bertha, is the book's central confrontation, an encounter – like Frances Crimsworth's fantasy about Lucia – not with her own sexuality but with her own imprisoned 'hunger, rebellion, and rage,' a secret dialogue of self and soul on whose outcome, as we shall see, the novel's plot, Rochester's fate, and Jane's coming-of-age all depend.

[...]

Detailed accounts of Jane's experiences at Gateshead, Lowood and Thornfield then follow.

[...]

That Rochester's character and life pose in themselves such substantial impediments to his marriage with Jane does not mean, however, that Jane herself generates none. For one thing, 'akin' as she is to Rochester, she suspects him of harboring all the secrets we know he does harbor, and raises defenses against them, manipulating her 'master' so as to keep him 'in reasonable check.' In a larger way, moreover, all the charades and masquerades – the secret messages – of patriarchy have had their effect upon her. Though she loves Rochester the man, Jane has doubts about Rochester the husband even before she learns about Bertha. In her world, she senses, even the equality of love between true minds leads to the inequalities and minor despotisms of marriage. 'For a little while,' she says cynically to Rochester, 'you will perhaps be as you are now, [but] ... I suppose your love will effervesce in six months, or less. I have observed in books written by men, that period assigned as the farthest to which a husband's ardor extends' (chap. 24). He, of course, vigorously repudiates this prediction, but his argument – 'Jane: you please me, and you master me [because] you seem to submit' – implies a kind of Lawrentian sexual tension and only makes things worse. For when he asks 'Why do you smile [at this], Jane? What does that inexplicable ... turn of countenance mean?' her peculiar, ironic smile, reminiscent of Bertha's mirthless laugh, signals an 'involuntary' and subtly hostile thought 'of Hercules and Samson with their charmers.' And that hostility becomes overt at the silk warehouse, where Jane notes that 'the more he bought me, the more my cheek burned with a sense of annoyance and degradation.... I thought his smile was such as a sultan might, in a blissful and fond moment, bestow on a slave his gold and gems had enriched' (chap. 24).

Jane's whole life-pilgrimage has, of course, prepared her to be angry in this way at Rochester's, and society's, concept of marriage. Rochester's loving tyranny recalls John Reed's unloving despotism, and the erratic nature of Rochester's favors ('in my secret soul I knew that his great kindness to me was balanced by unjust severity to many others' [chap. 15]) recalls Brocklehurst's hypocrisy. But even the dreamlike paintings that Jane produced early in her stay at Thornfield – art works which brought her as close to her 'master' as Helen Graham (in *The Tenant of Wildfell Hall*) was to hers – functioned ambiguously, like Helen's, to predict strains in this relationship even while they seemed to be conventional Romantic fantasies. The first represented a drowned female corpse; the second a sort of avenging mother goddess rising (like Bertha Mason Rochester or *Frankenstein*'s monster) in 'electric travail' (chap. 13); and the third a terrible paternal specter carefully designed to recall Milton's sinister image of Death. Indeed, this last, says Jane, quoting *Paradise Lost*, delineates 'the shape which shape had none,' the patriarchal shadow implicit even in the Father-hating gloom of hell.

Given such shadowings and foreshadowings, then, it is no wonder that as Jane's anger and fear about her marriage intensify, she begins to be symbolically drawn back into her own past, and specifically to reexperience the dangerous sense of doubleness that had begun in the red-room. The first sign that this is happening is the powerfully depicted, recurrent dream of a child she begins to have as she drifts into a romance with her master. She tells us that she was awakened 'from companionship with this baby-phantom' on the night Bertha attacked Richard Mason, and the next day she is literally called back into the past, back to Gateshead to see the dying Mrs. Reed, who reminds her again of what she once was and potentially still is: 'Are you Jane Eyre? ... I declare she talked to me once like something mad, or like a fiend' (chap. 21). Even more significantly, the phantom-child reappears in two dramatic dreams Jane has on the night before her wedding eve, during which she experiences 'a strange regretful consciousness of some barrier dividing' her from Rochester. In the first, 'burdened' with the small wailing creature, she is 'following the windings of an unknown road' in cold rainy weather, straining to catch up with her future husband but unable to reach him. In the second, she is walking among the ruins of Thornfield, still carrying 'the unknown little child' and still following Rochester; as he disappears around 'an angle in the road,' she tells him, 'I bent forward to take a last look; the wall crumbled; I was shaken; the child rolled from my knee, I lost my balance, fell, and woke' (chap. 25).

What are we to make of these strange dreams, or – as Jane would call them – these 'presentiments'? To begin with, it seems clear that the wailing child who appears in all of them corresponds to 'the poor orphan child' of Bessie's song at Gateshead, and therefore to the child Jane herself, the wailing Cinderella whose pilgrimage began in anger and despair. That child's complaint – 'My feet they are sore, and my limbs they are weary;/Long is the way, and the mountains are wild' – is still Jane's, or at least the complaint of that part of her which resists a marriage of inequality. And though consciously Jane wishes to be rid of the heavy problem her orphan self presents, 'I might not lay it down anywhere, however tired were my arms, however much its weight impeded my progress.' In other words, until she reaches the goal of her pilgrimage – maturity, independence, true equality with Rochester (and therefore in a sense with the rest of the world) – she is doomed to carry her orphaned alter ego everywhere. The burden of the past cannot be sloughed off so easily – not, for instance, by glamorous lovemaking, silk dresses, jewelry, a new name. Jane's 'strange regretful consciousness of a barrier' dividing her from Rochester is, thus, a keen though disguised intuition of a problem she herself will pose.

Almost more interesting than the nature of the child image, however, is the *predictive* aspect of the last of the child dreams, the one about the ruin of Thornfield. As Jane correctly foresees, Thornfield *will* within a year become 'a dreary ruin, the retreat of bats and owls.' Have her own subtle and not-so-subtle hostilities to its master any connection with the catastrophe that is to befall the house? Is her clairvoyant dream in some sense a vision of wish-fulfilment? And why, specifically, is she freed from the burden of the wailing child at the moment *she* falls from Thornfield's ruined wall?

The answer to all these questions is closely related to events which follow upon the child dream. For the apparition of a child in these crucial weeks preceding her marriage is only one symptom of a dissolution of personality Jane seems to be experiencing at this time, a fragmentation of the self comparable to her 'syncope' in the red-room. Another symptom appears early in the chapter that begins, anxiously, 'there was no putting off the day that advanced – the bridal day' (chap. 25). It is her witty but nervous speculation about the nature of 'one Jane Rochester, a person whom as yet I knew not,' though 'in yonder closet ... garments *said* to be hers had already displaced [mine]: *for not to me appertained that ... strange wraith-like apparel*' (chap. 25 [ital. ours]). Again, a third symptom appears on the morning of her wedding: she turns toward the mirror and sees 'a robed and veiled figure, so unlike my usual self that it seemed almost the image of a stranger' (chap. 26), reminding us of the moment in the red-room when all had 'seemed colder and darker in that visionary hollow' of the looking glass 'than in reality.' In view of this frightening series of separations within the self – Jane Eyre splitting off from Jane Rochester, the child Jane splitting off from the adult Jane, and the image of Jane weirdly separating from the body of Jane – it is not surprising that another and most mysterious specter, a sort of 'vampyre,' should appear in the middle of the night to rend and trample the wedding veil of that unknown person, Jane Rochester.

Literally, of course, the nighttime specter is none other than Bertha Mason Rochester. But on a figurative and psychological level it seems suspiciously clear that the specter of Bertha is still another – indeed the most threatening – avatar of Jane. What Bertha now *does*, for instance, is what Jane wants to do. Disliking the 'vapoury veil' of Jane Rochester, Jane Eyre secretly wants to tear the garments up. Bertha does it for her. Fearing the inexorable 'bridal day,' Jane would like to put it off. Bertha does that for her too. Resenting the new mastery of Rochester, whom she sees as '*dread* but adored,' (ital. ours), she wishes to be his equal in size and strength, so that she can battle him in the contest of their marriage. Bertha, 'a big woman, in stature almost equalling her husband,' has the necessary 'virile force' (chap. 26). Bertha, in other words, is Jane's truest and darkest double: she is the angry aspect of the orphan child, the ferocious secret self Jane has been trying to repress ever since her days at Gateshead. For, as Claire Rosenfeld points out, 'the novelist who consciously or unconsciously exploits psychological Doubles' frequently juxtaposes 'two characters, the one representing the socially acceptable or conventional personality, the other externalizing the free, uninhibited, often criminal self.'[9]

It is only fitting, then, that the existence of this criminal self imprisoned in Thornfield's attic is the ultimate legal impediment to Jane's and Rochester's marriage, and that its existence is, paradoxically, an impediment raised by Jane as well as by Rochester. For it now begins to appear, if it did not earlier, that Bertha has functioned as Jane's dark double *throughout* the governess's stay at Thornfield. Specifically, every one of Bertha's appearances – or, more accurately, her manifestations – has been associated with an experience (or repression) of anger on Jane's part. Jane's feelings of 'hunger, rebellion, and rage' on the battlements, for instance, were accompanied by Bertha's 'low, slow ha! ha!' and 'eccentric murmurs.' Jane's apparently secure response to Rochester's apparently egalitarian sexual confidences was followed by Bertha's attempt to incinerate the master in his bed. Jane's unexpressed resentment at Rochester's manipulative gypsy-masquerade found expression in Bertha's terrible shriek and her even more terrible attack on Richard Mason. Jane's anxieties about her marriage, and in particular her fears of her own alien 'robed and veiled' bridal image, were objectified by the image of

Bertha in a 'white and straight' dress, 'whether gown, sheet, or shroud I cannot tell.' Jane's profound desire to destroy Thornfield, the symbol of Rochester's mastery and of her own servitude, will be acted out by Bertha, who burns down the' house and destroys *herself* in the process as if she were an agent of Jane's desire as well as her own. And finally, Jane's disguised hostility to Rochester, summarized in her terrifying prediction to herself that 'you shall, yourself, pluck out your right eye; yourself cut off your right hand' (chap. 27) comes strangely true through the intervention of Bertha, whose melodramatic death causes Rochester to lose both eye and hand.

These parallels between Jane and Bertha may at first seem somewhat strained. Jane, after all, is poor, plain, little, pale, neat, and quiet, while Bertha is rich, large, florid, sensual, and extravagant; indeed, she was once even beautiful, somewhat, Rochester notes, 'in the style of Blanche Ingram.' Is she not, then, as many critics have suggested, a monitory image rather than a double for Jane? As Richard Chase puts it, 'May not Bertha, Jane seems to ask herself, be a living example of what happens to the woman who [tries] to be the fleshly vessel of the [masculine] *élan*?'[10] 'Just as [Jane's] instinct for self-preservation saves her from earlier temptations,' Adrienne Rich remarks, 'so it must save her from becoming this woman by curbing her imagination at the limits of what is bearable for a powerless woman in the England of the 1840s.'[11] Even Rochester himself provides a similar critical appraisal of the relationship between the two. 'That is *my wife*,' he says, pointing to mad Bertha,

> 'And *this* is what I wished to have ... this young girl who stands so grave and quiet at the mouth of hell, looking collectedly at the gambols of a demon. I wanted her just as a change after that fierce ragout.... Compare these clear eyes with the red balls yonder – this face with that mask – this form with that bulk....' [chap. 26]

And of course, in one sense, the relationship between Jane and Bertha is a monitory one: while acting out Jane's secret fantasies, Bertha does (to say the least) provide the governess with an example of how not to act, teaching her a lesson more salutary than any Miss Temple ever taught.

Nevertheless, it is disturbingly clear from recurrent images in the novel that Bertha not only acts *for* Jane, she also acts *like* Jane. The imprisoned Bertha, running 'backwards and forwards' on all fours in the attic, for instance, recalls not only Jane the governess, whose only relief from mental pain was to pace 'backwards and forwards' in the third story, but also that 'bad animal' who was ten-year-old Jane, imprisoned in the red-room, howling and mad. Bertha's 'goblin appearance' – 'half dream, half reality,' says Rochester – recalls the lover's epithets for Jane: 'malicious elf,' 'sprite,' 'changeling,' as well as his playful accusation that she had magically downed his horse at their first meeting. Rochester's description of Bertha as a 'monster' ('a fearful voyage I had with such a monster in the vessel' [chap. 27]) ironically echoes Jane's own fear of being a monster ('Am I a monster? ... is it impossible that Mr. Rochester should have a sincere affection for me?' [chap. 24]). Bertha's fiendish madness recalls Mrs. Reed's remark about Jane ('she talked to me once like something mad or like a fiend') as well as Jane's own estimate of her mental state ('I will hold to the principles received by me when I was sane, and not mad – as I am now' [chap. 27]). And most dramatic of all, Bertha's incendiary tendencies recall Jane's early flaming rages, at Lowood and at Gateshead, as well as that 'ridge of lighted heath' which she herself saw as emblematic of her mind in its rebellion against society. It is only fitting, therefore, that, as if to balance the child Jane's terrifying vision of herself as an alien figure in the 'visionary hollow' of the red-room looking glass, the adult Jane first clearly perceives her terrible double when Bertha puts on the wedding veil intended for the second Mrs. Rochester, and turns to the mirror. At that moment, Jane sees 'the reflection of the visage and features quite distinctly in the dark oblong glass,' sees them as if they were her own (chap. 25).

For despite all the habits of harmony she gained in her years at Lowood, we must finally recognize, with Jane herself, that on her arrival at Thornfield she only '*appeared* a disciplined and subdued character' [ital. ours]. Crowned with thorns, finding that she is, in Emily Dickinson's words, 'The Wife – without the Sign,'[12] she represses her rage behind a subdued facade, but her soul's impulse to dance 'like a Bomb, abroad,' to quote Dickinson again,[13] has not been exorcised and will not be exorcised until the literal and symbolic death of Bertha frees her from the furies that torment her and makes possible a marriage of equality – makes possible, that is, wholeness within herself. At that point, significantly, when the Bertha in Jane falls from the ruined wall of Thornfield and is destroyed, the orphan child too, as her dream predicts, will roll from her knee – the burden of her past will be lifted – and she will wake. In the meantime, as Rochester says, 'never was anything at once so frail and so indomitable ... consider the resolute wild free thing looking out of [Jane's] eye. ... Whatever I do with its cage, I cannot get at it – the savage, beautiful creature' (chap. 27).

[...]

An account of Jane's relations with the Rivers family at Marsh End is given here.

[...]

Jane's return to Thornfield, her discovery of Bertha's death and of the ruin her dream had predicted, her reunion at Ferndean with the maimed and blinded Rochester, and their subsequent marriage form an essential epilogue to that pilgrimage toward selfhood which had in other ways concluded at Marsh End, with Jane's realization that she could not marry St. John. At that moment, 'the wondrous shock of feeling had come like the earthquake which shook the foundations of Paul and Silas' prison; it had opened the doors of the soul's cell, and loosed its bands – it had wakened it out of its sleep' (chap. 36). For at that moment she had been irrevocably freed from the burden of her past, freed both from the raging specter of Bertha (which had already fallen in fact from the ruined wall of Thornfield) and from the self-pitying specter of the orphan child (which had symbolically, as in her dream, rolled from her knee). And at that moment, again as in her dream, she had *wakened* to her own self, her own needs. Similarly, Rochester, 'caged eagle' that he seems (chap. 37), has been freed from what was for him the burden of Thornfield, though at the same time he appears to have been fettered by the injuries he received in attempting to rescue Jane's mad double from the flames devouring his house. That his 'fetters' pose no impediment to a new marriage, that he and Jane are now, in reality, equals, is the thesis of the Ferndean section.

Many critics, starting with Richard Chase, have seen Rochester's injuries as 'a symbolic castration,' a punishment for his early profligacy and a sign that Charlotte Brontë (as well as Jane herself), fearing male sexual power, can only imagine marriage as a union with a diminished Samson. 'The tempo and energy of the universe can be quelled, we see, by a patient, practical woman,' notes Chase ironically.[14] And there is an element of truth in this idea. The angry Bertha in Jane *had* wanted to punish Rochester, to burn him in his bed, destroy his house, cut off his hand and pluck out his overmastering 'full falcon eye.' Smiling enigmatically, she had thought of 'Hercules and Samson, with their charmers.'

It had not been her goal, however, to quell 'the tempo and energy of the universe,' but simply to strengthen herself, to make herself an equal of the world Rochester represents. And surely another important symbolic point is implied by the lovers' reunion at Ferndean: when both were physically whole they could not, in a sense, *see* each other because of the social disguises – master/servant, prince/ Cinderella – blinding them, but now that those disguises have been shed, now that they are equals, they can (though one is blind) see and speak even beyond the medium of the flesh. Apparently sightless, Rochester – in the tradition of blinded Gloucester – now sees more clearly than he did when as a 'mole-eyed blockhead' he married Bertha Mason (chap. 27). Apparently mutilated, he is paradoxically stronger than he was when he ruled Thornfield, for now, like Jane, he draws his powers from within himself, rather than from inequity, disguise, deception. Then, at Thornfield, he was 'no better than the old lightning-struck chestnut tree in the orchard,' whose ruin foreshadowed the catastrophe of his relationship with Jane. Now, as Jane tells him, he is 'green and vigorous. Plants will grow about your roots whether you ask them or not' (chap. 37). And now, being equals, he and Jane can afford to depend upon each other with no fear of one exploiting the other.

Nevertheless, despite the optimistic portrait of an egalitarian relationship that Brontë seems to be drawing here, there is 'a quiet autumnal quality' about the scenes at Ferndean, as Robert Bernard Martin points out.[15] The house itself, set deep in a dark forest, is old and decaying: Rochester had not even thought it suitable for the loathsome Bertha, and its valley-of-the-shadow quality makes it seem rather like a Lowood, a school of life where Rochester must learn those lessons Jane herself absorbed so early. As a dramatic setting, moreover, Ferndean is notably stripped and asocial, so that the physical isolation of the lovers suggests their spiritual isolation in a world where such egalitarian marriages as theirs are rare, if not impossible. True minds, Charlotte Brontë seems to be saying, must withdraw into a remote forest, a wilderness even, in order to circumvent the strictures of a hierarchal society.

Does Brontë's rebellious feminism – that 'irreligious' dissatisfaction with the social order noted by Miss Rigby and *Jane Eyre's* other Victorian critics – compromise itself in this withdrawal? Has Jane exorcised the rage of orphanhood only to retreat from the responsibilities her own principles implied? Tentative answers to these questions can be derived more easily from *The Professor*, *Shirley*, and *Villette* than from *Jane Eyre*, for the qualified and even (as in *Villette*) indecisive endings of Brontë's other novels suggest that she herself was unable clearly to envision viable solutions to the problem of patriarchal oppression. In all her books, writing (as we have seen) in a sort of trance, she was able to act out that passionate drive toward freedom which offended agents of the status quo, but in none was she able consciously to define the full meaning of achieved freedom – perhaps because no one of her contemporaries, not even a Wollstonecraft or a Mill, could adequately describe a society so drastically altered that the matured Jane and Rochester could really live in it.

What Brontë could not logically define, however, she could embody in tenuous but suggestive imagery and in her last, perhaps most significant redefinitions of Bunyan. Nature in the largest sense seems now to be on the side of Jane and Rochester. *Ferndean*, as its name implies, is without artifice – 'no flowers, no garden-beds' – but it is green as Jane tells Rochester he will be, green and ferny and fertilized by soft rains. Here, isolated from society but flourishing in a natural order of their own making, Jane and Rochester will become physically 'bone of [each other's] bone, flesh of [each other's] flesh' (chap. 38), and here the healing powers of nature will eventually restore the sight of one of Rochester's eyes. Here, in other words, nature, unleashed from social restrictions, will do 'no miracle – but her best' (chap. 35). For not the Celestial City but a natural paradise, the country of Beulah 'upon the borders of heaven,' where 'the contract between bride and bridegroom [is] renewed,' has all along been, we now realize, the goal of Jane's pilgrimage.[16]

As for the Celestial City itself, Charlotte Brontë implies here (though she will later have second thoughts) that such a goal is the dream of those who accept inequities on earth, one of the many tools used by patriarchal society to keep, say, governesses in their 'place.' Because she believes this so deeply, she quite consciously concludes *Jane Eyre* with an allusion to *Pilgrim's Progress* and with a half-ironic apostrophe to that apostle of celestial transcendence, that shadow of 'the warrior Greatheart,' St. John Rivers. 'His,' she tells us, 'is the exaction of the apostle, who speaks but for Christ when he says – "Whosoever will come after me, let him deny himself and take up his cross and follow me"' (chap. 38). For it was, finally, to repudiate such a crucifying denial of the self that Brontë's 'hunger, rebellion, and rage' led her to write *Jane Eyre* in the first place and to make it an 'irreligious' redefinition, almost a parody, of John Bunyan's vision.[17] And the astounding progress toward equality of plain Jane Eyre, whom Miss Rigby correctly saw as 'the personification of an unregenerate and undisciplined spirit,' answers by its outcome the bitter question Emily Dickinson was to ask fifteen years later: '"My husband" – women say – /Stroking the Melody – /Is *this* – the way?"'[18] No, Jane declares in her flight from Thornfield, *that* is not the way. *This*, she says – this marriage of true minds at Ferndean – this is the way. Qualified and isolated as her way may be, it is at least an emblem of hope. Certainly Charlotte Brontë was never again to indulge in quite such an optimistic imagining.

Notes (cut and renumbered)

All references are to the Norton Critical Edition of *Jane Eyre*, ed. Richard J. Dunn (New York: Norton, 1971).

1. Matthew Arnold, *The Letters of Matthew Arnold*, ed. George W. E. Russell (New York and London: Macmillan, 1896), 1 : 34.
2. Matthew Arnold, *The Letters of Matthew Arnold to Arthur Hugh Clough*, ed. Howard Foster Lowry (London and New York: Oxford University Press, 1932), p. 132.
3. Significantly, in view of comments by other contemporary critics, Arnold added in the same letter that 'Religion or devotion or whatever it is to be called may be impossible for such people now: but they have at any rate not found a substitute for it, and it was better for the world when they comforted themselves with it.' It should of course be noted, however, that *Jane Eyre* (like *Villette*) was warmly praised by many reviewers, usually for what George Henry Lewes, writing in *Fraser's Magazine* 36 (December 1847), called its 'deep, significant reality.'
4. *Quarterly Review* 84 (December 1848): 173–74.
5. *The Christian Remembrancer* 25 (June 1853): 423–43.
6. *Blackwood's Magazine* 77 (May 1855): 554–68.
7. Richard Chase, 'The Brontës, or Myth Domesticated,' in *Jane Eyre*, ed. Richard J. Dunn (New York: Norton, 1971), pp. 468 and 464.
8. *Quarterly Review* 84 (December 1848): 173–74. That Charlotte Brontë was herself quite conscious of the 'revolutionary' nature of many of her ideas is clearly indicated by the fact that, as we shall see, she puts some of Miss Rigby's words into the mouth of the unpleasant and supercilious Miss Hardman in *Shirley*.
9. Claire Rosenfeld, 'The Shadow Within: The Conscious and Unconscious Use of the Double,' in *Stories of the Double*, ed. Albert J. Guerard (Philadelphia: J. B. Lippincott, 1967), p. 314. Rosenfeld also notes that 'When the passionate uninhibited self is a woman, she more often than not is dark.' Bertha, of course, is a Creole – swarthy, 'livid,' etc.
10. Chase, 'The Brontës, or Myth Domesticated,' p. 467.
11. Rich, 'Jane Eyre: The Temptations of a Motherless Woman,' *Ms.* 2, 4, Oct. 1973, p. 72. The question of what was 'bearable for a powerless woman in the England of the 1840s' inevitably brings to mind the real story of Isabella Thackeray, who went mad in 1840 and was often (though quite mistakenly) thought to be the original of Rochester's mad wife. Parallels are coincidental, but it is interesting that Isabella was reared by a Bertha Mason-like mother of whom it was said that 'wherever she went, "storms, whirlwinds, cataracts, tornadoes" accompanied her,' and equally interesting that Isabella's illness was signalled by mad inappropriate laughter and marked by violent suicide attempts, alternating with Jane Eyre-like docility. That at one point Thackeray tried to guard her by literally *tying* himself to her ('a riband round her waist, & to my waist, and this always woke me if she moved') seems also to recall Rochester's terrible bondage. For more about Isabella Thackeray, see Gordon N. Ray, *Thackeray: The Uses of Adversity, 1811–1846* (New York: McGraw-Hill, 1955), esp. pp. 182–85 (on Isabella's mother) and chap. 10, 'A Year of Pain and Hope,' pp. 250–77.
12. See Emily Dickinson, *Poems*, J. 1072, 'Title divine – is mine!/The Wife – without the Sign!'
13. See Emily Dickinson, *Poems*, J. 512, 'The Soul has Bandaged Moments.'
14. Chase, 'The Brontës, or Myth Domesticated,' p. 467.
15. Robert Bernard Martin, *The Accents of Persuasion: Charlotte Brontë's Novels* (New York: Norton, 1966), p. 90.
16. *The Pilgrim's Progress* (New York: Airmont Library, 1969), pp. 140–41.
17. It should be noted here that Charlotte Brontë's use of *The Pilgrim's Progress* in *Villette* is much more conventional. Lucy Snowe seems to feel that she will only find true bliss after death, when she hopes to enter the Celestial City.
18. See Emily Dickinson, *Poems*, J. 1072, 'Title divine – is mine!'

3.4   GAYATRI CHAKRAVORTY SPIVAK: FROM 'THREE WOMEN'S TEXTS AND A CRITIQUE OF IMPERIALISM' (1985)

Gayatri Spivak is currently Avalon Foundation Professor in the Humanities at Columbia University, New York. Of middle-class Bengali origin, Spivak presents herself as at once a 'Third-World woman', an American academic, and a 'visitor', 'guest' and 'anomaly' in all the cultural and intellectual locales she inhabits. She is a major contributor to international debates on migrancy and the position of women in postcoloniality. Her influential essays are collected in the following volumes: *In Other Worlds: Essays in Cultural Politics* (1987); *The Postcolonial Critic: Interviews, Strategies, Dialogues*, ed. Sarah Harasym (1990); and *Outside in the Teaching Machine* (1993). See also Donna Landry *et al.*, eds, *The Spivak Reader* (Routledge, 1995), and, for further initial discussion, *A Reader's Guide* 3/e, pp. 193–6. The translator (with important introduction) of Derrida's *Of Grammatology* (1976), she is clearly influenced by his work and by that of Lacan, but also sees herself as drawing on Marxism and feminism (of both of which she is, nevertheless, critical). Spivak's work is a strategically unstable and destabilizing amalgam of deconstruction, psychoanalysis, Marxism and feminism – marked also, as in the present essay, by an oblique manner of presentation which at once deconstructs the ways in which 'truth' is constructed and draws attention to its own complicity in what it is deconstructing. Her 'subject', then, is the unsynchronized and contradictory discourses of ethnicity, class and gender which compose the identities of individual human subjects (including her own). It is this which informs the present essay's project of subverting and criticizing the emergent dominant discourse of Western feminism – its tendency to privilege the metropolitan 'psychobiography of the militant female subject' and 'female individualism' – and its complicity in 'the axioms of imperialism' (pp. 134, 135, 133, below). She does this by deconstructing *Jane Eyre*, a 'cult text' of feminism though unrecognized by such to be so, as it is itself deeply implicated in imperialist ideology. Her reading of Rhys' revisionary 'life' of Bertha then helps to reveal *Jane Eyre* as representing 'an allegory of the general epistemic violence of imperialism', by transforming Bertha into the fictional (colonial) Other 'so that Jane Eyre can become the feminist individualist heroine of British fiction' (p. 139, below). The full essay goes on to offer a reading of Mary Shelley's *Frankenstein* which, by contrast, Spivak sees as not deploying the unquestioned axiomatics of imperialism.

Compare Spivak's critique with the earlier essays here of Anglo-American feminist criticism. Does she have a point? Try to identify the various constituent theoretical threads in the essay. How do they relate to, and support, each other? How, in particular, does the essay negotiate its relation to deconstruction and feminism? Compare Spivak's stance and method to those of other 'postcolonialist' critics featured in Ch. 9 on *Beloved*. Is it possible to deduce any common characteristics? How does this extract relate to Spivak's general project outlined earlier in the Headnote, and how might it point beyond the perceived limits of feminist literary criticism and of a self-reflexive deconstructionism?

For a further example of Spivak's work, and discussion of it, see the extract in Ch. 10 and Headnote, pp. 477–94.

The essay from which the following extract derives (title as above) was first published in H. L. Gates, ed., *'Race', Writing and Difference*, Chicago University Press, 1985, pp. 262–78; the first twelve pages are reproduced here.

Three Women's Texts and a Critique of Imperialism

It should not be possible to read nineteenth-century British literature without remembering that imperialism, understood as England's social mission, was a crucial part of the cultural representation of England to the English. The role of literature in the production of cultural representation should not be ignored. These two obvious 'facts' continue to be disregarded in the reading of nineteenth-century British literature. This itself attests to the continuing success of the imperialist project, displaced and dispersed into more modern forms.

If these 'facts' were remembered, not only in the study of British literature but in the study of the literatures of the European colonizing cultures of the great age of imperialism, we would produce a narrative, in literary history, of the 'worlding' of what is now called 'the Third World.' To consider the Third World as distant cultures, exploited but with rich intact literary heritages waiting to be recovered, interpreted, and curricularized in English translation fosters the emergence of 'the Third World' as a signifier that allows us to forget that 'worlding,' even as it expands the empire of the literary discipline.[1]

It seems particularly unfortunate when the emergent perspective of feminist criticism reproduces the axioms of imperialism. A basically isolationist admiration for the literature of the female subject in Europe and Anglo-America establishes the high feminist norm. It is supported and operated by an information-retrieval approach to 'Third World' literature which often employs a deliberately 'nontheoretical' methodology with self-conscious rectitude.

In this essay, I will attempt to examine the operation of the 'worlding' of what is today 'the Third World' by what has become a cult text of feminism: *Jane Eyre*.[2] I plot the novel's reach and grasp, and locate its structural motors.

[...]

I need hardly mention that the object of my investigation is the printed book, not its 'author.' To make such a distinction is, of course, to ignore the lessons of deconstruction. A deconstructive critical approach would loosen the binding of the book, undo the opposition between verbal text and the bio-graphy of the named subject 'Charlotte Brontë,' and see the two as each other's 'scene of writing.' In such a reading, the life that writes itself as 'my life' is as much a production in psychosocial space (other names can be found) as the book that is written by the holder of that named life – a book that is then consigned to what *is* most often recognized as genuinely 'social': the world of publication and distribution.[3] To touch Brontë's 'life' in such a way, however, would be too risky here. We must rather strategically take shelter in an essentialism which, not wishing to lose the important advantages won by U.S. mainstream feminism, will continue to honor the suspect binary oppositions – book and author, individual and history – and start with an assurance of the following sort: my readings here do not seek to undermine the excellence of the individual artist. If even minimally successful, the readings will incite a degree of rage against the imperialist narrativization of history, that it should produce so abject a script for her. l provide these assurances to allow myself some room to situate feminist individualism in its historical determination rather than simply to canonize it as feminism as such.

Sympathetic U.S. feminists have remarked that I do not do justice to Jane Eyre's subjectivity. A word of explanation is perhaps in order. The broad strokes of my presuppositions are that what is at stake, for feminist individualism in the age of imperialism, is precisely the making of human beings, the constitution and 'interpellation' of the subject not only as individual but as 'individualist.'[4] This stake is represented on two registers: childbearing and soul making. The first is domestic-society-through-sexual-reproduction cathected as 'companionate love'; the second is the imperialist project cathected as civil-society-through-social-mission. As the female individualist, not-quite/not-male, articulates herself in shifting relationship to what is at stake, the 'native female' as such (*within* discourse, *as* a signifier) is excluded from any share in this emerging norm.[5] If we read this account from an isolationist perspective in a 'metropolitan' context, we see nothing there but the psychobiography of the militant female subject. In a reading such as mine, in contrast, the effort is to wrench oneself away from the mesmerizing focus of the 'subject-constitution' of the female individualist.

To develop further the notion that my stance need not be an accusing one, I will refer to a passage from Roberto Fernández Retamar's 'Caliban.'[6] José Enrique Rodó had argued in 1900 that the model for the Latin American intellectual in relationship to Europe could be Shakespeare's Ariel.[7] In 1971 Retamar, denying the possibility of an identifiable 'Latin American Culture,' recast the model as Caliban. Not surprisingly, this powerful exchange still excludes any specific consideration of the civilizations of the Maya, the Aztecs, the Incas, or the smaller nations of what is now called Latin America. Let us note carefully that, at this stage of my argument, this 'conversation' between Europe and Latin America (without a specific consideration of the political economy of the 'worlding' of the 'native') provides a sufficient thematic description of our attempt to confront the ethnocentric and reverse-ethnocentric benevolent double bind (that is, considering the 'native' as object for enthusiastic information-retrieval and thus denying its own 'worlding') that I sketched in my opening paragraphs.

In a moving passage in 'Caliban,' Retamar locates both Caliban and Ariel in the postcolonial intellectual:

> There is no real Ariel-Caliban polarity: both are slaves in the hands of Prospero, the foreign magician. But Caliban is the rude and unconquerable master of the island, while Ariel, a creature of the air, although also a child of the isle, is the intellectual.
>
> The deformed Caliban – enslaved, robbed of his island, and taught the language by Prospero – rebukes him thus: 'You taught me language, and my profit on't / Is, I know how to curse.' ['C,' pp. 28, 11]

As we attempt to unlearn our so-called privilege as Ariel and 'seek from [a certain] Caliban the honor of a place in his rebellious and glorious ranks,' we do not ask that our students and colleagues should emulate us but that they should attend to us ('C,' p. 72).

If, however, we are driven by a nostalgia for lost origins, we too run the risk of effacing the 'native' and stepping forth as 'the real Caliban,' of forgetting that he is a name in a play, an inaccessible blankness circumscribed by an interpretable text.[8] The stagings of Caliban work alongside the narrativization of history: claiming to *be* Caliban legitimizes the very individualism that we must persistently attempt to undermine from within.

Elizabeth Fox-Genovese, in an article on history and women's history, shows us how to define the historical moment of feminism in the West in terms of female access to individualism.[9] The battle for female individualism plays itself out within the larger theater of the establishment of meritocratic individualism, indexed in the aesthetic field by the ideology of 'the creative imagination.' Fox-Genovese's presupposition will guide us into the beautifully orchestrated opening of *Jane Eyre*.

It is a scene of the marginalization and privatization of the protagonist: 'There was no possibility of taking a walk that day.... Out-door exercise was now out of the question. I was glad of it,' Brontë writes (*JE*, p. 9). The movement continues as Jane breaks the rules of the appropriate topography of withdrawal. The family at the center withdraws into the sanctioned architectural space of the withdrawing room or drawing room; Jane inserts herself – 'I slipped in' – into the margin – 'A small breakfast-room *adjoined* the drawing room' (*JE*, p. 9; my emphasis).

The manipulation of the domestic inscription of space within the upwardly mobilizing currents of the eighteenth- and nineteenth-century bourgeoisie in England and France is well known. It seems fitting that the place to which Jane withdraws is not only not the withdrawing room but also not the dining room, the sanctioned place of family meals. Nor is it the library, the appropriate place for reading. The breakfast room 'contained a book-case' (*JE*, p. 9). As Rudolph Ackerman wrote in his *Repository* (1823), one of the many manuals of taste in circulation in nineteenth-century England, these low bookcases and stands were designed to 'contain all the books that may be desired for a sitting-room without reference to the library.'[10] Even in this already triply off-center place, 'having drawn the red moreen curtain nearly close, I [Jane] was shrined in double retirement' (*JE*, pp. 9–10).

Here in Jane's self-marginalized uniqueness, the reader becomes her accomplice: the reader and Jane are united – both are reading. Yet Jane still preserves her odd privilege, for she continues never quite doing the proper thing in its proper place. She cares little for reading what is meant to be read: the 'letter-press.' *She* reads the pictures. The power of this singular hermeneutics is precisely that it can make the outside inside. 'At intervals, while turning over the leaves of my book, I studied the aspect of that winter afternoon.' Under 'the clear panes of glass,' the rain no longer penetrates, 'the drear November day' is rather a one-dimensional 'aspect' to be 'studied,' not decoded like the 'letter-press' but, like pictures, deciphered by the unique creative imagination of the marginal individualist (*JE*, p. 10).

Before following the track of this unique imagination, let us consider the suggestion that the progress of *Jane Eyre* can be charted through a sequential arrangement of the family/counter-family dyad. In the novel, we encounter, first, the Reeds as the legal family and Jane, the late Mr. Reed's sister's daughter, as the representative of a near incestuous counter-family; second, the Brocklehursts, who run the school Jane is sent to, as the legal family and Jane, Miss Temple, and Helen Burns as a counter-family that falls short because it is only a community of women; third, Rochester and the mad Mrs. Rochester as the legal family and Jane and Rochester as the illicit counter-family. Other items may be added to the thematic chain in this sequence: Rochester and Céline Varens as structurally functional counter-family; Rochester and Blanche Ingram as dissimulation of legality – and so on. It is during this sequence that Jane is moved from the counter-family to the family-in-law. In the next sequence, it is Jane who restores full family status to the as-yet-incomplete community of siblings, the Riverses. The final sequence of the book is a *community of families*, with Jane, Rochester, and their children at the center.

In terms of the narrative energy of the novel, how is Jane moved from the place of the counter-family to the family-in-law? It is the active ideology of imperialism that provides the discursive field.

(My working definition of 'discursive field' must assume the existence of discrete 'systems of signs' at hand in the socius, each based on a specific axiomatics. I am identifying these systems as discursive fields. 'Imperialism as social mission' generates the possibility of one such axiomatics. How the individual artist taps the discursive field at hand with a sure touch, if not with transhistorical clairvoyance, in order to make the narrative structure move I hope to demonstrate through the following example. It is crucial that we extend our analysis of this example beyond the minimal diagnosis of 'racism.')

Let us consider the figure of Bertha Mason, a figure produced by the axiomatics of imperialism. Through Bertha Mason, the white Jamaican Creole, Brontë renders the human/animal frontier as acceptably indeterminate, so that a good greater than the letter of the Law can be broached. Here is the celebrated passage, given in the voice of Jane:

> In the deep shade, at the further end of the room, a figure ran backwards and forwards. What it was, whether beast or human being, one could not ... tell: it grovelled, seemingly, on all fours; it snatched and growled like some strange wild animal: but it was covered with clothing, and a quantity of dark, grizzled hair, wild as a mane, hid its head and face. [*JE*, p. 295]

In a matching passage, given in the voice of Rochester speaking *to* Jane, Brontë presents the imperative for a shift beyond the Law as divine injunction rather than human motive. In the terms of my essay, we might say that this is the register not of mere marriage or sexual reproduction but of Europe and its not-yet-human Other, of soul making. The field of imperial conquest is here inscribed as Hell:

> 'One night I had been awakened by her yells ... it was a fiery West Indian night....
> 'This life,' said I at last, 'is hell! – this is the air – those are the sounds of the bottomless pit! *I have a right* to deliver myself from it if I can. ... Let me break away, and go home to God!' ...
> 'A wind fresh from Europe blew over the ocean and rushed through the open casement: the storm broke, streamed, thundered, blazed, and the air grew pure. ... It was true Wisdom that consoled me in that hour, and showed me the right path....

'The sweet wind from Europe was still whispering in the refreshed leaves, and the Atlantic was thundering in glorious liberty....

'"Go,"' said Hope, ' "and live again in Europe.... You have done all that God and Humanity require of you."' [*JE*, pp. 310–11; my emphasis]

It is the unquestioned ideology of imperialist axiomatics, then, that conditions Jane's move from the counter-family set to the set of the family-in-law. Marxist critics such as Terry Eagleton have seen this only in terms of the ambiguous *class* position of the governess.[11] Sandra Gilbert and Susan Gubar, on the other hand, have seen Bertha Mason only in psychological terms, as Jane's dark double.[12]

I will not enter the critical debates that offer themselves here. Instead, I will develop the suggestion that nineteenth-century feminist individualism could conceive of a 'greater' project than access to the closed circle of the nuclear family. This is the project of soul making beyond 'mere' sexual reproduction. Here the native 'subject' is not almost an animal but rather the object of what might be termed the terrorism of the categorical imperative.

I am using 'Kant' in this essay as a metonym for the most flexible ethical moment in the European eighteenth century. Kant words the categorical imperative, conceived as the universal moral law given by pure reason, in this way: 'In all creation every thing one chooses and over which one has any power, may be used *merely as means*; man alone, and with him every rational creature, is an *end in himself.*' It is thus a moving displacement of Christian ethics from religion to philosophy. As Kant writes: 'With this agrees very well the possibility of such a command as: *Love God above everything, and thy neighbor as thyself.* For as a command it requires respect for a law which *commands love* and does not leave it to our own arbitrary choice to make this our principle.'[13]

The 'categorical' in Kant cannot be adequately represented in determinately grounded action. The dangerous transformative power of philosophy, however, is that its formal subtlety can be travestied in the service of the state. Such a travesty in the case of the categorical imperative can justify the imperialist project by producing the following formula: *make* the heathen into a human so that he can be treated as an end in himself.[14] This project is presented as a sort of tangent in *Jane Eyre*, a tangent that escapes the closed circle of the *narrative* conclusion. The tangent narrative is the story of St. John Rivers, who is granted the important task of concluding the text.

At the novel's end, the *allegorical* language of Christian psychobiography – rather than the textually constituted and seemingly *private* grammar of the creative imagination which we noted in the novel's opening – marks the inaccessibility of the imperialist project as such to the nascent 'feminist' scenario. The concluding passage of *Jane Eyre* places St. John Rivers within the fold of *Pilgrim's Progress*. Eagleton pays no attention to this but accepts the novel's ideological lexicon, which establishes St. John Rivers' heroism by identifying a life in Calcutta with an unquestioning choice of death. Gilbert and Gubar, by calling *Jane Eyre* 'Plain Jane's progress,' see the novel as simply replacing the male protagonist with the female. They do not notice the distance between sexual reproduction and soul making, both actualized by the unquestioned idiom of imperialist presuppositions evident in the last part of *Jane Eyre*:

> Firm, faithful, and devoted, full of energy, and zeal, and truth, [St. John Rivers] labours for his race. ... His is the sternness of the warrior Greatheart, who guards his pilgrim convoy from the onslaught of Apollyon. ... His is the ambition of the high master-spirit[s] ... who stand without fault before the throne of God; who share the last mighty victories of the Lamb; who are called, and chosen, and faithful. [*JE*, p. 455]

Earlier in the novel, St. John Rivers himself justifies the project: 'My vocation? My great work? ... My hopes of being numbered in the band who have merged all ambitions in the glorious one of bettering their race – of carrying knowledge into the realms of ignorance – of substituting peace for war – freedom for bondage – religion for superstition – the hope of heaven for the fear of hell?' (*JE*, p. 376). Imperialism and its territorial and subject-constituting project are a violent deconstruction of these oppositions.

When Jean Rhys, born on the Caribbean island of Dominica, read *Jane Eyre* as a child, she was moved by Bertha Mason: 'I thought I'd try to write her a life.'[15] *Wide Sargasso Sea*, the slim novel published in 1965, at the end of Rhys' long career, is that 'life.'[16]

I have suggested that Bertha's function in *Jane Eyre* is to render indeterminate the boundary between human and animal and thereby to weaken her entitlement under the spirit if not the letter of the Law. When Rhys rewrites the scene in *Jane Eyre* where Jane hears 'a snarling, snatching sound, almost like a dog quarrelling' and then encounters a bleeding Richard Mason (*JE*, p. 210), she keeps Bertha's humanity, indeed her sanity as critic of imperialism, intact. Grace Poole, another character originally in *Jane Eyre*, describes the incident to Bertha in *Wide Sargasso Sea*: 'So you don't remember that you attacked this gentleman with a knife? ... I didn't hear all he said except "I cannot interfere legally between yourself and your husband". It was when he said "legally" that you flew at him' (*WSS*, p. 150). In Rhys' retelling, it is the dissimulation that Bertha discerns in the word 'legally' – not an innate bestiality – that prompts her violent *re*action.

In the figure of Antoinette, whom in *Wide Sargasso Sea* Rochester violently renames Bertha, Rhys suggests that so intimate a thing as personal and human identity might be determined by the politics of imperialism. Antoinette, as a white Creole child growing up at the time of emancipation in Jamaica, is caught between the English imperialist and the black native. In recounting Antoinette's development, Rhys reinscribes some thematics of Narcissus.

There are, noticeably, many images of mirroring in the text. I will quote one from the first section. In this passage, Tia is the little black servant girl who is Antoinette's close companion: 'We had eaten the same food, slept side by side, bathed in the same river. As I ran, I thought, I will live with Tia and I will be like her. ... When I was close I saw the jagged stone in her hand but I did not see her throw it. ... We stared at each other, blood on my face, tears on hers. It was as if I saw myself. Like in a looking glass' (*WSS*, p. 38).

A progressive sequence of dreams reinforces this mirror imagery. In its second occurrence, the dream is partially set in a *hortus conclusus*, or 'enclosed garden' – Rhys uses the phrase (*WSS*, p. 50) – a Romance rewriting of the Narcissus topos as the place of encounter with Love.[17] In the enclosed garden, Antoinette encounters not Love but a strange threatening voice that says merely 'in here,' inviting her into a prison which masquerades as the legalization of love (*WSS*, p. 50).

In Ovid's *Metamorphoses*, Narcissus' madness is disclosed when he recognizes his Other as his self: 'Iste ego sum.'[18] Rhys makes Antoinette see her *self* as her Other, Brontë's Bertha. In the last section of *Wide Sargasso Sea*, Antoinette acts out *Jane Eyre's* conclusion and recognizes herself as the so-called ghost in Thornfield Hall: 'I went into the hall again with the tall candle in my hand. It was then that I saw her – the ghost. The woman with streaming hair. She was surrounded by a gilt frame but I knew her' (*WSS*, p. 154). The gilt frame encloses a mirror: as Narcissus' pool reflects the selfed Other, so this 'pool' reflects the Othered self. Here the dream sequence ends, with an invocation of none other than Tia, the Other that could not be selfed, because the fracture of imperialism rather than the Ovidian pool intervened. (I will return to this difficult point.) 'That was the third time I had my dream, and it ended. ... I called "Tia" and jumped and woke' (*WSS*, p. 155). It is now, at the very end of the book, that Antoinette/Bertha can say: 'Now at last I know why I was brought here and what I have to do' (*WSS*, pp. 155–56). We can read this as her having been brought into the England of Brontë's novel: 'This cardboard house' – a book between cardboard covers – 'where I walk at night is not England' (*WSS*, p. 148). In this fictive England, she must play out her role, act out the transformation of her 'self' into that fictive Other, set fire to the house and kill herself, so that Jane Eyre can become the feminist individualist heroine of British fiction. I must read this as an allegory of the general epistemic violence of imperialism, the construction of a self-immolating colonial subject for the glorification of the social mission of the colonizer. At least Rhys sees to it that the woman from the colonies is not sacrificed as an insane animal for her sister's consolation.

Critics have remarked that *Wide Sargasso Sea* treats the Rochester character with understanding and sympathy.[19] Indeed, he narrates the entire middle section of the book. Rhys makes it clear that he is a victim of the patriarchal inheritance law of entailment rather than of a father's natural preference for the firstborn: in *Wide Sargasso Sea*, Rochester's situation is clearly that of a younger son dispatched to the colonies to buy an heiress. If in the case of Antoinette and her identity, Rhys utilizes the thematics of Narcissus, in the case of Rochester and his patrimony, she touches on the thematics of Oedipus. (In this she has her finger on our 'historical moment.' If, in the nineteenth century, subject-constitution is represented as childbearing and soul making, in the twentieth century psychoanalysis allows the West to plot the itinerary of the subject from Narcissus [the 'imaginary'] to Oedipus [the 'symbolic']. This subject, however, is the normative male subject. In Rhys' reinscription of these themes, divided between the female and the male protagonist, feminism and a critique of imperialism become complicit.)

In place of the 'wind from Europe' scene, Rhys substitutes the scenario of a suppressed letter to a father, a letter which would be the 'correct' explanation of the tragedy of the book.[20] 'I thought about the letter which should have been written to England a week ago. Dear Father ...' (WSS, p. 57). This is the first instance: the letter not written. Shortly afterward:

> Dear Father. The thirty thousand pounds have been paid to me without question or condition. No provision made for her (that must be seen to). ... I will never be a disgrace to you or to my dear brother the son you love. No begging letters, no mean requests. None of the furtive shabby manoeuvres of a younger son. I have sold my soul or you have sold it, and after all is it such a bad bargain? The girl is thought to be beautiful, she is beautiful. And yet ... [WSS, p. 59]

This is the second instance: the letter not sent. The formal letter is uninteresting; I will quote only a part of it:

> Dear Father, we have arrived from Jamaica after an uncomfortable few days. This little estate in the Windward Islands is part of the family property and Antoinette is much attached to it. ... All is well and has gone according to your plans and wishes. I dealt of course with Richard Mason. ... He seemed to become attached to me and trusted me completely. This place is very beautiful but my illness has left me too exhausted to appreciate it fully. I will write again in a few days' time. [WSS, p. 63]

And so on.

Rhys' version of the Oedipal exchange is ironic, not a closed circle. We cannot know if the letter actually reaches its destination. 'I wondered how they got their letters posted,' the Rochester figure muses. 'I folded mine and put it into a drawer of the desk. ... There are blanks in my mind that cannot be filled up' (WSS, p. 64). It is as if the text presses us to note the analogy between letter and mind.

Rhys denies to Brontë's Rochester the one thing that is supposed to be secured in the Oedipal relay: the Name of the Father, or the patronymic. In Wide Sargasso Sea, the character corresponding to Rochester has no name. His writing of the final version of the letter to his father is supervised, in fact, by an image of the loss of the patronymic: 'There was a crude bookshelf made of three shingles strung together over the desk and I looked at the books, Byron's poems, novels by Sir Walter Scott, Confessions of an Opium Eater ... and on the last shelf, Life and Letters of ... The rest was eaten away' (WSS, p. 63).

Wide Sargasso Sea marks with uncanny clarity the limits of its own discourse in Christophine, Antoinette's black nurse. We may perhaps surmise the distance between Jane Eyre and Wide Sargasso Sea by remarking that Christophine's unfinished story is the tangent to the latter narrative, as St. John Rivers' story is to the former. Christophine is not a native of Jamaica; she is from Martinique. Taxonomically, she belongs to the category of the good servant rather than that of the pure native. But within these borders, Rhys creates a powerfully suggestive figure.

Christophine is the first interpreter and named speaking subject in the text. 'The Jamaican ladies had never approved of my mother, "because she pretty like pretty self" Christophine said,' we read in the book's opening paragraph (WSS, p. 15). I have taught this book five times, once in France, once to students who had worked on the book with the well-known Caribbean novelist Wilson Harris, and once at a prestigious institute where the majority of the students were faculty from other universities. It is part of the political argument I am making that all these students blithely stepped over this paragraph without asking or knowing what Christophine's patois, so-called incorrect English, might mean.

Christophine is, of course, a commodified person. "'She was your father's wedding present to me'" explains Antoinette's mother, "'one of his presents'" (*WSS*, p. 18). Yet Rhys assigns her some crucial functions in the text. It is Christophine who judges that black ritual practices are culture-specific and cannot be used by whites as cheap remedies for social evils, such as Rochester's lack of love for Antoinette. Most important, it is Christophine alone whom Rhys allows to offer a hard analysis of Rochester's actions, to challenge him in a face-to-face encounter. The entire extended passage is worthy of comment. I quote a brief extract:

> 'She is Creole girl, and she have the sun in her. Tell the truth now. She don't come to your house in this place England they tell me about, she don't come to your beautiful house to beg you to marry with her. No, it's you come all the long way to her house – it's you beg her to marry. And she love you and she give you all she have. Now you say you don't love her and you break her up. What you do with her money, eh?' [And then Rochester, the white man, comments silently to himself] Her voice was still quiet but with a hiss in it when she said 'money.' [*WSS*, p. 130]

Her analysis is powerful enough for the white man to be afraid: 'I no longer felt dazed, tired, half hypnotized, but alert and wary, ready to defend myself' (*WSS*, p. 130).

Rhys does not, however, romanticize individual heroics on the part of the oppressed. When the Man refers to the forces of Law and Order, Christophine recognizes their power. This exposure of civil inequality is emphasized by the fact that, just before the Man's successful threat, Christophine had invoked the emancipation of slaves in Jamaica by proclaiming: 'No chain gang, no tread machine, no dark jail either. This is free country and I am free woman' (*WSS*, p. 131).

As I mentioned above, Christophine is tangential to this narrative. She cannot be contained by a novel which rewrites a canonical English text within the European novelistic tradition in the interest of the white Creole rather than the native. No perspective *critical* of imperialism can turn the Other into a self, because the project of imperialism has always already historically refracted what might have been the absolutely Other into a domesticated Other that consolidates the imperialist self.[21] The Caliban of Retamar, caught between Europe and Latin America, reflects this predicament. We can read Rhys' reinscription of Narcissus as a thematization of the same problematic.

Of course, we cannot know Jean Rhys' feelings in the matter. We can, however, look at the scene of Christophine's inscription in the text. Immediately after the exchange between her and the Man, well before the conclusion, she is simply driven out of the story, with neither narrative nor characterological explanation or justice. "'Read and write I don't know. Other things I know.' She walked away without looking back' (*WSS*, p. 133).

Indeed, if Rhys rewrites the madwoman's attack on the Man by underlining of the misuse of 'legality,' she cannot deal with the passage that corresponds to St. John Rivers' own justification of his martyrdom, for it has been displaced into the current idiom of modernization and development. Attempts to construct the 'Third World Woman' as a signifier remind us that the hegemonic definition of literature is itself caught within the history of imperialism. A full literary reinscription cannot easily flourish in the imperialist fracture or discontinuity, covered over by an alien legal system masquerading as Law as such, an alien ideology established as only Truth, and a set of human sciences busy establishing the 'native' as self-consolidating Other.

In the Indian case at least, it would be difficult to find an ideological clue to the planned epistemic violence of imperialism merely by rearranging curricula or syllabi within existing norms of literary pedagogy. For a later period of imperialism – when the constituted colonial subject has firmly taken hold – straightforward experiments of comparison can be undertaken, say, between the functionally witless India of *Mrs. Dalloway*, on the one hand, and literary texts produced in India in the 1920s, on the other. But the first half of the nineteenth century resists questioning through literature or literary criticism in the narrow sense, because both are implicated in the project of producing Ariel. To reopen the fracture without succumbing to a nostalgia for lost origins, the literary critic must turn to the archives of imperial governance.

[...]

The essay concludes with an analysis of *Frankenstein*; see Headnote, above.

Notes (cut and renumbered)
1. My notion of the 'worlding of a world' upon what must be assumed to be uninscribed earth is a vulgarization of Martin Heidegger's idea; see 'The Origin of the Work of Art,' *Poetry, Language, Thought*, trans. Albert Hofstadter (New York, 1977), pp. 17–87.
2. See Charlotte Brontë, *Jane Eyre* (New York, 1960); all further references to this work, abbreviated *JE*, will be included in the text.
3. I have tried to do this in my essay 'Unmaking and Making in *To the Lighthouse*,' in *Women and Language in Literature and Society*, ed. Sally McConnell-Ginet, Ruth Borker, and Nelly Furman (New York, 1980), pp. 310–27.
4. As always, I take my formula from Louis Althusser, 'Ideology and Ideological State Apparatuses (Notes towards an Investigation),' *'Lenin and Philosophy' and Other Essay*, trans. Ben Brewster (New York, 1971), pp. 127–86. For an acute differentiation between the individual and individualism, see V. N. Vološinov, *Marxism and the Philosophy of Language*, trans. Ladislav Matejka and I. R. Titunik, Studies in Language, vol. 1 (New York, 1973), pp. 93–94 and 152–53. For a 'straight' analysis of the roots and ramifications of English 'individualism,' see C. B. MacPherson, *The Political Theory of Possessive Individualism: Hobbes to Locke* (Oxford, 1962). I am grateful to Jonathan Rée for bringing this book to my attention and for giving a careful reading of all but the very end of the present essay.
5. I am constructing an analogy with Homi Bhabha's powerful notion of 'not-quite/not-white' in his 'Of Mimicry and Man: The Ambiguity of Colonial Discourse,' *October* 28 (Spring 1984): 132. I should also add that I use the word 'native' here in reaction to the term 'Third World Woman.' It cannot, of course, apply with equal historical justice to both the West Indian and the Indian contexts nor to contexts of imperialism by transportation.

6. See Roberto Fernández Retamar, 'Caliban: Notes towards a Discussion of Culture in Our America,' trans. Lynn Garafola, David Arthur McMurray, and Robert Márquez, *Massachusetts Review* 15 (Winter–Spring 1974): 7–72; all further references to this work, abbreviated 'C,' will be included in the text.

7. See José Enrique Rodó, *Ariel*, ed. Gordon Brotherston (Cambridge, 1967).

8. For an elaboration of 'an inaccessible blankness circumscribed by an interpretable text,' see my 'Can the Subaltern Speak?' *Marxist Interpretations of Culture*, ed. Cary Nelson (Urbana, Ill., 1988).

9. See Elizabeth Fox-Genovese, 'Placing Women's History in History,' *New Left Review* 133 (May–June 1982): 5–29.

10. Rudolph Ackerman, *The Repository of Arts, Literature, Commerce, Manufactures, Fashions, and Politics*, (London, 1823), p. 310.

11. See Terry Eagleton, *Myths of Power: A Marxist Study of the Brontës* (London, 1975); this is one of the general presuppositions of his book.

12. See Sandra M. Gilbert and Susan Gubar, *The Madwoman in the Attic: The Woman Writer and the Nineteenth-Century Literary Imagination* (New Haven, Conn., 1979), pp. 360–62.

13. Immanuel Kant, *Critique of Practical Reason, The 'Critique of Pure Reason,' the 'Critique of Practical Reason' and Other Ethical Treatises, the 'Critique of Judgement,'* trans. J. M. D. Meiklejohn et al. (Chicago, 1952), pp. 328, 326.

14. I have tried to justify the reduction of sociohistorical problems to formulas or propositions in my essay 'Can the Subaltern Speak?' The 'travesty' I speak of does not befall the Kantian ethic in its purity as an accident but rather exists within its lineaments as a possible supplement. On the register of the human being as child rather than heathen, my formula can be found, for example, in 'What Is Enlightenment?' in Kant, *'Foundations of the Metaphysics of Morals,' 'What Is Enlightenment?' and a Passage from 'The Metaphysics of Morals,'* trans. and ed. Lewis White Beck (Chicago, 1950). I have profited from discussing Kant with Jonathan Rée.

15. Jean Rhys, in an interview with Elizabeth Vreeland, quoted in Nancy Harrison, *An Introduction to the Writing Practice of Jean Rhys: The Novel as Women's Text* (Rutherwood, N. J., 1988). This is an excellent, detailed study of Rhys.

16. Jean Rhys, *Wide Sargasso Sea*, Penguin, 1966; all further references to this work, abbreviated *WSS*, are included in the text.

17. See Louise Vinge, *The Narcissus Theme in Western European Literature Up to the Early Nineteenth Century*, trans. Robert Dewsnap et al. (Lund, 1967), chap. 5.

18. For a detailed study of this text, see John Brenkman, 'Narcissus in the Text,' *Georgia Review* 30 (Summer 1976): 293–327.

19. See, e.g., Thomas F. Staley, *Jean Rhys: A Critical Study* (Austin, Tex. 1979), pp. 108–16; it is interesting to note Staley's masculist discomfort with this and his consequent dissatisfaction with Rhys' novel.

20. I have tried to relate castration and suppressed letters in my 'The Letter As Cutting Edge,' in *Literature and Psychoanalysis; The Question of Reading: Otherwise*, ed. Shoshana Felman (New Haven, Conn., 1981), pp. 208–26.

21. This is the main argument of my 'Can the Subaltern Speak?'

Chapter 4

George Eliot:
Middlemarch

GENERAL INTRODUCTION

Mary Ann Evans, writing under the male pseudonym George Eliot, published a number of successful novels between 1859 and 1876: *Adam Bede* (1859), *The Mill on the Floss* (1860), *Silas Marner* (1861), *Romola* (1863), *Felix Holt* (1866), *Middlemarch* (1871–2) and *Daniel Deronda* (1876). She is regarded as one of the great nineteenth-century realist novelists. Equally, *Middlemarch* – 'A Study of Provincial Life' – is usually taken to represent the peak of her achievement, the most developed expression of her humanist worldview and realist fictional technique, a judgement recently reconfirmed by the self-consciously 'faithful' BBC television six-part dramatization of the novel (1994). Characteristically, F. R. Leavis, in his immensely influential book, *The Great Tradition* (1948), places Eliot squarely amongst 'the [four] great English novelists' (the others are Jane Austen, Henry James and Joseph Conrad), and sees *Middlemarch* as the 'magnificent' product of her 'mature genius' (p. 146, below). Most later critics, whatever their theoretical and ideological orientation, have also given *Middlemarch* its due, and it has become a focus for critical debate – especially about fiction and history and the nature and function of realism. All the excerpts in the present exercise relate, more or less directly, to these issues: from Leavis' paean of praise (tempered by his criticism of the characterization of Dorothea and Ladislaw); through Williams' and Eagleton's variously Marxist readings of text, history and ideology; to Hillis Miller's deconstructive analysis of the novel's metaphoric discourse and MacCabe's now famous identification and definition of 'the classic realist text'.

What is at stake, in several of these extracts, in their varying responses to the character of Ladislaw? George Eliot's metaphor of the 'web' is at the centre of discussion in several essays; what is the informing stance of the critics in relation to her treatment of it? In what ways may Williams and Eagleton in particular be seen to be writing 'against' Leavis? Eagleton employs the notion of 'ideology' extensively (for his later discussion of this concept, see *Ideology: An Introduction*, 1993); consider why it has become central to discussions of literature and history – in this exercise and more generally. The importance of a *historical* dimension in literary study clearly informs some of the extracts (see also the discussions of similar issues in Ch. 9 on *Beloved*). It is equally clearly lacking in others; what are the implications of these different perspectives? What makes Hillis Miller's and MacCabe's pieces 'poststructuralist'? Taking MacCabe's concept of 'the classic realist text' as a starting-point, try to deduce the various definitions and theoretical models of realism which lie behind the five essays reprinted here. Consider also the relationship between humanism and realism, and the ideological implications of the different critical positions adopted. How does Hillis Miller's deconstructionism fit in to a debate about realism? Why does MacCabe need to define realism in the way he does? Analyse the textual strategies for reading *Middlemarch* deployed in the different extracts in relation to their different projects and theoretical premises. All five of the critics here are men, and none of the analyses seems to be influenced by feminism. Consider what a feminist reading of *Middlemarch* might look like (drawing, perhaps, on critical models exemplified in Chs 3 and 9 on *Jane Eyre* and *Beloved*).

Further Reading

Interesting collections of earlier critical essays on Eliot include George R. Creeger's 'Twentieth-Century Views' volume (Prentice Hall, 1970) and the 'Casebook' on *Middlemarch*, ed. Patrick Swinden (Macmillan, 1972). Recent collections which give an excellent sample of contemporary approaches and readings are: K. M. Newton, ed., *George Eliot* (Longman 'Critical Reader', 1991) and John Peck, ed., *Middlemarch* (Macmillan 'New Casebook', 1992). There is, of course, much feminist criticism on George Eliot (from Elaine Showalter's and Gilbert and Gubar's earlier work – see Headnotes in Ch. 3 – to an extensive debate on Eliot's own relation to feminism). Both recent critical Readers above contain examples of this – Kathleen Blake's essay, '*Middlemarch*: Vocation, Love and the Woman Question', and Gillian Beer's excerpt from her *George Eliot* (Harvester, 1986), '*Middlemarch* and "The Woman Question"', both in Peck, ed., being the most apposite here.

4.1   F. R. LEAVIS: FROM *THE GREAT TRADITION* (1948)

Leavis (1895–1975) has been one of the most influential English critics of the twentieth century. His teaching at Cambridge University, his editorship of the journal *Scrutiny* (1932–53), and his own extensive critical writing made him a formative figure in the development of English studies and literary criticism, especially in Great Britain. His works also include *New Bearings in English Poetry* (1932), *Revaluation* (1936) and *The Common Pursuit* (1962), as well as full-length studies of D. H. Lawrence and Dickens, and of minority and mass culture (see also his *Education and the University*, 1943, and Q. D. Leavis, *Fiction and the Reading Public*, 1932). A valuable general analysis of Leavis' work and influence is Francis Mulhern's *The Moment of 'Scrutiny'* (Verso, 1979); more recent books about him include M. Bell, *F. R. Leavis* (Routledge, 1988) and Anne Samson, *F. R. Leavis* (Harvester, 1992).

Profoundly influenced by Matthew Arnold and T. S. Eliot, Leavis combined a critical stance of direct reference to 'the text' (which relates him, in part, to 'practical criticism' and 'new criticism'; see Headnote to Cleanth Brooks, Ch. 2, p. 71) with a moral mission for literature (especially that 'discriminated' – in his terms – as Great Literature). Equally, the study of literature was at the heart of the defence and promotion of 'minority culture' in the face of a 'mass civilization'. In *The Great Tradition*, Leavis argues that the work of the 'great English novelists' is 'characterised by a vital capacity for experience, a kind of reverent openness before life, and a marked moral intensity'. In his resolutely untheorized (indeed anti-theoretical) critical discourse, these constitute key terms and notions. Try to find instances in the extract where they drive Leavis' criticism. What exactly is the 'weakness' in Dorothea's characterization for Leavis, and how does this relate to his larger project? Also note his criticism of Ladislaw – in preparation for Raymond Williams' defence of that character in the following excerpt. Leavis is now well known for several characteristic critical tactics and stylistic tropes: try to identify some of them (e.g. how does he use the literary text itself in his reading practice?) Why, on this evidence, should Leavis have become the prime target for critique by later Marxist and poststructuralist schools of criticism in Britain?

For a further example of Leavis' work, and discussion of it, see the extract in Ch. 6 and Headnote, pp. 244–50.

The following excerpt is pp. 74, 86–93 (Penguin edition, 1962) of Part ii of Ch. 2, '*Romola* to *Middlemarch*' – which deals with all of Eliot's major fiction.

The Great Tradition

Only one book can, as a whole (though not without qualification), be said to represent her mature genius. That is, of course, *Middlemarch*.

The necessary part of great intellectual powers in such a success as *Middlemarch* is obvious. The sub-title of the book is 'A Study of Provincial Life', and it is no idle pretension. The sheer informedness about society, its mechanism, the ways in which people of different classes live and (if they have to) earn their livelihoods, impresses us with its range, and it is real knowledge; that is, it is knowledge alive with understanding. George Eliot had said in *Felix Holt*, by way of apology for the space she devoted to 'social changes' and 'public matters': 'there is no private life which has not been determined by a wider public life'. The aim implicit in this remark is magnificently achieved in *Middlemarch,* and it is achieved by a novelist whose genius manifests itself in a profound analysis of the individual.

[...]

Here follow twelve pages of laudatory analysis of the characterization of Casaubon, Lydgate, Rosamond and Bulstrode, evidenced by many long quotations.

[...]

The weakness of the book, as already intimated, is in Dorothea. We have the danger-signal in the very outset, in the brief 'Prelude', with its reference to St Teresa, whose 'flame ... fed from within, soared after some illimitable satisfaction, some object which would never justify weakness, which would reconcile self-despair with the rapturous consciousness of life beyond self'. 'Many Teresas', we are told, 'have been born who found for themselves no epic life wherein there was a constant unfolding of far-resonant action....' In the absence of a 'coherent social faith and order which could perform the function of knowledge for the ardently willing soul' they failed to realize their aspiration: 'Their ardour alternated between a vague ideal and the common yearning of womanhood. ...' Their failure, we gather, was a case of 'a certain spiritual grandeur ill-matched with the meanness of opportunity....' It is a dangerous theme for George Eliot, and we recognize a far from reassuring accent. And our misgivings are not quieted when we find, in the close of the 'Prelude', so marked a reminder of Maggie Tulliver as this:

> Here and there a cygnet is reared uneasily among the ducklings in the brown pond, and never finds the living stream in fellowship with its own oary-footed kind. Here and there is born a Saint Teresa, a foundress of nothing, whose loving heart-beats and sobs after an unattained goodness tremble off and are dispersed among hindrances, instead of centring in some long-recognizable deed.

All the same, the first two chapters make us forget these alarms, the poise is so sure and the tone so right. When we are told of Dorothea Brooke that 'her mind was theoretic, and yearned by its nature after some lofty conception of the world which might fairly include the parish of Tipton, and her own rule of conduct there', we give that 'parish of Tipton' its full weight. The provinciality of the provincial scene that George Eliot presents is not a mere foil for a heroine; we see it in Dorothea herself as a callowness confirmed by culture: she and her sister had 'both been educated ... on plans at once narrow and promiscuous, first in an English family and afterwards in a Swiss family at Lausanne....' This is an education that makes little difference to Maggie Tulliver – who is now, we feel, seen by the novelist from the outside as well as felt from within. Dorothea, that is to say, is not exempted from the irony that informs our vision of the other characters in these opening chapters – Celia, Mr Brooke, Sir James Chettam, and Mr Casaubon. It looks as if George Eliot had succeeded in bringing within her achieved maturity this most resistant and incorrigible self.

Unhappily, we can't go on in that belief for long. Already in the third chapter we find reasons for recalling the 'Prelude'. In the description of the 'soul-hunger' that leads Dorothea to see Casaubon so fantastically as a 'winged messenger' we miss the poise that had characterized the presentment of her at her introduction:

> For a long while she had been oppressed by the indefiniteness which hung in her mind, like a thick summer haze, over all her desire to make her life greatly effective. What could she do, what ought she to do? ... The intensity of her religious disposition, the coercion it exercised over her life, was but one aspect of a nature altogether ardent, theoretic, and intellectually consequent: and with such a nature struggling in the bands of a narrow teaching, hemmed in by a social life which seemed nothing but a labyrinth of petty courses, a walled-in maze of small paths that led no whither, the outcome was sure to strike others as at once exaggeration and inconsistency.

Aren't we here, we wonder, in sight of an unqualified self-identification? Isn't there something dangerous in the way the irony seems to be reserved for the provincial background and circumstances, leaving the heroine immune? The doubt has very soon become more than a doubt. When (in Chapter VII) Dorothea, by way of illustrating the kind of music she enjoys, says that the great organ at Freiberg, which she heard on her way home from Lausanne, made her sob, we can't help noting that it is the fatuous Mr Brooke, a figure consistently presented for our ironic contemplation, who comments: 'That kind of thing is not healthy, my dear'. By the time we see her by the 'reclining Ariadne' in the Vatican, as Will Ladislaw sees her –

> a breathing, blooming girl, whose form, not shamed by the Ariadne, was clad in Quakerish grey drapery; her long cloak, fastened at the neck, was thrown backward from the arms, and one beautiful ungloved hand pillowed her cheek, pushing somewhat backward the white beaver bonnet which made a sort of halo to her face around the simply braided dark-brown hair.

– we are in a position to say that seeing her here through Will's eyes involves for us no adjustment of vision: this is how we *have* been seeing her – or been aware that we are meant to see her. And in general, in so far as we respond to the novelist's intention, our vision goes on being Will's.

The idealization is overt at the moment, finding its licence in the surrounding statuary and in Will's role of artist (he is with his German artist friend). But Will's idealizing faculty clearly doesn't confine itself to her outward form even here, and when, thirty or so pages farther on, talking with her and Casaubon, he reflects, 'She was an angel beguiled', we are clearly not meant to dissociate ourselves or the novelist. In fact, he has no independent status of his own – he can't be said to exist; he merely represents, not a dramatically real point of view, but certain of George Eliot's intentions – intentions she has failed to realize creatively. The most important of these is to impose on the reader her own vision and valuation of Dorothea.

Will, of course, is also intended – it is not really a separate matter – to be, in contrast to Casaubon, a fitting soul-mate for Dorothea. He is not substantially (everyone agrees) 'there', but we can see well enough what kind of qualities and attractions are intended, and we can see equally well that we are expected to share a valuation of them extravagantly higher than any we can for a moment countenance. George Eliot's valuation of Will Ladislaw, in short, is Dorothea's, just as Will's of Dorothea is George Eliot's. Dorothea, to put it another way, is a product of George Eliot's own 'soul-hunger' – another day-dream ideal self. This persistence, in the midst of so much that is so other, of an unreduced enclave of the old immaturity is disconcerting in the extreme. We have an alternation between the poised impersonal insight of a finely tempered wisdom and something like the emotional confusions and self-importances of adolescence.

It is given us, of course, at the outset, as of the essence of Dorothea's case, that she is vague in her exaltations, that she 'was oppressed by the indefiniteness which hung in her mind, like a thick summer haze, over all her desire to make her life greatly effective'. But the show of presenting this haze from the outside soon lapses; George Eliot herself, so far as Dorothea is concerned, is clearly in it too. That is peculiarly apparent in the presentment of those impossibly high-falutin' *tête-à-tête* – or soul to soul – exchanges between Dorothea and Will, which is utterly without irony or criticism. Their tone and quality are given fairly enough in this retrospective summary (it occurs at the end of Chapter LXXXII): 'all their vision, all their thought of each other, had been in a world apart, where the sunshine fell on tall white lilies, where no evil lurked, and no other soul entered'. It is Will who is supposed to be reflecting to this effect, but Will here – as everywhere in his attitude towards Dorothea – is unmistakably not to be distinguished from the novelist (as we have noted, he hardly exists).[1]

There is, as a matter of fact, one place where for a moment George Eliot dissociates herself from him (Chapter XXXIX):

> For the moment Will's admiration was accompanied with a chilling sense of remoteness. A man is seldom ashamed of feeling that he cannot love a woman so well when he sees a certain greatness in her; nature having intended greatness for men.

What she dissociates herself from, it will be noted, is not the valuation; the irony is not directed against that, but, on the contrary, implicitly endorses it. To point out that George Eliot identifies herself with Will's sense of Dorothea's 'subduing power, the sweet dignity, of her noble unsuspicious inexperience', doesn't, perhaps, seem a very damaging criticism. But when it becomes plain that in this self-identification such significant matters of valuation are involved the criticism takes on a different look.

> Men and women make such sad mistakes about their own symptoms, taking their vague uneasy longings, sometimes for genius, sometimes for religion, and oftener still for a mighty love.

– The genius of George Eliot is not questioned, but what she observes here in respect of Rosamond Vincy has obvious bearings on her own immature self, the self persisting so extraordinarily in company with the genius that is self-knowledge and a rare order of maturity.

Dorothea, with her 'genius for feeling nobly', that 'current' in her mind 'into which all thought and feeling were apt sooner or later to flow – the reaching forward of the whole consciousness towards the fullest truth, the least partial good' (end of Chapter XX), and with her ability to turn that current into a passion for Will Ladislaw, gives us Maggie's case again, and Maggie's significance: again we have the confusions represented by the exalted vagueness of Maggie's 'soul-hunger'; we have the unacceptable valuations and the day-dream self-indulgence.

The aspect of self-indulgence is most embarrassingly apparent in Dorothea's relations (as we are invited to see them) with Lydgate, who, unlike Ladislaw, is real and a man. Lydgate's reality makes the unreality of the great scene intended by George Eliot (or by the Dorothea in her) the more disconcerting: the scene in which to Lydgate, misunderstood, isolated, ostracized, there appears an unhoped-for angelic visitation, Dorothea, all-comprehending and irresistibly good (Chapter LXXVI):

> 'Oh, it is hard!' said Dorothea. 'I understand the difficulty there is in your vindicating yourself. And that all this should have come to you who had meant to lead a higher life than the common, and to find out better ways – I cannot bear to rest in this as unchangeable. I know you meant that. I remember what you said to me when you first spoke to me about the hospital. There is no sorrow I have thought more about than that – to love what is great, and try to reach it, and yet to fail.'
>
> 'Yes,' said Lydgate, feeling that here he had found room for the full meaning of his grief. ...
>
> 'Suppose,' said Dorothea meditatively. 'Suppose we kept on the hospital according to the present plan, and you stayed here though only with the friendship and support of the few, the evil feeling towards you would gradually die out; there would come opportunities in which people would be forced to acknowledge that they had been unjust to you, because they would see that your purposes were pure. You may still win a great fame like the Louis and Laennec I have heard you speak of, and we shall all be proud of you', she ended, with a smile.

We are given a good deal in the same vein of winning simplicity. Such a failure in touch, in so intelligent a novelist, is more than a surface matter; it betrays a radical disorder. For Lydgate, we are told, the 'childlike grave-eyed earnestness with which Dorothea said all this was irresistible – blent into an adorable whole with her ready understanding of high experience'. And lest we shouldn't have appreciated her to the full, we are told that

> As Lydgate rode away, he thought, 'This young creature has a heart large enough for the Virgin Mary. She evidently thinks nothing of her own future, and would pledge away half her income at once, as if she wanted nothing for herself but a chair to sit in from which she can look down with those clear eyes at the poor mortals who pray to her. She seems to have what I never saw in any woman before – a fountain of friendship towards men – a man can make a friend of her.'

What we have here is unmistakably something of the same order as Romola's epiphany in the plague-stricken village; but worse – or, at any rate, more painfully significant. Offered as it is in a context of George Eliot's maturest art, it not only matters more; it forces us to recognize how intimately her weakness attends upon her strength. Stressing the intended significance of the scene she says, in the course of it:

> The presence of a noble nature, generous in its wishes, ardent in its charity, changes the lights for us: we begin to see things again in their larger, quieter masses, and to believe that we too can be seen and judged in the wholeness of our character.

This is a characteristic utterance, and, but for the illustration we are being offered, we should say it came from her strength – the strength exhibited in her presentment of Casaubon, Rosamond, Lydgate, and Bulstrode. It is certainly her strength as a novelist to have a noble and ardent nature – it is a condition of that maturity which makes her so much greater an artist than Flaubert. What she says of Dorothea might have been said of herself:

> Permanent rebellion, the disorder of a life without some loving reverent resolve, was not possible to her.

But that she says it of Dorothea must make us aware how far from a simple trait it is we are considering, and how readily the proposition can slide into such another as this:

> No life would have been possible for Dorothea that was not filled with emotion.

Strength, and complacent readiness to yield to temptation – they are not at all the same thing; but we see how insidiously, in George Eliot, they are related. Intensely alive with intelligence and imaginative sympathy, quick and vivid in her realization of the 'equivalent centre of self' in others – even in a Casaubon or a Rosamond, she is incapable of morose indifference or the normal routine obtuseness, and it may be said in a wholly laudatory sense, by way of characterizing her at her highest level, that no life would have been possible for her that was not filled with emotion: her sensibility is directed outward, and she responds from deep within. At this level, 'emotion' is a disinterested response defined by its object, and hardly distinguishable from the play of the intelligence and self-knowledge that give it impersonality. But the emotional 'fulness' represented by Dorothea depends for its exalting potency on an abeyance of intelligence and self-knowledge, and the situations offered by way of 'objective correlative' have the day-dream relation to experience; they are generated by a need to soar above the indocile facts and conditions of the real world. They don't, indeed, strike us as real in any sense; they have no objectivity, no vigour of illusion. In this kind of indulgence, complaisantly as she abandons herself to the current that is loosed, George Eliot's creative vitality has no part.

Note

1. Though, significantly, it is he alone who is adequate to treating Rosamond with appropriate ruthlessness – see the episode (Chapter LXXVIII) in which he 'tells her straight' what his author feels about her.

4.2 RAYMOND WILLIAMS: FROM *THE ENGLISH NOVEL FROM DICKENS TO LAWRENCE* (1970)

Raymond Williams (1921–88), of working-class origins in the Welsh 'border country', spent most of his working life as a lecturer and then Professor of Drama at the University of Cambridge, producing his huge *oeuvre* of radical writings (including half a dozen novels); and was an internationally formative figure in literary, cultural and media studies. His critical writings include: *Culture and Society* (1958), *The Long Revolution* (1961), *Modern Tragedy* (1966), *The Country and the City* (1973), *Television, Technology and Cultural Form* (1974), *Marxism and Literature* (1977), *Problems in Materialism and Culture* (1980) and *Resources of Hope* (1989). The most helpful introduction to, and critical assessment of, his work remains the *New Left Review* interviews published as *Politics and Letters* (1979).

Williams' life-work was, in a sense, a radical theoretical construction of the whole domain of social meaning – 'culture' as 'a whole way of life' – and he developed this in studies of many different genres of cultural production. Firmly historical and materialist in all his work, he eventually defined his theoretical position as 'cultural materialism' (see Headnotes to Dollimore and Sinfield in Ch. 5) – only declaring a more direct relation to Marxism with *Marxism and Literature* in the later 1970s. Even so, in this period, younger Marxists of the new 'New Left', like Terry Eagleton, while recognizing Williams as their mentor, criticized him for his apparent residual humanism. Eagleton is now reconciled to Williams' project, but in an earlier critique, in *Criticism and Ideology* (1976), he characterized it as 'left Leavisism'. *The English Novel* is a relatively early work; does Eagleton's phrase usefully describe the present extract; what might differentiate it from Leavis' criticism? The notions 'structure of feeling' (see also the discussion of this in *Marxism and Literature*) and 'knowable community' – the latter treated at some length in the excerpts below – are central to Williams' thinking in this period. Try to define what he means by them, and how he puts them to work. Does this piece exemplify 'historical' criticism and 'cultural materialism'? Williams uses the notion of 'consciousness' a great deal; in what relation does this term stand to Eagleton's 'ideology' in the following essay? What are the implications for cultural politics of Williams' defence of the 'unconvincing' Ladislaw (and of *Daniel Deronda*) in the closing paragraphs? Williams' reading is generalized and at an apparent remove from the text of the novel; could his argument be supported by a close textual reading?

For a further example of Williams' work, and discussion of it, see the extract in Ch. 7 and Headnote, pp. 292–6.

The following extract is pp. 63–79, *passim* (Paladin edition, 1974) of Ch. 3, 'George Eliot', a more general study of her fiction.

The English Novel from Dickens to Lawrence

The opening one-and-a-half pages establish a link between the loneliness and frustration of Maggie Tulliver in *The Mill on the Floss* and Lucy Snowe in Charlotte Brontë's *Villette*.

[...]

What we must then examine is the relation – the very difficult relation – in George Eliot's development, between the intense feeling which is so often in practice separating and isolating, and the practical extension in observation and sympathy of the ordinary community of the novel.

Is the connection of these experiences, we might ask first, only historical: only the coincidence, in an actual adolescence and now in memory, of intense lonely feeling and a practical sharing of ordinary working life? Certainly the internal relation is simpler when the whole structure is retrospective. This has an obvious relevance to George Eliot's practice of setting most of her novels back in time. But the more critical question is about the kind of sharing of ordinary life that is actually achieved. This bears directly on a problem which seems to me to be central in the subsequent development of the English novel: the real relations, in feeling and in form, between *educated* and *customary* life and thought.

[...]

Williams makes the point here that the 'farmers and craftsmen' in *Adam Bede* and *The Mill on the Floss* are there more as a collective 'landscape' than as the 'separated individuals' the novels increasingly focus on.

[...]

This is a real history: indeed one of the clearest examples of literature enacting a history which is not otherwise, in any important way, articulated or recorded. It is very complicated once we take its full weight. There is the intense feeling of the isolated individual: isolated in the first instance by the structure of this feeling, because while the personal life is experienced the social life is mainly observed. Yet the more serious the observation, in a community that is taken as given – as there by the facts of birth and place – the more insistent the emphasis, the emphasis of want. And the way in which this very conflict between isolation and sympathy emerges is a matter of ideas: of consciousness, social consciousness, as a personal need –

she wanted some explanation of this hard real life.

We have already observed two positions: the intensity of isolated need and desire; the inherited sympathy of general observation. We must now add a third: the analytic consciousness, that ordinary product of individual and social development, which comes in to enlighten and to qualify but above all to mediate the isolated desire and the general observation. George Eliot's genius is that she is fully exposed – that she exposes herself – over this whole range. She has precedents for each faculty in the previous development of the novel, but for the combination of these faculties – the necessary combination for the next and difficult creative stage – she has no precedents. She has to create a new form on her own, under the pressures of what are not merely different but conflicting actions and methods. In the very texture of her writing, in the basic construction of her novels, she has to resolve a conflict of grammars: a conflict of 'I' and 'we' and 'they', and then of the impersonal constructions that in a way inevitably come to substitute for each.

That is the necessary contrast with Dickens: the contrast that has to be at the centre of any serious analysis of nineteenth-century English writing. The strength of Dickens's position is that he could base himself on an existing social formation: on an urban popular culture which in its amalgam of strengths and weaknesses had an available, a directly communicating, grammar. But George Eliot's social formation was at best only emerging: a guarantee of connection to our own world in which each of its separate processes has gone further and deeper, but in her own world conflicting, pulling different ways, setting conscious problems in each story, almost each sentence, she must write. She extends the community of the novel, as we have already seen. She develops the idiom of individual moral analysis into a world in which morality is both individual and social: the quality of a way of life in the qualities of persons. She faces the new problems of intense vision within, uneasily within, a hard real life.

But whereas the idiom of the novelist in Jane Austen was quite closely connected with the idiom of the characters, in George Eliot a disconnection is the most evident fact, and the novelist herself is very acutely aware of this. Or compare the idiom of Charlotte Brontë, sustaining intense feeling but cutting its connections with an intrusive or controlling consciousness; driving the single feeling through, but at the expense of any extended, any placing observation. George Eliot, by contrast, forces the feeling and the consciousness together, but of course uneasily. There is then a new kind of break in the texture of the novel: between the narrative idiom of the novelist and the recorded language of her characters; between the analytic idiom and the overwhelming emphasis of emotion.

Most novelists develop, but George Eliot, I would say, had almost to create a new form, each time, if she was to go on with this whole and uneasy experience. If in looking at this process we see, as we must, certain radical failures, we have to refer them in the end to this underlying and transforming growth and extension: a creative and experimental process which took all her great powers.

This is the right way, I think, to see the relation in her work between the consciousness of the writer and the knowable community: that relation which I see as the key to this history.

[...]

Williams quotes a paragraph from *The Mill on the Floss* beginning: 'In writing the history of unfashionable families'; notes Eliot's 'own brand of irony' in it; and quotes two other examples from *Adam Bede*.

[...]

In passages like these and in the novels from which they are taken, George Eliot has extended the real social range of the novel – its knowable community – and yet is more self-conscious than any of her predecessors; more uneasily placating and appealing to what seems a dominant image of a particular kind of reader. The knowable community is this common life, which she is pleased to record with a necessary emphasis. But the known community, creatively known, is something else again – an uneasy contract, in language, with another interest and another sensibility.

What is true of language is true of action. George Eliot extends the plots of her novels to include the farmers and the craftsmen, and also the disinherited. But just as she finds it difficult to individuate working people – falling back on a choral mode, a generalizing description, or an endowment with her own awkwardly translated consciousness – so she finds it difficult to conceive whole actions which spring from the substance of these lives, and which can be worked through in direct and controlling relation to who and what they are. *Adam Bede* is the nearest to this, but it is overridden, finally, by an external interest. Hetty is a subject till that last moment on the road, before she abandons her baby. From that point on she is an object: of confession and conversion, of *attitudes* towards suffering. This is the essential difference from Hardy's *Tess of the D'Urbervilles* which has the strength to keep to the subject to the end. Adam Bede and Dinah Morris – as one might say the dignity of self-respecting labour and religious enthusiasm – are more important in the end. Even the changed repentant Arthur is more important than the girl whom the novelist abandons, in a moral action more decisive than Hetty's own confused and desperate leaving of her child.

Yet still the history is active: the finding of continuity in the stress of learned feelings. *The Mill on the Floss* is the crisis of this determining history. It is an action from within the emphasis of want: in the guarded unattractive rituals of survival of the small farmers, the Dodsons; in the rash independence of Tulliver, broken by the complications of law and economic pressure that he does not understand. But in neither of those ways can any fullness of life be achieved, and there is no way through where the novelist's feelings really go; only the weak unwilled temporary escape of the trip on the river: the fantasy of comfort. What is then made to happen, because it is all that can happen, is a return to childhood and the river; a return, releasing feeling, to a transcending death. From the common history, which had been primary, the curve of feeling moves to a renunciation, an isolation; to the exposed and separated individual in whom the only action of value is located. And then what can be in these early novels an active desperate isolation becomes in her later work a sad though still intense resignation.

In the later novels, for all their evidence of growing maturity and control, the actions become more external to that common world in which the emphasis of want was decisive. As if overcome by the dead weight of the interests of a separated and propertied class – the supposed class of her readers, the educated class to which she now directly relates – the plots of the later works are in a different world. *Felix Holt*, a portrait of radicalism, is made to turn on of all things the inheritance of an estate. This is a surrender to that typical interest which preoccupied the nineteenth-century middle-class imagination. Of course Esther rejects the inheritance in the end. That is part of the real history. George Eliot's moral emphasis is too genuinely of an improving kind, of a self-making and self-made life, to permit Esther to accept the inheritance and find the fashionable way out. The corruption of that inheriting world, in which the price of security is intrigue and self-betrayal, is powerfully shown in Mrs Transome and in Jermyn. But the emphasis of want is now specialized to Felix Holt: to the exposed, separated, potentially mobile individual. It is part of a crucial history in the development of the novel, in which the knowable community – the extended and emphatic world of an actual rural and then industrial England – comes to be known primarily as a problem of relationship: of how the separated individual, with a divided consciousness of belonging and not belonging, makes his own moral history.

This is the source of the disturbance, the unease, the divided construction of the later George Eliot novels (the exception for reasons we shall see is *Middlemarch*).

[...]

There follows an extended comparison with her contemporary, Anthony Trollope, and his easy unprobing narration of the 'social mechanics' of the 'interaction of classes and interests'.

[...]

George Eliot, by contrast, questioning in a profoundly moral way the real and assumed relations between property and human quality, accepts the emphasis of inheritance as the central action and then has to make it external, contradictory and finally irrelevant, as her real interest transfers to the separated exposed individual, who becomes sadly resigned, or must go away. What happens to the Transomes' land, in *Felix Holt*, or to Grandcourt's, in *Daniel Deronda*, is no longer decisive; yet around the complications of that kind of interest a substantial part of each novel has been built. In this sense George Eliot's novels are transitional between that form which could end in a series of settlements, in which the social and economic solutions and the personal achievements were in a single dimension, and that new form which extending and complicating and then finally collapsing this dimension ends with a single person going away on his own, having achieved his moral growth by distancing or by extrication. It is a divided consciousness of belonging and not belonging. The social solutions – the common solutions – are still taken seriously up to the last point of personal crisis, and then what is achieved as a personal moral development has to express itself as some kind of physical or spiritual renewal; an emigration, at once resigned and hopeful, from what had originally been offered as a decisive social world.

It is worth considering this pattern in relation to *Middlemarch* which I have already suggested is in important ways an exception in her mature work. George Eliot became so conscious of history as a social and as a moral process that the problem of most of her work after *Mill on the Floss* is the discovery of an action which is capable of expressing it in its real connections. In the early novels the essential connections are *given*: one wants to say 'in retrospect' but that isn't at all how it feels. It isn't *looking* back, it's more like taking a whole experience straight out of the past, an experience already complete in itself, on which it is true the author makes marginal comments, but then the point is that the margin – the later consciousness – is visible and external.

[...]

Williams sees a shift in Eliot's fiction from a simpler vision of a value-laden past to one of historical *process* in which value has to be created: to one of 'radical disconnection' and 'intractable difficulty' – not 'network' but 'web'.

[...]

I drew attention, in *Culture and Society*, to George Eliot's use of these metaphors – 'network' and 'web', 'a tangled business' – to describe actual social relations. But I think we have to go on to distinguish the different bearings of this complicated image. The network, we might say, connects; the web, the tangle, disturbs and obscures. To discover a network, to feel human connection in what is essentially a knowable community, is to assert (I mean assert creatively, produce as an experience) a particular social value: a necessary interdependence. But to discover a web or a tangle is to see human relationships as not only involving but compromising, limiting, mutually frustrating. And this is of course a radically different consciousness: what is still called a modern consciousness; in fact the first phase of a post-liberal world: a period between cultures, in which the old confidence of individual liberation has gone and the new commitment to social liberation has not yet been made. George Eliot moves more powerfully than any of our novelists in that profoundly difficult transitional world. The ideas of *Felix Holt* and of *Daniel Deronda* are positive moves to surpass it; but the radicalism of the first ends by confirming the sense of a dead-lock; and the faith of the second is an effective emigration – not the functional emigration of earlier nineteenth-century novels, as in Elizabeth Gaskell or Kingsley, the guiding of loved characters to a simpler and happier land, but a spiritual emigration, a deeply felt, deeply desired transcendence.

Middlemarch stands between these attempts but its process is different. There is no overt dislocation, no pull inside the novel towards separable worlds across which accidental connections are made by the mechanics of plot. What is found in *Middlemarch* is a knowable community, but knowable in a new sense. Socially it is in some ways contracted. The country labourers talking of the railway are a brief chorus: 'this is the big folks's world'. The town craftsmen are also a chorus, characteristically heard in the pubs: 'Mr Gabbe the glazier' and other representative happy families, talking sharply but instrumentally about their social superiors, the main characters of the novel.

But then within this real circle Middlemarch is a remarkably integrated society. It is a provincial town with its necklace villages, or looked at the other way, the main way of the novel, it is a system of parishes with this new and growing organism somewhat ambiguously at its centre; 'municipal town and rural parish gradually made fresh threads of connexion', in a phase just preceding the full effect of industrialism. Middlemarch, like Coventry in the 1820s and 1830s, is a town of small textile manufacturers: braid-making, ribbon-making and dyeing; still employing some handloom weavers and outworkers; with a traditional county town and a new industrial town, Brassing, not far away. Vincy the manufacturer and Bulstrode the banker are there in the town, but the social consciousness begins and ends in the landed society into which these new forces are growing. It is Brooke, with his abstract ideas of reform, who brings the main characters together, not without some protest from Mrs Cadwallader; and the professional men – doctors and clergymen – moving about 'disregarding the Middlemarch discrimination of ranks' are also the 'threads of connexion'. George Eliot refers to the real processes within this sort of society – the steady rise and fall of families – as 'those less marked vicissitudes which are constantly shifting the boundaries of social intercourse and begetting new consciousness of interdependence'. This is a changing but still knowable community, except that something else is happening: what she calls 'the double change of self and beholder'. That I believe is what is really new in the novel, because it affects, profoundly, the novelist's essential method.

Middlemarch in every way is less given than taken: taken, consciously, in 'the double change of self and beholder'. An older mode of awareness is still present in the Garths; I mean in the way George Eliot sees the Garths, as we see our own families – present, whole, simply there, before anything needs to be said about them. Mary Garth is not formally described, given analysing discriminating features, until some time after she has been effectively present. It is as we might stare and reflect, in some moment of adverted attention, at someone we already effectively know, simply know and are with. But the dominant consciousness is quite different: a signifying consciousness: not of the known or the knowable but of the to-be-known; in a sense, a decisive sense, the *objects* of consciousness. Dorothea has elements of Maggie Tulliver, but she is now at arm's length being looked at. Virtually all the other characters and indeed the society are looked at, examined, in this public way: 'the double change in self and beholder'.

It is a consciousness, a fictional method, that has been widely recommended. It is referred back to the cool 'impersonality' of Jane Austen; forward to the wrought observation of Henry James and thence to what is often called, in a sweeping indeed overbearing dimension, maturity. The difference from Jane Austen, the deciding difference, is that not only the characters but the way of life they compose come under this conscious examination. The difference from many later examples is also this: for it is a method that when abstracted is a cold placing, a critic's fiction. Indeed, more than that, it is a social mode in which the observer, the signifier, is not himself at stake but is refined into a fictional process, indeed into a fiction. At its lower levels, which have been very popular, it is the mode of an anxious society – an anxious class preoccupied with placing, grading, defining: the sharp enclosing phrases about others as they leave the room, and a kind of willing forgetfulness that it will happen to the phrasers as they also leave. It's the staple of a familiar – sometimes witty, sometimes malicious – minor fiction, and of a whole world of small talk. As you'll have gathered, I don't really find it particularly mature, though when it bears down on you in a whole place – in a university for example – it has an apparent poise that takes some time to live through: a mode in which we are all signifiers, all critics and judges, and can somehow afford to be because life – given life, creating life – goes on where it is supposed to, elsewhere.

I've pushed it that far, from its much more substantial, more affirmed existence in *Middlemarch*, as a way of registering a profound unease – an unease that of course goes along with respect – about the coldness, the picking, of those parts of the novel. I think it was inevitable. It is a dislocation, not of an overt kind but very deep and substantial: the dislocation in consciousness, 'the double change in self and beholder'. *Middlemarch* as a whole is a superb presentation, a superb analysis: that *is* its consciousness. As a way of seeing, it is so powerfully composed that it creates its own conditions, enacts and re-enacts its own kind of achievement. It has been so praised so often in just that sense that I don't need to add any other tributary adjectives. I want only to say that as a kind of consciousness it is really a portent: reminding us of that other meaning of 'known' and 'knowable', where the knower has become a separated process in himself: a profoundly serious but also profoundly accepted alienation.

'Anyone watching keenly the stealthy convergence of human lots': that phrase from *Middlemarch* defines the method exactly and defines the relationships, the substantial relationships, that are now knowable and known. It is the web in a new sense; the web we are watching from outside. The profound satisfaction this seems actually to give isn't anything I can argue against; it is an earlier choice of one life or another. All I'd add for emphasis (though it may emphasize only the shock, the inevitable shock of the breach of that convention) is that George Eliot can be seen as trying to pull free, trying to reach beyond that connecting, interlocking, threaded consciousness. I believe she attempts this in Ladislaw, and it's very significant that we've had a parade of English critics disapproving of Ladislaw in very uniform ways. That he's unconvincing: that first ploy that is tried, but what is it, in a character, that 'convinces'?; it depends on general experience quite as much as on what is actually done with the fiction. Really, I suppose, that he's not 'one of us'; and that, listening, I'd grant. Indeed I think that's the point, and I'd add that some of these critics speaking with active distaste of Ladislaw sound remarkably like Mrs Cadwallader.

But it's more than old snobbery. It's what Ladislaw does. Lydgate fails; Casaubon fails; Brooke is inadequate; Chettam is limited; Rosamond is trivial; Bulstrode is exposed. The Garths are stable; they last from an older world. And that pattern is clear, very clearly acceptable. In that older world there was stability and value; in the newer world, only complication, the web, a tangled business. The record is then of failure, frustration, resignation. And human fineness, human insight, is also that; sadly, wisely that: a stealthy convergence of human lots that has this valuable by-product, a wise settling insight.

And what can then be made of Ladislaw and of Dorothea marrying him? He's an offence, an obvious offence against that kind of settlement. Perhaps you've noticed how often critics refer to his hair; the tone is exactly one we've heard often recently about young men in the sixties; and in fact there's a connection. For Ladislaw is a free man in the way the others are not; a free mind with free emotions; a man who is wholly responsive. He isn't tied by property, which he can reject in a principled way. He's not of 'good birth' and doesn't try to depend on it. He has nothing on his side but his own feelings, his own actions, yet he understands art and learning better than Casaubon and reforms much better than Brooke. He makes friends with everyone he meets, including the 'unimportant' people; and he suffers from the will of both kinds of property, the inherited and the commercial. But since unlike Lydgate he can accept poverty, he is not frustrated, is not corrupted, does not become resigned. Coming from 'nowhere', belonging 'nowhere', he is able to move, to relate and so to grow in ways that the others are not. And it is to this, after all, that Dorothea responds.

'Unconvincing'. It is convenient, surely, to conclude that. For this is George Eliot thinking beyond, feeling beyond, the restrictions and the limitations she has so finely recorded; thinking into mobility not as dislocating but as liberating; with some anxiety, certainly – some registered qualified anxiety – but following a thread to the future, as she tried in *Daniel Deronda*; a single thread that has come loose from the web, but that she insists is there, running beyond *Middlemarch* as she herself ran beyond it: a responsiveness and a courage to live in new ways, under the weight, the defining weight, of a limited and frustrating world.

The main point, in the end, is still the defining consciousness: the method that predominates, the method that was learned. She is a great novelist in precisely that mode: a mode she achieved, literally made, out of profound disturbance and tension. And if the tension is there to the end – a different thread to the future in that superbly observed, superbly managed and limiting, defining world—that too is as it should be. She is giving her last strength, her deep warmth, to a hope, a possibility beyond what she had to record in a hardening clearly seen world.

4.3   TERRY EAGLETON: FROM *CRITICISM AND IDEOLOGY* (1976)

Terry Eagleton is currently Warton Professor of English at Oxford University; and it is appropriate that he should appear in the same exercise as Leavis and Williams, since he is the other figure within British literary theory and criticism – certainly since the war – of similar formative impact. He has been equally productive, his books since *Criticism and Ideology* now including: *Walter Benjamin or Towards a Revolutionary Criticism* (1981); *The Rape of Clarissa* (1982); *Literary Theory: An Introduction* (1983); *The Function of Criticism* (1984); *Against the Grain: Essays 1975–85* (1986; including his important essay responding to the challenge postmodernism offers Marxism, 'Capitalism, Modernism and Postmodernism', 1985); *The Ideology of the Aesthetic* (1990); *Ideology: An Introduction* (1993); and *Heathcliff and the Great Hunger* (1995; for an extract from this, and discussion of it, see Ch. 5 on Oscar Wilde and Headnote, pp. 232–41). He has also written a novel, *Saints and Sinners* (1987), radio and stage drama (e.g. *Saint Oscar*), and the screenplay for Derek Jarman's film, *Wittgenstein*.

A feature of Eagleton's work has been its ability to change and develop in response to fresh intellectual and political challenges. From the Althusserian orientation of the present piece, he moved to a more politically revolutionary conception of cultural criticism (albeit taking in some of the subversive strategies of deconstruction along the way); he also registers the influence of Derrida and Lacan in his socialist and feminist re-reading of Richardson's *Clarissa*; more recently, a reorientation to Frankfurt, rather than Paris, has become perceptible; as has – in fiction, drama and the recent *Heathcliff* book – a commitment to Irish cultural politics. In the case of the present extract, however, Althusser and Macherey are the important influences (Eagleton's slightly earlier *Myths of Power*, 1975, belongs to the same phase; see Headnote to Ch. 3 on *Jane Eyre*, p. 108). This is a short piece from a long chapter, 'Ideology and Literary Form', which offers a critical re-reading of 'great tradition'/'culture and society' British writers from Matthew Arnold to D. H. Lawrence. Eagleton identifies the ideological location of each of the writers within an increasingly 'corporatist' nineteenth- and early twentieth-century capitalism, and shows how this shapes the textual contradictions in their work. Conversely, these textual disturbances can be used to reveal the ideological matrices which created them. What, then, does *Middlemarch* show us, in Eagleton's view? In what respects may this piece be seen as an extension, or indeed supersession, of Williams' reading; or how far may both be seen to be locked into a similar – if differently inflected – critical space (note how Eagleton, too, comments on Ladislaw and his 'realisation') compared, say, to Hillis Miller's essay? How does the concept of 'ideology' in Eagleton's discussion help to resolve the problematics of studying literature and/in/as history? For Eagleton, this is not merely *another* reading of *Middlemarch*, but one which goes far beyond textual criticism. Consider what larger project this kind of re-reading is geared to: how might it impact on 'Literary Studies', the status of 'Literature', and the notion of 'literary value', for example? Finally, how would you compare Eagleton's approach here to his reading of Oscar Wilde (Ch. 5, pp. 232–41)?

The following excerpts are taken from pp. 110–25, *passim* (Verso edition, 1978) of the section, 'George Eliot', in Ch. 4.

Criticism and Ideology

A short passage on mid-Victorian prosperity, corporatism and incorporation of the working class prefaces the section on Eliot.

[. . .]

The ideological matrix of George Eliot's fiction is set by the increasingly corporate character of Victorian capitalism and its political apparatus. Eliot's work attempts to resolve a structural conflict between two forms of mid-Victorian ideology: between a progressively muted Romantic individualism, concerned with the untrammelled evolution of the 'free spirit', and certain 'higher', corporate ideological modes. These higher modes (essentially, Feuerbachian humanism and scientific rationalism) seek to identify the immutable social laws to which Romantic individualism, if it is to avoid both ethical anarchy and social disruption, must conform. In principle, it is possible for Romantic individualism to do so without betraying its own values. For if it is true on the one hand that scientific rationalism, in judiciously curbing the disruptive tendencies of Benthamite egoism, also obstructs Romantic self-expression, it is also true that it reveals certain historically progressive laws with which the developing individual may imaginatively unite. Moreover, the Religion of Humanity imbues scientific law with Romantic humanist spirit, discovering that law inscribed in the very passions and pieties of men. Unlike the obsessively abstract, systemic symbology of Comtism, it can offer itself as a totalising doctrine without detriment to the 'personal' – to a lived relation with immediate experience. The Religion of Humanity protects Romantic values against an aggressive rationalism; but by rooting those values in the human collective, it defends them equally against an unbridled individualism. By virtue of this ideological conjuncture, the Romantic individualist may submit to the social totality without sacrifice to personal self-fulfilment.

In principle, that is; in practice, a potentially tragic collision between 'corporate' and 'individualist' ideologies is consistently defused and repressed by the forms of Eliot's fiction.

[...]

A passage follows on how the framing forms (e.g. 'pastoral') of Eliot's earlier fictions (e.g. *The Mill on the Floss*) ideologically resolve the historical contradictions at their heart.

[...]

Again, it is not difficult to see how in *Middlemarch* the realist form itself determines a certain 'ideology of the text'. In the earlier 'pastoral' novels, Eliot's realism is partly signified by her apologetic engagement with socially obscure destinies; yet that engagement does not necessarily extend to a fully 'internal' mode of characterisation. Once it does so, however, the novel-form is instantly decentred: since every destiny is significant, each is consequently relativised. Realism, as Eliot conceives of it, involves the tactful unravelling of interlaced processes, the equable distribution of authorial sympathies, the holding of competing values in precarious equipoise. The 'general' ideological correlative of this textual ideology is, naturally, liberal reformism; no other ideological effect could conceivably be produced by such an assemblage of fictional devices.

[...]

A cut of four pages here extends similar kinds of analysis to *Adam Bede, The Mill on the Floss*, and *Felix Holt*.

[...]

Liberal-minded working men like Felix Holt seem to propose one answer to that problem, blending 'culture' with moral discipline; yet after *Felix Holt* Eliot did not repeat the doomed experiment of centring such 'pastoral' figures within urban landscapes. The Bede–Holt character in *Middlemarch* is Caleb Garth, stock type of rural organicism, but decidedly muted and marginal within the novel's structure. As such figures decline in ideological impact, value shifts to an alternative oppositional standpoint: in the case of *Middlemarch*, to the cosmopolitan artist Will Ladislaw. If the traditionalist craftsman forms a pocket of spiritual resistance within bourgeois society, the cosmopolitan artist inhabits such a dissentient space outside it. He is, however, no complete compensation for the outmoded organicist type: if Ladislaw has the edge over Garth in liberal culture it is because he lacks his social rootedness. It is only with Daniel Deronda, who combines synoptic vision with settled allegiance, that this ideological dilemma can be finally dissolved.

This is not to say, however, that Garth's values do not finally triumph in *Middlemarch*. They do, but in the 'higher' mode of a wide-eyed liberal disillusionment which, with the collapse of more ambitious commitments, is compelled to find solace in the humble reformist tasks nearest to hand. The irony of *Middlemarch* is that it is a triumph of aesthetic totalisation deeply suspicious of ideological totalities. Each of the novel's four central characters represents such an historically typical totalisation: Casaubon idealism, Lydgate scientific rationalism, Bulstrode Evangelical Christianity, Dorothea Brooke Romantic self-achievement through a unifying principle of action. Each of these totalities crumbles, ensnared in the quotidian; and that ensnarement can be read in two ways. It is in part a salutary empiricist cheek to the tyranny of theoreticism; but it also signifies the bleak victory of an entrenched provincial consciousness over rationalist or Romantic drives to transcend it. That stalemate, the novel's title suggests, springs from a transitional phase of rural society at the time of the first Reform Bill; yet there is no doubt that the novel's judiciously muted disillusion, its 'end-of-ideologies' ambience, belongs to its post-second Reform Bill present. The problem which *Middlemarch* objectively poses, and fails to resolve, is how ideology is to be conceptually elaborate yet emotionally affective – how it is to nurture 'irrational' personal pieties while cohering them into a structure which surpasses mere empiricism and Romantic spontaneity. What is needed, according to Ladislaw, is 'a soul in which knowledge passes instantaneously into feeling, and feeling flashes back as a new organ of knowledge' – a question to which we have seen Matthew Arnold address himself. Confronted with the aggressive modes of working-class consciousness caricatured in *Felix Holt*, the cautious empiricism of the bourgeois liberal tradition must be reaffirmed; yet that empiricism is in itself an ideologically inadequate response to the historical moment of post-Reform Bill England, with its demand for a more intensively incorporating ideology.

This dilemma is figured in *Middlemarch* in one of its key images: that of the *web* as image of the social formation. The web is a *derivative* organic image, a mid-point between the animal imagery of *Adam Bede* and some more developed theoretical concept of *structure*. The complexity of the web, its subtle interlacing of relatively autonomous strands, its predatory overtones, the possibilities of local complication it permits, accommodate forms of conflict excluded by the more thoroughgoing organicist imagery of *Adam Bede*. But at the same time the web's symmetry, its 'spatial' de-historicising of the social process, its exclusion of levels of contradiction, preserve the essential unity of the organic mode. The web's complex fragility impels a prudent political conservatism: the more delicately interlaced its strands, the more the disruptive consequences of action can multiply, and so the more circumspect one must be in launching ambitiously totalising projects. Yet conversely, if action at any point in the web will vibrate through its filaments to affect the whole formation, a semi-mystical relationship to the totality is nevertheless preserved. Here, as in the novel's closing trope of the river, which in diffusing its force to tributaries intensifies its total impact, natural imagery is exploited to signify how a fulfilling relation to the social totality can be achieved, not by ideological abstraction, but by pragmatic, apparently peripheral work. And if *Middlemarch*'s natural metaphors perform this function, so does its aesthetic imagery. As Ladislaw remarks to Dorothea: 'It is no use to try and take care of all the world; that is being taken care of when you feel delight – in art or in anything else.' The problem of totality within the novel is effectively displaced to the question of aesthetic form itself, which gives structure to its materials without violating their empirical richness. The novel, in other words, formally answers the problem it thematically poses. Only the novelist can be the centred subject of her own decentred fiction, the privileged consciousness which at once supervenes on the whole as its source, and enters into empathetic relation with each part.

Middlemarch, one might say, is an historical novel in form with little substantive historical content. The Reform Bill, the railways, cholera, machine-breaking: these 'real' historical forces do no more than impinge on the novel's margins. The mediation between the text and the 'real' history to which it alludes is notably dense; and the effect of this is to transplant the novel from the 'historical' to the 'ethical'. *Middlemarch* works in terms of egoism and sympathy, 'head' and 'heart', self-fulfilment and self-surrender; and this predominance of the ethical at once points to an historical impasse and provides the means of ideologically overcoming it. History in the novel is officially in a state of transition; yet to read the text is to conclude that 'suspension' is the more appropriate term. What is officially offered as an ambivalent, intermediate era leading eventually to the 'growing good of the world' is in fact more of an historical vacuum; the benighted, traditionalist-minded Middlemarch seems little more responsive to historical development than does the Hayslope of *Adam Bede*. There is, then, a discrepancy between what the novel claims and what it shows: in aesthetically 'producing' the melioristic ideology intimated by its title, it betrays a considerably less sanguine view of historical progress. It reveals, in fact, an image of the early eighteen-thirties which belongs to the jaundiced viewpoint of where they actually led to – the early eighteen-seventies, where Will Ladislaw's pioneering reformist zeal 'has been much checked'. *Middlemarch* projects back onto the past its sense of contemporary stalemate; and since the upshot of this is a radical distrust of 'real' history, that history is effectively displaced into ethical, and so 'timeless', terms. Yet such displacement thereby provides Eliot with an ideological solution: for what cannot be resolved in 'historical' terms can be accommodated by a moralising of the issues at stake. This, indeed, is a mystification inherent in the very forms of realist fiction, which by casting objective social relations into interpersonal terms, constantly hold open the possibility of reducing the one to the other.[1] In *Middlemarch*, such an ethical reduction of history is achieved in the 'solution' of self-sacrifice, to which, in their various ways, Dorothea, Lydgate and (in a sense) Bulstrode struggle through. The suffering abnegation of the ego offers itself as the answer to the riddle of history.

Yet such a solution is ideologically insufficient, as Will Ladislaw's presence in the novel would suggest. For Ladislaw, while consenting to the course of social evolution, also retains an individualist verve which challenges such mature resignation. As a politically reforming artist, he suggests that empirical labour and Romantic self-afffirmation need not be incompatible; in Mr Brooke's words, he is 'a sort of Burke with a leaven of Shelley'. The novel's difficulty in 'realising' him springs from its incapacity to see how this desirable ideological conjuncture, yoking prudent gradualism to visionary Romanticism, can be achieved in the historical conditions it describes. At this point, therefore, a different kind of history becomes necessary. What cannot be effectively achieved in Ladislaw can be re-attempted on more propitious terms in that later amalgam of Romantic prophet and reformist politician, Daniel Deronda.

What is demanded, in fact, is a 'totalising' vision which binds the individual to the laws of a social formation, preserves the 'personal' pieties violated by such visions in *Romola* and *Middlemarch*, and romantically liberates the self.

[...]

Eagleton suggests that *Daniel Deronda* offers a 'magical' solution the the impasse – outside a 'real' historical England, but only, in effect, a 'fictional construct' bounded by its own aesthetic discourse.

[...]

Eliot's fiction, then, represents an attempt to integrate liberal ideology, in both its Romantic and empiricist forms, with certain pre-industrial, idealist or positivist organic models. It is an enterprise determined in the last instance by the increasingly corporate character of nineteenth-century capitalism during the period of her literary production. Yet this is not to argue for a simple homology between literary and historical systems, or for a reductively diachronic reading of Eliot's *oeuvre*. It is not a question of Eliot's work evolving from pre-industrial 'pastoral' to fully-fledged realism in response to some linear development of bourgeois ideology. On the contrary, it is a question of grasping at once the ideological synchronies and formal discontinuities of her texts – of theorising the set of disjunctures whereby distinct literary discourses produce a corporatist ideology which is present from the outset. The *differences* of Eliot's fiction are the effect of a continual repermutation of the literary forms into which it is inserted – a repermutation which in each of her texts 'privileges' a particular, dominant discourse which 'places' and deforms the others. Within this synchronic practice a significant development can be discerned: one from an essentially *metaphorical* closure of ideological conflict (social history as analogous to natural evolution) towards an essentially *metonymic* resolution of such issues ('personal' values, visions and relations as the solution to social ills).[2] The naturalising, moralising and mythifying devices of the novels effect such closures, but in the act of doing so lay bare the imprint of the ideological struggles which beset the texts. It is in the irregular transmutation of one fictional code into another, the series of formal displacements whereby turbulent issues are marginalised yet remain querulously present, that Eliot's organic closures betray their *constructing* functions. What threatens to subvert them is not a suppressed 'outside', but the absences and dislocations they internally produce.

The section ends with a suggestion that in Eliot's last work a much more reactionary voice can be heard.

Notes (renumbered)
1. A point made by Francis Mulhern in 'Ideology and Literary Form – a comment', *New Left Review* 91, May/June 1975.
2. For this general distinction in fiction, see Francis Mulhern, *art. cit.*

4.4 J. HILLIS MILLER: FROM 'OPTIC AND SEMIOTIC IN *MIDDLEMARCH*' (1975)

Hillis Miller is Professor of English and Comparative Literature at the University of California, Irvine. During the 1960s a proponent of 'phenomenological' criticism who produced a number of significant books on Victorian writing (including studies of Dickens and Hardy), Miller became an important figure in American deconstruction in the 1970s and beyond (strongly registering the influence of Derrida at Yale, where Miller also worked). His later books include: *Fiction and Repetition* (1982); *The Linguistic Moment* (1985); *The Ethics of Reading* (1987); *Versions of Pygmalion*; *Victorian Subjects*; and *Tropes, Parables and Performatives* (all 1990). Miller has written a number of times on George Eliot. His first deconstructive essay about her fiction was 'Narrative and History' (*English Literary History*, 41, 1974). Then follow the present essay; a deconstructive reading of *The Mill on the Floss*, 'The Two Rhetorics: George Eliot's Bestiary', in G. D. Atkins and B. Johnson, eds, *Writing and Reading Differently: Deconstruction and the Teaching and Composition of Literature* (Kansas University Press, 1985); and, on *Adam Bede*, 'Reading Writing: Eliot', in *The Ethics of Reading* (reprinted in Newton, ed., *op. cit.*).

Miller's line on Eliot is that, despite the apparently secure totalizing vision and textuality of the 'classic realist text', the novels continually deconstruct themselves by revealing their contradictions and disjunctions. In true deconstructive manner, Miller probes what Barbara Johnson has called 'the warring forces of signification within the text itself'. In this respect, Eliot's novels would refute the position MacCabe takes up (see following extract) of seeing them as self-confidently coherent reproductions of 'reality'. What is also at issue in Miller's work, however, is whether Eliot is knowingly in control of her fiction's self-deconstructing dimension. At times, in the earlier piece on *Middlemarch*, he finds evidence to suggest that she is. What is his position by the end of the present essay? Has his analysis of structuring metaphors shown them to be, in the end, an incoherent and destructive discourse in the novel's (futile) attempt to establish a totalizing vision of the world it is constructing? Or does Miller make Eliot complicit in a recognition of the incoherence and disunity of all texts? (The first half of the essay is a painstaking account of the 'families' of 'all-encompassing metaphors' on which *Middlemarch* is structured: web, stream and 'fragment as whole'.) Try to outline the stages in Miller's argument in the present extract. How does he use the text of *Middlemarch* in the process? Identify passages and tactics in Miller's approach which you would consider quintessentially 'deconstructive'. Does he offer his essay as a *criticism* or an *elucidation* of the novel; if not, what does it offer us? What might be its informing (cultural) politics? Deconstruction generally, and Miller's work on Eliot more specifically, has itself come in for criticism – both literary and political. Consider the validity of the following claims: that such work is ahistorical and apolitical, an 'irresponsible' expression of postmodern indeterminacy; that it precludes any possibility of language referring to the world; that the notions of the total uncertainty and incoherence of a text may be appropriate to postmodern writing, but merely impose an inappropriate late-twentieth-century mindset on nineteenth-century fiction; that it delights in textual contradiction and disunity only in and for itself (see *A Reader's Guide* 3/e, p. 157; Peck, ed., *op. cit.*, pp. 81–2; also Frank Lentricchia, *After the New Criticism*, Methuen, 1980, for a useful critique of deconstruction).

The following extract is the second half of the essay; first published in Jerome H. Buckley, ed., *The Worlds of Victorian Fiction*, Harvard University Press, 1975, pp. 125–45.

Optic and Semiotic in *Middlemarch*

See Headnote for a brief synopsis of the first half of the essay.

[...]

All this family of intertwined metaphors and motifs[1] – the web, the current, the minutely subdivided entity – make up a single comprehensive model or picture of Middlemarch society as being a complex moving medium, tightly interwoven into a single fabric, always in process, endlessly subdividable. This medium can be seen and studied objectively, as if there could be an ideal observer who does not change what he observes and who sees the moving web as it were from all perspectives at once, from close up and far away, with both gross and fine lenses, in a continual systole and diastole of inquiry. The storyteller in *Middlemarch* is in short the ideal observer of Victorian fiction, the 'omniscient' narrator. His aim is to do full representative justice to the complexity of the condition of man in his social medium. There are many admirable passages in *Middlemarch* giving examples of what the narrator sees, each a new application of the model I have been describing. None is perhaps so comprehensive an exploitation of the totalising implications of this family of metaphors as an admirable passage in chapter 11 describing 'old provincial society':

> Old provincial society had its share of this subtle movement: had not only its striking downfalls, its brilliant young professional dandies who ended by living up an entry with a drab and six children for their establishment, but also those less marked vicissitudes which are constantly shifting the boundaries of social intercourse, and begetting new consciousness of interdependence. Some slipped a little downward, some got higher footing: people denied aspirates, gained wealth, and fastidious gentlemen stood for boroughs; some were caught in political currents, some in ecclesiastical, and perhaps found themselves surprisingly grouped in consequence; while a few personages or families that stood with rocky firmness amid all this fluctuation, were slowly presenting new aspects in spite of solidity, and altering with the double change of self and beholder.
>
> Therefore speak I to them in parables: because they seeing see not; and hearing they hear not, neither do they understand.
>
> (Matthew 13:13)
>
> ... er hat das Auge nicht dafür, das Einmalige zu sehen; die Ähnlichseherei und Gleichmacherei ist das Merkmal schwacher Augen.[2]

'Double change of self and beholder'! I have said that my first family of metaphors in *Middlemarch* does not raise problems of perspective, or that in any case it presupposes the possibility of an ideal observer such as that assumed in much nineteenth-century science, in the days before operationalism, relativity, and the principle of indeterminacy. This is true, but in fact an optical or epistemological metaphor has already introduced itself surreptitiously into many of my examples. The narrator must concentrate 'all the light [he] can command' (ch. 15) on his particular web in order to see clearly how it is woven. Study of the web requires constant changes of the lens in the systole and diastole of inquiry. Any conceivable observer in Middlemarch will be changing himself along with all the other changes and so will change what he sees.

A pervasive figure for the human situation in *Middlemarch* is that of the seer who must try to identify clearly what is present before him. This metaphor contaminates the apparently clear-cut objectivist implications of the metaphor of the flowing web. As more and more examples of it accumulate, it struggles with a kind of imperialistic will to power over the whole to replace that objectivism with a fully developed subjectivism or perspectivisim. The 'omniscience' of the narrator, according to this alternative model for the human condition, can be obtained only because he is able to share the points of view of all the characters, thereby transcending the limited vision of any single person. 'In watching effects', as the narrator says, 'if only of an electric battery, it is often necessary to change our place and examine a particular mixture or group at some distance from the point where the movement we are interested in was set up' (ch. 40). The narrator can move in imagination from one vantage point to another, or from close up to far away. He can be, like the angel Uriel, 'watching the progress of planetary history from the Sun' (ch. 41), and at the same time share in that microscopic vision of invisible process, perceptible only to inward imaginative vision, so splendidly described in a passage about Lydgate's method as a scientist. It is a passage which also describes covertly the claims of Eliot's own fictional imagination. Lydgate, the narrator says, is endowed

> with the imagination that reveals subtle actions inaccessible by any sort of lens, but tracked in that outer darkness through long pathways of necessary sequence by the inward light which is the last refinement of Energy, capable of bathing even the ethereal atoms in its ideally illuminated space ... he was enamoured of that arduous invention which is the very eye of research, provisionally framing its object and correcting it to more and more exactness of relation; he wanted to pierce the obscurity of those minute processes which prepare human misery and joy...
>
> (ch. 16)

The metaphor of the complex moving web, the 'embroiled medium', is, one can see, further complicated, or even contradicted, by the metaphor of vision. Each of those nodes in the social web which is a separate human being is endowed with a power to see the whole. This power is defined throughout the novel as essentially distorting. Each man or woman has a 'centre of self, whence the lights and shadows must always fall with a certain difference' (ch. 31). The 'radiance' of Dorothea's 'transfigured girlhood', as the narrator says, 'fell on the first object that came within its level' (ch. 5). Her mistakes, as her sister Celia tells her, are errors in seeing, of which her literal myopia is a metonymy. 'I thought it right to tell you,' says Celia apropos of the fact that Sir James intends to propose to Dorothea, 'because you went on as you always do, never looking just where you are, and treading in the wrong place. You always see what nobody else sees; it is impossible to satisfy you; yet you never see what is quite plain' (ch. 4). Mr. Casaubon, however, is also 'the centre of his own world'. From that point of view he is 'liable to think that others were providentially made for him, and especially to consider them in the light of their fitness for the author of a "Key to all Mythologies"' (ch. 10). Of the inhabitants of Middlemarch generally it can in fact be said that each makes of what he sees something determined by his own idiosyncratic perspective, for 'Probabilities are as various as the faces to be seen at will on fretwork or paperhangings: every form is there, from Jupiter to Judy, if you only look with creative inclination' (ch. 32).

Seeing, then, is for Eliot not a neutral, objective, dispassionate, or passive act. It is the creative projection of light from an egotistic centre motivated by desire and need. This projected radiance orders the field of vision according to the presuppositions of the seer. The act of seeing is the spontaneous affirmation of a will to power over what is seen. This affirmation of order is based on the instinctive desire to believe that the world is providentially structured in a neat pattern of which one is oneself the centre, for 'we are all of us born in moral stupidity, taking the world as an udder to feed our supreme selves'. This interpretation of the act of seeing is most fully presented in the admirable and often discussed 'parable' of the 'pier-glass' at the beginning of chapter 27:

> An eminent philosopher among my friends, who can dignify even your ugly furniture by lifting it into the serene light of science, has shown me this pregnant little fact. Your pier-glass or extensive surface of polished steel made to be rubbed by a housemaid, will be minutely and multitudinously scratched in all directions; but place now against it a lighted candle as a centre of illumination, and lo! the scratches will seem to arrange themselves in a fine series of concentric circles round that little sun. It is demonstrable that the scratches are going everywhere impartially, and it is only your candle which produces the flattering illusion of a concentric arrangement, its light falling with an exclusive optical selection. These things are a parable. The scratches are events, and the candle is the egoism of any person now absent – of Miss Vincy, for example. Rosamond had a Providence of her own who had kindly made her more charming than other girls, and who seemed to have arranged Fred's illness and Mr. Wrench's mistake in order to bring her and Lydgate within effective proximity.[3]

This passage is perhaps more complicated than it at first appears. It begins with an example of what it describes, an example which implicitly takes note of the fact that Eliot's own 'parabolic' method, in this text, as in many other passages in *Middlemarch*, is a seeing of one thing in the 'light' of another. The word 'parable', like the word 'allegory', the word 'metaphor', or indeed all terms for figures of speech, is of course itself based on a figure. It means 'to set aside', from the Greek *para*, beside, and *ballein*, to throw. A parable is set or thrown at some distance from the meaning which controls it and to which it obliquely or parabolically refers, as a parobolic curve is controlled, across a space, by its parallelism to a line on the cone of which it is a section. The line and the cone may have only a virtual or imaginary existence, as in the case of a comet with a parabolic course. The parabola creates that line in the empty air, just as the parables of Jesus remedy a defect of vision, give sight to the blind, and make the invisible visible. In Eliot's parable of the pier glass the 'eminent philosopher' transfigures 'ugly furniture', a pier glass, by 'lifting it into the serene light of science', but also makes an obscure scientific principle visible. In the same way, the candle makes the random scratches on the pier glass appear to be concentric circles, and so Rosamond interprets what happens around her as being governed by her private providence, just as Eliot sees provincial society as like a woven web, or the ego of an individual person in the light of a comparison to a candle. The same projective, subjective, even egotistic act, seeing one thing as set or thrown, parabolically, beside another, is involved in all four cases.

At this point the reader may remember that the narrator, in a passage I earlier took as a 'key' expression[4] of Eliot's use of a model of objective scientific observation, says 'all the light I can command must be concentrated on this particular web'. With a slight change of formulation this could be seen as implying that the subjective source of light not only illuminates what is seen but also, as in the case of the candle held to the pier glass, determines the structure of what is seen. Middlemarch society perhaps appears to be a web only because a certain kind of subjective light is concentrated on it. The passage taken in isolation does not say this, but its near congruence with the passage about the pier glass, a slightly asymmetrical analogy based on the fact that the same metaphorical elements are present in each allows the contradictory meaning to seep into the passage about the web when the two texts are set side by side. Each is seen as a modulation of the other. The same key would not open both, though a 'master key' might.

In spite of the disquieting possibilities generated by resonances between two similar but not quite congruent passages, the narrator in various ways throughout *Middlemarch* is clearly claiming to be able to transcend the limitations of the self-centred ego by seeing things impersonally, objectively, scientifically: 'It is demonstrable that the scratches are going everywhere impartially.' This objective vision, such is the logic of Eliot's parable, shows that what is 'really there' has no order whatsoever, but is merely random scratches without pattern or meaning. The pier glass is 'minutely and multitudinously scratched in all directions'. The idea that reality is chaotic, without intrinsic order or form, and the corollary that any order it may appear to have is projected illicitly by some patterning ego, would seem to be contradicted by the series of totalising metaphors I have explored – web, flowing water, and so on – as well as by the generalising, rationalising, order-finding activity of the narrator throughout the book. It would seem hardly plausible, at this point at least, to say that reality for Eliot is a chaotic disorder. It might seem more likely that this is an irrelevant implication of the parable, an implication which has by accident, as it were, slipped in along with implications which are 'intended'. A decision about this must be postponed.

Among the 'intended' implications, however, may be one arising from the fact that a pier glass is a kind of mirror, while the examples of the 'flattering illusion' Eliot would have encountered in Herbert Spencer or in Ruskin lacked this feature. Ruskin, for example, speaks of the path of reflected moonlight seen across the surface of a lake by a spectator on the shore.[5] The pier glass would, after all, reflect what was brought near it, as well as produce its own interfering illusion of concentric circles, and the candle is a displacement or parable for the ego, of Rosamond or whomever. Rosamond would of course see her own image in the mirror, Narcissus-like. This implication of the parable links it with all those other passages, not only in *Middlemarch* but also in *Adam Bede*, for example, or in *Daniel Deronda*, where egotism is symbolised by the admiration of one's image in a mirror, or where the work of representation is expressed in the traditional image of holding a mirror up to reality. A passage in chapter 10, for example, apropos of the low opinion of Mr Casaubon held by his neighbours, says that even 'the greatest man of his age' could not escape 'unfavourable reflections of himself in various small mirrors'. This apparently uses the figure of the mirror in a way contradicting the parable of the pier glass. The mirror is now the ego rather than the external world. In fact, however, what is always in question when the mirror appears is narcissistic self-reflection. This may be thought of as seeing our own reflection in the mirroring world outside because we have projected it there. Or it may be thought of as our distortion of the world outside in our reflecting ego, so that it takes the configurations of our private vision of things. Any two subjectivities, according to this model, will face one another like confronting mirrors. If Casaubon was 'the centre of his own world', had 'an equivalent centre of self, whence the lights and shadows must always fall with a certain difference', the people in whom he seeks the reflection of his own sense of himself are not innocent mirrors, but are themselves instruments of distortion: 'even Milton, looking for his portrait in a spoon, must submit to have the facial angle of a bumpkin' (ch. 10). The projection of one's selfish needs or desires on reality orders that random set of events into a pattern, the image of the mirror would imply. This pattern is in fact a portrait of the ego itself, an objective embodiment of its subjective configurations. The terrible isolation of each person, for Eliot, lies in the way each goes through the world encountering only himself, his own image reflected back to him by the world because he (or she) has put it there in the first place, in the illusory interpretation of the world the person spontaneously makes.

The narrator of *Middlemarch*, it would seem, can escape from this fate only by using perspective to transcend perspective, by moving from the microscopic close-up to the panoramic distant view, and by shifting constantly from the point of view of one character to the point of view of another. Such shifts will give a full multidimensional picture of what is 'really there', as when the narrator, after a prolonged immersion within the subjective experience of Dorothea, asks: '– but why always Dorothea? Was her point of view the only possible one with regard to this marriage? I protest against all our interest, all our efforts at understanding being given to the young skins that look blooming in spite of trouble... In spite of the blinking eyes and white moles objectionable to Celia, and the want of muscular curve which was morally painful to Sir James, Mr. Casaubon had an intense consciousness within him, and was spiritually a-hungered like the rest of us' (ch. 29).

The word 'interpretation', however, which I used just above, will serve as a clue indicating the presence within the optical metaphors of an element so far not identified as such. This element contaminates and ultimately subverts the optical model in the same way that the optical model contaminates and makes more problematic the images of the web or of the current. All the optical passages in fact contain elements which show that for Eliot seeing is never 'merely' optical. Seeing is never simply a matter of identifying correctly what is seen, seeing that windmills are windmills and not giants, a washpan a washpan and not the helmet of Mambrino, to use the example from *Don Quixote* cited as an epigraph for chapter 2. Seeing is always interpretation, that is, what is seen is always taken as a sign standing for something else, as an emblem, a hieroglyph, a parable.

Superimposed on the models for the human situation of the objective scientist and the subjective perspectivist, interlaced with them, overlapping them in each of their expressions, is a model for the situation of the characters and of the narrator which says all human beings in all situations are like readers of a text. Moreover, if for Eliot all seeing is falsified by the limitations of point of view, it is an even more inevitable law, for her, that we make things what they are by naming them in one way or another, that is, by the incorporation of empirical data into a conventional system of signs. A corollary of this law is the fact that all interpretation of signs is false interpretation. The original naming was an act of interpretation which falsified. The reading of things made into signs is necessarily a further falsification, an interpretation of an interpretation. An important sequence of passages running like Ariadne's thread through the labyrinthine verbal complexity of *Middlemarch* develops a subtle theory of signs and of interpretation. Along with this goes a recognition of the irreducibly figurative or metaphorical nature of all language.

I have elsewhere discussed George Eliot's theory of signs, of interpretation, and of figurative language in *Middlemarch*.[6] Limitations of space would in any case forbid discussion of this third model for the human situation here. It is possible, however, to conclude on the basis of what I have said about two families of metaphors in *Middlemarch* that the models are multiple and incompatible. They are incompatible not in the sense that one is more primitive or naive and gives way to a more sophisticated paradigm, but in the sense that any passage will reveal itself when examined closely to be the battleground of conflicting metaphors. This incoherent, heterogeneous, 'unreadable', or nonsynthesisable quality of the text of *Middlemarch* jeopardises the narrator's effort of totalisation. It suggests that one gets a different kind of totality depending on what metaphorical model is used. The presence of several incompatible models brings into the open the arbitrary and partial character of each and so ruins the claim of the narrator to have a total, unified, and impartial vision. What is true for the characters of *Middlemarch*, that 'we all of us, grave or light, get our thoughts entangled in metaphors, and act fatally on the strength of them' (ch. 10), must also be true for the narrator. The web of interpretative figures cast by the narrator over the characters of the story becomes a net in which the narrator himself is entangled and trapped, his sovereign vision blinded.

George Eliot's insight into the dismaying dangers of metaphor is expressed already in an admirably witty and perceptive passage in *The Mill on the Floss*, published over a decade before *Middlemarch*, in 1860. Here already she formulates her recognition of the deconstructive powers of figurative language, its undoing of any attempt to make a complete, and completely coherent, picture of human life. This undoing follows from the fact that if we can seldom say what a thing is without saying it is something else, without speaking parabolically, then there is no way to avoid the ever present possibility of altering the meaning by altering the metaphor.

> It is astonishing what a different result one gets by changing the metaphor! Once call the brain an intellectual stomach, and one's ingenious conception of the classics and geometry as ploughs and harrows seems to settle nothing. But then it is open to some one else to follow great authorities, and call the mind a sheet of white paper or a mirror, in which case one's knowledge of the digestive process becomes quite irrelevant. It was doubtless an ingenious idea to call the camel the ship of the desert, but it would hardly lead one far in training that useful beast. O Aristotle! if you had had the advantage of being 'the freshest modern' instead of the greatest ancient, would you not have mingled your praise of metaphorical speech, as a sign of high intelligence, with a lamentation that intelligence so rarely shows itself in speech without metaphor – that we can so seldom declare what a thing is, except by saying it is something else?
>
> (Bk 2, ch. 1)[7]

Notes (cut and renumbered)

1. What, exactly, is the nature of the resemblance which binds together the members of this family and makes it seem of one genetic stock? Why, if Eliot's goal is to describe what is 'really there', objectively, must there be more than one model in order to create a total picture?

2. Friedrich Nietzsche, *Die Fröhliche Wissenschaft*, para. 228, in *Werke*, vol. 2, ed. Karl Schlecta (Munich, 1966), pp. 152–3; '... they lack eyes for seeing what is unique. Seeing things as similar and making things the same is the sign of weak eyes.' (*The Gay Science*, trans. Walter Kaufmann [New York, 1974], p. 212.)

3. Although several hypothetical originals, including G. H. Lewes, have been suggested for the 'eminent philosopher', N. N. Feltes argues persuasively that the philosopher was Herbert Spencer and that the image may be traced back from Spencer to a passage in Ruskin. See 'George Eliot's "Pier-Glass"; the Development of a Metaphor', *Modern Philology*, 67 (1969), 69–71.

4. The metaphor of the key, which I have borrowed for the language of the novel to use as language about the novel, contains exactly the ambiguity I am exploring here. A 'key' as in the 'Key to all Mythologies', is both an intrinsic pattern organising from within a large body of apparently heterogeneous material and at the same time something introduced from the outside which 'unlocks' an otherwise hidden pattern. A key is a formula which cracks a code, as when George Eliot in *Daniel Deronda* says, 'all meanings, we know, depend on the key of interpretation' (ch. 6). The meaning of a text is both intrinsic to that text and yet present in it only when it is projected by a certain extrinsic set of assumptions about the code or 'key'. This shifting from intrinsic to extrinsic definitions of 'key' is present in the various meanings of the word, which include mechanical, architectural, musical, and botanical senses.

5. See N. N. Feltes, 'George Eliot's "Pier-Glass" (details in note 3 above), p. 69, for a discussion of the passage from Ruskin's letter of February 1844 to the *Artist and Amateur's Magazine*, reprinted in *The Works of John Ruskin*, vol. 3, ed. E. T. Cook and Alexander Wedderburn (London, 1903), pp. 656–7.

6. In 'Narrative and History', *English Literary History*, 41 (1974), 455–73. I have also tried to indicate in this essay the alternative positive theories of history, of individual human life, and of the work of art with which Eliot, in *Middlemarch*, replaces the 'metaphysical' theories, governed by concepts of totality, of origin, of end, and of substantial analogy, which she so persuasively dismantles in the novel.

7. It is worth noting that George Eliot's rueful complaint about the proliferating contradictions of metaphor, which has arisen apropos of Tom Tulliver's difficulties in school, is followed almost immediately by an ostentatious and forceful metaphor, as if Eliot were compelled, in spite of herself, to demonstrate that we cannot say what a thing is except by saying that it is something else: 'At

present, in relation to this demand that he should learn Latin declensions and conjugations, Tom was in a state of as blank unimaginativeness concerning the cause and tendency of his sufferings, as if he had been an innocent shrewmouse imprisoned in the split trunk of an ash-tree in order to cure lameness in cattle.'

4.5 COLIN MACCABE: FROM *JAMES JOYCE AND THE REVOLUTION OF THE WORD* (1979)

Colin MacCabe is Head of Production at the British Film Institute and Professor of English at the University of Pittsburgh. He has been influential in introducing poststructuralist theory into literary and film study, especially in the British context. He was an editor of the journal *Screen* and is currently editor of *Critical Quarterly*. His publications include the study of Joyce from which the present extract is taken; an edited collection, *James Joyce: New Perspectives* (1982); *Godard* (1981); and *Theoretical Essays: Film, Linguistics, Literature* (1985).

MacCabe's principal subject in the present book is the modernist 'heteroglossic' discourse of Joyce's texts, but in the introduction he needs to set up a kind of prior stalking-horse tradition to which Joyce is in reaction. The 'classic realist texts' of George Eliot (*Middlemarch* here; and *Daniel Deronda* in later passages) supply this. Basically, MacCabe defines this concept as a kind of fictional sleight-of-hand which 'refuses to acknowledge its own status as writing' and 'functions simply as a window on reality' (p. 178, below). The authorial 'meta-language' is the dominant one in the hierarchy of discourses which comprise the text (no such meta-language is apparent in Joyce), and it is by this means that the author's worldview constitutes (and denies its presence as) the ostensibly unmediated 'reflection' of reality the world of the novel represents. The 'classic realist text', in other words, refuses to problematize the relation between language and reality.

Consider the influence of linguistic and psychoanalytic theory in MacCabe's work, and compare this with extracts included in Ch. 1 on Hamlet (by Lacan and Rose). How does Hillis Miller's (earlier) essay in effect rebut MacCabe's presentation of 'reflective' language in *Middlemarch*? How would Miller have read the two long quotations MacCabe uses to make his point? Does the admission that it would be 'a distortion' to present Eliot's texts as 'totally determined' by his governing concept (p. 180, below) call in question MacCabe's argument as a whole? (David Lodge, in '*Middlemarch* and the Idea of the Classic Realist Text', 1981, reprinted in both Newton, ed., *op. cit.* and Peck, ed., *op. cit.*, argues that the narration of the novel is by no means the unitary meta-language of MacCabe's thesis, and deploys Bakhtin to stress that it is, in fact, polyphonic and heteroglossic.) What might you deduce to be the larger project behind MacCabe's treatment of Eliot, and of his book as a whole? Is it about modernism rather than realism? (See also Chs 7 and 8 on Joyce and Brecht.) How meaningful would it be to characterize MacCabe's (and Hillis Miller's) essay as 'postmodernist' rather than merely 'poststructuralist'? (See Jameson on Joyce in Ch. 7, and essays on *Beloved* and Rushdie in Chs 9 and 10.)

The following excerpts comprise much of the first half, and some later passages, of the introduction (Macmillan, 1979, pp. 13–25, *passim*).

James Joyce and the Revolution of the Word

In order to carry out its task of interpretation, the discourse of literary criticism must always be able to identify what is represented, independently of the form of the representation. This identification is only possible if the discourse of the critic is in a position to transform the text into content, and, to undertake this transformation, the relation between the language of the text and the language of the critic must be that which obtains between an object- and a meta-language. A meta-language 'talks about' an object-language and transforms it into content by naming the object-language (accomplished through the use of inverted commas) and thus being able to identify both the object-language and its area of application.[1] It is from the position of the meta-language that correspondence between word and world can be established.

A text is made up of many languages, or discourses, and the critic's ability to homogenise these articulations is related to their prior organisation within the text.

[...]

A short passage is omitted here which observes the refusal of a 'meta-language' in Joyce's texts – signalled by the absence of what he called 'perverted commas'.

[...]

While those sections in a work which are contained in inverted commas may offer different ways of regarding and analysing the world, they are negated as real alternatives by the unspoken prose that surrounds and controls them. The narrative prose is the meta-language that can state all the truths in the object-language(s) (the marks held in inverted commas) and can also explain the relation of the object-language to the world. This relation of dominance allows the meta-language to understand how the object discourses obscurely figure truths which find clear expression in the meta-language. A meta-language regards its object discourses as material but itself as transparent. And this transparency allows the identity of things to shine through the window of words in the unspoken narrative whereas the spoken discourses which clothe meaning with material are necessarily obscure. At all costs the meta-language must refuse to admit its own materiality, for in so far as the meta-language is itself treated as material, it, too, can be re-interpreted; new meanings can be found for it in a further meta-language. The problem of the infinite regress of meta-languages brings us to the heart of the problem of meaning and interpretation. What the materiality of language constantly insists on, and what is insistently repressed in our society, is the separation between speech (or writing) and conscious-ness. This separation can be understood as the gap between the act of saying and what is said; a gap which occurs both temporally and spatially. For the time that it takes to traverse a page or listen to a sentence forbids any instantaneous grasping of meaning. Interpretation is perpetually deferred as each segment of meaning is defined by what follows. And in the space that separates eye from page or ear from mouth, there is a constant possibility of an interference, a misunderstanding, that similarly disrupts the presence of meaning. The problem arises from the fact that meaning is distributed through material and is constantly, therefore, open to further interpreta-tions, even though as we say or write a sentence the meaning seems fixed and evident. This formulation of the problem is itself misleading because it presupposes an original moment when there is strict coincidence between meaning and material. The difficulty is more radical because there is no such original moment. The act of enunciation and what is enounced, the saying and the said, are always separated.

It is to ignore this separation that a text uses inverted commas. The meta-language within such a text refuses to acknowledge its own status as writing – as marks of material difference distributed through time and space. The text outside the area of inverted commas claims to be the product of no articulation, it claims to be unwritten. This unwritten text can then attempt to staunch the haemorrhage of interpretations threatened by the material of language. Whereas other discourses within the text are considered as materials which are open to reinterpretation, the narrative discourse functions simply as a window on reality. This relationship between discourses can be taken as the defining feature of the *classic realist text*. The normal criterion for realism (whether a discourse is fully adequate to the real) merely accepts the conception of the real which the classic realist text proposes for its own project. Thus a traditional anti-realist position that no discourse can ever be adequate to the multifarious nature of the real assumes the classic realist division of language and reality. The classic realist text should not, however, be understood in terms of some homology to the order of things but as a specific hierarchy of discourses which places the reader in a position of dominance with regard to the stories and characters. However, this position is only achieved at the cost of a certain fixation, a certain subjection. George Eliot's texts provide an example of this discursive organisation.

In the scene in *Middlemarch* where Mr Brooke goes to visit Dagley's farm we are presented with two discourses. One is the educated, well-meaning, but not very intelligent discourse of Mr Brooke and the other is the uneducated, violent and very nearly unintelligible discourse of the drunken Dagley. But the whole dialogue is surrounded by a meta-language (which being unspoken is also unwritten) which places these discourses in inverted commas and can thereby discuss their relation to truth – a truth illuminatingly revealed in the meta-language. The meta-language reduces the object languages into a simple division between form and content and extracts the meaningful content from the useless form. Thus we find the following passage towards the end of the chapter:

> He [Mr Brooke] had never been insulted on his own land before, and had been inclined to regard himself as a general favourite (we are all apt to do so, when we think of our own amiability more than of what other people are likely to want of us). When he had quarrelled with Caleb Garth twelve years before he had thought that the tenants would be pleased at the landlord's taking everything into his own hands.
>
> Some who follow the narrative of his experience may wonder at the midnight darkness of Mr Dagley; but nothing was easier in those times than for an hereditary farmer of his grade to be ignorant, in spite somehow of having a rector in the twin parish who was a gentleman to the backbone, a curate nearer at hand who preached more learnedly than the rector, a landlord who had gone into everything, especially fine art and social improvement, and all the lights of Middlemarch only three miles off (George Eliot 1880, vol. 2, p. 188).

In this passage we are given the necessary interpretations for the discourses that we have just read. The words of Dagley and Mr Brooke are revealed as springing from two types of ignorance which the meta-language can expose and reveal. Thus we have Mr Brooke's attitude to his tenants contrasted with the reality which is available to us through the narrative prose. No discourse, except that charged with the narrative, is allowed to speak for itself, instead each speech must be placed in a context which will reduce it to a simple explicable content. The claim of the narrative prose to grant direct access to a final reality guarantees the claim of the realist novel to represent the invariable features of humanity. To reveal the truth about Mr Brooke permits the generalisations about human nature.

But it is not only the vanity of Mr Brooke that is laid bare; there is also the 'midnight darkness' of drunken Dagley. The metaphor employed contrasts the darkness of Dagley's discourse with the daylight clarity of the prose that surrounds and interprets it. Dagley's darkness has already been indicated through the attempt to render his accent phonetically. The emphasis on the material sounds of Dagley's discourse is directly in proportion to the difficulty in understanding it. The material of language is essentially a material that obscures. It is in so far as the narrative prose is not material that the truths of the world can shine through it.

The irony of the passage, which expresses its mock astonishment at the fact of Mr Dagley's ignorance when surrounded by such illuminating figures (and having 'all the lights of Middlemarch' only three miles away), works through the knowledge that the text has already conveyed and in no way damages the narrative's claim to be representing reality without intermediaries. There is a kind of irony (we will come to it later in our reading of Joyce) which works without any fixed rules for re-writing the ironic passage. This lack of interpretative rules is what makes for the difficulty of reading Joyce's texts. However, in this example from George Eliot we can read an example of classical irony. Classical irony is established in the distance between the original sentence and the sentence as it should be, given the knowledge of reality that the text has already conferred on us. For readers there is no astonishment that such midnight darkness as Mr Dagley's should exist not three miles from Middlemarch because the lights of that town have been exposed as shadows by the greater light of the text itself.

The conviction that the real can be displayed and examined through a perfectly transparent language is evident in George Eliot's Prelude to *Middlemarch*. In that Prelude she talks of those who care 'to know the history of man, and how the mysterious mixture behaves under the varying experiments of Time' and this language of empiricism runs through the text. The view of science as a matter of experiment is of a piece with a view of the immutable quality of human nature. For as language disappears and absents itself from the stage, we can clearly see the two-faced character Janus, the god of communication, one face that of human nature and the other that of the external physical world. To transform language into pure communicative absence is to transform the world into a self-evident reality where, in order to discover truth, we have only to use our eyes. This complete refusal to interrogate the form of the investigation, the belief in language's transparency, is evident on those occasions (frequent enough) when George Eliot reflects on that form. Thus in *Middlemarch* at the beginning of Chapter 15:

A great historian, as he insisted on calling himself, who had the happiness to be dead a hundred and twenty years ago, and so to take his place among the colossi whose huge legs our living pettiness is observed to walk under, glories in his copious remarks and digressions as the least imitable part of his work, and especially in those initial chapters to the successive books of his history, where he seems to bring his armchair to the proscenium and chat with us in all the lusty ease of his fine English. But Fielding lived when the days were longer (for time, like money, is measured by our needs), when summer afternoons were spacious, and the clock ticked slowly in the winter evenings. We belated historians must not linger after his example, and if we did so, it is probable that our chat would be thin and eager, as if delivered from a camp-stool in a parrot-house. I at least have so much to do in unravelling certain human lots, and seeing how they were woven and interwoven, that all the light I can command must be concentrated on this particular web, and not dispersed over the tempting range of relevancies called the universe (George Eliot 1880, vol. 1, pp. 213–214).

Although, at first sight, George Eliot would appear to be questioning her form, the force of the passage is to leave us convinced that we have finally abandoned forms to be treated to the simple unravelling of the real. Fielding's digressions, which, as it were, placed his fictions as fictions, are held to have been due to the 'lusty ease of his fine English'; that is, to a certain style. It should not go unremarked that George Eliot considers pleasure ('lusty ease' in language) as fatal as materiality to the transparency of language. If Fielding insisted on calling himself an historian, the passage demonstrates to us the impossibility of that claim. No author so preoccupied with his own position on the stage, 'the proscenium', can avoid the materiality and pleasure of language. It is only 'we belated historians' who no longer have any style, whose chat 'would be thin and eager', it is only such as these who can unravel the real.

The digression itself is no real digression because, situated in the middle of the narrative, its function is merely to efface itself; to testify to the reality of the story in which it is held. Where in Fielding the digression testifies to the written nature of the work, situating the narrative as construction, in Eliot the digression situates the narrative as pure representation, in which the author could not interfere because the author can no longer speak. In the same way the disclaimer of the 'tempting range of relevancies called the universe' does not affect the narrative's claim to be representing the world as it really is as long as the particular 'web' is fully illuminated. And significantly, once again, we find the metaphor of 'light', which is what the text is going to produce. These disclaimers have the function of ensuring, like the wealth of irrelevant detail which is heaped up in the text, the innocence and absence of a form and a language in which content might be distorted. We are persuaded that language and form have disappeared, allowing light to shine on the previously obscured world.

[…]

A further example from *Daniel Deronda* is given here.

[…]

It would be a distortion to consider George Eliot's texts as totally determined by that discursive organisation that I have defined as the classic realist text. Within her novels there are always images which counter the flat and univocal process which is the showing forth of the real. Casaubon's key to all the mythologies, Romola's blind father and, perhaps most powerfully of all, the Hebrew language which rests uninvestigable at the centre of *Daniel Deronda*, question and hold in suspense the project of Eliot's texts.

[...]

A little more on this disturbance of the meta-language follows here – mainly on the Hebrew language and poems in *Daniel Deronda*.

[...]

The problems and method of reading a realist text may be usefully compared to the problems an analyst faces in the analysis of a neurotic's discourses and the methods used to disengage significant interpretations from those discourses. Conflicts within the psyche combine and interact to produce dreams, symptoms, slips, etc. These psychic productions are described and explained by the neurotic in discourses which render the dreams coherent, the symptoms rational and the slips insignificant. The analyst is invited to offer the neurotic alternative explanations within these explanatory discourses. The analyst, however, has, as it were, to disengage the symptoms and the dreams from these explanatory discourses. Such a disengagement will demonstrate to the analysand not only how the conflicts have entered into the elaboration of the explanatory discourses but more importantly how the major conflict of neurosis can be located within the relationship between the explanatory discourses and the dreams, symptoms or slips.

Let us take, for example, the analysis of dreams and examine the formal structure of that analysis, remembering that this formal structure is realised in the analytic situation as a complex and dialectical process in which each element of the analysis interacts with the others. The patient relates a dream that sounds coherent. Starting from that element in the dream which lacks the coherence of the rest of the material (this might be an addition or a hesitation), the analyst attempts to disengage the dream from the operations of the secondary revision. The secondary revision renders coherent the material produced by the primary operations of the dream work (*displacement* and *condensation* limited by *considerations of representability*). The secondary revision thus provides the dream's own explanatory discourse. Therefore, when the analyst has stripped away the operations of the secondary revision from the dream, the dream has been transformed and it is this already transformed material which forms the basis for the next stage of the analysis.

In the course of an analysis certain key conflicts will repeat themselves. These conflicts are the result of unconscious desires which are denied access to consciousness. But, if the desires do not appear, their absence does. It is the gaps in the narrative of the dream that make evident the working of a censorship which suppresses those elements of the dream that would carry traces of the unconscious desires into consciousness. But the gaps themselves bear witness to an activity of repression and the existence of unconscious desire and it is in an attempt to refuse even the testimony of silence that the secondary revision recasts the dream in a new, coherent form. Now these unconscious desires will none the less affect the form and content of the secondary revision but, more importantly, it is in the need of the secondary revision to accomplish its work that one can locate the fundamental neurotic conflict. Independently of the content of the particular neurosis, one could aphoristically describe the condition of the neurotic as the refusal to recognise the existence of the unconscious.

This refusal naturally produces two stages within the neurotic's repression of the workings of the unconscious. We have the original repression of the desire because it is unacceptable to consciousness and then we have the further repression of the evidence of the original repression. The analyst, therefore, attempts in one and the same moment to bring the existence of unconscious desire to the attention of the neurotic and to persuade the neurotic to abandon those explanatory discourses which would link all the results of repression to reality. For the neurotic has constant recourse to reality in order to provide a coherent explanation of the troubling symptoms and slips, dreams and parapraxes that compose his or her being.

[...]

More on *Daniel Deronda* follows, illustrating that the meta-language of realism evinces 'neurosis' in its refusal to accept that meanings are constituted by difference and its demand for 'constant identities' unaffected by absence and loss.

[...]

The existence of a meta-language within the text allows the reader (and critic) to read from a position of dominance. It is not necessary for the reader to accept the identifications of the meta-language as long as he or she accepts its position. It is the position that is essential to this textual organisation and not the particular content that is given to reality. It is possible, however, as has already been suggested, to read against the position of the meta-language. To undertake such a challenge is to read against the alibi of reality and to enter into the world of fantasy where language figures and re-figures desire; where the letter is inscribed in the sex and the sex in the letter. It is such a reading that Joyce's texts invite.

[...]

Three pages follow which argue, by way of Benjamin, that the critic's job is to 'wrest tradition away from ... conformism', that Eliot's works – whether or not they are ineluctably 'classic realist texts' – have been institutionalized as such, and that Joyce's 'psychotic' texts offer a way of breaking that conformism. Such is the 'thesis' (or 'politics') of MacCabe's book.

[...]

George Eliot's texts are devoted to repressing the operations of the signifier by positing a meta-language which exists outside of materiality and production. The multitude of objects which appear in her texts do not bear witness to the activity of signification, to the constitutive reality of absence, but rather, in their massive identity, they deny the existence of such activity. And denying this activity, they deny the reality of absence. It is such a denial that constitutes the repression of desire.

The essay ends here.

Note

1. The definition of a meta-language is taken from Tarski's classic article on the semantic conception of truth (Tarski 1949). Throughout this work language (and its compounds) will be used as a synonym for discourse, that is to say as a term to refer to any system of lexical combination which has as effect a distinct subject position. It is thus not synonymous (except where the context demands it) with that everyday use of the word 'language' to refer to different national tongues, nor to Saussure's definition of language (*la langue*) as a system of differences, a definition which ignores any reference to subject position. An everyday use which approaches closely the sense desired can be identified in a phrase like 'They speak a different language', when the speaker is indicating differences of position and attitude amongst speakers of a single national language.

References

ELIOT, GEORGE (1880), *The Works of George Eliot* (Cabinet Edition), 20 vols. Edinburgh, 1878–80.
TARSKI, ALFRED (1949), 'The Semantic Conception of Truth', in *Readings in Philosophical Analysis*, ed. H. Feigl and W. Sellars. New York, pp. 52–84.

Chapter 5

Oscar Wilde:
The Picture of Dorian Gray and *The Importance of Being Earnest*

GENERAL INTRODUCTION

Wilde's novel, *The Picture of Dorian Gray*, was published in 1891, and his fourth play, *The Importance of Being Earnest*, was first performed at St James's Theatre, London on 14 February 1895 (it was published in 1899). In April and May of 1895 occurred the three trials regarding Wilde's relations with Lord Alfred Douglas, the son of the Marquess of Queensberry. He was found guilty of 'gross indecency' and sentenced to two years' imprisonment in solitary confinement with hard labour, which he mainly spent in Reading Gaol. Three-and-a-half years after his release, he died in Paris in 1900, a broken man in body and spirit. As the trials began, his two plays, *Earnest* and *An Ideal Husband*, running in London to packed audiences, were closed down. His other plays were *Lady Windermere's Fan* (1892/3); *A Woman of No Importance* (1893/4); and *Salome*, written in French (1893; English trans. 1894), and first performed in Paris, 1896. Amongst his many volumes of poems and essays, other well-known works include 'The Soul of Man Under Socialism' (1891), *De Profundis* (written in gaol in 1897, but published later) and 'The Ballad of Reading Gaol' (published in 1898 after his release). Both during his lifetime and for much of the twentieth century, Wilde and his work have been highly regarded (when not vilified) for their style and wit, for their 'quotable' epigrammatic brilliance, as examples of *fin de siècle* aestheticism, for their humane oppositional politics, and for the plays' stagecraft. More recently, with the development of gay and lesbian studies, gendered criticism and 'queer theory' on the one hand, and postcolonialism on the other, Wilde has become a focal figure for gay and lesbian criticism and for the newer Irish cultural history.

  The present chapter brings together five examples of these developments and is thus rather different from many of the others. Here, the contributions do not so clearly display markedly different kinds of theory in practice which often explicitly challenge or displace another or earlier movement, but present different inflections of, or directions within, the growing field of 'transgressive' theory and criticism. In one sense, they therefore challenge the perspectives of most contemporary theory and criticism, including the majority of essays presented elsewhere in this volume. As Eve Kosofsky Sedgwick, at the start of her book, *Epistemology of the Closet*, states: 'an understanding of virtually any aspect of modern Western culture must be, not merely incomplete, but damaged in its central substance to the degree that it does not incorporate a critical analysis of modern homo/heterosexual definition' (p. 1). The place to start, she says, is from 'the relatively decentred perspective of modern gay and anti-homophobic theory' (*ibid.*). Others here would broadly agree. Drawing on poststructuralism, psychoanalysis, feminism, deconstruction, cultural materialism and aspects of postcolonial theory, such work traces the structuring and fracturing caused by this (male) division, as it shapes the figuration of literary works, to reveal a 'dissident', 'transgressive' ('Wilde') political aesthetic with which to estrange and critique the natural, the conformist and the established. Oscar Wilde offers an exemplary text for such engaged criticism. And although Eagleton's essay is not driven by a transgressive *sexual* politics, Wilde's national identity and cultural insertion – his particular 'Irishness' – is mobilized in this reading to suggest another transgressive stance to the British upper classes.

Compare and contrast the different inflections of 'queer theory' in the first four extracts. Are they motivated by a common 'transgressive' aesthetics? In what ways, if any, do the essays offer specifically *homosexual* readings of Wilde's texts, and what specifically textual reading strategies do they deploy to this end? Gay and lesbian theory is demonstrably 'political' in aim and effect – as, indeed, is postcolonial cultural history; try, therefore, to define the political agenda which informs each of the extracts, and consider how it is mobilized on behalf of *present* ideological formations (in the 1990s). Identify the ways in which the criticism here inflects the various tributary theoretical movements listed in the preceding paragraph (poststructuralism, psychoanalysis, etc.) Does the theoretical criticism represented below 'dehistoricize' Wilde's texts? Does it free itself from the problematics surrounding notions of 'literary value'? Consider how, finally, in Sedgwick's phrase, other critical theory in other exercises is 'damaged' by its failure to incorporate the dimension of 'modern homo/heterosexual definition'. Taking one or two examples, explore how other essays in other exercises would be transformed if they were to include this dimension. Attempt, yourself, to make a reading of some of the other texts (e.g. *Hamlet*, *Heart of Darkness*, *Jane Eyre*, *Middlemarch*) based on the notion of a 'transgressive aesthetics'.

Further Reading
Gay and lesbian theory is a recent and expanding field, and a number of the central figures in it are those represented in this exercise; individual Headnotes, therefore, refer to further works by them. In addition, useful volumes include: Jeffrey Weeks, *Sexuality and its Discontents* (Routledge, 1985); Elaine Showalter, ed., *Speaking of Gender* (Routledge, 1989); Joseph Boone and Michael Cadden, eds, *Engendering Men* (Routledge, 1991); Judith Butler, *Gender Trouble* (Routledge, 1990); Diana Fuss, ed., *Inside/Out: Lesbian Theories, Gay Theories* (Routledge, 1992); Kaja Silverman, *Male Subjectivities at the Margins* (Routledge, 1992); Arthur and Marilouise Kroker, eds, *The Last Sex: Feminism and Outlaw Bodies* (Macmillan, 1993); Sally Munt, ed., *New Lesbian Criticism* (Harvester, 1992); and Sally Ledger, Josephine McDonagh and Jane Spencer, eds, *Political Gender: Texts and Contexts* (Harvester, 1994).

5.1   EVE KOSOFSKY SEDGWICK: FROM *EPISTEMOLOGY OF THE CLOSET* (1990)

Eve Kosofsky Sedgwick is Newman Ivey White Professor of English at Duke University, and the author of *Between Men: English Literature and Male Homosexual Desire* (1985); *Fat Art, Thin Art* (1994); and *Tendencies* (1994). *Epistemology of the Closet* has been a ground-breaking book in lesbian and gay studies, identifying, as do other essays here, the crucial moment towards the end of the nineteenth century when the word 'homosexual' entered the language and became the means by which the 'world-mapping' of all people went beyond the 'male/female' binarism and institutionalized the other binarized identity of homo/heterosexuality (p. 2). Being 'homosexual', in other words, had not been *named* before in this schismatic way. As the quotation from Sedgwick, above pp. 184–5, also makes clear, she sees the whole of twentieth-century Western culture as 'structured – indeed, fractured – by a chronic, now endemic crisis of homo/heterosexual definition' (p. 1). The notion of 'the closet' – 'the relations of the known and the unknown, the explicit and the inexplicit' around this definition – is the reflex of such a crisis, and the 'place' where twentieth-century homosexual men and women, especially, have lived their lives. Sedgwick's 'epistemology' of this is established by way of a series of readings of (primarily) literary texts whose 'performative aspects' (as with speech acts more generally) are 'peculiarly revealing' as 'sites of definitional creation, violence, and rupture'. '"Closetedness" itself', she adds, 'is a performance initiated as such by the speech act of a silence' (p. 3). Despite its primary focus on male homosexuality, she makes explicit that it is a 'feminist' book, drawing on 'considerably more advanced' feminist theory and practice to assist in the further development of gay male or anti-homophobic analysis (pp. 15–16). Although the result may look, she says, like a collection of 'unreconstructedly literary readings of essentially canonic texts', the notions of 'literary text' and 'literary reading' become 'more and more unstable' under the pressures set up by the cultural context of theoretical work in her own and other cognate areas (p. 13). The previous chapter has focused on Melville's *Billy Budd*; Sedgwick's argument in the present one is structured on a comparative reading of Wilde and Nietzsche. It is sectionalized with sub-headings, and these have been retained where appropriate; passages on Nietzsche have been omitted.

What is the *effect* of Sedgwick's reading of Wilde's texts (especially *Dorian Gray*) here? In what sense, if any, do the later pages represent a 'deconstructive' analysis of the text? How (given her statement above) does the essay avoid becoming a 'literary reading' of a 'canonic text'? Also, does Sedgwick's formation within feminism manifest itself in these extracts; compare her work with other feminist readings in other exercises (e.g. those on *Hamlet, Jane Eyre* and *Beloved*)? How, and to what end, does the essay relate Wilde to modernism; and how does it deal with Wilde in a national/colonial context? Compare it, in this respect, with Eagleton's commentary in this chapter and with Spivak's on *Jane Eyre* (Ch. 3).

The following excerpts are taken from Ch. 3, 'Some Binarisms (II). Wilde, Nietzsche, and the Sentimental Relations of the Male Body', in *Epistemology of the Closet* (1990), Harvester, 1991, pp. 131–81, *passim*.

Epistemology of the Closet

The chapter opens here.

For readers fond of the male body, the year 1891 makes an epoch. Chapter 1 of

Billy Budd opens, as we have noted, with a discussion of the Handsome Sailor – 'a superb figure, tossed up as by the horns of Taurus against the thunderous sky' (1354). As Chapter 1 of *The Picture of Dorian Gray* opens, 'in the centre of the room, clamped to an upright easel, stood the full-length portrait of a young man of extraordinary personal beauty.'[1] Like many Atget photographs, these two inaugural presentations of male beauty frame the human image high up in the field of vision, a singular apparition whose power to reorganize the visibility of more conventionally grounded figures is arresting and enigmatic.

For readers who hate the male body, the year 1891 is also an important one. At the end of *Dorian Gray* a dead, old, 'loathsome' man lying on the floor is the moralizing gloss on the other thing the servants find in Dorian Gray's attic: 'hanging upon the wall, a splendid portrait of their master as they had last seen him, in all the wonder of his exquisite youth and beauty' (248). The end of *Billy Budd* is similarly presided over by the undisfigured pendant: Billy noosed to the mainyard gallows 'ascended, and, ascending, took the full rose of the dawn' (80). The exquisite portrait, the magnetic corpse swaying aloft: iconic as they are of a certain sexual visibility, their awful eminence also signalizes that the line between any male beauty that's articulated as such and any steaming offal strung up for purchase at the butcher's shop is, in the modern dispensation so much marked by this pair of texts, a brutally thin one.

In this chapter I am undertaking to consider some more of the modern relations over which this male body presides in formative texts of the late nineteenth century. Through a broader application of the same deconstructive procedure of isolating particular nodes in a web of interconnected binarisms, I move here from the last chapter's treatment of one 1891 text, *Billy Budd*, to treating a group of other texts dating from the 1880s and early 1890s, including the contemporaneous *Picture of Dorian Gray*. This chapter moves outward in two other principal ways, as well: from the sentimental/antisentimental relations around the displayed male figure toward, on the one hand, the modernist crisis of individual identity and figuration itself; toward, on the other, the intersections of sexual definition with relatively new problematics of kitsch, of camp, and of nationalist and imperialist definition.

The two, roughly contemporaneous figures whom I will treat as representing and overarching this process are Wilde and Nietzsche, perhaps an odd yoking of the most obvious with the least likely suspect. Wilde is the obvious one because he seems the very embodiment of, at the same time, (1) a new turn-of-the-century homosexual identity and fate, (2) a modernist antisentimentality, and (3) a late-Victorian sentimentality. Interestingly, the invocation of Nietzsche's name has become a minor commonplace in Wilde criticism, though certainly not vice versa. It has served as a way, essentially, of legitimating Wilde's seriousness as a philosopher of the modern – in the face of his philosophically embarrassing, because narratively so compelling, biographical entanglements with the most mangling as well as the most influential of the modern machineries of male sexual definition. Needless to say, however, the opposite project interests me as much here: the project of looking at Nietzsche through a Wildean optic.

[...]

Three-and-a-half pages follow on the self-contradictions in Nietzsche's work around 'desire'.

The next excerpt is from a section sub-headed 'Greek/Christian'. It starts here.

For Nietzsche as for Wilde, a conceptual and historical interface between Classical and Christian cultures became a surface suffused with meanings about the male body. In both German and English culture, the Romantic rediscovery of ancient Greece cleared out – as much as recreated – for the nineteenth century a prestigious, historically underfurnished imaginative space in which relations to and among human bodies might be newly a subject of utopian speculation. Synecdochically represented as it tended to be by statues of nude young men, the Victorian cult of Greece gently, unpointedly, and unexclusively positioned male flesh and muscle as the indicative instances of 'the' body, of a body whose surfaces, features, and abilities might be the subject or object of unphobic enjoyment. The Christian tradition, by contrast, had tended both to condense 'the flesh' (insofar as it represented or incorporated pleasure) as the *female* body and to surround its attractiveness with an aura of maximum anxiety and prohibition. Thus two significant differences from Christianity were conflated or conflatable in thought and rhetoric about 'the Greeks': an imagined dissolving of the bar of prohibition against the enjoyed body, and its new gendering as indicatively male.

Dorian Gray, appearing in *The Picture of Dorian Gray* first as artist's model, seems to make the proffer of this liberatory vision – at least he evokes formulations of its ideology from his two admirers. The artist Basil Hallward says of him, 'Unconsciously he defines for me the lines of a fresh school, a school that is to have in it all the passion of the romantic spirit, all the perfection of the spirit that is Greek. The harmony of soul and body – how much that is! We in our madness have separated the two, and have invented a realism that is vulgar, an ideality that is void' (16–17). And Lord Henry Wotton addresses the immobilized sitter with a Paterian invocation:

> 'The aim of life is self-development. To realize one's nature perfectly – that's what each of us is here for. People are afraid of themselves nowadays. ... And yet ... I believe that if one man were to live out his life fully and completely, were to give form to every feeling, expression to every thought, reality to every dream – I believe that the world would gain such a fresh impulse of joy that we would forget all the maladies of medievalism, and return to the Hellenic ideal – to something finer, richer, than the Hellenic ideal, it may be. But the bravest man among us is afraid of himself. The mutilation of the savage has a tragic survival in the self-denial that mars our lives. We are punished for our refusals.' (25)

The context of each of these formulations, however, immediately makes clear that the conceptual divisions and ethical bars instituted by, or attributed to, Christianity are easier to condemn than to undo, or perhaps even wish to undo. The painter's manifesto for Dorian's ability to reinstitute a modern 'harmony of soul and body,' for instance, is part of his extorted confession – and confession is the appropriate word – to Lord Henry concerning 'this curious artistic idolatry, of which, of course, I have never cared to speak to [Dorian]. He knows nothing about it. He shall never know anything about it. But the world might guess it; and I will not bare my soul to their shallow prying eyes' (17). To delineate and dramatize a space of *the secret* also emerges as the project of Lord Henry's manifesto, an address whose performative aim is after all less persuasion than seduction. Like Basil, Lord Henry constructs *the secret* in terms that depend on (unnameable) prohibitions attached specifically to the beautiful male body; and like Basil's, Lord Henry's manifesto for the Hellenic unity of soul and body derives its seductive rhetorical force from a culmination that depends on their irreparable divorce through shame and prohibition.

> 'We are punished for our refusals. ... The only way to get rid of a temptation is to yield to it. Resist it, and your soul grows sick with longing for the things it has forbidden to itself, with desire for what its monstrous laws have made monstrous and unlawful. ... You, Mr Gray, you yourself, with your rose-red youth and your rose-white boyhood, you have had passions that have made you afraid, thoughts that have filled you with terror, day-dreams and sleeping dreams whose mere memory might stain your cheek with shame –'
>
> 'Stop!' faltered Dorian Gray, 'stop! you bewilder me. I don't know what to say. There is some answer to you, but I cannot find it.' (25–26)

The crystallization of desire as 'temptation,' of the young body as the always initiatory encroachment of rose-red on rose-white, gives the game of wholeness away in advance. Each of these enunciations shows that the 'Hellenic ideal,' insofar as its reintegrative power is supposed to involve a healing of the culturewide ruptures involved in male homosexual panic, necessarily has that panic so deeply at the heart of its occasions, frameworks, demands, and evocations that it becomes not only inextricable from but even a propellant of the cognitive and ethical compartmentalizations of homophobic prohibition. That it is *these* in turn that become exemplary propellants of homosexual desire seems an inevitable consequence.

[...]

One-and-a-half pages on Nietzsche's 'classicism' are cut here.

[...]

The assumption I have been making so far, that the main impact of Christianity on men's desire for the male body – and the main stimulus it offers to that desire – is prohibitive, is an influential assumption far beyond Wilde and Nietzsche. It is also an assumption that even (or especially) those who hold and wield it, including both Wilde (who was never far from the threshold of Rome) and Nietzsche (who, at the last, subscribed himself as 'The Crucified'), know is not true. Christianity may be near-ubiquitous in modern European culture as a figure of phobic prohibition, but it makes a strange figure for that indeed. Catholicism in particular is famous for giving countless gay and proto-gay children the shock of the possibility of adults who don't marry, of men in dresses, of passionate theatre, of introspective investment, of lives filled with what could, ideally without diminution, be called the work of the fetish. Even for the many whose own achieved gay identity may at last include none of these features or may be defined as against them, the encounter with them is likely to have a more or other than prohibitive impact. And presiding over all are the images of Jesus. These have, indeed, a unique position in modern culture as images of the unclothed or unclothable male body, often in extremis and/or in ecstasy, prescriptively meant to be gazed at and adored. The scandal of such a figure within a homophobic economy of the male gaze doesn't seem to abate: efforts to disembody this body, for instance by attenuating, Europeanizing, or feminizing it, only entangle it the more compromisingly among various modern figurations of the homosexual.

The nominal terms of the Greek/Christian contrast, as if between permission and prohibition or unity and dichotomy, questionable as (we have seen) they may be in themselves, have even less purchase on this aspect of Christianity by which, nonetheless, they are inevitably inflected. Both in Nietzsche and in Wilde – and, partly through them, across twentieth-century culture – this image is, I believe, one of the places where the extremely difficult and important problematic of sentimentality is centered. Let me take a little time to explore why it is so difficult to get hold of analytically and so telling for the twentieth century, on the way back to a discussion of its pivotal place in the homo/heterosexual definition struggles of Wilde and Nietzsche.

[...]

The opening five pages of a section entitled 'Sentimental/Antisentimental', which propose the recuperation of the former concept for gay male culture, are omitted. It then continues as follows.

[...]

How, then, through the issue of sentimentality can we bring to Nietzsche questions that Wilde and the reading of Wilde may teach us to ask? Gore Vidal begins a recent essay on Wilde: 'Must one have a heart of stone to read *The Ballad of Reading Gaol* without laughing?'[2] The opening points in only too many directions. Between it and the same remark made by Wilde himself, a century earlier, about the death of Little Nell, where to look for the wit-enabling relation? One story to tell is the historical/thematic one just sketched: that whereas in the nineteenth century it was images of women in relation to domestic suffering and death that occupied the most potent, symptomatic, and, perhaps, friable or volatile place in the sentimental *imaginaire* of middle-class culture, for the succeeding century – the century inaugurated by Wilde among others – it has been images of agonistic male self-constitution. Thus the careful composition of *The Ballad of Reading Gaol*, where Wilde frames his own image between, or even as, those of a woman-murdering man and the Crucified, sets in motion every conceivable mechanism by which most readers know how to enter into the circuit of the sentimental:

> Alas! it is a fearful thing
>   To feel another's guilt!
> For, right, within, the Sword of Sin

> Pierced to its poisoned hilt,
> And as molten lead were the tears we shed
> For the blood we had not spilt.
>
> . . . .
>
> And as one sees most fearful things
> In the crystal of a dream,
> We saw the greasy hempen rope
> Hooked to the blackened beam,
> And heard the prayer the hangman's snare
> Strangled into a scream.
>
> And all the woe that moved him so
> That he gave that bitter cry,
> And the wild regrets, and the bloody sweats,
> None knew so well as I:
> For he who lives more lives than one
> More deaths than one must die.[3]

Think of the cognate, ravishing lines of Cowper –

> We perished, each alone,
> But I beneath a rougher sea
> And whelmed in deeper gulfs than he[4]

– and the cognate sentimental markers (the vicariousness, the uncanny shifting first person of after death, the heroic self-pity) that give them their awful appropriateness, their appropriability, to the narrow, imperious, incessant self-reconstitution of, say, Virginia Woolf's paterfamilias Mr. Ramsay. Yet the author of *Reading Gaol* is also the creator of 'Ernest in town and Jack in the country' and of Mr. Bunbury, of men whose penchant for living more lives than one, and even dying more deaths, not to speak of having more christenings, seems on the contrary to give them a fine insouciance about such identity issues as the name of the father – which his sons, who have forgotten it, have to look up in the Army Lists. 'Lady Bracknell, I hate to seem inquisitive, but would you kindly inform me who I am?' (*Earnest*, in *Complete*, 181). At the same time, the precise grammatical matrix of even the most anarchic Wildean wit still tends toward the male first-person singular in the mode of descriptive self-definition. 'None of us are perfect. I myself am peculiarly susceptible to draughts.' 'I can resist anything except temptation.' 'I have nothing to declare except my genius.' The project of constructing the male figure is not made any the less central by being rendered as nonsense; in fact, one might say that it's the candor with which Wilde is often capable of centering this male project in the field of vision that enables him to operate so explosively on it.

The squeam-inducing power of texts like *De Profundis* and *Reading Gaol* – and I don't mean to suggest that they are a bit the less powerful for often making the flesh crawl – may be said to coincide with a thematic choice made in each of them: that the framing and display of the male body be placed in the explicit context of the displayed body of Jesus. One way of reading *The Picture of Dorian Gray* would tell the same story, since the fall of that novel from sublime free play into sentimental potency comes with the framing and hanging of the beautiful male body as a visual index of vicarious expiation.

[...]

Two pages on Nietzsche and 'sentimentality' are cut here, as is the sub-section 'Direct/ Vicarious; Art/Kitsch'.

The next extract is from the section 'Same/Different; Homo/Hetero', of which the opening two-and-a-half pages – refuting the notion that homosexuality *does* depend on a 'defining *sameness* between partners' – are cut.

[...]

How does a man's love of *other* men become a love of the *same*? The process is graphic in *Dorian Gray*, in the way the plot of the novel facilitates the translation back and forth between 'men's desire for men' and something that looks a lot like what a tradition will soon call 'narcissism.' The novel takes a plot that is distinctively one of male-male desire, the competition between Basil Hallward and Lord Henry Wotton for Dorian Gray's love, and condenses it into the plot of the mysterious bond of figural likeness and figural expiation between Dorian Gray and his own portrait. The suppression of the original defining *differences between* Dorian and his male admirers – differences of age and initiatedness, in the first place – in favor of the problematic of Dorian's *similarity* to the painted male image that is and isn't himself does several things. To begin with, the similarity trope does not, I believe, constitute itself strongly here as against an 'inversion' model, in which Wilde seldom seemed particularly interested and whose rhetoric is virtually absent from *Dorian Gray*. Rather, this plot of the novel seems to replicate the discursive eclipse in this period of the Classically based, *pederastic* assumption that male-male bonds of any duration must be structured around some diacritical difference – old/young, for example, or active/passive – whose binarizing cultural power would be at least comparable to that of gender. Initiating, along with the stigma of narcissism, the utopic modern vision of a strictly egalitarian bond guaranteed by the exclusion of any consequential difference, the new calculus of homo/hetero, embodied in the portrait plot, owes its sleekly utilitarian feel to the linguistically unappealable classification of anyone who shares one's gender as being 'the same' as oneself, and anyone who does not share one's gender as being one's Other.

It served, however, an additional purpose. For Wilde, in 1891 a young man with a very great deal to lose who was trying to embody his own talents and desires in a self-contradictory male-homosocial terrain where too much was not enough but, at the same time, anything at all might always be too much, the collapse of homo/ hetero with self/other must also have been attractive for the protective/expressive camouflage it offered to distinctively gay content. Not everyone has a lover of their own sex, but everyone, after all, has a self of their own sex.[5] (This camouflage, by the way, continues to be effective in institutions that connive with it: in a class I taught at Amherst College, fully half the students said they had studied *Dorian Gray* in previous classes, but not one had ever discussed the book in terms of any homosexual content: all of them knew it could be explained in terms of either the Theme of the Double – 'The Dividelf' – or else the Problem of Mimesis – 'Life and Art.')

For Wilde, the progression from *homo* to same to self resulted at least briefly, as we shall see, in a newly articulated modernist 'self'-reflexiveness and antifigurality, antirepresentationism, iconophobia that struggles in the antisentimental entanglements of *Dorian Gray* and collapses in the sentimental mobilizations of *Reading Gaol.*[6]

[...]

Again, two pages on Nietzsche in the same context are cut, as is the opening page of the next section, 'Abstraction/Figuration', on nineteenth-century 'gothic' inscription. It continues as follows.

The overtly Gothic *Dorian Gray*, insofar as its plot devolves, as we've seen, from a worldly one of complex intersubjective rivalries to a hermetic one of the Double *tout court*, drinks as deeply and much more conventionally of this nineteenth-century current by which the energies of a male-male desire by now complexly prohibited but still rather inchoately defined could be at once circulated, channeled, extended, and occluded. Chapter 4, on the historical creation and manipulation of male homosexual panic per se, will discuss these mechanisms more fully. What makes *Dorian Gray* so distinctively modern(ist) a book, however, is not the degree to which it partakes of the paranoid-associated homophobic alibi 'I do not *love* him; I *am* him.' It is a different though intimately related alibi that the *modernism* of *Dorian Gray* performs: the alibi of abstraction.

Across the turn of the century, as we know, through a process that became most visible in, but antedated and extended far beyond, the trials of Oscar Wilde, the discourse related to male homosexuality itself became for the first time extremely public and highly ramified through medical, psychiatric, penal, literary, and other social institutions. With a new public discourse concerning male homosexuality that was at the same time increasingly discriminant, increasingly punitive, and increasingly trivializing or marginalizing, the recuperative rhetoric that emerged had an oddly oblique shape. I would describe it as the occluded intersection between a minority rhetoric of the 'open secret' or glass closet and a subsumptive public rhetoric of the 'empty secret.'

The term 'open secret' designates here a very particular secret, a homosexual secret. As I explain in Chapter 1, I use it as a condensed way of describing the phenomenon of the 'glass closet,' the swirls of totalizing knowledge-power that circulate so violently around any but the most openly acknowledged gay male identity. The lavender button I bought the other day at the Oscar Wilde Memorial Bookstore, that laconically says, 'I KNOW YOU KNOW,' represents a playful and seductive version of the Glass Closet. Hitchcock's recently re-released Gothic film *Rope* is a good example of the murderous version. It opens with two men, clearly lovers, strangling a third man in a darkened penthouse; then pulling back the curtains from the skylight with orgasmic relief – 'Pity we couldn't have done it with the curtains open, in bright sunlight. Well, we can't have everything, can we? We did do it in daytime' – they put their friend's dead body in a large box which they place in the middle of the living room and use as the buffet table and centerpiece for a party, the guests to which include the fiancée, the father, the aunt, the best friend, and the prep-school ex-housemaster of the murdered man. Needless to say, the two lovers manage to make sure that the existence of A Secret, and the location of that secret in the big box in the middle of the room, does not remain A Secret for long.

The public rhetoric of the 'empty secret,' on the other hand, the cluster of aperçus and intuitions that seems distinctively to signify 'modernism' (at least, male high modernism), delineates a space bounded by hollowness, a self-reference that refers back to – though it differs from – nineteenth-century paranoid solipsism, and a split between content or thematics on the one hand and structure on the other that is stressed in favor of structure and at the expense of thematics. I will argue in the next chapter that this rhetoric of male modernism serves a purpose of universalizing, naturalizing, and thus substantively voiding – depriving of content – elements of a specifically and historically male homosexual rhetoric. But just as the gay male rhetoric is itself already marked and structured and indeed necessitated and propelled by the historical shapes of homophobia, for instance by the contingencies and geographies of the highly permeable closet, so it is also true that homophobic male modernism bears the structuring fossil-marks of and in fact spreads and reproduces the specificity of desire that it exists to deny.

The Picture of Dorian Gray occupies an especially symptomatic place in this process. Published four years before Wilde's 'exposure' as a sodomite, it is in a sense a perfect rhetorical distillation of the open secret, the glass closet, shaped by the conjunction of an extravagance of deniability and an extravagance of flamboyant display. It perfectly represents the glass closet, too, because it is in so many ways *out* of the purposeful control of its author. Reading *Dorian Gray* from our twentieth-century vantage point where the name Oscar Wilde virtually *means* 'homosexual,' it is worth reemphasizing how thoroughly the elements of even this novel can be read doubly or equivocally, can be read either as having a thematically empty 'modernist' meaning or as having a thematically full 'homosexual' meaning. And from the empty 'modernist' point of view, this full meaning – *any* full meaning, but, in some exemplary representative relation to that, *this* very particular full meaning – this insistence on narrative content, which means the insistence on *this* narrative content, comes to look like kitsch.

Basil Hallward perfectly captures the immobilizing panic that underlies this imperfect transformation of the open secret into the empty secret. He had been able, in decent comfort, to treat artistically of his infatuation with Dorian so long as he had framed it anachronistically, Classically – even while knowing that 'in such mad worships there is peril' (128) – but

> Then came a new development. I had drawn you as Paris in dainty armour, and as Adonis with huntsman's cloak and polished boatspear. ... And it had all been what art should be – unconscious, ideal, and remote. One day, a fatal day I sometimes think, I determined to

paint a wonderful portrait of you as you actually are, not in the costume of dead ages, but in your own dress and your own time. Whether it was the Realism of the method, or the mere wonder of your own personality, thus directly presented to me without mist or veil, I cannot tell. But I know that as I worked at it, every flake and film of colour seemed to me to reveal my secret. I grew afraid that others would know of my idolatry. I felt, Dorian, that I had told too much, that I had put too much of myself into it. ... Well, after a few days the thing left my studio, and as soon as I had got rid of the intolerable fascination of its presence it seemed to me that I had been foolish in imagining that I had seen anything in it, more than that you were extremely good-looking, and that I could paint. Even now I cannot help feeling that it is a mistake to think that the passion one feels in creation is ever really shown in the work one creates. Art is always more abstract than we fancy. Form and colour tell us of form and colour – that is all. (128–29)

Or, as Basil has put it earlier, interrupting his own confession of love and desire for Dorian: 'He is never more present in my work than when no image of him is there. He is a suggestion, as I have said, of a new manner. I find him in the curves of certain lines, in the loveliness and subtleties of certain colours. That is all.' (17)

Passages like these, as well as some of the important antinarrative projects that seem to shape the early parts of *Dorian Gray*, suggest the prefiguring manifesto of a modernist aesthetic according to which sentimentality inheres less in the object figured than in a prurient vulgarity associated with figuration itself. Postmodernism, in this view, the strenuous rematch between the reigning champ, modernist abstraction, and the deposed challenger, figuration, would thus *necessarily* have kitsch and sentimentality as its main spaces of contestation. But insofar as there is a case to be made that the modernist impulse toward abstraction in the first place owes an incalculable part of its energy precisely to turn-of-the-century male homo/heterosexual definitional panic – and such a case is certainly there for the making, in at any rate literary history from Wilde to Hopkins to James to Proust to Conrad to Eliot to Pound to Joyce to Hemingway to Faulkner to Stevens – to that extent the 'figuration' that had to be abjected from modernist self-reflexive abstraction was not the figuration of just *any* body, the figuration of figurality itself, but, rather, that represented in a very particular body, the desired male body. So as kitsch or sentimentality came to mean representation itself, what represented 'representation itself' came at the same time signally to be a very particular, masculine object and subject of erotic desire.

[...]

A section on 'decadence', mainly about Nietzsche, is omitted. The final extract is all but the first page of the following one: 'Voluntarity/Addiction; Cosmopolitan/National'. It opens with a passage on the relation of decadence to drugs and addiction in the period.

[...]

In *The Picture of Dorian Gray* as in, for instance, *Dr. Jekyll and Mr. Hyde*, drug addiction is both a camouflage and an expression for the dynamics of same-sex desire and its prohibition: both books begin by looking like stories of erotic tensions between men, and end up as cautionary tales of solitary substance abusers. The two new taxonomies of the addict and the homosexual condense many of the same issues for late nineteenth-century culture: the old antisodomitic opposition between something called nature and that which is *contra naturam* blends with a treacherous apparent seamlessness into a new opposition between substances that are *natural* (e.g., 'food') and those that are *artificial* (e.g., 'drugs'); and hence into the characteristic twentieth-century way of problematizing almost every issue of will, dividing desires themselves between the natural, called 'needs,' and the artificial, called 'addictions.' It seems as though the reifying classification of certain particular, palpable substances as unnatural in their (artificially stimulating) relation to 'natural' desire must necessarily throw into question the naturalness of any desire (Wilde: 'Anything becomes a pleasure if one does it too often'),[7] so that Nietzsche's hypostatization of Will 'itself,' for example, would necessarily be part of the same historical process as the nineteenth-century isolation of addiction 'itself.'[8] Inexorably, from this grid of overlapping classifications – a purported taxonomic system that in fact does no more than chisel a historically specific point of stress into the unresolved issue of voluntarity – almost no individual practice in our culture by now remains exempt. The development of recent thought related to food is a good example: the concept of addiction to food led necessarily to that of addiction to dieting and in turn to that of addiction to exercise: each assertion of *will* made voluntarity itself appear problematical in a new area, with the consequence that that assertion of will itself came to appear addictive. (In fact, there has recently been a spate of journalism asserting that antiaddiction programs such as Alcoholics Anonymous and others modeled on it are addictive.) Some of the current self-help literature is explicit by now in saying that every extant form of behavior, desire, relationship, and consumption in our culture can accurately be described as addictive. Such a formulation does not, however, seem to lead these analysts to the perception that 'addiction' names a counter-structure always internal to the ethicizing hypostatization of 'voluntarity'; instead, it drives ever more blindly their compulsion to isolate some new space of the purely voluntary.

The 'decadence' of drug addiction, in these late nineteenth-century texts, intersects with two kinds of bodily definition, each itself suffused with the homo/heterosexual problematic. The first of these is the national economic body; the second is the medical body. From the Opium Wars of the mid-nineteenth century up to the current details of U.S. relations with Turkey, Colombia, Panama, Peru, and the Nicaraguan Contras, the drama of "foreign substances' and the drama of the new imperialisms and the new nationalisms have been quite inextricable. The integrity of (new and contested) national borders, the reifications of national will and vitality, were readily organized around these narratives of introjection. From as far back as Mandeville, moreover, the opium product – the highly condensed, portable, expensive, commerce-intensive substance seen as having a unique ability to pry the trajectory of demand conclusively and increasingly apart from the homeostasis of biological need – was spectacularly available to serve as a representation for emerging intuitions about commodity fetishism. The commodity-based orientalism of *Dorian Gray*, for instance, radiates outward from 'a green paste, waxy in lustre, the odour curiously heavy and persistent' that represents an ultimate recourse for Dorian – outward through its repository, 'a small Chinese box of black and gold-dust lacquer, elaborately wrought, the sides patterned with curved waves, and the silken cords hung with round crystals and tasselled inplaited metal threads' – outward through the 'Florentine cabinet, made out of ebony, and inlaid with ivory and blue lapis,' from whose triangular secret drawer his fingers move 'instinctively' to extract the box (201–2). Like Wagnerian opera, *Dorian Gray* accomplished for its period the performative work of enabling a European community of gay mutual recognition and self-constitution at least partly by popularizing a consumerism that already derived an economic model from the traffic in drugs.

Take an example from the prodigally extravagant guide to lifestyle, interior decoration, and textiles offered in *Dorian Gray's* aptly titled Chapter 11. A whole set of epistemological compactions around desire, identification, and the responsive, all but paranoid mutuality attributed to gay recognition are condensed in the almost compulsive evocation there, even more than elsewhere in the novel, of the drug-tinged adjectives 'curious' and 'subtle,' two of the Paterian epithets that trace in *Dorian Gray* the homosexual-homophobic path of simultaneous epistemological heightening and ontological evacuation. Unlike the cognate labels attached so nearly inalienably to Claggart in *Billy Budd*, these adjectives float freely through the text: 'some curious dream' (8), 'this curious artistic idolatry' (17), 'throbbing to curious pulses' (26), 'a subtle magic' (26), 'his subtle smile' (27), 'a curious charm' (28), 'a subtle fluid or a strange perfume' (44), 'so curious a chance' (44), 'women … are curious' (55), 'a mad curiosity' (57), 'a curious influence' (61), 'some curious romance' (63), 'a subtle sense of pleasure' (64), 'poisons so subtle' (66), 'the curious hard logic of passion' (66), 'some curious race-instinct' (77), 'curious Renaissance tapestries' (102), 'pleasures subtle and secret' (119), 'the curious secret of his life' (136), 'curious unpictured sins whose very mystery lent them their subtlety and their charm' (137), 'metaphors as monstrous as orchids, and as subtle in colour' (140), 'subtle symphonic arrangements of exotic flowers' (144), 'that curious indifference that is not incompatible with a real ardour of temperament' (147), 'their subtle fascination' (148), 'a curious pleasure' (148), 'a curious delight' (150), and so on apparently endlessly. Besides being almost violently piquant and uninformative, 'curious' shares with 'subtle' a built-in epistemological indecision or doubling. Each of them can describe, as the *OED* puts it, 'an object of interest': among the *OED* meanings for this sense of 'curious' are 'made with care or art, delicate, *recherché*, elaborate, unduly minute, abstruse, subtle, exquisite, exciting curiosity … queer. (The ordinary current objective sense).' At the same time, however, each adjective also describes, and in almost the same terms, the quality of the perception brought by the attentive subject to such an object: for 'curious' 'as a subjective quality of persons,' the *OED* lists, e.g., 'careful, attentive, anxious, cautious, inquisitive, prying, subtle.' The thing known is a reflection of the impulse toward knowing it, then, and each describable only as the excess, 'wrought' intensiveness of that knowledge-situation.

In their usage in the fetish-wrought Chapter 11, the epithets record, on the one hand, the hungrily inventive raptness of the curious or subtle perceiving eye or brain; and, on the other, the more than answering intricacy of the curious or subtle objects perceived – imported or plundered artifacts, in these typifying cases, whose astonishing density of jewels and 'wrought' work such as embroidery testify, more than to taste, to the overt atrocities they sometimes depict, and most of all to the 'monstrous,' 'strange,' 'terrible' (I use the Wildean terms) exactions of booty in precious minerals, tedious labor, and sheer wastage of (typically female) eyesight, levied on the Orient by the nations of Europe. 'Yet, after some time, he wearied of them, and would sit in his box at the Opera, either alone or with Lord Henry, listening in rapt pleasure to "Tannhauser"' (150).

Still, it would be reductive to confine the national question embodied in the sexuality of *Dorian Gray* to an exercise in orientalism. Indeed, the very patency of Wilde's gay-affirming and gay-occluding orientalism renders it difficult to turn back and see the outlines of the sexual body and the national body sketched by his *occidentalism*. With orientalism so ready-to-hand a rubric for the relation to the Other, it is difficult (Wilde seems to want to make it difficult) to resist seeing the desired English body as simply the domestic Same. Yet the sameness of this Same – or put another way, the *homo-* nature of this sexuality – is no less open to question than the self-identicalness of the national borders of the domestic. After all, the question of the national in Wilde's own life only secondarily – though profoundly – involved the question of overseas empire in relation to European *patria*. To the contrary: Wilde, as an ambitious Irish man, and the son, intimate, and protégé of a celebrated Irish nationalist poet, can only have had as a fundamental element of his own sense of self an exquisitely exacerbated sensitivity to how by turns porous, brittle, elastic, chafing, embracing, exclusive, murderous, in every way contestable and contested were the membranes of 'domestic' national definition signified by the ductile and elusive terms England, Britain, Ireland. Indeed, the consciousness of foundational and/or incipient national *difference* already internal to national *definition* must have been part of what Wilde literally embodied, in the expressive, specularized, and symptomatic relation in which he avowedly stood to his age. As a magus in the worship of the 'slim rose-gilt soul' – the individual or generic figure of the 'slim thing, gold-haired like an angel' that stood at the same time for a sexuality, a sensibility, a class, and a narrowly English national type – Wilde, whose own physical make was of an opposite sort and (in that context) an infinitely less appetizing, desirable, and placeable one, showed his usual uncanny courage ('his usual uncanny courage,' *anglice* chutzpah) in foregrounding his own body so insistently as an index to such erotic and political meanings. Wilde's alienizing physical heritage of unboundable bulk from his Irish nationalist mother, of a louche swarthiness from his Celticizing father, underlined with every self-foregrounding gesture of his person and *persona* the fragility, unlikelihood, and strangeness – at the same time, the transformative reperceptualizing power – of the new '*homo-*' homosexual imagining of male-male desire. By the same pressure, it dramatized the uncouth nonequivalence of an English national body with a British with an Irish, as domestic grounds from which to launch a stable understanding of national/imperial relations.

[…]

The chapter ends with a three-page section, 'Health/Illness', on Nietzsche's figuration of decadence in terms of the human body.

Notes (cut and renumbered)

1. Oscar Wilde, *The Picture of Dorian Gray* (Harmondsworth, Middlesex: Penguin, 1949), p. 7. Further citations are incorporated in parentheses in the text.
2. Gore Vidal, 'A Good Man and a Perfect Play' (review of Richard Ellmann, *Oscar Wilde*), *Times Literary Supplement* (October 2–8, 1987): 1063.
3. *The Complete Works of Oscar Wilde* (Twickenham, Middlesex: Hamlyn, 1963), pp. 732, 735. Further quotations from this edition will cite it as *Complete* in the text.
4. William Cowper, 'The Castaway,' lines 64–66, in the *Complete Poetical Works of William Cowper*, ed. H. S. Milford (Oxford: Humphrey Milford, 1913), p. 652.
5. If, at any rate, under this new definitional possibility, that which I *am* and that which I *desire* may no longer be assumed to be distinct, then each one of those terms can be subjected to the operations of slippage. We have seen how both Wilde and Nietzsche camouflage what seem to be the male objects of male desire as, 'ultimately,' mere reflections of a divided 'self.' But it can work in the other direction: the *homo*-construction also makes a language in which a man who desires may claim to take on some of the lovable attributes of the man desired. In Nietzsche, for example, the unimaginable distance between the valetudinarian philosopher who desires, and the bounding 'masters of the earth' whom he desires, is dissolved so resolutely by the force of his rhetoric that it is startling to be reminded that 'Homer would not have created Achilles, nor Goethe Faust, if Homer had been an Achilles, or Goethe a Faust' (*Genealogy*, 235). And, as we shall see, Wilde presents a similar double profile.
6. For Nietzsche, whose literary impulses aren't in that sense modernist, the desired male figure never ceases to be visible as a male figure, except, as we've noted, in those instances where the sense of sight is willfully suppressed.
7. *Dorian Gray*, p. 236.
8. This discussion of will and addiction, and what follows on opium as a figure for imperialist relations, builds on the discussion in Chapter 10 of *Between Men* cf. Headnote above, 'Up the Postern Stair: *Edwin Drood* and the Homophobia of Empire,' pp. 180–200.

5.2 JONATHAN DOLLIMORE: FROM *SEXUAL DISSIDENCE* (1991)

Jonathan Dollimore is a professor in the School of English and American Studies at the University of Sussex. He has been among the foremost figures in promoting gay studies in the UK especially, and has written extensively (sometimes with Alan Sinfield) on homosexuality within cultural history. His other books include (with Alan Sinfield) ed., *Political Shakespeare: New Essays in Cultural Materialism* (1985), and *Radical Tragedy: Religion, Ideology and Power in the Drama of Shakespeare and his Contemporaries* (1989). With Sinfield and others (e.g. Catherine Belsey and Francis Barker), Dollimore has also been at the centre of the British inflection of 'new historicism' (see Headnotes in Chs 1 and 2, on *Hamlet* and the 'Ode', especially pp. 54, 91), focusing its principal area of study, like part of the American movement, on the literary culture of the English Renaissance and the early seventeenth century. Influenced by Althusser, Foucault and Raymond Williams (q.v.; from whom they took the term 'cultural materialism'), these critics have developed a more politically radical and less pessimistic analysis of the Renaissance ideological and cultural totality than the American version seems to present. They see all histories as containing 'resistances', as well as subjections, and therefore value marginalized and subversive elements as signs that the dominant ideologies' power to proscribe change will always be resisted. They also see the meanings of literary texts as never finally 'appropriated' by one interest, and therefore open to provisional appropriation by themselves as cultural materialists. A critical account of this school of criticism is Scott Wilson, *Cultural Materialism in Theory and in Practice* (Blackwell, 1995).

    Sexual Dissidence: Augustine to Wilde, Freud to Foucault is a wide-ranging study of the place and effects of homosexuality in literature and society, and appeared the year after Sedgwick's book above. Together they mark the coming-of-age of a sophisticated 'queer' theory and practice. Dollimore mounts an oblique and allusive argument, often combining analysis of Wilde with a discussion of André Gide. The present excerpts, which retain their sub-section headings, are taken from across the book, and are intended to bring into bold relief Dollimore's treatment of Wilde in terms of his foundational theoretical concept of a 'transgressive aesthetic'. He says (pp. 20–2) that he himself regards the book as an example of 'cultural materialism', despite being at an 'intersection of diverse perspectives', and that it is about the various transgressions of, and resistances to, the 'language, ideologies, and cultures of domination' – in particular, those of 'sexual dissidence'. Explore the two 'sides' of Dollimore's criticism. Are his cultural materialism and 'transgressive aesthetics' consonant with each other? What is the nature – and result – of Dollimore's reading of Wilde? What do you think is the rationale for his mode of presenting his argument as you perceive it here? Why does he have a sub-section on 'Wilde and English Studies'? What is the *historical* prerogative, in the last extract, for recuperating Wilde for modernism and postmodernism? Compare his work, finally, with that of Levinson, the North American 'new historicist' (see Ch. 2, pp. 91–106); and, in the immediate context, with Sedgwick; draw out similarities and differences between them. Attempt a reading – informed by the notion of a transgressive aesthetic – of another text in another exercise (e.g. by Salman Rushdie).

The following excerpts from *Sexual Dissidence*, Oxford University Press, 1991, are: Ch. 1 ('Wilde and Gide in Algiers'), pp. 10–11, 14–17; Ch. 4 – complete – pp. 64–73; and Ch. 20 ('Post/modern: On the Gay Sensibility, or the Pervert's Revenge on Authority–Wilde, Genet, Orton and Others'), pp. 308–10. For the parenthetical references throughout the text, see the list of 'Works Cited' at the end.

Sexual Dissidence

From Ch. I. Four short sections precede this excerpt.

Art versus Life
Key concepts in Wilde's aesthetic are protean and shifting, especially when paradoxically and facetiously deployed. When, for example, he speaks of life – 'poor, probable, uninteresting human life' ('Decay', 305) – or reality as that to which art is opposed, he means different things at different times. But one of the most interesting and significant referents of concepts like life and reality, as Wilde uses them, is not so much the pre-social, or what transcends the social, as the prevailing social order. Even nature, conceived as the opposite of culture and art, retains a social dimension (e.g. 'Critic', 394, 399), especially when it signifies nature as ideological mystification of the social; that is why, for Wilde, anyone trying to be natural is posing, and embarrassingly so, since they are trying to mystify the social as natural (*Dorian Gray*, 10–11).

Nature and reality signify a prevailing order which art wilfully, perversely, and rightfully ignores, and which the critic negates, subverts, and transgresses. Thus, for example, the person of culture is concerned to give 'an accurate description of what has never occurred', while the critic sees 'the object as in itself it really is not' ('Critic', 343, 368; Wilde is here inverting the proposition which opens Arnold's famous essay 'The Function of Criticism at the Present Time'). Not surprisingly then, criticism and art are aligned with individualism against a conservative social order; a passage which indicates this is important also in indicating the basis of Wilde's aesthetic of transgressive desire: 'Art is Individualism and Individualism is a *disturbing and disintegrating force*. Therein lies its immense value. For what it seeks to disturb is monotony of type, slavery of custom, tyranny of habit' ('Soul', 272, my emphasis). Art is also self-conscious and critical; in fact, 'self-consciousness and the critical spirit are one' ('Critic', 356). And art, like individualism, is orientated towards the realm of transgressive desire: 'What is abnormal in Life stands in normal relations to Art. It is the only thing in Life that stands in normal relations to Art' ('Maxims', 1203). One who inhabits that realm, 'the cultured and fascinating liar', is both an object and source of desire ('Decay', 292, 305). The liar is important because he or she contradicts not just conventional morality, but its sustaining origin, 'truth'. So art runs to meet the liar, kissing his 'false beautiful lips, knowing that he alone is in possession of the great secret of all her manifestations, the secret that Truth is entirely and absolutely a matter of style'. Truth, the epistemological legitimation of the real, is rhetorically subordinated to its antitheses – appearance, style, the lie – and thereby simultaneously both appropriated, perverted, and displaced. Reality, also necessarily devalued and demystified by the loss of truth, must imitate art, while life must meekly follow the liar (p. 305).

Further, life is at best an energy which can only find expression through the forms which art offers it. But form is another slippery and protean category in Wilde's aesthetic. In one sense Wilde is a proto-structuralist: 'Form is the beginning of things

... The Creeds are believed, not because they are rational, but because they are repeated ... Form is everything ... Do you wish to love? Use Love's Litany, and the words will create the yearning from which the world fancies that they spring' ('Critic', 399). Here form is virtually synonymous with culture, and the supposed natural cause shown to be cultural effect. Moreover, it is a passage in which Wilde recognizes the priority of the social and the cultural in determining not only public meaning but 'private' or subjective desire. This means that for Wilde, although desire is deeply at odds with society in its existing forms, it does not exist as a pre-social authenticity; it is always within, and informed by, the very culture which it also transgresses.

[...]

A two-page section on Gide is omitted here.

[...]

Paradox and Perversity
The contrast between Gide and Wilde is striking: not only are Wilde's conceptions of subjectivity and desire anti-essentialist but so too – and consequently – is his advocacy of transgression. It is as if deviant desire, rather than creating a new integrity of self, actually decentres or disperses the self, and the liberation is experienced as being, in part, just that. Wilde's experience of deviant desire, though no less intense than Gide's, leads him not to escape the repressive ordering of society, but to a reinscription within it, and an inversion of the binaries upon which that ordering depends; desire, and the transgressive aesthetic which it fashions, reacts against, disrupts, and displaces from within.[1]

For Gide transgression is in the name of a desire and identity rooted in the natural, the sincere, and the authentic; Wilde's transgressive aesthetic is the reverse: insincerity, inauthenticity, and unnaturalness become the liberating attributes of decentred identity and desire, and inversion becomes central to Wilde's expression of this aesthetic – as can be seen from a selection of his *Phrases and Philosophies for the Use of the Young* (1894):

> If one tells the truth, one is sure, sooner or later to be found out.
> Only the shallow know themselves.
> To be premature is to be perfect.
> It is only the superficial qualities that last.
> Man's deeper nature is soon found out.
> To love oneself is the beginning of a lifelong romance. (pp. 433–4)

In Wilde's writings a non-centred or vagrant desire is both the impetus for a subversive inversion, and what is released by it. Perhaps the most general inversion in his work operates on that most dominating of binaries, nature/culture; more specifically the attributes on the left are substituted for those on the right:

X	for	Y
surface		depth
lying		truth

change	stasis
difference	essence
persona/role	essential self
abnormal	normal
insincerity	sincerity
style/artifice	authenticity
facetious	serious
narcissism	maturity

For Michel in *The Immoralist* and to an extent for Gide himself, desire may be proscribed but this does not affect its authenticity or its naturalness; if anything it confirms them. It is society which is inauthentic. In a sense then, deviant desire is legitimated in terms of culture's opposite, nature, or, in a different but related move, in terms of something which is pre-cultural and so always more than cultural. So Gide shares with the dominant culture an investment in the *Y* column above; he appropriates its categories for the subordinate. In contrast, for Wilde transgressive desire is both rooted in culture and the impetus for affirming different/alternative kinds of culture (*X* column). From an essentialist point of view, Wilde's position might seem to rest on a confusion: how can the desire which culture outlaws itself be thoroughly cultural? In fact it is because and not in spite of this shared cultural dimension that Wilde can enact one of the most disturbing of all forms of transgression, namely that whereby the outlaw turns up as inlaw, and the other as proximate proves more disturbing than the other as absolute difference. That which society forbids, Wilde reinstates *through and within* some of its most cherished and central cultural categories – art, the aesthetic, art criticism, individualism. At the same time as he appropriates those categories he also transvalues them through perversion and inversion, thus making them now signify those binary exclusions (*X* column) by which the dominant culture knows itself (thus abnormality is not just the opposite, but the necessarily always present antithesis of normality). It is an uncompromising inversion, this being the (perversely) appropriate strategy for a transgressive desire which is of its 'nature', according to this culture, an 'inversion'.

Of inversion's specific targets, perhaps the most important is *depth*. As can be seen from the *Phrases and Philosophies* just quoted, Wilde insistently subverts those dominant categories which signify subjective depth. Such categories (*Y* column) are precisely those which ideologically identify (inform) the mature adult individual. And they too operate in terms of their inferior opposite: the individual knows what he – I choose the masculine pronoun deliberately – is in contrast to what he definitely is not or must not be. In Wilde's inversions, the excluded inferior term returns as the now superior term of a related series of binaries. Some further examples of Wilde's subversion of subjective depth:

A little sincerity is a dangerous thing, and a great deal of it is absolutely fatal. ('Critic', 393)

All bad poetry springs from genuine feeling. ('Critic', 398)

In matters of grave importance, style, not sincerity is the *vital* thing. (*Importance*, 83, my emphasis[2])

Only shallow people ... do not judge by appearances. (*Dorian Gray*, 29)

> Insincerity … is merely a method by which we can multiply our personalities. Such … was Dorian Gray's opinion. He used to wonder at the shallow psychology of those who conceived the Ego in man as a thing simple, permanent, reliable, and of one essence. To him man was a being with myriad lives and myriad sensations, a complex, multiform creature … (*Dorian Gray*, 158–9)

At work here is a transgressive desire which makes its opposition felt as a disruptive reaction upon, and inversion of, the categories of subjective depth which hold in place the dominant order which proscribes that desire.[3] As Wilde himself remarked, there was here an intimate connection between perversity and paradox: 'What the paradox was to me in the sphere of thought, perversity became to me in the sphere of passion' (*De profundis*, 466). It was a connection to have far-reaching cultural effects.[4]

In *The Importance of Being Earnest* there is a wonderful repudiation of the depth model, and with a rather different effect:

> CECILY. How dare you? This is no time for wearing the shallow mask of manners. When I see a spade I call it a spade.
> GWENDOLEN. I am glad to say that I have never seen a spade. It is obvious that our social spheres have been widely different. (II. 675–9)

Cecily tries to take over what we might call the high ground of the straightforward as opposed to the low ground of the shallow, the mannered and the duplicitous. But if being natural is only an infuriating pose (*Dorian Gray*, 10–11), so too is being straightforward, and especially since it too masquerades as naturalness. Gwendolen, in a response which shows so memorably that there may be more to snobbery than ignorant condescension, repudiates the implied opposition and kicks Cecily straight back into the domain of class, into the 'social sphere'. Never has a spade been so effectively 'defamiliarized'. Compare Wilde's use of the same idea in May 1892, when an alderman had praised him for calling a spade a spade. Wilde replied: 'I would like to protest against the statement that I have ever called a spade a spade. The man who did so should be condemned to use one' (Ellmann, *Oscar Wilde* (1987), 347).

[…]

A brief coda on Gide completes the chapter.

[…]

The following is Ch. 4 (complete).

Wilde's Transgressive Aesthetic and Contemporary Culture Politics

The politics of inversion
Wilde's transgressive aesthetic relates to contemporary theoretical debates in at least three respects: first, the dispute about whether the inversion of binary opposites

subverts, or, on the contrary, reinforces the order which those binaries uphold; second, the political importance – or irrelevance – of decentring the subject; third, post-modernism and one of its more controversial features: the so-called disappearance of the depth model, especially the model of a deep human subjectivity, and the cultural and political ramifications of this. Since the three issues closely relate to each other, I shall take them together.

It is said that Wildean inversion disturbs nothing; by merely reversing the terms of the binary, inversion remains within its limiting framework: an inverted world can only be righted, not changed. Moreover, the argument might continue, Wilde's paradoxes are superficial in the pejorative sense of being inconsequential, of making no difference. There are two responses to this, one theoretical, the other historical. I shall take the theoretical first, since it is necessarily both a general question about deconstruction, and a specific question about the binary and its inversion.

It is an achievement of deconstruction to show the limitations of binary logic in theory and its often pernicious effects in practice; to show how binaries, far from being eternal necessities of cultural organization, or essential, unavoidable attributes of human thought, are unstable constructs whose antithetical terms presuppose, and can therefore be used against, each other. Meaning becomes an effect of difference and deferral. Because its terms are vulnerable to inversion and its structure (via inversion) to displacement, the continued existence of the binary is never guaranteed; it has to be maintained, often in and through struggles over representation. In particular, the terms of the dominant/subordinate binary never denote homogeneous static blocs; the dominant is only ever the more powerful and (possibly) repressive side of a shifting relationship or series of relationships which interconnect, often asymmetrically. Thus any individual typically occupies diverse subject positions, some of which may be dominant, some subordinate.[5] All this is crucial for a study like this one, concerned as it is with several of the binaries which powerfully organize our cultures: natural/unnatural, masculine/feminine, hetero/homosexual; with what hold them in place socially, and what is necessarily disavowed in their political effectiveness – with, in other words, what enables them to endure and yet also renders them unstable.

But we should not deceive ourselves into thinking that to deconstruct these binaries somehow neutralizes their effect in history and/or the here and now. That is an instance of how the indispensability of theory can be deflected into a 'theoreticist' evasion of what it might most effectively challenge. Binaries remain fundamental to, and violently active within, social organization and discursive practices,[6] more so than we usually realize as we live and suffer them daily. But how, then, are they challenged?

Derrida has insisted that metaphysics can only be contested from within, by disrupting its structures and redirecting its force against itself. He defines the binary opposition as a 'violent hierarchy' (*Positions*, 41) where one of the two terms forcefully governs the other, and insists that a crucial stage in the deconstruction of binaries involves their inversion, an overturning, which brings low what was high. In effect inversion of the binary is a necessary stage in its displacement:

> I strongly and repeatedly insist on the necessity of the phase of reversal, which people have perhaps too swiftly attempted to discredit ... To neglect this phase of reversal is to forget that the structure of the opposition is one of conflict and subordination and thus to pass too swiftly, without gaining any purchase against the former opposition, to a *neutralization* which *in practice* leaves things in their former state and deprives one of any way of *intervening* effectively.[7]

Wilde's inversions, operating to subvert a deeply conservative authenticity and the deep subjectivity on which it is premissed, were overturnings in Derrida's sense.

Someone famous once said that people make their own history but not in conditions of their own choosing. I think Derrida is saying something similar when he adds that the political effect of failing to invert the binary opposition, of trying simply to jump beyond it into a world free of it, is simply to leave the binary intact in the only world we have. Despite this emphasis in Derrida, some of his adherents still want to make that jump, insisting that the inversion of a binary achieves nothing, and opting instead for its ahistorical, conceptual deconstruction. Thus in his account of sexual difference and homosexuality, Robert Young declares that the reversal of a binary 'only remains within its terms and does not challenge it – in fact it only perpetuates it' ('The Same Difference', especially p. 87).

Of course, inversion is only a stage in a process of resistance whose effects can never be guaranteed and perhaps not even predicted. (In)subordinate inversions, if at all successful, provoke reaction. The result is a cultural struggle between unevenly matched contenders, a struggle in which the dominant powers, which transgressive inversion fiercely disturbs, now react equally fiercely against it. But the case of Wilde suggests why, as a strategy of cultural struggle, binary inversion so often provokes such reaction. In actual historical instances, the inversion is not just the necessary precondition for the binary's subsequent displacement, but often already constitutes a displacement, if not directly of the binary itself, then certainly of the moral and political norms which cluster dependently around its dominant pole and in part constitute it. Because in any historical instance the binary holds in place more than it actually designates, its inversion typically has effects beyond itself: inversion may for instance give impetus to cultures denigrated by its subordinate term, and simultaneously throw into disarray the cultures officially sanctioned by its dominant term. Robert Young's article, even as it clearly indicates the importance of Derrida's concept of *différance* for issues of gender, is also an instance of the limitations of the deconstructive trope followed through in abstraction and independently of any historical reference. The limitation is especially marked here, where the most informative work on inversion as a strategy of sexual transgression has been historically grounded in the early modern period.[8]

Reconsidering inversion in the light of this history is also to restore to it dimensions absent from its sexological and psychoanalytic uses. Kunzle, for instance, discussing the iconography of the world-turned-upside-down broadsheets, offers a conclusion which registers the complex potential of inversion and is thereby nicely suggestive for understanding Wilde: 'Revolution appears disarmed by playfulness, the playful bears the seed of revolution. "Pure" formal fantasy and subversive desire, far from being mutually exclusive, are two sides of the same coin' ('World Turned Upside Down', 89).

Notoriously, some of Wilde's contemporaries were not disarmed by his playfulness. In the first of the three trials involving Wilde in 1895, he was cross-examined on his *Phrases and Philosophies* (cited above, Chapter 1), the implication of opposing counsel being that its elegant binary inversions, along with *Dorian Gray*, were 'calculated to subvert morality and encourage unnatural vice' (Hyde, *Oscar Wilde*, 271). There is a sense in which evidence cannot get more material than this, and it remains so whatever our retrospective judgement about the crassness of the thinking behind such a view. Observe also how quickly the spurious distinction I offered a moment ago between the theoretical and the historical responses has already broken down: the theoretical issue has already become a historical one, and in a way which I welcome given the objective of this study to argue for, and exemplify, a cross-reading between theory and history.

One of the many reasons why people were terrified by Wilde was because of a perceived connection between his aesthetic transgression and his sexual transgression. 'Inversion' was being used increasingly to define a specific kind of deviant sexuality inseparable from a deviant personality. As an aspect of this development Foucault has described the change I have had occasion to remark already, namely the way the homosexual had become a species of being whereas before sodomy had been an aberration of behaviour (*History*, 43; [...]). In fact, the transition he describes was more complicated than he allows, occurring over a greater period of time, and even then (and still now) with cultural and class distinctions. But it is true that, by the time of Wilde, homosexuality could be regarded as rooted in a person's identity and as pathologically pervading all aspects of his being. As such the expression of homosexuality might be regarded as the more *intentionally* insidious and subversive. Hence in part the animosity and hysteria directed at Wilde during and after his trial. He was attacked by the press (in the words of one editorial) for subverting the 'wholesome, manly simple ideals of English life'. Moreover his 'abominable vices ... were the natural outcome of his diseased intellectual condition'. Sexual perversion is inseparable from intellectual and moral corruption. No wonder the same editorial also imagined Wilde as the leader of a subculture in London, comprised of like-minded, but younger men (Hyde, *Trials*, 12).

This feared cross-over between discursive and sexual perversion, politics and pathology, has sanctioned terrible brutalities against the homosexual; at the same time, at least in this period, it was also becoming the medium for what, following Foucault, might be called a reverse or counter-discourse (*History*, 101, [...]), giving rise to what I explored in Wilde in Chapter 1 – a transgressive aesthetic working through a politics of inversion/perversion (again crossing over and between the different senses of these words).

We begin to see then why Wilde was hated with such an intensity, even though he rarely advocated in his published writings any explicitly immoral practice. What kept those 'wholesome, manly simple ideals of English life' in place were traditional and conservative ideas of what constituted human nature and human subjectivity, and it was these that Wilde attacked: not so much conventional morality itself as the ideological anchor points for that morality, namely notions of identity as subjective depth which manifest themselves in these newspaper reports as wholesomeness, right reason, seriousness, etc., and whose criteria appear in the *Y* column above (Chapter 1). Here, generally, as with Gide more specifically, Wilde's transgressive aesthetic subverted the dominant categories of subjectivity which kept desire in subjection, subverted the essentialist categories of identity which kept morality in place. And even though there may now be a temptation to patronize and indeed dismiss both the Victorians' wholesome, manly, simple ideals of English life and Wilde's inversion of them, the fact remains that, in successively reconstituted forms, those ideals, together with the subject positions which instantiate them, came to form the moral and ethical base of English Studies in our own century and indeed remain culturally central today.

Wilde and English Studies
I am thinking here not just of the organicist ideology so characteristic of an earlier phase of English Studies, one which led, for example, to the celebration of Shakespeare's alleged 'national culture, rooted in the soil and appealing to a multi-class audience', but more specifically of what Chris Baldick in his useful study goes on to call its more enduring 'subjective correlative', namely, the 'maintenance of the *doctrine of psychic wholeness in and through literature as an analogue for a projected harmony and order in society*' (Baldick, *Social Mission*, 213–18, my emphasis).

For I. A. Richards all human problems (continues Baldick) become problems of mental health with art as the cure, and literary criticism becomes 'a question of attaining the right state of mind to judge other minds, according to their degree of immaturity, inhibition, or perversion'. Richards advocates sincerity as 'the quality we most insistently require in poetry', and also 'the quality we most need as critics' (Richards, quoted from Baldick, *Social Mission*, 215). As a conception of both art and criticism, this is the reverse of Wilde's. Similarly with the Leavises, for whom an equally imperative concept was the related one of 'maturity', and one unhappy consequence of which was their promotion of the 'fecund' D. H. Lawrence against the 'perverse' W. H. Auden. As Baldick goes on to observe, 'this line of critics is not only judicial in tone but positively inquisitorial, indulging in a kind of perversion-hunting' which is itself rooted in 'a simple model of [pre- or anti-Freudian] normality and mental consistency' (Baldick, *Social Mission*, 217).

A more sophisticated development of this line of thought persists today. It addresses sexual deviation rather more directly, finding in its putative inadequacy the origin of a debilitating failure of aesthetic vision. As such this criticism bears out Michel Foucault's argument that there has emerged in recent times a belief in profound connections between sex and truth. This belief has two particular manifestations: first, that sexual deviation is thought to be a deviation from the truth; this is a truth embodied in, and really only accessible to, normality, with the result that, even if sexual deviants are to be tolerated, 'there is still something like an "error" involved in what they do ... a manner of acting that is not adequate to reality'. Its second manifestation is the conviction that 'it is in the area of sex that we must search for the most secret and profound truths about the individual' (*Herculine Barbin*, pp. x–xi).

Many instances of this belief might be cited from evidently dated literary criticism. Consider instead a couple of more recent examples. Jan B. Gordon brings the full weight of a 'phenomenological' perspective to bear on Wilde, finding that

> The homosexual in jail ... is the ultimate reduction of the self-contained, reflex image. And *De Profundis* is the confession of an individual no longer capable of distinguishing self from false self, where all subjects have become objects. Oscar Wilde's condition, in brief, is the one art form where parody, gossip, the epigram, failed development manifested in the denial of growth, and the dehumanization that is part of the pornographic experience all conspire in an utterance that is the pretence of a failed autobiography. ('Decadent Spaces', 53)

In another essay in the same volume, on Swinburne's 'circle of desire', Chris Snodgrass concludes that 'incest – with its correlate, homosexuality – is, of course, the paramount sexual symbol for "loss of difference"' (p. 82). Such criticism, even where it does not explicitly endorse it, relates to the critical perspective which sought to build an entire world view on the doctrine of psychic wholeness, personal maturity, a firm grasp of the actual, and, where appropriate, a defence of hetero/ sexual difference against the undifferentiation of sexual perversion. It is a perspective subjected to fairly relentless critiques in recent years. In particular, its belief in the ontological, epistemological, and ethical primacy of subjective integration, and in the profound connections between sex and truth, have been attacked by one or more of the major movements within contemporary critical theory.

And yet Wilde's challenge to this critical/ethical vision is still largely excluded from consideration; worse, he is still subjected to the judgement of that older vision in its updated yet hardly more discerning mode, as in the examples above. That 'theory' has not rediscovered Wilde is strange, given that we have passed beyond that heady and in many ways justified moment when it seemed that only Continental theory had the necessary force to displace the complacencies of our own tradition. It is also ironic, because even when looking so intently to the Continent, we failed to notice that Wilde was, and remains, a very significant figure there (Pfister, *Oscar Wilde*). And not only there: while the *Spectator* (February 1891) thought 'The Soul of Man under Socialism' was a joke in bad taste, the essay soon became extremely successful in Russia, appearing in many successive editions across the next twenty years. Perhaps, then, there exists or has existed a kind of 'muscular theory', one which shares with the critical movements it has displaced a significant blindness with regard to Wilde and what he represented. If so this almost certainly has something to do with the persistence of an earlier attempt to rid literature and English Studies of a perceived 'feminized' identity.[9] It may also be because, rather than in spite of, the legendary status of Wilde. Whatever, one aim of this book is to argue that Wilde needs to be rescued from some of his admirers and radically rethought by some at least of his critics.

Decentred subjectivity and the post-modern

Recent critics of post-modernism, including Fredric Jameson, Ihab Hassan, Dan Latimer, and Terry Eagleton,[10] have written intriguingly on one of its defining criteria: the disappearance of the depth model. Eagleton offers an important and provocative critique of post-modernism: 'confidently post-metaphysical [it] has outlived all that fantasy of interiority, that pathological itch to scratch surfaces for concealed depths'. With the post-modern there is no longer any subject to be alienated and nothing to be alienated from, 'authenticity having been less rejected than merely forgotten'. The subject of post-modern culture is 'a dispersed, decentred network of libidinal attachments, emptied of ethical substance and psychical interiority, the ephemeral function of this or that act of consumption, media experience, sexual relationship, trend or fashion'. Modernism, by contrast, is (or was) still preoccupied with the experience of alienation, with metaphysical depth and/or the psychic fragmentation and social wretchedness consequent upon the realization that there is no metaphysical depth or (this being its spiritual instantiation) authentic unified subject. As such, modernism is 'embarrassingly enmortgaged to the very bourgeois humanism it otherwise seeks to subvert'; it is 'a deviation still enthralled to a norm, parasitic on what it sets out to deconstruct'. But, concludes Eagleton, the subject of late capitalism is actually neither the 'self regulating synthetic agent posited by classical humanist ideology, nor merely a decentred network of desire [as posited by post-modernism] but a contradictory amalgam of the two'. And if in one respect the decentred, dispersed subject of post-modernism is suspiciously convenient to our own phase of late capitalism, it follows that those post-structuralist theorists who stake all on the assumption that the unified subject is still integral to contemporary bourgeois ideology, and that it is always a politically radical act to decentre and deconstruct that subject, need to think again (Eagleton, 'Capitalism, Modernism and Postmodernism', 143, 132, 145, 143–5).

   Eagleton's argument can be endorsed with yet further important distinctions. First, even though the unified subject was indeed an integral part of an earlier phase of bourgeois ideology, the instance of Gide and the tradition he represents must indicate that it was never even then exclusively in the service of dominant ideologies. Indeed, to the extent that Gide's essentialist legitimation of homosexual desire was primarily an affirmation of his own nature as pederast or paedophile, some critics might usefully rethink their own assumption that essentialism is fundamentally and always a conservative philosophy. In Gide we find essentialism in the service of a radical sexual nonconformity which was and remains largely outlawed by conventional and dominant sexual ideologies, be they bourgeois or socialist. Also, it needs only a glance at the complex and often contradictory histories of sexual liberation movements in our own time to see that they have sometimes (and necessarily) embraced a radical essentialism with regard to their own identity (as does Eagleton's contradictory subject of late capitalism), while simultaneously offering an equally radical critique of the essentializing sexual ideologies responsible for their oppression.

This is important: the implication of Eagleton's argument is not just that we need to make our theories of subjectivity a little more sophisticated, but rather that we need to be more historical in our practice of theory. Only then can we see the dialectical complexities of social process and social struggle. How, for example, the very centrality of an essentialist concept to dominant ideology (e.g. 'the natural'), has made an appropriation of it for a subordinate culture seem indispensable in that culture's struggle for legitimacy; roughly speaking, this corresponds to Gide's position as I am representing it here. Conversely we also see how other subordinate cultures and voices seek not to appropriate dominant concepts and values so much as to sabotage, invert, and displace them. This is something we can see in Wilde. Today the Wildean strategy has re-emerged albeit in a changed form, while the Gidean politics of selfhood have suffered something of an eclipse. That is all the more reason to engage with the histories of both.

Anti-essentialist politics

The decentred subject of post-modernism contrasts vividly with Berman's summary of the modern individual in quest of authenticity [...]. But whether this post-modern subject is subversive of, alternative to, or indeed actually produced by, late capitalism, is an intriguing and important area of debate. What is certain though is that there are those today who are advancing as criteria of the post-modern what Wilde was using to scandalize his contemporaries in the 1890s. And those contemporaries exacted a heavy price: in a very real sense, Wilde's exploration of decentred desire, and the transgressive aesthetic which emerged from it, cost him his life. In 1898, complaining of his inability to write, Wilde tells Robert Ross, 'Something is killed in me ... Of course my first year in prison destroyed me body and soul. It could not have been otherwise' (*Letters*, 760).[11]

At the very least the case of Wilde will lead us to rethink the antecedents of the modern and the post-modern. Wilde prefigures elements of each while remaining importantly different from – and not just obviously prior to – both. If his transgressive aesthetic anticipates post-modernism to the extent that it suggests a culture of the surface, the decentred and the different, it also anticipates modernism in being not just hostile to, but intently concerned with, its opposite: depth and exclusive integration as fundamental criteria of identity. Yet unlike some versions of the post-modern, Wilde's transgressive aesthetic includes an acute political awareness and often an uncompromising political commitment;[12] and in contrast to modernism, his critique of the depth model is accompanied not by *Angst* but something utterly different and reminiscent of Barthes's *jouissance*, or what Borges has perceptively called Wilde's 'negligent glee ... the fundamental spirit of his work [being] joy' (Ellmann (ed.), *Oscar Wilde: Critical Essays*, 174). Gide spoke of Wilde similarly, identifying him with the sculptor in one of Wilde s own parables, smashing the statue of Grief he had previously made in order to make from it that of Joy (*Oscar Wilde*, 56).

The following is from Ch. 20. The first two pages challenge the notion of a 'homosexual sensibility'.

[...]

Michel Foucault argues that in the modern period sex has become definitive of the truth of our being [...]. As such, sexuality in its normative forms constitutes a 'truth' connecting inextricably with other truths and norms not explicitly sexual. This is a major reason why sexual deviance is found threatening: in deviating from normative truth and the 'nature' which underpins it, such deviance shifts and confuses the norms of truth and being throughout culture. Wilde's transgressive aesthetic simultaneously confirmed and exploited this inextricable connection between the sexual and the (apparently) non-sexual, between sexual perversion and social subversion, and does so through Wilde's own version of that connection: 'what pardox was to me in the sphere of thought, perversity became to me in the sphere of passion' (Wilde, *De Profundis*, 466).

If I had to give a single criterion of that dubious category, the homosexual sensibility, it would be this connection between perversity and paradox – if only because it suggests why that sensibility does not exist as such. As we have seen [...], Wilde's transgressive aesthetic writes desire into a discourse of liberation inseparable from an inversion and displacement of dominant categories of subjective depth (the depth model). It is from just these categories that notions of sensibility traditionally take their meaning. Additionally for Wilde, perverse desire is not only an agency of displacement, it is partly constituted by that displacement and the transgressive aesthetic which informs it. Just as in reverse discourse the categories of subordination are turned back upon the regimes of truth which disqualify, so this 'other' sensibility is in part affirmed as an inversion and absence of sensibility's traditional criteria. Perverse desire is transvalued, socially, sexually, and aesthetically. *Dorian Gray* describes moments when 'the passion for sin, or for what the world calls sin' is utterly overwhelming

> and conscience is either killed, or, if it lives at all, lives but to give rebellion its fascination, and disobedience its charm. For all sins, as theologians weary not of reminding us, are sins of disobedience. When that high spirit, that morning-star of evil, fell from heaven, it was as a rebel that he fell. (p. 210)

Law and conscience are subjected to the perverse dynamic, being made to enable and intensify the rebellion they were supposed to prevent; likewise with Wilde's transgressive aesthetic in the realm of desire and culture.

Wilde lived an anarchic and a political homosexuality simultaneously. Richard Ellmann describes him as 'conducting, in the most civilized way, an anatomy of his society, and a radical reconsideration of its ethics. ... His greatness as a writer is partly the result of the enlargement of sympathy which he demanded for society's victims' (*Oscar Wilde*, p. xiv). I agree, and this can stand as a cogent if incomplete description of what is meant by a political homosexuality. But Wilde also fashioned his transgressive aesthetic into a celebration of anarchic deviance, and this is yet another factor which makes it difficult to identify the sensibility involved. There is a positive desire to transgress and disrupt, and a destructiveness, even a running to one's own destruction, paradoxically creative. Though in a different way, what we have seen to be true of Gide was also true of Wilde: 'running foul of the law in his sexual life was a stimulus to thought on every subject. ... His new sexual direction liberated his art. It also liberated his critical faculty' (Ellmann, *Oscar Wilde*, 270).

Conformity angered and bored Wilde. It is not clear which, the anger or the boredom, was thought to be the more insulting, but both were expressed as that arrogance for which he was often hated. Yeats recalls receiving a letter from Lionel Johnson 'denouncing Wilde with great bitterness'; Johnson believed that Wilde got a '"sense of triumph and power, at every dinner-table he dominated, from the knowledge that he was guilty of that sin which, more than any other possible to man, would turn all those people against him if they but knew"' (Yeats, *Autobiographies*, 285). Maybe Johnson was paranoid; that does not stop him being correct. Gide at the end of his life remarked that Wilde only began to live after dark as it were, away from most of those who knew him (*So Be It*, 27). But the point here is that Wilde also lived in terms of the discrepancy between his 'public' and 'private' selves, and took pleasure from it – from having a sexual identity elsewhere at the same time as being socially 'here'.

The anarchic and the political, the anger and the boredom, are all active in Wilde's transgressive aesthetic, and most especially when the survival strategies of subordination – subterfuge, lying, evasion – are aesthetically transvalued into weapons of attack, but ever working obliquely through irony, ambiguity, mimicry, and impersonation.

[...]

By way of the notion of 'camp', the chapter goes on to deal with the other figures in its title – see Headnote.

Notes (cut and renumbered)
1. Ellmann suggests that inversion, or the turning of things inside out, was also crucial for Gide, this being the most important lesson that he learned from Wilde as a result of the latter's spiritual seduction of him ('Corydon and Ménalque', 100). But Gide contains inversion within the same kind of essentialist conviction which Wilde uses inversion to displace, while at the same time of course radically redefining the referent of that conviction.
2. In matters of grave importance: at the risk of being laborious we might spell out the way the proposition works: there is a simultaneous fourfold procedure: (1) sincerity is displaced by style; (2) the natural link between gravity and sincerity is undermined; (3) gravity and vitality are appropriated *for* style; and, (4) in the process, transvalued.
3. Wilde exploited that confusion – often paranoia – consequent upon a breakdown of Victorian 'sincerity' deriving in part from the social mobility and emergence of a consumerist economy described by Regenia Gagnier in *Idylls and the Market Place*. See also Bowlby, 'Promoting Dorian Gray'.

4. On the importance of this connection for the so-called gay sensibility, see below, Ch. 20.
5. Sedgwick gives a persuasive theoretical formulation of this perspective, and readings to substantiate it, in 'Across Gender', esp. 53–61.
6. I use 'discursive practice' to indicate the inseparability of cultural formations and the languages used within them; specifically, to denote the interrelationship of (1) representation of the social, (2) interpretation of the social, and (3) praxis within the social.
7. *Positions*, 41–2, quoted from Culler's translation in *On Deconstruction*, 165–6, which includes a crucial passage in Derrida's original – the first sentence of this quotation – left out of the Alan Bass translation. See also Derrida, *Grammatology*, pp. lxxvi–lxxviii, and Terdiman, *Discourse/Counter Discourse*, esp. introduction.
8. I have in mind especially Kunzle, 'World Turned Upside Down'; Hill, *The World Turned Upside Down*; Davis, 'Women on Top'; Stallybrass and White, *The Politics and Poetics of Transgression*; and Clark, 'Inversion, Misrule and the Meaning of Witchcraft'.
9. See Sinfield, *Literature, Politics and Culture in Post-War Britain*, ch. 5, esp. 63–4, 77–8.
10. Jameson, 'Postmodernism and Consumer Society', and 'Postmodernism, or the Cultural Logic of Late Capitalism'; Hassan, 'Pluralism in Postmodern Perspective'; Latimer, 'Jameson and Postmodernism'; Eagleton, 'Capitalism, Modernism and Postmodernism'.
11. Wilde is also recorded as having said that he died in prison (*Letters*, 493 n. 2).
12. Woodcock, in his biography of Wilde, writes interestingly of Wilde's political involvements, including his refusal to support racial prejudices or anti-Semitism and his relation to the Chicago anarchists of 1886 (see Woodcock, *The Paradox of Oscar Wilde*, esp. 138, 148–9).

Works Cited

Primary Texts

R. Ellman, ed., *The Artist as Critic: Critical Writings of Oscar Wilde*, W. H. Allen, 1970. Includes: ('Decay') 'The Decay of Lying', 1889; ('Critic') 'The Critic as Artist', 1890; ('Soul') 'The Soul of Man under Socialism', 1891; 'Phrases and Philosophies for the Use of the Young', 1894.
R. Hart-Davis, ed., *The Letters of Oscar Wilde*, Harcourt Brace, 1962. Includes: 'De Profundis', 1897.
Vyvyan Holland, ed., *The Complete Works of Oscar Wilde*, Collins, 1948. Includes: ('Maxims') 'A Few Maxims for the Instruction of the Overeducated', pp. 1203–4.
Oscar Wilde, ('Dorian Gray') *The Portrait of Dorian Gray*, Penguin, 1949.
Oscar Wilde, *The Importance of Being Earnest* (ed. R. Jackson), Ernest Benn, 1980.

Secondary Texts

Chris Baldick, *The Social Mission of English Criticism, 1848–1932*, Clarendon Press, 1983.
Rachel Bowlby, 'Promoting Dorian Gray', *Oxford Literary Review*, 9 (1987), pp. 147–62.
Stuart Clark, 'Inversion, Misrule and the Meaning of Witchcraft', *Past and Present*, 87 (1980), pp. 98–127.
Jonathan Culler, *On Deconstruction: Theory and Criticism after Structuralism*, Routledge, 1983.
Natalie Z. Davis, 'Women on Top: Symbolic Sexual Inversion and Political Disorder in Early Modern Europe', in B. Babcock, ed., *The Reversible World*, Cornell University Press, 1978.
Jacques Derrida, *Of Grammatology* (1967), trans. Gayatri Spivak, Johns Hopkins University Press, 1976.
Jacques Derrida, *Positions*, trans. Alan Bass, Athlone, 1981.

Terry Eagleton, 'Capitalism, Modernism and Postmodernism', in *Against the Grain*, Verso, 1986.

R. Ellman, ed., *Oscar Wilde: A Collection of Critical Essays*, Prentice Hall, 1969.

R. Ellman, 'Corydon and Ménalque', in *Golden Codgers: Biographical Speculations*, Oxford University Press, 1973.

R. Ellman, *Oscar Wilde*, Hamish Hamilton, 1987.

Michel Foucault, *The History of Sexuality* (1978), Vintage Books, 1980.

Michel Foucault, *Herculine Barbine*, Harvester, 1980.

Regenia Gagnier, *Idylls of the Market Place: Oscar Wilde and the Victorian Public*, Scolar Press, 1987.

André Gide, *Oscar Wilde*, trans. B. Frechtman, William Kimber, 1951.

André Gide, *So Be It, or: The Chips are Down* (1952), trans. Justin O'Brien, Chatto, 1960.

Jan B. Gordon, 'Decadent Spaces: Notes for a Phenomenology of the *Fin de siécle*, in I. Fletcher, ed., *Decadence and the 1890's*, Arnold, 1979.

I. Hassan, 'Pluralism in Postmodern Perspective', *Critical Inquiry*, 12, 3 (1986), pp. 503–20.

H. M. Hyde, *The Trials of Oscar Wilde*, William Hodge, 1948.

H. M. Hyde, *Oscar Wilde: A Biography*, Methuen, 1982.

Fredric Jameson, 'Postmodernism and Consumer Society', in H. Foster, ed., *The Anti-Aesthetic: Essays on Postmodern Culture*, Bay Press, 1983.

Fredric Jameson, 'Postmodernism, or the Cultural Logic of Late Capitalism', *New Left Review*, 146 (1984), pp. 53–92.

D. Kunzle, 'World Turned Upside Down: The Iconography of a European Broadsheet Type', in B. Babcock, ed., 1978, *op. cit.* (see Davis above).

D. Latimer, 'Jameson and Postmodernism', *New Left Review*, 148 (1984), pp. 116–28.

Manfred Pfister, *Oscar Wilde: The Picture of Dorian Gray*, Wilhelm Fink, 1986.

Eve Kosofsky Sedgwick, 'Across Gender, Across Sexuality: Willa Cather and Others', *South Atlantic Quarterly*, 88, 1 (1989), pp. 53–72.

Alan Sinfield, *Literature, Politics and Culture in Post-War Britain*, Blackwell, 1989.

Chris Snodgrass, 'Swinburne's Circle of Desire: A Decadent Theme', in I. Fletcher, ed., 1979, *op. cit.* (see Gordon above).

R. Terdiman, *Discourse/Counter Discourse: Theory and Practice of Symbolic Resistance in Nineteenth-Century France*, Cornell University Press, 1985.

George Woodcock, *The Paradox of Oscar Wilde*, Boardman, 1949.

W. B. Yeats, *Autobiographies*, Macmillan, 1955.

Robert Young, 'The Same Difference', *Screen*, 28, 3 (1987), pp. 87–9.

5.3   JOSEPH BRISTOW: 'THE IMPORTANCE OF BEING EARNEST' (1992)

Joseph Bristow is a lecturer in English literature at the University of York. He has been at the forefront of the development of gay and lesbian studies for a number of years, specializing in the close analysis of both canonic and 'popular' texts to reveal how literature is central to the construction of notions of (especially white, British) masculinity and how it also enables 'forbidden' same-sex desires to be articulated (this is apparent in the extracts on Wilde below). Bristow's other books include *Empire Boys: Adventures in a Man's World* (1991); ed., *Sexual Sameness: Textual Difference in Lesbian and Gay Writing* (1992); and, ed., *The Oxford Book of Adventure Stories* (1995). As the series in which his volume appears is primarily for student use, the introduction also gives an account of Wilde's life and art, his politics, and the early theatre-history of *Earnest*; while the 'Critical Commentary' includes further analysis of other essays by Wilde such as 'The Critic as Artist' and 'The Soul of Man under Socialism'. In neither case is there explicit theoretical underpinning, but the extracts below clearly enact the notion of a 'transgressive aesthetics'.

Identify the above, and consider its implications in the reading of Wilde's play. What do you think is Bristow's aim in reading the play in the way he does? Is it based solely on 'sexual politics'? In the Headnote to the later piece by Alan Sinfield, Sinfield is quoted to the effect that looking for a homosexual scenario in *Earnest* 'doesn't really work'. Would Bristow agree? What is at issue here? Does Bristow's reading relate to Sedgwick's concept of the 'epistemology of the closet'? What kind of *literary* criticism does Bristow employ? Is it at all influenced by deconstruction? In this respect compare his approach here with essays revealing the 'not-said' – for example, in Ch. 3 on *Jane Eyre*. Finally, what kind of 'historical' dimension, if any, does this criticism involve?

The following excerpts are from 'Introduction' and 'Critical Commentary' in Bristow's edition of *The Importance of Being Earnest and Related Writings*, 'Routledge English Texts', 1992, pp. 17–20, 202–17, *passim*.

The Importance of Being Earnest

From 'Introduction'.

[…] journal articles from the mid-1890s frequently referred to 'morbid' sexuality, by which they probably meant homosexuality. It is worth bearing in mind that at this time 'homosexuality' was not known by that name. Historians have shown how the idea of the homosexual as a particular type of person was not established until the débâcle of the Wilde trials. It was the Criminal Law Amendment Act of 1885 that first legislated against acts of 'gross indecency' between men (even in private), and under which Wilde was tried. Prior to that, homosexuality was understood only in terms of the sexual act. Men were hanged for committing buggery or sodomy, rather than for being homosexuals, until 1836. Wilde's own homosexual liaisons probably began in the late 1880s but it is unlikely that he referred to himself as a homosexual. The word, in any case, was a pathological definition, very far removed from Wilde's celebratory attitude to male same-sex love. By 1890 his writing was already examining sexual desire between men, and it was for this reason that *Dorian Gray* incensed some reviewers. One of them, Charles Whibley, wrote in the Tory *Scots Observer*: 'if he [Wilde] can write for none but outlawed noblemen and perverted telegraph-boys, the sooner he takes to tailoring (or some other decent trade) the better for his own reputation and public morals'.[1] Whibley was alluding to the major homosexual scandals of the 1880s, notably the Cleveland Street affair where wealthy men employed the sexual services of young post office workers. The sexual subtext of *Dorian Gray* goes against such middle-class virtues as 'self-help' (to be noted in the idea of the 'decent' tailor working at an honest trade). It was Walter Pater who advised Wilde on how to revise the novel, which went on sale in an emended version in 1891. Certainly, Pater could see just as clearly as Wilde how Victorian society would be offended by the sexual interests of this novel.

Wilde moved in homosexual circles with literary ambitions. The poet, Lionel Johnson, was one of his main admirers. Johnson wrote a poem in Latin celebrating *Dorian Gray*. It was through Johnson that Wilde met Alfred Douglas, and it was within this network of contacts that the implicit homosexual allusions of *Earnest* would have been understood. Part of the origins of *Earnest* lie in an Oxford undergraduate magazine, the *Chameleon*, published in 1894, and which, for reasons that shall become obvious, ran to only one number. Wilde contributed his 'Phrases and Philosophies for the Use of the Young' to the *Chameleon*. These 'Phrases' were juxtaposed with Douglas's two poems on same-sex desire, 'The Love that Dare Not Speak Its Name' and 'In Praise of Shame'. Each of these works was brought up by Queensberry's counsel during the court proceedings of 1895. Amid the contents were items by two 'Uranian' (or boy-loving) writers. One was a story, 'The Priest and the Acolyte', by the editor, Jack Bloxam; the other was 'The Shadow of the End', a poem by John Gambril Nicholson. Two years earlier, in 1892, Nicholson had published a short collection of poems, *Love in Earnest*, which contained a homoerotic ballad entitled 'Of Boys' Names'. This is the closing quatrain:

> My little Prince, Love's mystic spell
> Lights all the letters of your name,
>   And you, if no one else, can tell
> Why Ernest sets my heart a-flame.

Timothy d'Arch Smith suggests that 'Ernest' is a carefully coded word for homosexual desire.[2] Certainly, Wilde's play makes the notion of being earnest into its complete opposite. He also makes a hilarious joke about the identity of 'Ernest'. Both the leading male characters pretend to be 'Ernest' at different points of the action, as they struggle to maintain their lives of deception. Since *Earnest* refers to living a 'double life' at key moments, it is possible to glimpse how the comedy addresses issues that only those closest to Wilde would comprehend. In any case, *Earnest* is full of private allusions. The editor of the *Chameleon* turns up in the name of Lady Bloxham (p. 41);[3] Lady Bracknell has the honour of naming the town where Douglas's mother lived; Jack Worthing (who really is Ernest at the end of the third act) has a surname referring to the town where Wilde wrote the play; and Jack's address, the Albany, was the residence of the homosexual emancipationist, George Ives.

Earnest, then, is a privately coded as well as publicly entertaining play. It is probable that most people in Wilde's audience saw the use of the name Ernest as a simple inversion of terms. Samuel Butler, who also engaged in an untiring attack on Victorian values, gave the same name to the hero of his novel, *The Way of All Flesh* (1903). Here Butler's narrator comments on the popularity of the name Ernest in the 1830s: 'The word "earnest" was just beginning to come into fashion, and he [Ernest's father] thought the possession of such a name might, like his having been baptised in water from the Jordan, have a permanent effect upon the boy's character.'[4] Ernest, then, meant moral earnestness. The sexual joke that Wilde, not Butler, was making therefore had all the more force. This rather daring play on the meaning of being Ernest had already occurred in 'The Critic as Artist', where Ernest is the name of the younger man in the Socratic dialogue that structures the essay. There are further connections between the play and the essay. 'The Critic as Artist' is subtitled 'With some remarks upon the importance of doing nothing'. It was not uncommon for Wilde to take his choicest phrasing from one work and then implant it in another. Most of his writings are, to varying degrees, verbally entwined.

Notes (cut and renumbered)

1. Charles Whibley, Review of *The Picture of Dorian Gray*, 5 July 1890, *Scots Observer*, reprinted in *Selected Letters of Oscar Wilde*, ed. Rupert Hart-Davis (Oxford: Oxford University Press, 1979), p. 81. Wilde made a spirited response to Whibley's attack.
2. Timothy d'Arch Smith, *Love in Earnest: Some Notes on the Lives and Writings of English 'Uranian' Poets from 1889 to 1930* (London: Routledge & Kegan Paul, 1970), p. viii.
3. Page numbers in the text, here and in the following piece, are to Bristow's own Routledge edition.
4. Samuel Butler, *The Way of All Flesh* (1903: Harmondsworth: Penguin Books, 1966), p. 106.

From 'Critical Commentary'.

Earnest starts and finishes with the hilarious relationship between two young bachelors whose identities, as the play progresses, grow more and more confused. At the outset, it is not entirely clear how and why these young men have come to know one another. In the first act, they meet in Algernon's opulent London flat. They loudly share jokes as if they were the best of friends. Obviously, they are enjoying the pleasures of high Society (the capital letter signalling, as it did in Wilde's day, the most luxurious life to be had). This is, indeed, a world of exceptional privileges: lashings of champagne, lavish parties, and the proprieties of high tea. Social rituals are certainly uppermost in their minds. In fact, among the first of the many ceremonies they lightheartedly discuss is courtship. 'Ernest' will soon be engaged to Algernon's cousin, Gwendolen. The odd thing is, 'Ernest' has been hiding his true identity from Algernon. Why?

This puzzling question is partly answered in the opening scene – with all sorts of implications for what turns into a very complex but perfectly fashioned plot. 'Ernest', it would seem, provides Jack with an excellent alibi: 'My name is Ernest in town and Jack in the country' (p. 32). Jack, posing as 'Ernest', is leading a somewhat precarious double life. In his country seat, he is obviously known to everyone by his real name, Jack Worthing. However, since he finds his life on his estate constraining, and relishes the 'pleasure' of London society, he has had to devise another identity for himself.

This, his alter ego, allows him to spend as much time as possible in the city. It is a complex ploy. To maintain these two identities, Jack tells different lies to different people. To his family in Hertfordshire, he claims that he has to go to London to see his irresponsible brother, 'Ernest'. When Jack reaches London and mixes with Algernon he actually becomes the 'brother' he is supposed to be visiting. The country bores Jack; the city excites 'Ernest'. Only now, it seems, has he been found out. In the first scene, Jack is trying hard to explain to Algernon why he has different names in different places. Jack (alias 'Ernest') anxiously declares: 'I don't know whether you will be able to understand my real motives' (p. 33). Although his motives may be hard to grasp, it becomes clear that this deception is a very careful piece of plotting.

Mistaken identities; subtle deceptions; rapid reversals in relationships: these form the substance of Wilde's agile comedy. Confusions between names and faces, as well as names and places, hereafter proliferate. In each of its three acts, the play turns its attention to all sorts of amusing structures of deceit. Throughout *Earnest*, people are never quite what they seem to be. For a start, they do not even seem to correspond with what we might expect of dramatic characters. If they are not deceiving one another, then they are talking in a way that hardly seems authentic. They quip, joke, and come out with ideas and expressions that would appear to be something other than their own. It is, indeed, difficult to find some kind of psychological insight into either Jack or Algernon or anyone else in the play for that matter. It is *what* they say, rather than *why* they are saying it, that captures our attention. Inventive word-play; brilliant dialogue; sparkling wit: these are the things which drive the drama forward. Their motives vanish behind the brilliant façade of verbal trickery.

Even in the opening scene, the levels of intricate deceit begin to multiply. 'Ernest' is not the only character who adopts a persona to disguise his identity when he goes in search of 'pleasure'. Algernon, too, plays a similar trick upon his own relations. Just as Jack has invented the imaginary 'Ernest', so does Algernon have his fictional alias, 'Bunbury'. Like 'Ernest', 'Bunbury' makes enormous demands upon his inventor. 'Bunbury', according to Algernon, is 'an invaluable permanent invalid' (p. 33) – and so Algernon's endless visits to 'Bunbury' would appear to be the actions of a kind-hearted individual. At least, that is how Algernon wants to be understood. 'Bunbury', with his chronic illnesses and ceaseless calls on Algernon's attentions, enables Algernon to 'go down into the country' whenever he so wishes. For some reason or other, Algernon frequently needs to make a quick escape from London. Again, we are not exactly clear why.

[…]

One paragraph on the 'country/city' contrast is cut here.

[…]

Jack is the one who seems most keen to escape in the name of 'pleasure', and the more we find out about him, the stranger he seems.

[…]

Part of a paragraph describing Jack's 'background' is omitted.

[...]

The man who first of all pretends to have a brother called 'Ernest', and tells his London friends he is 'Ernest', actually discovers, after many sudden reversals in the plot, that he really *is* Ernest. And by becoming truly Ernest in the end, Jack finds out that he is Algernon's brother. In other words, once falsely 'Ernest', Jack is eventually *Ernest* in *earnest*. The drama closes as soon as it has made dramatic sense of this pun.

This comedy, therefore, centres on what might appear a rather laboured play on words – with entirely unexpected consequences. Living a double life has, paradoxically, enabled the revelation of the far-fetched truth that 'Ernest' is, indeed, Ernest. Having sorted out who's who in the furious closing moments, we can see how *Earnest* elegantly turns upon two remarkable ironies. First, a man who has tried to deceive another turns out to be that man's brother. Second, a true identity (Ernest in earnest) is, simultaneously, a linguistic joke (E(a)rnest). Set up first as a manipulative *fiction*, 'Ernest' is ultimately a *fact* – but only through the workings of a most contrived piece of plotting. Given the strenuous lengths to which this piece of word-play on 'E(a)rnest' is taken, it should be abundantly evident that there is some point to it. It is not there just for the sake of fun. Indeed, all the jokes in *Earnest* have serious resonances to them. With this play on 'E(a)rnest' in mind, we can see how this lively and fast-moving comedy raises a number of related questions about who or what a person truly is. What is the difference between an authentic identity and a false one? When is 'Ernest' genuinely in earnest? To put this another way: who or what might be taken in earnest in *Earnest*? The significance of these questions will deepen as we witness the quick turn of dramatic events in detail.

As soon as we discover how 'Ernest' and 'Bunbury' serve as 'covers' for each of the young men, the action swiftly changes, and the imperious Lady Bracknell and her daughter, Gwendolen, sweep on to the stage. Already Algernon has signalled that his aunt is coming to tea. The butler, Lane, has laid the table with suitable things to eat: cucumber sandwiches for Lady Bracknell, and bread and butter for Gwendolen. The trouble is, Algernon finds the cucumber sandwiches irresistible. In fact, he is in danger of eating them all up before his aunt arrives, and indeed he does. The sandwiches are important, for two reasons. Firstly, they are a hallmark of polite society. A proper high tea has to be graced with such delicacies. But secondly, and far less respectably, the sandwiches are among the many edible items suggesting rapacious desires. *Earnest* makes a whole host of rather vulgar allusions to love, romance, and sexuality. At crucial and potentially embarrassing moments, the comedy turns to rituals of eating, and each of the many foods mentioned seems charged with sexual meaning. Cucumber sandwiches; muffins; bread and butter; tea-cake: every single slice points to the hungriest of sexual appetites. Food is where each character's frustrated wishes are indirectly expressed, and most of these wishes concern sex. In this very proper world of courtship, engagements, and sudden bursts of passion, food becomes the focus for all sorts of anxieties that cannot be expressed out loud. 'Gwendolen,' says Algernon, 'is devoted to bread and butter' (p. 30), while he is equally unable to stop eating the sandwiches his aunt expects to be served at tea. Noticeably, Jack's very first words to Algernon closely align 'pleasure' with 'eating' (p. 29). These two things, thereafter, are never sundered. For example, Lady Bracknell reports that she has just eaten crumpets with Lady Harbury 'who seems … to be living entirely for pleasure now' (p. 36). The full implications of the play's sexual subtext will be dealt with below.

[…]

One-and-a-half pages on Lady Bracknell's character as upper-class female follow here.

[…]

Early in the play, Lady Bracknell passes her disapproval on 'Mr Bunbury' whose ill-health, she says, is a sign of 'morbidity' (p. 76). Here, at least two carefully coded homosexual allusions can be detected. Once we recognize the importance of these names then it is possible to comprehend exactly why Jack has invented 'Ernest' and Algernon has made up 'Bunbury', and, moreover, how and why they have come to know one another in the first place. To begin with, the name Bunbury suggests sodomy, since it plays on the slang words 'buns' for 'buttocks', and 'bury' implies penetration. Second, the word 'morbid' was frequently used in the 1890s as a euphemism for same-sex desire, which was regarded as an increasingly dangerous and degenerating illness. As we saw earlier, 'Ernest' was a code-word for homosexual among a coterie of pederastic writers known to Wilde. At this time, it is important to remember, homosexuality was being discussed with greater intensity by medical writers and sexologists than ever before. It was a type of behaviour that escalated the worries of a society that feared sexual desire in all its multifarious forms. Taken together, then, 'Bunburying' and 'morbid' indicate that Algernon's life of deception has a rather sickening quality about it, and that is why Lady Bracknell would like him to bring it to an end. That said, very few among Wilde's West End theatre audience would have understood the full implications of these words. If they had, they would have been altogether outraged. It is fair to say that there is a lot more provocative sexual innuendo than most critics have been willing to observe in *Earnest*. And, certainly, Wilde's closest associates would have found all sorts of things to laugh about – especially when the majority of the audience could not see that 'the importance of being earnest' meant 'the importance of being homosexual'. The last laugh, then, was to be relished almost by Wilde alone.

In this light, Lady Bracknell seems to know what Algernon is doing when he leaves town to see 'Bunbury'. As she tells Algernon, she insists on the very highest standards of behaviour. Instead of 'Bunburying', Lady Bracknell would prefer Algernon to play the part of the perfect nephew by arranging her music – and he must arrange it according to her specifications. Rather than corrupt Gwendolen with French songs, Lady Bracknell wants the musical performance to take place in German. In this world of amusingly exaggerated propriety, Gwendolen has to be protected from things French; German is thought to be altogether more respectable.

Again, Wilde is poking fun at upper-class attitudes to these different European cultures in Britain at this time. In the 1880s and 1890s, French was commonly associated with morally degenerate fiction (such as Emile Zola's *Germinal*, 1885); German, by contrast, was venerated as the language of philosophy (exemplified in the work of such writers as Kant and Hegel). French suggested unleashed sexuality and vulgarity; German represented seriousness and common sense. But a further point comes out from the juxtaposition of these two languages. Once again, it highlights how this upper-class ethos is constructed along a division between healthy and unhealthy, desirable and undesirable things. Wilde, as ever, is laughing at a society based on polarized values particularly where questions of right and wrong are reduced to absurd prejudices concerning differing nationalities. It is as ridiculous to be ill-disposed to the French language as it is to treat a handbag with contempt. At a deeper level, it is perhaps just as foolish to hold same-sex desire in such disrepute. What does it matter if one was born in a handbag or desires someone of one's own sex? This is certainly one of the questions that emerges from a 'serious' consideration of this supposedly trivial play.

[...]

Five pages describing the action of the play are cut here.

[...]

Humour does not stop there. Once again, there is another potentially shocking joke to be found in the midst of these proceedings. Looking Cecily up and down, Lady Bracknell suggests a way of instantly improving the girl's appearance: 'A thoroughly experienced French maid produces a really marvellous result in a very brief space of time. I remember recommending one to young Lady Lancing, and after three months her own husband did not know her' (p. 78). On the face of it, she means that a well-trained servant will enhance a woman's attractiveness to the degree that her husband would no longer recognize her. But since all things French have been associated so far with harmful influences, there is some reason to believe this is an allusion to something that would have been thought sexually corrupt—like lesbianism. The French maid seemed to satisfy Lady Lancing to an extreme degree. Certainly, this implication is even more strongly accentuated when we hear Jack's prompt aside: 'And after six months nobody knew her' (p. 78). The 'marvellous result' seems to have excluded Lady Lancing from Society.

Earnest, as has already been shown, is peppered with risk-taking comments about same-sex desire, and these fall from the lips not just of Algernon, Jack, and Lady Bracknell but of almost every other character. In Act II it is Cecily who notes that 'Ernest' (on this occasion, Algernon) has probably been leading a 'double life', and that such an activity is 'wicked' (p. 52). And Gwendolen, in her conversation over tea with Cecily, remarks: 'men of the noblest possible moral character are extremely susceptible to the influence of the physical charms of others. Modern, no less than ancient history, supplies us with many most painful examples of what I refer to' (pp. 65–6). Gwendolen, either by design or default, is alluding to the cult of homosexuality in Ancient Greece, which was proving an increasing problem in the teaching of Plato to public schoolboys. Classical literature was, at one and the same time, considered the highest form of learning for young men, and yet it uncomfortably referred to the lowest form of vice. No wonder men of 'noble character' were 'susceptible' to undesirable activities.

The comedy allows Gwendolen another remark of this kind. Again when conversing with Cecily over tea, Gwendolen expresses her views on men's role in life: 'The home seems to me to be the proper sphere for the man. And certainly once a man begins to neglect his domestic duties he becomes painfully effeminate, does he not? And I don't like that. It makes men so very attractive' (p. 65). These comments, as usual, cut in two directions. Firstly, Victorians often stated that women had a 'proper sphere', and that was the home. Gwendolen, therefore, is turning this idea on its head. To her, men are best kept indoors. Outside the home, she implies, they may run into trouble. One implication is that husbands were often unfaithful to their wives, and so it is vital for men to attend to their 'domestic duties', namely their families. 'Domestic duties', however, are things generally ascribed to women. Yet there is a second, and somewhat more subtle, reading that may emerge from these lines. The notion that men become 'effeminate' once they stray from their 'proper sphere', and in so doing grow 'attractive', suggests that they are sexually active outside the home, not just with prostitutes, but with other men: 'effeminate' is a word closely connected with homosexuality. Gwendolen's statement, then, is complex and contradictory. Inside the home, men are both wifely (in women's 'proper sphere') and husbandly (attending to their families). Outside the home, men are 'attractive' (free from family constraints) and 'effeminate' (homosexual). However we choose to interpret these lines, we can see that the play is suggesting that there is something wrong with the way people are supposed to lead their lives. Everything that makes people 'attractive' or gives them 'pleasure' involves transgressing the limits laid down by society. A society run on narrow-minded morals that sets unfair limits on 'pleasure' can make for disaster. And it is on this note that the play rushes to its end.

Pleasure, it seems, leads the whole cast into temptation – whether that means eating someone else's sandwiches or going 'Bunburying' in the country. Miss Prism, as she admitted to Cecily earlier, indulged her pleasures when writing a three-volume novel. It was an activity that got her into considerable trouble. Little might we anticipate that her former novel-writing is responsible for Jack's abandonment as a baby on the Brighton line. Once Lady Bracknell hears Prism's name, the whole humilating story of the handbag is revealed. Lady Bracknell, when referring to Prism harshly as 'a female of repellent aspect, remotely connected with education', is airing an old upper-class prejudice against governesses, who were often thought untrustworthy. Governesses were seen as impostors from the lower ranks of the educated middle classes who were allowed into the homes of the rich to teach their children. For many members of the landed classes, it was important to ensure that young women teachers did not ingratiate themselves into the household. They were employees who should have no ambition to rise above their station – by, for example, trying to marry into a wealthy family. Wilde takes this demeaning attitude against middle-class educators such as Prism to new extremes to highlight the snobbery and ignorance of the rich. 'In a moment of mental abstraction, for which I never can forgive myself,' says Prism, 'I deposited the manuscript in the bassinette, and placed the baby in the handbag' (p. 83). Presented with the bag, Prism confirms that it was hers. Jack instantly – and most mistakenly – assumes Prism is his mother. Assured this is not the case, Jack then demands to know exactly who he is. After a quick turning of the pages of the Army Lists, his first name is revealed. Jack is told he is Algernon's brother. And so he discovers – in all its multifarious ways – the importance of being E(a)rnest.

If playful with its plotting and punning, *Earnest* remains a witty piece of social commentary, noting throughout how society is riven with prejudices and snobbery. There are, we may infer, pointless divisions between the classes, between the country and the city, and between men and women. As we have seen, Wilde never misses an opportunity to challenge conventional values, and it is through this dialectical principle that his energetic critique proceeds. Everything that might be taken for granted is turned upside-down so that fiction becomes fact, and fact an unlikely kind of fiction. This activity – of swapping or alternating real and imagined worlds – may make us wonder to what degree a play such as *Earnest* is any more or less authentic than the world it represents. What is the play suggesting about the real world? That our lives are the stuff of farce? That comedy is more serious than real life? It is hard to tell the difference between the sincere and the artificial. Perhaps we should not try to make any distinction between them at all?

[...]

The essay then focuses on 'The Critic as Artist'.

5.4   ALAN SINFIELD: 'PICTURING *DORIAN GRAY*' (1994)

Alan Sinfield is Professor of English in the School of Cultural and Community Studies at the University of Sussex, where he convenes the MA course in 'Sexual Dissidence and Cultural Change'. He has published widely in the fields of gay studies and cultural materialism (see Headnote on Dollimore above). His books include: *Political Shakespeare* (ed., with Dollimore, 1985); *Alfred Tennyson* (1986); *Literature, Politics and Culture in Post-war Britain* (1989); *Faultlines: Cultural Materialism and the Politics of Dissident Reading* (1992); and *Cultural Politics – Queer Reading* (1994). As with Dollimore, Sinfield's cultural materialism and sexual politics are inseparable elements of the same project: to prize open the 'faultlines' in dominant cultural ideologies so that marginalized, dissident and subversive voices are released to trouble and contest them. He has undertaken such readings for both the Renaissance and Modern periods, but perhaps more important in Sinfield's work is the continual interpenetration of past and present – one 'reading' the other in dialectical oscillation. *The Wilde Century: Effeminacy, Oscar Wilde and the Queer Moment* is a case in point. Starting from the recognition, like Sedgwick and Bristow, that homosexuality only becomes a 'condition' once it is 'named' in the later nineteenth century, Sinfield argues that Wilde and his writings 'look queer' because our stereotype of male homosexuality is based on our ideas about him: 'our interpretation is retroactive'; 'our present selves are formed out of continuity and difference; because Wilde and others were as they were, we are as we are' (pp. vii–viii). 'Effeminacy' is the key term in this process. Defining his project as 'constructionist' (i.e. that 'sexualities ... are not essential, but constructed within an array of prevailing social possibilities', p. 11), Sinfield at once explores the construction of twentieth-century male homosexuality in Wildean terms – effete, camp, aesthetic, amoral, decadent, insouciant, dandified – and shows the feedback in terms of how we read Wilde. This 'cultural materialist' theoretical model, which perceives the 'faultlines' ('inherent instabilities' and 'dissident action' which the dominant social order cannot fail to produce and which contest and disrupt its own criteria of plausibility, p. 17), allows Sinfield, in the later parts of his book, to mobilize Wilde on behalf of the agenda for a gay cultural politics a hundred years later.

A central observation of Sinfield's about Wilde, which stems from the notion of 'retroactivity' above, is that 'the place of homosexuality in his plays is by no means plain'; that – despite the assumption that 'there must be a gay scenario lurking somewhere in the depths of ... *Earnest*', and that Bunburying must mean 'cruising for rough trade' – 'it doesn't really work' (p. vi). And yet, he says, 'queerness' feels everywhere present. How would you relate this perception to Sinfield's reading of *Dorian Gray* in the following extract? What kind of a 'historical' perspective informs his reading? Compare Sinfield's views in this respect with Bristow's 'homosexual' reading of *Earnest*. Does Sinfield's analysis undercut Bristow's? Also, what kind of textual analysis do you think is operating in this essay? Is it, in any sense, 'poststructuralist'? Does some (underlying) notion of 'literary value' remain perceptible here? Finally, compare Sinfield's criticism with that of the feminist cultural materialist, Lisa Jardine, in Ch. 1 on *Hamlet*, and with Levinson's 'new historicism' on Wordsworth's 'Ode' (Ch. 2).

The following extract is the final sub-section of Ch. 4 ('Aestheticism and Decadence') in *The Wilde Century*, Cassell, 1994, pp. 98–105; two previous sections explore the correlation between the aesthetic and the effeminate in the late nineteenth century.

Picturing *Dorian Gray*

Wilde's self-fashioning took two phases. In his dress he stressed aestheticism until his return from the USA in 1882; then he took up the dandy manner. This shift, from aesthete to dandy, enacts a change in class identification. The aesthete – it is apparent in *Patience* and *Candida* – is almost a bohemian. He lives on the edge of society, and the dragoons are annoyed partly by his upstart status. However, the (perceived) effeminacy of the aesthete offered another possibility: a conflation with the (perceived) effeminacy of the leisure class. For Huysmans, the connection could be presumed; to Nordau it was a matter for complaint. For Wilde, it was the dream ticket: a conjunction of art and the leisure class, in opposition to middle-class, philistine, masculine practicality. The ground of the association would be uselessness and amorality, and above all, the stance that linked them through the idea of leisured idleness: effeminacy. To the Reverend Richard A. Armstrong, it was a potent combination. He inveighed against 'writers of elegant and glittering literature, that lies on drawing-room tables, who gloss over evil, and make vice seem pretty and refined ... There are plays upon the boards, patronised by rank and fashion, which deal a deadly blow at maiden modesty and manly purity.'[1]

Leisured decadence was more promising as a base for the artist than bohemian exclusion, Wilde must have thought. 'The best work in literature is always done by those who do not depend upon it for their daily bread,' he wrote to an aspiring writer, 'and the highest form of literature, poetry, brings no wealth to the singer.' Regenia Gagnier sees this as the key to Wilde's manner: 'The late-Victorian dandy in Wilde's works and in his practice is the human equivalent of aestheticism in art; he is the man removed from life, a living protest against vulgarity and means-end living.'[2] Wilde worked hard (paradoxically) to establish it. 'The condition of perfection is idleness,' he declared; 'Dandyism is the assertion of the absolute modernity of Beauty.' The aesthetic critic, in his account, sounds like an idealized version of the leisured gentleman: 'Calm, and self-centred, and complete, the aesthetic critic contemplates life, and no arrow drawn at a venture can pierce between the joints of his harness. He at least is safe. He has discovered how to live.'[3] The defensive tone in this assertion indicates that Wilde is engaged in an ambitious venture.

Of course, most aristocrats were not interested in art, except perhaps as conspicuous consumption; they were busy ordering other people around (occupying positions of responsibility), hunting, shooting and fishing, and trying to maintain their estates (often by marrying new money or adopting modern business practices). The overlap between art and class was produced by Wilde, especially, through his theory and his representations of leisured idleness, sensibility, luxury, insouciance and natural superiority. This idea may be observed in the making in *The Picture of Dorian Gray* (1890).

The artist, Basil Hallward, is not presented as a dandy, or as effeminate (though he has an artist's long hands); he is, in fact, thoroughly in earnest about art and life. He instantiates a pre-Wildean idea of the artist as intense and sincere. He insists that to him Dorian is 'simply a motive in art', and laments his inability to influence him for the better.[4] This places Hallward entirely at odds with the dandy, Wotton; so one of them claims art and the other leisure-class insouciance. Neither of them combines the two, in the manner that Wilde was proposing. Such a new combination, it seems, is to be the contribution of Dorian. He, apparently, is the third term, merging art and leisured accomplishment. It is Dorian who says: 'For the canons of good society are, or should be, the same as the canons of art. Form is absolutely essential to it' (p. 142). 'Life has been your art. You have set yourself to music. Your days are your sonnets,' Wotton tells him (p. 217). Many young men 'saw, or fancied that they saw,' in Dorian 'a type that was to combine something of the real culture of the scholar with all the grace and distinction and perfect manner of a citizen of the world' (p. 129). 'Or fancied that they saw' is an important qualification: Dorian is not actually the effortlessly graceful person the other characters imagine – any more than the frantic Alfred Douglas was to be.

Camille Paglia says 'Dorian *becomes* Lord Henry'; she imagines a sinister power of 'homosexual generation'.[5] However, dandy manipulations of young men are almost never successful in Wilde's writing. Dorian is urged by Wotton to adopt 'a new Hedonism', but he becomes stupidly infatuated with Sybil Vane and guilt-ridden after abandoning her. His troubles arise from sentimental self-indulgence and want of intelligence and self-control, not from aestheticism and amorality. The painting registers his guilt, but does not control it; it merely prevents it from showing in his body. So although Dorian seems to reject Hallward, he retains his spiritual intensity; that is why he cannot tolerate Hallward remaining alive. This is not the insouciance that Wotton himself instantiates and had wanted combined with art in the person of Dorian. Murder, Wotton remarks, 'is always a mistake. One should never do anything that one cannot talk about after dinner' (p. 213). Dorian arrives at disaster not because he abjures conventional moral principles but because he remains under their sway. The alignment of art and leisure is broached, but not attained.

To accomplish this theme, it is not necessary for Wilde to make any of his characters homosexual; that is the burden of my argument so far. In the nexus of aestheticism, decadence and leisure, as Wilde received it, that is an optional extra. In *Dorian Gray* no one exactly meets the bill – though, as I will argue in a moment, the whole book is pervaded with queerness. Lord Wotton has the aristocratic decadence and exercises over Dorian the strange influence that sets the plot going, but his sexual involvements seem to be with women (pp. 101–2). Basil Hallward is in love with Dorian, but apparently not in a sensual way.

> The love that he bore him – for it was really love – had nothing in it that was not noble and intellectual. It was not that mere physical admiration of beauty that is born of the senses, and that dies when the senses tire. It was such love as Michael Angelo had known, and Montaigne, and Winckelmann, and Shakespeare himself.

We might be inclined to read this list simply as a coded allusion to queerness, but Dorian adds: 'Yes, Basil could have saved him' (p. 119). This is the theory Pater draws out of Winckelmann: the same-sex lover is precisely opposed to sensual excess – Dorian kills Hallward because he can't cope with his steady virtue. Careful commentators have seen this. 'That Dorian might have had sexual relations with Lord Henry, or even with his portraitist, Basil Hallward,' Hans Mayer opines, 'seems excluded by the text.' Dorian's milieu, Dellamora observes, is homosocial rather than homosexual.[6]

Hallward comes closest to same-sex passion and is an artist, so we have one correlate in the Wildean queer image. But he is also idealistic and moralizing; other factors are disposed elsewhere – immoral debauchery (Dorian), and amoral, leisured insouciance (Wotton). The queer image refuses to cohere – refuses to meet our expectation that there will be a character in the twentieth-century Wildean image. This is an original move – more exciting than the more popular idea that Dorian, somehow, must be like gay men today.

Dorian is represented (in chapter 11) as repeating the debaucheries of Huysmans's protagonist in *Against Nature*, but there is no clear reference to anything that corresponds to the latter's same-sex experiences. He is accused of ruining the reputations of numerous women and of having corrupted young men, but the vice of one of these is specified as taking 'his wife from the streets', and of another as fraud. What Wilde had wanted, he said, was 'to surround Dorian Gray with an atmosphere of moral corruption. Otherwise the story would have had no meaning and the plot no issue. To keep this atmosphere vague and indeterminate and wonderful was the aim.'[7] Of course, that does not rule out same-sex passion, but neither does it make possible a secure labelling of Dorian's vice. Mayer thinks it has more to do with drugs than homosexuality; for Showalter, what happens to the picture suggests a venereal disease (she supposes that to be a special problem for homosexuals).[8]

A vice that would very well fit what happens to Dorian's picture is masturbation. His sins would 'mar its beauty, and eat away its grace. They would defile it, and make it shameful' (p. 119). Edward Thring said that as a consequence of masturbation 'the face loses its frank and manly expression'; Dean Farrar wrote, in 1862, of the masturbating boy: 'Within these two years he has lost – and his countenance betrays the fact in his ruined beauty – he has lost the true joys of youth, and known instead of them the troubles of the envious, the fears of the cowardly, the heaviness of the slothful, the shame of the unclean.'[9] Hallward can hardly believe the rumours about Dorian because such signs are absent: 'Sin is a thing that writes itself across a man's face. It cannot be concealed. People talk sometimes of secret vices. There are no such things. If a wretched man has a vice, it shows itself in the lines of his mouth, the droop of his eyelids, the moulding of his hands even' (pp. 149–50). The effects are of course shifted on to Dorian's picture. He is said to have been narcissistically drawn to it; now it will 'bear the burden of his shame' (p. 105); he recalls the erstwhile 'stainless purity of his boyish life' (p. 122). Henry Maudsley (generally a more advanced thinker) said 'these degenerate beings' – masturbators – become

> sullen, silent, and indisposed to converse at all; but if they do enter into conversation, they reveal delusions of a suspicious or obscure nature. They believe themselves subjected to strange influences, especially in the night, and sometimes that unnatural offences are

practised upon them. Their minds seem to dwell much on such disgusting subjects ... the body is usually much emaciated, notwithstanding they eat well.[10]

Wotton's initial challenge to Dorian is framed in similar terms, though with a different evaluation: he accuses Dorian of 'self-denial' which

> broods in the mind, and poisons us. ... The only way to get rid of a temptation is to yield to it. Resist it, and your soul grows sick with longing for the things it has forbidden to itself, with desire for what its monstrous laws have made monstrous and unlawful. ... you have had passions that have made you afraid, thoughts that have filled you with terror, day-dreams and sleeping dreams whose mere memory might stain your cheek with shame – (p. 18)

Masturbation was not generally linked with same-sex passion. The danger was said to be physical exhaustion and psychological self-absorption. In fact, the solitary secrecy, the evasion of surveillance, was the principal objection, Ed Cohen suggests.[11]

My aim here is not to find a new clue to the hidden mystery of Wilde's novel but to indicate how tricky it is to get any fix on Dorian Gray's vices. The Victorians placed emphases that we do not place, saw vices where we see trivia, allowed confusions where we would expect clarity. The book should be viewed not as the cunning masking of an already-known queerness, but as reaching out towards formulations of same-sex experience that were, we keep observing, as yet nameless. Wotton is intrigued by Hallward's worship of Dorian: 'how strange it all was! He remembered something like it in history. Was it not Plato, that artist in thought, who had first analysed it? Was it not Buonarroti who had carved it in the coloured marbles of a sonnet-sequence? But in our own century it was strange' (p. 36). In part, no doubt, the questioning manner is a strategy to introduce the topic cautiously to a general public. But also, in 1890, it displays Wotton entertaining a new possibility, exploring a new kind of sensibility. It is not reasonable to assume that any idealistic stance was either hypocrisy or self-deception on Wilde's part, or on that of other same-sex apologists. *Dorian Gray* is helping to constitute just those terms in which we might wish, subsequently, to read it.

These possibilities are the more enticing because of the way Wilde managed, continually, to anticipate himself. As Bartlett remarks, 'Dorian Gray was imagined in 1890. Wilde first met Douglas in January or June 1891. ... He was a fiction, one that already existed in his books.' And 'Dorian's fatal punishment, lying dead, a wrinkled husk of a man,' Joseph Bristow suggests, 'anticipates Wilde's own in Reading Gaol'.[12] This is not uncanny; it is because Wilde's culture and his writing were propelling him, and all of us, towards the coherence that we observe in his life and writing; towards an image which as yet he could only intuit.

The Picture of Dorian Gray invokes the queer image, to some readers at least, *despite at no point representing it.* Wilde strews around the elements in the emerging bricolage, and some readers at least were able to tot up the sum. When you put down the book, that is what it appears to have been about. 'It is not irrelevant that in the popular imagination,' Claude Summers remarks, 'the name Dorian Gray conjures not an image of evil but of preternaturally extended youth and beauty bought at the trivial price of a disfigured portrait.'[13] It is not a matter of this or that coded reference, but of the entire text being a displaced vision of the danger of, and to, the desirable youth. Despite the moralism of Hallward and the insouciance of Wotton, Wilde's fable is ultimately complicit with Dorian's narcissism in this respect: the disfigurement of the picture depends on a correlation of corruption with loss of youth and beauty. The ageing process is made to represent moral degeneracy; then, as now, this is a proposition that seems unethical in mainstream culture but which answers to a fantasy in gay male subculture.

Same-sex passion seems always on the point of getting said in the novel; its omission, indeed, seems significant – since it is a likely element in the career of the debauched aristocrat. 'In the course of his evil career he is proved guilty of adultery, debauchery, luxury, greed, vanity, murder and opium addiction. Only one of his vices is hidden, only one sin cannot be named.'[14] Same-sex passion is the impossible point of presence, at which the text might spring into miraculous coherence. It was there, almost, for some readers at least.

As commentators have suggested, we may envisage Wilde as seeking to extend the range of sexual awareness, of purposefully writing for both a knowing and an unknowing readership.[15] Initial reviewers manifest varying degrees of knowingness. The *Daily Chronicle* called *Dorian Gray* 'a poisonous book, the atmosphere of which is heavy with the mephitic odours of moral and spiritual putrefaction – a gloating study of the mental and physical corruption of a fresh, fair and golden youth, which might be horrible and fascinating but for its effeminate frivolity, its studied insincerity, its theatrical cynicism, its tawdry mysticism ...'.[16] The *Chronicle*'s reviewer was more specific: he disliked Dorian's 'pretty face, rosy with the loveliness that endeared youth of his odious type to the paralytic patricians of the Lower Empire;' in similar vein, *Punch* said Dorian is 'Ganymede-like'. In these instances, reaching for a classical referent holds the concept at arm's length from contemporary society. The *Scots Observer*, however, averred that Wilde 'can write for none but outlawed noblemen and perverted telegraph-boys' – a pointed reference to the Cleveland Street scandal of 1889–90.[17]

The potential of the book became clear to Wilde's prosecutors when, in a precise act of bricolage, they put all the evidence together. Suddenly queerness seemed of the essence. *Dorian Gray*, Queensberry's plea of justification asserted, 'was designed and intended' by Wilde 'and was understood by the readers thereof to describe the relations, intimacies, and passions of certain persons of sodomitical and unnatural habits, tastes, and practices'.[18] Some readers did understand it like that; after the trials it is impossible not to do so. On the one hand, it was not unreasonable for Wilde's counsel to complain that 'hidden meanings have been most unjustly read into the poetical and prose works of my client'; the prosecution was unable to cite any sodomitical passages.[19] On the other hand, meaning is contextual, and once Wilde enters the dock and his relations with Alfred Douglas are invoked, the book is deafeningly queer.

Notes (cut and renumbered)

For works cited without full reference, see list of 'Additional Works' below. Parenthetical references in the text to *The Picture of Dorian Gray* are to the Oxford University Press 'World's Classics' edition, 1981, ed. Isobel Murray.

1. The Reverend Richard A. Armstrong, *Our Duty in the Matter of Social Purity* (London: Social Purity Alliance, 1885), p. 10.
2. Rupert Hart-Davis, ed., *The Letters of Oscar Wilde* (New York: Harcourt, Brace, 1962), p. 179; Gagnier, *Idylls*, p. 7.
3. Oscar Wilde, *Complete Works*, intr. Holland (London and Glasgow: Collins, 1966): 'Phrases and philosophies for the use of the young', p. 1206; 'A few maxims for the instruction of the over-educated', p. 1204; 'The critic as artist', p. 1042.
4. Wilde, *Dorian Gray*, p. 11. Hallward's declarations of devotion to Dorian were toned down slightly when Wilde adjusted the story from the initial magazine version for publication in book form (Neil Bartlett, *Who Was That Man?* (London: Serpent's Tail, 1988), p. 112).
5. Camille Paglia, *Sexual Personae* (New Haven: Yale University Press, 1990), p. 518.
6. Hans Mayer, *Outsiders*, trans. Denis M. Sweet (Cambridge, MA: MIT Press, 1984), p. 223; Dellamora, *Masculine Desire*, pp. 207–8.
7. *Dorian Gray*, pp. 142, 150–2, 163, 204–5, 210–11; Wilde, letter to the *Scots Observer*, 9 July 1890, quoted in H. Montgomery Hyde, *The Trials of Oscar Wilde* (London: William Hodge, 1948), p. 158.
8. Mayer, *Outsiders*, pp. 223–4; Elaine Showalter, *Sexual Anarchy* (London: Bloomsbury, 1991), p. 177.
9. J. R. de S. Honey, *Tom Brown's Universe* (London: Millington, 1977), pp. 170–1; Joseph Bristow, *Empire Boys* (London: Harper-Collins, 1991), pp. 133–6.
10. *Journal of Medical Science*, 14 (1868), p. 149, quoted by Alex Comfort, *The Anxiety Makers* (London: Panther, 1968), p. 116; see also p. 96.
11. Cohen, *Talk*, pp. 43–68, 89–90.
12. Bartlett, *Who Was That Man?*, pp. 195–6; J. Bristow, 'Wilde, *Dorian Gray*, and gross indecency', in Bristow, ed., *Sexual Sameness* (London, Routledge, 1992), p. 61.
13. Claude J. Summers, *Gay Fictions* (New York: Continuum, 1990), p. 44.
14. Bartlett, *Who Was That Man?*, pp. 93–4.
15. Gagnier, *Idylls*, pp. 61–2; Behrendt, *Oscar Wilde*, p. 181; William A. Cohen, 'Willie and Wilde', *South Atlantic Quarterly*, 88 (1989), 219–45; Lawrence Dansen, 'Oscar Wilde, W. H. and the unspoken name of love', *ELH*, 58 (1991), 979–1000; Bristow, 'Wilde, *Dorian Gray*, and gross indecency'. I have tried to establish this kind of split reading for audiences of the plays of Noel Coward: see Alan Sinfield, 'Private lives/public theatre: Noel Coward and the politics of homosexual representation', *Representations*, 36 (fall 1991), 43–63.
16. Beckson, *Oscar Wilde*, p. 72; see Gagnier, *Idylls*, pp. 57–62.
17. Beckson, *Oscar Wilde*, pp. 73, 75, 76; also p. 69.
18. Hyde, *Trials*, p. 114; quoted from Cohen, *Talk*, p. 128.
19. Hyde, *Trials*, p. 229.

Additional Works

Karl Beckson, ed., *Oscar Wilde: The Critical Heritage*, Routledge, 1970.

Patricia Flanagan Behrendt, *Oscar Wilde: Eros and Aesthetics*, Macmillan, 1991.

Ed Cohen, *Talk on the Wilde Side*, Routledge, 1993.

Richard Dellamora, *Masculine Desire*, North Carolina University Press, 1990.

Regenia Gagnier, *Idylls of the Market Place: Oscar Wilde and the Victorian Public*, Scolar Press, 1987.

5.5   TERRY EAGLETON: 'OSCAR' (1995)

For further details of Terry Eagleton's work, see the Headnote in Ch. 4 on *Middlemarch*.

Heathcliff and the Great Hunger: Studies in Irish Culture is the result of Eagleton's more recent desire, while recognizing how fraught this is for a 'semi-outsider', to intervene in Irish cultural politics and historical debate. The tentative and highly self-conscious preface explains his reasons for entering this 'minefield', partly autobiographical and affinitive, but more particularly to contribute his 'stock-in-trade', cultural theory, in a 'sustained project', to the analysis of Irish history. He notes that 'culture ... in colonial conditions ... tends to assume a more central political significance than elsewhere', and therefore seeks 'to bring to bear on Ireland the language of contemporary cultural theory', while simultaneously seeking to challenge, by way of the material realities of Irish experience, the (postmodern) 'repressions and evasions of the latter' (pp. ix–x). The subsequent book is a series of readings, many of them of literary texts (by Emily Brontë, Swift, Maria Edgeworth, Le Fanu, Stoker, Burke, George Moore, Yeats, Joyce), which concludes with the present essay on two more Irish 'exiles and emigrés', George Bernard Shaw and Wilde. The chapter offers a comparative critique of their philosophical and political ideas, and seeks to establish (by way, *inter alia*, of Lamarck, Darwin, Herbert Spencer, Nietzsche and Pater) the intellectual matrix which shaped the profound contradictions and tensions of both their positions. This general introductory exposition, together with passages more exclusively on Shaw, has largely been omitted here.

How, in terms of the above, does Eagleton's 'cultural theory' contribute to Irish history in the present instance? What does he do for Wilde in the process? Does the essay insert Wilde into a colonial context, and is it then a recognizable inflection of postcolonial criticism (compare it with other such essays in other chapters)? What claims do you think the extract makes for 'art'? Does it privilege the latter and, if so, why? Unlike the other essays in this exercise, Eagleton's makes little of Wilde's sexual 'dissidence'. Is it possible, nevertheless, to regard the essay as identifying a 'transgressive aesthetic'? Is Eagleton's work, moreover, also a form of 'cultural materialism', similar in its approach and intentions to the political criticism of Dollimore and Sinfield? What, in another perspective, are the continuities/discontinuities between this essay and the example of his earlier work in Ch. 4 on George Eliot?

The following extract largely comprises the final part of Ch. 8 ('Oscar and George') in *Heathcliff and the Great Hunger*, Verso, 1995, pp. 326, 331–41.

Oscar

Six pages of introductory material on Lamarck *et al.* – cf. Headnote – are omitted here.

[...]

Oscar Wilde sprang from a failing class too; indeed his life-span is more or less coterminous with the decline of Ascendancy fortunes. He was born a few years after the Famine, at a time when the Catholic middle classes were starting out on their long march to political power. The Church of Ireland was disestablished in his adolescence; the first Home Rule Bill was drafted around the time of his early literary success; and his death in 1900 coincides with the passing of the Land Acts which were to destroy the Ascendancy's economic power. Wilde's origin, as Lady Bracknell remarks of Jack Worthing, is thus a kind of terminus: he was born in a cul-de-sac, if not exactly a railway station, and his own crisis of identity shares in the chronic insecurity of an Anglo-Irish caste who, like some of the characters of *The Importance of Being Earnest*, were never quite able to say who they were. His rake's progress through English society seems an image of this crumbling splendour. One can feel, in Wilde's too-brilliant career, the gathering hubris of a man who is riding too high, hanging on by his wits, and who seems at times to be perversely courting disaster. Like the effervescent wit and intoxicating high spirits of *Earnest*, written at a time when the policeman's hand was just about to feel his collar, his life seems giddily sustained by nothing but its own exhilarating momentum. As with his Anglo-Irish countryman Charles Stewart Parnell, he is at first admired, then thrust out as immoralist and sexual transgressor. Just as his own profligate class in Ireland finally pulled the roof down upon their own heads, so Wilde's spendthrift lifestyle and flamboyant flouting of convention seems a race towards self-destruction, as though he was intent on wresting the initiative from others even in this, cutting himself down before the Establishment stepped in and did it for him.

[...]

Four-and-a-half pages are cut here which establish the intellectual trajectory for Wilde's arrival at 'his full immaturity', when he is 'set free to treat the world as a work of art'.

[...]

Wilde, who hailed from the city his compatriot Joyce spelt as Doublin, is a fissured subject in all kinds of ways: English and Irish, socialite and sodomite, dandy and republican, upper-class and underdog, a respectable paterfamilias who consorted with rent boys, a shameless bon viveur who laid claim to the title of socialist. There is in any case something intriguingly divided about the aristocrat, who is at once overlord and immoralist, commanding and cavalier, an inverted anarchist with all the iconoclasm of those unquestionably in control. But beyond these purely social polarities, Wilde's work urges an ontological division between history and consciousness, one which splits the human subject down the middle as thoroughly as the Kantian self is strung out between phenomenal object and free subject. Vivian in 'The Decay of Lying' explicitly repudiates the historicist perspective on art which his author had learnt from Pater, and the essay contains a negative allusion to Herbert Spencer. If facts for 'The Rise of Historical Criticism' are the very locus of mighty cosmic laws, the later essay will dismiss them, in lofty Arnoldian vein, as usurping the domain of Fancy. 'The Rise of Historical Criticism' deploys an aesthetic image to assure us that Nature is inherently purposive: it is not, Wilde maintains, 'full of incoherent episodes like a bad tragedy'. 'The Critic as Artist' exploits the same theatrical metaphor to illustrate exactly the opposite point: life is deficient in form, its catastrophes happen in the wrong way, and its tragedies seem to culminate in farce.

To pit mind against reality, however, is not necessarily to pit the *individual* mind against it. 'The Critic as Artist' speaks of the determining law of heredity as having 'hemmed us round with the nets of the hunter, and written upon the wall the prophecy of our doom. We may not watch it, for it is within us'.[1] So necessity is not after all just external; on the contrary, it informs human consciousness from within, just as it did for the scientific evolutionism of 'The Rise of Historical Criticism'. If, then, subjectivity is just as determined as biology, where does freedom have its source? Wilde resolves this difficulty by mobilizing his earlier Hegelian idea of collective mind. Just as Samuel Butler resorts to the notion of race memory as the motivating force of human action, so 'The Critic as Artist' sees the imagination as distilling a kind of racial unconscious. It is this, not individual creativity, which lies at the origin of art; our soul is 'no single spiritual entity' but the precipitate of this collective history of spirit.[2] So creativity and determinism are preserved together – but only at the cost of sacrificing the uniqueness of the individual imagination, which is now decentred into the dreams of the species as a whole. For Wilde as for Butler, individual creativity is paradoxically quite as programmed as Nature itself, since it is merely the workings within us of a vital transindividual force. But whereas for the Creative Evolutionists this force is a dynamic within material history itself, for Wilde its creativity is increasingly confined to the mind. The very law of heredity which breeds exotic fantasies in the subjective sphere is also the force which enslaves us in the objective one. The evolutionary vitalism which, for Butler and Shaw, overcomes the distinction of mind and matter thus serves in Wilde's case to reinforce it. There is one great Necessity which works itself out in both mind and world; but this monism instantly bifurcates into a dualism, since the dreams it generates in the mind lead us blessedly away from material reality. The law of heredity 'can lead us away from surroundings whose beauty is dimmed to us by the mists of familiarity, or whose ignoble ugliness and sordid claims are marring the perfection of our development'.[3] It is in this way that Wilde can simultaneously cling to his determinism, open a space for the imagination, and deconstruct the individual psyche.

The tension in Wilde's work here is the sign of a familiar Romantic dilemma. If the human subject is integrated with Nature, it gains a secure foundation but sheds its freedom; if it breaks with Nature, it achieves an autonomy which is disturbingly ungrounded. The point of Creative Evolution (and, indeed, of Hegel's philosophy) is to have it both ways: if Nature is secretly a subject, then one can unite with it with no detriment to one's freedom. But there may also be a more specifically Irish context to Wilde's thought here. For the anti-mimetic aesthetic which his dualism involves – art must invent its own world, or at least transform Nature rather than slavishly reproducing it – has a venerable Irish lineage, all the way from the fantastic hyperbole of the ancient sagas to the myth and symbolism of the Revivalists. Like Yeats, Wilde carried over this anti-mimetic creed into life itself, denouncing heteronomy, refusing to submit to the law of another, taking himself as his own supreme model. 'There is no mode of action, no form of emotion, that we do not share with the lower animals', comments Gilbert in 'The Critic as Artist'. 'It is only by language that we rise above them, or above each other – by language, which is the parent, and not the child, of thought.'[4] Once again, Wilde retains his earlier scientific naturalism, but in the same gesture separates out human consciousness from it. A naturalistic anti-humanism, which regards humanity as just one more animal species, instantly breeds its own opposite – a humanism for which language is the mind's lonely edge over a determining environment. Language, as often in Irish history, compensates for a history in which you are more determined than determining, more object than agent.

The gap between consciousness and action is among other things a familiar Irish discrepancy between rhetoric and reality; and when Wilde speaks of language as the parent rather than the child of thought, he is adopting a performative rather than representational epistemology which has a lengthy Irish provenance. The more the body becomes the plaything of external forces, the more you must just keep talking, as Samuel Beckett's grotesque figures continue to stammer out the ghost of a narrative as the flesh disintegrates around the mouth. Language is the one frail enclave of freedom in an oppressive world; and its supreme form of expression, art, does not merely displace that world but actively wreaks vengeance upon it, refashions reality until fact is just the passing creation of fancy and life a slipshod imitation of art. 'Nature', comments Vivian, 'is our creation. It is in our brain that she quickens to life. Things are because we see them, and what we see, and how we see it, depends on the Arts that have influenced us.'[5] Like Yeats, Wilde dips back into Berkeleyan idealism in the teeth of a recalcitrant history, asserting with a certain Ascendancy arrogance of mind that the world is whichever way we wish it.[6] Or perhaps it would be more accurate to say that it is a way of seeing which combines the cavalierness of the Anglo-Irish with their sense of being under siege. It will be left to the even more audacious Shaw to suggest that the point of such mental acts is not only to interpret the world but to change it – that if only we will hard enough, life will deliver us our desire.

If Wilde despises Nature, it is also because, as for Roland Barthes and Michel Foucault, it suggests an oppressive normativity. Nature is the family, heterosexuality, stock notions, social convention; and Wilde had only to be presented with a convention to feel the irresistible urge to violate it. His whole instinct was to improvise, experiment, self-fashion; and if he disliked the natural it was because, as one who made a fetish of originality, he found it repetitive and predictable. One is tempted to speculate that one reason for his homosexuality is just the fact that he found heterosexuality intolerably clichéd; and Wilde was more terrified of a cliché than he was of appearing on Piccadilly in the wrong cut of waistcoat. So it is that he brandishes the epigram as a lethal weapon; for the epigram is the mind's momentary triumph over the dead matter of conventional wisdom, a piece of linguistic deviancy, a sagacious saying gone suddenly awry. 'A paradox', comments an early Wildean critic, 'is simply the truth of the minority, just as a commonplace is the truth of the majority.'[7] The epigram inverts, deconstructs, turns inside out, displays that capacity of the mind to dismantle and transmute the actual which we know as wit. This compulsion to invert runs much deeper in Wilde than sexuality, though the frisson of the epigram is erotic: 'What the paradox was to me in the sphere of thought', Wilde writes in *De Profundis*, 'perversity became to me in the sphere of passion.'[8] The Wildean epigram is a satiric cut, a negation of the given; but it also has the utopian dimension of the Freudian jest, which delights in its own exuberant play of spirit at the very moment it scores a deadly point. Both Wilde and Shaw are court jesters to the English upper classes, practitioners of paradox, estrangers of the tediously naturalized; but Shaw's more terse, cerebral wit, while quite as iconoclastic as Wilde's, is less languidly self-pleasuring, more briskly demystifying, more pointedly in the service of a hard-headed common sense. The Romantic and the rationalist, unified in Shaw's supposedly scientific theory of evolutionary vitalism, are also curiously commingled in his wit, which couples an intuitive flash of knowledge with a lethal shaft of realism. Shaw is brittle, bumptious, intolerably opinionated – though many of his opinions are admirably enlightened; Wilde presses through this cult of the ego to an extravagant extreme, raises it to the second power, so that its fictional or pose-like quality ironically qualifies it. The last person to whom it might have occurred that the subject was a fiction, for all his theories of the composite self, was George Bernard Shaw.

In what sense for Wilde, though, *was* the self a fiction? There is no doubt that he was a postmodernist *avant la lettre*, with his belief that interpretation is endless, criticism a form of creative writing, truth more aesthetic than cognitive, the human subject an ephemeral construct, the world a product of the sign, the body and its pleasures a subversive undoing of a pharisaical ideology. It is not hard for the émigré to perceive the constructed nature of social reality; if English stage comedy has been dominated by the Irish, it is partly because nobody is better placed to appreciate the comic arbitrariness of conventions than those who, while insiders enough to manipulate them with aplomb, never took them wholly for granted in the first place.[9] Wilde hijacked the social and theatrical forms of the English to demonstrate that he could deploy them even more dexterously than the natives, parodying their conventions by obeying them so exactly. Whether this was flattery or mockery was never easy to determine. If he was fascinated by the life of English high society, it was partly because its social forms seemed at once absolutely binding and flagrantly gratuitous; indeed in its meticulous formality of manners, English aristocratic society was for him a work of art all in itself. So it is that his formalism is at once an assault on bourgeois moralism, and a devotion to the truth of masks or substance of style on the part of one whose whole existence was a carefully wrought illusion.[10] But 'illusion' might suggest a concealed or distorted reality; and the question is whether Wilde believed that a true self lay behind his manifold masks, or whether he thought it merely an effect of them.

If there is a Nietzschean strain in his work which suggests that identity is a chimera, there is also an older Romantic drive to absolute self-realization. These need not be logical opposites: you can view identity as fluid, multiple, provisional, while holding that each of its passing phases demands complete expression. But such expression would seem to be of the essence of the self; and it is hard to see where this essence lies if the self, like truth, is just one's latest mood. Dorian Gray rejects 'the shallow psychology of those who conceive the Ego in man as a thing simple, permanent, reliable, and of one essence';[11] the self for him is protean, intertextual, composed (as for Samuel Butler) as much of the dead as of the living. Yet the narrative he belongs to works with the logic of the doubled, rather than decentred, subject, which is indeed essentialist: Dorian's hideous portrait signifies his true selfhood behind the alluring appearance. Guilt and remorse – the 'mediaeval emotions', as Henry Wotton scornfully dubs them – are a negative clue to who you are. Wilde pins together these conflicting views of the self by paradox: 'we are never more true to ourselves than when we are inconsistent ... through constant change, and through constant change alone, will [the individual] find his true unity'.[12] But if the essence of the self is evolution, this still does not resolve the Kantian problem of how this particular development comes to be mine rather than someone else's. The unity of the self may persist through change, but it cannot logically be identical with it.

Wilde's problem here is that he values the non-identical, but is committed to a notion of individualism which depends on self-identity.[13] The Schillerian and Arnoldian language of self-perfecting he inherits posits the very unified self which his more Nietzschean doctrines seek to undermine. On the one hand, he calls for a multiplication of personalities; on the other hand, he values the individual who is 'perfectly and absolutely himself', and imagines true personality as a simple, flower-like growth.[14] The self is pose, mask, persona; yet true individuality 'comes naturally and inevitably out of man', and 'The Soul of Man under Socialism' will even reach back to its author's early flirtation with Spencer by imagining this progressive differentiation as a force inherent in life itself. There is still a conflict, in other words, between evolutionary naturalism and its alternatives – only now this is one between different images of the self, not just a conflict between its unity with and separation from Nature. 'The Critic as Artist' tells us on one page that 'we are never more true to ourselves than when we are inconsistent', and portrays the critic as a decentred subject, a practitioner of negative capacity able to evaluate the object from every point of view. On the next page it speaks up for a strongly partisan self, remarking that 'the man who sees both sides of a question is a man who sees absolutely nothing at all'. 'Man', comments Gilbert, 'is least himself when he talks in his own person. Give him a mask, and he will tell you the truth.'[15] Does the image identify mask and true selfhood, or is the former merely a means to the latter?

Wilde adopts an idealist language of authenticity, while being mightily suspicious of the whole idea. It is, in part, a conflict between the European Romanticism to which he was heir, and the self-ironizing consciousness of the colonial mimic man, for whom truth can only mean the wry knowledge of one's own fictionality. Wilde was an accomplished impersonator of himself, holding that the posture created the subject as surely as you could fall in love by lingering over the vowels of a love poem. In Brechtian or Wittgensteinian fashion, he believes that interiority is a product of the signifier. If he was a phoney, then he would justify the fact by setting out to expose all identity as ungrounded and evanescent; the outsider would become the fifth columnist in the enemy camp, unmasking his own apparently assured identity for the poor pretence it was. The misery of colonial non-identity could thus be turned to advantage, converted into a utopian alternative to the politics which had produced it. But Wilde was also a sexually, ethnically and socially divided subject who for that very reason felt, like Yeats, the allures of absolute self-identity, and exemplified that condition in *De Profundis* in his aestheticized portrait of Christ.

'Truth in art is the unity of a thing with itself', Wilde comments.[16] If the human subject really is fluid, multiple, diffuse, then it is hard to see how it can have the self-identity of the work of art; yet Wilde's whole ambition is to aestheticize that subject. Art is not a substitute for life, as in the more stereotyped forms of aestheticism, but the very model of it. Gilbert remarks in Kantian vein that the sphere of art and that of ethics are absolutely distinct;[17] but this just means that the aesthetic should be kept free from the clutches of bourgeois morality. Wilde does not seem to realize that he himself has conflated the ethical and the aesthetic by aestheticizing ethics. To live well is to conduct yourself like a work of art, which means realizing one's creative potential, savouring each sensation with the intensity of a poem, valuing experience as an end in itself, and bowing to no authority but the law of one's own being. Anarchism and the aesthetic consort naturally together, the antinomianism of the one mirrored by the autonomism of the other. Every impulse which is truly of the self must find expression; but if the self is nothing but its impulses, how can it transcend them sufficiently to judge which ones are really authentic? If the answer is 'all of them' – if the only crime is the stifling of the self's free development – then one must either hold in naively libertarian fashion that all human desire is positive, or explain away why one has just enshrined the right to murder. 'Whatever is realised is right', Wilde comments dangerously in *De Profundis*. Moreover, if the subject's moods are diverse and conflictive, the imperative to express them all will lead to a contradictory selfhood, not a unified one.

Wilde has no real solutions to these problems, and neither does the Romantic lineage he inherits. Ethically speaking, he is a consequentialist who believes that morally right conduct is whatever promotes the non-moral good of free individual self-realization. In this, he is more or less at one with Karl Marx. But Marx himself qualified such consequentialism with certain deontological imperatives – the claim, for example, that such self-realization must take a form which allows it to be universalized.[18] For Marx, it must be a matter of mutuality, such that the self-realization of each is the condition for the self-realization of all. Wilde accepts the universalizing, but not the reciprocity. He is aware that his own liberty is deformed by its offensively privileged character, in a society where so many others are oppressed. This is why socialism is for him the pre-condition of genuine individual-ism: under socialism, everyone will live as he lives now. He is not thereby prepared to abandon that freedom, partly because he is enjoying himself too much, partly because one needs proleptic images of utopia. Just lie on the couch all day and be one's own communist society. But though Wilde wishes, like Marx, to universalize individual self-development, this will not for him be achieved through mutuality. On the contrary, it will be achieved by each individual leaving the others alone. It is in this sense that his political vision is finally more anarchist than socialist, and in this sense too that his individualism is at once a spiritualized version of commonplace bourgeois egoism, and one which threatens to subvert that ideology by pressing it to an outrageous extreme.[19] The self for Wilde may be mutable, pluralist, decentred; but it is not at root relational, and so is in the end more Nietzschean than Marxist. The self is indeed relational for the early Wilde of the Oxford commonplace book, who in Hegelian fashion views ego and non-ego as interdependent. It is also relational in so far as it is the product of a whole racial unconscious, a mere intertextual tangle in the evolution of *Geist*. But Wilde rarely views the human subject as constituted by its practical relations to others of its kind. The human being under socialism stands essentially alone, but will reap joy from sympathizing with others; and this is exactly the situation of Nietzsche's *Übermensch*, who recognizes no moral claims on his compassion but will exercise it, if he so chooses, for essentially aesthetic reasons.

Wilde's socialism is sometimes a naturalistic affair, in the manner of nineteenth-century libertarianism. There is a force at work in Nature making for individual freedom, and if only it were to be prised loose from artificial political institutions it would lead us by its own momentum into a higher social state. Resonances of this doctrine, which is in effect Spencer's Law of Equal Freedom, can be found in 'The Soul of Man under Socialism', and they hark back to the evolutionary naturalism of 'The Rise of Historical Criticism'. But the essay can also be read in a way more consonant with Wilde's later, more dualistic thought. The argument of 'The Soul of Man under Socialism' is that socialism, by automating labour and abolishing poverty, will release men and women from the claims of others and allow them to evolve as genuine individualists. This case, for all its perverse panache, is closer to Marx than to William Morris, whose *News from Nowhere* Wilde would probably have read in serialized form. Morris believed in making labour creative, whereas Marx believed in doing away with it as far as possible, so that individuals could fulfil their powers and capacities in some more fruitful way.

Both Marx and Wilde recognized that an economic revolution was necessary if economics were to cease binding so much precious human energy. Socialism for Wilde is a way of escaping the material world by reorganizing it; and the consequent division between self and society is a social version of the ontological duality we have examined earlier. Just as, for 'The Decay of Lying', Nature operates by certain laws from which the mind must keep its disdainful distance, so for 'The Soul of Man under Socialism' socialism will convert society into a 'thoroughly healthy organism', an automated sphere which the individual can then thankfully leave to look after itself. Society for Wilde is 'blind' and 'mechanical',[20] which is how Nature is too; but the point of socialism is to mechanize it even further, not to transform it into a creative medium. History is not, *pace* the Lamarckian vitalists, to become an expression of mind; instead, subjectivity must detach itself from the tedium of social life, relieved of all fatiguing responsibility for it. Just as Wilde argues in 'The Critic as Artist' that an awareness of determinism frees us from responsibility for our actions and allows us to dream, so his essay on socialism transplants this doctrine to the political sphere. Socialism will liberate us from the demands of altruism, which for Wilde is as much the flip side of possessive egoism as sentimentality is of cynicism. Few were as well placed as he to appreciate the selfish delights of self-sacrifice.

For Theodor Adorno, the identity of the subject, if one can speak in those terms, lies in suffering. This is what Wilde means in *De Profundis* when he remarks that pain, unlike pleasure, has no mask. But the work undercuts its own pronouncement. The Wilde of Reading Gaol, who urges meekness, simplicity, spontaneity, has simply discovered a fascinating new persona. The Jesus whose artistic genius and 'charm of personality' prove so seductive bears a remarkable resemblance to Oscar Wilde, a man now so humbled that he remakes the Son of God in his own image. *De Profundis* is all about how deeply its author has changed, and how utterly self-identical he remains. Bernard Shaw was quick to note this fact, remarking approvingly of the essay that Wilde 'comes out the same man he went in'.[21] In the very crisis of conversion, there must be no revolutionary break with a past self: it is just that whereas he previously fingered the flowers of evil, he will now, for the sake of Hellenic completeness, extend his aesthetic sympathies to the good. His prose is hushed, grave, tremulous with pathos, even as the old wisecracks keep breaking through. This spiritually chastened penitent is all he ever was, only more so: having unaccountably overlooked the aesthetic delights of moral virtue, he is now resolved to savour them to the full.

For all his exquisitely calculated pathos, Wilde is a genuinely tragic figure; and it is here, finally, that he has the edge over Shaw. Shaw praised *De Profundis* as exhilaratingly comic, commenting that 'it annoys me to have people degrading the whole affair to the level of sentimental tragedy'.[22] There can be no real waste or breakdown for the hubristic philosophy of evolutionary vitalism, with its callow insensitivity to the material limitations of the human creature.[23] Sin, crime, failure will all finally be recycled as success, in a perspective to which the equally anti-tragic Yeats was in his own way no stranger. Wilde sometimes flirts with this idea too, adopting the theory (a kind of evolutionary deism) that evil is misperceived good; but in him, in contrast to Shaw, Romanticism has confronted Darwinism rather than taking the Lamarckian detour around it. The universe is not spontaneously on the side of the individual, and neither, as Wilde was to discover, is society. The imaginary bond between mind and world has been ruptured, and the mind must now turn back on its own resources in that gesture of cosmic defiance we know as art. One would not wish Oscar Wilde's calamity on Bernard Shaw; but his art would no doubt have been the better for it.

Notes (cut and renumbered)

1. 'The Critic as Artist', in G. F. Maine, ed., *The Works of Oscar Wilde*, London, 1949, p. 979.
2. Wilde may have derived this doctrine from the anthropology of Edward Tylor, with which he seems to have been familiar. See Tylor's *Primitive Culture* (London 1871). For his interest in heredity, see John Wilson Foster, 'Against Nature? Science and Oscar Wilde', *University of Toronto Quarterly*, vol. 63, no. 2 (Winter 1993/4).
3. 'The Critic as Artist', *Works*, p. 980.
4. Ibid., p. 962. The thought is probably Max Muller's, with whom Wilde studied at Oxford. For Muller, language was 'the one great barrier between the brute and man: Man speaks, and no brute

has ever uttered a word. Language is our Rubicon, and no brute will dare to cross it ...' (quoted by Philip E. Smith and Michael S. Helfand, eds, *Oscar Wilde's Oxford Notebooks*, New York and Oxford, 1989, p. 9).

5. 'The Decay of Lying', *Works*, p. 925.
6. An emphasis on the creative mind which can be found as far back in Irish thought as the ninth-century theology of John Scottus Eriugena. For Eriugena, humanity is an image of God in the boundlessness of its mind, free from all external authority and necessity. Eriugena's term for such boundlessness is *anarchos*: the human individual is entirely free because he or she is ruled only by the utter freedom of the divine will. Just as art for Wilde is the intervention of the mind in Nature, so for the idealist Eriugena knowledge is less an adequation to the real than an absorption of reality into thought. See Dermot Moran, 'Nature, Man and God in the Philosophy of John Scottus Eriugena', in Richard Kearney, ed., *The Irish Mind* (Dublin 1985).
7. Ernest Newman, 'Oscar Wilde: A Literary Appreciation', reprinted in Karl Beckson, ed., *Oscar Wilde: The Critical Heritage* (London 1970), p. 203.
8. *De Profundis, Works*, p. 857.
9. For a discussion of the Irish influence on the English comic stage, see Thomas Kilroy, 'Anglo-Irish Playwrights and Comic Tradition', in M. P. Hederman and R. Kearney, eds, *The Crane Bag Book of Irish Studies* (Dublin 1982).
10. Wilde's formalist bent anticipates the doctrines of Russian Formalism: when he writes in 'The Critic as Artist' that the poet's idea follows from his choice of the sonnet form, he is very close to the Formalists' notion of content as the mere 'motivation' of form.
11. *The Picture of Dorian Gray, Works*, p. 112.
12. 'The Critic as Artist', *Works*, pp. 984, 987.
13. It is not clear why a view of the self as non-identical should be thought of in our own time as inherently radical. If this is so, then David Hume was certainly a radical.
14. 'The Soul of Man under Socialism', *Works*, pp. 1026, 1023.
15. 'The Critic as Artist', *Works*, p. 984.
16. *De Profundis, Works*, p. 864.
17. Wilde is also Kantian in his belief, recorded in 'The Soul of Man under Socialism', that new works of art cannot be measured by the standards of the past – precisely Kant's argument in *The Critique of Judgement*.
18. See on this topic R. G. Peffer, *Marxism, Morality, and Social Justice* (Princeton 1990), Part 1.
19. The same may be said of his homosexuality, which is at once a radical strike against convention and a covertly accepted part of Victorian ruling-class male practice.
20. *De Profundis, Works*, p. 882.
21. Letter to Robert Ross of 1905, reprinted in Beckson, ed., *Oscar Wilde: The Critical Heritage*, p. 244.
22. Ibid., p. 244.
23. For an eloquent statement of this theme, see Sebastiano Timpanaro, *On Materialism* (London 1975), Ch. 1.

Chapter 6

Joseph Conrad:
Heart of Darkness

GENERAL INTRODUCTION

Joseph Conrad (1857–1924) was born Jozef Teodor Konrad Korzeniowski in Russian Poland. He joined the merchant marine in 1874, learned English three years later, and in 1886 became a British subject. He began writing fiction in London in 1889. His first novel, *Almayer's Folly* (1895), was followed by – amongst other works – *The Nigger of the Narcissus* (1898), the 'Preface' of which contains an important artistic credo; *Lord Jim* (1900); *Nostromo* (1904); *The Secret Agent* (1907) and *Under Western Eyes* (1911). In 1890 Conrad travelled to the Congo Free State, ruled by King Leopold II of Belgium, to take charge of a steamer 230 miles up river for a Belgian trading company. He kept a diary of his short visit (between mid-June and August 1890) and drew on the experience for the story 'An Outpost of Progress' (1897) as well as for the *Heart of Darkness*. This was serialized in 1899 and published in a single edition in 1902.

The following four essays present quite marked differences in styles of reading and commentary as well as both underlying and explicit differences in moral, philosophical and political perspective. One way of assessing these differences is to see how their authors understand a common feature or theme. As we suggest in the Headnotes below, the references to 'emptiness' in these arguments provide a revealing instance of this. A further difference is that these critics are in turn British, French, American-Palestinian and Nigerian. They therefore offer a set of international perspectives upon a canonic author and text and show how the status and meanings of this text have altered as new critical and ideological positions have come to assert themselves – while reminding us that Conrad's story was never perhaps taken for granted. Try in assessing the essays to identify these differences in perspective and to track the changing valuations of the story.

    If, at the same time, some of the critical methods and cultural assumptions at work in these essays are quite different, they are all noticeably by male critics. Does this mean that they to any extent share a perspective? Fairly clearly, the question of gender is of interest, 'internally', in Conrad's story itself. Thus, readers of *Heart of Darkness* have often acknowledged the important role of Kurtz's 'Intended' and noted the pairing of this white woman and the African who appears to be his mistress in the Congo. The essays sometimes refer along these lines to the 'Intended', or to both women. But generally they refer to neither.

Is this a significant omission? Would it require a fundamentally different approach to rectify it? Also, if we were to consider questions of gender and sexuality, as well as, or along with, imperialism – which is the major ideological theme these essays address – would this produce a different perspective not only upon women characters but the relation of Kurtz to Marlow or the male company aboard the *Nellie*? Again, would the essays by the present company of male critics need to shift their ground radically to accommodate this aspect of the story?

Further Reading

Jocelyn Baines, *Joseph Conrad. A Critical Biography* (Weidenfeld & Nicolson, 1960).
Avrom Fleishman, *Conrad's Politics* (Johns Hopkins University Press, 1967).
Wilson Harris, 'The Frontier on Which *Heart of Darkness* Stands', in *Explorations. A Selection of Talks and Articles* (Dagaroo Press, 1981).
Benita Parry, *Conrad and Imperialism* (Macmillan, 1983).

Useful study aids

Heart of Darkness. Text Plus, Introduction by Craig Raine, Notes by Jim Porteus (Hodder & Stoughton, 1990), includes relevant statements from letters and Conrad's Congo diary as well as biographical, historical and critical material.
D. Tallack (ed.), *Literary Theory at Work* (Batsford, 1987) contains three essays demonstrating structuralist, dialogic and Marxist readings of Conrad's tale.
Ross C. Murfin, *Heart of Darkness* (Macmillan 'Case Studies' in Contemporary Criticism, 1992) contains the text of Conrad's story and five essays representing different critical perspectives.

Francis Ford Coppola's film of the Vietnam war, *Apocalypse Now* (1979), draws consciously on Conrad's story. For further related viewing and commentary, see *Hearts of Darkness: A Filmmaker's Apocalypse* (Eleanor Coppola's documentary on the making of *Apocalypse Now*), directed by Fax Bahr and George Hickenlooper, USA, 1991; Cesare Casarino, 'Historical Critique in *Heart of Darkness* and *Apocalypse Now*', *Polygraph* (Duke University Press) Nos. 2/3 (1989), pp. 94–113 and Anthony Easthope, 'Realism and its Subversion', in Louvre and Walsh, eds, *Tell Me Lies* (Oxford University Press), 1988.

6.1   F. R. LEAVIS: FROM *THE GREAT TRADITION* (1948)

For further details on F. R. Leavis see Ch. 4, p. 146.

In *The Great Tradition*, Leavis argues that the work of Jane Austen, George Eliot, Henry James and Joseph Conrad comprises a tradition sharing 'a vital capacity for experience, a kind of reverent openness before life, and a marked moral intensity' (p. 17). He introduces his reflections on the *Heart of Darkness* – which form part of a chapter on the 'Minor Works and *Nostromo*' – with an observation, supported by remarks by E. M. Forster on Conrad's misleading philosophical manner: 'that the greatness attributed to him tended to be identified with an imputed profundity and that this "profundity" was not what it was taken to be, but quite other, and the reverse of a strength' (p. 192). Since Leavis begins the discussion below with an illustration of 'strength', it is worth considering what meaning and value this term holds for him and what might be meant by its opposite.

Above all, this judgement rests on the matter of Conrad's phrasing (his use of terms such as 'inscrutable', 'unfathomable' and 'inconceivable'). What is Leavis' objection to this vocabulary and what does this reveal of his sense of literary value or 'strength'? At one point he accuses Conrad of 'borrowing the arts of the magazine-writer'. How do you think later critics might choose to think of this 'borrowing'; and how might they view the relation of presence and absence (Conrad's 'insistence on the presence of what he can't produce') which Leavis detects? The air of mystery in the story, he says finally, applies not only to Kurtz and the wilderness but to the sea and to 'Woman'. What is Leavis' point here, and how, in relation to the question raised in the General Introduction above, might a feminist critic explore these associations and their treatment, in both Leavis and Conrad?

Readers will also note the extent to which Leavis depends on direct and lengthy quotations from Conrad's story. This practice was characteristic of his method and of the American-based 'new criticism' and, as such, highly influential upon Anglo-American literary teaching and study (see Ch. 2, pp. 69–71). What attitudes and assumptions (towards literature and the reader) does this suggest, and how is it related, do you think, to the aesthetic and moral values which otherwise direct Leavis' commentary?

Compare Leavis' discussion of George Eliot, Ch. 4, pp. 146–51. Does this support your findings on the present essay?

The following extract is taken from *The Great Tradition* (Chatto & Windus, 1948), pp. 193–202.

The Great Tradition

Heart of Darkness is, by common consent, one of Conrad's best things – an appropriate source for the epigraph of *The Hollow Men*: 'Mistah Kurtz – he dead.' That utterance, recalling the particularity of its immediate context, represents the strength of *Heart of Darkness*:

> He cried in a whisper at some image, at some vision – he cried out twice, a cry that was no more than a breath –
> 'The horror! The horror!'
> I blew the candle out and left the cabin. 'The pilgrims were dining in the mess-room, and I took my place opposite the manager, who lifted his eyes to give me a questioning glance,

which I successfully ignored. He leaned back, serene, with that peculiar smile of his sealing the unexpressed depth of his meanness. A continuous shower of small flies streamed upon the lamp, upon the cloth, upon our hands and faces. Suddenly the manager's boy put his insolent face in the doorway, and said in a tone of scathing contempt –

'Mistah Kurtz – he dead.'

All the pilgrims rushed out to see. I remained, and went on with my dinner. I believe I was considered brutally callous. However, I did not eat much. There was a lamp in there – light, don't you know – and outside it was so beastly, beastly dark.

This passage, it will be recognized, owes its force to a whole wide context of particularities that gives the elements here – the pilgrims, the manager, the manager's boy, the situation – their specific values. Borrowing a phrase from Mr Eliot's critical writings, one might say that *Heart of Darkness* achieves its over-powering evocation of atmosphere by means of 'objective correlatives'. The details and circumstances of the voyage to and up the Congo are present to us as if we were making the journey ourselves and (chosen for record as they are by a controlling imaginative purpose) they carry specificities of emotion and suggestion with them. There is the gunboat dropping shells into Africa:

There wasn't even a shed there, and she was shelling the bush. It appears the French had one of their wars going on thereabouts. Her ensign dropped limp like a rag; the muzzles of the long six-inch guns stuck out all over the low hull; the greasy, slimy swell swung her up lazily and let her down, swaying her thin masts. In the empty immensity of earth, sky and water, there she was, incomprehensible, firing into a continent. Pop, would go one of the six-inch guns; a small flame would dart and vanish, a tiny projectile would give a feeble screech – and nothing happened. Nothing could happen. There was a touch of insanity in the proceeding, a sense of lugubrious drollery in the sight; and it was not dissipated by somebody on board assuring me earnestly there was a camp of natives – he called them enemies! – hidden out of sight somewhere.

We gave her her letters (I heard the men in that lonely ship were dying of fever at the rate of three a day) and went on. We called at some more places with farcical names, where the merry dance of death and trade goes on in the still and earthy atmosphere as of an overheated catacomb. ...

There is the arrival at the Company's station:

I came upon a boiler wallowing in the grass, then found a path leading up the hill. It turned aside for the boulders, and also for an undersized railway-truck lying there on its back with its wheels in the air. One was off. The thing looked as dead as the carcass of some animal. I came upon more pieces of decaying machinery, a stack of rusty nails. To the left a clump of trees made a shady spot, where dark things seemed to stir feebly. I blinked, the path was steep. A horn tooted to the right, and I saw black people run. A heavy, dull detonation shook the ground, a puff of smoke came out of the cliff, and that was all. No change appeared on the face of the rock. They were building a railway. The cliff was not in the way of anything; but this objectless blasting was all the work going on.

A slight clanking behind me made me turn my head. Six black men advanced in a file, toiling up the path. They walked erect and slow, balancing small baskets full of earth on their heads, and the clink kept time with their footsteps. Black rags were wound round their loins, and the short ends behind waggled to and fro like tails. I could see every rib, the joints of their limbs were like knots in a rope; each had an iron collar on his neck, and all were connected together with a chain whose bights swung between them, rhythmically clinking. Another report from the cliff made me think suddenly of that ship of war I had seen firing into a continent. It was the same kind of ominous voice; but these men could by no stretch of imagination be called enemies. They were called criminals. ...

There is the grove of death:

At last I got under the trees. My purpose was to stroll into the shade for a moment; but no sooner within it than it seemed to me that I had stepped into the gloomy circle of some Inferno. The rapids were near, and an uninterrupted, uniform, headlong, rushing noise filled the mournful stillness of the grove, where not a breath stirred, not a leaf moved, with a mysterious sound – as though the tearing pace of the launched earth had suddenly become audible.

Black shapes crouched, lay, sat beneath the trees, leaning against the trunks, clinging to the earth, half coming out, half effaced within the dim light, in all the attitudes of pain, abandonment, and despair. Another mine of the cliff went off, followed by a slight shudder of the soil under my feet. The work was going on. The work! And this was the place where some of the helpers had withdrawn to die.

They were dying slowly – it was very clear. They were not enemies, they were not criminals, they were nothing earthly now – nothing but black shadows of disease and starvation, lying confusedly in the greenish gloom. ... These moribund shapes were free as air and nearly as thin. I began to distinguish the gleam of the eyes under the trees. There, glancing down, I saw a face near my hand. The black bones reclined at full length with one shoulder against the tree, and slowly the eyelids rose and the sunken eyes looked up at me, enormous and vacant, a kind of blind, white flicker in the depths of the orbs, which died out slowly.

By means of this art of vivid essential record, in terms of things seen and incidents experienced by a main agent in the narrative, and particular contacts and exchanges with other human agents, the overwhelming sinister and fantastic 'atmosphere' is engendered. Ordinary greed, stupidity, and moral squalor are made to look like behaviour in a lunatic asylum against the vast and oppressive mystery of the surroundings, rendered potently in terms of sensation. This means lunacy, which we are made to feel as at the same time normal and insane, is brought out by contrast with the fantastically secure innocence of the young harlequin-costumed Russian ('son of an arch-priest ... Government of Tambov'), the introduction to whom is by the way of that copy of Tower's (or Towson's) *Inquiry into Some Points of Seamanship*, symbol of tradition, sanity, and the moral idea, found lying, an incongruous mystery, in the dark heart of Africa.

Of course, as the above quotations illustrate, the author's comment cannot be said to be wholly implicit. Nevertheless, it is not separable from the thing rendered, but seems to emerge from the vibration of this as part of the tone. At least, this is Conrad's art at its best. There are, however, places in *Heart of Darkness* where we become aware of comment as an interposition, and worse, as an intrusion, at times an exasperating one. Hadn't he, we find ourselves asking, overworked 'inscrutable', 'inconceivable', 'unspeakable' and that kind of word already? – yet still they recur.

Is anything added to the oppressive mysteriousness of the Congo by such sentences as:

> It was the stillness of an implacable force brooding over an inscrutable intention – ?

The same vocabulary, the same adjectival insistence upon inexpressible and incomprehensible mystery, is applied to the evocation of human profundities and spiritual horrors; to magnifying a thrilled sense of the unspeakable potentialities of the human soul. The actual effect is not to magnify but rather to muffle. The essential vibration emanates from the interaction of the particular incidents, actions, and perceptions that are evoked with such charged concreteness. The legitimate kind of comment, that which seems the inevitable immediate resonance of the recorded event, is represented here:

> And then I made a brusque movement, and one of the remaining posts of that vanished fence leaped into the field of my glass. You remember I told you I had been struck at the distance by certain attempts at ornamentation, rather remarkable in the ruinous aspect of the place. Now I had suddenly a nearer view, and its first result was to make me throw my head back as if before a blow. Then I went carefully from post to post with my glass, and I saw my mistake. Those round knobs were not ornamental but symbolic; they were expressive and puzzling, striking and disturbing – food for thought and also for the vultures if there had been any looking down from the sky; but at all events for such ants as were industrious enough to ascend the pole. They would have been even more impressive, those heads on the stakes, if their faces had not been turned to the house. Only one, the first I had made out, was facing my way. I was not so shocked as you may think. The start back I had given was really nothing but a movement of surprise. I had expected to see a knob of wood there, you know. I returned deliberately to the first I had seen – and there it was, black, dried, sunken, with closed eyelids – a head that seemed to sleep at the top of that pole, and, with the shrunken dry lips showing a narrow white line of the teeth, was smiling too, smiling continuously at some endless and jocose dream of that eternal slumber.
>
> I am not disclosing any trade secrets. In fact, the manager said afterwards that Mr Kurtz's methods had ruined the district. I have no opinion on that point, but I want you clearly to understand that there was nothing exactly profitable in those heads being there. They only showed that Mr Kurtz lacked restraint in the gratification of his various lusts, that there was something wanting in him – some small matter which, when the pressing need arose, could not be found under his magnificent eloquence. Whether he knew of this deficiency himself I can't say. I think the knowledge came to him at last – only at the very last, but the wilderness had found him out early, and had taken on him a terrible vengeance for the fantastic invasion. I think it had whispered to him things about himself which he did not know, things of which he had no conception till he took counsel with this great solitude – and the whisper had proved irresistibly fascinating. It echoed loudly within him because he was hollow at the core. ... I put down the glass, and the head that had appeared near enough to be spoken to seemed at once to have leaped away from me into inaccessible distance.

– That the 'admirer of Mr Kurtz', the companion of the narrator here, should be the fantastically sane and innocent young Russian is part of the force of the passage.

By such means as it illustrates we are given a charged sense of the monstrous hothouse efflorescences fostered in Kurtz by solitude and the wilderness. It is a matter of such things as the heads on posts – a direct significant glimpse, the innocent Russian's explanations, the incidents of the progress up the river and the moral and physical incongruities registered; in short, of the charge generated in a variety of highly specific evocations. The stalking of the moribund Kurtz, a skeleton crawling through the long grass on all fours as he makes his bolt towards the fires and the tomtoms, is a triumphant climax in the suggestion of strange and horrible perversions. But Conrad isn't satisfied with these means; he feels that there is, or ought to be, some horror, some significance he has yet to bring out. So we have an adjectival and worse than supererogatory insistence on 'unspeakable rites', 'unspeakable secrets', 'monstrous passions', 'inconceivable mystery', and so on. If it were only, as it largely is in *Heart of Darkness*, a matter of an occasional phrase it would still be regrettable as tending to cheapen the tone. But the actual cheapening is little short of disastrous. Here, for instance, we have Marlow at the crisis of the episode just referred to:

> I tried to break the spell – the heavy, mute spell of the wilderness – that seemed to draw him to its pitiless breast by the awakening of forgotten and brutal instincts, by the memory of gratified and monstrous passions. This alone, I was convinced, had driven him out to the edge of the forest, towards the gleam of the fires, the throb of drums, the drone of weird incantations; this alone had beguiled his unlawful soul beyond the bounds of permitted aspirations. And, don't you see, the terror of the position was not in being knocked on the head – though I had a very lively sense of that danger too – but in this, that I had to deal with a being to whom I could not appeal in the name of anything high or low. ... I've been telling you what we said – repeating the phrases we pronounced – but what's the good? They were common everyday words – the familiar vague sounds exchanged on every waking day of life. But what of that? They had behind them, to my mind, the terrific suggestiveness of words heard in dreams, of phrases spoken in nightmares. Soul! If anybody had ever struggled with a soul, I am the man. And I wasn't arguing with a lunatic either. ... But his soul was mad. Being alone in the wilderness, it had looked within itself, and, by heavens! I tell you, it had gone mad. I had – for my sins, I suppose – to go through the ordeal of looking into it myself. No eloquence could have been so withering to one's belief in mankind as his final burst of sincerity. He struggled with himself too, I saw it – I heard it. I saw the inconceivable mystery of a soul that knew no restraint, no faith, and no fear, yet struggling blindly with itself.

– Conrad must here stand convicted of borrowing the arts of the magazine-writer (who has borrowed his, shall we say, from Kipling and Poe) in order to impose on his readers and on himself, for thrilled response, a 'significance' that is merely an emotional insistence on the presence of what he can't produce. The insistence betrays the absence, the willed 'intensity' the nullity. He is intent on making a virtue out of not knowing what he means. The vague and unrealizable, he asserts with a strained impressiveness, is the profoundly and tremendously significant:

> I've been telling you what we said – repeating the phrases we pronounced – but what's the good? They were common everyday words – the familiar vague sounds exchanged on every waking day of life. But what of that? They had behind them, to my mind, the terrific suggestiveness of words heard in dreams, of phrases spoken in nightmares.

– What's the good, indeed? If he cannot through the concrete presentment of incident, setting and image invest the words with the terrific something that, by themselves, they fail to convey, then no amount of adjectival and ejaculatory emphasis will do it.

> I saw the inconceivable mystery of a soul – etc.

– That, of course, is an ambiguous statement. I see that there is a mystery, and it remains a mystery for me; I can't conceive what it is; and if I offer this inability to your wonder as a thrilling affair of 'seeing an inconceivable mystery', I exemplify a common trait of human nature. Actually, Conrad had no need to try and inject 'significance' into his narrative in this way. What he shows himself to have successfully and significantly seen is enough to make *Heart of Darkness* a disturbing presentment of the kind he aimed at. By the attempt at injection he weakens, in his account of Kurtz's death, the effect of that culminating cry:

> He cried in a whisper at some image, at some vision – he cried out twice, a cry that was no more than a breath – 'The horror! The horror!'

– The 'horror' there has very much less force than it might have had if Conrad had strained less.

This final account of Kurtz is associated with a sardonic tone, an insistent irony that leads us on to another bad patch, the closing interview in Brussels with Kurtz's 'Intended':

> The room seemed to have grown darker, as if all the sad light of the cloudy evening had taken refuge on her forehead. This fair hair, this pale visage, this pure brow, seemed surrounded by an ashy halo from which the dark eyes looked out at me. Their glance was guileless, profound, confident, and trustful. She carried her sorrowful head as though she were proud of that sorrow, as though she would say, I – I alone know how to mourn for him as he deserves.

It is not part of Conrad's irony that there should be anything ironical in this presentment of the woman. The irony lies in the association of her innocent nobility, her purity of idealizing faith, with the unspeakable corruption of Kurtz; and it is developed (if that is the word) with a thrilled insistence that recalls the melodramatic intensities of Edgar Allan Poe:

> I felt like a chill grip on my chest. 'Don't,' I said in a muffled voice.
> 'Forgive me. I – I – have mourned so long in silence – in silence. ... You were with him – to the last? I think of his loneliness. Nobody near to understand him as I would have understood. Perhaps no one to hear. ...'
> 'To the very end,' I said shakily. 'I heard his very last words. ...' I stopped in a fright.
> 'Repeat them,' she murmured in a heart-broken tone. 'I want – I want – something – something to live with.'
> I was on the point of crying at her 'Don't you hear them?' The dark was repeating them in a persistent whisper all around us, in a whisper that seemed to swell menacingly, like the first whisper of a rising wind. 'The horror! the horror!'
> 'His last words – to live with,' she insisted. 'Don't you understand I loved him – I loved him – I loved him!'

I pulled myself together and spoke slowly.

'The last word he pronounced was – your name.'

I heard a light sigh and then my heart stood still, stopped dead short by an exulting and terrible cry, by the cry of inconceivable triumph and of an unspeakable pain.

'I knew it – I was sure!' ... She knew. She was sure.

Conrad's 'inscrutable', it is clear, associates with Woman as it does with the wilderness, and the thrilling mystery of the Intended's innocence is of the same order as the thrilling mystery of Kurtz's corruption: the profundities are complementary. It would appear that the cosmopolitan Pole, student of the French masters, who became a British master-mariner, was in some respects a simple soul. If anyone should be moved to question the propriety of this way of putting it, perhaps the following will be found something of a justification:

> Woman and the sea revealed themselves to me together, as it were: two mistresses of life's values. The illimitable greatness of the one, the unfathomable seduction of the other, working their immemorial spells from generation to generation fell upon my heart at last: a common fortune, an unforgettable memory of the sea's formless might and of the sovereign charm in that woman's form wherein there seemed to beat the pulse of divinity rather than blood.

This comes from a bad novel, one of Conrad's worst things, *The Arrow of Gold*. It is a sophisticated piece of work, with a sophistication that elaborates and aggravates the deplorable kind of naïvety illustrated in the quotation. Not that the author's talent doesn't appear, but the central theme – and the pervasive atmosphere – is the 'unfathomable seduction' of the 'enigmatic' Rita; a glamorous mystery, the avocation of which (though more prolonged and elaborated) is of the same order as the evocation of sinister significance, the 'inconceivable' mystery of Kurtz, at the close of *Heart of Darkness*. If any reader of that tale had felt that the irony permitted a doubt regarding Conrad's attitude towards the Intended, the presentment of Rita should settle it.

6.2   TZVETAN TODOROV: '*HEART OF DARKNESS*' (1978, TRANS. 1990)

Tzvetan Todorov is known chiefly for his contribution to the structuralist theory of narrative (see *A Reader's Guide* 3/e, pp. 109–13). He was born in Bulgaria and has lectured extensively in the USA and in France – he has held posts at the Ecole Pratique des Hautes Etudes and the Centre Nationale de la Recherche Scientifique in Paris, where he is currently Director of Research. His works in publication include *The Fantastic. A Structuralist Approach to a Literary Genre* (1975), *The Poetics of Prose* (1977) and *Mikhail Bakhtin. The Dialogic Principle* (1984).

Todorov's chapter on Conrad appears in *Genres in Discourse*, which consists of a group of theoretical essays on narrative and reading, followed by studies on texts exemplifying the genres of the poetic novel, prose poetry and short story. Conrad's novella he considers in relation to the conventions of the adventure story. Its action, he concludes, however, is disappointing; its 'mythological' narrative a pretext for a 'gnoseological' narrative of the search for truth. The *Heart of Darkness*, that is to say, emerges, in his terms, as less an adventure story than a narrative of interpretation and about interpretation. How does this mean Todorov views the 'inscrutability', emptiness and absence other critics comment upon? Is his own reading a 'structuralist' or 'poststructuralist' one? How does it comment on the search for meaning by other critics here and how do their more expressly evaluative and political readings comment in turn upon his own approach?

'*Heart of Darkness*' is from Tzvetan Todorov, *Genres in Discourse* (1978, trans. Catherine Porter, Cambridge University Press, 1990), pp. 103–12.

Heart of Darkness

On the surface, Joseph Conrad's *Heart of Darkness* resembles an adventure story. As a little boy, Marlow daydreams about the blank spaces on a map. When he grows up he decides to explore the largest of these spaces: the heart of the dark continent, reached by a serpentine river. He is assigned the task of reaching Kurtz, an agent of an ivory-collecting company. He is warned of dangers. This conventional beginning does not keep its promises, however. The risks suggested by the Company's doctor are internal: he measures the cranium of those who set out to travel and asks if there is madness in the family. Similarly, the Swedish captain who takes Marlow to the first station is pessimistic about the future, but he has in mind a man who went off alone and hung himself. Danger lies within; adventures are played out in the explorer's mind, not in the situations he encounters.

What follows only confirms this impression. When Marlow finally reaches the Central Station, he is condemned to inactivity by the shipwreck of the steamboat he is supposed to command. Long months go by during which his only activity is waiting for the arrival of some missing rivets. Nothing happens. And when something finally does happen, the narrative neglects to tell us about it. Kurtz's departure for the station, his meeting with the manager of the Central Station, Marlow's return and his relations with the 'pilgrims' after Kurtz's death – all these go unnarrated. During the decisive scene in which Kurtz is found, Marlow remains on board the boat in conversation with a peculiar Russian fellow; we never do find out what happened on land.

Or let us take the traditionally climactic moment in adventure stories, the battle scene: here it takes place between blacks and whites. The only death deemed worthy of mention is the helmsman's, and Marlow speaks of it only because the dying man's blood fills his shoes, which he then flings overboard. The outcome of the battle is derisory: the whites' fire reaches no one and only produces smoke ('I had seen, from the way the tops of the bushes rustled and flew, that almost all the shots had gone too high' [52–3]).[1] As for the blacks, the mere sound of the boat's whistle sends them flying: 'The tumult of angry and warlike yells was checked instantly ... The retreat ... was caused by the screeching of the steamwhistle' (47, 53).

The same is true of the one other culminating moment in the story: the unforgettable image of the black woman emerging from the jungle while Kurtz is being lifted into the board: 'Suddenly she opened her bared arms and threw them up rigid about her head, as though in an uncontrollable desire to touch the sky ...' (62). The gesture is powerful but finally just an enigmatic sign, not an act.

If there is adventure in this story, it is not where we expected to find it. The events that ought to have gripped our attention cannot do so for, contrary to all laws of suspense, their outcome is announced well in advance, and repeatedly. At the very beginning of the voyage, Marlow forewarns his listeners: 'I foresaw that in the blinding sunshine of that land I would become acquainted with a flabby, pretending, weak-eyed devil of a rapacious and pitiless folly' (17). We are reminded on several occasions not only of Kurtz's death but also of Marlow's subsequent destiny ('as it turned out, it was to have the care of his memory' [51]).

The facts are unimportant; only their interpretation will count. Marlow's voyage had but one goal: 'I had travelled all this way for the sole purpose of talking with Mr. Kurtz. Talking with ...' (48). Talking in order to comprehend, not to act. That is doubtless why Marlow goes looking for Kurtz after Kurtz has fled from the pilgrims, though Marlow disapproves of the pilgrims' kidnapping: it is because Kurtz has escaped from sight, from earshot, has not allowed himself to be known. The trip up the river is thus a way of approaching truth. Space symbolizes time; the story's adventures foster understanding. 'Going up that river was like travelling back to the earliest beginnings of the world ...' (34). 'We were travelling in the night of first ages ...' (36).

The 'mythological' narrative (of action) is present only to allow the deployment of a 'gnoseological' narrative (of knowledge). *Acts* are insignificant here because all efforts are focused on the search for *being*. (As Conrad noted in a 1918 article on British seamen: 'There is nothing more futile under the sun than a mere adventurer.'[2]) Conrad's adventurer – if we want to keep on calling him that – has transformed the direction of his search: he no longer seeks to win but to know.

Countless details strewn throughout the story confirm the predominance of knowing over doing, for the overall design has its repercussions on an infinite number of specific acts that all tend in the same direction. The characters never stop meditating on the hidden meaning of the words they hear, the impenetrable signification of the signals they perceive. The manager ends all his sentences with a smile that resembles 'a seal applied on the words to make the meaning of the commonest phrase appear absolutely unscrutable' (*Heart of Darkness*, 22). The message from the Russian, which is supposed to help the travelers, is for no obvious reason written in a telegraphic style that renders it incomprehensible. Kurtz knows the language of the blacks, yet to the question: 'Do you understand this?' he merely produces 'a smile of indefinable meaning' (68), a smile as enigmatic as the words spoken in an unknown language.

If words require interpretation, the nonverbal symbols exchanged need it even more. During the boat trip up the river, 'at night sometimes the roll of drums behind the curtain of trees would run up the river and remain sustained faintly, as if hovering in the air high over our heads, till the first break of day. Whether it meant war, peace, or prayer we could not tell' (35–6). Other symbolic nonintentional phenomena – events, behavior, situations – are just as hard to decipher. The steamer sank to the bottom of the river: 'I did not see the real significance of that wreck at once' (21). The pilgrims strolled about aimlessly at the Central Station: 'I asked myself sometimes what it all meant' (23). Moreover, Marlow's profession – steering a boat – is nothing but an ability to interpret signs: 'I had to keep guessing at the channel; I had to discern, mostly by inspiration, the signs of hidden banks; I watched for sunken stones ... I had to keep a look-out for the signs of dead wood we could cut up in the night for next day's steaming. When you have to attend to things of that sort, to the mere incidents of the surface, the reality – the reality, I tell you – fades. The inner truth is hidden – luckily, luckily' (34). Truth, reality, essences remain intangible; life wears itself out in the interpretation of signs.

Human relationships can be summed up as hermeneutic research. The Russian, for Marlow, is 'inexplicable,' 'an insoluble problem' (55). Yet Marlow himself becomes an object of interpretation for the brickmaker. And the Russian in turn, speaking of the relationship between Kurtz and his wife, has to admit defeat: 'I don't understand' (63). The jungle itself appears to Marlow 'so dark, so impenetrable to human thought' (56; note that the reference is to the mind and not the body) that he thinks he detects in it the presence of a 'mute spell' (67).

Several emblematic episodes add to the evidence that we are dealing with a narrative in which the interpretation of symbols predominates. At the beginning, at the gates of the Company, in a European city, two women are found: 'Often far away there I thought of these two, guarding the door of Darkness, knitting black wool as for a warm pall, one introducing, introducing continuously to the unknown, the other scrutinizing the cheery and foolish faces with unconcerned old eyes' (11). The one seeks (passively) to know; the other directs inquirers toward a knowledge that eludes her: these two figures of knowledge announce the unfolding of the narrative to come. At the very end of the story, we find another symbolic image: Kurtz's Intended dreams of what she could have done if she had been with him: 'I would have treasured every sigh, every word, every sign, every glance' (78): she would have made a collection of signs.

Marlow's narrative opens, moreover, with a parable featuring not Kurtz and the dark continent but an imaginary Roman, conqueror of England in the Year One. The

Roman encounters the same savagery, the same mystery, what he confronts is beyond comprehension. 'He has to live in the midst of the incomprehensible, which is also detestable. And it has a fascination, too, that goes to work upon him' (6). The tale that follows, illustrating the general case, is thus a tale of apprenticeship in the art of interpretation.

The ample and obvious metaphorics of black and white, light and dark, is clearly not unrelated to the problem of knowing. In principle, and in keeping with the metaphors inscribed in the English language, darkness is equivalent to ignorance, light to knowledge. England in its obscure beginnings is summed up in the word 'darkness.' The manager's enigmatic smile produces the same effect. 'He sealed the utterance with that smile of his, as though it had been a door opening into a darkness he had in his keeping' (22). Conversely, Kurtz's story illuminates Marlow's existence: 'It seemed somehow to throw a kind of light on everything about me – and into my thoughts. It was sombre enough too – and pitiful – not extraordinary in any way – not very clear either. No, not very clear. And yet it seemed to throw a kind of light' (7).

The title of the story has the same metaphoric resonance. The expression 'heart of darkness' recurs several times in the text; it designates the interior of the unknown continent where the steamer is headed ('We penetrated deeper and deeper into the heart of darkness' [35]) or from which it is returning ('The brown current ran swiftly out of the heart of darkness' [69]). It also is used in a restrictive sense to designate the man who embodies the continent's untouchable core – Kurtz as he lives in Marlow's memory while Marlow is crossing the threshold of the Intended's house (75). It appears again in the last sentence of the text, referring by generalization to the place of unconsciousness toward which another river flows: 'into the heart of an immense darkness' (79). In its metonymic usage, darkness also symbolizes danger or despair.

The status of darkness is actually more ambiguous than one might think at first, for it becomes an object of desire; light, in turn, is identified with presence in all its frustrating aspects. Kurtz, the object of desire of the entire narrative, is himself an 'impenetrable darkness.' He identifies to such an extent with the darkness that, when there is a light beside him, he does not notice it. '"I am lying here in the dark waiting for death." The light was within a foot of his eyes' (70). And when a light is on in the night, Kurtz cannot be present: 'A light was burning within, but Mr. Kurtz was not there' (65). This ambiguity of light is best revealed in Kurtz's death scene. Watching him die, Marlow blows out the candles: Kurtz belongs to darkness. Yet immediately afterward, Marlow takes refuge in the lighted cabin and refuses to leave, even though the others may accuse him of insensitivity: 'There was a lamp in there – light, don't you know – and outside it was so beastly, beastly dark' (71). Light is reassuring when darkness escapes.

The same ambiguity characterizes the division between black and white. In harmony, once again, with the metaphors of the language, the unknown is described as black. We have already observed the two women at the entrance to the Company knitting with black wool. The unknown continent is black ('the edge of a colossal jungle, so dark-green as to be almost black' [13]), as is the skin of its inhabitants.

Significantly, those blacks who enter into contact with whites are contaminated: inevitably, they have some spot of whiteness. This is the case with the paddlers who go in small boats between the continent and the steamer: the boats were 'paddled by black fellows. You could see from afar the white of their eyeballs glistening' (13–14). Or those who work for the whites: 'It looked startling round his black neck, this bit of white thread from beyond the seas' (18). Danger is black, too, even to the point of comedy: a Danish captain gets killed because of two hens. 'Yes, two black hens' (9).

And yet whiteness is not a straightforward object of desire, any more than light is: blackness is desired, and whiteness is only the disappointing result of a desire that proclaims itself satisfied. Whiteness will be disavowed, as a truth that is either deceptive (as with the white spaces on the map, which hide the black continent) or illusory: the whites think that ivory, white, is the ultimate truth; but Marlow exclaims: 'I've never seen anything so unreal in my life' (23). Whiteness may be an obstacle to knowledge, as with the white fog, 'more blinding than the night' (40), which impedes the approach to Kurtz. White, finally, is the white man confronting the black: and all Conrad's paternalistic ethnocentrism (which could pass for anticolonialism in the nineteenth century) cannot keep us from seeing that his sympathy lies with the indigenous inhabitants of the black continent: whites are cruel and stupid. Kurtz, ambiguous with respect to light and darkness, is equally so with respect to white and black. For on the one hand, believing that he possesses the truth, he advocates white domination of the blacks, in his report; and even the head of this tireless ivory hunter has become 'like a ball – an ivory ball" (49). On the other hand, he flees from whites, and wants to stay with the blacks; it is not a coincidence that Marlow, speaking of his meeting with Kurtz, alludes to 'the peculiar blackness of that experience' (66).

The narrative is thus impregnated with black and white, obscurity and clarity, for these shades are coordinated with the process of acquiring knowledge – and with its converse, ignorance, with all the nuances that these two terms can include. It all comes down to knowing, even colors and shadows. But nothing reveals the power of knowing better than Kurtz's role in the story. For the text is in fact the account of the search for Kurtz: the reader learns this little by little, and retrospectively. Knowledge of Kurtz provides the gradation on which the story is constructed. Just after the transition from the first chapter to the second, Marlow says: 'As for me, I seemed to see Kurtz for the first time' (32); and the transition from the second chapter to the third is marked by Marlow's encounter with the Russian, of all the characters in the book the one who knew Kurtz best. Moreover, Kurtz is far from being the only subject of the first chapter, whereas he dominates the second; in the third, finally, we encounter episodes that have nothing to do with the river voyage but that contribute to our knowledge of Kurtz, for example Marlow's subsequent encounters with Kurtz's next of kin, and the inquiries of all those who are trying to find out who he was. Kurtz is the pole of attraction of the narrative as a whole; however, it is only after the fact that we discover just how this attraction works. Kurtz is darkness, the object of desire of the narration; the heart of darkness is 'the barren darkness of his heart' (69). As we might have guessed, when he takes up painting, he paints darkness and light: 'a small sketch in oils, on a panel, representing a woman, draped and blindfolded, carrying a lighted torch. The background was sombre – almost black' (25).

Kurtz is indeed the focal point of the narrative, and knowledge of Kurtz is the driving force of the plot. Yet Kurtz's status within the story is quite peculiar. We have virtually no direct perception of him at all. Throughout most of the text his presence is anticipated, like that of a creature one is striving to reach but cannot yet see. After Marlow first hears about him, several sequential narratives describe him – the accountant's, the manager's, the bricklayer's. These narratives, whether they are grounded in admiration or terror, all make us want to know Kurtz, but they do not tell us much beyond the fact that there is something to be told. Then comes the trip upriver, supposed to lead us to the real Kurtz. Obstacles proliferate, however: darkness first of all, the attack by the blacks, the thick fog that prevents the travelers from seeing anything. At this point in the text, specifically narrative obstacles compound those thrown up by the jungle: instead of pursuing his tale of progressive knowledge of Kurtz, Marlow interrupts himself abruptly and sketches in a retrospective portrait, as if Kurtz can only be present in the tenses of absence, past and future. This is made explicit, moreover, after Marlow, who has just seen Kurtz, declares: '"I think Mr. Kurtz is a remarkable man,"' the manager responds: '"he *was*"' (63). When we return from portrait to narrative, new disappointments await us: in place of Kurtz we find the Russian, the author of a new story about the absent hero. Even when Kurtz finally appears, we do not learn very much. In the first place, he is dying, already partaking more of absence than of presence. Furthermore, we see him from afar, and fleetingly. When we are finally allowed into his presence, he is reduced to mere voice – thus to words, which are just as subject to interpretation as were the stories others had told about him. Yet another wall has arisen between Kurtz and ourselves. 'Kurtz discoursed. A voice! a voice! It rang deep to the last' (69). It is hardly surprising that this voice is particularly impressive: 'The volume of tone he emitted without effort, almost without the trouble of moving his lips, amazed me. A voice! a voice! It was grave, profound, vibrating, while the man did not seem capable of a whisper' (61). But even this enigmatic presence does not last, and soon a 'veil' descends over his face, rendering it impenetrable. Death changes almost nothing, so impossible had knowledge proved during Kurtz's life. We have merely moved from speculating to remembering.

Thus not only does the process of coming to know Kurtz dominate Marlow's narrative, but the knowledge sought is unattainable. Kurtz has become familiar to us, but we do not know him, we do not know his secret. Conrad expresses this frustration in dozens of different ways. In the end, Marlow has only been able to pursue a shadow, 'the shade of Mr. Kurtz' (50): 'a shadow darker than the shadow of the night, and draped nobly in the folds of a gorgeous eloquence' (75). The heart of darkness is 'Nowhere,' and it cannot be reached. Kurtz fades away before it is possible to know him ('all that had been Kurtz's had passed out of my hands: his soul, his body, his station, his plans, his ivory, his career. There remained only his memory ...' [74]). His name, Kurtz, 'short,' is only superficially misleading. When Marlow sees him for the first time, he remarks: 'Kurtz – Kurtz – that means short in German – don't it? Well, the name was as true as everything else in his life – and death. He looked at least seven feet long' (60). Kurtz is not small, as his name might suggest, it is our knowledge of him that falls short, remains forever inadequate, and it is no accident that he resists the whites' efforts to drag him out of his obscurity. Marlow has not understood Kurtz, even though he becomes his confidant at the end ('this ... wraith ... honoured me with its amazing confidence' [50]); similarly, after Kurtz's death, Marlow's efforts to understand him come to nothing: 'even the cousin ... could not tell me what he had been – exactly' (73).

Kurtz is the heart of darkness and his heart is empty. One can only dream about the ultimate moment, at the threshold of death, when one acquires absolute knowledge ('that supreme moment of complete knowledge' [71]). What Kurtz actually utters at that moment are words that express the void, canceling out knowledge: 'The horror! The horror!' (ibid.). An absolute horror whose object we shall never know.

Nothing is better proof of the derisory nature of knowledge than the final scene of the story, Marlow's meeting with the Intended. It is she who says '"I knew him best"' (76); yet we know that her knowledge is hopelessly incomplete, even illusory. Nothing remains of Kurtz but his memory, and this memory is false. When the Intended exclaims: '"How true! How true!"' (ibid.), it is in response to a lie. '"His words, at least, have not died"' (78), she says to console herself; and a moment later she extracts from Marlow another lie, about Kurtz's last words: '"The last word he pronounced was – your name" ... "I knew it – I was sure!"' (79), the Intended replies. Is that why, in the course of the conversation, 'with every word spoken, the room was growing darker' (76)?

Knowledge is impossible; the heart of darkness is itself obscure: this is the burden of the text as a whole. The voyage takes us indeed to the very center, the interior, the bottom, the core: 'I felt as though, instead of going to the centre of a continent, I were about to set off for the centre of the earth' (13); Kurtz's station is appropriately called the Inner Station; Kurtz himself is indeed 'at the very bottom of there' (19). But the center is empty: 'An empty stream, a great silence, an impenetrable forest' (34). According to the manager, '"Men who come out here should have no entrails"' (22); this rule proves to be followed to the letter. Marlow says of the brickmaker: 'It seemed to me that if I tried I could poke my forefinger through him, and would find nothing inside ...' (26). The manager himself, as we recall, stamps everything with an enigmatic smile; but perhaps his secret is impenetrable because it does not exist: 'He never gave that secret away. Perhaps there was nothing within him' (22).

The interior does not exist, any more than does ultimate meaning, and Marlow's experiences are all inconclusive. In this context, the very act of knowing is called into question. 'Droll thing life is – that mysterious arrangement of merciless logic for a futile purpose. The most you can hope from it is some knowledge of yourself – that comes too late – a crop of unextinguishable regrets' (71). The machine functions perfectly – but it is empty, and the fullest knowledge of others tells us only about ourselves. That the process of acquiring knowledge unfolds in an irreproachable matter in no way proves that the object of this knowledge may be reached; one is tempted to say indeed that just the opposite is true. E. M. Forster failed to understand this, for he remarked about Conrad, in perplexity: 'What is so elusive about him is that he is always promising to make some general philosophical statement about the universe, and then refraining in a gruff declaimer ... There is a central obscurity about him, something noble, heroic, inspiring half-a-dozen great books, but obscure! Obscure!'[3] We already know what to make of this obscurity. And Conrad himself wrote elsewhere: 'The aim of art ... is not in the clear logic of a triumphant conclusion; it is not in the unveiling of one of those heartless secrets which are called the Laws of Nature.'[4]

Speech, as we have seen, plays a decisive role in the process of acquiring knowledge: that is the light that ought to dispel darkness but in the end fails to do so. This we learn from Kurtz's example. 'Of all his gifts the one that stood out preeminently, that carried with it a sense of real presence, was his ability to talk, his words – the gift of expression, the bewildering, the illuminating, the most exalted and the most contemptible, the pulsating stream of light, or the deceitful flow from the heart of an impenetrable darkness' (*Heart of Darkness*, 48). But Kurtz only exemplifies something much more general, which is the possibility of constructing a reality, of stating a truth by means of words; Kurtz's adventure is at the same time a parable of narrative. It is no coincidence that Kurtz is also, as the occasion warrants, a poet, painter, and musician as well. It is not an accident that countless analogies are set up between the two narratives, the embedded tale and the framing tale, between the two rivers, finally between Kurtz and Marlow the narrator (the only two characters that have proper names in this story; all the others, such as the manager and the accountant – whom we meet moreover both in the framing story and in the embedded one – are reduced to their functions), and, correlatively, between Marlow the character and his listeners (whose role is played by ourselves, the readers). Kurtz is a voice. 'I made the strange discovery that I had never imagined him as doing, you know, but as discoursing. I didn't say to myself, "Now I will never see him," or "Now I will never shake him by the hand," but "now I will never hear him." The man presented himself as a voice' (ibid.). But is not the same thing true of Marlow the narrator? 'For a long time already he, sitting apart, had been no more to us than a voice' (28). 'The artist ... is so much of a voice that, for him, silence is like death,' Conrad wrote in a 1905 article on Henry James.[5] Marlow does the job of making the relation between the two series explicit in an interruption in his narrative: 'Kurtz ... was just a word for me. I did not see the man in the name any more than you do. Do you see him? Do you see the story? Do you see anything?' (27). Both explorer and reader are concerned only with signs, on the basis of which they have to construct, respectively, the referent (the reality that lies all around) or the reference (what the story is about). The reader (any reader) desires to know the object of the story just as Marlow desires to know Kurtz.

And just as this latter desire will be frustrated, so readers or listeners will never be able to reach the reference of the narrative, as we would have liked; its heart is quite absent. Is it not revealing that the story, begun at sunset, coincides in its development with the deepening dusk? 'It had become so pitch dark that we listeners could hardly see one another' (28). And just as knowledge of Kurtz is impossible in Marlow's account, so too is any construction on the basis of words, any attempt to grasp things through language. 'No, it is impossible; it is impossible to convey the life-sensation of any given epoch of one's existence – that which makes its truth, its meaning – its subtle and penetrating essence. It is impossible' (ibid.). The essence, the truth – the heart of the story – is inaccessible, the reader will never reach it. 'You can't understand' (50). Words do not allow us even to transmit other words: 'I've been telling you what we said – repeating the phrases we pronounced – but what's the good? They were common everyday words – the familiar, vague sounds exchanged on every waking day of life. But what of that? They had behind them, to my mind, the terrific suggestiveness of words heard in dreams, of phrases spoken in nightmares' (67). This aspect of words can never be reproduced.

It is impossible to accede to the reference; the heart of the story is empty, just as is the heart of man. For Marlow, 'the meaning of an episode was not inside like a kernel but outside, enveloping the tale which brought it out only as a glow brings out a haze, in the likeness of one of these misty halos that sometimes are made visible by the spectral illumination of moonshine' (5). The story's light is the hesitant light of the moon.

Thus Kurtz's story symbolizes the fact of fiction, construction on the basis of an absent center. Let us make no mistake: Conrad's writing is indeed allegorical, as numerous details attest (if only the absence of proper names, a way of generalizing), but not all allegorical interpretations of *Heart of Darkness* are equally welcome. To reduce the trip up the river to a descent into hell or to the discovery of the unconscious is an assertion for which the critic who utters it must take full responsibility. Conrad's allegorism is intertextual: if the search for Kurtz's identity is an allegory of reading, this allegory in turn symbolizes every quest for knowledge – knowledge of Kurtz being one example. The symbolized becomes in turn the symbolizer for what was formerly symbolizing; the symbolization is reciprocal. A final meaning, ultimate truth is nowhere to be found, for there is no interior and the heart is empty. What was true for things remains so, and more so, for signs; there is only referral, circular and nonetheless imperative, from one surface to another, from words to words.

Notes

1. Joseph Conrad, *Heart of Darkness: An Authoritative Text; Backgrounds and Sources; Essays in Criticism*, ed. Robert Kimbrough (New York: W. W. Norton, 1963). All passages cited are from this edition.
2. Joseph Conrad, 'Well Done' (*The Daily Chronicle*, 1918), in *Notes on Life and Letters* (Garden City, NY and Toronto: Doubleday, Page & Company, 1921) 190. Cited in *Heart of Darkness* (Kimbrough ed.) 138.
3. E. M. Forster, cited in *Heart of Darkness* (Kimbrough ed.) 164.

4. Joseph Conrad, Preface, *The Nigger of the 'Narcissus,'* in *The Works of Joseph Conrad*, vol. 3 (London: William Heinemann, 1921) xi–xii.
5. Joseph Conrad, 'Henry James: An Appreciation' (*North American Review*, 1905), in *Notes on Life and Letters*, 14. Cited in *Heart of Darkness* (Kimbrough ed.) 148.

6.3   CHINUA ACHEBE: 'AN IMAGE OF AFRICA: RACISM IN CONRAD'S *HEART OF DARKNESS*' (1988)

Chinua Achebe is a Nigerian-born writer best known for his first novel *Things Fall Apart* (1958). He was one of the first graduates of the University College of Ibadan and became Director of External Broadcasting in the Nigerian Broadcasting Corporation before embarking on a career of teaching and writing. He is currently Professor at Bard College, New York. His other novels include *No Longer at Ease* (1960), *Arrow of God* (1964) and *Anthills of the Savannah* (1987). For further reading, see Lynn Innes, *Chinua Achebe* (Cambridge University Press, 1990).

As suggested above, the question of 'emptiness' is a consistent theme of the essays collected here, whether in relation to Conrad's story itself or to its criticism – in the sense of what this discusses, or fails to discuss. Achebe responds to the assumption that it is Africa which is empty, 'that African history did not exist' (p. 262, below.) Conrad's story, by contrast, he sees as being about the 'fullness' of Western presuppositions. He quotes a passage from the middle of the story in illustrating this point (pp. 263–4, below). What is your reading of this passage? Would you find the 'meaning of *Heart of Darkness*' here? Achebe goes on to emphasize Conrad's wanting to see things 'in their place'. Compare this with other accounts of the 'inscrutability' and 'mystery' engendered by the story.

There are other points of comparison (on the significance given to the narrator and narrative structure, for example) but, above all, students will need to consider Achebe's negative criticism of the story. What is his charge? That Conrad (or Marlow?) is an example, as Achebe puts it, of 'those advanced and humane views appropriate to the English liberal tradition' (but to what extent is this an ironic description?), or that he 'was a thoroughgoing racist' (p. 267, below)? Is either view, and the second in particular, convincing? Achebe is led finally to ask another important question: whether a novel which 'celebrates' the dehumanization of Africa and Africans can be considered a 'great work of art'. His own answer is clear. How would you respond to this question?

Achebe's essay appears in his *Hopes and Impediments: Selected Essays 1965–1987* (Cambridge University Press, 1988), pp. 1–13.

An Image of Africa: Racism in Conrad's *Heart of Darkness*

In the fall of 1974 I was walking one day from the English Department at the University of Massachusetts to a parking lot. It was a fine autumn morning such as encouraged friendliness to passing strangers. Brisk youngsters were hurrying in all directions, many of them obviously freshmen in their first flush of enthusiasm. An older man going the same way as I turned and remarked to me how very young they came these days. I agreed. Then he asked me if I was a student too. I said no, I was a teacher. What did I teach? African literature. Now that was funny, he said, because he knew a fellow who taught the same thing, or perhaps it was African *history*, in a certain community college not far from here. It always surprised him, he went on to say, because he never had thought of Africa as having that kind of stuff, you know. By this time I was walking much faster. 'Oh well,' I heard him say finally, behind me: 'I guess I have to take your course to find out.'

A few weeks later I received two very touching letters from high-school children in Yonkers, New York, who – bless their teacher – had just read *Things Fall Apart*. One of them was particularly happy to learn about the customs and superstitions of an African tribe.

I propose to draw from these rather trivial encounters rather heavy conclusions which at first sight might seem somewhat out of proportion to them. But only, I hope, at first sight.

The young fellow from Yonkers, perhaps partly on account of his age but I believe also for much deeper and more serious reasons, is obviously unaware that the life of his own tribesmen in Yonkers, New York, is full of odd customs and superstitions and, like everybody else in his culture, imagines that he needs a trip to Africa to encounter those things.

The other person being fully my own age could not he excused on the grounds of his years. Ignorance might be a more likely reason; but here again I believe that something more wilful than a mere lack of information was at work. For did not that erudite British historian and Regius Professor at Oxford, Hugh Trevor-Roper, also pronounce that African history did not exist?

If there is something in these utterances more than youthful inexperience, more than a lack of factual knowledge, what is it? Quite simply it is the desire – one might indeed say the need – in Western psychology to set Africa up as a foil to Europe, as a place of negations at once remote and vaguely familiar, in comparison with which Europe's own state of spiritual grace will be manifest.

This need is not new; which should relieve us all of considerable responsibility and perhaps make us even willing to look at this phenomenon dispassionately. I have neither the wish nor the competence to embark on the exercise with the tools of the social and biological sciences but do so more simply in the manner of a novelist responding to one famous book of European fiction: Joseph Conrad's *Heart of Darkness*, which better than any other work that I know displays that Western desire and need which I have just referred to. Of course there are whole libraries of books devoted to the same purpose but most of them are so obvious and so crude that few people worry about them today. Conrad, on the other hand, is undoubtedly one of the great stylists of modern fiction and a good story-teller into the bargain. His contribution therefore falls automatically into a different class – permanent literature – read and taught and constantly evaluated by serious academics. *Heart of Darkness* is indeed so secure today that a leading Conrad scholar has numbered it 'among the half-dozen greatest short novels in the English language'.[1] I will return to this critical opinion in due course because it may seriously modify my earlier suppositions about who may or may not he guilty in some of the matters I will now raise.

Heart of Darkness projects the image of Africa as 'the other world', the antithesis of Europe and therefore of civilization, a place where man's vaunted intelligence and refinement are finally mocked by triumphant bestiality. The book opens on the River Thames, tranquil, resting peacefully 'at the decline of day after ages of good service done to the race that peopled its banks'.[2] But the actual story will take place on the River Congo, the very antithesis of the Thames. The River

Congo is quite decidedly not a River Emeritus. It has rendered no service and enjoys no old-age pension. We are told that 'going up that river was like travelling back to the earliest beginning of the world'.

Is Conrad saying then that these two rivers are very different, one good, the other bad? Yes, but that is not the real point. It is not the differentness that worries Conrad but the lurking hint of kinship, of common ancestry. For the Thames too 'has been one of the dark places of the earth'. It conquered its darkness, of course, and is now in daylight and at peace. But if it were to visit its primordial relative, the Congo, it would run the terrible risk of hearing grotesque echoes of its own forgotten darkness, and falling victim to an avenging recrudescence of the mindless frenzy of the first beginnings.

These suggestive echoes comprise Conrad's famed evocation of the African atmosphere in *Heart of Darkness*. In the final consideration his method amounts to no more than a steady, ponderous, fake-ritualistic repetition of two antithetical sentences, one about silence and the other about frenzy. We can inspect samples of this on pages 103 and 105 of the New American Library edition: (a) 'It was the stillness of an implacable force brooding over an inscrutable intention' and (b) 'The steamer toiled along slowly on the edge of a black and incomprehensible frenzy.' Of course there is a judicious change of adjective from time to time, so that instead of 'inscrutable', for example, you might have 'unspeakable', even plain 'mysterious', etc., etc.

The eagle-eyed English critic F. R. Leavis[3] drew attention long ago to Conrad's 'adjectival insistence upon inexpressible and incomprehensible mystery'. That insistence must not be dismissed lightly, as many Conrad critics have tended to do, as a mere stylistic flaw; for it raises serious questions of artistic good faith. When a writer while pretending to record scenes, incidents and their impact is in reality engaged in inducing hypnotic stupor in his readers through a bombardment of emotive words and other forms of trickery, much more has to be at stake than stylistic felicity. Generally normal readers are well armed to detect and resist such underhand activity. But Conrad chose his subject well – one which was guaranteed not to put him in conflict with the psychological predisposition of his readers or raise the need for him to contend with their resistance. He chose the role of purveyor of comforting myths.

The most interesting and revealing passages in *Heart of Darkness* are, however, about people. I must crave the indulgence of my reader to quote almost a whole page from about the middle of the story when representatives of Europe in a steamer going down the Congo encounter the denizens of Africa:

> We were wanderers on a prehistoric earth, on an earth that wore the aspect of an unknown planet. We could have fancied ourselves the first of men taking possession of an accursed inheritance, to be subdued at the cost of profound anguish and of excessive toil. But suddenly, as we struggled round a bend, there would be a glimpse of rush walls, of peaked grass-roofs, a burst of yells, a whirl of black limbs, a mass of hands clapping, of feet stamping, of bodies swaying, of eyes rolling, under the droop of heavy and motionless foliage. The steamer toiled along slowly on the edge of the black and

incomprehensible frenzy. The prehistoric man was cursing us, praying to us, welcoming us – who could tell? We were cut off from the comprehension of our surroundings; we glided past like phantoms, wondering and secretly appalled, as sane men would be before an enthusiastic outbreak in a madhouse. We could not understand because we were too far and could not remember because we were travelling in the night of first ages, of those ages that are gone, leaving hardly a sign – and no memories.

The earth seemed unearthly. We are accustomed to look upon the shackled form of a conquered monster, but there – there you could look at a thing monstrous and free. It was unearthly, and the men were – No, they were not inhuman. Well, you know, that was the worst of it – this suspicion of their not being inhuman. It would come slowly to one. They howled and leaped, and spun, and made horrid faces; but what thrilled you was just the thought of their humanity – like yours – the thought of your remote kinship with this wild and passionate uproar. Ugly. Yes, it was ugly enough; but if you were man enough you would admit to yourself that there was in you just the faintest trace of a response to the terrible frankness of that noise, a dim suspicion of there being a meaning in it which you – you so remote from the night of first ages – could comprehend.[4]

Herein lies the meaning of *Heart of Darkness* and the fascination it holds over the Western mind: 'What thrilled you was just the thought of their humanity – like yours ... Ugly.'

Having shown us Africa in the mass, Conrad then zeros in, half a page later, on a specific example, giving us one of his rare descriptions of an African who is not just limbs or rolling eyes:

And between whiles I had to look after the savage who was fireman. He was an improved specimen; he could fire up a vertical boiler. He was there below me, and, upon my word, to look at him was as edifying as seeing a dog in a parody of breeches and a feather hat, walking on his hind legs. A few months of training had done for that really fine chap. He squinted at the steam gauge and at the water gauge with an evident effort of intrepidity – and he had filed his teeth, too, the poor devil, and the wool of his pate shaved into queer patterns, and three ornamental scars on each of his cheeks. He ought to have been clapping his hands and stamping his feet on the bank, instead of which he was hard at work, a thrall to strange witchcraft, full of improving knowledge.[5]

As everybody knows, Conrad is a romantic on the side. He might not exactly admire savages clapping their hands and stamping their feet but they have at least the merit of being in their place, unlike this dog in a parody of breeches. For Conrad things being in their place is of the utmost importance.

'Fine fellows – cannibals – in their place,' he tells us pointedly. Tragedy begins when things leave their accustomed place, like Europe leaving its safe stronghold between the policeman and the baker to take a peep into the heart of darkness.

Before the story takes us into the Congo basin proper we are given this nice little vignette as an example of things in their place:

Now and then a boat from the shore gave one a momentary contact with reality. It was paddled by black fellows. You could see from afar the white of their eyeballs glistening. They shouted, sang; their bodies streamed with perspiration; they had faces like grotesque masks – these chaps; but they had bone, muscle, a wild vitality, an intense energy of movement, that was as natural and true as the surf along their coast. They wanted no excuse for being there. They were a great comfort to look at.[6]

Towards the end of the story Conrad lavishes a whole page quite unexpectedly on an African woman who has obviously been some kind of mistress to Mr Kurtz and now presides (if I may be permitted a little liberty) like a formidable mystery over the inexorable imminence of his departure:

> She was savage and superb, wild-eyed and magnificent ... She stood looking at us without a stir and like the wilderness itself, with an air of brooding over an inscrutable purpose.

This Amazon is drawn in considerable detail, albeit of a predictable nature, for two reasons. First, she is in her place and so can win Conrad's special brand of approval; and second, she fulfils a structural requirement of the story: a savage counterpart to the refined, European woman who will step forth to end the story:

> She came forward, all in black with a pale head, floating toward me in the dusk. She was in mourning ... She took both my hands in hers and murmured, 'I had heard you were coming' ... She had a mature capacity for fidelity, for belief, for suffering.[7]

The difference in the attitude of the novelist to these two women is conveyed in too many direct and subtle ways to need elaboration. But perhaps the most significant difference is the one implied in the author's bestowal of human expression to the one and the withholding of it from the other. It is clearly not part of Conrad's purpose to confer language on the 'rudimentary souls' of Africa. In place of speech they made 'a violent babble of uncouth sounds'. They 'exchanged short grunting phrases' even among themselves. But most of the time they were too busy with their frenzy. There are two occasions in the book, however, when Conrad departs somewhat from his practice and confers speech, even English speech, on the savages. The first occurs when cannibalism gets the better of them:

> 'Catch 'im,' he snapped, with a bloodshot widening of his eyes and a flash of sharp white teeth – 'catch 'im. Give 'im to us.' 'To you, eh?' I asked; 'what would you do with them?' 'Eat 'im!' he said curtly.[8]

The other occasion was the famous announcement: 'Mistah Kurtz – he dead'.[9]

At first sight these instances might be mistaken for unexpected acts of generosity from Conrad. In reality they constitute some of his best assaults. In the case of the cannibals the incomprehensible grunts that had thus far served them for speech suddenly proved inadequate for Conrad's purpose of letting the European glimpse the unspeakable craving in their hearts. Weighing the necessity for consistency in the portrayal of the dumb brutes against the sensational advantages of securing their conviction by clear, unambiguous evidence issuing out of their own mouth Conrad chose the latter. As for the announcement of Mr Kurtz's death by the 'insolent black head in the doorway', what better or more appropriate *finis* could be written to the horror story of that wayward child of civilization who wilfully had given his soul to the powers of darkness and 'taken a high seat amongst the devils of the land' than the proclamation of his physical death by the forces he had joined?

It might he contended, of course, that the attitude to the African in *Heart of Darkness* is not Conrad's but that of his fictional narrator, Marlow, and that far from endorsing it Conrad might indeed be holding it up to irony and criticism. Certainly Conrad appears to go to considerable pains to set up layers of insulation between himself and the moral universe of his story. He has, for example, a narrator behind a narrator. The primary narrator is Marlow but his account is given to us through the filter of a second, shadowy person. But if Conrad's intention is to draw a cordon sanitaire between himself and the moral and psychological *malaise* of his narrator his care seems to me totally wasted because he neglects to hint, clearly and adequately, at an alternative frame of reference by which we may judge the actions and opinions of his characters. It would not have been beyond Conrad's power to make that provision if he had thought it necessary. Conrad seems to me to approve of Marlow, with only minor reservations – a fact reinforced by the similarities between their two careers.

Marlow comes through to us not only as a witness of truth, but one holding those advanced and humane views appropriate to the English liberal tradition which required all Englishmen of decency to be deeply shocked by atrocities in Bulgaria or the Congo of King Leopold of the Belgians or wherever.

Thus Marlow is able to toss out such bleeding-heart sentiments as these:

> They were all dying slowly – it was very clear. They were not enemies, they were not criminals, they were nothing earthly now – nothing but black shadows of disease and starvation, lying confusedly in the greenish gloom. Brought from all the recesses of the coast in all the legality of time contracts, lost in uncongenial surroundings, fed on unfamiliar food, they sickened, became inefficient, and were then allowed to crawl away and rest.[10]

The kind of liberalism espoused here by Marlow/Conrad touched all the best minds of the age in England, Europe and America. It took different forms in the minds of different people but almost always managed to sidestep the ultimate question of equality between white people and black people. That extraordinary missionary, Albert Schweitzer, who sacrificed brilliant careers in music and theology in Europe for a life of service to Africans in much the same area as Conrad writes about, epitomizes the ambivalence. In a comment which has often been quoted Schweitzer says: 'The African is indeed my brother but my junior brother.' And so he proceeded to build a hospital appropriate to the needs of junior brothers with standards of hygiene reminiscent of medical practice in the days before the germ theory of disease came into being. Naturally he became a sensation in Europe and America. Pilgrims flocked, and I believe still flock even after he has passed on, to witness the prodigious miracle in Lamberene, on the edge of the primeval forest.

Conrad's liberalism would not take him quite as far as Schweitzer's, though. He would not use the word 'brother' however qualified; the farthest he would go was 'kinship'. When Marlow's African helmsman falls down with a spear in his heart he gives his white master one final disquieting look:

> And the intimate profundity of that look he gave me when he received his hurt remains to this day in my memory – like a claim of distant kinship affirmed in a supreme moment.[11]

It is important to note that Conrad, careful as ever with his words, is concerned not so much about 'distant kinship' as about someone *laying a claim* on it. The black man lays a claim on the white man which is well-nigh intolerable. It is the laying of this claim which frightens and at the same time fascinates Conrad, 'the thought of their humanity – like yours … Ugly.'

The point of my observations should be quite clear by now, namely that Joseph Conrad was a thoroughgoing racist. That this simple truth is glossed over in criticisms of his work is due to the fact that white racism against Africa is such a normal way of thinking that its manifestations go completely unremarked. Students of *Heart of Darkness* will often tell you that Conrad is concerned not so much with Africa as with the deterioration of one European mind caused by solitude and sickness. They will point out to you that Conrad is, if anything, less charitable to the Europeans in the story than he is to the natives, that the point of the story is to ridicule Europe's civilizing mission in Africa. A Conrad student informed me in Scotland that Africa is merely a setting for the disintegration of the mind of Mr Kurtz.

Which is partly the point. Africa as setting and backdrop which eliminates the African as human factor. Africa as a metaphysical battlefield devoid of all recognizable humanity, into which the wandering European enters at his peril. Can nobody see the preposterous and perverse arrogance in thus reducing Africa to the role of props for the break-up of one petty European mind? But that is not even the point. The real question is the dehumanization of Africa and Africans which this age-long attitude has fostered and continues to foster in the world. And the question is whether a novel which celebrates this dehumanization, which depersonalizes a portion of the human race, can be called a great work of art. My answer is: No, it cannot. I do not doubt Conrad's great talents. Even *Heart of Darkness* has its memorably good passages and moments:

> The reaches opened before us and closed behind, as if the forest had stepped leisurely across the water to bar the way for our return.

Its exploration of the minds of the European characters is often penetrating and full of insight. But all that has been more than fully discussed in the last fifty years. His obvious racism has, however, not been addressed. And it is high time it was!

Conrad was born in 1857, the very year in which the first Anglican missionaries were arriving among my own people in Nigeria. It was certainly not his fault that he lived his life at a time when the reputation of the black man was at a particularly low level. But even after due allowances have been made for all the influences of contemporary prejudice on his sensibility there remains still in Conrad's attitude a residue of antipathy to black people which his peculiar psychology alone can explain. His own account of his first encounter with a black man is very revealing:

> A certain enormous buck nigger encountered in Haiti fixed my conception of blind, furious, unreasoning rage, as manifested in the human animal to the end of my days. Of the nigger I used to dream for years afterwards.[12]

Certainly Conrad had a problem with niggers. His inordinate love of that word itself should be of interest to psychoanalysts. Sometimes his fixation on blackness is equally interesting as when he gives us this brief description: 'A black figure stood up, strode on long black legs, waving long black arms'[13] – as though we might expect a black figure striding along on black legs to wave white arms! But so unrelenting is Conrad's obsession.

As a matter of interest Conrad gives us in *A Personal Record* what amounts to a companion piece to the buck nigger of Haiti. At the age of sixteen Conrad encountered his first Englishman in Europe. He calls him 'my unforgettable Englishman' and describes him in the following manner:

> [his] calves exposed to the public gaze ... dazzled the beholder by the splendour of their marble-like condition and their rich tone of young ivory ... The light of a headlong, exalted satisfaction with the world of men ... illumined his face ... and triumphant eyes. In passing he cast a glance of kindly curiosity and a friendly gleam of big, sound, shiny teeth ... his white calves twinkled sturdily.[14]

Irrational love and irrational hate jostling together in the heart of that talented, tormented man. But whereas irrational love may at worst engender foolish acts of indiscretion, irrational hate can endanger the life of the community. Naturally Conrad is a dream for psychoanalytic critics. Perhaps the most detailed study of him in this direction is by Bernard C. Meyer, MD. In his lengthy book Dr Meyer follows every conceivable lead (and sometime inconceivable ones) to explain Conrad. As an example he gives us long disquisitions on the significance of hair and hair-cutting in Conrad. And yet not even one word is spared for his attitude to black people. Not even the discussion of Conrad's antisemitism was enough to spark off in Dr Meyer's mind those other dark and explosive thoughts. Which only leads one to surmise that Western psychoanalysts must regard the kind of racism displayed by Conrad as absolutely normal despite the profoundly important work done by Frantz Fanon in the psychiatric hospitals of French Algeria.

Whatever Conrad's problems were, you might say he is now safely dead. Quite true. Unfortunately his heart of darkness plagues us still. Which is why an offensive and deplorable book can be described by a serious scholar as 'among the half-dozen greatest short novels in the English language'. And why it is today perhaps the most commonly prescribed novel in twentieth-century literature courses in English departments of American universities?

There are two probable grounds on which what I have said so far may he contested. The first is that it is no concern of fiction to please people about whom it is written. I will go along with that. But I am not talking about pleasing people. I am talking about a book which parades in the most vulgar fashion prejudices and insults from which a section of mankind has suffered untold agonies and atrocities in the past and continues to do so in many ways and many places today. I am talking about a story in which the very humanity of black people is called in question.

Secondly, I may be challenged on the grounds of actuality. Conrad after all, did sail down the Congo in 1890 when my own father was still a babe in arms. How could I stand up more than fifty years after his death and purport to contradict him? My answer is that as a sensible man I will not accept just any traveller's tales solely on the grounds that I have not made the journey myself. I will not trust the evidence even of a man's very eyes when I suspect them to be as jaundiced as Conrad's. And we also happen to know that Conrad was, in the words of his biographer, Bernard C. Meyer, 'notoriously inaccurate in the rendering of his own history'.[15]

But more important by far is the abundant testimony about Conrad's savages which we could gather if we were so inclined from other sources and which might lead us to think that these people must have had other occupations besides merging into the evil forest or materializing out of it simply to plague Marlow and his dispirited band. For as it happened, soon after Conrad had written his book an event of far greater consequence was taking place in the art world of Europe. This is how Frank Willett, a British art historian, describes it:

> Gauguin had gone to Tahiti, the most extravagant individual act of turning to a non-European culture in the decades immediately before and after 1900, when European artists were avid for new artistic experiences, but it was only about 1904–5 that African art began to make its distinctive impact. One piece is still identifiable; it is a mask that had been given to Maurice Vlaminck in 1905. He records that Derain was 'speechless' and 'stunned' when he saw it, bought it from Vlaminck and in turn showed it to Picasso and Matisse, who were also greatly affected by it. Ambroise Vollard then borrowed it and had it cast in bronze ... The revolution of twentieth century art was under way![16]

The mask in question was made by other savages living just north of Conrad's River Congo. They have a name too: the Fang people, and are without a doubt among the world's greatest masters of the sculptured form. The event Frank Willett is referring to marked the beginning of cubism and the infusion of new life into European art that had run completely out of strength.

The point of all this is to suggest that Conrad's picture of the peoples of the Congo seems grossly inadequate even at the height of their subjection to the ravages of King Leopold's International Association for the Civilization of Central Africa.

Travellers with closed minds can tell us little except about themselves. But even those not blinkered, like Conrad with xenophobia, can he astonishingly blind. Let me digress a little here. One of the greatest and most intrepid travellers of all time, Marco Polo, journeyed to the Far East from the Mediterranean in the thirteenth century and spent twenty years in the court of Kublai Khan in China. On his return to Venice he set down in his book entitled *Description of the World* his impressions of the peoples and places and customs he had seen. But there were at least two extraordinary omissions in his account. He said nothing about the art of printing, unknown as yet in Europe but in full flower in China. He either did not notice it at all or, if he did, failed to see what use Europe could possibly have for it. Whatever the reason, Europe had to wait another hundred years for Gutenberg. But even more spectacular was Marco Polo's omission of any reference to the Great Wall of China, nearly four thousand miles long and already more than one thousand years old at the time of his visit. Again, he may not have seen it; but the Great Wall of China is the only structure built by man which is visible from the moon![17] Indeed travellers can be blind.

As I said earlier Conrad did not originate the image of Africa which we find in his book. It was and is the dominant image of Africa in the Western imagination and Conrad merely brought the peculiar gifts of his own mind to bear on it. For reasons which can certainly use close psychological inquiry the West seems to suffer deep anxieties about the precariousness of its civilization and to have a need for constant reassurance by comparison with Africa. If Europe, advancing in civilization, could cast a backward glance periodically at Africa trapped in primordial barbarity it could say with faith and feeling: There go I but for the grace of God. Africa is to Europe as the picture is to Dorian Gray – a carrier on to whom the master unloads his physical and moral deformities so that he may go forward, erect and immaculate. Consequently Africa is something to be avoided just as the picture has to be hidden away to safeguard the man's jeopardous integrity. Keep away from Africa, or else! Mr Kurtz of *Heart of Darkness* should have heeded that warning and the prowling horror in his heart would have kept its place, chained to its lair. But he foolishly exposed himself to the wild irresistible allure of the jungle and lo! the darkness found him out.

In my original conception of this essay I had thought to conclude it nicely on an appropriately positive note in which I would suggest from my privileged position in African and Western cultures some advantages the West might derive from Africa once it rid its mind of old prejudices and began to look at Africa not through a haze of distortions and cheap mystifications but quite simply as a continent of people – not angels, but not rudimentary souls either – just people, often highly gifted people and often strikingly successful in their enterprise with life and society. But as I thought more about the stereotype image, about its grip and pervasiveness, about the wilful tenacity with which the West holds it to its heart; when I thought of the West's television and cinema and newspapers, about books read in its schools and out of school, of churches preaching to empty pews about the need to send help to the heathen in Africa, I realized that no easy optimism was possible. And there was in any case something totally wrong in offering bribes to the West in return for its good opinion of Africa. Ultimately the abandonment of unwholesome thoughts must be its own and only reward. Although I have used the word 'wilful' a few times here to characterize the West's view of Africa it may well be that what is happening at this stage is more akin to reflex action than calculated malice. Which does not make the situation more but less hopeful.

The *Christian Science Monitor*, a paper more enlightened than most, once carried an interesting article written by its Education Editor on the serious psychological and learning problems faced by little children who speak one language at home and then go to school where something else is spoken. It was a wide-ranging article taking in Spanish-speaking children in America, the children of migrant Italian workers in Germany, the quadrilingual phenomenon in Malaysia and so on. And all this while the article speaks unequivocally about language. But then out of the blue sky comes this:

> In London there is an enormous immigration of children who speak Indian or Nigerian dialects, or some other native language.[18]

I believe that the introduction of 'dialects', which is technically erroneous in the context, is almost a reflex action caused by an instinctive desire of the writer to downgrade the discussion to the level of Africa and India. And this is quite comparable to Conrad's withholding of language from his rudimentary souls. Language is too grand for these chaps; let's give them dialects!

In all this business a lot of violence is inevitably done not only to the image of despised peoples but even to words, the very tools of possible redress. Look at the phrase 'native language' in the *Science Monitor* excerpt. Surely the only *native* language possible in London is Cockney English. But our writer means something else – something appropriate to the sounds Indians and Africans make!

Although the work of redressing which needs to be done may appear too daunting, I believe it is not one day too soon to begin. Conrad saw and condemned the evil of imperial exploitation but was strangely unaware of the racism on which it sharpened its iron tooth. But the victims of racist slander who for centuries have had to live with the inhumanity it makes them heir to have always known better than any casual visitor, even when he comes loaded with the gifts of a Conrad.

Notes

1. Albert J. Guerard, introduction to *Heart of Darkness*, New York, New American Library, 1950, p. 9.
2. Joseph Conrad, *Heart of Darkness* and *The Secret Sharer*, New York, New American Library, 1950, p. 66.
3. F. R. Leavis, *The Great Tradition*, London, Chatto and Windus, 1948; second impression 1950, p. 177.
4. Conrad, *Heart of Darkness*, op. cit., pp. 105–6.
5. Ibid., p. 106.
6. Ibid., p. 78.
7. Ibid.
8. Ibid., p. 148.
9. Ibid., p. 153.
10. Ibid., p. 82.
11. Ibid., p. 124.
12. Conrad, quoted in Jonah Raskin, *The Mythology of Imperialism*, New York, Random House, 1971, p. 143.
13. Conrad, *Heart of Darkness*, op. cit., p. 142.
14. Conrad, quoted in Bernard C. Meyer, MD, *Joseph Conrad: A Psychoanalytic Biography*, Princeton University Press, 1967, p. 30.
15. Ibid., p. 30.
16. Frank Willett, *African Art*, New York, Praeger, 1971, pp. 35–6.
17. About the omission of the Great Wall of China I am indebted to 'The Journey of Marco Polo' as recreated by artist Michael Foreman, published by *Pegasus* magazine, New York, 1974.
18. *Christian Science Monitor*, Boston, 25 November 1974, p. 11.

6.4   EDWARD SAID: 'TWO VISIONS IN *HEART OF DARKNESS*' (1994)

Edward Said was born in Palestine and educated there and in Egypt before moving to live and work in the United States, where he is Parr Professor of English and Comparative Literature at Columbia University, New York. His first critical work was *Joseph Conrad and the Fiction of Autobiography* (1966), followed by *Beginnings* (1973) and *The World, The Text and The Critic* (1983), which also contains a discussion of Conrad. These studies show an influential move, inspired in part by the writings of Michel Foucault, towards an accessible, politically located form of literary study and intellectual work. Said's reputation was chiefly established, however, by *Orientalism* (1978), a study of the West's ideas and ideology of the East. This and related essays have given a lead to the field of studies known in the late 1980s and 1990s as postcolonialism. (See *A Practical Guide* 3/e, Ch. 7, 'Postcolonialism', especially pp. 190–3, and essays in Chs 9 and 10 in the present volume.)

Said is concerned in the following discussion primarily with the theme of imperialism. He describes a 'many-sided imperial experience' and includes several contemporary literary and political references in his account (to Naipaul, Rushdie, the Islamic revolution, the Gulf war). What is the relevance of this discussion to Conrad's story and to the 'two visions' of Said's chapter title? Consider the meaning he gives to 'emptiness' in this connection and how this differs from the meanings and attributes this term has in Leavis and others. Said's perception, secondly, of the 'conjunctures' of 'politics with culture and aesthetics' leads him to see the modern writer or intellectual as adopting a necessarily commited cultural and political role. Does Said's own evident partisanship make his approach more, or less, appropriate to literary study? Chinua Achebe (see above) is an equally political critic (whom Said refers to in his essay). How would you summarize their differences?

'Two Visions in *Heart of Darkness*' is from Edward Said, *Culture and Imperialism* (Chatto & Windus, 1994), pp. 20–35.

Two Visions in *Heart of Darkness*

Domination and inequities of power and wealth are perennial facts of human society. But in today's global setting they are also interpretable as having something to do with imperialism, its history, its new forms. The nations of contemporary Asia, Latin America, and Africa are politically independent but in many ways are as dominated and dependent as they were when ruled directly by European powers. On the one hand, this is the consequence of self-inflicted wounds, critics like V. S. Naipaul are wont to say: *they* (everyone knows that 'they' means coloureds, wogs, niggers) are to blame for what 'they' are, and it's no use droning on about the legacy of imperialism. On the other hand, blaming the Europeans sweepingly for the misfortunes of the present is not much of an alternative. What we need to do is to look at these matters as a network of interdependent histories that it would be inaccurate and senseless to repress, useful and interesting to understand.

The point here is not complicated. If while sitting in Oxford, Paris, or New York you tell Arabs or Africans that they belong to a basically sick or unregenerate culture, you are unlikely to convince them. Even if you prevail over them, they are not going to concede to you your essential superiority or your right to rule them despite your evident wealth and power. The history of this stand-off is manifest throughout colonies where white masters were once unchallenged but finally driven out. Conversely, the triumphant natives soon enough found that they needed the West and that the idea of *total* independence was a nationalist fiction designed mainly for what Fanon calls the 'nationalist bourgeoisie', who in turn often ran the new countries with a callous, exploitative tyranny reminiscent of the departed masters.

And so in the late twentieth century the imperial cycle of the last century in some way replicates itself, although today there are really no big empty spaces, no expanding frontiers, no exciting new settlements to establish. We live in one global environment with a huge number of ecological, economic, social, and political pressures tearing at its only dimly perceived, basically uninterpreted and uncomprehended fabric. Anyone with even a vague consciousness of this whole is alarmed at how such remorselessly selfish and narrow interests – patriotism, chauvinism, ethnic, religious, and racial hatreds – can in fact lead to mass destructiveness. The world simply cannot afford this many more times.

One should not pretend that models for a harmonious world order are ready at hand, and it would be equally disingenuous to suppose that ideas of peace and community have much of a chance when power is moved to action by aggressive perceptions of 'vital national interests' or unlimited sovereignty. The United States' clash with Iraq and Iraq's aggression against Kuwait concerning oil are obvious examples. The wonder of it is that the schooling for such relatively provincial thought and action is still prevalent, unchecked, uncritically accepted, recurringly replicated in the education of generation after generation. We are all taught to venerate our nations and admire our traditions: we are taught to pursue their interests with toughness and in disregard for other societies. A new and in my opinion appalling tribalism is fracturing societies, separating peoples, promoting greed, bloody conflict, and uninteresting assertions of minor ethnic or group particularity. Little time is spent not so much in 'learning about other cultures' – the phrase has an inane vagueness to it – but in studying the map of interactions, the actual and often productive traffic occurring on a day-by-day, and even minute-by-minute basis among states, societies, groups, identities.

No one can hold this entire map in his or her head, which is why the geography of empire and the many-sided imperial experience that created its fundamental texture should be considered first in terms of a few salient configurations. Primarily, as we look back at the nineteenth century, we see that the drive toward empire in effect brought most of the earth under the domination of a handful of powers. To get hold of part of what this means, I propose to look at a specific set of rich cultural documents in which the interaction between Europe or America on the one hand and the imperialized world on the other is animated, informed, made explicit as an experience for both sides of the encounter. Yet before I do this, historically and systematically, it is a useful preparation to look at what still remains of imperialism in recent cultural discussion. This is the residuum of a dense, interesting history that is paradoxically global and local at the same time, and it is also a sign of how the imperial past lives on, arousing argument and counter-argument with surprising intensity. Because they are contemporary and easy at hand, these traces of the past in the present point the way to a study of the histories – the plural is used advisedly – created by empire, not just the stories of the white man and woman but also those of the non-whites whose lands and very being were at issue, even as their claims were denied or ignored.

One significant contemporary debate about the residue of imperialism – the matter of how 'natives' are represented in the Western media – illustrates the persistence of such interdependence and overlapping, not only in the debate's content but in its form, not only in what is said but also in how it is said, by whom, where, and for whom. This bears looking into, although it requires a self-discipline not easily come by, so well-developed, tempting, and ready at hand are the confrontational strategies. In 1984, well before *The Satanic Verses* appeared, Salman Rushdie diagnosed the spate of films and articles about the British Raj, including the television series *The Jewel in the Crown* and David Lean's film of *A Passage to India*. Rushdie noted that the nostalgia pressed into service by these affectionate recollections of British rule in India coincided with the Falklands War, and that 'the rise of Raj revisionism, exemplified by the huge success of these fictions, is the artistic counterpart to the rise of conservative ideologies in modern Britain'. Commentators responded to what they considered Rushdie's wailing and whining in public and seemed to disregard his principal point. Rushdie was trying to make a larger argument, which presumably should have appealed to intellectuals for whom George Orwell's well-known description of the intellectual's place in society as being inside and outside the whale no longer applied; modern reality in Rushdie's terms was actually 'whaleless, this world without quiet corners [in which] there can be no easy escapes from history, from hullabaloo, from terrible, unquiet fuss'.[1] But Rushdie's main point was *not* the point considered worth taking up and debating. Instead the main issue for contention was whether things in the Third World hadn't in fact declined after the colonies had been emancipated, and whether it might not be better on the whole to listen to the rare – luckily, I might add, extremely rare – Third World intellectuals who manfully ascribed most of their present barbarities, tyrannies, and degradations to their own native histories, histories that were pretty bad before colonialism and that reverted to that state after colonialism. Hence, ran *this* argument, better a ruthlessly honest V. S. Naipaul than an absurdly posturing Rushdie.

One could conclude from the emotions stirred up by Rushdie's own case, then and later, that many people in the West came to feel that enough was enough. After Vietnam and Iran – and note here that these labels are usually employed equally to evoke American domestic traumas (the student insurrections of the 1960s, the public anguish about the hostages in the 1970s) as much as international conflict and the 'loss' of Vietnam and Iran to radical nationalisms – after Vietnam and Iran, lines had to be defended. Western democracy had taken a beating, and even if the physical damage had been done abroad, there was a sense, as Jimmy Carter once rather oddly put it, of 'mutual destruction'. This feeling in turn led to Westerners rethinking the whole process of decolonization. Was it not true, ran their new evaluation, that 'we' had given 'them' progress and modernization? Hadn't we provided them with order and a kind of stability that they haven't been able since to provide for themselves? Wasn't it an atrocious misplaced trust to believe in their capacity for independence, for it had led to Bokassas and Amins whose intellectual correlates were people like Rushdie? Shouldn't we have held on to the colonies, kept the subject or inferior races in check, remained true to our civilizational responsibilities?

I realize that what I have just reproduced is not entirely the thing itself, but perhaps a caricature. Nevertheless it bears an uncomfortable resemblance to what many people who imagined themselves speaking for the West said. There seemed little scepticism that a monolithic 'West' in fact existed, any more than an entire ex-colonial world described in one sweeping generalization after another. The leap to essences and generalizations was accompanied by appeals to an imagined history of Western endowments and free hand-outs, followed by a reprehensible sequence of ungrateful bitings of that grandly giving 'Western' hand. 'Why don't they appreciate us, after what we did for them?'[2]

How easily so much could be compressed into that simple formula of unappreciated magnanimity! Dismissed or forgotten were the ravaged colonial peoples who for centuries endured summary justice, unending economic oppression, distortion of their social and intimate lives, and a recourseless submission that was the function of unchanging European superiority. Only to keep in mind the millions of Africans who were supplied to the slave trade is to acknowledge the unimaginable cost of maintaining that superiority. Yet dismissed most often are precisely the infinite number of traces in the immensely detailed, violent history of colonial intervention – minute by minute, hour by hour – in the lives of individuals and collectivities, on both sides of the colonial divide.

The thing to be noticed about this kind of contemporary discourse, which assumes the primacy and even the complete centrality of the West, is how totalizing is its form, how all-enveloping its attitudes and gestures, how much it shuts out even as it includes, compresses, and consolidates. We suddenly find ourselves transported backward in time to the late nineteenth century.

This imperial attitude is, I believe, beautifully captured in the complicated and rich narrative form of Conrad's great novella *Heart of Darkness*, written between 1898 and 1899. On the one hand, the narrator Marlow acknowledges the tragic predicament of all speech – that 'it is impossible to convey the life-sensation of any given epoch of one's existence – that which makes its truth, its meaning – its subtle and penetrating essence ... We live, as we dream – alone'[3] – yet still manages to convey the enormous power of Kurtz's African experience through his own overmastering narrative of his voyage into the African interior towards Kurtz. This narrative in turn is connected directly with the redemptive force, as well as the waste and horror, of Europe's mission in the dark world. Whatever is lost or elided or even simply made up in Marlow's immensely compelling recitation is compensated for in the narrative's sheer historical momentum, the temporal forward movement – with digressions, descriptions, exciting encounters, and all. Within the narrative of how he journeyed to Kurtz's Inner Station, whose source and authority he now becomes, Marlow moves backward and forward materially in small and large spirals, very much the way episodes in the course of his journey up-river are then incorporated by the principal forward trajectory into what he renders as 'the heart of Africa'.

Thus Marlow's encounter with the improbably white-suited clerk in the middle of the jungle furnishes him with several digressive paragraphs, as does his meeting later with the semi-crazed, harlequin-like Russian who has been so affected by Kurtz's gifts. Yet underlying Marlow's inconclusiveness, his evasions, his arabesque meditations on his feelings and ideas, is the unrelenting course of the journey itself, which, despite all the many obstacles, is sustained through the jungle, through time, through hardship, to the heart of it all, Kurtz's ivory-trading empire. Conrad wants us to see how Kurtz's great looting adventure, Marlow's journey up the river, and the narrative itself all share a common theme: Europeans performing acts of imperial mastery and will in (or about) Africa.

What makes Conrad different from the other colonial writers who were his contemporaries is that, for reasons having partly to do with the colonialism that turned him, a Polish expatriate, into an employee of the imperial system, he was so self-conscious about what he did. Like most of his other tales, therefore, *Heart of Darkness* cannot just be a straightforward recital of Marlow's adventures: it is also a dramatization of Marlow himself, the former wanderer in colonial regions, telling his story to a group of British listeners at a particular time and in a specific place. That this group of people is drawn largely from the business world is Conrad's way of emphasizing the fact that during the 1890s the business of empire, once an adventurous and often individualistic enterprise, had become the empire of business. (Coincidentally we should note that at about the same time Halford Mackinder, an explorer, geographer, and Liberal Imperialist, gave a series of lectures on imperialism at the London Institute of Bankers:[4] perhaps Conrad knew about this.) Although the almost oppressive force of Marlow's narrative leaves us with a quite accurate sense that there is no way out of the sovereign historical force of imperialism, and that it has the power of a system representing as well as speaking for everything within its dominion, Conrad shows us that what Marlow does is contingent, acted out for a set of like-minded British hearers, and limited to that situation.

Yet neither Conrad nor Marlow gives us a full view of what is *outside* the world-conquering attitudes embodied by Kurtz, Marlow, the circle of listeners on the deck of the *Nellie*, and Conrad. By that I mean that *Heart of Darkness* works so effectively because its politics and aesthetics are, so to speak, imperialist, which in the closing years of the nineteenth century seemed to be at the same time an aesthetic, politics, and even epistemology inevitable and unavoidable. For if we cannot truly understand someone else's experience and if we must therefore depend upon the assertive authority of the sort of power that Kurtz wields as a white man in the jungle or that Marlow, another white man, wields as narrator, there is no use looking for other, non-imperialist alternatives; the system has simply eliminated them and made them unthinkable. The circularity, the perfect closure of the whole thing is not only aesthetically but also mentally unassailable.

Conrad is so self-conscious about situating Marlow's tale in a narrative moment that he allows us simultaneously to realize after all that imperialism, far from swallowing up its own history, was taking place in and was circumscribed by a larger history, one just outside the tightly inclusive circle of Europeans on the deck of the *Nellie*. As yet, however, no one seemed to inhabit that region, and so Conrad left it empty.

Conrad could probably never have used Marlow to present anything other than an imperialist world-view, given what was available for either Conrad or Marlow to see of the non-European at the time. Independence was for whites and Europeans; the lesser or subject peoples were to be ruled; science, learning, history emanated from the West. True, Conrad scrupulously recorded the differences between the disgraces of Belgian and British colonial attitudes, but he could only imagine the world carved up into one or another Western sphere of dominion. But because Conrad also had an extraordinarily persistent residual sense of his own exilic marginality, he quite carefully (some would say maddeningly) qualified Marlow's narrative with the provisionality that came from standing at the very juncture of this world with another, unspecified but different. Conrad was certainly not a great imperialist entrepreneur like Cecil Rhodes or Frederick Lugard, even though he understood perfectly how for each of them, in Hannah Arendt's words, to enter 'the maelstrom of an unending process of expansion, he will, as it were, cease to be what he was and obey the laws of the process, identify himself with anonymous forces that he is supposed to serve in order to keep the whole process in motion, he will think of himself as mere function, and eventually consider such functionality, such an incarnation of the dynamic trend, his highest possible achievement'.[5] Conrad's realization is that if, like narrative, imperialism has monopolized the entire system of representation – which in the case of *Heart of Darkness* allowed it to speak for Africans as well as for Kurtz and the other adventurers, including Marlow and his audience – your self-consciousness as an outsider can allow you actively to comprehend how the machine works, given that you and it are fundamentally not in perfect synchrony or correspondence. Never the wholly incorporated and fully acculturated Englishman, Conrad therefore preserved an ironic distance in each of his works.

The form of Conrad's narrative has thus made it possible to derive two possible arguments, two visions, in the post-colonial world that succeeded his. One argument allows the old imperial enterprise full scope to play itself out conventionally, to render the world as official European or Western imperialism saw it, and to consolidate itself after World War Two. Westerners may have physically left their old colonies in Africa and Asia, but they retained them not only as markets but as locales on the ideological map over which they continued to rule morally and intellectually. 'Show me the Zulu Tolstoy', as one American intellectual has recently put it. The assertive sovereign inclusiveness of this argument courses through the words of those who speak today for the West and for what the West did, as well as for what the rest of the world is, was, and may be. The assertions of this discourse exclude what has been represented as 'lost' by arguing that the colonial world was in some ways ontologically speaking lost to begin with, irredeemable, irrecusably inferior. Moreover, it focuses not on what was shared in the colonial experience, but on what must never be shared, namely the authority and rectitude that come with greater power and development. Rhetorically, its terms are the organization of political passions, to borrow from Julien Benda's critique of modern intellectuals, terms which, he was sensible enough to know, lead inevitably to mass slaughter, and if not to literal mass slaughter then certainly to rhetorical slaughter.

The second argument is considerably less objectionable. It sees itself as Conrad saw his own narratives, local to a time and place, neither unconditionally true nor unqualifiedly certain. As I have said, Conrad does not give us the sense that he could imagine a fully realized alternative to imperialism: the natives he wrote about in Africa, Asia, or America were incapable of independence, and because he seemed to imagine that European tutelage was a given, he could not foresee what would take place when it came to an end. But come to an end it would, if only because – like all human effort, like speech itself – it would have its moment, then it would have to pass. Since Conrad *dates* imperialism, shows its contingency, records its illusions and tremendous violence and waste (as in *Nostromo*), he permits his later readers to imagine something other than an Africa carved up into dozens of European colonies, even if, for his own part, he had little notion of what that Africa might be.

To return to the first line out of Conrad, the discourse of resurgent empire proves that the nineteenth-century imperial encounter continues today to draw lines and defend barriers. Strangely, it persists also in the enormously complex and quietly interesting interchange between former colonial partners, say between Britain and India, or between France and the Francophone countries of Africa. But these exchanges tend to be overshadowed by the loud antagonisms of the polarized debate of pro- and anti-imperialists, who speak stridently of national destiny, overseas interests, neo-imperialism, and the like, drawing like-minded people – aggressive Westerners and, ironically, those non-Westerners for whom the new nationalist and resurgent Ayatollahs speak – away from the other ongoing interchange. Inside each regrettably constricted camp stand the blameless, the just, the faithful, led by the omnicompetent, those who know the truth about themselves and others; outside stands a miscellaneous bunch of querulous intellectuals and wishy-washy sceptics who go on complaining about the past to little effect.

An important ideological shift occurred during the 1970s and 1980s, accompanying this contraction of horizons in what I have been calling the first of the two lines leading out of *Heart of Darkness*. One can locate it, for instance, in the dramatic change in emphasis and, quite literally, direction among thinkers noted for their radicalism. The later Jean-François Lyotard and Michel Foucault, eminent French philosophers who emerged during the 1960s as apostles of radicalism and intellectual insurgency, describe a striking new lack of faith in what Lyotard calls the great legitimizing narratives of emancipation and enlightenment. Our age, he said in the 1980s, is post-modernist, concerned only with local issues, not with history but with problems to be solved, not with a grand reality but with games.[6] Foucault also turned his attention away from the oppositional forces in modern society which he had studied for their undeterred resistance to exclusion and confinement – delinquents, poets, outcasts, and the like – and decided that since power was everywhere it was probably better to concentrate on the local micro-physics of power that surround the individual. The self was therefore to be studied, cultivated, and, if necessary, refashioned and constituted.[7] In both Lyotard and Foucault we find precisely the same trope employed to explain the disappointment in the politics of liberation: narrative, which posits an enabling beginning point and a vindicating goal, is no longer adequate for plotting the human trajectory in society. There is nothing to look forward to: we are stuck within our circle. And now the line is enclosed by a circle. After years of support for anti-colonial struggles in Algeria, Cuba, Vietnam, Palestine, Iran, which came to represent for many Western intellectuals their deepest engagement in the politics and philosophy of anti-imperialist decolonization, a moment of exhaustion and disappointment was reached.[8] One began to hear and read how futile it was to support revolutions, how barbaric were the new regimes that came to power, how – this is an extreme case – decolonization had benefited 'world communism'.

Enter now terrorism and barbarism. Enter also the ex-colonial experts whose well-publicized message was: these colonial peoples deserve only colonialism or, since 'we' were foolish to pull out of Aden, Algeria, India, Indochina, and everywhere else, it might be a good idea to reinvade their territories. Enter also various experts and theoreticians of the relationship between liberation movements, terrorism, and the KGB. There was a resurgence of sympathy for what Jeane Kirkpatrick called authoritarian (as opposed to totalitarian) regimes who were Western allies. With the onset of Reaganism, Thatcherism, and their correlates, a new phase of history began.

However else it might have been historically understandable, peremptorily withdrawing 'the West' from its own experiences in the 'peripheral world' certainly was and is not an attractive or edifying activity for an intellectual today. It shuts out the possibility of knowledge and of discovery of what it means to be outside the whale. Let us return to Rushdie for another insight:

> We see that it can be as false to create a politics-free fictional universe as to create one in which nobody needs to work or eat or hate or love or sleep. Outside the whale it becomes necessary, and even exhilarating, to grapple with the special problems created by the incorporation of political material, because politics is by turns farce and tragedy, and sometimes (e.g., Zia's Pakistan) both at once. Outside the whale the writer is obliged to accept that he (or she) is part of the crowd, part of the ocean, part of the storm, so that objectivity becomes a great dream, like perfection, an unattainable goal for which one must struggle in spite of the impossibility of success. Outside the whale is the world of Samuel Beckett's famous formula: *I can't go on, I'll go on.*[9]

The terms of Rushdie's description, while they borrow from Orwell, seem to me to resonate even more interestingly with Conrad. For here is the second consequence, the second line leading out of Conrad's narrative form; in its explicit references to the outside, it points to a perspective outside the basically imperialist representations provided by Marlow and his listeners. It is a profoundly secular perspective, and it is beholden neither to notions about historical destiny and the essentialism that destiny always seems to entail, nor to historical indifference and resignation. Being on the inside shuts out the full experience of imperialism, edits it and subordinates it to the dominance of one Eurocentric and totalizing view; this other perspective suggests the presence of a field without special historical privileges for one party.

I don't want to overinterpret Rushdie, or put ideas in his prose that he may not have intended. In this controversy with the local British media (before *The Satanic Verses* sent him into hiding) he claimed that he could not recognize the truth of his own experience in the popular media representations of India. Now I myself would go further and say that it is one of the virtues of such conjunctures of politics with culture and aesthetics that they permit the disclosure of a common ground obscured by the controversy itself. Perhaps it is especially hard for the combatants directly involved to see this common ground when they are fighting back more than reflecting. I can perfectly understand the anger that fuelled Rushdie's argument because like him I feel outnumbered and outorganized by a prevailing Western consensus that has come to regard the Third World as an atrocious nuisance, a culturally and politically inferior place. Whereas we write and speak as members of a small minority of marginal voices, our journalistic and academic critics belong to a wealthy system of interlocking informational and academic resources with newspapers, television networks, journals of opinion, and institutes at its disposal. Most of them have now taken up a strident chorus of rightward-tending damnation, in which they separate what is non-white, non-Western, and non-Judeo-Christian from the acceptable and designated Western ethos, then herd it all together under various demeaning rubrics such as terrorist, marginal, second-rate, or unimportant. To attack what is contained in these categories is to defend the Western spirit.

Let us return to Conrad and to what I have been referring to as the second, less imperialistically assertive possibility offered by *Heart of Darkness*. Recall once again that Conrad sets the story on the deck of a boat anchored in the Thames; as Marlow tells his story the sun sets, and by the end of the narrative the heart of darkness has reappeared in England; outside the group of Marlow's listeners lies an undefined and unclear world. Conrad sometimes seems to want to fold that world into the imperial metropolitan discourse represented by Marlow, but by virtue of his own dislocated subjectivity he resists the effort and succeeds in so doing, I have always believed, largely through formal devices. Conrad's self-consciously circular narrative forms draw attention to themselves as artificial constructions, encouraging us to sense the potential of a reality that seemed inaccessible to imperialism, just beyond its control, and that only well after Conrad's death in 1924 acquired a substantial presence.

This needs more explanation. Despite their European names and mannerisms, Conrad's narrators are not average unreflecting witnesses of European imperialism. They do not simply accept what goes on in the name of the imperial idea: they think about it a lot, they worry about it, they are actually quite anxious about whether they can make it seem like a routine thing. But it never is. Conrad's way of demonstrating this discrepancy between the orthodox and his own views of empire is to keep drawing attention to how ideas and values are constructed (and deconstructed) through dislocations in the narrator's language. In addition, the recitations are meticulously staged: the narrator is a speaker whose audience and the reason for their being together, the quality of whose voice, the effect of what he says – are all important and even insistent aspects of the story he tells. Marlow, for example, is never straightforward. He alternates between garrulity and stunning eloquence, and rarely resists making peculiar things seem more peculiar by surprisingly misstating them, or rendering them vague and contradictory. Thus, he says, a French warship fires 'into a continent'; Kurtz's eloquence is enlightening as well as fraudulent; and so on – his speech so full of these odd discrepancies (well discussed by Ian Watt as 'delayed decoding'[10]) that the net effect is to leave his immediate audience as well as the reader with the acute sense that what he is presenting is not quite as it should be or appears to be.

Yet the whole point of what Kurtz and Marlow talk about is in fact imperial mastery, white Europeans *over* black Africans and their ivory, civilization *over* the primitive dark continent. By accentuating the discrepancy between the official 'idea' of empire and the remarkably disorienting actuality of Africa, Marlow unsettles the reader's sense not only of the very idea of empire but of something more basic, reality itself. For if Conrad can show that all human activity depends on controlling a radically unstable reality to which words approximate only by will or convention, the same is true of empire, of venerating the idea, and so forth. With Conrad, then, we are in a world being made and unmade more or less all the time. What appears stable and secure – the policeman at the corner, for instance – is only slightly more secure than the white men in the jungle, and requires the same continuous (but precarious) triumph over an all-pervading darkness, which by the end of the tale is shown to be the same in London and in Africa.

Conrad's genius allowed him to realize that the ever-present darkness could be colonized or illuminated – *Heart of Darkness* is full of references to the *mission civilisatrice*, to benevolent as well as cruel schemes to bring light to the dark places and peoples of this world by acts of will and deployments of power – but that it also had to be acknowledged as independent. Kurtz and Marlow acknowledge the darkness, the former as he is dying, the latter as he reflects retrospectively on the meaning of Kurtz's final words. They (and of course Conrad) are ahead of their time in understanding that what they call 'the darkness' has an autonomy of its own, and can reinvade and reclaim what imperialism had taken for *its* own. But Marlow and Kurtz are also creatures of their time and cannot take the next step, which would be to recognize that what they saw, disablingly and disparagingly, as a non-European 'darkness' was in fact a non-European world *resisting* imperialism so as one day to regain sovereignty and independence, and not, as Conrad reductively says, to reestablish the darkness. Conrad's tragic limitation is that even though he could see clearly that on one level imperialism was essentially pure dominance and land-grabbing, he could not then conclude that imperialism had to end so that 'natives' could lead lives free from European domination. As a creature of his time, Conrad could not grant the natives their freedom, despite his severe critique of the imperialism that enslaved them.

The cultural and ideological evidence that Conrad was wrong in his Eurocentric way is both impressive and rich. A whole movement, literature, and theory of resistance and response to empire exists [the subject of Chapter Three of *Culture and Imperialism*] and in greatly disparate post-colonial regions one sees tremendously energetic efforts to engage with the metropolitan world in equal debate so as to testify to the diversity and differences of the non-European world and to its own agendas, priorities, and history. The purpose of this testimony is to inscribe, reinterpret, and expand the areas of engagement as well as the terrain contested with Europe. Some of this activity – for example, the work of two important and active Iranian intellectuals, Ali Shariati and Jalal Ali i-Ahmed, who by means of speeches, books, tapes, and pamphlets prepared the way for the Islamic Revolution – interprets colonialism by asserting the absolute opposition of the native culture: the West is an enemy, a disease, an evil. In other instances, novelists like the Kenyan Ngugi and the Sudanese Tayib Salih appropriate for their fiction such great *topoi* of colonial culture as the quest and the voyage into the unknown, claiming them for their own, post-colonial purposes. Salih's hero in *Season of Migration to the North* does (and is) the reverse of what Kurtz does (and is): the Black man journeys north into white territory.

Between classical nineteenth-century imperialism and what it gave rise to in resistant native cultures, there is thus both a stubborn confrontation and a crossing over in discussion, borrowing back and forth, debate. Many of the most interesting post-colonial writers bear their past within them – as scars of humiliating wounds, as instigation for different practices, as potentially revised visions of the past tending towards a new future, as urgently reinterpretable and redeployable experiences, in which the formerly silent native speaks and acts on territory taken back from the empire. One sees these aspects in Rushdie, Derek Walcott, Aimé Césaire, Chinua Achebe, Pablo Neruda, and Brian Friel. And now these writers can truly read the great colonial masterpieces, which not only misrepresented them but assumed they were unable to read and respond directly to what had been written about them, just as European ethnography presumed the natives' incapacity to intervene in scientific discourse about them.

Notes (renumbered)

1. Salman Rushdie, 'Outside the Whale,' in *Imaginary Homelands: Essays and Criticism, 1981–1991* (London: Viking/Granta, 1991), pp. 92, 101.
2. This is the message of Conor Cruise O'Brien's 'Why the Wailing Ought to Stop', *The Observer*, June 3, 1984.
3. Joseph Conrad, 'Heart of Darkness,' in *Youth and Two Other Stories* (Garden City: Doubleday, Page, 1925), p. 82.
4. For Mackinder, see Neil Smith, *Uneven Development: Nature, Capital and the Production of Space* (Oxford: Blackwell, 1984), pp. 102–3. Conrad and triumphalist geography are at the heart of Felix Driver, 'Geography's Empire: Histories of Geographical Knowledge,' *Society and Space*, 1991.

5. Hannah Arendt, *The Origins of Totalitarianism* (1951; new ed., New York: Harcourt Brace Jovanovich, 1973), p. 215. See also Fredric Jameson, *The Political Unconscious: Narrative as a Socially Symbolic Act* (Ithaca: Cornell University Press, 1981), pp. 206–81.
6. Jean-François Lyotard, *The Postmodern Condition: A Report on Knowledge*, trans. Geoff Bennington and Brian Massumi (Minneapolis: University of Minnesota Press, 1984), p. 37.
7. See especially Foucault's late work, *The Care of the Self*, trans. Robert Hurley (New York: Pantheon, 1986). A bold new interpretation arguing that Foucault's entire *oeuvre* is about the self, and his in particular, is advanced in *The Passion of Michel Foucault* by James Miller (New York: Simon & Schuster, 1993).
8. See, for example, Gérard Chaliand, *Revolution in the Third World* (Harmondsworth: Penguin, 1978).
9. Rushdie, 'Outside the Whale,' pp. 100–101.
10. Ian Watt, *Conrad in the Nineteenth Century* (Berkeley: University of California Press, 1979), pp. 175–79.

Chapter 7

James Joyce:
Ulysses

GENERAL INTRODUCTION

James Augustine Joyce (1882–1941) was born and educated in Dublin, which he left permanently in 1904 to live in Trieste (between 1904 and 1915) and, from 1920, in Zurich and Paris. *Dubliners* was published in 1914 and *A Portrait of the Artist as a Young Man* in 1916. *Ulysses* was serialized in the *Little Review* from 1918 and published in Paris in 1922, but banned in the United States and Great Britain respectively until 1934 and 1936. *Finnegans Wake* was begun in 1923 and published in 1939.

The text of *Ulysses* has been unstable since its first printing by Shakespeare & Company in 1922. Hans Walter Gabler produced a 'critical and synoptic' edition in 1984 which was published by Random House and Penguin as the 'corrected' text in 1986, but this has been challenged, in particular by the US scholar John Kidd. The most useful text is the Oxford University Press edition which reprints the 1922 text of the novel with notes, including full information on the text's publishing history and present-day disputes.

In their introduction to *Post-Structuralist Joyce. Essays From the French* (Cambridge University Press, 1984), Derek Attridge and Daniel Ferrer remind us of Joyce's knowledge of Paris and of how he set its supposed decadent excess against the censorious norms of England and Dublin. The French have been more receptive to Joyce, they say, and this generosity has continued in poststructuralist criticism, which has sought neither to serve nor to master Joyce's text, by elucidating its difficulties or uncovering its meanings in the conventional way. Poststructuralist readings do not stand clear of the text but are none the less embedded, Attridge and Ferrer say, in 'a social space filled with texts' (p. 4); responsive to changed historical conditions and the new conditions for reading and meaning these produce. Modernist texts, they argue, were accommodated to the canon, and made acceptable to dominant literary taste, through 'transcendentalist' or 'empiricist' interpretations, the first emphasizing the structure of myth in *Ulysses*, the second the novel's realism. From a poststructuralist point of view, the more interesting readings have been the less recuperative interpretations by figures such as Wyndham Lewis, Carl Jung and Samuel Beckett.

In Attridge and Ferrer's assessment Anglophone literary criticism remained unaltered, quite noticeably in Joyce studies, by shifts in European literary theory which were in part prompted by Joyce's work. It is time, they conclude, 'to take the full measure' of Joyce's 'literary revolution – to produce Joyce's texts in ways designed to challenge rather than comfort, to antagonise instead of assimilate' (p. 7). This, they feel, is evidenced by essays on Joyce by, amongst others. Stephen Heath, Hélène Cixous and Jacques Derrida.

The following examples of Joyce criticism include an extract from Cixous and an essay by Derrida. Are these readings challenging in the way Attridge and Ferrer suggest? And what, in the light of their argument, are we to make of the essays by Raymond Williams, Fredric Jameson and Wolfgang Iser? Are these essays proof that non-poststructuralist readings seek to accommodate Joyce to a humanist orthodoxy, or are they a sign that there are other ways of taking the 'full measure' of Joyce'?

This leads to some further important, but difficult, questions. Do these essays employ significantly different theories of literature and of reading? If so, which position are you inclined to take? Do you find convincing grounds, for example, for making judgements of interpretative value, for preferring the earlier to the later Joyce (or the reverse)? Are you persuaded that a difficult text can be made accessible, its world and way of seeing reconstructed; or do you view this kind of critical mastery as inappropriate and see the task of reading as being, instead, to deconstruct a text, to explore and further activate its 'infinite productivity'?

Further reading
In the present context, students might usefully consult the selections in Richard Brown, ed., *Ulysses* ('New Casebook' Series, Macmillan, 1995), the essays in D. Attridge, ed., *The Cambridge Companion to James Joyce* (Cambridge University Press, 1990) and the survey of critical approaches in Alan Roughley, *Joyce and Critical Theory* (Harvester, 1991).

For more extensive background reading, see the following:

Frank Budgen, *James Joyce and the Making of Ulysses* (1934, reprinted Oxford University Press, 1972).

Richard Ellman, *James Joyce* (1959, rev. edn, 1982, corr., Oxford University Press, 1983).

Suzette A. Henke, *James Joyce and the Politics of Desire* (Routledge, 1990).

Dominic Manganiello, *Joyce's Politics* (Routledge, 1980).

Franco Moretti, 'The Long Goodbye. *Ulysses* and the End of Liberal Capitalism', in *Signs Taken for Wonders* (Verso, 1988), pp. 182–208.

Bonnie Kime Scott, *Joyce and Feminism* (Harvester, 1984).

7.1 HÉLÈNE CIXOUS: FROM 'JOYCE: THE (R)USE OF WRITING' (1970, TRANS. 1984)

Hélène Cixous is Chair of the Centre of Research in Feminine Studies at the University of Paris VIII (Saint Denis). She is a leading figure in 'French feminism' and a major contributor to debates on the question of 'feminine writing'. She has explored the themes of writing, the body, and sexual difference in a number of highly influential critical works as well as in avant-garde fictional and dramatic texts. Important works in translation include: 'The Laugh of the Medusa' in Elaine Marks and Isabelle de Courtivron, eds, *New French Feminisms* (1980); *The Newly Born Woman*, with Catherine Clement (1986) – an extract from which, 'Sorties', is also included in Marks and de Courtivron; and *Reading with Clarice Lispector*, ed., trans. and introduced by Verana Andermatt Conley (Prentice Hall/ Harvester, 1990). See also Susan Sellers, ed., *The Hélène Cixous Reader* (Routledge, 1994). A thorough and accessible introduction to Cixous' work, including some discussion of her readings of Joyce, is provided by Morag Shiach, *Hélène Cixous. A Politics of Writing* (Routledge, 1991).

Cixous has written a number of times on Joyce and he has proved an important measure for her developing exploration of writing, sexual difference, and subjectivity. Her doctoral thesis, *The Exile of James Joyce*, trans S. Purcell (John Calder, 1972), examined his writing in a biographical context, and has been followed by commentary on *Dubliners* and *A Portrait of the Artist*, notably in the collection *Prénoms de personne* (Paris, 1974) which contains four texts on Joyce's work; and by two essays, more directly on *Finnegans Wake* and questions of sexual difference, published in *Entre l'écriture* (Paris, 1986). In translation, the volume *Readings: The Poetics of Blanchot, Joyce, Kafka, Kleist, Lispector and Tsvetayeva*, ed., trans. and introduced by Verana Andermatt Conley (Prentice Hall/ Harvester 1992), includes a psychoanalytic reading of the 'embryonic' opening of Joyce's *A Portrait of the Artist*.

Above all, perhaps, Cixous is drawn, in Joyce's work, to the theme of the making of the artist, seeing a development from the desire to unify this figure in *A Portrait* to Joyce's later recognition of the necessarily internally split subject as represented in the experimental, multi-voiced forms of *Ulysses* and, most dramatically, *Finnegans Wake*. This strategic decentring of the subject is Cixous' main theme in the following. Joyce sets the artist-subject or self upon a quest 'with never a definitive way out, with no conclusion' (p. 287 below). A poststructuralist reading of Joyce would seem therefore to make him a poststructuralist before the advent of poststructuralism, just as the psychological narrative of *Ulysses* presents 'an implicit theory of the authorial unconscious, and of the textual unconscious' (p. 288, below) before, or without an acknowledged debt to, Freud. As suggested in the 'General Introduction' above, it is the implications of this perspective, as against one which values direction and coherence (in relation to the 'I, the Artist, the Word' as Cixous puts it), and seeks these in Joyce, which is at issue. Note, in considering these differences, the tensions Cixous detects in Joyce's writing itself, what she understands by the rhetoric (or ruse) of his writing, and how she addresses the dilemma (or riddle) it presents the reader.

The essay, 'Joyce: la (r)use de l'écriture', first appeared in *Poétique* 4 (1970). It was reprinted in *Prénoms de personne* (Paris, 1974) and in translation in D. Attridge and M. Ferrer, eds, *Post-Structuralist Joyce. Essays from the French* (Cambridge University Press,

1984), pp. 15–30, from which the following extract is taken. The essay is principally concerned with the story 'The Sisters' from Joyce's *Dubliners*, but opens with the more general discussion and comments on *Ulysses* reproduced here.

Joyce: The (R)use of Writing

Discrediting the Subject

> Joyce: 'I am the foolish author of a wise book.'
> 'The Catholic Church was built on a pun. It ought to be good enough for me.'

After a long theoretical disquisition on the engendering of writing, on paternity and maternity, on the relationship between Shakespeare's life and his work, and on the mythical kinship between Shakespeare, Hamlet, and the ghost of the dead father, Stephen Dedalus replies to the question posed by an irritated listener:

> – Do you believe your own theory?
> – No, Stephen said promptly.
> [...]
> I believe, O Lord, help my unbelief. That is, help me to believe or help me to unbelieve? Who helps to believe? *Egomen.* Who to unbelieve? Other chap.
> <div align="right">(<i>U</i> 213–14, 'Scylla and Charybdis' chapter)</div>

Here begins a reading of Joyce which will point out by means of certain fragments of *Dubliners* [*D*], of *A Portrait* [*P*], or of *Ulysses* [*U*] how Joyce's work has contributed to the discrediting of the subject; how today one can talk about Joyce's modernity by situating him 'on that breach of the self'[1] opened up by other writings whose subversive force is now undermining the world of western discourse; how his writing, which is justly famed for its system of mastering signs, for its control over grammar (including its transgressions and dislocations which cut across a language which is too much a 'mother' tongue, too alienating, a captive language which must be made to stumble), how this writing takes the risk of upsetting the literary institution and the Anglo-Saxon lexicon: by hesitating over the interpretation of signs, by the vitiation of metaphor, by putting a question mark over the subject and the style of the subject.

Joyce's work is crossed right through by a subject-waiting-for-itself which assumes the formal appearance of a quest, an apprenticeship, a journey, of all those literary genres where the advent of the self finds its niche and is proclaimed – *Bildungsroman* or Dantesque path – with never a definitive way out, with no conclusion. Sudden appearance of the self continually announced, continually cancelled, in books made up of beginnings and exits on top of other beginnings and other exits.

Book of departure: 'That lies in space which I in time must come to, ineluctably' (*U* 217); departures from the Book of departure: 'I go to encounter for the millionth time the reality of experience and to forge in the smithy of my soul the uncreated conscience of my race' (*P* 252).

The penultimate note of the Artist's diary projects the image of the creator in the paternal figure of Daedalus, who melts into Icarus in the last sentence of the book: 'Old father, old artificer, stand me now and ever in good stead.' Cry of the son taking wing, the surge of the *created*, the flight of the work, with, between father and son, the same flesh of writing; and from the father to the son, the sea, the drowning; and from *A Portrait* to *Ulysses*: 'Fabulous artificer, the hawklike man. You flew. Whereto? Newhaven–Dieppe, steerage passenger. Paris and back. Lapwing. Icarus. *Pater, ait.* Seabedabbled.' (*U* 210).

Between Daedalus and Icarus: *Ulysses*. And: 'My will: his will that fronts me. Seas between' (*U* 217). From father unto son, via the mother, always, begun again. This delayed birth constitutes the movement of a work which playfully undermines gestation, the delay inscribing itself in the various falls, losses, repeated and unexpected exiles, which are all the more astounding in that the goal seems accessible, is named, puts itself forward, fascinates, is not hidden but rather pointed out (I, the Artist, the Word), is not forbidden but rather promised, and in that the subject, held in suspense, pursues it with the foolhardiness, the stubbornness, the perfidious will of a hero, with the weapons of the self (silence, exile, cunning), marking out its passage with theories, incorporated hypotheses of formalization: one or two ideas from Aristotle, a pinch of St Thomas; a chapter on poetics and literary history; several chapters on the problems of autobiography; and, in a pre-Freudian context, an implicit theory of the authorial unconscious, and of the textual unconscious, in a blasphemous analogy with the Arian heresy, showing in the Trinity the three-sided, divinely ordered production that allows the Father to see through the Son's eyes, where the Holy Spirit would be like the chain linking the Name of the Father to the Name of the Son, the scriptor to writing: the breath of the unconscious on the text. And all this reverberating from book to book, till lost from sight but held in memory, as an echo, a leitmotiv, a reiteration, for the greater glory of a Word whose power is elevated on the absence or decline of the notion of a *unified* subject. Quest, odyssey, with a plural hero, question whose answer is only ever what is already known in the questioning, question which, while not answering itself, has as an answer the answer's aberration and as effect the eternal revival of the question whose point will no longer know where to put itself, will no longer put itself. Point which is looking for its departure point, whose invisible pointillage divides up *Finnegans Wake* into explosions and a crazy coalescence of the subject which undoes itself at the very moment when it constitutes itself in the new fragmentation of the word become word-tale or word-book, become one-plural.

[...]

Cixous here introduces her reflections on Joyce's story 'The Sisters' from *Dubliners*. The opening paragraph of the story, she says, shows 'the first manifestation of the slide from the One to the plural', presenting the 'scene of the decentering of the subject as it immediately strikes the readers of the text (in the text)'. She is led to the general comments on Joyce included here before returning to a detailed phrase-by-phrase reading of this opening paragraph.

[...]

(R)used writing, writing governed by ruse: which is therefore luxury writing, because in order to play tricks and to sow seeds, you have to produce wild-goose chases, you have to modify the traditional mode of the narrative which claims to offer a coherent whole, utilizable down to its smallest detail, the author being tacitly bound to produce an account of his expenditure. This is writing which is prodigal and therefore disconcerting because of its economy, which refuses to regulate itself, to give itself laws: sometimes restrained, finely calculated, strategic, intending by the systematic use of networks of symbols and correspondences to impose a rigid grid on the reader, to produce an effect of mastery; sometimes, on the other hand, within the same textual web, surreptitiously, perversely, renouncing all demands, opening itself up without any resistance to the incongruous, introducing metaphors which never end, hypnotic and unanswerable riddles, a proliferation of false signs, of doors crafted without keys: in other words (spoken in jest), it is an extraordinarily free game, which should shatter *any habits* of reading, which should be continually shaking the reader up, and thus committing this reader to a double apprenticeship: the necessary one which is reading – writing a text whose plurality explodes the painstakingly polished surface: and the one which is, in the very practice of a reading not condemned to linearity, an incessant questioning of the codes which appear to function normally but which are sometimes suddenly rendered invalid, and then the next moment are revalidated, and, in the inexhaustible play of codes, there slips in, indecipherable and hallucinatory by definition, the delirious code, a lost code, a kind of reserve where untamed signifiers prowl, but without the space of that reserve being delimited. We may expect to feel tricked, deceived, abandoned, and therefore enchanted (or exasperated) when, having thought that we heard a key turn, it is finally clear to us that the key had no door, and was supported only by its sound as a key. Thus in *Ulysses*, plumb in the middle of a majestic episode ('Nestor') which bears the meaning of History, which resounds with the echoes of battles, with questions concerning a country's past and its political heritage, and in general with a weighty examination of the fate of humanity, there slips onto the scene of representation and into a network of correspondences tightly worked by the idea of historical causality, a riddle posed by Stephen.[2]

It is posed to his pupils at the end of a History lesson (the world of science and objectivity). The context forces the reader into a dumbfounded identification with the pupils; everything combines to make you 'take seriously' the existence of an answer: the very genre of the riddle, a literary and detective-story genre, which assumes as a fundamental convention that there should be a solution somewhere, the one who asks being in theory the one who possesses the knowledge. Stephen, as the one who asks, is indeed the master of knowledge: however, his answer reveals not a positive knowledge, but the gap in knowledge, the knowledge of non- knowledge, the author abandoning his rights over language, and thus the desacralization of reading in the sense that reading is implicitly the rite of passage into culture.

> – This is the riddle, Stephen said.

> *The cock crew*
> *The sky was blue:*
> *The bells in heaven*
> *Were striking eleven.*
> *Tis time for this poor soul*
> *To go to heaven.*

> – What is that?
> – What, sir?
> – Again, sir. We didn't hear.
> Their eyes grew bigger as the lines were repeated. After a silence Cochrane said:
> – What is it, sir? We give it up.
> Stephen, his throat itching, answered:
> – The fox burying his grandmother under a hollybush.
> He stood up and gave a shout of nervous laughter to which their cries echoed dismay.

$$(U\ 32-3/26-7)$$

(Listen to the sound effects in the background of this passage: intensification, echo upon echo which calls to and then disappoints the ear; repetition of the puzzle which doubles the thickness of the lure, miming tension, – eyes – ears – open – the preciseness of the terms of the question, and the answer which apes scientificity or the absolute: eleven o'clock and not twelve. *The* fox and not a fox, his grandmother etc. And the play: poetic rhythm/silence/shout of laughter/exclamations, which makes a sonorous commentary on his disturbing words. Privilege slipping from the cock to the fox, without any apparent reason to support it. There remains the untamed subject: the fox. That is all. Stephen's nervous laughter is indeed, provided that you listen to it, the laughter of the perverse text. But it is hard to bear, just as it is difficult to accept that frustration is normal, especially in the intellectual sphere, where it is experienced as the subterfuge of castration: yet it is at this point that you must stop demanding meaning. It is also at this point that academic discourse is brought to its limit, or its 'dismay' ('dismay' → according to the etymology, *dis* is privative, indicating division, dispersion in all directions; *may* (from *magnan* O.H.G.), to possess potency, the power to ...; → discouragement, loss of heart, of moral fibre, of potency, in the face of danger or difficulty). The position of the critic, the reader whose reading is the received version for another reader, is in deep trouble here, unless there is a constant rethinking based on a continual calling back into question, and on a renunciation of all conclusions. There are two possible courses of action: the first trusting to the known facts about Joyce's work, particularly his intensive use of symbols, and his obsessive and often explicit concern to control word-order, thus prejudging the book as a 'full' text, governed by 'the hypostasis of the signified',[3] a text which conceals itself but which has something to conceal, which is findable. This reassuring position is in fact almost necessary, granted the conscious or unconscious fashion of pushing Joyce back into the theological world from which he wanted to escape, by squeezing him 'through the back door' (cf. the versions of Joyce as a Catholic, Medieval Joyce, Irish Joyce, Joyce the Jesuit in reverse and hence the right way round as well, etc.). On the other hand one can imagine a reading which would accept 'discouragement', not in order to 'recuperate' it by taking it as a metaphor for the Joycean occult (which would, by the way, be right but would only be taking account of the formal aspect of that effect of privation), but rather by seeing in that trap which confiscates signification the sign of the willed imposture which crosses and double-crosses the *whole* of Joyce's work, making that betrayal the very breath (the breathlessness) of the subject. Nothing will have been signified save the riddle, referral of a referral beneath a letter which, besides, is not beyond the pretence of having spirit. That fox worries us. And there are quite a few more of them in *Ulysses*.[4] He breaks (with his grandmother and with all that the simple relation animal + bond of kinship suggests, even on the level of the signifier) the circle of the 'readable',[5] of the causal chain which guarantees the continuation of metaphysics.

This farce of breaking-up which interferes directly with the order of *Ulysses*, indicating the vulnerability of that order, is easy to spot because it is isolated almost as a symptom in the extensive textual network in which thousands of apparently detached elements actually excuse their air of being *unemployed* by allusion, analogy, metonymy ... or by being reemployed in motifs or figures: the unattached element is indirectly granted a transgressive violence which it does not possess in previous texts (*Dubliners*, *A Portrait*) in which a *gratuitousness* which is more discreet, if not less dangerous, comes to the surface and makes significance quiver as if it were the *nervous laughter of writing*.

Notes (renumbered)

1. Julia Kristeva, 'Introduction' to Mikhail Bakhtin, *La Poétique de Dostoievski* (Paris: Seuil, 1970), p. 15.
2. The character of the artist, substitute for the author, 'thinker' who produces one of the ideological axes of *Ulysses*, and, as it happens, master in a public school, where the relationship teacher–taught is a concrete representation of dialogue, research, reflection, a symbol of the relationships master/ disciple – knowledge/ignorance, authority/submission, father/son, said/forbidden, master/servant, etc.
3. Julia Kristeva, 'Le discours sur la littérature', Colloque de Cluny, 1970.
4. We can cite, among others, the riddle of Macintosh: person? article of clothing? cover for archaisms? or the parable of Mount Pisgah...
5. The readerly (here translated as 'readable'), as defined by Barthes, *S/Z* (New York: Hill & Wang, 1974), p. 156.

7.2 RAYMOND WILLIAMS: FROM *THE COUNTRY AND THE CITY* (1973)

For further details on Raymond Williams see Ch. 4, p. 152.

In *The Country and the City*, Williams analyzes the changing perceptions, primarily through literature, of the county and city from classical times to the late twentieth century. In this account, he sees *Ulysses* as having realized the altered conditions and perceptions of the early twentieth century in an exemplary way; expressing this new state or structure of conscious-ness in an appropriately innovative prose or 'structure of language'. Consider what further relation he suggests between this new urban consciousness and forms of community, history and 'myth'. (Note that this last term refers chiefly here, not to Joyce's use of Homeric parallels in the novel, but to Carl Jung's notion of the 'collective unconscious' – Jung's 1932 essay on Joyce is included in Robert H. Denning, ed., *James Joyce, The Critical Heritage*, Routledge, 1970.) Williams also connects this state of consciousness with 'language itself' (p. 294 below) and Joyce's modernist technique. How would you compare this view of language and Joyce's prose style with Derrida's discussion below, or with Wolfgang Iser's?

Students might usefully consult Williams' definition of the notion of a 'structure of feeling' in his *Culture and Society* (1958) and *Marxism and Literature* (1977). He also develops the general theme of the relation between modernism and the modern city in the later essay 'The Metropolis and the Emergence of Modernism' (in Brooker, ed., *Modernism/ Postmodernism*, Longman, 1992, pp. 82–94).

The following extract is from *The Country and the City* (Chatto & Windus, 1973), pp. 242–7.

The Country and the City

There is [...] a direct relation between the motion picture, especially in its develop-ment in cutting and montage, and the characteristic movement of an observer in the close and miscellaneous environment of the streets. But this should remind us that the perceptual experience itself does not necessarily imply any particular mood, let alone an ideology. This experience of urban movement has been used, at all levels of seriousness and of play, to express a gamut of feelings from despair to delight. The single vision of Eliot's characteristic imagery, of smoke, scraps, grime, dinginess, has been very powerful but not overwhelming. We can see this most clearly if we look at Joyce's *Ulysses*, which is the most extended and memorable realisation in our literature of these fundamentally altered modes of perception and identity.

Wordsworth, near the beginning, had lost his familiar bearings:

> All laws of acting, thinking, speaking man
> Went from me, neither knowing me nor known.

But as the experience was prolonged it became clear that for 'laws' we must read 'conventions'. Generations of men and women learned to see in new ways, though it needed the genius of Joyce to take these new ways into the deep substance of literary method itself. In Joyce, the laws and the conventions of traditional observation and communication have apparently disappeared. The consequent awareness is intense and fragmentary, subjective primarily, yet in the very form of its subjectivity including others who are now with the buildings, the noises, the sights and smells of the city, parts of this single and racing consciousness. We can participate in just this experience as Bloom walks through Dublin:

> He crossed to the bright side, avoiding the loose cellarflap of number seventyfive. The sun was nearing the steeple of George's church. Be a warm day I fancy. Specially in these black clothes feel it more. Black conducts, reflects (refracts is it?) the heat. But I couldn't go in that light suit. Make a picnic of it. His eyelids sank quietly often as he walked in happy warmth. Boland's breadvan delivering with trays our daily but she prefers yesterday's loaves turnovers crisp crowns hot. Makes you feel young. Somewhere in the east: early morning: set off at dawn, travel round in front of the sun, steal a day's march on him. Keep it up for ever never grow a day older technically. Walk along a strand, strange land, come to a city gate, sentry there, old ranker too, old Tweedy's big moustaches learning on a long kind of a spear. Wander through awned streets. Turbaned faces going by. Dark caves of carpet shops, big man, Turko the terrible, seated crosslegged smoking a coiled pipe. Cries of sellers in the streets. Drink water scented with fennel, sherbet. Wander along all day. Might meet a robber or two. Well, meet him. Getting on to sundown. The shadows of the mosques along the pillars: priest with a scroll rolled up. A shiver of the trees, signal, the evening wind. I pass on. Fading gold sky. A mother watches from her doorway. She calls her children home in their dark language. High wall: beyond strings twanged. Night sky moon, violet, colour of Molly's new garters. Strings. Listen. A girl playing one of those instruments what do you call them: dulcimers. I pass

Here the fantasy of the Oriental city begins from the smell of bread in Boland's van, but each sight or sound or smell is a trigger to Bloom's private preoccupations. Under the pressure of his needs, the one city as it passes is as real as the other.

This is the profound alteration. The forces of the action have become internal and in a way there is no longer a city, there is only a man walking through it. Elizabeth Gaskell, we remember, went from the window of the druggist to 'Aladdin's garden of enchanted fruits', but within a rigidly controlled objective frame: 'the tales of our childhood' – writer and reader can share this memory; 'no such associations had Barton' – the objectively seen character, separate in situation and in culture, is made sharply distinct. In *Ulysses* the relation between action and consciousness, but also the relation between narrator and character, has been modulated until the whole shape of the language has changed:

> He approached Larry O'Rourke's. From the cellar grating floated up the flabby gush of porter. Through the open doorway the bar squirted out whiffs of ginger, teadust, biscuitmush. Good house, however: just the end of the city traffic. For instance M'Auley's down there: n.g. as position. Of course if they ran a tramline along the North Circular from the cattle market to the quays value would go up like a shot.
>
> Bald head over the blind. Cute old codger. No use canvassing him for an ad. Still he knows his own business best. There he is, sure enough, my bold Larry, leaning against the sugarbin in his shirtsleeves watching the aproned curate swab up with mop and bucket. Simon Dedalus takes him off to a tee with his eyes screwed up. Do you know what I'm going to tell you? What's that Mr O'Rourke? Do you know what? The Russians, they'd only be an eight o'clock breakfast for the Japanese.

Stop and say a word: about the funeral perhaps. Sad thing about poor Dignam, Mr O'Rourke.

Turning into Dorset Street he said freshly in greeting through the doorway:

- Good day Mr O'Rourke.
- Good day to you.
- Lovely weather, sir.
- 'Tis all that.

Here the contrast of dimensions is direct: the substance of Bloom's observations, speculations and memories – on a thread of narrative action – is an active exchange, even an active community, within the imagined speech of thought, whereas what is actually said when he reaches O'Rourke is flat and external: what the received conventions have become. The substantial reality, the living variety of the city, is in the walker's mind:

He walked along the curbstone. Stream of life. ...

... Cityful passing away, other cityful coming, passing away too: other coming on, passing on. Houses, lines of houses, streets, miles of pavements, piledup bricks, stones. Changing hands. This owner, that. Landlord never dies they say. Other steps into his shoes when he gets his notice to quit. They buy the place up with gold and still they have all the gold. Swindle in it somewhere. Piled up in cities, worn away age after age. Pyramids in sand. Built on bread and onions. Slaves. Chinese wall. Babylon. Big stones left. Round towers. Rest rubble, sprawling suburbs, jerrybuilt, Kerwan's mushroom houses, built of breeze. Shelter for the night.

No one is anything.

Joyce's originality in these parts of his work is remarkable. It is a necessary innovation if this way of seeing – fragmentary, miscellaneous, isolated – is to be actualised on the senses in a new structure of language.

The genius of *Ulysses* is that it dramatises three forms of consciousness (and in this sense three characters) – Bloom, Stephen and Molly. Their interaction but also their lack of connection is the tension of composition of the city itself. For what each enacts for the other is a symbolic role, and the reality to which they may ultimately relate is no longer a place and a time, for all the anxious dating of that day in Dublin. It is an abstracted or more strictly an immanent pattern of man and woman, father and son; a family but not a family, out of touch and searching for each other through a myth and a history. The history is not in this city but in the loss of a city, the loss of relationships. The only knowable community is in the need, the desire, of the racing and separated forms of consciousness.

Yet what must also be said, as we see this new structure, is that the most deeply known human community is language itself. It is a paradox that in *Ulysses*, through its patterns of loss and frustration, there is not only search but discovery: of an ordinary language, heard more clearly than anywhere in the realist novel before it; a positive flow of that wider human speech which had been screened and strained by the prevailing social conventions: conventions of separation and reduction, in the actual history. The greatness of *Ulysses* is this community of speech. That is its difference from *Finnegans Wake* in which a single voice – a voice offering to speak for everyone and everything, 'Here Comes Everybody' – carries the dissolution to a change of quality in which the strains already evident in the later sections of *Ulysses* (before the last monologue) have increased so greatly that the interchange of voices – public and private, the voices of a city heard and overheard – has given way to a surrogate, a universal isolated language. Where *Ulysses* was the climax, *Finnegans Wake* is the crisis of the development we have been tracing: of the novel and the city; the novel of 'acting, thinking, speaking' man.

But this development has another significance. It takes us back to Hardy's observation of London, where

each individual is conscious of *himself*, but nobody conscious of themselves collectively.

The intense self-consciousness, the perceptual subjectivity, was, as we have seen, very powerfully developed, as a literary mode. It relates, directly, not only to what is called 'stream of consciousness' or 'internal monologue', but also to that modernist version of 'symbolism' in which the isolation and projection of significant objects is a consequence of the separated subjectivity of the observer. These processes compose a powerful response to what is known, even conventionally, as city experience, but even when they are held at what appear directly aesthetic levels they are profoundly related to underlying models of life and society; quite as clearly, in the end, as when they explicitly overlap with ideological versions of an essential isolation, alienation, loss of community. It is then ironic that most modern versions of the rural past have been conventional and subsidiary elements of just these methods and ideologies: rhetorical projections of connection or community or belief.

Yet there is another kind of development, which relates more to Joyce. Given the facts of isolation, of an apparently impassable subjectivity, a 'collective consciousness' reappears, but in an altered form. This is the 'collective consciousness' of the myth, the archetype; the 'collective unconscious' of Jung. In and through the intense subjectivities a metaphysical or psychological 'community' is assumed, and characteristically, if only in abstract structures, it is universal; the middle terms of actual societies are excluded as ephemeral, superficial, or at best contingent and secondary. Thus a loss of social recognition and consciousness is in a way made into a virtue: as a condition of understanding and insight. A direct connection is then forged between intense subjectivity and a timeless reality: one is a means to the other and alternative terms are no more than distractions. The historically variable problem of 'the individual and society' acquires a sharp and particular definition, in that 'society' becomes an abstraction, and the collective flows only through the most inward channels. Not only the ordinary experiences of apparent isolation, but a whole range of techniques of self-isolation, are then gathered to sustain the paradoxical experience of an ultimate collectivity which is beyond and above community. Social versions of community are seen as variants of the 'myth' – the encoded meaning – which in one or other of its forms is the only accessible collective consciousness. There is a language of the mind – often, more strictly, of the body – and there is this assumed universal language. Between them, as things, as signs, as material, as agents, are cities, towns, villages: actual human societies.

In the twentieth century there has been a deep and confused and unfinished conflict between this reappearance of the collective, in its metaphysical and psychological forms, and that other response, also within the cities, which in new institutions and in new social ideas and movements offered to create what Hardy and others had seen as lacking: a collective consciousness which could see not only individuals but also their altered and altering relationships, and in seeing the relationships and their social causes find social means of change.

Out of the cities, in fact, came these two great and transforming modern ideas: myth, in its variable forms; revolution, in its variable forms. Each, under pressure, offers to convert the other to its own terms. But they are better seen as alternative responses, for in a thousand cities, if in confused forms, they are in sharp, direct and necessary conflict.

7.3   WOLFGANG ISER: 'DOING THINGS IN STYLE: AN INTERPRETATION OF "THE OXEN OF THE SUN" IN JAMES JOYCE'S *ULYSSES*' (1974)

Wolfgang Iser and his colleague Hans Robert Jauss have been regarded as the leading exponents of the German school of 'reception theory'. Philosophically this approach is endebted to phenomenology (in the tradition of Husserl, Roman Ingarden and Hans-Georg Gadamer) and shares its emphasis on the role of consciousness in the production of meaning. In reading literary texts, Iser argues, readers 'formulate the unformulated', constructing meanings from the gaps and silences of the text. His reception theory appears in *The Implied Reader* (1974), which also contains a five-part essay, 'Patterns of Communication in Joyce's *Ulysses*' and, in more developed form, in *The Act of Reading: A Theory of Aesthetic Response* (1976, trans. 1978). (See *A Reader's Guide* 3/e, Ch. 3, especially pp. 55–7; and Robert Holub, *Reception Theory. A Critical Introduction*, Routledge, 1984.)

   In recent years Iser's work has shifted into the area of what he terms 'literary anthropology'. For this development, see his *Prospecting. From Reader Response to Literary Anthropology* (1989) and *The Fictive and the Imaginary. Charting Literary Anthropology* (1993).

In the following essay, Iser uses the famous statement by T. S. Eliot on the function of Joyce's use of Homeric parallels in *Ulysses* to open the question of the relevance of this analogy or framework to an intepretation of the novel. To begin with, therefore, we might ask how his view of this 'mythological' criticism compares with Fredric Jameson's. Iser then turns his attention to 'The Oxen of the Sun' chapter because Joyce's stylistic experiment is most on display here. Other critics also clearly see the linguistic and literary play of the novel as being of crucial importance: as exemplifying a modernist attention to the medium itself, as an expression of urban community and consciousness (Williams), as the mark of an open unmasterable productivity (Derrida). What is Iser's view? Consider his comments throughout the chapter on the relation – including the distance and deformation – between style and theme. What, in this connection, is the implication of the multiple styles and points of view adopted by Joyce in the novel as a whole and, conspicuously, in this chapter? And how in particular – though Iser does not comment directly on this – do you think this discussion places the reader of Joyce's text ? Notice too, in relation to the issues raised above in the 'General Introduction', that Iser's own reading is presented explicitly as 'an interpretation'.

Iser's essay appears in *The Implied Reader* (Johns Hopkins University Press, 1974), pp. 179–95. The following extract omits some supporting quotations and some of Iser's notes.

Doing Things in Style: An Interpretation of 'The Oxen of the Sun' in James Joyce's *Ulysses*

I

Shortly after Joyce's *Ulysses* was published in 1922, T. S. Eliot saw in the multifarious allusions to the literature of the past the fabric indispensable to the literature of the future. 'In using the myth, in manipulating a continuous parallel between contemporaneity and antiquity, Mr. Joyce is pursuing a method which others must pursue after him. They will not be imitators, any more than the scientist who uses the discoveries of an Einstein in pursuing his own, independent, further investigations. It is simply a way of controlling, of ordering, of giving a shape and a significance to the immense panorama of futility and anarchy which is contemporary history.'[1] If the Homeric myth in *Ulysses* is to be regarded as a means of giving shape to a world of futility and anarchy, then clearly a link must be established between past and present that will enable the myth to exercise its 'ordering' function. The nature of this link is something that has caused many a headache to Joyce critics down through the years. Is the Homeric epic to be viewed as an 'objective correlative'[2] – as defined by Eliot in his 'Hamlet' essay – that enables us to grasp the modern situation in the first place? Or does the literary parallel reveal a structural principle that moulds the modern world just as it did the ancient? These two lines of thought represent the two basic approaches to the function of the Homeric parallel. According to both, the apparent chaos of the 'Welt-Alltag' (World Week-day) of June 16, 1904, is related to the sequence of adventures in the *Odyssey*, and through this connection is to bring to life in the reader's mind the outlines of an order which is to be read into the events of that day. This view has gained currency through the fact that in the modern world we are denied direct insight into the meaning of events, so that the Homeric parallel appears to offer a way of projecting a hidden meaning onto the chaos of everyday life. But herein lies the inherent weakness of this approach, for it says nothing about the way in which myth and the present day can be brought together.

If Homer's epic contains the meaning, and Joyce's novel contains only a confusing plethora of appearances interspersed with allusions to Homer, such a view must lead ultimately to a Platonizing interpretation of the modern novel. The *Odyssey* will then act as the ideal, while Bloom's wanderings are nothing but the copy of a homecoming which for Ulysses means completion, but for Bloom entails just one more grind in the ceaseless monotony of everyday life. Whenever interpretation is dominated by the idea of an analogy, one is bound to be dogged by the consequences inherent in the old conception of the *analogia entis*.

There is, however, another possible interpretation of the Homeric parallel to *Ulysses*, and Joyce himself offered certain indications of this. He called the *Odyssey* 'the most beautiful, all-embracing theme' in all world literature.[3] Going into details, he suggests that Ulysses embodies the most vivid conglomeration of all human activities, so that for him the Homeric hero becomes an archetype for humanity. Some Joyce scholars have tried to couple this statement with the idea that the modern novel is an attempt to renew Homeric archetypes. And so the concept of literary permanence comes to the fore whenever the critic concerned makes a fetish of the 'unbroken tradition' of Western literature. But such a naive view of permanence demands a blind eye for all the differences between Joyce's novel and Homer's epic. Even though the permanence interpretation of *Ulysses* does not insist that Bloom is nothing but a return of Ulysses, it does insist that he *is* a Ulysses in modern dress.[4] Such a metaphor, however, obscures rather than illuminates the intention of Joyce's novel. Indeed both 'schools of thought' – that of analogy and that of permanence – even though they are backed up by some of Joyce's own statements, by existing parallels, and by the actual grouping of the episodes in the novel, shed light only on starting-points and not on intentions.

A hint as to the intention might be found in the oft quoted conclusion of Joyce's *A Portrait of the Artist as a Young Man*: 'Welcome, O life! I go to encounter for the millionth time the reality of experience and to forge in the smithy of my soul the uncreated conscience of my race.'[5] This corresponds to what we have come to expect in modern times of our novel-writers. [...] In the light of such an expecta-tion, the Homeric parallel takes on a very precise function. If the novel is to uncover a new dimension of human existence, this can only present itself to the conscious mind of the reader against a background made recognizable by allusions and references which will thus provide a sufficient amount of familiarity. But the 'uncreated conscience,' which the novel is to formulate, cannot be the return of something already known – in other words, it must not coincide purely and simply with the Homeric parallel. Harry Levin has rightly pointed out that the links between Joyce and Homer are parallels 'that never meet.'[6] While the Homeric allusions incorporate into the text a familiar literary repertoire, the parallels alluded to seem rather to diverge than to converge. Here we have the conditions for a rich interplay that goes far beyond the lines of interpretation laid down by the analogy or permanence theories. Indeed there arises a certain tension out of the very fact that there is no clearly formulated connection between the archaic past and the everyday present, so that the reader himself is left to motivate the parallelism indicated as it were by filling in the gaps between the lines.

This process only comes to the fore if one in fact abandons the idea of the parallels and instead takes the modern world and the Homeric world as figure and ground – the background acting as a sort of fixed vantage point from which one can discern the chaotic movements of the present. By means of the allusions, Bloom's and Stephen's experiences are constantly set off against this background, which brings home to the reader the great gulf between Joyce's characters and those of Homer. If Bloom is, so to speak, viewed through Ulysses, and Stephen through Telemachus,[7] the reader who knows his Homer will realize what is missing in these two modern men. Thus greater emphasis is thrown on those features which do not coincide with Homer, and in this way the individuality is given its visible outline. Individuality is therefore constituted as the reverse side of what is suggested by the Homeric allusions; being conditioned by the very nonfulfillment of the expectations arising from these allusions. Joyce's characters begin to take on a life of their own the moment we, the readers, begin to react to them, and our reactions consist of an attempt to grasp and hold fast to their individuality – a process that would be quite unnecessary if they were immediately recognizable types representing an immediately recognizable frame of reference. Here the reader is compelled to try and find the frame of reference for himself, and the more intensively he searches, the more inescapably he becomes entangled in the modern situation, which is not explained for him but is offered to him as a personal experience.

The Homeric repertoire is not, however, only a background enabling us to grasp the theme of modern everyday life. The interaction can also be two-way, with Ulysses occasionally being viewed through the perspective of Bloom. This is significant in the light of the fact that for Joyce, Homer's hero epitomized humanity.[8] How, then, could he lack something which Bloom has simply by not being identical with Ulysses? Obviously because humanity never coincides completely with any of its historical manifestations – it is a potential which is realized differently at different times. Even if Ulysses is an ideal manifestation, this only becomes apparent through the Bloom perspective, which mirrors not just the ideality of Ulysses but also – and much more significantly – the fact that humanity, whatever its outward circumstances, can only be apprehended as individual manifestations arising out of reactions to historical situations. And so the Homeric myth itself takes on another dimension against the foreground-turned-background of the 'Welt-Alltag' – a dimension aptly described by S. L. Goldberg as follows: 'Once divorced from their origin in implicit, pious belief – and that is the only condition under which we now know the myths of Greece and, for most of us, the myths of Christianity as well – their meanings are perpetually created in our experience, are the colouring they take on from the material into which we project them. The myth is like a potentiality of meaning awaiting actualization in the world we recognize as real, in a specific "now and here".'[9]

II

The actualization of this potential is not left to the discretion of the individual reader. On the contrary, the manner in which he perceives and conceives events will be guided by the stylistic technique with which they are represented. In *Ulysses* the function of style is so important that a whole chapter is devoted to it. For Joyce, style as the technique of communication was of prime significance. When Stanislaus wanted to discuss fascism with his brother, Joyce remarked laconically: 'Don't talk to me about politics. I'm only interested in style.'[10] The chapter entitled 'The Oxen of the Sun' sheds a good deal of light on this obsession, although Joyce critics generally have tended to look on it with a certain amount of embarrassment, regarding the linguistic experiments as an obvious digression from the novel's apparent subject matter – everyday life in Dublin. The most acceptable explanation for this widespread unease is given by Goldberg, though he too has certain qualms about this chapter:

> 'The 'symbolic' scheme so violently obtruded into these chapters from 'Wandering Rocks' to 'Oxen of the Sun' attempts much the same effect as the Homeric parallel, but without its foundation and enactment in the characters' own lives and in the reader's belief in the abiding poetic truth of the original myth. The trouble with these chapters in short is that their order is not 'aesthetic' enough. [...] Given the strategic need to bring himself, as artist, into the action of his book, Joyce could hardly use the old tactic of direct authorial commentary. [...] What he did, however, is in its way very like intruded authorial comment.[11]

If Joyce's 'failure' lies in the fact that here he discloses his technique instead of continuing the dramatization of individual attitudes, by unraveling this technique we should be able to gain a good deal of insight into its function within the novel's overall framework of presentation. Here we might bear in mind Ezra Pound's pronouncement: 'I believe in technique as the test of a man's sincerity.'[12]

The subject of this chapter is Bloom's visit to a maternity hospital. There he and his friends wait for Mrs. Purefoy's confinement. The conversation is mainly about love, procreation, and birth.[13] The linguistic presentation of these themes takes place on different, contrasting levels of style. The chapter begins with an enigmatic invocation, and this is followed by an equally cryptic succession of long and tortuous sentences, which seem to lose their meaning as they progress. Immediately after these comes the sequence of historical styles that takes up the whole of the chapter. The subjects of love, procreation, and birth are dealt with in all the characteristic styles of English literature, from alliterative prose right through to pidgin English. 'The Oxen of the Sun' starts with three sentences, each of which is repeated three times. An impression of some sort of magic arises out of these triads. The sentences are: 'DESHIL HOLLES EAMUS. Send us, bright one, light one, Horhorn, quickening and wombfruit.' And finally the Dada sounding 'Hoopsa, boyaboy, hoopsa.'[14] These three sentences, deciphered, convey the following: Bloom feels an urge to go to Holles Street, where Dr. Horne's maternity hospital is situated. There is an invocation to the art of Dr. Horne to help the fruit of the womb to come into the world. And finally we have the threefold delight of the midwife as she holds the newborn babe in her hands.[15] These banal contents leap to life through the use of Latin words, Latin-sounding turns of phrase, a rhythmic beat, and an incantatory evocativeness. But they also take on a peculiar sort of tension, for the simplicity of the content and the complexity of the presentation seem out of all proportion. Are linguistic montages and magic incantations necessary to make us aware of ordinary, everyday events? This question, right at the beginning of the chapter, is symptomatic of the whole, and indeed here we have a technique which Joyce uses frequently in *Ulysses*: individual chapters begin with a sort of codified theme which is then orchestrated by the narrative process. The invocation then gives way to a completely different style. With long-drawn-out, mainly unpunctuated sentences, an attempt is made to describe the nature and significance of a maternity hospital. But it is only after very careful study that the reader begins to discern this intention. The lack of punctuation excludes any logical linguistic pattern, and behind this there obviously lies the fear of making any concrete statement about the object to be described. Joyce himself gives voice to this fear: 'For who is there who anything of some significance has apprehended but is conscious that that exterior splendour may be the surface of a downward-tending lutulent reality.'[16] His awareness of the danger that he will capture only the surface view of things, makes him approach the object as it were from all linguistic sides, in order to avoid a perspective foreshortening of it. And so the long appositions are not set out as such, and dependent clauses are left unmarked, for divisions of this kind would involve premature definition of the object concerned. At the same time, however, the language makes wide use of specialized vocabulary and precise nuances of meaning, and this gives rise to the impression that the institution is to be described with the utmost exactitude, although in fact it tends to become more and more blurred. Through this effort to depict the object from as many sides as possible, the maternity hospital seems almost to become something living and moving. And this is a stylistic feature typical not only of the chapter in question, but also of important sections of the whole novel: language is used not to fix an object, but to summon it to the imagination. The multiplication of perspectives will blur the outline, but through it the object will begin to grow, and this growth would be stunted if one were to try and define, since definition involves restriction to a chosen viewpoint which, in turn, involves a stylization of the reality perceived. It is therefore scarcely surprising that practically every chapter of *Ulysses* is written in a different style, in order – as Broch puts it – to transfer 'the object from one stylistic illumination to another,' for only in this way is 'the highest degree of reality'[17] to be achieved. The constant change of perspective modifies the definition inherent in each stylistic variant, and so reveals the object as something continually expanding. In this way, even the most commonplace things seem potentially illimitable.

From the invocation that opens this chapter, we may conclude that only a cryptic form of language can succeed in making statements about even the simplest of things. The relation between language and object becomes a mystery, and the tension arising from this is extended by the next stylistic form which, as it were, sets the object in motion through its changing nuances of observation. Thus the basis is laid for the subsequent array of styles emanating from the history of English literature. If one bears in mind the fact that the two different levels of style at the start of the chapter seek only to set us on the road to the maternity hospital and to evoke the nature of such institutions, whereas now we are to be confronted with the great themes of love, procreation, and birth, one might expect the gap between language and object to reach unbridgeable proportions. If the simple themes at the beginning were difficult to deal with linguistically, surely these much broader subjects will totally exceed the capacity of language. And yet, surprisingly, this is not so. Although he may be confused at first, the reader actually needs only a basic knowledge of English literature in order to understand completely all that is going on. Without doubt, Stuart Gilbert's commentary offers some very useful guidelines on this,[18] but critics have never really accepted the parallelism he suggests between the sequence of period styles and the development of the embryo, or the many other references and cross-symbols he worked out as a ground plan for *Ulysses*. Goldberg ends his critique of Gilbert's book with the question: 'But if Mr. Gilbert's way of interpreting it [i.e., *Ulysses*] is generally felt to be wrong, what is the right way, and why?'[19] As far as 'The Oxen of the Sun' is concerned, a provisional answer must be: because Gilbert's equation of the individual styles with embryonic development is too rigid – not unlike the analogy theory that always seeks to establish precise equivalents in *Ulysses* and the *Odyssey*. Gilbert overlooks the latent comedy that runs through the imitations and shows up the degree of deformation brought about by each individual style.

We can gain a closer insight into the nature of the historical sequence of styles by having a look at a few examples: first, in imitation of old English poetry, we are given an alliterative prose impression of Dr. Horne's maternity hospital. A mainly substantial style captures the outside of things and sets them side by side *en bloc* and unconnected. It seems as if the articles of equipment described are simply there for their own sake, although the alliteration does hint at certain unformulated connections.[20] The function of the individual items remains hidden from perception, so that they take on an element of incomprehensibility which transforms their practical value into some secret sort of reference. The style itself brings about an effect of contrast, insofar as this austere, alliterative prose follows on directly from the attempt, through extreme nuances of language, to describe the nature and importance of a maternity hospital. The consequences of the next style are quite different: events in the maternity hospital are recounted in the form of a late medieval travel book. Everything seems somehow to be tinged with excitement. The surface description of things is conditioned by the need to understand the new in terms of the familiar. However, this technique gets into severe difficulties when the traveler is confronted by a tin of sardines in olive oil. The resultant comedy derives from the incongruity between a style rigidly seeking to define the object in its own gallant terms, and the mundane object itself. The determinant pressure exerted by this style is so great that the advertising agent Leopold Bloom suddenly becomes the medieval 'traveller Leopold.'[21] Then the language changes again: the characters waiting in the hall of the maternity hospital converse in the style of Sir Thomas Malory.[22] Once again the unifying tendency of the style affects the very identity of the characters. The medieval traveler Leopold of a moment ago now becomes 'Sir Leopold.' The highly stylized discussion concerns traditional moral problems connected with birth (e.g., whether a wife should be allowed to die for her baby), and then suddenly Stephen raises the subject of contraception. Now neologisms creep into the conversation as signs of human independence defining man's interference with the God-given order of things. Here it becomes evident that the style shaped by the ideal of Christian knighthood is no longer capable of coping with the multifarious problems under discussion – namely, of love and procreation. Nevertheless, the attempt is made to use the system of references inherent in the ideal of the Christian knight in order to work out an idea of love that cannot be fitted into this system. This incongruity between style and object is apparent all through the series of imitations from one century to another. After a love passage in the language of the Arcadian shepherds, there arises an inner indignation against the trend of the conversation, and this is expressed in the form of a Bunyan allegory.[23] The spiritual conflict transforms the maternity hospital and its trappings into 'the land of Phenomenon,'[24] with an unreal outer world giving way to the reality of the inner. The hidden thoughts and feelings of the people concerned are externalized as allegorical characters that enact the ensuing conflict. But here, too, the relation between object and style becomes absurdly unbalanced, as the lusts of the characters are suddenly allegorized, bringing about an extraordinary sort of psychomachia. In medieval literature, allegory personified the Christian moral code. The personification of sexual urges, carried to extremes by Joyce, destroys the whole principle of the form as it had been used up to and including Bunyan.

As a sort of relief from all this personified 'inwardness', there now follows a minute description of the external events of the evening, in the diction of Samuel Pepys.[25] The most insignificant trifles are so lovingly observed that they seem over life-size, and every detail becomes a whole world in itself. After this, the central subject of the chapter enters into the realm of Utopian projects, conveyed in the style of the moral weeklies.[26] In pseudoscientific detail the characters discuss various practical methods of controlling with mechanical perfection all the processes of intimacy. This latent Utopianism is conveyed through a number of tales which are intended to establish the illusion that these special cases actually happened in the lives of particular people. Through these stories, the reader is meant to accept as perfectly natural the life planned for him on a 'national fertilising farm.'[27] In order to bring about this acceptance, the style imitates the narrative form of the moral weeklies, which were designed to create intimate contact with the public. But here the style sets out projects which destroy all intimacy; again we have total incongruity.

The stylistic idiosyncrasies of the great eighteenth-century novelists offer plenty of variations on the love theme through the individualization of speech, while the nineteenth-century parodies nearly all hypostatize the moods and emotions associated with love. All these overblown treatments of the subject show an extremely one-sided view, for each style reveals a latent ideology, constantly reducing the reality to the scope of individual principles. In the language of Landor, the unseemly side of love is again glossed over, this time through the respectability of mythological characters.[28] There is a similar sweet innocence to be found in the homely Dickensian passage that follows a little later. Love is peace and domestic bliss.[29] But in between, there is a detailed section on sex determination and infant mortality that is couched in the scientific terminology of hygiene and biology, with the apparent claim of being able to define these phenomena within the theory of scientific positivism.[30] Again, the relation between subject and treatment is grotesque, and the overall parody is enhanced here by the actual sequence of the styles. Next we come to theological interpretations in the style of Ruskin, Carlyle, and Newman, setting the world of appearances against its metaphysical background – though here, too, we have different definitions of love and the world under perception. After this series of rich and varied styles, the language at the end of the chapter seems to explode into a chaos of possibilities, and in this confused linguistic hodgepodge meaning finally seems to go by the board; it fades away in the elusiveness of language.

III

From these briefly sketched examples we may draw certain conclusions which together will give us a degree of insight into the Joycean technique of style. Although the various consequences are very closely connected with one another, we shall gain a clearer understanding of them by first examining them separately. To begin with, this stylistic historical tour of English literature is designed to grasp a particular subject through language. Each individual style projects a clearly recognizable idea of love, procreation, or birth. Joyce's style imitations therefore fulfill the demands summarized by John Middleton Murry as follows: 'Style is a quality of language which communicates precisely emotions or thoughts, or a system of emotions or thoughts, peculiar to the author. ... Style is perfect when the communication of the thought or emotion is exactly accomplished; its position in the scale of absolute greatness, however, will depend upon the comprehensiveness of the system of emotions and thoughts to which the reference is perceptible.'[31] The styles imitated by Joyce are dominated by such thoughts or thought systems, and the predetermined, predetermining nature of all style is demonstrated quite unmistakably through the individual variations. The judgments inherent in each style create a uniform picture of the subject presented, choosing those elements of the given reality that correspond to the frame of reference essential to all observation.[32] The particular point of view, then, determines which individual phenomena out of all those present are, or are not to be presented. And this, for Joyce, is the whole problem of style. Presentability or nonpresentability is not a quality inherent to any observable reality, but has to be imposed on that reality by the observer.

[...]

Iser rehearses the dilemma explored by Joyce's chapter. A 'historical sequence of styles' designed 'to comprehend the subject matter from every conceivable angle' could not present 'the object itself' but only 'the frame of reference' by which it was viewed.

[...]

And it is such frames of references that are in fact presented by the ensuing series of imitations. Joyce's aim, however, was not solely to show up the limitations of all styles through the systems of thought underlying them but also to evoke those aspects of an object that are kept concealed by the perspective mode of observation. Hence the fact that virtually every chapter of *Ulysses* is written in a different style.[33] Herein lies a basic difference between Joyce and all other modern writers. Joyce wanted to bring out, if not actually to overcome, the inadequacy of style as regards the presentation of reality, by constant changes of style, for only by showing up the relativity of each form could he expose the intangibility and expansibility of observable reality. And so in 'The Oxen of the Sun' we have the themes of love, procreation, and birth discussed in a series of historically sequent styles which each convey a single, one-sided viewpoint.

This leads us to the second conclusion to be drawn from the examples given. If style reproduces only aspects of reality and not – in contrast to its implicit claims – reality itself, then it must be failing in its intention. This idea is worked up through the element of parody in the stylistic impersonations. Joyce caricatures the formal restrictions of each style, so that Leopold Bloom, the main character in the novel, finds himself taking on a corresponding variety of identities. The resultant distortion is one that the reader can scarcely ignore, since he already knows a good deal about Bloom's character from the preceding chapters. We find the same distortion in the treatment of the main theme of the chapter, for it is not love itself that is presented, but only the way in which Malory, Bunyan, Addison, and the other writers understood it. Indeed one has the impression that the different views presented by the different styles exclude rather than supplement one another. With each author, the theme takes on a different shape, but each treatment seems to assume that it is offering *the* reality. And so there emerges a latent naïveté underlying every style. One might perhaps wonder which of the views comes closest to the truth, but it is patently obvious that every one of the authors has cut reality to the shape of a particular meaning not inherent in that reality. By parodying the styles, Joyce has exposed their essentially manipulative character. The reader gradually becomes conscious of the fact that style fails to achieve its ends, in that it does not capture reality but imposes upon it an historically preconditioned form. [...]

This brings us to our third conclusion. With his historical panoply of individual and period styles, Joyce exposes the characteristic quality of style – namely, that it imposes form on an essentially formless reality. Thus in the various views of love that are presented, the decisive influence is the historical conditions which shaped the understanding of the subject during the period concerned. Clearly, then, the theme itself is so multifarious that it can encompass every possible historical reflection of it, and the more clearly defined the judgment, the more historically conditioned is the style. Out of the series of parodies, then, emerges the fact that not only are the styles one-sided but they are also conditioned by sets of values that will change from period to period. In other words, the same subject (in this case, love) will take on a different form when viewed under different conditions or at different times. Which style can best capture the reality of the subject? The answer, clearly, is none, for all styles are relative to the historical conditions that shape them.

This brings us to a fourth and last conclusion: if the factors that shape a style are essentially historical, the resultant definition of the object to be described can only be a pragmatic one, since it depends on everchanging historical conditions. But the pragmatic nature of style can only be exposed through some sort of comparative survey – in this case, the historical sequence – since none of the authors Joyce parodies would have regarded their own form of presentation as a merely pragmatic view of the subjects they were dealing with. Now if style can only accomplish a pragmatic definition, its function in illuminating observed reality must be figurative, or metaphorical, for the limited system of references that forms it is applied to the unlimited reality it is attempting to convey. This is the only way, of course, in which style can build up a uniform picture. But if style can only capture objects in a metaphorical manner, it must be counted simply as one of those rhetorical devices of which Lessing once said: 'that they never stick strictly to the truth; that at one moment they say too much, and at another too little.'[34] Joyce's chronological exhibition of styles shows clearly that they are all metaphorical and can only offer a preconditioned, one-sided view of their subject matter. The intrinsic aim of style is to capture a phenomenon as accurately as possible, but being only a metaphor, it cannot help but miss out a whole range of aspects of that phenomenon.

[…]

Iser quotes Roman Ingarden to support this conclusion.

[…]

If we take up Goldberg's view of 'The Oxen of the Sun' as the author's commentary on his novel,[35] we may reasonably extend our findings to the use of style throughout the whole book. While the theme of this one chapter is love, the theme of *Ulysses* itself is everyday human life, and the stylistic presentation of this varies from chapter to chapter, because it can never be grasped as a whole by any one individual style. Only by constantly varying the angle of approach is it possible to convey the potential range of the 'real-life' world, but in literature the 'approach' is what gives rise to the style. By constantly changing the style, Joyce not only conveys the preconditioned, one-sided nature of each approach but also seems to set both object and observer in motion, thus accumulating an assembly of mobile views that show the essential expansiveness of reality. In this sense, 'The Oxen of the Sun' epitomizes the technique of the whole novel. The sequence of styles brings out the one-sidedness of each and the constant expansion of the subject. One aspect after another appears within the mirror of style, but 'hey, presto, the mirror is breathed on' and that seemingly all-important facet 'recedes, shrivels, to a tiny speck within the mist.'[36]

[…]

Iser ends with a quotation from Joyce that the 'hidden aspects of reality' may 'rise up … in the most various circumstances'. This insight he believes is developed in 'The Oxen of the Sun' and throughout the novel.

Notes (cut and renumbered)

1. T S. Eliot, 'Ulysses, Order and Myth,' in *James Joyce: Two Decades of Criticism*, ed. Seon Givens (New York, 1948), p. 201. (The essay was published originally in 1923).
2. T. S. Eliot, *Selected Essays* (London, 1951), p. 145. (The 'Hamlet' essay was published originally in 1919.)
3. Richard Ellman, *James Joyce* (New York, 1953), p. 430.
4. See for instance Ellman, 'Ulysses: the Divine Nobody' in *Twelve Original Essays on Great English Novels*, ed. Ch. Shapiro (Detroit, 1960), pp. 246 ff and H. Broch, *Dichten and Erkennen* (Zurich, 1955), p. 193.
5. James Joyce, *A Portrait of the Artist as a Young Man* (London, 1952), p. 288.
6. Harry Levin, *James Joyce: A Critical Introduction* (New York, 1960, 1941), p. 71.
7. It goes without saying that the Hamlet parallel also plays an important part for Stephen. But in principle the reference to Hamlet – or the elucidation of Stephen through Hamlet – serves to bring out his special situation, and so is very similar to the Homeric parallel.
8. See the statement reproduced in Ellmann's *Joyce*, p. 430.
9. S. L. Goldberg, *The Classical Temper: A Study of James Joyce's Ulysses* (London, 1961), p. 202.
10. Quoted by Ellmann in his introduction to Stanislaus Joyce, *My Brother's Keeper* (London, 1958), p. 23.

11. Goldberg, *The Classical Temper*, p. 288.
12. Ezra Pound, *Literary Essays*, ed. T. S. Eliot (London, 1960), p. 9.
13. For the purposes of this essay, the discussion is confined to the one central theme. Other themes are brought in from time to time, and these, too, have their form imposed on them by the style of the individual authors Joyce imitates.
14. James Joyce, *Ulysses* (London: Bodley Head, 1958), p. 366.
15. See also Gilbert, *James Joyce's Ulysses*, p. 296. For the purposes of this interpretation, discussion of the other parallels has deliberately been avoided.
16. Joyce, *Ulysses*, p. 366.
17. Broch, *Dichten und Erkennen*, p. 191 However, he does not discuss the subject any further.
18. See Gilbert, *James Joyce's Ulysses* (New York, 1955), pp. 298 ff.
19. Goldberg, *The Classical Temper*, p. 212.
20. Joyce, *Ulysses*, p. 368.
21. Ibid., p. 369.
22. Ibid., pp. 370 ff. For the key to the sequence of styles, see Gilbert, *James Joyce's Ulysses*, pp. 298 ff; Frank Budgen, *James Joyce and the Making of Ulysses* (1934, 1960), pp. 215 ff, and Stanislaus Joyce, *My Brother's Keeper*, p. 104. No account has been taken here of the other parallels Gilbert mentions for this chapter. For an account of these see, esp., A. Walton Litz, *The Art of James Joyce* (London, 1961), pp. 34 f.
23. See Joyce, *Ulysses*, pp. 377 f.
24. Ibid., p. 378.
25. Ibid., p. 379.
26. Ibid., pp. 384 ff.
27. Ibid., p. 384.
28. Ibid., pp. 396 ff.
29. Ibid., pp. 402 ff.
30. Ibid., pp. 399 ff.
31. John Middleton Murry, *The Problem of Style* (Oxford, 1960; 1922), p. 65.
32. Ibid., p. 65.
33. See Jacques Mercanton, 'The Hours of James Joyce. Part 1,' *Kenyon Review* 24 (1962): 701 f., who reproduces the following statement by Joyce concerning the style of *Ulysses*: 'The hallucinations in *Ulysses* are made up out of elements from the past, which the reader will recognize if he has read the book five, ten, or twenty times. Here is the unknown. There is no past, no future; everything flows in an eternal present. All the languages are present, for they have not yet been separated. It's a tower of Babel. Besides, in a dream, if someone speaks Norwegian to you, you are not surprised to understand it. The history of people is the history of language.'
34. G. E. Lessing, *Gesammelte Werke*, VII, ed. Paul Rilla (Berlin, 1956), p. 233.
35. See Goldberg, *The Classical Temper*, p. 288.
36. Joyce, *Ulysses*, p. 395.

7.4   FREDRIC JAMESON: '*ULYSSES* IN HISTORY' (1982)

Fredric Jameson has held several posts in American universities and is currently Professor of Comparative Literature and Director of the graduate programme in literature and theory at Duke University. His assimilation of European theory and broad cultural commentary, especially upon developments in postmodernism, have made his writings of central importance to radical literary and cultural studies. His works include: *Marxism and Form* (1971), *The Political Unconscious* (1981), *Late Marxism: Adorno and the Persistence of Dialectic* (1990) and the award-winning *Postmodernism, or, the Cultural Logic of Late Capitalism* (1991). His most recent work is *The Seeds of Time* (1994).

Joyce's novel, says Jameson, has always already been read for a new reader by generations of mythical, psychoanalytical and ethical interpretations. Obviously he means to distance his own reading from these traditional approaches. From the outset his interpretation has two striking features: his judgement that the Eumaeus and Ithaca chapters are 'boring', and that a radically transformed 'social and global situation' requires something other than more 'canonical' readings of the novel.

Jameson is known as a Marxist critic. His account employs some of the key concepts of Marxism (class, reification, the mode of production, capitalism), but what kind of Marxist reading – if this is indeed an appropriate description – does he offer? Does his idea, for example, of the text of *Ulysses* as a 'network of cross references' which cause us to read 'backwards and forwards' resemble Derrida's 'poststructuralist' idea of the novel as a switchboard, or does he view the novel's textuality – since sections of it are 'depersonalised' and 'boring' – in a significantly different way? A crucial concept in his interpretation, and in relation to these issues, is 'dereification'. What does he mean by this and in what ways does *Ulysses* illustrate or exemplify it? Finally, what is the force of the 'in history' of Jameson's title? He describes a 'radically different' contemporary 'social and global situation' (and speaks in this connection of 'the bankruptcy of modernism', the 'depthlessness' of consumer society, 'the essential surface logic of our world of simulacra', p. 311 below). What part does this view of contemporary history play in producing a new reading of the novel? Would we do better to think of this as a 'postmodern' reading?

Two writers who comment on this last question in Joyce are Terry Eagleton in *The Ideology of the Aesthetic* (Blackwell, 1990, pp. 317–22, 375–7) and Patricia Waugh, *Practising Postmodernism, Reading Modernism* (Edward Arnold, 1994, pp. 148–63). Waugh offers an explicitly postmodernist reading of the novel.

Jameson's essay is taken from W. J. McCormack and Alistair Stead, eds, *James Joyce and Modern Literature* (Routledge, 1982), pp. 126–41.

Ulysses in History

> One does not read Joyce today, let alone write about him, without remembering the fifteen-year-long struggle for freedom of the people of Northern Ireland; the following, then, for whatever it is worth, must necessarily be dedicated to them.

I had it in mind, in what follows, to say something about the two most boring chapters of 'Ulysses': most people would agree that these are surely the Eumaeus and the Ithaca chapters, the scene in the cabmen's shelter and the catechism. I have found, however, that in order to do that properly one must necessarily speak about the rest in some detail so that finally those parts are greatly reduced. One of the things such a subject leads you to consider, however, is boredom itself and its proper use when we are dealing with literary texts of this kind, and in particular the classical texts of high modernism or even postmodernism. I will still say something about that – I think there is a productive use of such boredom, which tells us something interesting about ourselves as well as about the world in which we live today – but I also mean to use this word in a far less positive sense, so I will do that first and say that if there are boring chapters of 'Ulysses', with which we must somehow learn to live, there are also boring interpretations of 'Ulysses', and those we can really make an effort to do without, sixty years after its publication, and in a social and global situation so radically different from that in which the canonical readings of this text were invented.

It would be surprising indeed if we were unable to invent newer and fresher ways of reading Joyce; on the other hand, the traditional interpretations I am about to mention have become so sedimented into our text – 'Ulysses' being one of those books which is 'always-already-read', always seen and interpreted by other people before you begin – that it is hard to see it afresh and impossible to read it as though those interpretations had never existed.

They are, I would say, threefold, and I will call them the mythical, the psychoanalytical, and the ethical readings respectively. These are, in other words, the readings of 'Ulysses', first in terms of the Odyssey parallel; second, in terms of the father-son relationship; and third, in terms of some possible happy end according to which this day, Bloomsday, will have changed everything, and will in particular have modified Mr Bloom's position in the home and relationship to his wife.

Let me take this last reading first. I will have little to say here about Molly's monologue, and only want now to ask not merely why we are so attached to the project of making something decisive happen during this representative day, transforming it in other words into an Event; but also and above all to ask why we should be committed to this particular kind of event, in which Mr Bloom is seen as reasserting his authority in what can therefore presumably once again become a vital family unit. (You will recall that he has asked Molly to bring him breakfast in bed the next day – the triumph over the suitors!) In this day and age, in which the whole thrust of a militant feminism has been against the nuclear and the patriarchal family, is it really appropriate to recast 'Ulysses' along the lines of marriage counselling and anxiously to interrogate its characters and their destinies with a view towards saving this marriage and restoring this family? Has our whole experience of Mr Bloom's Dublin reduced itself to this, the quest for a 'happy ending' in which the hapless protagonist is to virilise himself and become a more successful realisation of the dominant, patriarchal, authoritarian male?

Still, it will be said that this particular reading is part of the more general attempt to fit ' Ulysses' back into the Odyssey parallel. As for the mythical interpretation – the Odyssey parallel undoubtedly underscored for us by the text itself as well as by generations of slavish interpreters – here too it would be desirable to think of something else. We are today, one would hope, well beyond that moment of classical modernism and its ideologies in which, as Sartre said somewhere, there was a 'myth of myth', in which the very notion of some mythic unity and reconciliation was used in a mythical, or as I would prefer to say, a fetishised way. The bankruptcy of the ideology of the mythic is only one feature of the bankruptcy of the ideology of modernism in general; yet it is a most interesting one, on which (had we more time) it might have been instructive to dwell. Why is it that, in the depthlessness of consumer society, the essential surface logic of our world of simulacra – why is it that the mythic ideal of some kind of depth integration is no longer attractive and no longer presents itself as a possible or workable solution? There is a kinship here, surely, between this waning of the mythic ideal or mirage and the disappearance of another cherished theme and experience of classical or high modernism, namely that of temporality, 'durée', lived time, the passage of time. But perhaps the easiest way to dramatise the breakdown of myth and myth criticism is simply to suggest that we suddenly, with anthropologists like Lévi-Strauss, discovered that myths were not what we thought they were in the first place: not the place of some deep Jungian integration of the psyche, but quite the opposite, a space preceding the very construction of the psyche or the subject itself, the ego, personality, identity and the like: a space of the pre-individualistic, of the collective, which could scarcely be appealed to to offer the consolations that myth criticism had promised us.

On the other hand, as I stated previously, we can scarcely hope to read 'Ulysses' as though it were called something else. I would suggest, then, that we displace the act or the operation of interpretation itself. The Odyssey parallel can then be seen as one of the organisational frameworks of the narrative text: but it is not itself the interpretation of that narrative, as the ideologues of myth have thought. Rather it is itself – qua organisational framework – what remains to be interpreted. In itself, the Odyssey parallel – like so much of that whole tradition of the classical pastiche from Cocteau or even from 'La Belle Hélène' all the way to Giraudoux or Sartre or even John Updike – functions as wit: a matching operation is demanded of us as readers, in which the fit of the modern detail to its classical overtext is admired for its elegance and economy, as when, in 'Ulysses', Odysseus' long separation from Penelope is evoked in terms of a ten-year period of coitus interruptus or anal intercourse between the partners of the Bloom household. You will agree, however, that the establishment of the parallel is scarcely a matter of interpretation – that is, no fresh meaning is conferred either on the classical Homeric text, nor on the practices of contemporary birth control, by the matching of these two things.

Genuine interpretation is something other than this, and involves the radical historisation of the form itself: what is to be interpreted is then the historical necessity for this very peculiar and complex textual structure or reading operation in the first place. We can make a beginning on this, I think, by evoking the philosophical concept, but also the existential experience, called 'contingency'. Something seems to have happened at a certain point in modern times to the old unproblematic meaning of things, or to what we could call the content of experience; and this particular event is as so often first most tangibly detectable and visible on the aesthetic level. There is something like a crisis of detail, in which we may, in the course of our narrative, need a house for our characters to sleep in, a room in which they may converse, but nothing is there any longer to justify our choice of this particular house rather than that other, or this particular room, furniture, view, and the like. It is a very peculiar dilemma, which Barthes described as well as anyone else, when he accounted for the fundamental experience of the modern or of modernity in terms of something like a dissociation between meaning and existence

[...]

Jameson quotes Barthes on the 'mythic opposition between the *vecu*', or lived experience, 'and the intelligible'. His point is that the symbolism characterizing high modernism's – but not Joyce's – attempt to give existing things meaning is now discredited.

[...]

Yet before I try to describe what is really going on in the text of 'Ulysses', let me do something Barthes did not care to do, in the passage I quoted, and designate the historical reasons for that modernist crisis, that dissociation of the existent and the meaningful, that intense experience of contingency in question here. We must explain this experience historically because it is not at all evident, and particularly not in the ideological perspective – existential or Nietzschean – which is that of Roland Barthes, among many others, and for which the discovery of the absurd and of the radical contingency and meaninglessness of our object world is simply the result of the increasing lucidity and self-consciousness of human beings in a post-religious, secular, scientific age.

But in previous societies (or modes of production) it was Nature that was meaningless or anti-human. What is paradoxical about the historical experience of modernism is that it designates very precisely that period in which Nature – or the in- or anti-human – is everywhere in the process of being displaced or destroyed, expunged, eliminated, by the achievements of human praxis and human production. The great modernist literature – from Baudelaire and Flaubert to 'Ulysses' and beyond – is a city literature: its object is therefore the anti-natural, the humanised, par excellence, a landscape which is everywhere the result of human labour, in which everything – including the formerly natural, grass, trees, our own bodies – is finally produced by human beings. This is then the historical paradox with which the experience of contingency confronts us (along with its ideologies – existentialism and nihilism – and its aesthetics – modernism): how can the city be meaningless? How can human production be felt to be absurd or contingent, when in another sense one would think it was only human labour which created genuine meaning in the first place?

Yet it is equally obvious that the experience of contingency is a real or 'objective' one, and not merely a matter of illusion or false consciousness (although it is that too). The missing step here – the gap between the fact of the human production of reality in modern times and the experience of the results or products of that production as meaningless – this essential mediation is surely to be located in the work process itself, whose organisation does not allow the producers to grasp their relationship to the final product; as well as in the market system, which does not allow the consumer to grasp the product's origins in collective production. I am assuming, rightly or wrongly, that I do not have to insert a general lecture on alienation and reification, on the dynamics of capital and the nature of exchange value, at this point: I do want to dwell at somewhat greater length on one of the basic forms taken by reification as a process, and that is what can be called the analytical fragmentation of older organic or at least 'naturwüchsige' or traditional processes. [1] Such fragmentation can be seen on any number of levels: on that of the labour process first of all, where the older unities of handicraft production are broken up and 'taylorised' into the meaningless yet efficient segments of mass industrial production; on that of the psyche or psychological subject, now broken up into a host of radically different mental functions, some of which – those of measurement and rational calculation – are privileged and others – the perceptual senses and aesthetic generally – are marginalised; on that of time, experience, and storytelling, all of which are inexorably atomised and broken down into their most minimal unities, into that well-known 'heap of fragments where the sun beats'; the fragmentation, finally, of the older hierarchical communities, neighbour-hoods, and organic groups themselves, which, with the penetration of the money and market system, are systematically dissolved into relations of equivalent individuals, 'free but equal' monads, isolated subjects equally free to sell their labour power, yet living side by side in a merely additive way within those great agglomerations which are the modern cities. It is incidentally this final form of reification which accounts, be it said in passing, for the inadequncy of that third conventional interpretation of 'Ulysses' mentioned above, namely the fetishisation of the text in terms of 'archetypal' patterns of father-son relationships, the quest for the ideal father or for the lost son, and so forth. But surely today, after so much prolonged scrutiny of the nuclear family, it has become apparent that the obsession with these relationships and the privileging of such impoverished interpersonal schemas drawn from the nuclear family itself are to be read as break-down products and as defence mechanisms against the loss of the knowable community. The efforts of Edward Said and others to demonstrate the omnipresence of such familial schemes in modern narrative should surely not be taken as an affirmation of the ultimate primacy of such relationships, but rather exactly the reverse, as sociopathology and as diagnosis of the impoverishment of human relations which results from the destruction of the older forms of the collective. [2] The father-son relationships in 'Ulysses' are all miserable failures, above all others the mythical ultimate 'meeting' between Bloom and Stephen; and if more is wanted on this particular theme, one might read into the record here the diatribes against the very notion of an Oedipus complex developed in Deleuze and Guattari's 'Anti-Oedipus', which I do not necessarily endorse but which should surely be enough to put an end to this particular interpretive temptation.

But the psychoanalytic or Oedipal interpretation was itself only a sub-set of the Odyssey parallel or mythological temptation, to which, after this digression, I promised to return. What I wanted to suggest about the kind of reading determined by the

Odyssey parallel in 'Ulysses' is that this parallelism, and the kind of matching it encourages between the two levels of written and over-text, functions as something like an empty form. Like the classical unities, it offers a useful but wholly extrinsic set of limits against which the writer works, and which serve as a purely mechanical check on what risks otherwise becoming an infinite proliferation of detail. [3] The point is that, as we suggested a moment ago, the older traditional narrative unities have disappeared, been destroyed in the process of universal fragmentation: the organic unity of the narrative can thus no longer serve as a symbol for the unity of experience, nor as a formal limit on the production of narrative sentences: the single day – that overarching formal unity of 'Ulysses' – is a meaningful unit neither in human experience nor in narrative itself. But at that point, if what used to be experience, human destiny and the like, is shattered into such components as taking a walk at lunchtime from your place of business to a restaurant, buying a cake of soap, or having a drink, or visiting a patient in a hospital – each of these components being then in itself infinitely subdivisible – then there is absolutely no guarantee that the transformation of these segments into narrative sentences might not be infinitely extended and indeed last forever. The Odyssey parallel helps avoid this unwelcome development and sets just such external limits, which ultimately become those of Joyce's minimal units of composition – the individual chapters themselves.

But what I wanted to show you was that alongside the type of reading encouraged by the mythic parallels – which I have called a matching up – there is a rather different form of reading which resists that one in all kinds of ways, and ends up subverting it. This is a type of reading which interrupts the other, consecutive kind, and moves forward and backwards across the text in a cumulative search for the previous mention or the reference to come: as Kenner and others have pointed out, it is a type of reading, a mental operation, peculiarly inconceivable before printing, before numbered pages, and more particularly before the institutionalisation of those unusual objects called dictionaries or encyclopedias. [4] Now one is tempted to assimilate this kind of reading to the more customary thematic or thematising kind, where we compile lists of recurrent motifs, such as types of imagery, obsessive words or terms, peculiar gestures or emotional reactions; but this is not at all what happens in 'Ulysses', where the object of the cross-referencing activity is always an event: taking old Mrs Riordan for a walk, the borrowed pair of tight trousers worn by Ben Dollard at a memorable concert, or the assassination in Phoenix Park twenty-two years before. This is to say that these seemingly thematic motifs are here always referential: for they designate content beyond the text, beyond indeed the capacity of any of the given textual variants to express or exhaust them. In such cross-referencing, indeed, one can say that the referent itself is produced, as something which transcends every conceivable textualisation of it.

[...]

Jameson cites the destabilizing return of characters in Balzac's *Comédie Humaine*.

[...]

What I want to suggest is that the [...] recurrence of events and characters throughout 'Ulysses' can equally be understood as a process whereby the text itself is unsettled and undermined, a process whereby the universal tendency of its terms, narrative tokens, representations, to solidify into an achieved and codified symbolic order as well as a massive narrative surface, is perpetually suspended. I will call this process 'dereification', and I first want to describe its operation in terms of the city itself. The classical city is not a collection of buildings, nor even a collection of people living on top of one another; nor is it even mainly or primarily a collection of pathways, of the trajectories of people through those buildings or that urban space, although that gets us a little closer to it. No, the classical city, one would think – it always being understood that we are now talking about something virtually extinct, in the age of the suburb or megalopolis or the private car – the classical city is defined essentially by the nodal points at which all those pathways and trajectories meet, or which they traverse: points of totalisation, we may call them, which make shared experience possible, and also the storage of experience and information, which are in short something like a synthesis of the object (place) and the subject (population), focal points not unlike those possibilities of unifying perspectives and images which Kevin Lynch has identified as the signs and emblems of the successful, the non-alienating city. [5]

But to talk about the city in this way, spatially, by identifying the collective transit points and roundabouts of temple and agora, pub and post office, park and cemetery, is not yet to identify the mediation whereby these spatial forms are at one with collective experience. Unsurprisingly that mediation will have to be linguistic, yet it will have to define a kind of speech which is neither uniquely private nor forbiddingly standardised in an impersonal public form, a type of discourse in which the same, in which repetition, is transmitted again and again through a host of eventful variations, each of which has its own value. That discourse is called gossip: and from the upper limits of city life – the world of patronage, machine politics, and the rise and fall of ward leaders – all the way down to the most minute aberrations of private life, it is by means of gossip and through the form of the anecdote that the dimensions of the city are maintained within humane limits and that the unity of city life is affirmed and celebrated.

[...]

Jameson finds a supporting reference for this in John Berger's *Pig Earth*.

[...]

So in that great village which is Joyce's Dublin, Parnell is still an anecdote about a hat knocked off, picked up and returned, not yet a television image nor even a name in a newspaper; and by the same token, as in the peasant village itself, the ostensibly private or personal – Molly's infidelities, or Mr Bloom's urge to discover how far the Greek sculptors went in portraying the female anatomy – all these things are public too, and the material for endless gossip and anecdotal transmission.

Now for a certain conservative thought, and for that heroic fascism of the 1920s for which the so-called 'masses' and their standardised city life had become the very symbol of everything degraded about modern life, gossip – Heidegger will call it 'das Gerede' – is stigmatised as the very language of inauthenticity, of that empty and stereotypical talking pour rien dire to which these ideologues oppose the supremely private and individual speech of the death anxiety or the heroic choice. But Joyce – a radical neither in the left-wing nor the reactionary sense – was at least a populist and a plebeian. 'I don't know why the communists don't like me,' he complained once, 'I've never written about anything but common people.' Indeed, from the class perspective, Joyce had no more talent for or interest in the representation of aristocrats than Dickens; and no more experience with working-class people or with peasants than Balzac (Beckett is indeed a far sounder guide to the Irish countryside or rural slum than the essentially urban Joyce.) In class terms, then, Joyce's characters are all resolutely petty-bourgeois: what gives this apparent limitation its representative value and its strength is the colonial situation itself. Whatever his hostility to Irish cultural nationalism, Joyce's is the epic of the metropolis under imperialism, in which the development of bourgeoisie and proletariat alike is stunted to the benefit of a national petty-bourgeoisie: indeed, precisely these rigid constraints imposed by imperialism on the development of human energies account for the symbolic displacement and flowering of the latter in eloquence, rhetoric and oratorical language of all kinds; symbolic practices not particularly essential either to businessmen or to working classes, but highly prized in precapitalist societies and preserved, as in a time capsule, in ' Ulysses' itself. And this is the moment to rectify our previous account of the city and to observe that if 'Ulysses' is also for us the classical, the supreme representation of something like the Platonic idea of city life, this is also partly due to the fact that Dublin is not exactly the full-blown capitalist metropolis, but like the Paris of Flaubert, still regressive, still distantly akin to the village, still un- or under-developed enough to be representable, thanks to the domination of its foreign masters.

Now it is time to say what part gossip plays in the process of what I have called dereification, or indeed in that peculiar network of cross-references which causes us to read 'Ulysses' backwards and forwards like a handbook. Gossip is indeed the very element in which reference – or, if you prefer, the 'referent' itself – expands and contracts, ceaselessly transformed from a mere token, a notation, a short-hand object, back into a full-dress narrative. People as well as things are the reified markers of such potential story-telling: and what for a high realism was the substantiality of character, of the individual ego, is here equally swept away into a flux of anecdotes – proper names on the one hand, an intermittent store of gossip on the other. But the process is to be sure more tangible and more dramatic when we see it at work on physical things: the statues, the commodities in the shopwindows, the clanking trolleylines that link Dublin to its suburbs (which dissolve, by way of Mr Deasy's anxieties about foot-and-mouth disease, into Mr Bloom's fantasy projects for tramlines to move cattle to the docks); or the three-master whose silent grace and respectability as an image is at length dissolved into the disreputable reality of its garrulous and yarn-spinning crewman; or, to take a final example, that file of sandwichmen whose letters troop unevenly through the text, seeming to move towards that ultimate visual reification fantasised by Mr Bloom virtually in analogue to Mallarmé's 'livre':

> Of some one sole unique advertisement to cause passers to stop in wonder, a poster novelty, with all extraneous accretions excluded, reduced to its simplest and most efficient terms not exceeding the span of casual vision and congruous with the velocity of modern life. ('Ulysses', p. 641)

The visual, the spatially visible, the image, is, as has been observed, the final form of the commodity itself, the ultimate terminus of reification. Yet even so strikingly reified a datum as the sandwichboard ad is once again effortlessly dereified and dissolved when, on his way to the cabman's shelter, Stephen hears a down-and-out friend observe: 'I'd carry a sandwichboard only the girl in the office told me they're full up for the next three weeks, man. God, you've to book ahead!' ('Ulysses', p. 538). Suddenly the exotic picture-postcard vision of a tourist Dublin is transformed back into the dreary familiar reality of jobs and contracts and the next meal: yet this is not necessarily a dreary prospect; rather it opens up a perspective in which, at some ideal outside limit, everything seemingly material and solid in Dublin itself can presumably be dissolved back into the underlying reality of human relations and human praxis.

Yet the ambulatory letters of the sandwichmen are also the very emblem of textuality itself, and this is the moment to say the price 'Ulysses' must pay for the seemingly limitless power of its play of reification and dereification; the moment, in other words, to come to terms with Joyce's modernism. Stated baldly, that price is radical depersonalisation, or in other words, Joyce's completion of Flaubert's programme of removing the author from the text – a programme which also removes the reader, and finally that unifying and organising mirage or aftermirage of both author and reader which is the 'character', or better still, 'point of view'. What happens at that point can perhaps oversimply be described this way: such essentially idealistic (or ideal, or imaginary) categories formerly served as the supports for the unity of the work or the unity of the process. Now that they have been withdrawn, only a form of material unity is left, namely the printed book itself, and its material unity as a bound set of pages within which the cross-references mentioned above are contained. One of the classic definitions of modernism is of course the increasing sense of the materiality of the medium itself (whether in instrumental timbre or oil painting), the emergent foregrounding of the medium in its materiality. It is paradoxical, of course, to evoke the materiality of language; and as for the materiality of print or script, that particular material medium is surely a good deal less satisfying or gratifying in a sensory, perceptual way than the materials of oil paint or of orchestral coloration; none the less, the role of the book itself is functionally analogous, in Joyce, to the materialist dynamics of the other arts.

Now in one sense textualisation may be seen as a form or subset of reification itself: but if so, it is a unique type of reification, which unbinds fully as much as it fixes or crystallises. They may, indeed, offer the most appropriate contemporary way of dealing with the phenomena Joseph Frank described in his now classical essay as 'spatial form'. I am thinking, for instance, of the moment in which a remarkable and ingenious method for cabling news of the Phoenix Park murders across the Atlantic is described: the reporter takes an ad (Mr Bloom's 'one sole unique advertisement') and uses its spatial features to convey the trajectory of the killers and the map of the assassination ('Ulysses', pp. 137–8). This is to institute a peculiarly fluid relationship between the visually reified and the historically eventful, since here these categories pass ceaselessly back and forth into one another.

The climax of this development is in many ways reached in the Nighttown section [...]

[...]

Jameson compares this with the 'space of hallucination' created by Flaubert in *La Tentation de Saint Antoine*.

[...]

The instability of space or experience of this kind lies in the failure of the discrete or isolated image to generate any background or depth, any worldness in which it can take root. On the printed page, this essentially means that the ground, the anticipatory-retrospective texture, of narrative – what Greimas calls its isotopies, its ana- and cata-phoric relationships – is ruptured: it therefore falls to the typographic and material mechanisms of theatrical and scenic directions to bind (or rebind) these discontinuous images together. Typography thus becomes an event within the text among others. Or, if you prefer, since it is the reified sense of the visual which has here been solicited and stimulated, this sense will now begin to function as it were in the void, taking as its object the material signifiers, the printed words themselves, and no longer the latter's signifieds or representations or meanings.

At any rate, this peculiar climax of 'Ulysses' in the seeming immediacy of a theatrical representation which is in reality the unmediated experience of the printed book will now help us to understand two kinds of things: the peculiarly anticlimactic nature of the chapters that follow it (I'm getting to them, at last!), and the ground on which the depersonalised textualisation of the narrative of 'Ulysses' takes place, what one is tempted to call a kind of 'autistic textualisation', the production of sentences in a void, moments in which the book begins to elaborate its own text, under its own momentum, with no further need of characters, point of view, author or perhaps even reader:

> Mr Bloom reached Essex bridge. Yes, Mr Bloom crossed bridge of Yessex. ('Ulysses', p. 260)

> Love loves to love love. Nurse loves the new chemist. Constable 14A loves Mary Kelly. Gerty MacDowell loves the boy that has the bicycle. M. B. loves a fair gentleman. Li Chi Han lovey up kissy Cha Pu Chow. Jumbo, the elephant, loves Alice, the elephant. Old Mr Verschoyle with the ear trumpet loves old Mrs Verschoyle with the turnedin eye. ... You love a certain person. And this person loves that other person because everybody loves somebody but God loves everybody. ('Ulysses', pp. 331–2)

The point I want to make about passages like these, and they are everywhere in 'Ulysses', is that 'point of view' theory does not *take* on them, nor any conceivable notion of the Implied Author, unless the I. A. is an imbecile or a schizophrenic. No one is speaking these words or thinking them: they are simply, one would want to say, printed sentences.

And this will be my transition to the two most boring chapters of 'Ulysses', and thence to a close. Because what happens in the Eumaeus chapter is that, so to speak, Joyce lapses back into more traditional narrative 'point of view': that is, for the first time in 'Ulysses' we once again get the 'he thought/she thought' form of indirect discourse, what I will call the third person indistinct, and a henceforth conventional belief in that central reflective consciousness which is both appropriate and ironic in the chapter in which Bloom and Stephen are finally able to sit down together, two closed or solipsistic monads projecting that most boring theme of our own time, namely 'lack of communication'. Indeed, I am tempted to say, judging from the sentence structure, the elaborate periphrases, the use of occasional foreign expressions as well as cautiously isolated 'colloquial' ones, that this chapter really constitutes Joyce's attempt at a parody or pastiche of a writer he had no particular sympathy or respect for, namely Henry James. (If so, it is not a very good pastiche, and only our supreme belief in Joyce's power of mimicry, in his ability to do anything stylistically, has prevented us from noticing it.) Or better still, this chapter deploys the stylistic mannerisms of Henry James in order to record a social and psychological content characteristic, rather, of James's enemy brother and archetypal rival, H. G. Wells – that is, an essentially petty-bourgeois content whose comfortable fit with the Jamesian narrative apparatus is somehow humiliating for both of them and sends both off back to back, as though their well-known differences on the form and function of the novel were less the taking of incompatible positions than – to use a more contemporary expression – mere variants within a single problematic, the problematic of the centred subject, of the closed monad, of the isolated or privatised subjectivity. The theory and practice of narrative 'point of view', as we associate it with Henry James, is not simply the result of a metaphysical option, a personal obsession, nor even a technical development in the history of form (although it is obviously also all those things): point of view is rather the quasi-material expression of a fundamental social development itself, namely the increasing social fragmentation and monadisation of late capitalist society, the intensifying privatisation and isolation of its subjects.

We have already touched on one aspect of this development – reification – which can now be characterised in another way, as the increasing separation, under capitalism, between the private and the public, between the personal and the political, between leisure and work, psychology and science, poetry and prose, or to put it all in a nutshell, between the subject and the object. The centred but psychologised subject and the reified object are indeed the respective orientations of these two concluding chapters, Eumaeus and Ithaca: and it is as though Joyce meant here to force us to work through in detail everything that is intolerable about this opposition. What we have been calling boredom is not Joyce's failure, then, but rather his success, and is the signal whereby we ourselves as organisms register a situation but also forms that are finally stifling for us.

This is perhaps a little easier to show in the Ithaca or catechism sequence: the format – question and answer – is not really, I think, a return to the experimentation – better still, the textualisation – of the earlier chapters. It is rather that quite different thing – the construction of a form of discourse from which the subject – sender or receiver – is radically excluded: a form of discourse, in other words, that would be somehow radically objective, if that were really possible. And if it is observed that even this seemingly sterilised alternation of question and answer turns increasingly, towards the end of the chapter, around Mr Bloom's private thoughts and fantasies, in other words, around the subjective rather than the objective, then I will reply by noting the degree to which those fantasies, Mr Bloom's 'bovarysme' (tactfully called 'ambition' by Joyce), are henceforth inextricably bound up with objects, in the best consumer society tradition. These are falsely subjective fantasies: here, in reality, commodities are dreaming about themselves through us.

These two final Bloom chapters, then, pose uncomfortable problems, and not least about narrative itself: the subjective or point-of-view chapter, Eumaeus, asks us why we should be interested in stories about private individuals any longer, given the extraordinary relativisation of all individual experience, and the transformation of its contents into so many purely psychological reactions. Meanwhile, the objective chapter, Ithaca, completes an infinite subdivision of the objective contents of narrative, breaking 'events' into their smallest material components and asking whether, in that form, they still have any interest whatsoever. Two men have a discussion over cocoa, and that may be interesting at a pinch: but what about the act of putting the kettle on to boil – that is a part of the same event, but is it still interesting? The elaborate anatomy of the process of boiling water ('Ulysses', pp. 591–4) is boring in three senses of the word: (1) it is essentially non-narrative; (2) it is inauthentic, in the sense in which these mass-produced material instruments (unlike Homer's spears and shields) cannot be said to be organic parts of their users' destinies; finally, (3) these objects are contingent and meaningless in their instrumental form, they are recuperable for literature only at the price of being transformed into symbols. Such passages thus ask three questions:

1. Why do we need narrative anyway? What are stories and what is our existential relation to them? Is a non-narrative relationship to the world and to Being possible?
2. What kind of lives are we leading and what kind of world are we living them in, if the objects that surround us are all somehow external, extrinsic, alienated from us? (It is a question about the simulacra of industrial society, essentially a question about the city, but in this form at least as old as the interrogation of the 'wholeness' of Greek culture by German romanticism.)
3. (A question I have already raised but which remains seemingly unanswered, namely) How can the products of human labour have come to be felt as meaningless or contingent?

Yet to this last question at least, Joyce's form has a kind of answer, and it is to be found in that great movement of dereification I have already invoked, in which the whole dead grid of the object world of greater Dublin is, in the catechism chapter, finally, disalienated and by the most subterranean detours traced back ... less to its origins in Nature, than to the transformation of Nature by human and collective praxis deconcealed. So to the vitalist ideology of Molly's better known final affirmation, I tend rather to prefer this one:

> What did Bloom do at the range?
> He removed the saucepan to the left hob, rose and carried the iron kettle to the sink in order to tap the current by turning the faucet to let it flow.
> Did it flow?
> Yes. From Roundwood reservoir in county Wicklow of a cubic capacity of 2,400 million gallons, percolating through a subterranean aqueduct of filter mains of single and double pipeage constructed at an initial plant cost of £5 per linear yard. ... ('Ulysses', p. 591)

Notes (cut and renumbered)

1. See for a more detailed account of reification my 'The Political Unconscious; Narrative as a Socially Symbolic Act' (London: Methuen; Ithaca: Cornell University Press, 1981), esp. pp. 62–4, 225–37, and 249–52.
2. Edward Said, 'Beginnings' (New York: Basic Books, 1975), pp. 137–52.
3. For further remarks on the proliferation of sentences see my 'Fables of Aggression: Wyndham Lewis, the Modernist as Fascist' (Berkeley: University of California Press, 1979).
4. See Hugh Kenner, 'Flaubert, Joyce, Beckett: the Stoic Comedians' (Boston: Beacon, 1962). Also the work of MacLuhan and Walter Ong.
5. Kevin Lynch, 'The Image of the City' (Cambridge (Mass.): Harvard University Press, 1960).

7.5   JACQUES DERRIDA: FROM 'ULYSSES GRAMOPHONE: HEAR SAY YES IN JOYCE' (1988)

Jacques Derrida is a celebrated French philosopher associated chiefly with the movement of deconstruction. He is the author of, amongst many other texts, *Writing and Difference* (1967, trans. 1978), *Of Grammatology* (1967, trans. 1973), *The Postcard. From Socrates to Freud and Beyond* (1980, trans. 1987), and *Spectres of Marx* (1994). New readers will find his *Positions* (1981) most useful. His writings include two essays on James Joyce, 'Two Words for Joyce', translated in Derek Attridge and Daniel Ferrer, eds, *Post-Structuralist Joyce. Essays from the French* (Cambridge University Press, 1984) and 'Ulysse Gramophone: Oui-dire de Joyce', translated by Tina Kendall in Bernard Benstock, ed., *James Joyce. The Augmented Ninth* (New York State University Press, 1988) and also in Peggy Kamuf, ed., *A Derrida Reader* (1991).

Derrida's essay was first presented as an introductory lecture to the Ninth International James Joyce Symposium. It is likely that students will find it a challenging but amusing and playful piece, and recognize the conscious affinity, noted by Attridge and Ferrer, between author and poststructuralist reader. Derrida remarks, for example, on having recently visited certain places – Tokyo, Ohio, Ithaca – mentioned by Bloom in the novel, and in a closer act of homage and identification places his signature beside and beneath Joyce's and the 'signature' of Molly's last words: 'Yes I said yes I will yes.' But how, precisely, are we to think of the relationship of such a reader to such a text? Derrida sees *Ulysses* as an intertextual scene of random play, a 'polytelephonic structure' in which 'everything has already happened ... and has been signed in advance by Joyce' (p. 328 below). He sees Bloom as expressing its essence. Does Bloom's being 'at the telephone', waiting for a call, therefore describe Derrida's relation to *Ulysses*? Does he seek some personal authentication from the text? Is this relationship – in terms of the telegraphic metaphor of his essay – a person-to-person call? Or is there a more general affinity? Does the idea of the text as a switchboard through which the scraps and permutations or echoes of *all* languages, itineraries and personalities pass, mean that it anticipates and authenticates a Derridean model of language? Is *Ulysses* the text of deconstruction or, switching the emphasis, is deconstruction only a later name for Joyce's modernism?

Deconstruction also has a more obvious, but still self-reflexive, bearing on the essay. Derrida sees the method of deconstruction as instigating a double reversal and dispersal of binary opposites. He draws attention, in the course of the essay, to distinctions of this kind between the internal and external, the legitimate and illegitimate, and to an evidently hierachical distinction, involving himself, between incompetence and expertise. Thus his own incompetence is 'the profound truth of his relation to this work' and is contrasted with the professional expertise of the Joycean critical industry whose representatives he is addressing. Is this distinction between amateurism and expertise retained or deconstructed, and if so how? Indeed, in the spirit of the above, are we to think that its deconstruction has already occurred in *Ulysses*?

There is an important final emphasis upon the word 'yes'. This Derrida associates with affirmation, living presence and with women. Molly Bloom's speech is framed by this 'yes', but her speech is a monologue. How, therefore, does Derrida relate this to the model of exchange and interchangeability, of waiting for a call, which governs his reading?

For further initial commentary and suggestions for reading on Derrida and poststructuralism see *A Reader's Guide* 3/e, Ch. 6. See also Christopher Norris, *Derrida* (Fontana, 1987) and *Deconstruction. Theory and Practice* (Routledge, 2nd edn, 1991).

The following is taken from the selection in Peggy Kamuf, ed., *A Derrida Reader. Between the Blinds* (Prentice Hall/Harvester, 1991), pp. 569–98, and includes Kamufs editorial notes. Additional cuts are indicated by a summarizing comment in the text.

Ulysses Gramophone: Hear Say Yes in Joyce

[...]

If I am not mistaken, the first phone call sounds with Bloom's words: 'Better phone him up first' in the sequence entitled 'AND IT WAS THE FEAST OF THE PASSOVER.'[1] A little before, he had somewhat mechanically, like a record, repeated this prayer, the most serious of all prayers for a Jew, the one that should never be allowed to become mechanical, to be gramophoned: *Shema Israel Adonai Elohanu.* If, more or less legitimately (for everything and nothing is legitimate when we lift out segments as examples of narrative metonymy), we cut out this element from the most obvious thread of the narrative, then we can speak of the telephonic *Shema Israel* between God, who is infinitely removed (a long-distance call, a collect call from or to the 'collector of prepuces'), and Israel. *Shema Israel* means, as you know, call to Israel, listen Israel, hello Israel, to the address of the name of Israel, a person-to-person call.[2] The 'Better phone him up first' scene takes place in the offices of *The Telegraph* (and not *The Tetragram*) newspaper and Bloom has just paused to watch a kind of typewriter, or rather a composing machine, a typographic matrix: 'He stayed in his walk to watch a typesetter neatly distributing type.' And as he first of all reads it backwards ('Reads it backwards first'), composing the name of Patrick Dignam, the name of the father, Patrick, from right to left, he remembers his own father reading the hagadah in the same direction. In the same paragraph, around the name of Patrick, you can follow the whole series of fathers, the twelve sons of Jacob, et cetera, and the word 'practice' crops up twice to scan this patristic and perfectly paternal litany ('Quickly he does it. Must require some practice that.' And twelve lines lower, 'How quickly he does that job. Practice makes perfect'). Almost immediately after this we read, 'Better phone him up first': '*plutôt un coup de téléphone pour commencer,*' the French translation says. Let's say: a phone call, rather, to begin with. In the beginning, there must have been some phone call.

Before the act or the word, the telephone. In the beginning was the telephone. There would be much to say about the apparently random figures that this *coup de téléphone*[3] plays on; we hear it resonate unceasingly. And it sets off within itself this *yes* toward which we slowly, moving in circles around it, return. There are several modalities or tonalities of the telephonic *yes*, but one of them, without saying anything else, amounts to marking, simply, that one is *there*, present, listening, on the other end of the line, ready to respond but not for the moment responding anything other than the preparation to respond (hello, yes: I'm listening, I can hear that you are there, ready to speak just when I am ready to speak to you). In the beginning the telephone, yes, in the beginning of the *coup de téléphone*

[...]

Telephonic spacing is particularly superimprinted in the scene entitled 'A DISTANT VOICE.' The scene crosses all the lines in our network, the paradoxes of competence and institution, represented here in the shape of the professor, and, in every sense of the word, the *repetition* of the 'yes' between eyes and ears. All these telephonic threads can be drawn from one paragraph:

A DISTANT VOICE
  – I'll answer it, the professor said going. ...
  – Hello? *Evening Telegraph* here ... Hello? ... Who's there? ... Yes ... Yes ... Yes ...
    The professor came to the inner door.
  – Bloom is at the telephone, he said. (*U*, 137–38)

Bloom-is-at-the-telephone. In this way, the professor defines a particular situation at a certain moment in the novel, no doubt, but as is always the case in the stereophony of a text that gives several levels to each statement, always allowing for metonymic extracts – and I am not the only reader of Joyce to indulge in this pursuit, at once legitimate and abusive, authorized and illegitimate – the professor is also naming the permanent essence of Bloom. It can be read by means of this particular paradigm: *he is at the telephone*, he is always there, he belongs to the telephone, he is both riveted and destined there. His being is a being-at-the-telephone. He is hooked up to a multiplicity of voices and answering machines. His being-there is a being-at-the-telephone, a being for the telephone, in the way that Heidegger speaks of a being for death of *Dasein*. And I am not playing with words when I say this: Heideggerian *Dasein* is also a being-called, it is always, as we are informed in *Sein und Zeit*, and as my friend Sam Weber reminded me,[4] a *Dasein* that accedes to itself only on the basis of the Call (*der Ruf*), a call which has come from afar, which does not necessarily use words, and which, in a certain way, does not say anything. The whole of chapter 57 of *Sein und Zeit* on the subject of *der Ruf*, down to the last detail, could be adjusted to this analysis, drawing, for example, on phrases like the following: *Der Angerufene ist eben dieses Dasein; aufgerufen zu seinem eigensten Seinkönnen (Sich-vorweg ...) Und aufgerufen ist das Dasein durch den Anruf aus dem Verfallen in das Mann.* ... The called one is precisely *this Dasein*; convoked, provoked, interpellated toward its possibility of being the most proper (before itself). And in this way the Dasein is hailed by this call, called out to, called out of the collapse into the 'One'. Unfortunately, we do not have the time to enter further into this analysis, within or beyond the jargon of *Eigentlichkeit*, which this university (Frankfurt) may well remember.

  – Bloom is at the telephone, he said.
  – Tell him to go to hell, the editor said promptly. X is Burke's public house, see? (*U*, 138)

Bloom is at the telephone, hooked up to a powerful network to which I shall return in a moment. He belongs in his essence to a polytelephonic structure. But he is at the telephone in the sense that one also waits on the telephone. When the professor says, 'Bloom is at the telephone, and I shall shortly say, 'Joyce is at the telephone,' he is saying: he is waiting for someone to respond to him, waiting for an answer, which the editor, who decides the future of the text, its safekeeping or its truth, does not want to give – and who at this point sends him to hell, into the depths, in the *Verfallen*, the hell of censured books.[5] Bloom is waiting for an answer, for someone to say, 'hello, yes,' that is, for someone to say, 'Yes, yes,' beginning with the telephonic *yes* indicating that there is indeed another voice, if not an answering machine, on the other end of the line. When, at the end of the book, Molly says, 'yes, yes,' she is answering a request, but a request that she requests. She is at the telephone, even when she is in bed, asking, and waiting to be asked, on the telephone (since she is alone) to say, 'yes, yes.' And the fact that she asks 'with my eyes' does not prevent this demand from being made by telephone; on the contrary: 'well as well him as another and then I asked him with my eyes to ask again yes and then he asked me would I yes to say yes my mountain flower and first I put my arms around him yes and drew him down to me so he could feel my breasts all perfume yes and his heart was going like mad and yes I said yes I will Yes' (*U*, 704).

The final 'Yes,' the last word, the eschatology of the book, gives itself up only to *reading*, since it distinguishes itself from the others by an inaudible capital letter, an inaudible, only visible remains, the literal incorporation of the yes in the eye of the language, of the *yes* in the *eyes*. Language of eyes, of ayes. *Langue d'oeil*.[6]

We still do not know what yes means and how this small word, if it is one, operates in language and in what we glibly refer to as speech acts. We do not know whether this word shares anything at all with any other word in any language, even with the word *no*, which is most certainly not symmetrical to it. We do not know if a grammatical, semantic, linguistic, rhetorical, or philosophical concept exists that is capable of this event marked *yes*. Let us leave that aside for the moment. Let us, and this is not merely a fiction, act *as if* this did not prevent us, on the contrary, from hearing what the word *yes* governs. We will move on to the difficult questions later, if we have time.

Yes on the telephone can be crossed, in one and the same occurrence, by a variety of intonations whose differential qualities are potentialized on long stereophonic waves. They may appear to be limited to interjection, to the mechanical quasi signal that indicates either the mere presence of the interlocutory *Dasein* at the other end of the line (Hello, yes?), or the passive docility of a secretary or a subordinate who, like some archiving machine, is ready to record orders (*yes sir*) or who is satisfied with purely informative answers (*yes, sir*; *no, sir*). Here is just one example among many. I have deliberately chosen the section where a typewriter and the trade name H. E. L. Y.'S lead us to the last piece of furniture in this vestibule or this techno-telecommunication preamble, to a certain gramophone, at the same time as they connect us to the network of the prophet Elijah. So here we are, though of course I have sectioned and selected, filtering the noise on the line:

> Miss Dunne hid the Capel street library copy of *The Woman in White* far back in her drawer and rolled a sheet of gaudy notepaper into her typewriter.
> Too much mystery business in it. Is he in love with that one, Marion? Change it and get another by Mary Cecil Haye.
> The disk shot down the groove, wobbled a while, ceased and ogled them: six.
> Miss Dunne clicked at the keyboard:
> – 16 June 1904. [almost eighty years.]

Five tallwhitehatted sandwichmen between Monypeny's corner and the slab where Wolfe Tone's statue was not, eeled themselves turning H. E. L. Y.'S and plodded back as they had come. ...

The telephone rang rudely by her ear.

– Hello. Yes, sir. No, sir. Yes, sir. I'll ring them up after five. Only those two, sir, for Belfast and Liverpool. All right, sir. Then I can go after six if you're not back. A quarter after. Yes, sir. Twentyseven and six. I'll tell him. Yes: one, seven, six.

She scribbled three figures on an envelope.

– Mr Boylan! Hello! That gentleman from *Sport* was in looking for you. Mr Lenehan, yes. He said he'll be in the Ormond at four. No, sir. Yes, sir. I'll ring them up after five. (*U*, 228–29)

It is not by accident that the repetition of yes can be seen to assume mechanical, servile forms, often bending the woman to her master, even if any answer to the other as a singular other must, it seems, escape those forms. In order for the *yes* of affirmation, assent, consent, alliance, of engagement, signature, or gift to have the value it has, it must carry the repetition within itself. It must *a priori* and immediately confirm its promise and promise its confirmation. This essential repetition lets itself be haunted by an intrinsic threat, by an internal telephone which acts like a parasite, like its mimetic, mechanical double, its incessant parody. We shall return to this fatality. But we can already hear a gramophony which records writing in the liveliest voice. *A priori* it reproduces it, in the absence of all intentional presence of the affirmer. Such gramophony responds, of course, to the dream of a reproduction which *preserves* as its truth the living *yes*, archived in the form of the most living voice. But by the very same token, it gives way to the possibility of parody, of a *yes* technique that persecutes the most spontaneous, the most giving desire of the *yes*. To meet (*répondre à*) its destination, this *yes* must reaffirm itself immediately. Such is the condition of a signed commitment. The *yes* can only speak *itself* if it promises itself its own memory. [*Le oui ne peut se dire que s'il se promet la mémoire de soi.*] The affirmation of the *yes* is the affirmation of memory. *Yes* must preserve itself, and thus reiterate itself, archive its voice in order to give it once again to be heard and understood.

This is what I call the gramophone effect. *Yes* gramophones itself and, *a priori*, telegramophones itself.

The desire for memory and the mourning of the word *yes* set in motion the anamnesic machine. And its hypermnesic overacceleration. The machine reproduces the quick [*le vif*], it doubles it with its automaton.

[...]

I was telling you about my travel experiences, my round trip, and about a few phone calls. If I am telling stories, it is to put off speaking about serious things and because I am too intimidated. Nothing intimidates me more than a community of experts in Joycean matters. Why? I wanted first of all to speak to you about this, to speak to you about authority and intimidation. The page that I am going to read was written on the plane to Oxford, Ohio, a few days before my trip to Tokyo. I had decided at that time to put before you the question of competence, of legitimacy, and of the Joycean institution. Who has a recognized right to speak of Joyce, to write on Joyce, and who does this well? What do competence and performance consist of here?

When I agreed to speak before you, before the most intimidating assembly in the world, before the greatest concentration of knowledge on such a polymathic work, I was primarily aware of the honor that was being paid me. I wondered by what claim I had managed to make people think I deserved it, if only to a minor degree. I do not intend to answer this question here. But I know, as you do, that I do not belong to your large, impressive family. I prefer the word family to that of foundation or institute. Someone answering, yes, in Joyce's name, to Joyce's name, has succeeded in linking the future of an institution to the singular adventure of a proper name and a signature, a *signed* proper name, for writing out one's name is not yet signing. In a plane, if you write out your name on the identity card which you hand in on arrival in Tokyo, you have not yet signed. You sign when the gesture whereby, in a certain place, preferably at the end of a card or a book, you inscribe your name again, takes on the sense of a *yes*, this is my name, I certify this, and, yes, yes, I will be able to attest to this again, I will remember later, I promise, that it is indeed I who signed. A signature is always a *yes*, *yes*, the *synthetic* performative of a promise and a memory that conditions every commitment. We shall return to this obligatory departure point of all discourse, following a circle which is also that of the *yes*, of the 'so be it' – of the amen and the hymen.

I did not feel worthy of honor that had been bestowed on me, far from it, but I must have been nourishing some obscure desire to be part of this mighty family which tends to sum up all others, including their hidden narratives of bastardy, legitimation, and illegitimacy. If I have accepted, it is mainly because I suspected some perverse challenge in a legitimation so generously offered. You know better than I that the worried concern regarding familial legitimation is what makes *Ulysses*, as well as *Finnegans Wake*, vibrate. I was thinking, in the plane, of the challenge and the trap: Experts, I said to myself, with the lucidity and experience that a long acquaintance with Joyce confers on them, ought to know better than most to what extent, beneath the simulacrum of a few signs of complicity, of references or quotations in each of my books, Joyce remains a stranger to me, as if I did not know him. They realize that incompetence is the profound truth of my relationship to this work which I know finally only indirectly, through hearsay, through rumors, through what people say, second hand exegeses, always partial readings. For these experts, I said to myself, the time has come for the deception to be exposed, and how better to expose or denounce it than at the opening of a large symposium?

So, in order to defend myself against this hypothesis, which was almost a certainty, I asked myself: but in the end what does competence come down to in the case of Joyce? And what can a Joycean institution or family, a Joycean international be? I do not know how far we can speak of the modernity of Joyce, but if this exists, beyond the apparatus for postal and programophonic technologies, it consists in the fact that the declared project of keeping generations of university scholars at work for centuries of babelian edification must itself have been drawn up using a technological model and the division of university labor that could not be that of former centuries. The scheme of bending vast communities of readers and writers to this law, of detaining them by means of an interminable transferential chain of translation and tradition, can equally well be attributed to Plato and Shakespeare, to Dante and Vico, without mentioning Hegel or other finite divinities. But none of these was able to calculate, as well as Joyce did, his move, by regulating it on certain types of world research institutions prepared to use not only means of transport, of communication, or organizational programming that allow an accelerated capital-ization, a crazy accumulation of interest in terms of knowledge blocked in Joyce's name, even as he lets you all sign in his name as Molly would say ('1 could often have written out a fine cheque for myself and write his name on it' *U*, 702), but also modes of archivization and consultation of data unheard of for all the grandfathers whom I have just named, omitting Homer.

Hence the intimidation: Joyce experts are the representatives as well as the effects of the most powerful project for programming the totality of research in the onto-logico-encyclopedic field for centuries, all the while commemorating its own, proper signature. A Joyce scholar has the right to dispose of the totality of competence in the encyclopedic field of the *universitas*. He has at his command the computer of all memory, he plays with the entire archive of culture – at least of what is called Western culture, and of that which in this culture returns to itself according to the Ulyssean circle of the encyclopedia; and this is why one can always at least dream of writing *on* Joyce and not *in* Joyce from the fantasy of some Far Eastern capital, without, in my case, having too many illusions about it.

The effects of this preprogramming, which you know better than I, are admirable and terrifying, and sometimes intolerably violent. One of them has the following form: nothing can be invented *on the subject* of Joyce. Everything we can say about *Ulysses*, for example, has already been anticipated there, including, as we have seen, the scene about academic competence and the ingenuousness of metadiscourse. We are caught in this net. All the gestures by which we might attempt to take the initiative are already announced in an overpotentialized text that will remind you, at a given moment, that you are captive in a network of language, writing, knowledge, and *even narration*. That is one of the things I wanted to demonstrate earlier, in recounting all these stories, which were moreover true. [....] We have verified that all this had its narrative paradigm and was *already* recounted in *Ulysses*. Everything that happened to me, including the narrative that I would attempt to make of it, was already predicted and pre-narrated in its dated singularity, prescribed in a sequence of knowledge and narration, within *Ulysses*, to say nothing of *Finnegans Wake*, by a hypermnesic machine capable of storing in an immense epic work, along with the memory of the West and virtually all the languages in the world *up to and including traces of the future*. Yes, everything has already happened to us with *Ulysses* and has been signed in advance by Joyce.

It remains to be seen what happens to this signature in these conditions, and this is one of my questions.

This situation is one of reversal, stemming from the paradox of the *yes*. Moreover, the question of the *yes* is always linked to that of the *doxa*, to what is opined in opinion. So this is the paradox: just when the work of such a signature starts operating – some might say subjugating, at any rate relaunching *for itself*, so that there might be a return – the most competent and reliable production and reproduction machine, it simultaneously ruins its model. Or, at least, it threatens its model with ruin. Joyce laid stakes on the modern university, but he challenges it to reconstitute itself after him. He marks its essential limits. Basically, there can be no Joycean competence, in the certain and strict sense of the concept of competence, with the criteria of evaluation and legitimation that are attached to it. There can be no Joycean foundation, no Joycean family; there can be no Joycean legitimacy. What is the relation between this situation, the paradox of the *yes*, or the structure of a signature?

The classical concept of competence supposes that one can rigorously disassociate knowledge (in its act or in its position) from the event that one is dealing with, and especially from the ambiguity of written or oral marks – let's call them gramophonies. Competence implies that a metadiscourse is possible, neutral and univocal with regard to a field of objectivity, whether or not it has the structure of a text. Performances ruled by this competence must in principle lend themselves to translation with nothing left over on the subject of the corpus that is itself translatable. Above all they should not be essentially of a narrative type. In principle, one doesn't tell stories in the university; one does history, one recounts in order to know and to explain; one speaks about narrations or epic poems, but events and histories (stories) must not be produced there under the heading of institutionalizable knowledge. Now with the event signed by Joyce, a *double bind* has become at least explicit (for we have been caught in it since Babel and Homer and everything else that follows): on the one hand, we must write, we must sign, we must bring about new events with untranslatable marks – and this is the frantic call, the distress of a signature that is asking for a *yes* from the other, the pleading injunction for a counter-signature; but on the other hand, the singular novelty of every other *yes*, of every other signature, finds itself already phonoprogrammed in the Joycean corpus.

I do not notice the effects of the challenge of this double bind on myself alone, in the terrified desire I might have to belong to a family of Joycean representatives among whom I will always remain an illegitimate son; I also notice these effects on you.

On the one hand, you are legitimately assured of possessing, or being in the process of constructing a supercompetence, which would measure up to a corpus that includes virtually all the corpuses treated in the university (sciences, technical domains, religion, philosophy, literature, and, co-extensive to all this, languages). With regard to this hyperbolic competence, nothing is transcendent. Everything is *internal*, mental telephony; everything can be integrated into the domesticity of this programmotelephonic encyclopedia.

But, on the other hand, one must realize at the same time, and *you do realize this*, that the signature and the *yes* that occupy you are capable – it is their destination – of destroying the very root of this competence, of this legitimacy, of its domestic interiority, capable of deconstructing the university institution, with its internal or interdepartmental divisions, as well as its contract with the extra-university world.

Hence the mixture of assurance and distress that one can sense in 'Joyce scholars.' From one point of view, they are as crafty as Ulysses, knowing, as did Joyce, that they know more, that they always have one more trick up their sleeve. Whether it is a question of totalizing resumption or of subatomistic micrology (what I call 'divisibility of the letter'), one can do no better; everything can be integrated in the 'this is my body' of the corpus. But, from another point of view, this hypermnesic interiorization can never be closed on itself. For reasons that have to do with the structure of the corpus, the project, and the signature, there can be no assurance of any principle of truth or legitimacy.

Given that nothing new can take you by surprise from the inside, you also have the feeling that something might eventually happen to you from an unforseeable outside. And you have guests.

You are awaiting the passage or the second coming of Elijah. And, as in all good Jewish families, you always have a place set for him. Waiting for Elijah, even if his coming is already gramophoned in *Ulysses*, you are prepared to recognize, without too many illusions, I think, the external competence of writers, philosophers, psychoanalysts, linguists. You even ask them to open your colloquia.

[...]

The uncertain identity of the 'community' of Joyce scholars, says Derrida, means that they call on strangers like himself to give them recognition. He adds that he is also called Elijah (Derrida's Hebrew name).

[...]

So where are we going with the alliance of this Joycean community? What will become of it at this pace of accumulation and commemoration in one or two centuries, taking into account new technologies for archiving and storing information? Finally, Elijah is not me, nor some stranger come to say this thing to you, the news from outside, even the apocalypse of Joycean studies, that is, the truth, the final revelation (and you know that Elijah was always associated with an apocalyptic discourse). No, Elijah is you: you are the Elijah of *Ulysses*, who is presented as a large telephone exchange ('HELLO THERE, CENTRAL!' *U*, 149), the marshalling yard, the network through which all information must transit. We can imagine that there will soon be a giant computer of Joycean studies ('operating all this trunk line. ... Book through to eternity junction' *U*, 473). It would capitalize all publications, coordinate and teleprogram all communication, colloquia, theses, papers, and would draw up an index in all languages. We would be able to consult it any time by satellite or by 'sunphone,' day and night, taking advantage of the reliability of an answering machine. 'Hello, yes, yes, what are you asking for? Oh, for all the occurrences of the word *yes* in *Ulysses*? Yes.' It would remain to be seen if the basic language of this computer would be English and if its patent would be American, given the overwhelming and significant majority of Americans in the trust of the

Joyce Foundation. It would also remain to be seen if we could consult this computer on the word *yes*, and if the *yes*, in particular, the one involved in consulting operations, can be counted, calculated, numbered. A circle will shortly lead me back to this question.

In any case, the figure of Elijah, whether it be that of the prophet or the circumciser, of polymathic competence, or of telematic mastery, is only a synecdoche of Ulyssean narration, at once smaller and greater than the whole.

We should, then, get rid of a double illusion and a double intimidation. (1) No truth can come from outside the Joycean community, that is, without the experience, the cunning, and the knowledge amassed by overtrained readers. But (2) inversely, or symmetrically, there is no model for 'Joycean' competence, no interiority and no closure possible for the concept of such a competence. There is no absolute criterion for measuring the relevance of a discourse on the subject of a text signed 'Joyce.' The very concept of competence finds itself shaken by this event. For we must write, write in one language, while we respond to the *yes* and countersign in another language. The very discourse of competence (that of neutral, metalinguistic knowledge immune from all untranslatable writing, etc.) is thus incompetent, the least pertinent there is on the subject of Joyce, who, moreover, also finds himself in the same situation whenever he speaks of his 'work'.

Instead of pursuing these generalities, and bearing in mind time passing, I return to the *yes* in *Ulysses*. For a very long time, the question of the *yes* has mobilized or traversed everything that I have been trying to think, write, teach, or read. To cite only the example of readings, I had devoted seminars and texts to the *yes*, to the double *yes* in Nietzsche's *Zarathustra* ('Thus spake Zarathustra,' Mulligan moreover says – *U*, 29), the *yes*, *yes* of the hymen, which is still the best example, the *yes* of the great midday affirmation, and then the ambiguity of the double *yes*: one of them comes down to the Christian assumption of one's burden, the *Ja, Ja* of the donkey overloaded as Christ was with memory and responsibility; and the other *yes*, *yes* that is light, airy, dancing, solar is also a yes of reaffirmation, of promise, and of oath, a *yes* to the eternal recurrence.[7] The difference between the two *yes*es, or rather between the two repetitions of the *yes*, remains unstable, subtle, sublime. One repetition haunts the other. For Nietzsche, who, like Joyce, anticipated that one day professorships would be set up to study his *Zarathustra*, the *yes* always finds its chance with a certain kind of woman. In the same way, in Blanchot's *La folie du jour*, the quasi-narrator attributes the power to say *yes* to women, to the beauty of women, beautiful insofar as they say *yes*: '*J'ai pourtant rencontré des êtres qui n'ont jamais dit à la vie, tais-toi, et jamais à la mort, va-t-en. Presque toujours des femmes, de belles créatures*' (Yet I have met people who have never said to life, 'Quiet!', who have never said to death, 'Go away!' Almost always women, beautiful creatures.)

The *yes* then, would be of woman – and not just of the mother, the flesh, the earth, as is so often said of Molly's *yes*es in the majority of readings devoted to her: 'Penelope, bed, flesh, earth, monologue,' said Gilbert, and many others after him and even before him, and here Joyce is no more competent than anyone else. This is not false, it is even the truth of a certain truth, but it is not all, and it is not so simple. The law of gender *[genre]*[8] seems to me to be largely overdetermined and infinitely more complicated, whether we are speaking of sexual or grammatical gender, or again of rhetorical technique. To call this a monologue is to display a somnambulistic carelessness. So I wanted to listen again to Molly's *yes*es. But could one do this without making them resonate with all the *yes*es that prepare the way for them, correspond to them, and keep them hanging on the other end of the line throughout the whole book? So, last summer in Nice I read *Ulysses* again, first in French, then in English, pencil in hand, counting the *oui*'s and then the *yes*es and sketching out a typology of them. As you can imagine, I dreamt of hooking up to the Joyce Foundation computer, and the result is not the same from one language to the other.

Molly is not Elijah (*Elie*), is not *Moelie* (for you know that the Moy'l is the circumciser), and Molly is not Joyce, but even so: her *yes* circumnavigates and circumscribes, encircling the last chapter of *Ulysses*, since it is at once her first and her last word, her send-off *[envoi]* and her closing cadence *[chute]*: 'Yes because he never did' and finally 'and yes I said yes I will Yes' (*U*, 704). The last, eschatological 'Yes' occupies the place of the signature at the bottom right of the text. Even if one distinguishes, as one must, Molly's 'yes' from that of *Ulysses*, in which she is but a figure and a moment, even if one distinguishes, as one also must do, these two signatures (that of Molly and that of *Ulysses*) from that of Joyce, even so they read each other and call out to *[s'appellent]* each other. They call to each other precisely through a *yes*, which always inaugurates a scene of call and request: it confirms and countersigns. Affirmation demands *a priori* confirmation, repetition, the safekeeping, and the memory of the *yes*. A certain narrativity is to be found at the simple core *[coeur simple]* of the simplest yes: 'I asked him with my eyes to ask again yes and then he asked me would I yes to say yes' (*U*, 704), and so on. A *yes* never comes alone, and one is never alone in saying *yes*. Nor do we laugh alone, as Freud says, and we shall come back to this. And Freud also stresses that the unconscious never says *no*.

[...]

Derrida reflects on the question of Joyce's signature: '*Who* is signing? Who is signing *what* in Joyce's name?' he asks, and sees this as connected to another question: 'Who is laughing and how does one laugh *with* Joyce ...?'

[...]

But why laugh and why laughter? No doubt, everything has already been said on laughter in Joyce, on parody, satire, derision, humor, irony, mockery. And on his Homeric laughter and his Rabelaisian laughter. It remains perhaps to think of laughter, precisely, as a remains. What does laughter want to say? What does laughter want? *[Qu'est-ce que ça veut dire, le rire? Qu'est-ce que ça veut rire?]* Once one recognizes that, in principle, in *Ulysses* the virtual totality of experience, of meaning, of history, of the symbolic, of language, and of writing, the great cycle and the great encyclopedia of cultures, scenes, and affects, in sum, the sum total of all sum totals tends to unfold itself and reconstitute itself by playing out all its possible combinations, while writing seeks to occupy virtually all the spaces, well, the totalizing hermeneutic that makes up the task of a worldwide and eternal institution of Joyce studies will find itself confronted with what I hesitate to call a dominant affect, a *Stimmung* or a *pathos*, a tone that re-traverses all the others and that nevertheless is not part of the series of the others since it *re-marks* all of them, adds itself to them without allowing itself to be added in or totalized, in the manner of a remains that is at once quasi-transcendental and supplementary. And it is this *yes-laughter [oui-rire]* that overmarks not only the totality of the writing, but all the qualities, modalities, genres of laughter whose differences might be classified into some sort of typology.

[…]

Derrida remarks further on the omnipotence of this 'yes-laughter' and on Joyce's laughter at this omnipotence.

[…]

This yes-laughter of encircling reappropriation, of all-powerful Odyssean recapitulation, accompanies the installation of a structure virtually capable of impregnating in advance its patented signature, even that of Molly, with all the countersignatures to come, even after the death of the artist as an old man, who moves off with only the empty shell, the accident of a substance. The machine of filiation – legitimate or illegitimate – functions well and is ready for anything, ready to domesticate, circumcise, circumvent everything; it lends itself to the encyclopedic reappropriation of absolute knowledge which gathers itself up close to itself, as Life of the Logos, that is, also in the truth of natural death. We are here in Frankfurt to bear witness to this in commemoration.

But the eschatological tone of this yes-laughter also seems to me to be worked over or traversed – I prefer to say *haunted* – joyously ventriloquized by a completely different music, by the vowels of a completely different song. I can hear it too, very close to the other one, as the yes-laughter of a gift without debt, the light almost amnesic, affirmation, of a gift or an abandoned event, which in classical language is called 'the work,' a lost signature without a proper name that only shows and names the cycle of reappropriation and domestication of all the paraphs in order to delimit their phantasm, to contrive the break-in necessary for the coming of the other, an other whom one can always call Elijah, if Elijah is the name of the unforeseeable other for whom a place must be kept, and no longer Elijah, head of the megaprogramotelephonic network, Elijah, the great switchboard operator, but the other Elijah: Elijah, the other. But there we are, this is a homonym: Elijah can always be one and the other at the same time, we cannot invite the one without the risk of the other turning up. But this is a risk that must forever be run. I return then, in this final movement, to the risk or the chance of this contamination of one yes-laughter by the other, of the parasiting of one Elijah, that is to say of one me, by the other.

Why have I linked the question of laughter, of a laughter which *remains* as the fundamental and quasi-transcendental tonality, to that of the 'yes'?

In order to ask oneself what happens with *Ulysses*, or with the arrival of whatever, whomever – Elijah for example – it is necessary to try to think the singularity of the event, and therefore the uniqueness of the signature, or rather of an irreplaceable mark that cannot necessarily be reduced to the phenomenon of copyright, legible in the patronym after circumcision. It is necessary to try to think circumcision, if you like, beginning with a possibility of the mark, that of a trait that precedes and provides its figure. Now if laughter is a fundamental or abyssal tonality in *Ulysses*, if its analysis is not exhausted by any of the forms of knowledge available precisely because it laughs at knowledge and from knowledge, then laughter bursts out in the event of signature itself. And there is no signature without *yes*. If the signature does not amount to the manipulation or the mention of a name, it supposes the irreversible commitment of the person confirming, who *says* or *does* yes, the token of some mark left behind. Before asking oneself who is doing the signing, whether Joyce is or Molly is, or what is the status of the difference between the author's signature and that of a figure or a fiction signed by an author; before conversing about sexual difference as duality and expressing one's conviction of the 'onesidedly womanly woman' (and here I am quoting Frank Budgen and others after him) of Molly's character, the beautiful plant, the herb or *pharmakon*[9] or of the 'onesidedly masculine' character of James Joyce; before taking into consideration what Joyce says about the non-stop monologue as 'the indispensable countersign to Bloom's passport to eternity' (and once again, the competence of Joyce in letters and conversations does not seem to me to enjoy any privilege); before manipulating clinical categories and a psychoanalytical knowledge that are largely derivative in view of the possibilities we are talking about here, it is necessary to ask oneself what a signature is: It requires a *yes* more 'ancient' than the question 'what is?' since the latter presupposes it; it is thus 'older' than knowledge. It is necessary to ask for what reason the yes always comes about as a *yes, yes*. I say the yes and not the word '*yes*,' for there can be a *yes* without the word, which is precisely our problem.

One ought, then, to have preceded all of this with a long, knowledgeable, and thoughtful meditation on the meaning, the function, the presupposition above all of the *yes*: before language, in language, but also in an experience of the plurality of languages that perhaps no longer belongs to linguistics in the strict sense. The expansion toward a pragmatics seems to me to be necessary but inadequate so long as it does not open itself up to a thinking of the trace, of writing, in a sense that I have tried to explain elsewhere and which I cannot go into here.

What is it that is spoken, written, what occurs *[advient]* with yes?

Yes can be implied without the word being said or written. This explains, for example, the multiplication of *yes*es everywhere in the French version when it is assumed that a *yes* is marked by English sentences from which the word *yes* is in fact absent. But at the limit, given that *yes* is co-extensive with every statement, there is a great temptation, in French but first of all in English, to double up everything with a kind of continuous *yes*, even to double up the *yes*es articulated simply to mark the rhythm, intakes of breath in the from of pauses or murmured interjections, as sometimes happens in *Ulysses*. This *yes* comes – from me to me, from me to the other in me, from the other to me – to confirm the primary telephonic 'Hello': yes, that's right, that's what I'm saying, I am, in fact, speaking, yes, there we are, I'm speaking, yes, yes you can hear me, I can hear you, yes, we are in the process of speaking, there is language, you are receiving me, it's like this, it takes place, happens, is written, is marked, yes, yes.

But let's set out again from the *yes phenomenon*, the manifest *yes* patently marked as a *word*, spoken, written, or phonogramed. Such a word says but says nothing in itself, if by saying we mean designating, showing, describing some thing to be found outside language, outside marking *[hors marque]*. Its only references are other marks, which are also marks of the other. Given that *yes* does not say, show, name anything that is beyond marking, some would be tempted to conclude that *yes* says nothing: an empty word, barely an adverb, since all adverbs, in which grammatical category *yes* is situated in our languages, have a richer, more determined semantic charge than the *yes* they always presuppose. In short, *yes* would be transcendental adverbiality, the ineffaceable supplement to any verb: in the beginning was the adverb, yes, but as an interjection, still very close to the inarticulated cry, a preconceptual vocalization, the perfume of a discourse.

But can one sign with a perfume? Just as we can replace *yes* neither by a thing which it would be supposed to describe (it describes nothing, states nothing, even if it is a sort of performative implied in all statements: yes, I am stating, it is stated, etc.), nor even by the thing it is supposed to approve or affirm, likewise one cannot replace the *yes* by the names of the concepts supposed to describe this act or operation, if indeed this is an act or operation. The concept of activity or of actuality does not seem to me apt to account for a *yes*. And this quasi-act cannot be replaced by *approval, affirmation, confirmation, acquiescence, consent*. The word *affirmative* used by the military to avoid all kinds of technical risks, does not replace the *yes*; it supposes it once again: yes, I am saying *affirmative*.

What does this *yes* lead us to think, this *yes* that names, describes, designates nothing, and that has no reference outside marking (and not outside language, for *yes* can get by without words, or at least the word *yes*)? In its radically nonconstative or nondescriptive dimension, even if it is saying 'yes' to a description or a narration, *yes* is *par excellence* and through and through a performative. But this characterization seems to me inadequate. First because a performative must be a *sentence* and one which is sufficiently endowed with meaning by itself, in a given conventional context, if it is to bring about a determined event. Now I believe, yes, that – to put it in a classical philosophical code – *yes* is the transcendental condition of all performative dimensions. A promise, an oath, an order, a commitment always implies a *yes, I sign*. The *I* of *I sign* says *yes* and says *yes* to itself, even if it signs a simulacrum. Any event brought about by a performative mark, any writing in the widest sense of the word involves a *yes*, whether or not it is phenomenalized, that is, verbalized or adverbalized as such. Molly says *yes*, she remembers *yes*, the *yes* that she spoke with her eyes to ask for *yes* with her eyes, et cetera.

We are in an area which is *not yet* the space where the big questions of the origin of negation, affirmation or denegation can and must be deployed. Nor are we even in the space where Joyce was able to reverse '*Ich bin der Geist, der stets verneint*' by saying that Molly is the flesh that always says *yes*. The *yes* we are talking about now is 'anterior' to all these reversing alternatives, to all these dialectics. They suppose it and envelop it. Before the *Ich* in *Ich bin* affirms or negates, it poses itself or pre-poses itself: not as *ego*, as the conscious or unconscious self, as masculine or feminine subject, spirit or flesh, but as a pre-performative force that, for example, in the form of the 'I' marks that 'I' as addressing itself to some other, however undetermined he or she is: 'Yes-I,' or 'Yes-I-say-to-the-other,' even if *I* says *no* and even if *I* addresses itself without speaking. The minimal, primary *yes*, the telephonic 'hello' or tap *[coup]* through a prison wall, marks, before meaning or signifying: *I-here*, listen answer, there is some mark, there is some other. Negativities may ensue, but even if they completely take over, this *yes* can no longer be erased.

I have had to yield to the rhetorical necessity of translating this minimal and undetermined, almost virgin, address into words, into words such as 'I,' 'I am,' 'language,' at a point where the position of the *I*, of being, and of language still remains derivative with regard to this *yes*. This is the whole problem for anyone wishing to speak on the subject of the *yes*. A metalanguage will always be impossible here insofar as it will itself suppose the event of the *yes* which it will be unable to comprehend. The situation will be the same for any accountancy or computation, for any calculation aiming to regulate a series of *yeses* according to the principle of reason and its machines. *Yes* marks that there is address to the other. This address is not necessarily a dialogue or an interlocution, since it supposes neither voice nor symmetry, but the haste, in advance, of a response that is already asking. For if there is some other, if there is some *yes*, then the other no longer lets itself be produced by the same or by the self. *Yes*, the condition of any signature and any performative, addresses itself to some other that it does not constitute, and to whom it can only begin by *asking*, in response to a request that is always anterior, to *ask him/her* to say yes. Time appears only with this singular anachrony. These commitments may remain fictitious, fallacious, and always reversible, and the address may remain invisible or undetermined; this does not change anything in the necessity of the structure. *A priori* it breaks off all possible monologue. Nothing is less a monologue than Molly's 'monologue,' even if, within certain conventional limits, we have the right to consider it as deriving from the genre or type known as the 'monologue.' But a discourse comprised between two *Yes*es of different quality, two *Yes*es with capital letters, and therefore two gramophoned *Yes*es, could not be a monologue, but at the very most a soliloquy.

But we can see why the appearance of a monologue imposes itself here, precisely because of the yes, yes. The yes says nothing and asks only for another *yes*, the *yes* of an other, which, as we will shortly see, is analytically – or by *a priori* synthesis – implied in the first *yes*. The latter only situates itself, advances itself, marks itself in the call for its confirmation, in the *yes, yes*. It begins with the *yes, yes*, with the second *yes*, with the other *yes*, but as this is still only a *yes* that *recalls*, (and Molly is remembering, is recalling to herself *[se rappelle]* from the other yes), we might always be tempted to call this anamnesis monologic. And tautological. The *yes* says nothing but the *yes*, another *yes* that resembles it even if it says *yes* to the advent of an altogether other *yes*. It appears monotautological or specular, or imaginary, because it opens up the position of the *I*, which is itself the condition of all performativity. Austin reminds us that the performative grammar *par excellence* is that of a sentence in the first person of the present indicative: yes, I promise, I accept, I refuse, I order, I do, I will, and so on. 'He promises' is not an explicit performative and cannot be so unless an *I* is understood, as, for example, in 'I swear to you that he promises.'

The self-affirmation of the *yes* can address itself to the other only by recalling itself to itself *[se rappelant à soi]*, in saying to itself *yes, yes*. The circle of this universal presupposition, fairly comic in itself, is like a dispatch [envoi] to oneself, a sending back *[renvoi]* of self to self which *both never leaves itself and never arrives* at itself. Molly says to herself (apparently talking to herself), reminds herself, that she says *yes* in asking the other to ask her to say *yes*, and she starts or finishes by saying *yes* to the other in herself, but she does so in order to say to the other that she will say *yes* if the other asks her, yes, to say *yes*. This sending back and forth *[envois et renvois]* always mimics the situation of questions and answers in scholastics. And the scene of 'sending oneself to oneself, getting it off with oneself' is repeated many times in *Ulysses* in its literally postal form.[10] And it is always marked with scorn, like the phantasm and failure themselves. The circle does not close.

[...]

Derrida finds further examples of 'self-sending' in the text of *Ulysses*.

[...]

To be more and more aphoristic and telegraphic, I will say in conclusion that the Ulyssean circle of self-sending commands a reactive yes-laughter, the manipulatory operation of hypermnesic reappropriation, whenever the phantasm of a signature wins out, a signature gathering the dispatch together near itself. But when (and it is only a question of rhythm) the circle opens, reappropriation is renounced, the specular gathering together of the dispatch lets itself be joyfully dispersed in a multiplicity of unique yet innumerable dispatches, then the other *yes* laughs, the other, yes, laughs.

But here's the thing: The relationship of one *yes* to the Other, of one *yes* to the other, and of one *yes* to the other *yes*, must be such that the contamination of the two *yeses* remains inevitable. And not only as a threat: but also as a chance. With or without words, taken as a minimal event, a *yes* demands *a priori* its own repetition, its own memorizing, demands that a *yes* to the *yes* inhabit the arrival of the first *yes*, which is therefore never simply originary. We cannot say yes without promising to confirm it and to remember it, to keep it safe, countersigned in another *yes*; we cannot say *yes* without promise and memory, without the promise of memory. Molly remembers, recalls herself to herself. This memory of a promise begins the circle of appropriation, bringing with it all the risks of technical repetition, of automatized archives, of gramophony, of simulacrum, of wandering deprived of address and destination. A yes must entrust itself to memory. Having come already from the other, in the dissymmetry of the demand, and from the other of whom it is requested to request a *yes*, the *yes* entrusts itself to the memory of the other, of the *yes* of the other and of the other yes. All the risks already crowd around from the first breath of *yes*. And the first breath hangs on the breath of the other, already, always a second breath. It remains there out of sound and out of sight, linked up in advance to some 'gramophone in the grave.'

We cannot separate the twin *yeses*, and yet they remain completely other. Like Shem and Shaun, like writing and the post. Such a coupling seems to me to ensure not so much the signature of *Ulysses* but the *vibration* of an event which *succeeds only in/by asking*. A differential vibration of several tonalities, several qualities of yes-laughter which do not allow themselves to be stabilized in the indivisible simplicity of one sole dispatch, of self to self, or of one sole consigning, but which call for the counter-signature of the other, for a *yes* which would resonate in a completely other writing, an other language, an other idiosyncrasy, stamped with an other *timbre*.

[...]

Notes (cut and renumbered)

1. *Ulysses* (London: Penguin, 1968), p. 124. All further references to this edition will be indicated by *U*, followed by the page number.

2. Elsewhere, in the brothel, it is the circumcised who say the 'Shema Israel,' and once again the dead sea, the *Lacus Morte*, shows up: 'THE CIRCUMCISED: (In a dark guttural chant as they cast dead fruit upon him, no flowers) Shema Israel Adonai Elohena Adonai Echad' (*U*, 496).

   And since we are talking about Ulysses, the dead sea, the gramophone, and soon laughter, here is *Remembrance of Things Past*: 'He stopped laughing; I should have liked to recognize my friend, but, like Ulysses in the Odyssey when he rushes forward to embrace his dead mother, like the spiritualist who tries in vain to elicit from a ghost an answer which will reveal its identity, like the visitor at an exhibition of electricity who cannot believe that the voice which the gramophone restores unaltered to life is not a voice spontaneously emitted by a human being, I was obliged to give up the attempt.' Earlier we read: 'The familiar voice seemed to be emitted by a gramophone more perfect than any I had ever heard.' *The Past Recaptured*, Andreas Mayor, trans. (New York: Vintage Books, 1971), pp. 188–89.

3. Derrida calls attention here to the word *coup* in the expression *coup de téléphone*, telephone call, and thus to the resonance with figures of chance and randomness (*coup de dés*, throw of the dice; *coup de chance*, stroke of luck) as well as the arbitrary imposition of an order or a law (e.g. *coup d'état*). The word *coup* has been given a large field of play throughout Derrida's writing; cf., in particular, *Glas* and *Dissemination*. – ED.

4. See Samuel Weber, 'The Debts of Deconstruction and Other, Related Assumptions' in William Kerrigan and Joseph H. Smith, eds., *Taking Chances: Derrida, Psychoanalysis, and Literature* (Baltimore: The Johns Hopkins University Press, 1984), pp. 59 ff. – ED.

5. In the French *Bibliothèque Nationale*, certain materials considered scandalous are shelved in an area called *l'enfer* (hell). – ED.

6. Literally, language of the eye, but one hears and sees as well *langue d'oïl*, the medieval northern language from which modern French derives for the most part. The latter was distinguished from the

southern language – *langue d'oc* – by the different words for yes: *oïl* (*oui*) and *oc*. Earlier in the essay, Derrida noted that Italian was also sometimes called the 'langue de *si*.' – ED.

7. On Nietzsche and affirmation see especially *The Ear of the Other* [1982] ; also *Spurs*. – ED.

8. 'The Law of Genre' is the title of one of Derrida's essays (in *Parages*) on the Blanchot text mentioned here, *La folie du jour*; see as well 'Living On,' above. – ED.

9. On this word, see 'Plato's Pharmacy,' *A Derrida Reader*, pp. 185–87. – ED.

10. Literally, *s'envoyer* would mean to send oneself something. But this form of the verb is used colloquially in the expressions: *s'envoyer quelqu'un* (literally to send oneself someone), to make it with someone, to have it off with someone, to get laid; *s'envoyer en l'air* (literally, to send oneself into the air), also to have it off, get some, or get laid. The only point at which colloquial English might be seen to approach such a use would be in expressions like 'You send me,' 'That really sends me.' – ED.

Chapter 8

Bertolt Brecht:
Theory and Late Plays

GENERAL INTRODUCTION

Bertolt Brecht (1896–1956) was a highly influential German playwright, poet and theorist of political theatre. His major early success was the *Threepenny Opera* (1928), at which time he began to develop his conception of an anti-illusionist 'epic' theatre and its allied 'alienation effects' under the combined influence of Marxist theory, Soviet art, Noh theatre, music hall, cabaret and early cinema. His best-known plays, including *Galileo*, *The Caucasian Chalk Circle* and *Mother Courage*, belong to the period of the late 1930s and 1940s during which time he lived and worked in Scandinavia and Hollywood. He returned to East Berlin in 1947, there to become creator and director of the celebrated Berliner Ensemble.

Most criticism of Brecht has concentrated on his work in the theatre (rather than his poetry, for example) and has had at some point to address his explicitly Marxist beliefs and his political theory of acting and of the theatre's social function. In one response (notably in Martin Esslin's much reprinted *Brecht: A Choice of Evils*, 1959), it is thought that Brecht's political convictions hampered and impaired his dramatic art and that the second is at its best when it transcends the first. This was, in fact, the dominant approach in the immediately post-war period to the modernist canon and the politics – whether of the Left or Right – of such writers as Eliot, Yeats and Ezra Pound as well as Brecht. The attempt to separate art and political conviction is now more readily seen as itself an example of a particular critical ideology; one that is profoundly at odds with Brecht's own declared position. This does not disqualify such critics from commenting on or judging Brecht's work, of course, but it does suggest that the terms of the discussion of his work will be not only aesthetic but in different ways 'committed' on all sides.

With one exception, the critics grouped below were all (at least at the time of the selected essay by Roland Barthes) 'Marxist' critics. It might, therefore, be thought that they were equally sympathetic to Brecht and viewed the relation of his art and beliefs in a similar way. As these essays show, however, this was plainly not the case.

In addition, readers will notice that, unlike most other exercises in this volume, this set of essays does not focus on a single common text. Though they refer to particular play-texts and performances, they tend to present these in terms of the more general issues raised by Brecht's work: the question of art's autonomy and political function, for example, or the relevance of artistic theory and form, ideas of character and consciousness, or the role of the spectator. This is partly because Brecht's work itself directly raises these more theoretical and political questions, and partly an expression of the broad interests characterizing Marxist criticism – or, more specifically, the examples of European Marxism represented here, for whom Brecht remained a continuing point of reference. In effect, this selection provides an introduction to a range of work in this tradition and will, we hope, give the student some material evidence both of Marxism's shared assumptions and its internal differences.

The most recent controversy concerning Brecht's work has been introduced not from within Marxist criticism, nor by a supposed 'non-political' criticism, but through the influence of feminism, here represented by selections from John Fuegi's study of Brecht's use of the work of women collaborators. This raises many fresh questions, amongst them a question about Marxism itself and what, for all its internal debates, it has traditionally failed to discuss. Taking the essays together – ranging in date from the 1930s to the 1990s – we see how notions of political art, and the agenda for a political criticism, have changed over time; and how therefore not only Brecht in this instance, but criticism too, needs to be understood as occurring in history and ideology.

For further discussion and reading of Marxist literary theory, see *A Reader's Guide* 3/e, Ch. 4. For further reading on Brecht, see the following:

Ernst Bloch *et al.*, *Aesthetics and Politics* (New Left Books/Verso, 1977).

Peter Brooker, *Bertolt Brecht. Dialectics, Poetry, Politics* (Croom Helm, 1988).

Stephen Heath, 'Lessons from Brecht', in Francis Mulhern, ed., *Contemporary Marxist Literary Criticism* (Longman, 1992).

Peter Thomson and Glendyr Sacks, eds, *The Cambridge Companion to Brecht* (Cambridge University Press, 1994).

John Willett, trans. and ed., *Brecht on Theatre* (Methuen, 1964).

Elizabeth Wright, *Postmodern Brecht. A Re-Presentation* (Routledge, 1989).

8.1   WALTER BENJAMIN: FROM *UNDERSTANDING BRECHT* (1938, 1966, TRANS. 1973)

Walter Benjamin (1892–1940) is one of the most enigmatic and original thinkers in the Marxist tradition, combining the influences of Adorno and the Frankfurt school with those of Brecht, Kafka and the Kabbala. He met Brecht in the late 1920s and often visited him in the 1930s during the period of Brecht's exile in Svenborg, Denmark. He committed suicide in September 1940 when confronted by the Gestapo while attempting to make his way from France to Spain and thence to the United States. In addition to his essays on Brecht, Benjamin's key works in translation are *Illuminations* (1970), *Charles Baudelaire, A Lyric Poet in the Era of High Capitalism* (1973) and *The Origin of German Tragic Drama* (1977).

The commentaries below represent Benjamin's exposition of Brecht's epic theatre – a topic he returned to and revised in other essays – and his reflections on a specific play, the cycle usually translated as *Fear and Misery in the Third Reich*, a selection of which Benjamin saw premiered in Paris in May 1938. As these pieces show, Benjamin was a champion of Brecht's revolutionary aesthetic. In his view, Brecht presented the model for a new relation of art and modern technology in a fast-changing capitalist economy and a period of fascist hegemony in Europe. Hence his stress on the fragmentary and transitory, and on Brecht's introduction of the *Verfremdungseffekt* (the 'alienation device') whose critical force gave hope in a time of oppression. At the same time, Benjamin clearly wrote as Brecht's contemporary, companion and ally. Does this personal association and the historical occasion of the essays mean that his response reads now as a limited one, confined to the particular circumstances of the 1930s? Does what he says have an application to the role of art in later or present-day societies?

The following two selections (the first from a manuscript unpublished in Benjamin's lifetime, the second published in June 1938) appear with other of Benjamin's essays on Brecht, including the important 'The Author as Producer', in *Understanding Brecht* (1966, trans. Anna Bostock, introduction by Stanley Mitchell, New Left Books/Verso, 1973), pp. 23–5, 37–41.

Understanding Brecht

Studies for a Theory of Epic Theatre
Epic theatre is gestural. Strictly speaking, the gesture is the material and epic theatre its practical utilization. If we accept this then two questions come to hand. First, from where does epic theatre obtain its gestures? Second, what do we understand by the 'utilization' of gestures? The third question which would then follow is: What methods does the epic theatre use in its treatment and critique of gestures?

In answer to the first question: the gestures are found in reality. More precisely – and this is an important fact very closely related to the nature of theatre – they are found only in the reality of today. Suppose that someone writes a historical play: we maintain that he will succeed in his task only to the extent that he is able to coordinate past events, in a meaningful and intelligible way, with gestures a man might make today. From this stipulation certain insights into the possibilities and limitations of historical drama might follow. In the first place, imitated gestures are worthless unless the point to be made is, precisely, the gestural process of imitation. Also, the gesture of, say, a pope as he crowns Charlemagne, or of Charlemagne as he receives the crown, can no longer occur today except as imitation. Hence the raw material of epic theatre is exclusively the gesture as it occurs today – the gesture either of an action or of the imitation of an action.

In answer to the second question: the gesture has two advantages over the highly deceptive statements and assertions normally made by people, and over their many-layered and opaque actions. First, the gesture is falsifiable only up to a point; and the more inconspicuous it is, the more habitually it is repeated, the more difficult it is to falsify. Secondly, unlike people's actions and endeavours, it has a definable beginning and a definable end. Indeed, this strict, frame-like, enclosed nature of each moment of an attitude which, after all, is as a whole in a state of living flux, is one of the basic dialectical characteristics of the gesture. This leads to an important conclusion: the more frequently we interrupt someone engaged in an action, the more gestures we obtain. Hence, the interrupting of action is one of the principal concerns of epic theatre. It is here that the importance of the songs for the 'economy' of the drama as a whole resides. Without anticipating the difficult study, yet to be made, of the function of the text in epic theatre, we can at least say that often its main function is not to illustrate or advance the action but, on the contrary, to interrupt it: not only the action of others, but also one's own. Incidentally, it is the retarding quality of these interruptions and the episodic quality of this framing of action which allow gestural theatre to become epic theatre.

A possible subject for further discussion might be the way in which the raw material (the gesture) thus prepared is processed on the stage. Action and text serve here as nothing more than variable elements in an experiment. But where does the result of the experiment point?

The answer to the second question, put in this way, cannot be separated from the problem of the third: what are the methods used in processing gestures?[1] These questions reveal the true dialectic of epic theatre. We shall only point here to a few of its basic concepts. For a start, the following relationships are dialectical: that of the gesture to the situation, and *vice versa*; that of the actor to the character represented, and *vice versa*; that of the attitude of the actor, as determined by the authority of the text, to the critical attitude of the audience, and *vice versa*; that of the specific action represented to the action implied in any theatrical representation. This list is sufficient to show that all the dialectical moments are subordinated here to the supreme dialectic – now rediscovered after being forgotten for a long time – namely, the dialectic between recognition and education. All the recognitions achieved by epic theatre have a directly educative effect; at the same time, the educative effect of epic theatre is immediately translated into recognitions – though the specific recognitions of actors and audience may well be different from one another.

The Country Where it is Forbidden to Mention the Proletariat[2]

Only political drama can be the proper concern of theatre in emigration. Most of the plays which attracted a political audience ten or fifteen years ago have since been overtaken by events. The theatre of emigration must start again at the beginning; not just its stage, but also its plays must be built anew.

It was a sense of this historical situation which united the audience at the Paris première of parts of a new drama cycle by Brecht. The audience was recognizing itself for the first time as a dramatic audience. Taking account of this new audience and this new situation of the theatre, Brecht introduces a new dramatic form. He is an expert in fresh starts. In the years between 1920 and 1930 he never tired of testing his dramas against the example of contemporary history. In doing so he tried out numerous forms of theatre and the most varied types of public. He worked for the theatre of the public platform as well as for opera; he exhibited his products before the proletariat of Berlin as well as the bourgeois avant-garde of the West.

Thus, like no one else, Brecht started at the beginning again and again. And this, incidentally, is the distinguishing mark of the dialectician. (There is a dialectician hidden in every master of an art.) Make certain, says Gide, that the impetus you have once achieved never benefits your subsequent work. Brecht has proceeded in accordance with this maxim – and particularly in the new plays intended for the theatre of emigration.

To sum up briefly: the 'attempts' (*Versuche*) of the earlier years yielded, in the end, a distinct and well-founded standard of Brechtian theatre. It described itself as epic, and, by this description, set itself up in opposition to the dramatic theatre whose theory was first formulated by Aristotle. That is why Brecht introduced his theory as 'non-Aristotelian', just as Riemann once introduced a 'non-Euclidean' geometry. Riemann rejected the axiom of parallels; what was rejected in this new drama was the Aristotelian 'catharsis', the purging of the emotions through identification with the hero's turbulent destiny: a destiny made turbulent by the movement of a wave which sweeps the audience along with it. (The famous *peripeteia* is the crest of the wave which, breaking, rolls forward to the end.)

Epic theatre, by contrast, advances by fits and starts, like the images on a film strip. Its basic form is that of the forceful impact on one another of separate, distinct situations in the play. The songs, the captions included in the stage decor, the gestural conventions of the actors, serve to separate each situation. Thus distances are created everywhere which are, on the whole, detrimental to illusion among the audience. These distances are meant to make the audience adopt a critical attitude, to make it think. (In a similar way the French classical stage made room among its actors for persons of high rank, whose arm-chairs were placed upon the open stage.)

Epic theatre overthrew certain crucial positions of bourgeois theatre by productions which were superior in method and precision to productions of the bourgeois theatre. But the victories it won were *ad hoc* ones. The epic stage was not yet so firmly established, and the circle of those trained to act upon it not yet so large, that it could be built up anew in emigration. Recognition of this fact lies at the root of Brecht's new work.

Terror and Misery of the Third Reich is a cycle formed of twenty-seven one-act plays constructed according to the precepts of traditional dramaturgy. Sometimes the dramatic element blazes out like a magnesium flare at the end of an apparently idyllic development. (Those who come in at the kitchen door are the Winter Aid[3] people with a sack of potatoes for the little household; those who walk out are storm troopers leading between them the daughter of the family, whom they have arrested.) Other parts of the cycle have fully developed dramatic plots (e.g. in *The Chalk Cross* a worker tricks a storm-trooper into revealing one of the methods which the Gestapo's accomplices use in fighting the underground). Sometimes it is the tension of a contradiction in social relations which, almost without transposition, is revealed dramatically on the stage. (Two prisoners taking exercise in the prison-yard under the eyes of the warder whisper among themselves; both are bakers; one is in gaol because he did not put any bran in his bread, the other was arrested a year later because he did.)

These and other plays were performed for the first time in S.Th. Dudow's well thought-out production on 21 May 1938 before an audience which followed them with passionate interest. At last, after five years of exile, the special political experience which unites this public found expression on a theatre stage. Steffi Spira, Hans Altmann, Günter Ruschin, Erich Schoenlank, actors who until then had not always been able to release their full potential when performing in individual numbers in political cabaret, now succeeded in playing off their talents against one another, and they showed to what good use they had put the experience which most of them had acquired nine months earlier in Brecht's *Señora Carrar's Rifles*.

Helene Weigel did justice to the tradition which, in spite of everything, has survived from Brecht's earlier work in this new kind of theatre. She maintained the kind of European authority established in the earlier Brechtian theatre. We would have given a great deal to see her in the last play of the cycle, *Referendum*, in which, as a proletarian woman (a part reminiscent of her unforgettable role in *The Mother*), she embodies the spirit of the underground struggle in times of persecution.

The cycle represents for the theatre of German emigration a political and artistic opportunity which palpably demonstrates, for the first time, the necessity for that theatre. The two elements, political and artistic, here merge into one. It is easy to see that to play a storm-trooper or a member of the 'people's courts' is a very different task for a refugee actor than it is, say, for a good-hearted actor to play Iago. For the former, empathy is no more suitable than it would be for a political fighter to identify himself with his comrades' murderer. A different mode of acting – the epic mode, to be plain – may find a new justification here and achieve a new kind of success.

The cycle – and here again its epic quality is apparent, though in a different form – can appeal to a reading public as much as to theatre audiences. As long as the conditions which Brecht depicts upon the stage prevail, it is unlikely that the means will be available for producing more than a fairly limited selection from the cycle.

Such a selection is open to critical objections, and this goes for the Paris production. Not all the spectators were able to grasp what a reader would recognize as the determining thesis of all these short plays. The thesis can be summed up in a sentence from Kafka's prophetic *Trial*: 'The lie is transformed into a world order.'

Each of these short plays demonstrates one thing: how ineluctably the rule of terror which parades before the nations as the Third Reich makes all relationships between human beings subject to the law of the lie. A declaration under oath before a court of law is a lie (*Legal Finding*); a science whose teachings may not be applied in practice is a lie (*Occupational Disease*); what is shouted from the rooftops is a lie (*Referendum*) and what is whispered in a dying man's ears is still a lie (*The Sermon on the Mount*). A lie is brutally injected into what husband and wife have to say to one another in the last instants of their life together (*The Jewish Wife*); a lie is the mask which pity herself puts on when she still dares to give a sign of life (*In the Service of the People*). We are in the country where the name of the proletariat may not be mentioned. Brecht shows us how things have come to such a pass in that country that a peasant cannot even any longer feed his beasts without endangering 'state security' (*The Farmer Feeds his Sow*).

The truth, which will one day consume this State and its order like a purifying fire, is today only a feeble spark. It is fanned by the worker who, in front of the microphone, shows up for the lies that they are the words he is being forced to speak; it is kept alive by the silence of those who cannot, except with the greatest circumspection, meet their comrade who has suffered martyrdom; whilst the referendum leaflet whose entire text is 'NO' is nothing other than that tiny glowing spark itself.

It is to be hoped that the cycle will soon be available in book form. For the stage it offers an entire repertoire. For the reader it is a drama such as Kraus created in his *Last Days* of *Mankind*. It is only this kind of drama which can perhaps contain the still glowing reality of the present moment and carry it down to posterity like a testament of iron.

Notes (renumbered)
1. In the original typescript, the following passage appears in manuscript in the margin adjoining this paragraph: 'The gesture demonstrates the social significance and applicability of dialectics. It tests relations on men. The production difficulties which the producer meets while rehearsing the play cannot – even if they originate in the search for "effect" – be separated any longer from concrete insights into the life of society.'
2. On the world première of eight one-act plays by Brecht.
3. *Winterhilfe*: a spurious charity campaign mounted by the Nazi Party to ingratiate itself with the workers (Translator's note).

8.2   GEORG LUKÁCS: FROM *THE MEANING OF CONTEMPORARY REALISM* (1963)

Georg Lukács (1885–1971) was a Hungarian-born Marxist critic and a continuing influence on the Marxist tradition, as is evident in the work of figures such as Lucien Goldmann, Raymond Williams and Fredric Jameson. He is best known for his defence of 'critical realism' (of which the leading examples were Balzac and Thomas Mann) and his attack on the subjectivism and decadence of expressionism and modernist literary forms in general. His most sustained critique of modernism appears in *The Meaning of Contemporary Realism*. Other works include *The Theory of the Novel* (1916, 1971), *History and Class Consciousness* (1923, 1971), and *The Historical Novel* (1947, 1962).

Lukács and Brecht engaged in a debate on the issues of realism and popular art in the 1930s in what has become a major reference point in Marxist aesthetics. Brecht's position is set out in his essay, 'The Popular and the Realistic' (1938, reprinted in John Willett, ed., *Brecht on Theatre*, Hill & Wang; Eyre Methuen, 1964). Relevant essays by both Brecht and Lukács, with some useful background discussion, can also be found in the volume *Aesthetics and Politics* (Verso, 1977).

In the following extract, as will be seen, Lukács praises the realism of certain of Brecht's plays. However, Brecht's own essays (see Willett, above) make it clear that he viewed realism and political art in different terms. What are Lukács's criteria? Is he mistaken in not adhering to Brecht's own ideas?

Lukács's comments should be compared not only with Brecht's own, however, but with those of other critics presented here. Consider his views on the role of theory and the 'alienation effect' with the commentary by Barthes and Althusser, and on character and the 'humanist realism' of the late plays with the discussion by John Fuegi.

The following extract is from *The Meaning of Contemporary Realism* (Merlin, 1963), pp. 87–9.

The Meaning of Contemporary Realism

In Brecht's development, [...] traditional realism played an important role. I have no space here to examine Brecht's work at length. We must begin with Brecht's middle period, the period of his turning towards communism, of *The Measures Taken* and of his adaptation of Gorky's *Mother*. Brecht's political didacticism, his attempt to impose intellectual schemata on the spectator, turned his characters into mere spokesmen. He based his new aesthetic on a contempt for cheap theatrical emotionalism. The full blast of his hatred was directed towards the 'culinary' aspects of the contemporary bourgeois theatre. And he seized on the theory of *Einfühlung* as the source of much of the bad art of the time. Now there is no doubt that Brecht, despite his exaggerations, was right to reject this particular theory. But he made the then not uncommon mistake – implicit in Wilhelm Worringer's original formulation of the theory – of assuming that *Einfühlung* was fundamental to traditional aesthetics. The boss's secretary may 'identify', through *Einfühlung*, with her opposite number on the screen; and the young man about town may identify with, say, Schnitzler's *Anatol*. But no one surely has ever, in this sense, 'identified' with Antigone or King Lear. The truth is, Brecht's dramatic theories were the product of an – at the time, quite justified – local polemic. Brecht's actual dramatic practice changed radically after the rise to power of Hitler, during his long years of exile. But he never subjected his theories to revision. I have no space to investigate the problem in detail. But two poems, written during that exile, may serve to indicate the changes I have in mind:

> A wooden Japanese mask hangs on my wall
> The mask of an angry demon, covered with gold.
> With fellow-feeling I see
> The swollen veins in the forehead, showing
> What a strenuous business it is to be angry.

Or these lines from the marvellous poem *To Posterity*:

> Yet we know too well,
> Hatred of evil
> Can distort the features,
> Rage at injustice
> Make the voice hoarse. Alas, we
> Who wished to make room for friendliness
> Could not ourselves be friendly.

We see here how ethical preoccupations, a concern for the inner life and motivation of his characters, began to loom larger in Brecht's mind. Not that his central political and social preoccupations were displaced. On the contrary, the effect of this change was to give them greater depth, range and intensity. And even the greatest admirers of Brecht's dramaturgy must admit that many plays of this period – *The Rifles of Señora Carrar* or *The Life of Galileo* – evidence a partial return to despised Aristotelean aesthetics. Be that as it may, let us briefly turn our attention to those plays – *Mother Courage, The Caucasian Chalk Circle, The Good Woman of Setzuan* – which do not thus return to traditional norms. These plays are indeed *Lehrstücke*, products of epic theatre; the anti-Aristotelean intention, the calculated use of alienation-effects, is undeniable. But if we compare these plays with, say, *The Measures Taken* we see that the over-simplified schema of that play has given way to a complex dialectic of good and evil. Problems of society have become problems of humanity, subsuming the inner conflicts and contradictions of the warring parties. Where Brecht's characters had once been spokesmen for political points of view, they are now multi-dimensional. They are living human beings, wrestling with conscience and with the world around them. Allegory has acquired flesh and blood; it has been transformed into a true dramatic typology. Alienation-effect ceases to be the instrument of an artificial, abstract didacticism; it makes possible literary achievement of the highest order. All great drama, after all, must find means to transcend the limited awareness of the characters presented on the stage. It must express the general philosophical theme, represented in concrete terms by the action, in adequate poetic form (this is the function of the chorus in Aeschylus and Sophocles, and of the monologue in *Hamlet*, *Othello*, and *Lear*). It is this aspect that predominates in the later Brecht, a direct consequence of his new concern for ethical complexity, of his search for a multi-dimensional typology. That Brecht clung to his earlier theories should not conceal from us this fundamental change. Even the scenic structure of Brecht's plays begins to approximate to the Shakespearean model. The break with the '*milieu*-theatre', with the 'atmospheric' ambience of the older stage, is really a break with naturalism. It is a return to a dramaturgy aiming both at a typology that displays the full range of human complexity and at the creation of living human beings grappling with the forces of their environment. The mature Brecht, by overcoming his earlier, one-sided theories, had evolved into the greatest realistic playwright of his age. And the most influential, too, for good and for bad. Indeed, Brecht's influence shows once again how misleading it is to argue from the theory to the work and not from the work, its structure and intellectual content, to the theory. For Brecht's theories lead both to the pretentious, empty experimentalism of Ionesco and to topical, realistic drama like Dürrenmatt's *The Visit*. The confusion to which this gave rise – the result of a formalistic over-emphasis on one element abstracted from literature – is still remarkably widespread and influential (that Brecht was a socialist writer, both in personal ideology and literary practice, in no way contradicts what I have said here. His influence has been, and is, chiefly effective in the struggle between critical realism and modernist anti-realism).

8.3   THEODOR ADORNO: FROM 'COMMITMENT' (1965)

Theodor Wiesengrund Adorno (1903–69) was a distinguished philosopher and leading member of the Institute for Social Research (the 'Frankfurt school'), established at the University of Frankfurt in the 1930s and subsequently in New York before its return to Frankfurt in 1950. He is known above all for his critique of Enlightenment rationalism (in *The Dialectic of Enlightenment*, 1972, with Max Horkheimer), which he saw as complicit in the creation of the 'administered' societies of late capitalism; for his denunciation of the standardizing banalities of mass culture (an argument advanced in the much reprinted chapter, 'The Culture Industry: Enlightenment as Mass Deception', in the above volume); and as a champion of the necessary difficulty and autonomy of modern art. The fullest exposition of this view appears in *Aesthetic Theory* (1984), but also informs additional, individual essays on Kakfa, Proust and Beckett (available in the volumes *Prisms*, 1967, and *Notes to Literature*, 1958, trans. Sherry Weber Nicholson, ed. Rolf Tiedemann, Columbia University Press, 1991) as well as the comments below on Brecht.

In the following selection, Adorno challenges many of the common assumptions regarding committed art. Brecht would appear to be an obvious, even model type of the committed artist for a Marxist philosopher and defender – as Adorno was – of literary modernism. However, Adorno finds Brecht's works simplistic and reductive, and thus an easily assimilable caricature of the real social relations under capitalism and the true horrors of recent history. He disagrees profoundly, therefore, with his associate Walter Benjamin and with Barthes and Althusser on Brecht. This is less a matter of different interpretations of particular texts than of their ideas on the relation of (in particular Brecht's) theory to artistic practice (on which Adorno appears to agree with Lukács) and of their different conceptions of the nature, social function and effectivity of art.

It is therefore to Adorno's conception of art in this essay that we should pay particular attention. He refers here to 'art for art's sake', to propaganda and 'tendency' literature, as well as to committed and 'autonomous' art. In what terms does he distinguish between these? And what of the further distinction he indicates between types of committed art: between Brecht and Sartre, for example, and another type, invoked by statements such as 'committed art in the proper sense', 'the office of art', 'the ideal of the committed work of art' (pp. 352, 359 below)? What does he mean by this type of art, what idea of artistic form and function does it imply, and who are his examples? Is this argument, and the implications it has for his judgement of Brecht, a convincing one?

The essay raises a number of other broad, and equally contentious, issues: on the relation, for example, not so much of art to politics but of art to 'bad' politics ('bad politics becomes bad art', Adorno writes, p. 356). Do you agree? Can there be or has there been a 'great' fascist or sexist work of art? (Consider this question in relation to Fuegi's verdict on Brecht's conduct below.) Secondly, Adorno questions not only the role but the very possibility of an ethical art in a bad society. We might turn this around to ask what it is in contemporary society which leads Adorno to this conclusion and thus to his judgements on Brecht, Sartre, Picasso, Kafka and Beckett. Does the social and political analysis underlying his views have to result in this particular aesthetic theory?

The essay 'Commitment' was published as 'Engagement' in *Noten zur Literatur III* (Suhrkamp Verlag, 1965) and in translation by Francis McDonagh in the collection *Aesthetics and Politics* (New Left Books/Verso, 1977), pp. 177–95. The following is taken from this translation. Several minor cuts have been made, where Adorno introduces supporting philosophical or artistic references. More substantial cuts, often of his discussion of J.-P. Sartre, are indicated in the text.

Commitment

Since Sartre's essay *What is Literature*? there has been less theoretical debate about committed and autonomous literature. Nevertheless, the controversy over commitment remains urgent, so far as anything that merely concerns the life of the mind can be today, as opposed to sheer human survival. Sartre was moved to issue his manifesto because he saw – and he was certainly not the first to do so – works of art displayed side by side in a pantheon of optional edification, decaying into cultural commodities. In such coexistence, they desecrate each other. If a work, without its author necessarily intending it, aims at a supreme effect, it cannot really tolerate a neighbour beside it. This salutary intolerance holds not only for individual works, but also for aesthetic genres or attitudes such as those once symbolized in the now half-forgotten controversy over commitment.

There are two 'positions on objectivity' which are constantly at war with one another, even when intellectual life falsely presents them as at peace. A work of art that is committed strips the magic from a work of art that is content to be a fetish, an idle pastime for those who would like to sleep through the deluge that threatens them, in an apoliticism that is in fact deeply political. For the committed, such works are a distraction from the battle of real interests, in which no one is any longer exempt from the conflict between the two great blocs. The possibility of intellectual life itself depends on this conflict to such an extent that only blind illusion can insist on rights that may be shattered tomorrow. For autonomous works of art, however, such considerations, and the conception of art which underlies them, are themselves the spiritual catastrophe of which the committed keep warning. Once the life of the mind renounces the duty and liberty of its own pure objectification, it has abdicated. Thereafter, works of art merely assimilate themselves to the brute existence against which they protest, in forms so ephemeral (the very charge made against autonomous works by committed writers) that from their first day they belong to the seminars in which they inevitably end. The menacing thrust of the antithesis is a reminder of how precarious the position of art is today. Each of the two alternatives negates itself with the other. Committed art, necessarily detached as art from reality, cancels the distance between the two. 'Art for art's sake' denies by its absolute claims that ineradicable connection with reality which is the polemical *a priori* of the attempt to make art autonomous from the real. Between these two poles the tension in which art has lived in every age till now is dissolved.

Contemporary literature itself suggests doubts as to the omnipotence of these alternatives. For it is not yet so completely subjugated to the course of the world as to constitute rival fronts. The Sartrean goats and the Valéryan sheep will not be separated. Even if politically motivated, commitment in itself remains politically polyvalent so long as it is not reduced to propaganda, whose pliancy mocks any commitment by the subject. On the other hand, its opposite, known in Russian catechisms as formalism, is not decried only by Soviet officials or libertarian existentialists; even 'vanguard' critics themselves frequently accuse so-called abstract texts of a lack of provocation and social aggressivity. Conversely, Sartre cannot praise Picasso's *Guernica* too highly; yet he could hardly be convicted of formalist sympathies in music or painting. He restricts his notion of commitment to literature because of its conceptual character: 'The writer deals with meanings'.[1] Of course, but not only with them. If no word which enters a literary work ever wholly frees itself from its meaning in ordinary speech, so no literary work, not even the traditional novel, leaves these meanings unaltered, as they were outside it. Even an ordinary 'was', in a report of something that was not, acquires a new formal quality from the fact that it was not so. The same process occurs in the higher levels of meaning of a work, all the way up to what once used to be called its 'Idea'.

[...]

Adorno comments here on Sartre. The demand for a relevant 'content' or for 'literary realism', says Adorno, is as much a conservative as a progressive criterion and likely to reinforce artistic conformism.

[...]

In aesthetic theory, 'commitment' should be distinguished from 'tendency'. Committed art in the proper sense is not intended to generate ameliorative measures, legislative acts or practical institutions – like earlier propagandist plays against syphilis, duels, abortion laws or borstals – but to work at the level of fundamental attitudes. For Sartre its task is to awaken the free choice of the agent which makes authentic existence possible at all, as opposed to the neutrality of the spectator. But what gives commitment its aesthetic advantage over tendentiousness also renders the content to which the artist commits himself inherently ambiguous. In Sartre the notion of choice – originally a Kierkegaardian category – is heir to the Christian doctrine 'He who is not with me is against me', but now voided of any concrete theological content. What remains is merely the abstract authority of a choice enjoined, with no regard for the fact that the very possibility of choosing depends on what can be chosen. [...] his plays are nevertheless bad models of his own existentialism, because they display in their respect for truth the whole administered universe which his philosophy ignores: the lesson we learn from them is one of unfreedom. Sartre's theatre of ideas sabotages the aims of his categories. This is not a specific shortcoming of his plays. It is not the office of art to spotlight alternatives, but to resist by its form alone the course of the world, which permanently puts a pistol to men's heads. In fact, as soon as committed works of art do instigate decisions at their own level, the decisions themselves become interchangeable. Because of this ambiguity, Sartre has with great candour confessed that he expects no real changes in the world from literature – a scepticism which reflects the historical mutations both of society and of the practical function of literature since the days of Voltaire. The principle of commitment thus slides towards the proclivities of the author, in keeping with the extreme subjectivism of Sartre's philosophy, which for all its materialist undertones, still echoes German speculative idealism. In his literary theory the work of art becomes an appeal to subjects, because it is itself nothing other than a declaration by a subject of his own choice or failure to choose.

[...]

Adorno comments further on Sartre. Sartre's emphasis on an author's intention is invalid, he says. Motivation is 'irrelevant to the finished work, the literary product'. Ignoring the demands of formal composition, 'The content of his art becomes philosophy'.

[...]

Brecht, in some of his plays, such as the dramatization of Gorky's *The Mother* or *The Measures Taken*, bluntly glorifies the Party. But at times, at least according to his theoretical writings, he too wanted to educate spectators to a new attitude that would be distanced, thoughtful, experimental, the reverse of illusory empathy and identification. In tendency to abstraction, his plays after *Saint Joan* trump those of Sartre. The difference is that Brecht, more consistent than Sartre and a greater artist, made this abstraction into the formal principle of his art, as a didactic poetics that eliminates the traditional concept of dramatic character altogether. He realized that the surface of social life, the sphere of consumption, which includes the psychologically motivated actions of individuals, conceals the essence of society – which, as the law of exchange, is itself abstract. Brecht rejected aesthetic individuation as an ideology. He therefore sought to translate the true hideousness of society into theatrical appearance, by dragging it straight out of its camouflage. The people on his stage shrink before our eyes into the agents of social processes and functions, which indirectly and unknowingly they are in empirical reality. Brecht no longer postulates, like Sartre, an identity between living individuals and the essence of society, let alone any absolute sovereignty of the subject. Nevertheless, the process of aesthetic reduction that he pursues for the sake of political truth, in fact gets in its way. For this truth involves innumerable mediations, which Brecht disdains. What is artistically legitimate as alienating infantilism – Brecht s first plays came from the same milieu as Dada – becomes merely infantile when it starts to claim theoretical or social validity. Brecht wanted to reveal in images the inner nature of capitalism. In this sense his aim was indeed what he disguised it as against Stalinist terror – realistic. He would have refused to deprive social essence of meaning by taking it as it appeared, imageless and blind, in a single crippled life. But this burdened him with the obligation of ensuring that what he intended to make unequivocally clear was theoretically correct. His art, however, refused to accept this *quid pro quo*: it both presents itself as didactic, and claims aesthetic dispensation from responsibility for the accuracy of what it teaches.

Criticism of Brecht cannot overlook the fact that he did not – for objective reasons beyond the power of his own creations – fulfil the norm he set himself as if it were a means to salvation. *Saint Joan* was the central work of his dialectical theatre. (*The*

Good Woman of Szechuan is a variation of it in reverse: where Joan assists evil by the immediacy of her goodness, Shen Te, who wills the good, must become evil). The play is set in a Chicago half-way between the Wild West fables of *Mahagonny* and economic facts. But the more preoccupied Brecht becomes with information, and the less he looks for images, the more he misses the essence of capitalism which the parable is supposed to present. Mere episodes in the sphere of circulation, in which competitors maul each other, are recounted instead of the appropriation of surplus-value in the sphere of production, compared with which the brawls of cattle dealers over their shares of the booty are epiphenomena incapable of provoking any great crisis. Moreover, the economic transactions presented as the machinations of rapacious traders are not merely puerile, which is how Brecht seems to have meant them; they are also unintelligible by the criteria of even the most primitive economic logic. The obverse of the latter is a political naiveté which could only make Brecht's opponents grin at the thought of such an ingenuous enemy. They could be as comfortable with Brecht as they are with the dying Joan in the impressive final scene of the play. Even with the broadest-minded allowance for poetic licence, the idea that a strike leadership backed by the Party could entrust a crucial task to a non-member is as inconceivable as the subsequent idea that the failure of that individual could ruin the whole strike.

Brecht's comedy of the resistible rise of the great dictator *Arturo Ui* exposes the subjective nullity and pretence of a fascist leader in a harsh and accurate light. However, the deconstruction of leaders, as with all individuals in Brecht, is extended into a reconstruction of the social and economic nexus in which the dictator acts. Instead of a conspiracy of the wealthy and powerful, we are given a trivial gangster organization, the cabbage trust. The true horror of fascism is conjured away; it is no longer a slow end-product of the concentration of social power, but mere hazard, like an accident or a crime. This conclusion is dictated by the exigencies of agitation: adversaries must be diminished. The consequence is bad politics, in literature as in practice before 1933. Against every dialectic, the ridicule to which Ui is consigned renders innocuous the fascism that was accurately predicted by Jack London decades before. The anti-ideological artist thus prepared the degradation of his own ideas into ideology. Tacit acceptance of the claim that one half of the world no longer contains antagonisms is supplemented by jests at everything that belies the official theodicy of the other half. It is not that respect for historical scale forbids laughter at house-painters, although the use of that term against Hitler was itself a painful exploitation of bourgeois class-consciousness. The group which engineered the seizure of power in Germany was also certainly a gang. But the problem is that such elective affinities are not extra-territorial: they are rooted within society itself. That is why the buffoonery of fascism, evoked by Chaplin as well, was at the same time also its ultimate horror. If this is suppressed, and a few sorry exploiters of greengrocers are mocked, where key positions of economic power are actually at issue, the attack misfires. *The Great Dictator* loses all satirical force and becomes obscene when a Jewish girl can hit a line of storm-troopers on the head with a pan without being torn to pieces. For the sake of political commitment, political reality is trivialized: which then reduces the political effect.

Sartre's frank doubt whether *Guernica* 'won a single supporter for the Spanish cause' certainly also applies to Brecht's didactic drama. Scarcely anyone needs to be taught the *fabula docet* to be extracted from it – that there is injustice in the world; while the moral itself shows few traces of the dialectical theory to which Brecht gave cursory allegiance. The trappings of epic drama recall the American phrase 'preaching to the converted'. The primacy of lesson over pure form, which Brecht intended to achieve, became a formal device itself. [...] The substance of Brecht's artistic work was the didactic play as an artistic principle. His method, to make immediately apparent events into phenomena alien to the spectator, was also a medium of formal construction rather than a contribution to practical efficacy. It is true that Brecht never spoke as sceptically as Sartre about the social effects of art. But, as an astute and experienced man of the world, he can scarcely have been wholly convinced of them. He once calmly wrote that, to be honest, the theatre was more important to him than any changes in the world it might promote. Yet the artistic principle of simplification not only purged politics of the illusory distinctions projected by subjective reflection into social objectivity, as Brecht intended, but it also falsified the very objectivity which didactic drama laboured to distil. If we take Brecht at his word and make politics the criterion by which to judge his committed theatre, then politics proves his theatre untrue. [...]

Contemporary literary Germany is anxious to distinguish Brecht the artist from Brecht the politician. The major writer must be saved for the West, if possible placed on a pedestal as an All-German poet, and so neutralized *au-dessus de la mêlée*. There is truth in this to the extent that both Brecht's artistic force, and his devious and uncontrollable intelligence, went well beyond the official credos and prescribed aesthetics of the People's Democracies. All the same, Brecht must be defended against this defence of him. His work, with its often patent weaknesses, would not have had such power, if it were not saturated with politics. Even its most question-able creations, such as *The Measures Taken*, generate an immediate awareness that issues of the utmost seriousness are at stake. To this extent Brecht's claim that he used his theatre to make men think was justified. It is futile to try to separate the beauties, real or imaginary, of his works from their political intentions. The task of immanent criticism, which alone is dialectical, is rather to synthesize assessment of the validity of his forms with that of his politics. Sartre's chapter 'Why write?' contains the undeniable statement that: 'Nobody can suppose for a moment that it is possible to write a good novel in praise of anti-semitism'.[2] Nor could one be written in praise of the Moscow Trials, even if such praise were bestowed before Stalin actually had Zinoviev and Bukharin murdered.[3] The political falsehood stains the aesthetic form. Where Brecht distorts the real social problems discussed in his epic drama in order to prove a thesis, the whole structure and foundation of the play itself crumbles. *Mother Courage* is an illustrated primer intended to reduce to absurdity Montecuccoli's dictum that war feeds on war. The camp follower who uses the Thirty Years' War to make a life for her children thereby becomes responsible for their ruin. But in the play this responsibility follows rigorously neither from the fact of the war itself nor from the individual behaviour of the petty profiteer; if Mother

Courage had not been absent at the critical moment, the disaster would not have happened, and the fact that she has to be absent to earn some money, remains completely generic in relation to the action. The picture-book technique which Brecht needs to spell out his thesis prevents him from proving it. A socio-political analysis, of the sort Marx and Engels sketched in their criticism of Lassalle's play *Franz von Sickingen*, would show that Brecht's simplistic equation of the Thirty Years' War with a modern war excludes precisely what is crucial for the behaviour and fate of Mother Courage in Grimmelshausen's novel. Because the society of the Thirty Years' War was not the functional capitalist society of modern times, we cannot even poetically stipulate a closed functional system in which the lives and deaths of private individuals directly reveal economic laws. But Brecht needed the old lawless days as an image of his own, precisely because he saw clearly that the society of his own age could no longer be directly comprehended in terms of people and things. His attempt to reconstruct the reality of society thus led first to a false social model and then to dramatic implausibility. Bad politics becomes bad art, and vice-versa. But the less works have to proclaim what they cannot completely believe themselves, the more telling they become in their own right; and the less they need a surplus of meaning beyond what they are. For the rest, the interested parties in every camp would probably be as successful in surviving wars today as they have always been.

Aporia of this sort multiply until they affect the Brechtian tone itself, the very fibre of his poetic art. Inimitable though its qualities may be – qualities which the mature Brecht may have thought unimportant – they were poisoned by the untruth of his politics. For what he justified was not simply, as he long sincerely believed, an incomplete socialism, but a coercive domination in which blindly irrational social forces returned to work once again. When Brecht became a panegyrist of its harmony, his lyric voice had to swallow chalk, and it started to grate. Already the exaggerated adolescent virility of the young Brecht betrayed the borrowed courage of the intellectual who, in despair at violence, suddenly adopts a violent practice which he has every reason to fear. The wild roar of the *The Measures Taken* drowns out the noise of the disaster that has overtaken the cause, which Brecht convulsively tries to proclaim as salvation. Even Brecht's best work was infected by the deceptions of his commitment. Its language shows how far the underlying poetic subject and its message have moved apart. In an attempt to bridge the gap, Brecht affected the diction of the oppressed. But the doctrine he advocated needs the language of the intellectual. The homeliness and simplicity of his tone is thus a fiction. It betrays itself both by signs of exaggeration and by stylized regression to archaic or provincial forms of expression. It can often be importunate, and ears which have not let themselves be deprived of their native sensitivity cannot help hearing that they are being talked into something. It is a usurpation and almost a contempt for victims to speak like this, as if the author were one of them. All roles may be played, except that of the worker. The gravest charge against commitment is that even right intentions go wrong when they are noticed, and still more so, when they then try to conceal themselves. Something of this remains in Brecht's later plays in the linguistic *gestus* of wisdom, the fiction of the old peasant sated with epic experience as the poetic subject. No one in any country of the world is any longer capable of the earthy experience of South German muzhiks: the ponderous delivery has become a propaganda device to make us believe that the good life is where the Red Army is in control. Since there is nothing to give substance to this humanity as presented, which we have to take on trust, Brecht's tone degenerates into an echo of archaic social relations, lost beyond recall.

The late Brecht was not so distant from official humanism. A journalistically minded Westerner could well praise *The Caucasian Chalk Circle* as a hymn to motherhood, and who is not touched when the splendid girl is finally held up as an example to the querulous lady beset with migraine? Baudelaire, who dedicated his work to the coiner of the motto *l'art pour l'art*, would have been less suited to such a catharsis. Even the grandeur and virtuosity of such poems as *The Legend of the Origin of the Book of Tao Te Ch'ing on Lao-Tzu's Journey into Exile* are marred by the theatricality of total plain-spokenness. What his classical predecessors once denounced as the idiocy of rural life, Brecht, like some existential ontologist, treats as ancient truth. His whole oeuvre is a Sisyphean labour to reconcile his highly cultivated and subtle taste with the crudely heteronomous demands which he desperately imposed on himself.

I have no wish to soften the saying that to write lyric poetry after Auschwitz is barbaric; it expresses in negative form the impulse which inspires committed literature. The question asked by a character in Sartre's play *Morts Sans Sépulture*, 'Is there any meaning in life when men exist who beat people until the bones break in their bodies?', is also the question whether any art now has a right to exist; whether intellectual regression is not inherent in the concept of committed literature because of the regression of society. But Enzensberger's retort also remains true, that literature must resist this verdict, in other words, be such that its mere existence after Auschwitz is not a surrender to cynicism. Its own situation is one of paradox, not merely the problem of how to react to it. The abundance of real suffering tolerates no forgetting; Pascal's theological saying, *On ne doit plus dormir*, must be secularized. Yet this suffering, what Hegel called consciousness of adversity, also demands the continued existence of art while it prohibits it; it is now virtually in art alone that suffering can still find its own voice, consolation, without immediately being betrayed by it. The most important artists of the age have realized this. The uncompromising radicalism of their works, the very features defamed as formalism, give them a terrifying power, absent from helpless poems to the victims of our time. But even Schoenberg's *Survivor of Warsaw* remains trapped in the aporia to which, autonomous figuration of heteronomy raised to the intensity of hell, it totally surrenders. There is something embarrassing in Schoenberg's composition – not what arouses anger in Germany, the fact that it prevents people from repressing from memory what they at all costs want to repress – but the way in which, by turning suffering into images, harsh and uncompromising though they are, it wounds the shame we feel in the presence of the victims. For these victims are used to create something, works of art, that are thrown to the consumption of a world which destroyed them. The so-called artistic representation of the sheer physical pain of people beaten to the ground by rifle-butts contains, however remotely, the power to elicit enjoyment out of it. The moral of this art, not to forget for a single instant, slithers into the abyss of its opposite. The aesthetic principle of stylization, and even the solemn prayer of the chorus, make an unthinkable fate appear to have had some meaning; it is transfigured, something of its horror is removed. This alone does an injustice to the victims; yet no art which tried to evade them could confront the claims of justice. Even the sound of despair pays its tribute to a hideous affirmation. Works of less than the highest rank are also willingly absorbed as contributions to clearing up the past. When genocide becomes part of the cultural heritage in the themes of committed literature, it becomes easier to continue to play along with the culture which gave birth to murder.

There is one nearly invariable characteristic of such literature. It is that it implies, purposely or not, that even in so-called extreme situations, indeed in them most of all, humanity flourishes. [...]

Today, the adherents of a philosophy which has since degenerated into a mere ideological sport, fulminate in pre-1933 fashion against artistic distortion, deformation and perversion of life, as though authors, by faithfully reflecting atrocities, were responsible for what they revolt against. The best example of this attitude, still prevalent among the silent majority in Germany, is the following story about Picasso. An officer of the Nazi occupation forces visited the painter in his studio and, pointing to *Guernica*, asked: 'Did you do that?'. Picasso is said to have answered, 'No, you did'. Autonomous works of art too, like this painting, firmly negate empirical reality, destroy the destroyer, that which merely exists and, by merely existing, endlessly reiterates guilt. It is none other than Sartre who has seen the connection between the autonomy of a work and an intention which is not conferred upon it but is its own gesture towards reality. 'The work of art', he has written, '*does not have* an end; there we agree with Kant. But the reason is that it *is* an end. The Kantian formula does not account for the appeal which issues from every painting, every statue, every book.'[4] It only remains to add there is no straightforward relationship between this appeal and the thematic commitment of a work. The uncalculating autonomy of works which avoid popularization and adaptation to the market, involuntarily becomes an attack on them. The attack is not abstract, not a fixed attitude of all works of art to the world which will not forgive them for not bending totally to it. The distance these works maintain from empirical reality is in itself partly mediated by that reality. The imagination of the artist is not a creation *ex nihilo*; only dilettanti and aesthetes believe it to be so. Works of art that react against empirical reality obey the forces of that reality, which reject intellectual creations and throw them back on themselves. There is no material content, no formal category of artistic creation, however mysteriously transmitted and itself unaware of the process, which did not originate in the empirical reality from which it breaks free.

It is this which constitutes the true relation of art to reality, whose elements are regrouped by its formal laws. Even the *avant-garde* abstraction which provokes the indignation of philistines, and which has nothing in common with conceptual or logical abstraction, is a reflex response to the abstraction of the law which objectively dominates society. This could be shown in Beckett's works. These enjoy what is today the only form of respectable fame: everyone shudders at them, and yet no-one can persuade himself that these eccentric plays and novels are not about what everyone knows but no one will admit. Philosophical apologists may laud his works as sketches from an anthropology. But they deal with a highly concrete historical reality: the abdication of the subject. Beckett's *Ecce Homo* is what human beings have become. As though with eyes drained of tears, they stare silently out of his sentences. The spell they cast, which also binds them, is lifted by being reflected in them. However, the minimal promise of happiness they contain, which refuses to be traded for comfort, cannot be had for a price less than total dislocation, to the point of worldlessness. Here every commitment to the world must be abandoned to satisfy the ideal of the committed work of art – that polemical alienation which Brecht as a theorist invented, and as an artist practised less and less as he committed himself more firmly to the role of a friend of mankind. This paradox, which might be charged with sophistry, can be supported without much philosophy by the simplest experience: Kafka's prose and Beckett's plays, or the truly monstrous novel *The Unnameable*, have an effect by comparison with which officially committed works look like pantomines. Kafka and Beckett arouse the fear which existentialism merely talks about. By dismantling appearance, they explode from within the art which committed proclamation subjugates from without, and hence only in appearance. The inescapability of their work compels the change of attitude which committed works merely demand. He over whom Kafka's wheels have passed, has lost for ever both any peace with the world and any chance of consoling himself with the judgment that the way of the world is bad; the element of ratification which lurks in resigned admission of the dominance of evil is burnt away.

[...]

Adorno condemns the idle rejection of 'objective representation' and reflects on the ideas of commitment in French and German aesthetics. Autonomous works 'are knowledge as non-conceptual objects. ... This is why today autonomous rather than committed art should be encouraged in Germany'.

[...]

The notion of a 'message' in art, even when politically radical, already contains an accommodation to the world: the stance of the lecturer conceals a clandestine entente with the listeners, who could only be rescued from deception by refusing it.

   The type of literature that, in accordance with the tenets of commitment but also with the demands of philistine moralism, exists for man, betrays him by traducing that which could help him, if only it did not strike a pose of helping him. But any literature which therefore concludes that it can be a law unto itself, and exist only for itself, degenerates into ideology no less. Art, which even in its opposition to society remains a part of it, must close its eyes and ears against it: it cannot escape the shadow of irrationality. But when it appeals to this unreason, making it a *raison d'être*, it converts its own malediction into a theodicy. Even in the most sublimated work of art there is a hidden 'it should be otherwise'. When a work is merely itself and no other thing, as in a pure pseudo-scientific construction, it becomes bad art – literally pre-artistic. The moment of true volition, however, is mediated through nothing other than the form of the work itself, whose crystallization becomes an analogy of that other condition which should be. As eminently constructed and produced objects, works of art, including literary ones, point to a practice from which they abstain: the creation of a just life. This mediation is not a compromise between commitment and autonomy, nor a sort of mixture of advanced formal elements with an intellectual content inspired by genuinely or supposedly progressive politics. The content of works of art is never the amount of intellect pumped into them: if anything, it is the opposite.

Nevertheless, an emphasis on autonomous works is itself socio-political in nature. The feigning of a true politics here and now, the freezing of historical relations which nowhere seem ready to melt, oblige the mind to go where it need not degrade itself. Today every phenomenon of culture, even if a model of integrity, is liable to be suffocated in the cultivation of kitsch. Yet paradoxically in the same epoch it is to works of art that has fallen the burden of wordlessly asserting what is barred to politics.

[...]

Adorno concludes that, 'This is not a time for political art, but politics has migrated into autonomous art' and cites finally the examples of Kafka and Paul Klee.

Notes (cut and renumbered)
1. Jean-Paul Sartre, *What is Literature?*, London 1967, p. 4.
2. *What is Literature?*, p. 46.
3. Reference in *The Measures Taken*, written in 1930, which contained an implicit justification in advance of the Moscow Trials. Zinovicv and Bukharin were condemned in 1938.
4. *What is Literature?*, p. 34.

8.4   ROLAND BARTHES: 'THE TASKS OF BRECHTIAN CRITICISM' AND 'LITERATURE AND SIGNIFICATION' (1956, 1963, TRANS. 1972)

Roland Barthes (1915–80) helped introduce both structuralism and poststructuralism to literary study. His early work, *Writing Degree Zero* (1953, trans. 1972) and especially *The Elements of Semiology* (1964, trans. 1967) – together with seminal essays on narrative, advertising, fashion and photography – sought to develop a systematic science of literary and cultural semiology inspired by the structural linguistics of Ferdinand de Saussure. In a further early work, *Mythologies* (1957, trans. 1973), he produced a series of Marxist-inspired essays on popular French culture which demystified the operations of bourgeois ideology. By the time of their translation, however, Barthes had passed to the post-structuralist stage of his writing, influenced by Derrida and Lacan, and marked by a more self-reflexive and playful style. The key works of this later mode were *S/Z* (1970), a study of the multi-levelled codes and meanings of Balzac's story 'Sarrasine', and *The Pleasure of the Text* (1975). The distinction, initiated by the first work, between the 'lisible' ('readerly', 'classic realist') text and the 'scriptable' ('writerly', modern) text has been highly influential. (See MacCabe on George Eliot, Ch. 4, pp. 176–83.) The most provocative inauguration of Barthes' poststructuralist phase, however, remains the essay 'The Death of the Author' (reprinted with other essays, including 'Diderot, Brecht, Eisenstein', in *Image–Music–Text* (Fontana, 1977).

For further commentary, see *A Reader's Guide* 3/e, pp. 104–9, 130–6; and, for a recent study of Barthes, Rick Rylance, *Roland Barthes* (Harvester, 1994).

The essays on Brecht below were written in 1956 and 1963, the second as the first part of Barthes' answer to a nine-point questionnaire in the journal *Tel Quel*, and published in *Critical Essays* (1972). This volume contains three further essays or notices on Brecht (from 1955 and 1960) which show what an important point of reference he remained for Barthes in this decade. Barthes' translator says this volume 'marks an apparently decisive conversion to structuralism understood in its strictest sense' (p. ix). At the same time, Barthes' thinking in the essays on Brecht is quite evidently politically committed. Is there any tension between these approaches, do you think? Consider, for example, the categories, 'sociology', 'ideology' and 'semiology', which Barthes identifies in the first essay. If the first two are more obviously 'political' (and more conventionally 'Brechtian'), the last is more evidently 'structuralist'. Does Barthes reconcile these? And what role does the fourth category 'morality' – and the concept of 'responsibility' – play in this?

We might detect a further discourse in these essays in Barthes' discussion, in the later essay particularly, of 'signification'. His remarks here suggest a more *post*structuralist interest in the open, active production of meanings. Does this introduce a further tension, between a view of signification as 'dispersed in fragments' – as he writes at the end of the essay – and the more strictly structuralist interest in the systematic encoding of meaning? Consider Barthes' talk of a 'polyphonic' *system* of meanings, of how Brecht '*affirmed* meaning but did not *fulfill* it', and the 'friction between a (fulfilled) meaning and a (suspended) signification' (p. 366 below). This friction is assigned to Brecht, but is it also in, or produced by, Barthes' own approach?

Finally, what 'Brecht' emerges from these essays? And how are we to understand Barthes' own critical project? The title of the first essay is already ambiguous; thus, does a 'Brechtian criticism' imply an assessment *of* Brecht, or a criticism in the style of Brecht? And have the 'tasks' of this criticism altered by the time of the second essay?

The following essays are from *Critical Essays* (trans. Richard Howard, Northwestern University Press, 1972), pp. 71–6, 261–4.

The Tasks of Brechtian Criticism

It is safe to predict that Brecht's work will become increasingly important for us; not only because it is great, but because it is exemplary as well; it shines, today at least, with an exceptional luster amid two deserts: the desert of our contemporary theater, where aside from his there are no great names to cite; and the desert of revolutionary art, sterile since the beginnings of the Zhdanovian impasse. Any reflection on theater and on revolution must come to terms with Brecht, who brought about this situation himself: the entire force of his work opposes the reactionary myth of unconscious genius; its greatness is the kind which best suits our period, the greatness of responsibility; it is a work which is in a state of 'complicity' with the world, with our world: a knowledge of Brecht, a reflection on Brecht, in a word, Brechtian criticism is by definition extensive with the problematics of our time. We must tirelessly repeat this truth: knowing Brecht is of a different order of importance from knowing Shakespeare or Gogol; because it is for us, precisely, that Brecht has written his plays, and not for eternity. Brechtian criticism will therefore be written by the spectator, the reader, the consumer, and not the exegete: it is a criticism of a *concerned* man. And if I myself were to write the criticism whose context I am sketching here, I should not fail to suggest, at the risk of appearing indiscreet, how this work touches me and helps me, personally, as an individual. But to confine myself here to the essentials of a program of Brechtian criticism, I shall merely suggest the levels of analysis which such criticism should successively investigate.

(1) *Sociology.* Generally speaking, we do not yet have adequate means of investigation to define the theater's public, or publics. Furthermore, in France at least, Brecht has not yet emerged from the experimental theaters (except for the TNP's *Mother Courage*, a production so misconceived that the case is anything but instructive). For the moment, therefore, we can study only the press reactions.

There are four types to distinguish. By the extreme right, Brecht's work is totally discredited because of its political commitment: Brecht's theater is mediocre *because* it is communist. By the right (a more complicated right, which can extend to the 'modernist' bourgeoisie of *L'Express*), Brecht is subjected to the usual political denaturation: the man is dissociated from the work, the former consigned to politics (emphasizing successively and contradictorily his independence and his servility with regard to the Party), and the latter enlisted under the banners of an eternal theater: Brecht's work, we are told, is great in spite of Brecht, against Brecht.

On the left, there is first of all a humanist reading: Brecht is made into one of those giant creative figures committed to a humanitarian promotion of man, like Romain Rolland or Barbusse. This sympathetic view unfortunately disguises an anti-intellectualist prejudice frequent in certain far-left circles: in order to 'humanize' Brecht, the theoretical part of his work is discredited or at least minimized: the plays are great *despite* Brecht's systematic views on epic theater, the actor, alienation, etc.: here we encounter one of the basic theorems of *petit-bourgeois* culture, the romantic contrast between heart and head, between intuition and reflection, between the ineffable and the rational – an opposition which ultimately masks a magical conception of art. Finally, the communists themselves express certain reservations (in France, at least) with regard to Brecht's opposition to the positive hero, his epic conception of theater, and the 'formalist' orientation of his dramaturgy. Apart from the contestation of Roger Vailland, based on a defense of French tragedy as a dialectical art of crisis, these criticisms proceed from a Zhdanovian conception of art.

I am citing a dossier from memory; it should be examined in detail. The point, moreover, is not to refute Brecht's critics, but rather to approach Brecht by the means our society spontaneously employs to digest him. Brecht reveals whoever speaks about him, and this revelation naturally concerns Brecht to the highest degree.

(2) *Ideology*. Must we oppose the 'digestions' of the Brechtian canon by a canonical truth of Brecht? In a sense and within certain limits, yes. There is a specific ideological content, coherent, consistent, and remarkably organized, in Brecht's theater, one which protests against abusive distortions. This content must be described.

In order to do this, we possess two kinds of texts: first of all, the theoretical texts, of an acute intelligence (it is no matter of indifference to encounter a man of the theater who is intelligent), of a great ideological lucidity, and which it would be childish to underrate on the pretext that they are only an intellectual appendage to an essentially *creative* body of work. Of course Brecht's theater is made to be performed. But before performing it or seeing it performed, there is no ban on its being understood: this intelligence is organically linked to its constitutive function, which is to transform a public even as it is being entertained. In a Marxist like Brecht, the relations between theory and practice must not be underestimated or distorted. To separate the Brechtian theater from its theoretical foundations would be as erroneous as to try to understand Marx's action without reading *The Communist Manifesto* or Lenin's politics without reading *The State and the Revolution*. There is no official decree or supernatural intervention which graciously dispenses the theater from the demands of theoretical reflection. Against an entire tendency of our criticism, we must assert the capital importance of Brecht's systematic writings: it does not weaken the creative value of this theater to regard it as a reasoned theater.

Moreover, the plays themselves afford the chief elements of Brechtian ideology. I can indicate here only the principal ones: the historical and not 'natural' character of human misfortunes; the spiritual contagion of economic alienation, whose final effect is to blind the very men it oppresses as to the causes of their servitude; the correctible status of Nature, the tractability of the world; the necessary adequation of means and situations (for instance, in a bad society, the law can be re-established only by a reprobate judge); the transformation of ancient psychological 'conflicts' into historical contradictions, subject as such to the corrective power of men.

We must note here that these truths are never set forth except as the consequence of concrete situations, and these situations are infinitely plastic. Contrary to the rightist prejudice, Brecht's theater is not a thesis theater, not a propaganda theater. What Brecht takes from Marxism are not slogans, an articulation of arguments, but a general method of explanation. It follows that in Brecht's theater the Marxist elements always seem to be recreated. Basically, Brecht's greatness, and his solitude, is that he keeps inventing Marxism. The ideological theme, in Brecht, could be precisely defined as a dynamic of events which combines observation and explanation, ethics and politics: according to the profoundest Marxist teaching, each theme is at once the expression of what men want to be and of what things are, at once a protest (because it unmasks) and a reconciliation (because it explains).

(3) *Semiology.* Semiology is the study of signs and significations. I do not want to engage here in a discussion of this science, which was postulated some forty years ago by the linguist Saussure and which is generally accused of formalism. Without letting ourselves be intimidated by the words, we might say that Brechtian dramaturgy, the theory of *Episierung*, of alienation, and the entire practice of the Berliner Ensemble with regard to sets and costumes, propose an explicit semiological problem. For what Brechtian dramaturgy postulates is that today at least, the responsibility of a dramatic art is not so much to express reality as to signify it. Hence there must be a certain distance between signified and signifier: revolutionary art must admit a certain arbitrary nature of signs, it must acknowledge a certain 'formalism,' in the sense that it must treat form according to an appropriate method, which is the semiological method. All Brechtian art protests against the Zhdanovian confusion between ideology and semiology, which has led to such an esthetic impasse.

We realize, moreover, why this aspect of Brechtian thought is most antipathetic to bourgeois and Zhdanovian criticism: both are attached to an esthetic of the 'natural' expression of reality: art for them is a false Nature, a *pseudo-Physis*. For Brecht, on the contrary, art today – i.e., at the heart of a historical conflict whose stake in human disalienation – art today must be an *anti-Physis*. Brecht's formalism is a radical protest against the confusions of the bourgeois and *petit-bourgeois* false Nature: in a still-alienated society, art must be critical, it must cut off all illusions, even that of 'Nature': the sign must be partially arbitrary, otherwise we fall back on an art of expression, an art of essentialist illusion.

(4) *Morality.* Brechtian theater is a moral theater, that is, a theater which asks, with the spectator: what is to be done in such a situation? At this point we should classify and describe the archetypical situations of the Brechtian theater; they may be reduced, I think, to a single question: how to be good in a bad society? It seems to me very important to articulate the moral structure of Brecht's theater: granted that Marxism has had other more urgent tasks than to concern itself with problems of individual conduct; nonetheless capitalist society endures, and communism itself is being transformed: revolutionary action must increasingly cohabit, and in an almost institutional fashion, with the norms of bourgeois and *petit-bourgeois* morality: problems of conduct, and no longer of action, arise. Here is where Brecht can have a great cleansing power, a pedagogical power.

Especially since his morality has nothing catechistic about it, being for the most part strictly interrogative. Indeed, some of his plays conclude with a literal interrogation of the public, to whom the author leaves the responsibility of finding its own solution to the problem raised. Brecht's moral role is to infiltrate a question into what seems self-evident (this is the theme of the exception and the rule). For what is involved here is essentially a morality of invention. Brechtian invention is a tactical process to unite with revolutionary correction. In other words, for Brecht the outcome of every moral impasse depends on a more accurate analysis of the concrete situation in which the subject finds himself: the issue is joined by representing in explicit terms the historical particularity of this situation, its artificial, purely conformist nature. Essentially, Brecht's morality consists of a correct reading of history, and the plasticity of the morality (*to change Custom when necessary*) derives from the very plasticity of history.

Literature and Signification

What is theater? A kind of cybernetic machine. When it is not working, this machine is hidden behind a curtain. But as soon as it is revealed, it begins emitting a certain number of messages. These messages have this peculiarity, that they are simultaneous and yet of different rhythm; at a certain point in the performance, you receive at the same time six or seven items of information (proceeding from the set, the costumes, the lighting, the placing of the actors, their gestures, their speech), but some of these remain (the set, for example) while others change (speech, gestures); what we have, then, is a real informational polyphony, which is what theatricality is: *a density of signs* (in relation to literary monody and leaving aside the question of cinema). What relations do these counterpointed signs (i.e., at once dense and extensive, simultaneous and successive) have among themselves? They do not have the same signifiers (by definition); but do they always signify the same thing? Do they combine in a single meaning? What is the relation which unites them during an often very long interval to that final meaning which is, one may say, retrospective, since it is not contained in the last speech and yet is not clear until the play is over? Further, how is the theatrical signifier formed? What are its models? We know that the linguistic sign is not 'analogical' (the word 'cow' does not resemble a cow), it is formed by reference to a digital code; but what about the other signifiers – let us call them, for simplicity's sake, the *visual* signifiers – which prevail on the stage? Every performance is an extremely dense semantic act: the nature of the theatrical sign, whether analogical, symbolic, or conventional, the significant variations of this sign, the constraints of linkage, the denotation and connotation of the message – all these fundamental problems of semiology are present in the theater; one can even say that the theater constitutes a privileged semiological object since its system is apparently original (polyphonic) in relation to that of language (which is linear).

Brecht has brilliantly illustrated – and justified – this semantic status of the theater. First of all he understood that the theatrical phenomenon might be treated in cognitive and not purely emotive terms; he was able to conceive the theater intellectually, abolishing the (stale but still tenacious) mythic distinction between creation and reflection, nature and system, the spontaneous and the rational, the 'heart' and the 'head'; his theater is neither pathetic nor cerebral: it is a *justified* theater. Next he decided that the dramatic forms had a political responsibility; that the placing of a spotlight, the interruption of a scene by a song, the use of placards, the degree to which a costume was made to look threadbare, the way an actor spoke, *signified* a certain choice, not with regard to art but with regard to man and the world; in short, that the materiality of the spectacle derived not only from an esthetic or a psychology of emotion, but also and chiefly from a technique of signification; in other words, that the meaning of a theatrical work (generally an insipid notion identified with the author's 'philosophy') depended not on a sum of intentions and 'discoveries,' but on what we must call an intellectual system of signifiers. Finally, Brecht divined the variety and relativity of semantic systems: the theatrical sign does not appear as a matter of course; what we call the *naturalness* of an actor or the *truth* of a performance is merely one language among others (a language fulfills its function, which is to communicate, by its validity not by its truth), and this language depends on a certain mental context, i.e., a certain history, so that to change the signs (and not just what they say) is to give nature a new apportionment (an enterprise which precisely defines art), and to base this apportionment not on 'natural' laws but, quite the contrary, on man's freedom to make things signify.

But above all, precisely when he was linking this theater of signification to political thought, Brecht *affirmed* meaning but did not *fulfill* it. Of course his theater is ideological, more openly so than many others: it takes sides with regard to nature, labor, racism, fascism, history, war, alienation; yet it is a theater of consciousness not of action, of problems not of answers; like every literary language, it serves to 'formulate' not to 'execute'; all Brecht's plays end on an implicit 'find the solution' addressed to the spectator in the name of that decipherment to which the spectacle's materiality must lead him: *consciousness of unconsciousness*, consciousness the audience must have of the unconsciousness prevailing on the stage – that is Brecht's theater. It doubtless explains why this theater signifies so powerfully and preaches so little; the role of the system here is not to transmit a positive message (this is not a theater of the signified) but to show that the world is an object to be deciphered (this is a theater of the signifier). Brecht thus elaborates the tautological status of all literature, which is a message of the signification of things and not of their meaning (by *signification* I refer to the process which produces the meaning and not this meaning itself). What makes Brecht's enterprise exemplary is that it takes more risks than others: Brecht proceeds to the extreme of a certain meaning (which we may call, roughly, a Marxist meaning), but precisely when it 'takes' (solidifies into a positive signified) he suspends this meaning as a question (a suspension we encounter in the particular quality of historical time represented in Brecht's theater, a time of the not-yet). This very subtle friction between a (fulfilled) meaning and a (suspended) signification is an enterprise which far surpasses, in audacity, in difficulty, in necessity, too, the suspension of meaning which the *avant-garde* believed it had produced by a pure subversion of ordinary language and of theatrical conformism. A vague question (the kind which a philosophy of the 'absurd' could ask the world) has much less power (disturbs less) than a question whose answer is imminent yet arrested (like Brecht's): in literature, which is an order of connotation, there is no pure question: a question is never anything but its own scattered answer, dispersed in fragments among which meaning erupts and escapes at the same time.

8.5   LOUIS ALTHUSSER: FROM 'THE "PICCOLO TEATRO":
BERTOLAZZI AND BRECHT. NOTES ON A MATERIALIST THEATRE'
(1962, TRANS. 1977).

Louis Althusser (1918–90) was a celebrated philosopher, teacher and life-long member of the French Communist Party, known chiefly for his interventionist reading of Marx propounded in *Reading Capital* (with Etienne Balibar, 1970) and the works *Lenin and Philosophy* (1971) and *For Marx* (1977). His influence on literary studies has been indirect but considerable. In the main, this has derived from his theory of ideology and reconfiguration of the relation of the (economic) base and (cultural-ideological) superstruc-ture as conceived in traditional Marxism. Ideology Althusser defined as an 'imaginary' version of real social relations, communicated through the assumptions and routinized practices of state and cultural institutions, including education, and hence literature. He therefore viewed literature as inescapably ideological, but as working upon or exposing ideology rather than simply reproducing it. This the critic could in turn reveal by attending less to a work's ordered unity than to its silences and ideological suppressions. This 'symptomatic reading' of a text's framing presuppositions has affinities with Barthes' early work and is clearly important to Althusser's admiration for Brecht.

For the most sustained development of these ideas in criticism see Pierre Macherey's *A Theory of Literary Production* (1966, trans. 1978) and Terry Eagleton's *Criticism and Ideology* (1976, see the extract from this volume in Ch. 4, pp. 161–6, and the essay in Ch. 3 by the Marxist-Feminist Literature Collective). For further commentary, see *A Reader's Guide* 3/e, pp. 86–90, and Gregory Elliot, ed., *Althusser. A Critical Reader* (Blackwell, 1994).

Althusser's essay below (dated August 1962) mounts a double discussion of Bertolazzi's *El Nost Milan* and Brecht (principally of the late plays, *Galileo* and *Mother Courage*). Most importantly, he sees in the plays of both 'a latent asymmetrical-critical structure' (p. 369, below) – a dynamic of two temporalities, one non-dialectical and one dialectical, one internal (and false or partial) and one historical (and real). This 'asymmetrical, decentred structure', he says, is the basis not only of the ideological critique at work in Brecht's plays but is essential to any materialist (i.e. revolutionary Marxist) theatre. A poststructuralist vocabulary (the decentred, marginalized and 'not-said') joins a materialist Marxist project. In Althusser's case, this philosophical-political position is aligned with a particular view of formal or aesthetic structure. There are many points of affinity and difference between Althusser and the other essays here on these matters, but the most striking contrast is surely with Lukács and Fuegi and their discussion of the same late plays. What ideological and aesthetic critieria would you say inform the latter's views? Would it be fair to say, for example, that they read Brecht through the model of 'classical' art in Althusser's terms? Also, compare these positions with Lukács' comments on 'traditional aesthetics' and on 'great drama', including Shakespeare.

Althusser goes on to discuss the 'alienation effect' and the production of a new consciousness in the spectator (see again Lukács on how Brecht's mature plays 'overcame' his earlier theory and didacticism, as well as Barthes on consciousness and the production of new meaning). The creation of estrangement or 'critical distance', Althusser argues, must be understood as 'structural' to the play. What does he mean by this, and how does he arrive at his conclusion that the spectator becomes 'this distance itself, the distance which is simply active and living critique' (p. 373, below)? How, if you were to consider one of Brecht's plays closely, would you judge this process and its effects? (Althusser's own discussion is largely theoretical – and the role of theory is itself an important question in this group of essays – but note that his closing remarks return to Bertolazzi's play, and present its effects upon himself as an example of this theory in practice.)

The following extract is taken from *For Marx* (trans. Ben Brewster, New Left Books/Verso, 1977), pp. 142–51.

The 'Piccolo Teatro': Bertolazzi and Brecht. Notes on a Materialist Theatre

Althusser's discussion of Brecht follows his commentary on Strehler's production of Bertolazzi's *El Nost Milan*. He concludes that this production provided the play with a meaning beyond the characters' reflections on its action, beyond the conscious understanding of the audience, and possibly 'even ... beyond its author' (*For Marx*, p. 142).

[...]

If this reflection on an 'experience' is acceptable, we might use it to illuminate other experiences by an investigation into their meaning. I am thinking of the problems posed by Brecht's great plays, problems which recourse to such concepts as the alienation effect or the epic theatre has perhaps not in principle perfectly solved. I am very struck by the fact that a latent asymmetrical-critical structure, the dialectic-in-the-wings structure found in Bertolazzi's play, is in essentials also the structure of plays such as *Mother Courage* and (above all) *Galileo*. Here again we also find forms of temporality that do not achieve any mutual integration, which have no relation to one another, which coexist and interconnect, but never meet each other, so to speak; with lived elements which interlace in a dialectic which is localized, separate and apparently ungrounded; works marked by an internal dissociation, an unresolved alterity.

The dynamic of this specific latent structure, and in particular, the coexistence without any explicit relation of a dialectical temporality and a non-dialectical temporality, is the basis for a true critique of the illusions of consciousness (which always believes itself to be dialectical and treats itself as dialectical), the basis for a true critique of the false dialectic (conflict, tragedy, etc.) by the disconcerting reality which is its basis and which is waiting for recognition. Thus, the war in *Mother Courage*, as opposed to the personal tragedies of her blindness, to the false urgency of her greed; thus, in *Galileo* the history that is slower than consciousness impatient for truth, the history which is also disconcerting for a consciousness which is never able to 'take' durably on to it within the period of its short life. This silent confrontation of a consciousness (living its own situation in the dialectical–tragic mode, and believing the whole world to be moved by its impulse) with a reality which is indifferent and strange to this so-called dialectic – an apparently undialectical reality, makes possible an immanent critique of the illusions of consciousness. It hardly matters whether these things are said or not (they are in Brecht, in the form of fables or songs): in the last resort it is not the words that produce this critique, but the internal balances and imbalances of forces between the elements of the play's structure. For there is no true critique which is not immanent and already real and material before it is conscious. I wonder whether this asymmetrical decentred structure should not be regarded as essential to any theatrical effort of a materialist character. If we carry our analysis of this condition a little further we can easily find in it Marx's fundamental principle that it is impossible for any form of ideological consciousness to contain in itself, through its own internal dialectic, an escape from itself, that, *strictly speaking, there is no dialectic of consciousness*: no dialectic of consciousness which could reach reality itself by virtue of its own contradictions; in short, there can be no 'phenomenology' in the Hegelian sense: for consciousness does not accede to the real through its own internal development, but by the radical discovery of what is *other than itself*.

It was in precisely this sense that Brecht overthrew the problematic of the classical theatre – when he renounced the thematization of the meaning and implications of a play in the form of a consciousness of self. By this I mean that, to produce a new, true and active consciousness in his spectators, Brecht's world must necessarily exclude any pretensions to exhaustive self-recovery and self-representation in the form of a consciousness of self. The classical theatre (though Shakespeare and Molière must be excepted, and this exception explained) gave us tragedy, its conditions and its 'dialectic', completely reflected in the speculative consciousness of a central character – in short, reflected its total meaning in a consciousness, in a talking, acting, thinking, developing human being: what tragedy is for us. And it is probably no accident that this formal condition of 'classical' aesthetics (the central unity of a dramatic consciousness, controlling the other, more famous 'unities') is closely related to its material content. I mean that the material, or the themes, of the classical theatre (politics, morality, religion, honour, 'glory', 'passion', etc.) are precisely ideological themes, and they remain so, without their ideological nature ever being questioned, that is, criticized ('passion' itself, opposed to 'duty' or 'glory' is no more than an ideological counterpoint – never the effective dissolution of the ideology). But what, concretely, is this uncriticized ideology if not simply the 'familiar', 'well-known', transparent myths in which a society or an age can recognize itself (but not know itself), the mirror it looks into for self-recognition, precisely the mirror it must break if it is to know itself? What is the ideology of a society or a period if it is not that society's or period's consciousness of itself, that is, an immediate material which spontaneously implies, looks for and naturally finds its forms in the image of a consciousness of self living the totality of its world in the transparency of its own myths? I am not asking why these myths (the ideology as such) were not *generally* questioned in the classical period. I am content to be able to infer that a time without real self-criticism (with neither the means nor the need for a real theory of politics, morality and religion) should be inclined to represent itself and recognize itself in an uncritical theatre, that is, a theatre whose (ideological) material presupposed the formal conditions for an aesthetic of the consciousness of self. Now Brecht can only break with these formal conditions because he has already broken with their material conditions. His principal aim is to produce a critique of the spontaneous ideology in which men live. That is why he is inevitably forced to exclude from his plays this formal condition of the ideology's aesthetics, the consciousness of self (and its classical derivations: the rules of unity). For him (I am still discussing the 'great plays'), no character consciously contains in himself the totality of the tragedy's conditions. For him, the total, transparent consciousness of self, the mirror of the whole drama is never anything but an image of the ideological consciousness, which does include the whole world in its own tragedy, save only that this world is merely the world of morals, politics and religion, in short, of myths and drugs. In this sense these plays are decentred precisely because they can have no centre, because, although the illusion-wrapped, naive consciousness is his starting-point, Brecht refuses to make it that centre of the world it would like to be. That is why in these plays the centre is always to one side, if I may put it that way, and in so far as we are considering a demystification of the consciousness of self, the centre is always deferred, always in the beyond, in the movement going beyond illusion towards the real. For this basic reason the critical relation, which is a real production, cannot be thematized for itself: that is why no character is in himself 'the morality of history' – except when one of them comes down to the footlights, takes off his mask and, the play over, 'draws the lessons' (but then he is only a spectator reflecting on it from the outside, or rather prolonging its movement: 'we have done our best, now it is up to you').

It should now be clear why we have to speak of the dynamic of the play's latent structure. It is the structure that we must discuss in so far as the play cannot be reduced to its actors, nor to their explicit relations – only to the dynamic relation existing between consciousnesses of self alienated in spontaneous ideology (Mother Courage, her sons, the cook, the priest, etc.) and the real conditions of their existence (war, society). This relation, abstract in itself (abstract with respect to the consciousness of self – for this abstract is the true concrete) can only be acted and represented as characters, their gestures and their acts, and their 'history' only as a relation which goes beyond them while implying them; that is, as a relation setting to work abstract structural elements (e.g. the different forms of temporality in *El Nost Milan* – the exteriority of dramatic crowds, etc.), their imbalance and hence their dynamic. This relation is necessarily latent in so far as it cannot be exhaustively thematized by any 'character' without ruining the whole critical project: that is why, even if it is implied by the action as a whole, by the existence and movements of all the characters, it is their deep meaning, beyond their consciousness – and thus hidden from them; visible to the spectator in so far as it is invisible to the actors – and therefore visible to the spectator in the mode of a perception which is not given, but has to be discerned, conquered and drawn from the shadow which initially envelops it, and yet produced it.

Perhaps these remarks give us a more precise idea of the problem posed by the Brechtian theory of the alienation-effect. By means of this effect Brecht hoped to create a new relation between the audience and the play performed: a critical and active relation. He wanted to break with the classical forms of identification, where the audience hangs on the destiny of the 'hero' and all its emotional energy is concentrated on theatrical catharsis. He wanted to set the spectator at a distance from the performance, but in such a situation that he would be incapable of flight or simple enjoyment. In short, he wanted to make the spectator into an actor who would complete the unfinished play, but in real life. This profound thesis of Brecht's has perhaps been too often interpreted solely as a function of the technical elements of alienation: the abolition of all 'impressiveness' in the acting, of all lyricism and all 'pathos': *al fresco* acting; the austerity of the set, as if to eliminate any eye-catching relief (cf. the dark ochre and ash colours in *Mother Courage*); the 'flat' lighting; the commentary-placards to direct the readers' attention to the external context of the conjuncture (reality), etc. The thesis has also given rise to psychological interpretations centred around the phenomenon of identification and its classical prop: the hero. The disappearance of the hero (whether positive or negative), the object of identification, has been seen as the very precondition of the alienation-effect (no more hero, no more identification – the suppression of the hero being also linked to Brecht's 'materialist' conception – it is the masses who make history, not 'heroes'). Now, I feel that these interpretations are limited to notions which may well be important, but which are not determinant, and that it is essential to go beyond the technical and psychological conditions to an understanding that this very special critique must be constituted in the spectator's consciousness. In other words, if a distance can be established between the spectator and the play, it is essential that in some way this distance should be produced within the play itself, and not only in its (technical) treatment, or in the psychological modality of the characters (are they really heroes or non-heroes? Take the dumb daughter on the roof in *Mother Courage*, shot because she beat her infernal drum to warn the unknowing city that an enemy was about to fall on it, is she not, in fact, a 'positive hero'? Surely we do temporarily 'identify' with this secondary character?). It is within the play itself, in the dynamic of its internal structure, that this distance is produced and represented, at once criticizing the illusions of consciousness and unravelling its real conditions.

This – that the dynamic of the latent structure produces this distance within the play itself – must be the starting-point from which to pose the problem of the relation between the spectator and the performance. Here again Brecht reverses the established order. In the classical theatre it was apparently quite simple: the hero's temporality was the sole temporality, all the rest was subordinate to it, even his opponents were made to his measure, they had to be if they were to be *his* opponents; they lived *his* time, *his* rhythm, they were dependent on him, they were merely his dependants. The opponent was really *his* opponent: in the struggle the hero belonged to the opponent as much as the opponent did to the hero, the opponent was the hero's double, his reflection, his opposite, his night, his temptation, his own unconscious turned against him. Hegel was right, his destiny was consciousness of himself as of an enemy. Thereby the content of the struggle was identified with the hero's consciousness of himself. And quite naturally, the spectator seemed to 'live' the play by 'identifying' himself with the hero, that is, with his time, with his consciousness, the only time and the only consciousness offered him. In Bertolazzi's play and in Brecht's great plays this confusion becomes impossible, precisely because of their dissociated structure. I should say, not that the heroes have disappeared because Brecht has banished them from his plays, but that even as the heroes they are, and in the play itself, the play makes them impossible, abolishes them, their consciousness and its false dialectic. This reduction is not the effect of the action alone, nor of the demonstration which certain popular figures are fated to make of it (on the theme: neither God nor Caesar); it is not even merely the result of the play appreciated as an unresolved story; it is not produced at the level of detail or of continuity, but at the deeper level of the play's structural dynamic.

At this point close attention is essential: up till now only the play has been discussed – now we must deal with the spectator's consciousness. I should like to show in a few words that this is not, as might have been thought, a new problem, but really the same one. However, if this is to be accepted, two classical models of the spectatorial consciousness which cloud our reflection must first of all be relinquished. The first of these misleading models is once again a consciousness of self, this time the spectator's. It accepts that the spectator should not identify with the 'hero'; he is to be kept at a distance. But is he not then outside the play judging, adding up the score and drawing the conclusions? Mother Courage is presented to you. It is for her to act. It is for you to judge. On the stage the image of blindness – in the stalls the image of lucidity, led to consciousness by two hours of unconsciousness. But this division of roles amounts to conceding to the house what has been rigorously excluded from the stage. Really, the spectator has no claim to this absolute consciousness of self which the play cannot tolerate. The play can no more contain the 'Last Judgement' on its own 'story' than can the spectator be the supreme Judge of the play. He also sees and lives the play in the mode of a questioned false consciousness. For what else is he if not the brother of the characters, caught in the spontaneous myths of ideology, in its illusions and privileged forms, as much as they are? If he is kept at a distance from the play by the play itself, it is not to spare him or to set him up as a Judge – on the contrary, it is to take him and enlist him in this apparent distance, in this 'estrangement' – to make him into this distance itself, the distance which is simply an active and living critique.

But then, no doubt, we must also reject the second model of the spectatorial consciousness – a model that will haunt us until it has been rejected: the identification model. I am unable to answer this question fully here, but I shall try to pose it clearly: surely the invocation of a conception of identification (with the hero) to deal with the status of the spectatorial consciousness is to hazard a dubious correlation? Rigorously speaking, the concept of identification is a psychological, or, more precisely, a psychoanalytic concept. Far be it from me to contest the effectivity of psychological processes in the spectator seated in front of the stage. But it must be said that the phenomena of projection, sublimation, etc., that can be observed, described and defined in controlled psychological situations cannot by themselves account for complex behaviour as specific as that of the spectator-attending-a-performance. This behaviour is primarily social and cultural-aesthetic, and as such it is also ideological. Certainly, it is an important task to elucidate the insertion of concrete psychological processes (such as identification, sublimation, repression, etc., in their strict psychological senses) in behaviour which goes beyond them. But this first task cannot abolish the second – the definition of the specificity of the spectatorial consciousness itself – without lapsing into psychologism. If the consciousness cannot be reduced to a purely psychological consciousness, if it is a social, cultural and ideological consciousness, we cannot think its relation to the performance solely in the form of a psychological identification. Indeed, before (psychologically) identifying itself with the hero, the spectatorial consciousness recognizes itself in the ideological content of the play, and in the forms character-istic of this content. Before becoming the occasion for an identification (an identifi-cation with self in the species of another), the performance is, fundamentally, the occasion for a cultural and ideological recognition.

We should not imagine that this self-recognition escapes the exigencies which, in the last instance, command the destiny of the ideology. Indeed, art is as much the desire for self-recognition as self-recognition itself. So, from the beginning, the unity I have assumed to be (in essentials) achieved so as to restrict the analysis, the stock of common myths, themes and aspirations which makes representation possible as a cultural and ideological phenomenon – this unity is as much a desired or rejected unity as an achieved unity. In other words, in the theatrical world, as in the aesthetic world more generally, ideology is always in essence the site of a competition and a struggle in which the sound and fury of humanity's political and social struggles is faintly or sharply echoed. I must say that it is very odd to put forward purely psychological processes (such as identification) as explanations of spectatorial behaviour, when we know that the effects of these processes are sometimes radically absent – when we know that there are professional and other spectators who do not want to understand anything, even before the curtain rises or who, once the curtain has been raised, refuse to recognize themselves in the work presented to them, or in its interpretation. [...] This self-recognition presupposes as its principle an essential identity (which makes the processes of psychological identification themselves possible, in so far as they are psychological): the identity uniting the spectators and actors assembled in the same place on the same evening. Yes, we are first united by an institution – the performance, but more deeply, by the same myths, the same themes, that govern us without our consent, by the same spontaneously lived ideology. Yes, even if it is the ideology of the poor *par excellence*, as in *El Nost Milan*, we still eat of the same bread, we have the same rages, the same rebellions, the same madness (at least in the memory where stalks this ever-imminent possibility), if not the same prostration before a time unmoved by any History. Yes, like Mother Courage, we have the same war at our gates, and a handsbreadth from us, if not in us, the same horrible blindness, the same dust in our eyes, the same earth in our mouths. We have the same dawn and night, we skirt the same abysses: our unconsciousness. We even share the same history – and that is how it all started. That is why we were already ourselves in the play itself, from the beginning – and then what does it matter whether we know the result, since it will never happen to anyone but ourselves, that is, still in our world. That is why the false problem of identification was solved from the beginning, even before it was posed, by the reality of recognition. The only question, then, is what is the fate of this tacit identity, this immediate self-recognition, what has the author already done with it? What will the actors set to work by the Dramaturg, by Brecht or Strehler, do with it? What will become of this ideological self-recognition? Will it exhaust itself in the dialectic of the consciousness of self, deepening its myths without ever escaping from them? Will it put this infinite mirror at the centre of the action? Or will it rather displace it, put it to one side, find it and lose it, leave it, return to it, expose it from afar to forces which are external – and so drawn out – that like those wine-glasses broken at a distance by a physical resonance, it comes to a sudden end as a heap of splinters on the floor.

To return finally to my attempt at definition, with the simple aim of posing the question anew and in a better form, we can see that the play itself *is* the spectator's consciousness – for the essential reason that the spectator has no other consciousness than the content which unites him to the play in advance, and the development of this content in the play itself: the new result which the play *produces* from the self-recognition whose image and presence it is. Brecht was right: if the theatre's sole object were to be even a 'dialectical' commentary on this eternal self-recognition and non-recognition – then the spectator would already know the tune, it is his own. If, on the contrary, the theatre's object is to destroy this intangible image, to set in motion the immobile, the eternal sphere of the illusory consciousness's mythical world, then the play is really the development, the production of a new consciousness in the spectator – incomplete, like any other consciousness but moved by this incompletion itself, this distance achieved, this inexhaustible work of criticism in action; the play is really the production of a new spectator, an actor who starts where the performance ends, who only starts so as to complete it, but in life.

I look back, and I am suddenly and irresistibly assailed by *the* question: are not these few pages, in their maladroit and groping way, simply that unfamiliar play *El Nost Milan*, performed on a June evening, pursuing in me its incomplete meaning, searching in me, despite myself, now that all the actors and sets have been cleared away, for the *advent* of its silent discourse?

8.6   HERBERT MARCUSE: FROM *THE AESTHETIC DIMENSION* (1977)

Herbert Marcuse (1898–1979) was born in Berlin and is known chiefly for his contributions (with Adorno and Horkheimer) to the work of the Institute for Social Research (the former Frankfurt school), which he joined in New York in the war years, and for his celebrated writings and influence in the 1960s upon the New Left in America. The key texts of this period were *Eros and Civilisation* (1955), *One Dimensional Man* (1964) and *An Essay on Liberation* (1969) in which he identified the repressive nature of modern liberal societies and promoted students and other sectors of the new 'social movements' as a new revolutionary elite.

The following short extract relates to this thinking and shows how Marcuse sought still to draw upon sources in traditional Marxism, including Brecht, in formulating a more broadly libertarian populism which might now be described as post-Marxist. In particular, Marcuse questions how there can be a Marxist aesthetic which looks to the expression of a proletarian class-consciousness when the proletariat has been absorbed by late capitalism and is no longer its 'negation'. He draws upon the Marxist critic and philosopher Lucien Goldmann in making this argument, but the general situation he describes, and the implication it has for the apparent loss of art's critical force or distance upon capitalist society, has become more familiar to us as a description of the postmodern condition, especially in the writings of Fredric Jameson (q.v.).

Marcuse's references here to the culture and situation of the Left in the 1960s would confirm that he, too, is responding to the changed conditions of this period. In the process he evokes both Adorno and Brecht. We see once more, therefore, how Brecht figures as a key marker and model in a Marxist tradition and not simply as a playwright of interest to the Marxist critic or philosopher. Adorno's essay above gives us some idea, however, of how different, if not directly opposed, his own and Brecht's ideas of revolutionary and popular art were. In Adorno's terms, an autonomous, modernist art and a Brechtian style of engaged theatre practice were incompatible, and the second was likely to be seriously compromised. Does Marcuse side with one rather than the other of these positions? Or does he successfully recruit both to a new programme for 'revolutionary art'? What view of art, and what view of revolutionary social forces, does this idea imply?

The following extract is from *The Aesthetic Dimension. Towards a Critique of Marxist Aesthetics* (Beacon Press, 1977), pp. 30–5.

The Aesthetic Dimension

[...]

Lucien Goldmann has stated the central problem of Marxist aesthetics in the period of advanced capitalism. If the proletariat is not the negation of the existing society but to a great extent integrated into it, then Marxist aesthetics is confronted with a situation where 'authentic forms of cultural creations' exist 'though they cannot be attached to the consciousness – even a potential one – of a particular social group.' The decisive question therefore is: how the 'link is made between the economic structures and literary manifestations in a society where this link occurs *outside the collective consciousness*,' i.e., without being grounded in a progressive class consciousness, without expressing such consciousness?[1]

Adorno answered: in such a situation the autonomy of art asserts itself in extreme form – as uncompromising estrangement. To both the integrated consciousness and also to reified Marxist aesthetics, the estranged works may well appear as elitist or as symptoms of decadence. But they are nevertheless authentic forms of contradictions, indicting the totality of a society which draws everything, even the estranging works, into its purview. This does not invalidate their truth nor deny their promise. To be sure, the 'economic structures' assert themselves. They determine the use value (and with it the exchange value) of the works but not what they are and what they say.

Goldmann's text refers to a specific historical condition – the integration of the proletariat under advanced monopoly capitalism. But even if the proletariat were not integrated, its class consciousness would not be the privileged or the sole force which could preserve and reshape the truth of art. If art 'is' for any collective conscious-ness at all, it is that of individuals united in their awareness of the universal need for liberation – regardless of their class position. Nietzsche's *Zarathustra* dedication 'Für Alle und Keinen' (For All and None) may apply also to the truth of art.

Advanced capitalism constitutes class society as a universe administered by a corrupt and heavily armed monopolistic class. To a large extent this totality also includes the socially coordinated needs and interests of the working class. If it is at all meaningful to speak of a mass base for art in capitalist society, this would refer only to pop art and best sellers. In the present, the subject to which authentic art appeals is socially anonymous; it does not coincide with the potential subject of revolutionary practice. And the more the exploited classes, 'the people,' succumb to the powers that be, the more will art he estranged from 'the people.' Art can preserve its truth, it can make conscious the necessity of change, only when it obeys its own law as against that of reality. Brecht, not exactly a partisan of the autonomy of art, writes 'A work which does not exhibit its sovereignty vis à vis reality and which does not bestow sovereignty upon the public vis à vis reality is not a work of art.'[2]

But what appears in art as remote from the praxis of change demands recognition as a necessary element in a future praxis of liberation – as the 'science of the beautiful,' the 'science of redemption and fulfillment.' Art cannot change the world, but it can contribute to changing the consciousness and drives of the men and women who could change the world. The movement of the sixties tended toward a sweeping transformation of subjectivity and nature, of sensibility, imagination, and reason. It opened a new vista of things, an ingression of the superstructure into the base. Today the movement is encapsulated, isolated, and defensive, and an embarrassed leftist bureaucracy is quick to condemn the movement as impotent, intellectual elitism. Indeed, one prefers the safe regression to the collective father figure of a proletariat which is (understandably) not very interested in these problems. One insists on the commitment of art to a proletarian *Weltanschauung* oriented toward 'the people'. Revolutionary art is supposed to speak the 'language of the people.' Brecht wrote in the thirties: 'There is only one ally against the growing barbarism, the people who suffer so much under it. Only from them can we expect something. Therefore it is incumbent [upon the writer] to turn to the people.' And it is more necessary than ever to speak their language.[3] Sartre shares these sentiments: the intellectual must 'regain as fast as possible the place that awaits him among the people.'[4]

But who are 'the people'? Brecht gives a very stringent definition: 'the people who not only participate fully in the development but actually usurp it, force it, determine it. We envision a people which makes history, which changes the world and itself. We have a fighting people before our eyes …'.[5] But in the advanced capitalist countries this 'part of the people' is not '*the* people,' not the large mass of the dependent population. Rather, 'the people' as defined by Brecht would be a minority of the people, opposed to this mass, a militant minority. If art is supposed to be committed not only to this minority but to *the* people, then it is not clear why the writer must speak its language – it would not yet be the language of liberation.

It is characteristic that the texts just quoted commit art to 'the people,' that 'the people' appear as the sole allies against barbarism. In both Marxist aesthetics and in the theory and propaganda of the New Left there is a strong tendency to speak of 'the people' rather than of the proletariat. This tendency expresses the fact that under monopoly capitalism the exploited population is much larger than the 'proletariat' and that it comprises a large part of previously independent strata of the middle class. If 'the people' are dominated by the prevailing system of needs then only the rupture with this system can make 'the people' an ally against barbarism. Prior to this rupture there is no 'place among the people' which the writer can simply take up and which awaits him. Writers must rather first create this place, and this is a process which may require them to stand against the people, which may prevent them from speaking their language. In this sense 'elitism' today may well have a radical content. To work for the radicalization of consciousness means to make explicit and conscious the material and ideological discrepancy between the writer and 'the people' rather than to obscure and camouflage it. Revolutionary art may well become 'The Enemy of the People.'

Notes (renumbered)
1. Lucien Goldmann, *Towards a Sociology of the Novel* (London: Tavistock, 1975), pp. 10f.
2. Brecht, *Gesammelte Werke* (Frankfurt: Suhrkamp, 1967), Vol. VIII, p. 411.
3. *Ibid.*, p. 323.
4. Jean-Paul Sartre, *On a raison de se révolter* (Paris: Gallimard, 1974), p. 96.
5. Brecht, *Gesammelte Werke, op. cit.*, pp. 324f.

8.7   JOHN FUEGI: FROM *THE LIFE AND LIES OF BERTOLT BRECHT* (1994)

John Fuegi was born in Great Britain and is now Professor of Comparative, Germanic and Slavic Literature at the University of Maryland. He was the founder of the International Brecht Society and the editor of fourteen volumes of its *Proceedings*, and is author of *The Essential Brecht* (1972) and *Brecht: Chaos According to Plan* (1987). He has also co-directed a film, *Red Ruth*, on Ruth Berlau.

Fuegi's central thesis in *The Life and Lies of Bertolt Brecht* is that without due acknowledgement or payment Brecht used or stole the work of, amongst others, his three female collaborators and sometime lovers, Elisabeth Hauptman, Margarete Steffin and Ruth Berlau. In the most remarkable and 'indisputable' case, Hauptman, he believes, was responsible for eighty per cent of *The Threepenny Opera*. This exploitation and duplicity on Brecht's part also extended, Fuegi argues, as in the following extracts, to many other works both early and late in Brecht's career. His concern is to explode the Brechtian myth, to 'substitute historical fact for Brechtian fictions', as he puts it (p. 616), while at the same time confirming Brecht's reputation as a major dramatist of genius. The terms in which he applauds the plays are worth close attention and comparison with those above (compare Fuegi's comments on *Galileo* and *Mother Courage*, especially, with Lukács', for example). But so too are the terms in which he establishes a case against Brecht. What kind of historical fact does Fuegi adduce? What is the status of the interviews he conducted with Elisabeth Hauptman in 1966 and 1970, for example; or of Margarete Steffin's volume *Confucius Understands Nothing of Women*, published in 1991, which he both quotes and indirectly draws on, below, to present her inner reflections on Brecht? Does it alter Fuegi's case if we see these and other sources – such as documents in the Brecht archive – not as 'facts' but as 'texts', no less open to interpretation than the heavily 'intertextual' plays themselves?

Fuegi's argument raises a further general question. What – if we accept his view – is the relevance of his judgement on Brecht the 'man' to a judgement of Brecht the 'artist'? Are the two separable? What connection does Fuegi himself suggest between the personal relations of Brecht, Hauptman and Steffin and the themes of the plays? (See, for example, his discussion of *Saint Joan*, and his remarks on the consistently gendered types in the plays, including *Galileo*.) What does he suggest, secondly, of the relations between the *writings* of these figures (see, in this respect, his discussion of Margarete Steffin's poem in relation to Brecht's own work)? Are you convinced by this more texual side of his argument? Finally, Fuegi refers in his discussion to the circumstances of Steffin's family background and to the artistic and political climate of the 1930s. Does this background detail reinforce his case? Could it be read differently?

Students can pursue the debate Fuegi's study engendered in other related writings. His argument provided a major source, for example, for Elaine Feinstein's *Loving Brecht* (1993), a work of 'faction' which sets the fictional young woman actor and writer 'Frieda Bloom' in the world of Brecht and the Brechtian circle in the pre- and post-war years. Feinstein appears convinced by Fuegi's argument. The Brecht critic and scholar John Willett appears less so, referring (in a reply to a review of Brecht's journals by Feinstein) to the 'creeping campaign to discredit Brecht's writings via his affairs, real or imagined' (*Guardian*, 18 October 1993).

The following extracts are from *The Life and Lies of Bertolt Brecht* (HarperCollins, 1994), pp. 261–4, 267–73, 369–70, 380–1.

The Life and Lies of Bertolt Brecht

[...]

In 1931, the Berlin subscription theater the Volksbühne had staged Maxim Gorky's novel *Mother* in an adaptation by Günther Weisenborn and Günther Stark. Set in Russia in 1902, the novel told of a deeply religious woman who becomes convinced that the only realistic way to carry out the Christian principle of helping the poor was to join the Communist party. Relying on a film adaptation by the great Russian filmmaker Vsevolod Pudovkin, Stark and Weisenborn had boiled the sprawling novel down into a series of short, dramatic scenes in the same naturalist or representational manner as the novel itself. Changing it to a more presentational style, Hauptmann worked with Brecht, Hungarian director Slatan Dudow, and Hanns Eisler, who composed the music.[1] Where the original novel had ended with the unsuccessful uprising of 1905, the new German version brought events to the brink of the successful revolution of 1917. The central character, Pelegea Wlassowa, leads a march against the czarist forces, carrying in her own hand the banner of revolution.

Formally, *Die Mutter*, or *The Mother*, borrows heavily from the stage devices Hauptmann had introduced to the collective from her work with Japanese medieval drama. She told me in 1966 that she suggested opening the play with a direct address to the audience. This was the key to the construction of the whole play as characters come to the stage apron and say who they are and what they are going to do. Again, borrowing from the Japanese choral forms, at crucial points in the text (using words that directly point to Nikolai Bukharin's *The ABCs of Communism*), the ABCs of communism are presented in verse form half-recited, half-sung to Hanns Eisler's stirring music.[2]

While the work on turning *Mother* into a 'Brecht' play moved along and Hauptmann's name was dropped as one of its authors, Brecht developed an interest in an experimental film about unemployed Berlin workers. His co-workers on this project were Slatan Dudow and a shadowy, ex-right-wing spy named Ernst Ottwalt.[3] Once a strutting Freikorps member who had helped with the military eradication of the Spartacists in 1919–20, Ottwalt had now taken on similarly sinister tasks on the left. Immediately upon becoming a party member in September 1931, Ottwalt joined a group called the BB-Familie, a military-industrial espionage unit run by Moscow and the CPG. In his role as agent and as part of the Brecht ménage, Ottwalt fit in well.

According to Ilse Bartels and Ernst Busch (who were present), much of the writing of the *Kuhle Wampe* script was done by Ottwalt. Though this was known at the time, for publicity purposes – after all, was Brecht not the famous author of *The Threepenny Opera*? – the work was published as though Brecht were mainly responsible for it. The film was shot at the camp called Kuhle Wampe from which the film took its name. It featured the 'Red' campers, people who were out of work and homeless but who had banded together to create a tent community on the shores of a large lake. From here, the unemployed streamed forth daily on bicycles, trying to land any job advertised that day in the newspaper. As part of the 'Red' campers' entertainment in real life and in the film, an agitprop group presented skits on problems of the unemployed.

Among the crowds of unemployed workers who participated in the film was twenty-three-year-old Margarete Steffin. At the time she joined the *Kuhle Wampe* project, Steffin had recently been fired from her job as a bookkeeper 'because of political interests of a Communist nature.'[4] Steffin had contracted tuberculosis not long before but still had attended the Marxist Worker School where Helene Weigel was giving a practicum in stage vocal work. This would bring Steffin into the immediate Brecht circle.

While work on *Kuhle Wampe* moved from the shooting to the editing stage, and the adaptation of Gorky's *Mother* was completed and circulated among potential producers, work moved forward with the *Saint Joan of the Stockyards* project. The surviving records of the play give an unusually clear picture of how it came into being. Jan Knopf one of the editors of the newest Brecht edition, notes: 'From the work materials one can determine that *no small part – including the text – of the preparatory work was provided by Emil Burri and Elisabeth Hauptmann who were also responsible for the plot*; Brecht's work consisted primarily of checking up on suggestions, editing and expanding the text' (italics added).[5] After saying Burri and Hauptmann are responsible for the central elements of the play, however, Knopf does not address the question of authorship itself.[6] Ignoring all the thematically related writings published under Hauptmann's own name, he adds this work to the *Collected Works of Brecht*. Who wrote what is a matter of marginal concern for Knopf.[7] *Saint Joan of the Stockyards* is thought by some critics, who also ignore the question of authorship, to be one of Brecht's best works. One says: 'Viewed from an artistic perspective, the play represents a peak in Brecht's achievement.'[8]

The play's strength, in my own view, is traceable to two radically different, wholly irreconcilable points of view. Without reducing the play only to reflections of the strong personalities who participated in its creation, there is little doubt that they are reflected here. The central drama of the work (as with *The Threepenny Opera*) is the conflict between the title character, who is a typical Hauptmann creation, and her opponent, the arch-Brechtian figure of Mauler. As we have repeatedly seen, Hauptmann's own work presents strong, independent, intelligent, capable women characters trying to maintain their pride and independence in a world dominated by men. A typical central character in a Hauptmann work cares about other people, puts her own life on the line, and works to change the world for the better. When Brecht writes on his own, or where one finds the clearest traces that his was the primary hand in creating a text, we find figures like Baal, Garga, 'poor Bébé,' Fatzer, Macheath, or a figure he had now begun to write about, the mysterious and often brutal Herr Keuner. Consistently, his own male characters are arrogant, egocentric, ruthless, charismatic men who boastfully exploit and denigrate anyone unwise enough to enter their powerful orbits.

Nowhere is this clear-cut opposition quite as readily visible as in *Saint Joan of the Stockyards*. In what is basically a return to the devices of the old morality play, the Hauptmann figure, Joan Dark (d'Arc), is an orator and leader, a woman of great courage who uses all her daring, intelligence, and hope to fight against the representative of everything evil, brutal, and cunning. Often alone, but willing like her great historical predecessor to fight anyway, Joan Dark faces off against the quintessential Brecht figure of Pierpoint Mauler.[9]

It is no accident that the most famous single quote from Goethe's *Faust*, 'There are two souls in my breast,' is omnipresent in semiserious-semiparodic form in the *Saint Joan*. There are two souls in the *Saint Joan* play itself, and they are locked in deadly battle. The split apparent in *Measures* between the Young Comrade and the Moscow Control Chorus is played out in *Saint Joan* in a way that clearly anticipates the divided characters who will appear in many later Brecht plays.

The dramatic opposition of Joan Dark, who tries through direct human persuasion to change humanity for the better, and the clever, vicious Mauler is the greatest strength and most serious weakness of the play today. Joan, carefully and plausibly developed, learns the hard way that in the long run her work with the Salvation Army will not benefit the poor. (It is worth noting that Joan's demonstration that the Salvation Army cannot permanently help the poor is a gloss on Friedrich Engels's classic text on this subject.[10]) So lucid is her final analysis that Mauler must silence her and twist her legacy as quasi-saint to suit his own profoundly amoral and reactionary purposes.

Joan's opponent is so corrupt that even his heart and stomach (as his rival Criddle learns too late) give him guidance as to how to better play the market and extract greater profit. With the arch-villain Mauler representing capitalism, the *Saint Joan* play works only if we find his villainy plausible. In today's mixed, free market–social democratic models that usually attempt to ameliorate at least the most glaring inhumanities toward the poor, Mauler seems more caricature than dramatic character.

Though this play echoes persistent concerns both of Brecht and Hauptmann, there is perhaps another biographical reference in it. The religious, proto-Communist Joan Dark is, at the play's conclusion, 'twenty-three years old' and dying from 'something wrong with her lungs.'[11] Margarete Steffin, who entered the Brecht circle at precisely this time, was twenty-three years old, had tuberculosis, and was a committed Communist who also felt a strong pull toward religion.

This dark, personally revealing work was published by Peter Suhrkamp in the paperback *Versuche* series. However, when it was delivered to Wreede in late 1931, no one dared tackle it on a major stage in Germany. Had it been completed when first proposed in 1929, it would have been both playable and influential. Now it was useless. But astoundingly, again simply overwhelmed by Brecht's personality, Wreede agreed to continue to pay the one thousand gold mark monthly advance. Brecht promised Wreede that a very playable German version of *Measure for Measure* would soon be completed.

[...]

On the first day of rehearsals [of *The Mother*] Steffin arrived early.[12] She had been told that Ernst Ottwalt would write some new material for her, and she was anxious to meet Ernst Busch, the handsome male lead, and Burri, the director. She cared less at that time about Brecht's arrival. She knew him largely by reputation, and what she knew did not make him attractive. To her, a dedicated Communist party member, he was the opportunist who had become wealthy from *The Threepenny Opera* play and film. She remembered reading somewhere that he had stolen *Threepenny* 'from A to Z.' She also knew he had a bad reputation among Berlin workers as a man who spared little time for workers' groups.

Brecht arrived late at the rehearsal of *Mother*. To Steffin, he looked tired, his mind elsewhere. He seemed to be both shy and modest, with an attitude that many would have taken as rude, but which she saw as a lack of self-confidence. If he had made a lot of money from *Threepenny*, it did not look to her as if he had invested any of it into clothes: his suit was shabby, and his hair poked out from under a cap that he never bothered to take off. No sooner had he arrived than he was gone again.

Later, at those rehearsals when Brecht did bother to turn up, it became obvious to Weigel and others that something was going on between him and Margarete Steffin. He could not seem to see enough of this slender, vivacious, intelligent woman with her blond hair cut in the fashionable bob of the liberated women. He arranged private 'working' sessions with her and, despite her objections, tried to grope under her skirt. Steffin was not prudish. She was a Communist who believed in free sexual expression, but she wanted to get to know her partner first.

Born in a loud, filthy, smelly, tiny, damp Berlin slum flat in 1908, Grete Steffin had grown up in a family where both her mother, Johanna, and father, August, were active in the Communist party. Grete was committed to communism but had a low opinion of the CPG itself. Grete's younger sister, Herta, and her fiancé, Herbert Hanisch, were in the anarcho-syndicalist wing of the party. 'Things were very poor for us at home,' Herta told one interviewer later. 'Father drank a lot. Mother had to sew all the time. She sewed trousers for forty-eight pfennig, workers' trousers.'[13] But though Johanna Steffin had a full-time job and was often out on party business in the evening and weekends, her husband expected her to do all the housework and serve meals at his convenience.

August Steffin himself was erratically employed in the building trades. He never told his wife what he earned and drank up most of it anyway. Drunk, his behavior to family members was not, said Herta years later, 'very nice.' When the family was out together, socialism or no socialism, Herr Steffin required his wife and daughters to walk three steps behind him. Whenever he felt his authority as 'head of the family' challenged in any way, he became violent, threatening to smash the whole household. His personal hygiene included relieving himself in front of everybody in the kitchen sink.

At a school with eight hundred pupils, Grete established a brilliant academic record. Very religious, and trying hard to combine Christian compassion for the poor with her family's brand of socialism, she established a religious study circle. She bribed kids to attend by completing homework assignments for them. Her creative writing was so good that she won a Berlin-wide competition and was a published author before her teens. She showed such great promise both as a writer and linguist that when she did not have the money to enter gymnasium and prepare for the university, her teachers offered to pay for her; but her father would not allow it. He argued that education would alienate her from her own class and forced her to go to work at age fourteen. She quickly taught herself to become a superb typist and stenographer, and got a secretarial job with a Berlin book publisher. Here she was so outspoken in her Communist beliefs that she was fired and had to then rely on short-term jobs.

Even in her teens, Steffin showed signs of the tuberculosis that would eventually kill her. Often ill by the late 1920s, she remained active in socialist theatrical groups as a singer and narrator. As a teenager, she began to teach herself Russian so she could read Lenin in the original. At eighteen, she began to spend more and more time at the flat of a young male friend. In one of her erotic poems, she recalled lying with her friend on top of her as she wondered, 'Ob der Junge nicht bald fertig ist' (Is the kid not finished yet?)[14] The kid did finish, and she soon found herself pregnant. With abortions illegal, she made an expensive deal with a local pharmacist. After twenty hours of excruciating pain, she saw two bloody blobs at her feet.[15] After recovering from this, she volunteered as a singer and narrator in agitprop productions of the kind included in the *Kuhle Wampe* film.

While Burri rehearsed *Mother* with Weigel, Busch, and Steffin, *Mahagonny* rehearsals continued upstairs. The whores' chorus of *Mahagonny* began to be modeled on the shows with high-kicking, scantily clad dancers then popular in Berlin and Paris. Neher created his usual series of sexually frank pictures to be projected over the stage, together with a picture of a moving arrow representing the hurricane that threatened to sweep away the latter-day Sodom and Gomorrah Mahagonny. Aufricht liked the pictures and the arrow, but not Neher's use of titles projected between scenes. Aufricht insisted on having these texts read aloud by a master of ceremonies in an evening jacket.

Downstairs, Burri worked on a simple, stark production of *Mother*. The Hauptmann-Brecht adaptation shows a simple Russian woman taking a leadership role, promoting rebellion, and defying the police, finally, at the cost of her life. Here the Communist goal is literally worth any sacrifice, and exerts a force even greater than the bond between any two individuals – including mother and son, or lover and lover. This something-greater-than-both-of-them, their main hope of eventual salvation, is referred to in the text of the play as 'The Third Thing,'[16] an echo of the Holy Trinity itself, presented as a holy of holies. Songs such as 'Arise, the Party Is in Danger' and 'In Praise of Communism' were to be delivered, as Eisler instructed, in a triple fortissimo that shook the rehearsal room.

The final touches were put on *Mahagonny* so it could open to take advantage of Christmas-time business. *Mother* was being readied to open on January 15, the anniversary of Rosa Luxemburg's murder. The two productions precisely reflect Berlin theater in late 1931. Upstairs, scantily clad women kicked in unison while 'In Praise of Communism' was sung with passion and conviction in triple fortissimo in the cellar. Outside the theater, armed and uniformed Nazi thugs openly marched with ever-less fear of police reprisals. Franz Pfeffer von Salomon's standing orders to his fighting Nazi detachments read: 'The only form in which the SA displays itself to the public must be en masse. This is one of the most powerful forms of propaganda.

The sight of a large body of disciplined men, inwardly and outwardly alike, makes the most profound impression upon every German and speaks to his heart in a more convincing and persuasive language than writing and oratory and logic ever can. Calm composure and matter-of-factness emphasizes the impression of the strength of marching columns.'[17]

Mahagonny did excellently at the box office, running for fifty performances. Lenya later recalled: 'Today, I have but to meet a true Berliner of that time, a survivor of that truly glorious public, to hear him say: "Yes, yes, *The Threepenny Opera* was wonderful of course, but *Mahagonny*", and there follows a silence, a meaning beyond words that I do understand. There were those who came night after night, *Mahagonny* addicts, who tell me that they would leave the theatre in a kind of trance and walk the streets, Kurt's insidious bittersweet melodies repeating over and over inside their heads.'[18]

Aufricht would later remember the *Mahagonny* production as 'a Witches' Sabbath of injustice, horror, and brutality, that announced themselves as elements of the approaching future.'[19] Night after night, on Neher's huge screen mounted above the stage, a map of Mahagonny was shown. On the screen, a moving arrow marked the advance of an enormous hurricane, as Weill's music thundered and as a 'radio announcer' warned constantly of impending doom. Each night, at the last instant, the arrow marking the hurricane on the big screen would miraculously and inexplicably swerve, and each night the city would be spared.

At the progressive Volksbühne, it was a tough time for Weigel. Not only did she have to deal daily with her husband's latest young lover but as a Jewish woman and committed party member, every day she had to face the anti-Semitic thugs outside the theater who constituted a threat to her very life. At the opening, noted Ihering, Weigel was visibly ill at ease at first but settled down later.[20]

Of her rival in the cast of *Mother*, 'Steffin was very good,' said Weigel of her actress colleague. 'She looked marvelous for the part.'[21] Every night, Steffin sang of the need for revolution. Later, doctors would tell Steffin that her rehearsals and performances in the winter of 1931–32 in usually unheated theaters had hastened the progress of the tuberculosis that was to kill her at age thirty-two. Some nights, when the show ended, the rich, charismatic director would be waiting for her; and in his large car, he would drive her through the Nazi-patrolled streets to her tiny room in 'Red' Wedding. Soon he gave her copies of the 'special sonnets,' the erotic works he had had privately printed years ago in Augsburg.

What Steffin, the self-educated twenty-three-year-old, wrote in response to Brecht's sonnets is astounding. In content, sexual frankness, and, above all, in quality, much of Steffin's writing so matches his that to this day Brecht experts argue as to what is his and what is hers. With the lower-case style that Brecht had himself taken over from Arnolt Bronnen, a typical poem is addressed to Brecht:

> *when you asked me the first time*
> *whether i was wet, i asked myself, what does that mean?*
> *when you asked whether you should check to see*
> *i was ashamed of myself. i was wet.*

and when you asked whether i would come
as you took me the first time.
i didn't know that i could come.
but i said nothing and i came, i came, i love you.

i behaved like an inexperienced girl even though i had lived
with a man for four and a half years.
but only through you did i become a woman.

i also began through you to love myself
and i didn't ask anymore: what will come next?
finally i learned to enjoy the present
without fear of future changes between us.

when i come to you let it be in such a way
as if i came to you every day,
in the few hours i spend with you
let me have no wishes of my own.

when i am with you you must
tell me what has been going on for you
but do not tell me about the other women.
and may i myself say only: yes.[22]

Her appreciation of Brecht's sexual superiority to the 'kid,' her earlier sexual partner, explains something of the hold Brecht was taking on Steffin's life. In this poem Steffin's successful mimicking of the tone of Brechtian verse also shows the immediate influence he had on her as a writer. But though this poem – like other verse, prose, and plays of Steffin – is very similar to Brecht's work, it is also something quite different. Steffin radically inverts Brechtian language. Where he consistently speaks of a brutal world seen from a male perspective, Steffin expresses her own, non- or antimasculine vision of the world. This is, like the achievement of Hauptmann before her, a form of poetic ventriloquism. We hear what seems to be Brecht's voice. But the words spoken in that voice are hers. Steffin neither accepts a male visual or aural perspective unchallenged, nor does she accept a male-oriented system in determining the emotional, social, and ethical value of an event.

In Steffin's writing, as with Hauptmann's, the basic orientation exactly corresponds to what is described by Carol Gilligan in her book *In a Different Voice*.[23] The emphasis is always on maintaining warm social connections rather than on some abstract principle of law or logic. Hers is a world where one person feels responsibility for another, a world at a very far remove from Brecht's 'I am a person on whom you cannot rely.' Hers is not a world of winner and losers dominated by deception and violence. Steffin's and Hauptmann's writing consistently finds a way to express 'a different voice,' whereas Brecht's own writing hardly ever does.

Brecht quickly recognized that the voice used by Steffin blended in such a way with his writing that it could be marketed as his own. He welcomed such contributions in the way that Canetti had observed at the time *Threepenny* was being stitched together in late 1928. For the young, largely uneducated Steffin, it was deeply flattering that her work could blend indistinguishably with that of an acknowledged master of modern literature. And, at the practical, everyday level, as Steffin was taken into the collective, she found him and the circles in which he moved irresistible attractions.

After her unheated, tiny tenement, his large apartment was heaven. There she found a warm, dry, well-lit world with a piano and hundreds of books – including his impressive, if little read, volumes of Marxist thought – and a maid to keep everything in order and make sure he was fed his favorite meals. Not only was the place extremely comfortable but it was also exciting, both politically and intellectually. She met there the economist Karl Korsch as he argued passionately that in true communism, unlike what was now being created in the Soviet Union under Stalin, the state would wither away, and personal relations would be sufficiently harmonious that no government as such would be needed. She also met Walter Benjamin and Hanns Eisler, and formed friendships with both of them. And, less happily, she met the stream of other women in his life.

Still, most of Grete's nights in Berlin were apparently spent alone at her tiny flat as Brecht maintained a kind of Mack the Knife routine of going from one partner to another on a schedule that he alone determined. Steffin never knew when he might arrive, and whether he would want immediate sexual gratification or casually declare that he could not function sexually just then as he had come from another partner. She found herself tortured by images of him with other women. The situation was further complicated when she discovered that she was pregnant with Brecht's child. She worried whether she should have the child or again attempt to get an illegal abortion. This, as she knew from her earlier brutal experience, would be hard and expensive to arrange. She had little money of her own since in the low-budget production of *Mother*, often played for the unemployed, the cast was lucky if they took home two marks per night. It was not enough to live on even by herself, and certainly not enough, even if her own health were better, for her to think of trying to feed and clothe a baby also. Despite being a Communist, and supposedly not believing at all in the supernatural, she went to see a fortune teller who told her she would not outlive her thirty-third year. Believing both that she did not have long to live and that she would never be able to count on Brecht, she decided to not have the baby.

[...]

With *Galileo*, Brecht and Steffin have returned to the world of the classic drama with its towering but flawed central hero. The rise and fall of the action, with its deliberate retardation as we are forced to wait to discover whether Galileo will stand up to the Inquisition, is constructed in the prescribed Aristotelian manner. The play is as carefully constructed as a watch, each cog precisely driving the other. In its free use of historical sources, its use of music and dance, and its chronicle structure, it clearly echoes precisely the devices used by Shakespeare in his great history plays. It should not surprise us perhaps that Eric Bentley, arguably the keenest eye and ear of drama criticism in the twentieth century, should sum up his view of *Galileo* as 'theatre on the grandest scale,'[24] and that he should include the play in his two-volume anthology of the greatest drama the world has so far produced. We might wish to remember also that the great actor Charles Laughton would seriously compare this work with the plays of Shakespeare.[25] I believe the comparison is apt. In my view, *Galileo* is one of the two (*Mother Courage* is the other) greatest Elizabethan-style chronicle plays written in the twentieth century. Both in *Galileo* and *Mother Courage*, the techniques of exposition that served Shakespeare so well enjoy a radical renaissance in these two carefully rounded (in the end is the beginning), archly 'modern,' yet wholly classical, plays. Brecht was surely right in noting of the play that, in contrast to his earlier writing about 'epic' modern subjects, 'technically, *Galileo* is a large step backwards.'[26] It was a step back to the late sixteenth century. Again, the way to the drama of the future lay in the past (as it had with *Measures Taken* and other *Lehrstücke*, with their explicit medieval antecedents).

For all of the great dramatic strength of *Galileo*, women in the play (as is so often the case in other major classics) are presented mainly as caretakers, beings whose lives are dictated by the whims and wanderings of a 'great' man. Galileo is a man alone. He does not appear to express any real concern for the lives of those closest to him. His daughter's life is wholly sacrificed to his own. If, as Steffin claimed of Confucius-Brecht, they 'understood nothing of women,' the figure of Galileo is cut from the same cloth. In Steffin's intense work on this play, we see how she worked dialectically as she had in the poem archly speaking of how 'Denmark wept' when the 'great master' Brecht left for America in late 1935. For Steffin, these figures that history might present as great were, no matter how great their talents, deeply, deeply flawed human beings. It is, I think, the central human weakness of Galileo, as Steffin and Brecht present it, that, in dramatic terms, paradoxically constitute one of the play's greatest, and specifically Aristotelian, strengths.

[...]

The earliest extant version of *Mother Courage* reflects joint work; it has innumerable handwritten notes by both Steffin and Brecht.[27] The second extant version, both from the typing style and from its thematic content, appears not to be by Brecht though it takes lots of Brecht from the earlier version.[28] In the text that now emerged, the sheer brutality of Courage's mercantilism is offset by her mute daughter, Kattrin, who deliberately gives her life for others when, under the cocked guns of soldiers down below, she climbs on the roof of a peasant hut and powerfully beats a drum to awaken a city about to be attacked by marauders. As she is shot down, the cannons of the nearby city that she has awakened with her drumming are heard in the distance. The scene in which Kattrin is shot down would be described by Eric Bentley later as 'possibly the most powerful scene, emotionally, in twentieth-century drama.'[29] Such scenes of personal heroism are not usually found in work that we know for certain was written by Brecht. Structurally, the play is unusually strong for a Brecht play. *Mother Courage*, like *Galileo*, follows a line of dramatic development consciously taken from Shakespeare's chronicle, or history, plays.[30] Organized episodically, each episode sets up the next one, so that the work builds to tremendous dramatic force with the death of Kattrin and the horror of a woman whose children have all died violently.

The opposition of the life-destroying values of Mother Courage and the life-affirming values of Kattrin serves to dramatically supercharge the play. *Mother Courage* is a supreme example of how productive it can be to combine radically different points of view in a work. Courage acts in the over-dead-bodies-to-get-one's-own-way style so characteristic of virtually all Brecht's own writing. In contrast, Kattrin reflects the values of Steffin and Berlau. Kattrin puts her life on the line to help change the world. She is *not* willing to allow brutal mercenaries to get things their own way through rape and murder. She is *not* willing to postpone goodness, waiting for some never-never land of the future. She is *not* willing to cooperate with the forces of evil in order to save her own skin.

Whether aware or not of the full grandeur of what had been created with *Mother Courage*, a play that would help reshape the modern stage, Steffin shipped it off in November to Switzerland and the United States. At the same time, Wifstrand attempted to put together a production for Scandinavia, but none of the Scandinavian countries would risk it. Only tiny Switzerland, surrounded on every side by fascism, would dare to do so. The play's world premiere would be in Zurich on April 19, 1941.

Notes (cut and renumbered)

1. For a detailed examination of the play as text and performance, see John Fuegi, *The Essential Brecht* (Los Angeles: Hennessey and Ingalls, 1972), chap. 3.
2. As Bukharin was later murdered and made a nonperson by Stalin, references to this major figure in the spread of international communism are usually not included in discussions of the Brecht version of *Mother*.
3. See Reinhard Müller, ed., *Die Säuberung, Moskau 1936, Stenogramm einer geschlossenen Parteiversammlung* (Reinbeck bei Hamburg: Rowohlt, 1991), 68–70, 309–10, 552–56. Hereafter: Müller, *Säuberung*.
4. Margarete Steffin, *Konfutse versteckt nichts von Frauen* (Berlin: Rowohlt, 1991), 176 ff.
5. Jan Knopf, *Brecht, Theater Handbuch* (Stuttgart: Metzler, 1980), 107.
6. Ibid., 105.
7. A few examples may suffice here. Work of Elisabeth Hauptmann, Margarete Steffin, Ruth Berlau, and Martin Pohl has been routinely taken over in so-called Brecht editions without any prior authorization and despite protests made about unauthorized, unrecognized, and unpaid-for use. When Martin Pohl and Ruth Berlau protested to the publisher, their claims were dismissed out of hand. In the case of Steffin, the fact that she was dead and her family was too poor and ill-informed helped make decades of deception possible.
8. Helfried W. Seliger, *Das Amerikabild Bertolt Brechts* (Bonn: Bouvier, 1974), 183.
9. In the Fat Ham story, it is Hauptmann who saves the Ark. In her own stories and *Happy End*, she had dealt in detail with the Salvation Army.
10. The connection to an 1892 text of Engels is noted in Karl-Heinz Schoeps, *Bertolt Brecht und Bernard Shaw* (Bonn: Bouvier, 1974), 47. In addition to the Engels reference, Schoeps provides excellent materials on the myriad other sources used by the collective.
11. Bertolt Brecht Archive, Berlin (hereafter BBA) 117/13. 'Johanna D'ark dreiundzwanzig Jahre alt, gestorben an Lungenentzunung'.
12. For details on her recollections, see Steffin, *Konfutse*, 166 ff.
13. Interview with Herta Hanisch conducted by Rudy Hassing and Hans and Gudrun Bunge, Berlin, 17 November 1986, and kindly made available to me. In December 1987,1 spoke directly with Frau Hanisch in the village of Fredersdorf to the east of Berlin.
14. Steffin, *Konfutse*, 204.

15. Steffin described the abortion in a poem that she wrote in November 1932, at a time when she had had another abortion, this time of a child by Brecht.
16. Brecht, *Gesammelte Werke* (Frankfurt am Main: Suhrkamp Verlag, 1967), 2: 878.
17. Joachim Fest, *Hitler*, trans. Richard and Clara Winston (New York: Vintage Books, 1975), 244.
18. Lotte Lenya's jacket notes to her 1956 Columbia recording of *Mahagonny*.
19. Ernst Josef Aufricht, *Erzahle damit du dein Recht erweist* (Berlin: Propylaen Verlag, 1966), 128.
20. Werner Hecht, ed., *Materialien zu Bertolt Brechts 'Die Mutter'* (Frankfurt am Main: Suhrkamp Verlag, 1969), 27.
21. Ibid., 32.
22. Steffin, *Konfutse*, 202–3. The original typescript of the poem was one that Steffin showed to Brecht. He penciled in a few changes. He wanted the poem to read throughout as follows: Not, 'When he asked me the first time ...,' but rather, 'When you asked me the first time ...' The poem as finally printed in *Konfutse* in 1991 is, quite properly I feel, given in its original version.
23. Carol Gilligan, *In a Different Voice* (Cambridge: Harvard University Press, 1982). Using 'Jake' to represent a typical boy's reaction and 'Amy' as the 'different voice' of a girl, Gilligan writes: 'Jake sets himself apart from the world by his abilities, his beliefs, and his height. Although Amy also enumerates her likes, her wants, and her beliefs, she locates herself in relation to the world, describing herself through actions that bring her into connection with others, elaborating ties through her ability to provide help' (35). I see 'Jake' as a reflection of the core values of Brecht, and 'Amy' as reflecting the core values of Hauptmann and Steffin.
24. Eric Bentley, *Seven Plays by Bertolt Brecht* (New York: Grove Press, 1961), xxvi.
25. In a letter cited in Eric Bentley, *The Brecht Memoir* (New York: PAJ Publications, 1985), 35–6, Laughton, who had just played the lead role in *Galileo*, explicitly compares Brecht's greatness to that of Shakespeare.
26. BBA 275/14.
27. See BBA 490.
28. In *Bertolt Brechts schwedisches Exil* (Ph.D. diss., University of Lund, Sweden, 1969), Jan E. Olsson says flatly of this typescript (BBA 1989) that it is 'nicht von Brecht '(108).
29. Eric Bentley, *Seven Plays, op. cit.*, xii.
30. In Bertolt Brecht, *Arbeitsjournal*, 3 vols., ed. Werner Hecht (Frankfurt am Main: Surkamp Verlag, 1973), Vol. 1, 205, Brecht muses, reflectively on an imagined Shakespeare collective, 'I find only that purely technically the plays are so constructed that I believe I recognise the work of a collective.' He then goes on, 'The collective did not need always to be made up of the same people; it could have worked in a very loose way. Shakespeare could have been the decisive personality; he could have periodically had co-workers, etc.'

Chapter 9

Toni Morrison:
Beloved

GENERAL INTRODUCTION

Toni Morrison is Robert F. Goheen Professor, Council of the Humanities, Princeton University, but is better known as the author of six highly regarded novels: *The Bluest Eye* (1972), *Sula* (1974), *Song of Soloman* (1978) – which won the 1978 National Book Critics' Circle Award for fiction, *Tar Baby* (1981), *Beloved* (1987) – winner of the 1988 Pulitzer Prize for fiction, and *Jazz* (1992). She has also published a collection of essays, *Playing in the Dark: Whiteness and the Literary Imagination* (1992) and edited the collection *Race-ing Justice, En-gendering Power* (1992/3). In 1993, she was awarded the Nobel Prize for Literature. *Beloved* is extraordinary, if for nothing else, than for the wide critical acclaim it has received and its almost instant elevation to canonic status; and it is for this reason amongst others that it constitutes one of the exercises in this Reader. Dedicated to the 'Sixty Million and more' black people who died under slavery, it gives voice to the 'unspeakable thoughts, unspoken' of the women of 124 Bluestone Road in immediately post-bellum Cincinnati, thus at once writing the unwritten history of African Americans and offering a profound psychological analysis of its protagonists. To do this, *Beloved* develops a highly sophisticated narrative strategy (Morrison calls it a 'kind of literary archeology'), and draws on black oral cultural traditions to find a voice for a silent/silenced people. For some, the novel's formal invention and self-consciousness make it a postmodernist text. Whatever else, it clearly contains much of its own theory or, perhaps more to the point, encourages theoretically informed criticism in its contemporary commentators. This exercise brings together five extracts driven by theoretical concerns of marked and different kinds. Most employ the characteristic inflections of poststructuralism: psychoanalysis, feminism, postmodernism, postcolonialism, Marxism and dialogics. However, these tributary strands are not unilaterally 'represented' by any one piece, nor are they in competition in the sense that one method or school challenges or supersedes another. Rather, they register a common conspectus of concerns which also derive from, or circulate around, *Beloved* itself: the decentredness of the human subject, for example; the loss or recovery of history; the ambivalence of a condition of marginality; the transgression of textual, social or ethnic boundaries; and the appearance of heteroglossic story-telling in place of discredited 'grand narratives'.

Attempt to identify the theoretical models and strategies in each of the essays. How do they explore the contemporary concerns indicated above? Mae Henderson (p. 395, below) says her essay attempts 'a reading that links historiography and psychoanalysis'; and this is an issue lying behind several of the extracts. Consider how these 'links' are made, and how these might take the criticism beyond some of the polarities and impasses of earlier theoretical positions. Compare notions of 'transgression' here with those articulated in Ch. 5 on Oscar Wilde, and notions of 'historical' reading with the positions and approaches of cultural materialists or 'new historicists' in other chapters. In what sense, if any, are the approaches here properly defined as 'postcolonial' (see *A Reader's Guide* 3/e, pp. 188–90, on meanings of this term). Do *you* think *Beloved* determines its own readings? Are the readings here anything more than expository interpretations? What are the advantages of theoretical criticism as exemplified here? Is it possible to read *Beloved* critically, or 'against the grain'? Are any of the essays 'textual' or 'literary' in their critical strategies, or are we past all that? How and why is *Beloved* so valued? Is it possible to articulate convincingly evaluative judgements? Should it be?

Further Reading
Further reading will be found in the Headnotes to the extracts below. For general reading in postcolonial and black feminist theory and criticism, the student is directed to the biblio-graphies in sections 7 and 8 of *A Reader's Guide* 3/e. Further useful volumes specifically on postcolonialism and African-American writing are: P. Williams and L. Chrisman, eds, *Colonial Discourse and Post-Colonial Theory: A Reader* (Harvester, 1993); Eva Lennox Birch, *Black American Women's Writing* (Harvester, 1994 – chapter on Morrison); S. M. James and A. P. A. Busia, eds, *Theorizing Black Feminisms* (Routledge, 1993); Firdous Azim, *The Colonial Rise of the Novel* (Routledge, 1993); and Henry Louis Gates, ed., *Black Literature and Literary Theory* (1984; Routledge, 1990 – contains an essay on Morrison's novels prior to *Beloved* by Susan Willis, 'Eruptions of Funk: Historicizing Toni Morrison').

9.1   MAE G. HENDERSON: 'TONI MORRISON'S *BELOVED*: RE-MEMBERING THE BODY AS HISTORICAL TEXT' (1991)

Mae Henderson is Associate Professor in the African American Studies Program and the Department of English at the University of Illinois, Chicago. Her other works include *Anti Slavery Newspapers and Periodicals: An Annotated Index of Letters, 1817–1871* (5 vols; author and co-editor, 1980); ed., *Borders, Boundaries and Frameworks* (1994); and a number of articles on black and women's literature.

As noted in the General Introduction above, Henderson's project is to link historiography and psychoanalysis in a reading of *Beloved*, and to construct a kind of narratalogical homology between social and psychic subjectivities (p. 398, below). In the process, she draws on feminism and theories of discourse and narrativity. Analyse closely the complex interweaving of the various theoretical strands in Henderson's essay, and assess how they reinforce each other. What are the (sexual/racial) politics of the essay? How does Henderson use 'History' as a theoretical tool here? In what ways does her essay differ in approach from such schools of criticism as 'new historicism' and cultural materialism? The essay refers on a number of occasions to the Freudian notion of 'the return of the repressed'; Peter Nicholls (p. 443, below), while commending Henderson's reading, is unhappy with its dependence on this. Why? Compare his psychoanalytic reading with hers. Is hers more a 'close reading' of the novel, in terms of its textual strategies, than a 'deconstructive' one? Does the novel *control* her exposition, when other readings press for its 'not-said' – for what, even here, remains 'unspeakable' and 'unspoken'?

The following extract comprises much of Ch. 4 in Hortense J. Spillers, ed., *Comparative American Identities: Race, Sex and Nationality in the Modern Text*, Routledge, 1991, pp. 63–86, *passim*. Five opening epigraphs from Zora Neal Hurston, Paul Ricoeur, Derrida, Kristeva and Michel de Certeau are omitted.

Toni Morrison's *Beloved*: Re-membering the Body as Historical Text

Describing the nineteenth-century slave narratives, Toni Morrison observes, 'No slave society in the history of the world wrote more – or more thoughtfully – about its own enslavement.' Yet, for Morrison, the narratives with their 'instructive' and 'moral' force are incomplete:

> Over and over, the writers pull the narrative up short with a phrase such as, 'but let us drop a veil over these proceedings too terrible to relate.' In shaping the experience to make it palatable to those who were in a position to alleviate it, they were silent about many things, and they 'forgot' many other things. ...[1]

We should note that 'things too terrible to relate' were most often the sexual exploitation of slave women by white men. Convention allowed, indeed almost demanded, that these violations be named but not described. Morrison continues, 'But most importantly, – at least for me – there was no mention of their *interior life*' (emphasis mine). The writer's 'job' – as Morrison sees it – 'becomes how to rip that veil drawn over proceedings too terrible to relate ...,' to 'find and expose a truth about the interior life of people who didn't write it,' to 'fill in the blanks that the slave narratives left, to part the veil that was so frequently drawn,' and, finally, 'to implement the stories that [she has] heard' (110–113).

In utilizing the image of the veil, we note that Morrison draws on and revises a DuBoisian metaphor that was originally intended to suggest the division between blacks and whites in American society.[2] Rather than measuring a division *between* the races, however, Morrison's use of the veil as metaphor measures a division *within* the race – a psychic and expressive boundary separating the *speakable* from the *unspeakable* and the *unspoken*.[3] Her task as a writer, therefore, is to transgress these discursive boundaries by setting up a complementary and dialogic relationship between the 'interiority' of her own work and the 'exteriority' of the slave narrative.

Morrison, then, aims to restore a dimension of the repressed personal in a manifestly political discourse. In some ways, the texts of the slave narratives can be regarded as classic examples of the 'return of the repressed,' primarily because the events relating to violence and violation (which are self-censored or edited out) return again and again in 'veiled allusions.' To the degree that her work is intended to *resurrect* stories *buried* and *express* stories *repressed*, Morrison's relationship to the slave narrators, as well as the relationship of her text to its precursor narratives, can be profitably compared not only to the relationship of the historian to his or her informant, but also the analyst to the analysand.

Dedicating her novel *Beloved* to the 'Sixty Million and more' who failed to survive the Middle Passage, Morrison sets out to give voice to the 'disremembered and unaccounted for' – the women and children who left no written records. The epigraph from Romans 9:25 prefigures the writer's purpose to reclaim this 'lost tribe':

> *I will call them my people,*
> *which were not my people;*
> *and her beloved,*
> *which was not beloved.*

In her citation of a New Testament passage that repeats with little difference a passage from the Old Testament, the author not only problematizes the nature of the relationship between the past and the present, but also thematizes the importance of historical Reclamation and Repossession. As Jehovah reclaimed the Israelites after their apostasy (figured in Hosea as spiritual adultery), so Morrison seeks to repossess the African and slave ancestors after their historic violation (figured in *Beloved* as physical rape). Further, Morrison reinscribes the tension between Old Testament Law and New Testament spirit. Significantly, it is the epistles of Paul (Romans and Galatians, in particular) which announce that the doctrine of justification by deeds under the Old Dispensation of the Law is revised through justification by grace under the New Dispensation of the Spirit.[4] Engaging the Scriptures as a kind of intertext, Morrison enacts in her novel an opposition between the Law and the Spirit, redeeming her characters from the 'curse of the law' as figured in the master's discourse. In her rewriting of Scripture, Morrison ushers in an ironic new dispensation figured not by the Law of the (white) Father, but the Spirit of the (black and female) child, Beloved. Thus Morrison challenges the hegemonic status of the (primarily male) slave narratives as well as the 'canonical' history embodied in the master('s) narratives in a project which seeks to make both more accountable to the 'disremembered and unaccounted for.'

Like several of her contemporaries, Morrison seeks to achieve these ends in a novel that both historicizes fiction and fictionalizes history.[5]

[...]

A paragraph comprising quotations from Morrison, about the 'real' events on which *Beloved* is based, is omitted here.

[...]

Morrison's project, then, is twofold: the exploration of the black woman's sense of self, and the imaginative recovery of black women's history.

Describing her narrative strategy as a 'kind of literary archeology,' Morrison explains that, for her, 'the approach that's most productive and most trustworthy ... is the recollection that moves from the image to ... text.' Her task, as she defines it, is to '[move] that veil aside' in order to penetrate the 'memories within.' Although these memories – personal and collective – constitute the 'subsoil of [her] work,' she informs us that these alone cannot give 'total access to the unwritten interior life. ...' For Morrison, it is 'only the act of the imagination' that can provide such access:

> [O]n the basis of some information and a little bit of guesswork you journey to a site to see what remains were left behind and to reconstruct the world that these remains imply. What makes it fiction is the nature of the imaginative act: my reliance on the image – on the remains – in addition to recollection, to yield up a kind of truth. By 'image,' of course, I don't mean 'symbol'; I simply mean 'picture' and the feelings that accompany the picture.[6]

Elaborating on the relationship between picture and meaning, Morrison contrasts her own literary method (to move from image to text) to that of writers who move 'from event to the image that it left': 'My route is the reverse: the image comes first and tells me what the "memory" is about.'[7]

The notion of 'literary archeology' – the imaginative and reconstructive recovery of the past which characterizes Morrison's fictive process – can be usefully compared with R.G. Collingwood's description of the historical process: if the novelist relies upon the *a priori* imagination to construct the *possible* story in which characters and incidents develop 'in a manner determined by a necessity internal to themselves,' the historian relies upon the same inferential process to construct 'his' story of the *past*.

[...]

A quotation from Collingwood on the affinity of history and fiction 'as works of imagination' follows here.

[...]

The present essay will examine Morrison's novel in the context of some contemporary historical theory on discourse and narrativity, suggesting, where novelistic considerations warrant, a reading that links historiography and psychoanalysis.

Like Morrison, the principal character in *Beloved* is in struggle with a past that is part of white/male historical discourse. Lacking a discourse of her own, Sethe's task is to transform the residual images ('rememories') of her past into a historical discourse shaped by narrativity. These images, however, remain for a time disembodied – without form, sequence, or meaning. The challenge of the slave as victim of enforced illiteracy is similar to that of the highly literate contemporary historian or novelist – and that is to discover a way of organizing memory, of contriving a narrative configuration in the absence of written records. If it is true, as Henry Louis Gates, Jr. argues, that our sense of the self, as we have defined it in the West since the Enlightenment, 'turns in part upon written records,' if 'our idea of the self ... is ... inextricably interwoven with our ideas ... of [writing],' then what are the consequences of an absence of written records? Quite simply and perhaps startlingly, as a slave 'one's sense of one's existence ... depended upon memory.' 'It was memory, above all else,' according to Gates, 'that gave shape to being itself.'[8] What these remarks do not address, however, is how one formally shapes and derives meaning from disparate memories. In other words, how does one extract a configuration from a cluster of images or diversity of events? How does one, finally, transpose memories from a visual to a diegetic, or narrative, register? Like Morrison, Sethe must learn to represent the unspeakable and unspoken in language – and more precisely, as narrative.

Morrison figures both the interiority and the exteriority of memory, that is, memory as thought and memory as material inscription.[9] In the novel, 'Beloved' is the public inscription of a private memorial – seven letters chiseled into the pink headstone of a child-victim of 'mother-love,' a word Sethe had remembered from the preacher's funeral eulogy. If the inscription of Beloved is the trace ('the mark left behind') that initiates the novel's plot, it is also an image that haunts the text in the multiple guises of the character Beloved. As a term, 'beloved' is an address conferred by the lover on the object of affection, and used in matrimonial and eulogistic discourse, both commemorative, linguistic events: the former prefiguring the future, the latter refiguring the past. The action of the novel, however, attends to the novelistic present – a present problematized by an unresolved past and an unantici-pated future, a present which the past does not prefigure nor the future refigure.

When we meet Sethe at the outset of the novel, her 'future was a matter of keeping the past at bay' (42).[10] Her aim has been to protect her children from 'rememory' – which she describes as follows:

> Someday you be walking down the road and you hear something or see something going on. So clear. ... It's when you bump into a rememory that belongs to somebody else. Where I was before I came here, that place [Sweet Home] is real. It's never going away. Even if the whole farm – every tree and grass blade of it dies. The picture is still there and what's more, if you go there – you who never was there – if you go there and stand in the place where it was, it will happen again; it will be there for you, waiting for you. (36)

'Rememory,' it would seem, is something which possesses (or haunts) one, rather than something which one possesses. (It is, in fact, that which makes the past part of one's present.) Yet, despite her best efforts to '[beat] back the past,' Sethe remains, in her words, 'full of it.' 'Every mention of her past life hurt. Everything in it was painful or lost'(58). Hayden White's description of Ibsen's Hedda Gabler would also seem apt for Morrison's Sethe: She 'suffers [from] the incubus [or, in this case, the succubus] of the past – a surfeit of history compounded by, or reflected in, a pervasive fear of the future.'[11]

Thus, unable to contrive a meaningful or appropriate configuration for her memories, Sethe finds herself tyrannized by unconfigured and literally disfiguring images. As a consequence of an attempted escape, she receives a savage beating, leaving her back 'a clump of scars.' These scars function as signs of ownership inscribing her as property, while the mutilation signifies her diminishment to a less-than-human status. Traces of the past that Sethe represses (but can neither remember nor forget) have been gouged onto her back by the master's whip and bear the potential burden of both *hi*story and *her*story. Like the inscription of Beloved and the pictorial images of the past, the scars function as an archeological site or memory trace.

If the master has inscribed the master('s) code on Sethe's back, a white woman and a black man, in an effort to decipher it offer her alternative readings. Although initially 'struck dumb' at the sight of Sethe's scars, Amy, a runaway white girl who saves the fugitive's life and midwives the delivery of her second daughter, sees Sethe's back as a 'chokecherry tree':

> See, here's the trunk – it's red and split wide open, full of sap, and this here's the parting for the branches. ... Leaves, too, look like, and dern if these ain't blossoms. Tiny little cherry blossoms, just as white. Your back got a whole tree on it. In bloom. (79)

Amy describes an image, but an image which prompts her to wonder 'what God have in mind.' In her reverie, Sethe's back remains the trace of an event whose meaning, motivation, and consequence are largely unreadable.

Alternative readings are provided by Baby Suggs, Sethe's mother-in-law, and Paul D, the last survivor of the men from Sweet Home, the Kentucky plantation where he and Sethe had met before the War. Baby Suggs perceives her daughter-in-law's back as a pattern of 'roses of blood,' stenciled onto the bedsheet and blanket. Paul D, however, remarks on 'the sculpture [Sethe's] back had become, like the decorative work of an ironsmith too passionate for display. ...' (By the time Paul D arrives, the open wounds have healed into an intricate filigree whose private meaning is concealed from public exposure.) Notably, the distance between these sugges-tively gendered readings – the chokecherry tree and blood roses on the one hand, and the wrought-iron maze on the other – signifies the distance between so-called 'natural' and culturally inscribed meanings attributed to the sign.

It is the white man who inscribes; the white woman, the black man, and the black woman may variously read, but not write. Because it is her back (symbolizing the *presence* of her *past*) that is marked, Sethe has only been able to read herself through the gaze of others. The challenge for Sethe is to learn to read herself – that is, to configure the history of her body's text. If, as Paul Ricoeur contends, 'the past survives by leaving its trace,' then Sethe must learn how to link these traces (marks of her passage through slavery) to the construction of a personal and historical discourse.[12] Sethe's dilemma is that as a female slave without the benefit of literacy, she finds herself the written object of a white male discourse and the spoken subject of a black male and white female discourse. Significantly, Baby Suggs does *not* speak of the wounds on Sethe's back. 'Baby Suggs hid her mouth with her hand' (93). Instead, she concentrates on the ritual of healing: '[W]ordlessly, the older woman greased the flowering back and pinned a double thickness of cloth to the inside of the newly stitched dress' (emphasis mine, 93). The presumption is, of course, that black women have no voice, no text, and consequently no history. They can be written and written upon precisely because they exist as the ultimate Other whose absence or (non)being only serves to define the being or presence of the white or male subject. The black woman, symbolizing a kind of double negativity, becomes a *tabula rasa* upon which the racial/sexual identity of the other(s) can be positively inscribed.

Sethe's back is numb ('the skin on her back had been dead for years'), signifying her attempts to repress the past. (But the return of Paul D and, later Beloved, signal the return of the repressed.) For Sethe, these scars constitute traces of past deeds too horrible and violent either to forget or remember (a situation which Morrison describes elsewhere as 'a perfect dilemma'). The brutal whipping she receives as punishment for her attempt to run away is only part of a cluster of events which Sethe vainly seeks to forget.

If Morrison formalizes and thematizes the operation of imaginative construction, she also dramatizes, in the character of 'Schoolteacher' (as he is called by the slaves), the consequences of an alternative approach. The scenes with Schoolteacher are paradigmatic for reading the methodology of the white male as scholar and master.

[...]

A paragraph describing the Schoolteacher's characteristics is cut here.

[...]

Morrison's schoolteacher espouses a concept of difference and 'otherness' as a form of subhumanity that serves, through a process of negative self-identification, to confirm his own sense of superiority. It is Sethe's 'savagery' which confirms Schoolteacher's 'civilization,' her 'bestiality' which confirms his 'humanity.' Schoolteacher's sense of history is defined by the struggle between culture and nature, and questions of meaning and interpretation turn upon this opposition.[13]

The dismemberment of Schoolteacher's method is the discursive analog to the dismemberment of slavery. Just as his pupils measure and divide Sethe according to Schoolteacher's instructions, so Schoolteacher himself, speaking with the slave catchers, reveals to Paul D 'his worth.' Overhearing the men talking, Paul D, who 'has always known, or believed he did, his value – as a hand, a laborer who could make profit on a farm … now [discovers] his worth, which is to say he learns his price. The dollar value of his weight, his strength, his heart, his brain, his penis, and his future' (226). As both slaveholder and scholar, Schoolteacher is involved with the *dis-membering* of slaves from their families, their labor, their selves. It is against these forms of physical, social, and scholarly dismemberment that the act of (re)memory initiates a reconstitutive process in the novel. If dismemberment deconstitutes the whole, fragmenting it into various discrete and heterogeneous parts, then re-memory functions to re-collect, re-assemble, and organize into a meaningful sequential whole through, as we shall see, the process of narrativization.

The scenes of Paul D's figurative dismemberment both refigure the earlier scene of Schoolteacher's anatomical dismemberment of Sethe and prefigure a later scene which Sethe vainly attempts to forget: 'I am full God damn it of two boys with mossy teeth, one sucking on my breast the other holding me down, their book-reading teacher watching and writing it up' (70). Like Paul D, who is forced to go around with a horse's 'bit' in his mouth, Sethe is forced to submit to the bovine-like humiliation of 'being milked.' In this grotesque parody of Madonna and child, Sethe's milk, like her labor and the fruits of her womb, is expropriated. But the theft of her 'mother's milk' suggests the expropriation of her future – her ability to nurture and ensure the survival of the future embodied in the next generation.

With some irony we learn that Sethe herself has mixed Schoolteacher's ink,

> [Schoolteacher liked] how [she] mixed it and it was important to him because at night he sat down to write in his book. It was a book about [the slaves] ... He commenced to carry round a notebook and write down what we said. (37)

The image of Schoolteacher's ink conflates with the expropriation of Sethe's milk in a symbol that evokes Hélène Cixous's metaphor for 'écriture féminine' – namely, women writing a language of the body in the white ink of the mother's milk. It is not only the pages of his notebook, but also the literal inscription of Sethe's back with the markings of Schoolteacher's whip(pen) that constitute the ironically perverse fulfillment of Cixous's call.[14] Appropriating Sethe's 'milk' through a process of phallic substitution, Schoolteacher uses the pen – the symbol and instrument of masculine 'authority' in the sense that Sandra Gilbert and Susan Gubar use the term – to 're-mark' the slave woman with the signature of his paternity.[15] Sethe must discover some way of regaining control of her story, her body, her progeny, her milk, her ability to nurture the future.

Schoolteacher's association with 'the prison-house of language,' figured not only in his private ledger, but in the public slave codes as well, refigures the New Testament's personification of the Decalogue. St. Paul tells the churches in Galatia that 'the law was our schoolmaster,' or (alternatively translated) 'we were held prisoners by the law.'[16] It is this white/male construction of the law according to the authority of the master discourse that Sethe must first dismantle in order to construct her own story.

For Schoolteacher, history is a confining activity; for Sethe, it must become a liberating activity. She must accomplish precisely what Morrison does in the act of historicizing fiction – namely, 'to free retrospectively, certain possibilities that were not actualized in the historical past,' and to detect 'possibilities buried in the ... past.'[17] As historian, Sethe must liberate her present from the 'burden of the past' as constructed in '*history*.' She must learn to remap the past so that it becomes, for her, a blueprint for the future. Her job is to reconstitute the past through personal narrative, or storytelling. Collingwood has argued that the historian is primarily 'a story teller,' suggesting that 'historical sensibility is manifested in the capacity to make a plausible story out of congeries of "facts" which, in their unprocessed form, made no sense at all.'[18] Like Morrison, Sethe uses the memory of personal experience and what Collingwood calls the 'constructive imagination' as a means of re-membering a dis-membered past, and as a means of re-membering a dis-membered family and community.

If Morrison moves 'from image to text,' Sethe, too, begins with the image and, through a process of narrativization described by Ricoeur as *configuration* and White as *emplotment*, she shapes and animates 'rememories' of the past, endowing them with form, drama, and meaning. Narrativization enables Sethe to construct a meaningful life-story from a cluster of images, to transform separate and disparate events into a whole and coherent story.[19]

For Sethe, the past has the power either to make her captive or free. Her feelings, hopes, desires, perceptions – all colored by past incidents and events, culminating in what to her remain unspeakable acts and actions: physical violation and infanticide. Expressing her situation, Sethe thinks, 'Freeing yourself was one thing; claiming ownership of that freed self was another' (95). It is her preoccupation with the past that makes it impossible for her to process any new experiences except through the distant lens of the particular events in question. What Gates describes as 'this brilliant substructure of the system of slavery' – the dependence of the slave upon her memory – had the potential of making the slave [and later the ex-slave], in some respects, 'a slave to [her]self, a prisoner of [her] own power to recall.'[20]

If certain events remain unconfigured, others are overly and inappropriately configured. Thus an alternative reading of Sethe's dilemma might be 'overemplotment.' Using White's model, one might say that she has 'overemplotted' the events of her past, that she has 'charged them with a meaning so intense that … they continue to shape both [her] perceptions and [her] responses to the world long after they should have become "past history."' The problem for Sethe, then, is to configure or emplot on the one hand, but to '*re*configure' or '*re*emplot' on the other. She must imaginatively reconstitute, or 're-member,' her history 'in such a way as to change the *meaning* of those events for [her] and their *significance* for the economy of the whole set of events that make up [her] life.'[21] If Gates's assertion that 'the act of writing for the slave [narrator] constitute[s] the act of creating a public … self,' then I propose that the act of re-membering, for the unlettered slave, constitutes the act of constructing a private self.[22] As Ricoeur argues, it is the (re)configuration of the past which enables one to refigure the future – and such is Sethe's task.

If memory is *materialized* in Beloved's reappearance, it is *maternalized* in Sethe's (re)configuration. Sethe gives *birth to her past and to her future*: first to the baby with no name whose angry and sad spirit comes back to haunt 124 Bluestone Road, and later to the incarnate Beloved, the young woman with 'flawless skin and feet and hands soft and new.' The return of Beloved, therefore, becomes not only a psychological projection, but also a physical (rather than spiritual) manifestation. Her 'rebirth' represents, as it were, the uncanny return of the dead to haunt the living, the return of the past to shadow the present.

Yet it is the notion of 'self-distanciation' that intrigues Morrison in this as in other works: 'What is it that really compels a good woman to displace the self, her self?,' asks Morrison. What interests her is not only the nobility and generosity of these actions, but also the fact that such love ('the best thing that is in us') 'is ... the thing that makes us [as women] sabotage ourselves, sabotage in the sense [of perceiving] that our life ["the best part of ourselves"] is not as worthy.' Her method of characterization is intended to suggest this process of displacement – 'to project the self not into the way we say "yourself" but to put a space between those words, as though the self were really a *twin* or a thirst or a friend or something that sits right next to you and watches you. ...' What Morrison has done is to '[project] the dead out into the earth' in the character of Beloved, so that Beloved becomes the twin self or mirror of Sethe and other women in the novel.[23] Morrison's critical reflections, however, point to another dimension of Sethe's dilemma, a dilemma which combines the private and the public functions of 'rememory.' If the individual is defined as a conduit of communal consciousness, then (drawing on Teresa de Lauretis) the events of Sethe's life can be emplotted through historiography; conversely, if the community is defined as a conduit of individual consciousness, then the events of Sethe's psychic life can be encoded in psychoanalytic discourse.[24]

It is at the point of this intersection between the personal and the social that we begin to conflate the psychic and the historical. In other words, what I have been describing in terms of a kind of social subjectivity emplotted by historiography can also be figured in terms of psychic subjectivity and represented in the discourse of psychoanalysis.

[...]

A paragraph of short quotations from Norman Brown on the relation between the psychoanalytical and historical consciousness is cut here.

[...]

Linking history and psychoanalysis, then the events in Sethe's life can be encoded in an alternate plot structure. Sethe's past, the sources of her 'complex' or dis-ease, manifest themselves in her endless efforts to avoid the past and avert the future. The events in her past – namely, her own violation and the ensuing decision to take her daughter's life – have become sources of both repression and obsession. Sethe must 'conjure up' her past – symbolized by Beloved – and confront it as an antagonist. Drawing on Freud's 'recommendations on the technique of psychoanalysis,' one might say that Sethe must learn to regard her problematic past as an 'enemy worthy of [her] mettle, a piece of [her] personality, which has solid ground for its existence and out of which things of value for [her] future life have to be derived.' It is her communication with Beloved – and the events of the past which Beloved both symbolizes and evokes – that affords Sethe the opportunity 'to become ... conversant with this resistance over which [she] has now become acquainted, to *work through* it, to overcome it, by continuing, in defiance of it, the analytic work. ...'[25] Thus, the psychoanalytic process becomes, for Sethe, the means by which she must free herself from the burden of her past and from the burden of *hi*story.

In fact, psychoanalysis, as Michel de Certeau points out, is based on the theme which preoccupies Morrison's novel: the return of the repressed. 'This "mechanism,"' writes de Certeau, 'is linked to a certain conception of time and memory, according to which consciousness is both the deceptive *mask* and the operative *trace* of events that organize the present.' 'If the past ... is *repressed*,' he continues, '*it returns* in the present from which it was excluded. ...' The figuration of this 'detour-return,' and its consequences in the lives of individual characters as well as the community as a whole, structures Morrison's novel.[26]

It is in the 'poetic' chapters of the novel that the reader senses the full implications of Beloved (as well as the younger daughter, Denver) in relation to Sethe. The retreat of Sethe and her daughters behind the closed doors of 124 Bluestone represents a familial figuration of what Alfred Schutz calls 'the succession of generations: contemporaries, predecessors, and successors,' associated with the present, past, and future respectively. The connection of Sethe's present with her past is figuratively embodied in her relationship to Beloved while the connection with[27] her future is figuratively embodied in her relationship with Denver. The family thus becomes the site in which to explore notions of 'time and being.' As a historical field, it represents the complex and intimate interdependence of past, present, and future; as an ontological field, it represents the complexity of the relationship between Self and Other. The family, in other words, becomes a historically constituted social site in which individual subjectivity is constructed.

Further, Beloved symbolizes women in both the contemporaneous and historical black communities. Affiliated with the experiences of various women in the novel, Beloved represents the unsuccessfully repressed 'other' of Sethe as well as other women in and associated with the community – including Ella, whose 'puberty was spent in a house where she was abused by a father and son'; Vashti (the wife of Stamp Paid, who had ferried Sethe and others across the Ohio River to free land), who was concubined by her young master, and the girl who (as rumor had it) was locked up by a 'whiteman' who had used her to his own purpose 'since she was a pup'. Beyond this, however, Beloved is associated with her maternal and paternal grandmothers and the generation of slave women who failed to survive the 'middle passage.' As trace of 'the disremembered and unaccounted for,' Beloved's symbolic function of otherness connects the individual to repressed aspects of the self, as well as to contemporaneous and historical others. It is, in fact, Beloved's implication in the lives of the collectivity of women that makes it necessary that all the women in the community later participate in the ritual to exorcise her.

Central to Morrison's vision, as we have seen, is the reconstitution of self and other through re-memory in the act of storytelling, an act which imposes sequence and meaning on the welter of images and memories which shape and define one's sense of self. Yet, Sethe must not only narrativize her life in White's sense of rendering to her past the formal coherence of story; she must also be able to continue the process of metamorphosis by 'metaphorizing' her experiences within narrative.[28] Morrison uses the metaphor of maternity to establish an alternative to the metaphor of paternity common in white/male historical discourse. This recurrent and structuring metaphor complements and amplifies the images of the female body that are encoded in the text. In her remarks in 'Site of Memory,' Morrison provides a *cognitive* metaphor for representing her reconstructive methods as a novelist. The images of interiority which she privileges suggest specifically female images associated with the 'interior' rather than the 'exterior' life, with the personal rather than the public representation of experience. Ultimately, such a metaphor suggests that the object of our understanding is *inside* rather than *outside*, and thus can be reached only by what Morrison describes as her method of 'literary archeology.'[29]

Secondly, Sethe's birthing of the past and future appropriately figures Morrison's use of *depictive* metaphor. If the act of birthing figures Sethe's life-story in a metaphor of maternity, then, the womb functions as an image of corporeal interiority, the counterpart to Sethe's psychic interiority and Morrison's diegetic interiority. As a narrative metaphor, maternity privileges interiority and marks Sethe's entry into subjectivity. Perhaps the best example of this function is found in the scene describing Sethe's reaction upon seeing the incarnate Beloved for the first time:

> [F]or some reason she could not immediately account for, the moment she got close enough to see [Beloved's face], Sethe's bladder filled to capacity. ... She never made the outhouse. Right in front of its door she had to lift her skirts, and the water she voided was endless. Like a horse, she thought, but as it went on and on she thought, No, more like flooding the boat when Denver was born. So much water Amy said, 'Hold on ... You going to sink us you keep that up.' But there was no stopping water breaking from a breaking womb and there was no stopping now. (51)

Notably, Sethe rejects, on second thought, the equine metaphor. Further, in a radical reconception of history and culture, her ritual of birthing figures motherhood as a primary metaphor of history and human culture. The postdeluvian connotation of 'breaking of the water' historicizes the event and, at the same time, signifies a maternal delivery which becomes a means of 'deliverance' from the dominant conception of history as a white/paternal metaphor. Morrison seems to figure here a second immaculate conception, if you will, in which black motherhood becomes self-generative – a process which, in effect, reconstitutes black womanhood. By shifting the dominant metaphor from white to black and from paternity (embodied in the figure of the slavemaster) to maternity (figured and literally embodied in the black female slave), Morrison has shifted meaning and value. It is through this process of destructuring and restructuring, of decoding and recoding, that Morrison redefines notions of genesis and meaning as they have served to constitute black womanhood in the dominant discourse.

To return to the last in our typology of metaphor, the images of motherhood function *heuristically* to explain or 'trace' Sethe's history and that of the community along 'motherlines.' Her past, birthed from a womblike matrix, is read back through motherlines, motherlines tracked through four generations of marked slave women. It is Beloved's 'thirst' for these stories that gives her mother 'an unexpected pleasure' in *speaking* things which 'she and Baby Suggs had agreed without saying so ... [were] *unspeakable*' (emphasis mine). In speaking, that is, in storytelling, Sethe is able to construct an alternate text of black womanhood. This power to fashion a counternarrative, thereby rejecting the definitions imposed by the dominant other(s) finally provides Sethe with a self – a past, present, and future.

It is Beloved's persistent questions that enable Sethe to re-member long forgotten traces of her own mother, traces carried through memory as well as through the body. Sethe remembers that her own mother bore a mark, 'a circle and a cross burnt right in the skin' on her rib. It was the mark of ownership by the master who had as much as written 'property' under her breast. Yet like Sethe (as well as Hawthorne's Hester Prynne), her mother had transformed a mark of mutilation, a sign of diminished humanity, into a sign of recognition and identity. Sethe recalls her mother's words: 'This is your ma'am. ..., I am the only one got this mark now. The rest dead. If something happens to me and you can't tell me by my face, you can know me by this mark' (61). Indeed, it is her own markings which help her to decode the meaning of her mother's remarks. Sethe tells her own daughters, Denver and Beloved, 'I didn't understand it then. Not till I had a mark of my own.'

Constructed and metaphorized along motherlines, Sethe's retelling of her childhood story also enables her to decipher meaning encoded in a long forgotten 'mother tongue,' meaning which she passes on to her own daughter. Equally important, Sethe's story enables her to reread or reemplot her own experiences in the context of sacrifice, resistance, and motherlove. Although Sethe knows that the 'language her ma'am spoke ... would never come back,' she begins to recognize 'the message – that was and had been there all along,' and she began 'picking meaning out of a code she no longer understood.' Like the historian confronted with a plethora of documents who seeks to configure a probable story, Sethe seeks to reconfigure events based on 'words. Words Sethe understood then but could neither recall nor repeat now' (62). Remembering the story told her by Nan, 'the one she knew best, who was around all day, who nursed babies, cooked, had one good arm and half of another' – Nan, who spoke 'the same language her ma'am spoke,' Sethe is able to reconstruct her own story:

> Nighttime. Nan holding her with her good arm, waving the stump of the other in the air. 'Telling you. I am telling you, small girl Sethe,' and she did that. She told Sethe that her mother and Nan were together from the sea. Both were taken up many times by the crew. 'She threw them all away but you. The one from the crew she threw away on the island. The others from more whites she also threw away. Without names, she threw them. You she gave the name of the black man. She put her arms around him. The others she did not put her arms around. Never. Never. Telling you. I am telling you, small girl Sethe.' (62)

Interestingly Sethe's name recalls the Old Testament Hebrew name of 'Seth,' meaning 'granted' or 'appointed.' (Eve named her third born Seth, saying, 'God has granted me another child in the place of Abel.')[30] In this instance, it would seem that

Sethe signifies the child whose life was spared or 'granted' by her mother, who did not keep the offspring of the white men who forced themselves upon her. The story told her as a child about her mother by Nan, another mutilated mother, ironically prefigures Sethe's own actions, but at the same time, challenges her to some accountability. For although Beloved, like Sethe and her mother, bears a mark of mutilation, the scar across Beloved's throat is the mark of Sethe's own hand. And it is the fingerprints on Beloved's forehead as well as the scar under her chin ('the little curved shadow of a smile in the kootchy-koochy-coo place') that enables Sethe to recognize her daughter returned from 'the other side.'

In light of her recognition Sethe reconstitutes a family story of infanticide, a story of repetition, but repetition with a marked difference. Sethe's story of motherlove would seem to overwrite a story of rejection, and Sethe's task as historian is to find a narrative form that speaks to that difference. But it is her mother's story which refamiliarizes her own story. She receives from her mother that which she had hoped to discover with Paul D: 'Her story was bearable' – *not* because it was Paul D's, but *her mother's* – 'to tell, to refine and tell again' (99). The maternal discourse becomes a testimonial one for Sethe. What both mother and daughter share is protection of their own children – the one by saving a life and the other by taking a life.

But there are competing configurations as well. The first full representation of the events surrounding the infanticide are figured from a collective white/male perspective, represented by Schoolteacher and the sheriff:

> Inside [the shed], two boys bled in the sawdust and dirt at the feet of a nigger woman holding a blood-soaked child to her chest with one hand and an infant by the heels in the other. She did not look at them; she simply swung the baby toward the wall planks, missed and tried to connect a second time … Right off it was clear, to schoolteacher especially, that there was nothing there to claim. The three (now four – because she'd had the one coming when she cut) pickaninnies they had hoped were alive and well enough to take back to Kentucky, take back and raise properly to do the work Sweet Home desperately needed, were not … He could claim the baby struggling in the arms of the mewing old man, but who'd tend her? Because the woman – something was wrong with her. She was looking at him now, and if his other nephew could see that look he would learn the lesson for sure: you just can't mishandle *creatures* and expect success. (emphasis mine, 149–150)

In Schoolteacher's narrative, Sethe is 'the woman [who] … made fine ink, damn good soup, pressed his collars the way he liked besides having at least ten breeding years left …' In his words, 'she's gone wild, due to mishandling of the nephew' (149). The white sheriff reads these events as a cautionary tale on 'the results of a little so-called freedom imposed on people who needed every care and guidance in the world to keep them from the cannibal life they preferred'(151). Granting authority to the white newspaper's account, Stamp Paid concludes that '… while he and Baby Suggs were looking the wrong way, a pretty little slavegirl had recognized [her former master's hat], and split to the woodshed to kill her children' (158). Paul D, who suddenly 'saw what Stamp Paid wanted him to see,' summarizes events by insisting, 'You got two feet, Sethe, not four' (164–165).

Sethe must compete with the dominant metaphors of the master('s) narrative – wildness, cannibalism, animality, destructiveness. In radical opposition to these constructions is Sethe's reconceptualized metaphor of self based on motherhood, motherlines, and motherlove – a love described by Paul D as 'too thick.' Convinced that 'the best thing she was, was her children,' Sethe wants simply to stop Schoolteacher:

> Because the truth was ... [s]imple: she was squatting in the garden and when she saw them coming and recognized schoolteacher's hat, she heard wings. Little hummingbirds stuck their needle beaks right through her headcloth into her hair and beat their wings. And if she thought anything, it was No. No. Nono. Nonono. Simple. She just flew. Collected every bit of life she had made, all the parts of her that were precious and fine and beautiful, and carried, pushed, dragged them through the veil, out, away, over there where no one could hurt them (163).

'I took and put my babies where they'd be safe,' she tells Paul D (164). And in this way, she explains to Beloved, '[N]o one, nobody on this earth, would list her daughter's characteristics on the animal side of the paper' (251).

Sethe, in effect, creates a counternarrative that reconstitutes her humanity and demonstrates the requirements of motherlove. By shifting the dominant white and male metaphor to a black and maternal metaphor for self and history, Sethe effectively changes the plot and meaning of the story – and finally, the story itself. A story of oppression becomes a story of liberation; a story of inhumanity has been overwritten as a story of higher humanity. It is this process of destructuring and restructuring the dominant discourse and its organizing tropes that enables Sethe (and Morrison) to subvert the master code of the master('s) text. By privileging specifically female tropes in her narrative, Sethe is able to reconstitute her self and herstory within the context of intergenerational black women's experiences as represented in memory and narrative. By placing her life-history within a maternal family history and, by implication, placing her family history within a broader tradition of racial history, Morrison demonstrates not only the strength of motherlines in the slave community, but also how ontogeny followed black and female phylogeny. (It is the absence of Sethe's two runaway sons which, in effect, leaves Denver as sole heir and guarantor of the family's future.)

In accordance with Collingwood's notion of 'history as reenactment' of past experience, Sethe is able, finally, to 're-enact' a critical moment in her life.

[...]

A quotation from Collingwood on the process by which knowledge of the self is recovered is omitted.

[...]

Like the historian, Sethe is able to 're-act' or 're-think' a critical moment from the past, and is consequently able to perform an action which has the effect of altering her own life-history. In one of the final scenes in the novel, Sethe re-enacts the past, an act which provides an occasion for her to demonstrate her possession *of* rather than *by* the past. Sethe's actions, moreover, demonstrate that the present is bound to the past and the past to the future, and it is precisely the (re)configuration of the past that enables her to refigure the future.[31]

What has in the past been enacted in the psychic field is re-enacted, and dramatically and therapeutically re-worked, in the social field. The 'rememory' and repetition of actions which have imprisoned the 'patient' in the bonds of the past are broken in a scene of re-enactment in which Sethe rethinks and revises her previous (re)action. In a final and climactic scene of the novel, Sethe is able to 'relive' or re-enact the past.

Beloved is, in fact, exorcised during the course of this re-enactment. With the support of 'thirty neighborhood women,' Sethe is released from possession by the spirit of a now speakable past. Unable to 'countenance the possibility of sin moving on in the house,' the community performs a ritual of exorcism which 'frees' Sethe from the burden of her past:

> Instantly the kneelers and the standers joined [Sethe]. They stopped praying and took a step back to the beginning. *In the beginning there were no words. In the beginning was the sound*, and they all knew what that sound sounded like. (emphasis mine, 259)

Evoking 'the beginning' in which there were 'no words' – only 'the sound' – black women's voices revise Scripture ('In the beginning was the word') in such a way that the semiotic (rather than the symbolic) is associated with creation and creativity. In its revision of Scripture, this 'key,' this 'code,' this 'sound that broke the back of words' represents a challenge to the dominant white and male discourse in which the text of black womanhood is constructed. Sethe is, moreover, 'born again' in her reclamation by the community ('[The voices] broke over Sethe and she trembled like baptized in its wash') as much as by the community's exorcism of Beloved. The communal voice of black women, then, possesses the power not only to destroy, but also to create. In fact, Sethe's 're-birth' is predicated upon the rupture of the master('s) discourse. Thus, not only is Sethe 'delivered' from the 'errors' of her past, but her discourse is 'delivered' from the constraints of the master('s) discourse.

It is during the course of the communal exorcism that Sethe espies the 'black hat wide-brimmed enough to hide [Schoolteacher's] face but not his purpose. He is coming into her yard and he is coming for her best thing. She hears wings. Little hummingbirds stick needle beaks right through her headcloth into her hair and beat their wings. And if she thinks anything, it is no. No no. Nonono. She flies. The ice pick is not in her hand; it is her hand' (262). Sethe, in effect, re-enacts the original event – remembering, repeating, and working-through the 'primal scene' in a process that emblematizes the psychoanalytic process. This time, however, Sethe directs her response to the threatening Other rather than to 'her best thing' – her children. But it is not only Sethe who re-enacts the earlier scene; the community itself participates in the re-enactment. Because the community had failed to send warning of the slave captors' approach the first time, its 'sin of omission' makes it no less responsible for Beloved's death than Sethe's 'sin of commission.' In a scene of collective re-enactment, the women of the community intervene at a critical juncture, to save not Beloved, but Sethe. Thus, by revising her actions, Sethe is able to preserve the community, and the community in turn, is able to protect one of its own.

Returning once more to Ricoeur's model, prefiguration denotes the temporality of the world of human action; configuration the world of the narrative emplotment of these events; and refiguration the moment at which these two worlds interact and affect each other. It is Sethe's actions which constitute the prefigurative aspect; her storytelling which constitutes the configurative aspect; and finally, the re-enactment which constitutes the refigurative aspect.[32] Moreover, Morrison enables the reader to connect with the otherness of these past generations – especially as it relates to the experiences of slave women – in a process made possible by 'the intersection of the world of the text with the world of the reader.' Just as Nan's story of the generational mother enables Sethe to (re)configure her past, so Morrison's story of the historical m(other) enables the reader to do likewise. Moreover, the reader, like Sethe, learns that she must claim and surrender the past in order to refigure the future.[33]

The question of Sethe's accountability, however, must be addressed. Does Morrison, finally, indict or defend Sethe's 'too thick' motherlove? Is Sethe truly redeemed from an unspeakable past? If so, by what means? Wherein lies Sethe's 'redemption' from the 'sins' of the past – both those perpetuated *upon* her and *by* her? Is grace achieved through the spirit of Beloved (the past generations she symbolizes) or by its exorcism? Characteristically, Morrison draws out the paradoxes and ambiguities of this 'perfect dilemma.' I would suggest that the author, in fact, neither condemns nor condones, but rather 'delivers' her protagonist. For Sethe achieves redemption through *possession* by the spirit as well as *exorcism* of the spirit. Significantly, for Morrison, it is not through the Law ('Because the Law worketh wrath'), but the spirit (its reclamation and relinquishment) that the individual achieves 'deliverance' from the 'sins' of the past.[34] *Beloved*, then, (re)inscribes the conditions of the promise in the New Testament. What is important for Morrison, however, is the mediation between remembering (possession) and forgetting (exorcism). It is the process of 'working-through' which the author finally affirms. As in previous novels, Morrison focuses less on 'what' and 'why,' and more on 'how.' That is, she privileges the journey rather than the destination, the means rather than the end – a process which enables Sethe to achieve redemption through the creation of a cohesive psychoanalytical and historical narrative.

Like Sethe, Morrison herself seeks to achieve some mediation between 'resurrecting' the past and 'burying' it. Expressing her desire to provide a proper and artistic burial to the historical ancestors figured by Beloved, Morrison says:

> There's a lot of danger for me in writing ... The effort, the responsibility as well as the effort, the effort of being worth it. ... The responsibility that I feel for ... all of these people; these unburied, or at least unceremoniously buried, people made literate in art. But the inner tension, the artistic inner tension those people create in me, the fear of not properly, artistically, burying them, is extraordinary.[35]

Intent, it would seem, is to pay the historian's debt to the past, in Ricoeur's sense of rendering to the past its due and, in the process, putting it to rest.

What, then, is Morrison's final legacy to us as readers, and what is her own relationship to the past? Does Sethe become for the reader what Beloved is for Sethe – an embodiment of the past and the experiences of previous generations? What are we to make of the final haunting injunction at the end of the novel that this is NOT a story to 'be passed on' – that is, to remember, to be retold? Must Morrison's story, along with Sethe's past, be put behind? Must the reader rid herself of the burden of the past by exorcising from historical consciousness the violence and violation experienced by her ancestresses? If we were to take this injunction seriously, how, then, can we explain Morrison's own commitment to a project of recovery and 'rememory'? Clearly, such an injunction would threaten to contradict the motive and sense of the entire novel.

In a 1989 interview, Morrison tells us that *Beloved* is a book 'about something that the characters don't want to remember, I don't want to remember, black people don't want to remember, white people don't want to remember.'[36] The author's remarks speak to a public desire to repress the personal aspects of the story of slavery. Returning to Morrison's role as historian and analyst, however, we see that her accomplishment in this novel is precisely *not* to allow for the continuation of a 'national amnesia' regarding this chapter in America's history. For Morrison, the absent (like the historical) is only the 'other' of the present – just as the repressed is only the 'other' of the conscious. Read in this context, the narrator's final and thrice-repeated enjoinder resonates with ambivalence and ambiguity. Suggesting that that which is absent is not necessarily 'gone' (leaving behind no 'name,' no 'print,' no 'trace'), the narrator's closing reflections ensure the novel's open-endedness subverting any monologic reading of the final injunction. Is it possible that the narrator means, indeed must she mean, that this is not a story to be PASSED ON – not in the sense of being retold, but in the sense of being forgotten, repressed, or ignored? For if Richard Hofstadter is correct when he says that 'Memory is the thread of personal identity, history of public identity,' then it would follow that the importance of our private memories becomes, ultimately, the basis for a reconstructed public history.[37]

Notes (cut and renumbered)

1. Toni Morrison, 'Site of Memory' in William Zinsser, ed., *Inventing the Truth: The Art and Craft of Memoir* (Boston: Houghton-Mifflin, 1987), 109–110.
2. See W. E. B. Du Bois, 'The Forethought,' *The Souls of Black Folk* (Chicago: A.C. McClurg, 1903), viii.
3. See Toni Morrison's 'Unspeakable Things Unspoken,' *Michigan Quarterly Review* Vol. 28, No. 1 (Winter 1989).
4. 'Therefore we conclude that a man is justified by faith without the deeds of the law' (Romans 3:28); 'But that no man is justified by the law in the sight of God, *it is* evident: for, The just shall live by faith' (Galatians 3:11).
5. Contemporary black writers whose work fictionalizes history include, among others, Margaret Walker (*Jubilee*), Ernest Gaines (*The Autobiography of Miss Jane Pittman*), David Bradley (*The Chaneysville Incident*), Alice Walker (*The Color Purple*), Sherley Anne Williams (*Dessa Rose*), and Barbara Chase Riboud (*Sally Hemings* and *The Echo of Lions*).

6. Morrison, 'Site of Memory,' 111–112.

7. *Ibid*, 113–114.

8. Henry Louis Gates, Jr., 'Frederick Douglass and the Language of Self,' *The Yale Review*, Vol. 70, No. 4 (July 1981).

9. See Jacques Derrida's *Memoires for Paul de Man* (New York: Columbia University Press, 1986), 102–150 *passim*.

10. Toni Morrison, *Beloved* (New York: Afred Knopf, 1987). Page references for this work are given in the text.

11. Hayden White, *Tropics of Discourse: Essays in Cultural Criticism* (Baltimore: Johns Hopkins University Press, 1979), 33–34.

12. Paul Ricoeur, *The Reality of the Historical Past* (Milwaukee: Marquette University Press, 1984), 11.

13. Cf. Sherley Anne Williams' unnamed narrator in 'Meditations on History' and Adam Nehemiah in *Dessa Rose*. Both Williams and Morrison share reservations concerning disciplinary behaviors. Their works constitute a critique of certain aspects of both the praxis as well as the practitioners of these activities. Like Williams's characters, Morrison's investigator (who might be as appropriately designated ethnographer-as-historian), represents the author's indictment of the kind of 'scholarly' and 'scientific' discourse and representation in which the preconceptions and presuppositions of the inquirer subject the results of the inquiry to gross distortions. For critical treatments of Williams's work from this perspective, see my '(W)Riting *The Work* and Working *The Rites*,' in Linda Kauffman, ed., *Feminism and Institutions: Dialogues on Feminist Theory* (London: Basil Blackwell, 1989) and 'Speaking in Tongues: Dialogics, Dialectics, the Black Woman Writer's Literary Tradition' in Cheryl Wall, ed., *Changing Our Own Words: Essays on Criticism. Theory and Writing by Black Women* (New Brunswick: Rutgers University Press, 1989).

14. See Hélène Cixous, 'The Laugh of the Medusa,' eds. Elaine Marks and Isabelle de Courtivron, *New French Feminisms: An Anthology* (Amherst: The University of Massachusetts Press, 1980) 251.

15. See Sandra Gilbert and Susan Gubar, *The Madwoman in the Attic: The Woman Writer and the Nineteenth-Century Literary Imagination* (New Haven: Yale University Press, 1979).

16. The above represent alternative translations of Galatians 3:24.

17. See Paul Ricoeur, *Time and Narrative* (Chicago: University of Chicago Press 1988), Vol. 3, 191–192.

18. See White on Collingwood, *Tropics of Discourse*, 83.

19. According to Ricoeur, emplotment 'brings together diverse and heterogeneous story elements ... agents, goals, means, interactions, [and] circumstances ... [A]n event must be more than just a singular occurrence. It gets its definition from its contribution to the development of the plot. A story, too, must be more than just an enumeration of events in serial order; it must organize them into an intelligible whole, of a sort such that we can always ask what is the "thought" of this story. In short, emplotment is the operation that draws a configuration out of a simple succession.' See Ricoeur, *Time and Narrative*, (1984) Vol. 1, 65.

20. Gates, 'Frederick Douglass and the Language of Self,' 593.

21. See White, *Tropics of Discourse*, 87.

22. Gates, 'Frederick Douglass and the Language of Self,' 599.

23. Naylor and Morrison, 'A Conversation,' 585.

24. Teresa de Lauretis, *Alice Doesn't: Feminism, Semiotics, Cinema* (Bloomington: Indiana University Press, 1984).

25. Sigmund Freud, 'Remembering, Repeating and Working-Through,' *Standard Edition of the Works of Sigmund Freud*, ed. James Strachey (London: Hogarth Press, 1914), Vol. 12, 146–157.

26. Michel de Certeau, *Heterologies: Discourse on the Other*, Theory and History of Literature, Vol. 17 (Minneapolis: University of Minnesota Press, 1986), 3.

27. Alfred Schutz as quoted in Ricoeur, *Time and Narrative*, Vol. 3, 109.

28. Although White's work speaks eloquently to a 'classification of discourses based on tropology' (*Tropics*, 22), it is Philip Stambovsky whose work on metaphor and historical writing addresses my

concerns more specifically in this instance. Using Maurice Mandelbaum's 'three historical forms – explanatory, sequential, and interpretive' as a 'context for determining the functioning ... of ... metaphor in historical discourse,' Stambovsky identifies three functions of metaphor: heuristic, depictive, and cognitive. See Philip Stambovsky, 'Metaphor and Historical Understanding,' *History and Theory*, Vol. 27, No. 2 (1988), 125–134.

29. See Kaja Silverman, *The Acoustic Mirror: The Female Voice in Psychoanalysis and Cinema* (Bloomington: Indiana University Press, 1988) for an interesting discussion of the notions of interiority and exteriority.

30. Genesis 5:25. Interestingly, Seth was also the name of the Egyptian god of confusion, described as a trickster-like marginal figure located 'beyond or between the boundaries of social definition ... [who] gleefully breaks taboos and violates the limits that preserve order.' See Anna K. Nardo's 'Fool and Trickster' in *Mosaic* Vol. 22, (Winter 1989), 2.

31. We use Collingwood's term advisedly with the admonitions of Ricoeur that although the 're-enactment' of the past in the present operates under the sign of the same, 'to re-enact does not consist in reliving what happened,' primarily because it involves the notion of 'rethinking.' And according to Ricoeur, 'rethinking already contains the critical moment that requires us to detour by way of the historical imagination.' See Ricoeur, *Time and Narrative*, Vol. 3, 144–145. Rather than locate this process under the sign of the same, which implies repetition, I would rather locate it under both the same and the other – repetition with a difference.

32. Ricoeur designates these modes alternatively as mimesis 1, mimesis 2, and mimesis 3 (note that his formulation of mimesis includes what we normally (after Aristotle) call diegesis as well – thus expanding the notion of the imitation of an action to description. Ricoeur makes it clear that refiguration (or mimesis) is a stage which 'marks the intersection of the world of the text and the world of the hearer or reader,' thereby relating the world configured by the text to the world of 'real action.' I have modified and extended his model by using the term to describe both the intersection of the inner world of the character and the outer world of her actions as well as the intersection of the world of the text and the world of the reader. See Ricoeur, *Time and Narrative*, Vol. 1, 54–76.

33. 'The basic thesis [of refiguration] from which all the others are derived holds that the meaning of a literary work rests upon the dialogical relation established between the work and its public in each age. This thesis, similar to Collingwood's notion that history is but a reenactment of the past in the mind of the historian, amounts to including the effect produced by the work – in other words, the meaning the public attributes to it – within the boundaries of the work itself.' Ricoeur, *Time and Narrative*, Vol. 3, 171.

34. See Romans 4:15.

35. Naylor and Morrison, 'A Conversation,' 585.

36. Toni Morrison, 'The Pain of Being Black,' *Time* (May 22, 1989), 120.

37. Richard Hofstadter, *The Progressive Historians* (New York: Alfred A. Knopf, 1968), 3.

9.2   PAUL GILROY: FROM '"NOT A STORY TO PASS ON": LIVING MEMORY AND THE SLAVE SUBLIME' (1993)

Paul Gilroy is Professor of Sociology at Goldsmiths' College, University of London. He is the author of *There Ain't No Black in the Union Jack: The Cultural Politics of Race and Nation* (1987); he has published widely on issues around black modernity; and his collection, *Small Acts* (1994), contains an interview with Morrison entitled 'Living Memory: Meeting Toni Morrison'. Gilroy has been at the forefront of theorizing black studies in Britain in particular, concentrating on the contemporary construction of a national culture in the UK, on the damaging closure which all cultural nationalisms are prone to, and on the problems and potentialities of the 'double consciousness' of being both black and European. The book from which the present excerpt is taken, *The Black Atlantic: Modernity and Double Consciousness*, is a study which combines these concerns with an analysis of the 'embeddedness' of black experience in modernity and, indeed, in postmodernity. The 'black Atlantic' is Gilroy's term for the essential modernity of 'the intercultural and transnational formation' constituting black experience – unbounded by 'materialist paradigms for thinking about cultural history' (Preface, p. ix), including those of black nationalist thinking. This formation is both celebrated for its potential to transcend nationality and ethnicity, and monitored for its (negative) capacity to slip back into notions of 'purity' and separatism. The 'politics' of the book, then (overdetermining its otherwise characteristically postmodern promotion of 'the inescapability and legitimate value of mutation, hybridity and intermixture en route to better theories of racism and of black political culture', p. 417, below), are to ensure that this 'openness' will energize our political lives in the new century and to demonstrate that 'the history of the black Atlantic yields a course of lessons as to the instability and mutability of identities which are always unfinished, always being remade' (p. xi). In the last chapter, prior to the present extract, Gilroy offers a critique of 'Africentrism' and makes pointed parallels between black and Jewish experience (via the concepts of the diaspora and the holocaust) in an attempt to heal rifts and to promote positive exchanges between them. The sub-section from which the extract comes is significantly titled 'Black Culture and Ineffable Terror', and repudiates the criticism that *Beloved* is merely 'a blackface holocaust novel' which seeks to 'enter American slavery in the big-time martyr ratings contest'.

How would you relate Gilroy's treatment of *Beloved* to his general project as outlined above? In what respects is his work properly described as 'postcolonialist' or 'postmodernist'? Does its clear political drive differentiate it from the latter in significant ways? Compare this piece with Homi Bhabha's below, and consider especially the implications of their both focusing on the transgressing of 'boundaries'. Is it helpful to make a comparison with the notion of a 'transgressive aesthetic' in gay and lesbian criticism (see Ch. 5 on Oscar Wilde)? Finally, much discussion of *Beloved* is concerned with its treatment of history. How does Gilroy approach this issue, and what conception of history informs his approach?

The following excerpt is the concluding six pages of Ch. 6 (entitled as this extract), the final one in *The Black Atlantic* (Verso, 1993), pp. 218–23.

'Not a Story to Pass On': Living Memory and the Slave Sublime

In conclusion, I want to try to approach *Beloved* and some other parallel texts which share its interest in history and social memory in an experimental and openly political spirit. I want to draw attention to the ways in which some black writers have already begun the vital work of enquiring into terrors that exhaust the resources of language amidst the debris of a catastrophe which prohibits the existence of their art at the same time as demanding its continuance. I want to repeat and extend the argument frequently stated above that even when these writers are black Americans their work should not be exclusively assimilated to the project of building an ethnically particular or nationalist cultural canon, because the logic of the great political movement in which these texts stand and to which they contribute operates at other levels than those marked by national boundaries. These texts belong also to the web of diaspora identities and concerns that I have labelled the black Atlantic.

In turning away from anti-textual, vernacular forms and towards literature, it is essential to appreciate that different genres in black expressive culture have responded to the aporetic status of post-emancipation black art in quite different ways. Scepticism about the value of trying to revisit the sites of ineffable terror in the imagination is probably most valid in relation to the novel – a precariously placed latecomer in the spaces of black vernacular culture, if it can be placed there at all. Benjamin's warning that 'what draws the reader to the novel is the hope of warming his shivering life with a death he reads about'[1] should definitely be borne in mind when assessing the intermittent taste for fiction revealed by black Atlantic readerships from abolitionism onwards. However, this warning is principally an argument about the form of the novel and the different types of memory and remembrance which it solicits from its readers. The clutch of recent African-American novels which deal explicitly with history, historiography, slavery, and remembrance all exhibit an intense and ambivalent negotiation of the novel form that is associated with their various critiques of modernity and enlightenment. Charles Johnson's *Middle Passage*, which addresses these questions head on through the experiences of Rutherford Calhoun, an African-American crewman on a slaving voyage, has a neat intertextual relationship with Delany's *Blake* but, unlike its antecedent, presents itself in the guise of a journal. Sherley Anne Williams's *Dessa Rose* and David Bradley's *The Chaneysville Incident* both incorporate the antagonistic relationship between different kinds of inscription directly into their own structures, while Toni Morrison describes *Beloved* as 'outside most of the formal constricts of the novel.'[2] These remarks reveal a common degree of discomfort with the novel and a shared anxiety about its utility as a resource in the social processes that govern the remaking and conservation of historical memory. The source of these concerns may be equally located in the shift between oral and written culture and a response to the dominance of autobiographical writing within the vernacular mode of black literary production. Morrison describes these issues clearly:

> My sense of the novel is that it has always functioned for the class or group that wrote it. The history of the novel as a form began when there was a new class, a middle class, to read it; it was an art form that they needed. The lower classes didn't need novels at that time because they had an art form already: they had songs and dances, and ceremony and gossip and celebrations. The aristocracy didn't need it because they had the art that they had patronized, they had their own pictures painted, their own houses built, and they made

sure their art separated them from the rest of the world ... For a long time, the art form that was healing for black people was music. That music is no longer exclusively ours; we don't have exclusive rights to it. Other people sing and play it, it is the mode of contemporary music everywhere. So another form has to take its place, and it seems to me that the novel is needed ... now in a way that it was not needed before.[3]

Beloved was being written at the time these words were recorded, and it is especially relevant to the overall argument of this book because it is partly a retelling of the Margaret Garner story discussed in Chapter 2. Black women's experiences, and in particular the meanings they attach to motherhood, are central themes in the book, which makes important arguments for congruence between the integrity of the racial group as a whole and the status of its female members. For Morrison, these issues cannot be divorced from a different contradiction, constituted by the tension between the racial self and the racial community. Speaking of the Garner story, she explained: 'It occurred to me that the questions about community and individuality were certainly inherent in that incident as I imagined it. When you are the community, when you are your children, when that is your individuality, there is no division ... Margaret Garner didn't do what Medea did and kill her children because of some guy. It was for me this classic example of a person determined to be responsible.'[4] The Garner story illustrates more than just the indomitable power of slaves to assert their human agency in closely restricted circumstances. In Morrison's version, it encapsulates the confrontation between two opposed yet interdependent cultural and ideological systems and their attendant conceptions of reason, history, property, and kinship. One is the dilute product of Africa, the other is an antinomian expression of western modernity. Their meeting ground is the system of plantation slavery. It is thus the relationship between masters and slaves that supplies the key to comprehending the position of blacks in the modern world. The desire to return to slavery and to explore it in imaginative writing has offered Morrison and a number of other contemporary black writers a means to restage confrontations between rational, scientific, and enlightened Euro-American thought and the supposedly primitive outlook of prehistorical, cultureless, and bestial African slaves.

The desire to pit these cultural systems against one another arises from present conditions. In particular, it is formed by the need to indict those forms of rationality which have been rendered implausible by their racially exclusive character and further to explore the history of their complicity with terror systematically and rationally practised as a form of political and economic administration. Sherley Anne Williams offers a notable expression of these themes in her novel *Dessa Rose* where Dessa, a pregnant slave convicted of rebellion and awaiting the death that will follow the birth of her child, is intrusively interviewed by a white man preparing a scientific manual of slave husbandry: 'The Roots of Rebellion in the Slave Population and Some Means of Eradicating Them.'[5] Williams is primarily concerned with the differences between the marks inscribed on paper by Nehemiah's pen and the marks inscribed on or rather incorporated into Dessa's body by the brands and chains her slavery has required her to bear. Each supports a distinct system of meaning with its own characteristic forms of memory, rules, and racialised codes. They cross each other in Dessa herself. As a black writer looking backwards, over her shoulder, at slavery and making it both intelligible and legible, mediating terror by means of narrative, Williams is revealed to be the heir to both.

These imaginative attempts to revisit the slave experience and sift it for resources with which to bolster contemporary political aspirations do not point towards a simple disassociation (Africentric or otherwise) from the West and its distinctive understandings of being, thinking, and thinking about thinking and being. To be sure, the misguided association of slavery with antiquity and precapitalist systems of production and domination is broken, but the break indicates the opportunity to reconceptualise so that capitalist, racial slavery becomes internal to modernity and intrinsically modern. The same break is underscored in *Beloved* by Morrison's introduction of Schoolteacher, a slaveholder whose rational and scientific racism replaces the patrimonial and sentimental version of racial domination practiced at 'Sweet Home' by his predecessor: 'Schoolteacher was standing over one of them [his nephews] with one hand behind his back ... when I heard him say No, no. That's not the way. I told you to put her human characteristics on the left; her animal ones on the right. And don't forget to line them up.'[6]

In Charles Johnson's novels the tendency towards polarising two pure essences, African and European, is complicated by the insertion of African-American protagonists whose 'creolised' double consciousnesses[7] belie the force of that fundamental dualism which Johnson fears might be 'a bloody structure of the mind.'[8] Andrew Hawkins, the picaresque hero of *Oxherding Tale*, is another ex-coloured man who can pass for white. He has been trained in metaphysics by a transcendentalist. In *Middle Passage* his successor, Calhoun, is morally compromised not just by his position as a crew member on a slaver but by his estrangement from his biological kin and by his conspicuous non-identity with the Allmuseri tribespeople who stand in both books as persuasive symbols of an Africa that remains stubbornly incompatible with the modern world.

These literary assertions of the emphatic modernness of western black experience in slavery and since are strikingly reminiscent of C. L. R James's arguments in *The Black Jacobins*[9] and W. E. B. Du Bois's in *Black Reconstruction*.[10] It is being suggested that the concentrated intensity of the slave experience is something that marked out blacks as the first truly modern people, handling in the nineteenth century dilemmas and difficulties which would only become the substance of everyday life in Europe a century later. Morrison states this argument with special force:

> ... modern life begins with slavery ... From a women's point of view, in terms of confronting the problems of where the world is now, black women had to deal with post-modern problems in the nineteenth century and earlier. These things had to be addressed by black people a long time ago: certain kinds of dissolution, the loss of and the need to reconstruct certain kinds of stability. Certain kinds of madness, deliberately going mad in order, as one of the characters says in the book, 'in order not to lose your mind.' These strategies for survival made the truly modern person. They're a response to predatory western phenomena. You can call it an ideology and an economy, what it is is a pathology. Slavery broke the world in half, it broke it in every way. It broke Europe. It made them into something else, it made them slave masters, it made them crazy. You can't do that for

hundreds of years and it not take a toll. They had to dehumanize, not just the slaves but themselves. They have had to reconstruct everything in order to make that system appear true. It made everything in world war two possible. It made world war one necessary. Racism is the word that we use to encompass all this.[11]

All these books, though especially *Beloved*, deal with the power of history on several levels: with the contending conceptions of time that make its enregisterment possible,[12] with the necessity of socialised historical memory, and with the desire to forget the terrors of slavery and the simultaneous impossibility of forgetting. Morrison is once again acute: 'The struggle to forget which was important in order to survive is fruitless and I wanted to make it fruitless.'[13] These interlocking themes are rendered with great force in David Bradley's *The Chaneysville Incident*,[14] where the need for hermeneutic resources capable of unlocking the metaphysical choices of modern slaves is posed through an enquiry into the meaning of mass suicide by slaves cornered by the slave catchers. The protagonist here is John Washington, an academic historian who has to first master and then set aside his formal training in the discipline so that he can comprehend the significance of the slaves' preference for death rather than continued bondage.

In seeking to explain why she and other African-American novelists made this decisive turn to history Morrison suggests an interesting motivation which accentuates the source of this desire in a present which places little value on either history or historicity:

> It's got to be because we are responsible. I am very gratified by the fact that black writers are learning to grow in that area. We have abandoned a lot of valuable material. We live in a land where the past is always erased and America is the innocent future in which immigrants can come and start over, where the slate is clean. The past is absent or it's romanticized. This culture doesn't encourage dwelling on, let alone coming to terms with, the truth about the past. That memory is much more in danger now than it was thirty years ago.[15]

Morrison's emphasis on the imaginative appropriation of history and concern with the cultural contours of distinctively modern experience make her harsh on those who believe that being a black writer requires dogged adherence to orthodox narrative structures and realist codes of writing. Her work points to and celebrates some of the strategies for summoning up the past devised by black writers whose minority modernism can be defined precisely through its imaginative proximity to forms of terror that surpass understanding and lead back from contemporary racial violence, through lynching, towards the temporal and ontological rupture of the middle passage. Here Morrison and the others are drawing upon and reconstructing the resources supplied to them by earlier generations of black writers who allowed the confluence of racism, rationality, and systematic terror to configure both their disenchantment with modernity and their aspirations for its fulfilment.[16]

Their work accepts that the modern world represents a break with the past, not in the sense that premodern, 'traditional' Africanisms don't survive its institution, but because the significance and meaning of these survivals get irrevocably sundered from their origins. The history of slavery and the history of its imaginative recovery through expressive, vernacular cultures challenge us to delve into the specific dynamics of this severance.

The conclusion of this book is that this ought to be done not in order to recover hermetically sealed and culturally absolute racial traditions that would be content forever to invoke the premodern as the anti-modern. It is proposed here above all as a means to figure the inescapability and legitimate value of mutation, hybridity, and intermixture en route to better theories of racism and of black political culture than those so far offered by cultural absolutists of various phenotypical hues. The extreme circumstances out of which this obligation has grown only add to the urgency and the promise of this work. The history of blacks in the West and the social movements that have affirmed and rewritten that history can provide a lesson which is not restricted to blacks. They raise issues of more general significance that have been posed within black politics at a relatively early point. There is, for example, a potentially important contribution here towards the politics of a new century in which the central axis of conflict will no longer be the colour line but the challenge of just, sustainable development and the frontiers which will separate the overdeveloped parts of the world (at home and abroad) from the intractable poverty that already surrounds them. In these circumstances, it may be easier to appreciate the utility of a response to racism that doesn't reify the concept of race, and to prize the wisdom generated by developing a series of answers to the power of ethnic absolutism that doesn't try to fix ethnicity absolutely but sees it instead as an infinite process of identity construction. It merits repeating that this labour is valuable for itself and for the general strategy it can be shown to exemplify. At its most valuable, the history of contending racial identities affords a specific illustration of the general lessons involved in trying to keep the unstable, profane categories of black political culture open. Equally importantly, it can reveal a positive value in striving to incorporate the problems of coping with that openness into the practice of politics.

Notes (cut and renumbered)

1. Walter Benjamin, *Illuminations* (London: Fontana, 1973), p. 101.
2. Interview with Morrison, published as 'Living Memory: Meeting Toni Morrison,' in Paul Gilroy, *Small Acts* (London: Serpent's Tail, 1994), ch. 13.
3. Mari Evans, ed., *Black Women Writers: Arguments and Interviews* (London: Pluto Press, 1983), p. 340.
4. Gilroy, 'Living Memory.'
5. *Dessa Rose* (London: Futura, 1988), p. 23. A useful exploration of the nineteenth-century American literature on slave management is provided by James O. Breeden, ed., *Advice among Masters: The Ideal in Slave Management in the Old South* (Westport, Conn.: Greenwood Press, 1980).
6. Morrison, *Beloved* (London: Cape, 1988), p. 193.
7. 'The "I" that I was, was a mosaic of many countries, a patchwork of others and objects stretching backwards to perhaps the beginning of time. What I felt, seeing this, was indebtedness. What I felt, plainly, was a transmission to those on deck of all I had pilfered, as though I was but a conduit or window through which my pillage and booty of "experience" passed.' Charles Johnson, *Middle Passage* (New York: Atheneum, 1990), p. 162.
8. 'Dualism is a bloody structure of the mind. Subject and object, perceiver and perceived, self and other – these ancient twins are built into mind like the stem piece of a merchantman.' Ibid., p. 98.

9. 'When three centuries ago the slaves came to the West Indies, they entered directly into the large-scale agriculture of the sugar plantation, which was a modern system. It further required that the slaves live together in a social relation far closer than any proletariat of the time. The cane when reaped had to be rapidly transported to what was factory production. Even the cloth the slaves wore and the food they ate was imported. The Negroes, therefore, from the very start lived a life that was in its essence a modern life. That is their history – as far as I have been able to discover, a unique history.' James, *The Black Jacobins* (London: Allison and Busby, 1980), appendix, p. 392.

10. 'Negro slaves in America represented the worst and lowest conditions among *modern* labourers. One estimate is that the maintenance of a slave in the South cost the master $19 a year, which means that they were among the poorest paid labourers in the *modern* world' (emphasis added). W. E. B. Du Bois, *Black Reconstruction in America* (New York: Atheneum, 1977), p. 9.

11. 'Living Memory.'

12. Homi Bhabha, 'Post-colonial Authority and Post-modern Guilt,' in L. Grossberg et al., eds., *Cultural Studies* (New York: Routledge, 1992).

13. 'Living Memory.'

14. David Bradley, *The Chaneysville Incident* (London: Serpent's Tail, 1986).

15. 'Living Memory.'

16. Charles Chesnutt's *The Marrow of Tradition* (Boston and New York: Houghton, Mifflin, 1901) and Arna Bontemps's *Black Thunder* (New York: Macmillan, 1936) are two older books that come to mind here, the former through its treatment of lynching, the latter through its reconstruction of a slave rebellion.

9.3   HOMI K. BHABHA: FROM *THE LOCATION OF CULTURE* (1994)

Homi Bhabha is currently Wayne C. Booth Professor of English and Philosophy at the University of Chicago, and is one of the best-known postcolonial theorists and critics. He is editor of *Nation and Narration* (1990) and author of *The Location of Culture*, which brings together most of his own major essays since 1985. The 'Acknowledgements' which preface the book represent a roll-call of the international intellectual community (e.g. Said, Spivak, Eagleton, Stuart Hall, H. L. Gates, and ex-colleagues – Sinfield, Rose, Dollimore and Bowlby – at Sussex University) which Bhabha sees as sustaining his own work. He points specifically, however, to Toni Morrison (and to Salman Rushdie) as being 'formative in my thinking on narrative and historical temporality' (p. ix). A useful profile-interview of Bhabha, on the publication of his book, appeared in the *Times Higher Education Supplement* (11 February 1994, p. 17). In it, he describes his work as explaining 'why the culture of Western modernity must be re-located from the post-colonial perspective', and states that his primary theoretical concepts of hybridity and ambivalence seek to go beyond 'the traditional polarities East and West, Self and Other which have formed much of the post-colonial debate'. In focusing on the 'culture of relocation and migration, these hybrid cultural moments ... [which comprise] a great theme for the late-modern age', he finds himself 'really writing at the edge of my own powers of expression'. Hence, the tentativeness and 'openness' of his discursive style. Further, in the attempt to counteract the Western (self-) definition of modernity and contemporaneity, and to articulate the different kind of 'newness' experienced by 'minority, post-colonial people', he finds himself also treading 'the boundaries of different disciplines': 'your object is on the border of those disciplines ... and that border splits the object itself', so that the very borders of the object to be explained are transformed in the interdisciplinary reading. Crossing borders, then, 'newness', 'hybridity' and 'relocation' are all key terms in Bhabha's work (note the title of the first sub-section of the present extract).

Clearly, Bhabha's treatment of *Beloved* forms part of his larger argument (much of which extends this to other examples: most particularly to Nadine Gordimer's novel, *My Son's Story*, 1990, which Bhabha counterpoints with *Beloved*). Given his acknowledgement of Morrison's influence above, and his statement in the *THES* interview that 'to talk about the continuity of a concept is not about its return to its origins. I'm interested in the way in which, when you return to a concept, you rewrite, and displace it', consider both the ways in which Morrison has influenced his work, and how he reads her novel. What other post-structuralist influences (e.g. Derrida, Foucault, psychoanalysis) do you detect at work in his writing? Compare and contrast his deployment of psychoanalysis with that in Henderson's and Nicholls' essays here. Finally, consider Bhabha's commentary in relation to Gilroy's above, and to Spivak's essays in Chs 3 and 10 (pp. 132–43, 477–94). What do you learn of 'postcolonial' criticism from these essays? What challenge do they propose to other critical theories and practices? Do they have any elements in common with 'queer theory'?

The following excerpts are from the Introduction ('Locations of Culture') to *The Location of Culture*, Routledge, 1994, pp. 1–18, *passim*.

The Location of Culture

> A boundary is not that at which something stops but, as the Greeks recognized, the boundary is that from which something begins its presencing.
>
> Martin Heidegger, 'Building, dwelling, thinking'

Border Lives: The Art of the Present

It is the trope of our times to locate the question of culture in the realm of the *beyond*. At the century's edge, we are less exercised by annihilation – the death of the author – or epiphany – the birth of the 'subject'. Our existence today is marked by a tenebrous sense of survival, living on the borderlines of the 'present', for which there seems to be no proper name other than the current and controversial shiftiness of the prefix 'post': *postmodernism, postcolonialism, postfeminism. …*

The 'beyond' is neither a new horizon, nor a leaving behind of the past. … Beginnings and endings may be the sustaining myths of the middle years; but in the *fin de siècle*, we find ourselves in the moment of transit where space and time cross to produce complex figures of difference and identity, past and present, inside and outside, inclusion and exclusion. For there is a sense of disorientation, a disturbance of direction, in the 'beyond': an exploratory, restless movement caught so well in the French rendition of the words *au-delà* – here and there, on all sides, *fort/da*, hither and thither, back and forth.[1]

The move away from the singularities of 'class' or 'gender' as primary conceptual and organizational categories, has resulted in an awareness of the subject positions – of race, gender, generation, institutional location, geopolitical locale, sexual orientation – that inhabit any claim to identity in the modern world. What is theoretically innovative, and politically crucial, is the need to think beyond narratives of originary and initial subjectivities and to focus on those moments or processes that are produced in the articulation of cultural differences. These 'in-between' spaces provide the terrain for elaborating strategies of selfhood – singular or communal – that initiate new signs of identity, and innovative sites of collaboration, and contestation, in the act of defining the idea of society itself.

It is in the emergence of the interstices – the overlap and displacement of domains of difference – that the intersubjective and collective experiences of *nationness*, community interest, or cultural value are negotiated. How are subjects formed 'in-between', or in excess of, the sum of the 'parts' of difference (usually intoned as race/class/gender, etc.)? How do strategies of representation or empowerment come to be formulated in the competing claims of communities where, despite shared histories of deprivation and discrimination, the exchange of values, meanings and priorities may not always be collaborative and dialogical, but may be profoundly antagonistic, conflictual and even incommensurable?

[…]

Two pages are omitted here which develop these issues of hybridity, contingency and contradiction in cultural difference – in relation, especially, to the African-American artist, Renée Green.

[…]

'Beyond' signifies spatial distance, marks progress, promises the future; but our intimations of exceeding the barrier or boundary – the very act of going *beyond* – are unknowable, unrepresentable, without a return to the 'present' which, in the process of repetition, becomes disjunct and displaced. The imaginary of spatial distance – to live somehow beyond the border of our times – throws into relief the temporal, social differences that interrupt our collusive sense of cultural contemporaneity. The present can no longer be simply envisaged as a break or a bonding with the past and the future, no longer a synchronic presence: our proximate self-presence, our public image, comes to be revealed for its discontinuities, its inequalities, its minorities. Unlike the dead hand of history that tells the beads of sequential time like a rosary, seeking to establish serial, causal connections, we are now confronted with what Walter Benjamin describes as the blasting of a monadic moment from the homogenous course of history, 'establishing a conception of the present as the "time of the now"'.[2]

If the jargon of our times – postmodernity, postcoloniality, postfeminism – has any meaning at all, it does not lie in the popular use of the 'post' to indicate sequentiality – *after*-feminism; or polarity – *anti*-modernism. These terms that insistently gesture to the beyond, only embody its restless and revisionary energy if they transform the present into an expanded and ex-centric site of experience and empowerment. For instance, if the interest in postmodernism is limited to a celebration of the fragmentation of the 'grand narratives' of postenlightenment rationalism then, for all its intellectual excitement, it remains a profoundly parochial enterprise.

The wider significance of the postmodern condition lies in the awareness that the epistemological 'limits' of those ethnocentric ideas are also the enunciative boundaries of a range of other dissonant, even dissident histories and voices – women, the colonized, minority groups, the bearers of policed sexualities. For the demography of the new internationalism is the history of postcolonial migration, the narratives of cultural and political diaspora, the major social displacements of peasant and aboriginal communities, the poetics of exile, the grim prose of political and economic refugees. It is in this sense that the boundary becomes the place from which *something begins its presencing* in a movement not dissimilar to the ambulant, ambivalent articulation of the beyond that I have drawn out: 'Always and ever differently the bridge escorts the lingering and hastening ways of men to and fro, so that they may get to other banks. ... The bridge *gathers* as a passage that crosses.'[3]

[...]

A paragraph giving contemporary examples of the way national cultures, historical traditions and ethnic communities are in dissolution, and of a more transnational sense of hybridity emerging, is cut here.

[...]

What is striking about the 'new' internationalism is that the move from the specific to the general, from the material to the metaphoric, is not a smooth passage of transition and transcendence. The 'middle passage' of contemporary culture, as with slavery itself, is a process of displacement and disjunction that does not totalize experience. Increasingly, 'national' cultures are being produced from the perspective of disenfranchised minorities. The most significant effect of this process is not the proliferation of 'alternative histories of the excluded' producing, as some would have it, a pluralist anarchy. What my examples show is the changed basis for making international connections. The currency of critical comparativism, or aesthetic judgement, is no longer the sovereignty of the national culture conceived as Benedict Anderson proposes as an 'imagined community' rooted in a 'homogeneous empty time' of modernity and progress. The great connective narratives of capitalism and class drive the engines of social reproduction, but do not, in themselves, provide a foundational frame for those modes of cultural identification and political affect that form around issues of sexuality, race, feminism, the lifeworld of refugees or migrants, or the deathly social destiny of AIDS.

The testimony of my examples represents a radical revision in the concept of human community itself. What this geopolitical space may be, as a local or transnational reality, is being both interrogated and reinitiated. Feminism, in the 1990s, finds its solidarity as much in liberatory narratives as in the painful ethical position of a slavewoman, Morrison's Sethe, in *Beloved*, who is pushed to infanticide. The body politic can no longer contemplate the nation's health as simply a civic virtue; it must rethink the question of rights for the entire national, and international, community, from the AIDS perspective. The Western metropole must confront its postcolonial history, told by its influx of postwar migrants and refugees, as an indigenous or native narrative *internal to its national identity*; and the reason for this is made clear in the stammering, drunken words of Mr 'Whisky' Sisodia from *The Satanic Verses*: 'The trouble with the Engenglish is that their hiss hiss history happened overseas, so they dodo don't know what it means.'[4]

Postcoloniality, for its part, is a salutary reminder of the persistent 'neo-colonial' relations within the 'new' world order and the multinational division of labour. Such a perspective enables the authentication of histories of exploitation and the evolution of strategies of resistance. Beyond this, however, postcolonial critique bears witness to those countries and communities – in the North and the South, urban and rural – constituted, if I may coin a phrase, 'otherwise than modernity'. Such cultures of a postcolonial *contra-modernity* may be contingent to modernity, discontinuous or in contention with it, resistant to its oppressive, assimilationist technologies; but they also deploy the cultural hybridity of their borderline conditions to 'translate', and therefore reinscribe, the social imaginary of both metropolis and modernity.

[...]

Two-and-half pages follow giving examples of 'creative' interventions by postcolonial voices from within the interstices of Western 'modernity.'

[...]

Unhomely Lives: The Literature of Recognition

Fanon recognizes the crucial importance, for subordinated peoples, of asserting their indigenous cultural traditions and retrieving their repressed histories. But he is far too aware of the dangers of the fixity and fetishism of identities within the calcification of colonial cultures to recommend that 'roots' be struck in the celebratory romance of the past or by homogenizing the history of the present. The negating activity is, indeed, the intervention of the 'beyond' that establishes a boundary: a bridge, where 'presencing' begins because it captures something of the estranging sense of the relocation of the home and the world – the unhomeliness – that is the condition of extra-territorial and cross-cultural initiations. To be unhomed is not to be homeless, nor can the 'unhomely' be easily accommodated in that familiar division of social life into private and public spheres. The unhomely moment creeps up on you stealthily as your own shadow and suddenly you find yourself with Henry James's Isabel Archer, in *The Portrait of a Lady*, taking the measure of your dwelling in a state of 'incredulous terror'.[5]

[...]

A few lines are cut which expand on this 'unhomeliness' in James' novel.

[...]

Although the 'unhomely' is a paradigmatic colonial and post-colonial condition, it has a resonance that can be heard distinctly, if erratically, in fictions that negotiate the powers of cultural difference in a range of transhistorical sites. You have already heard the shrill alarm of the unhomely in that moment when Isabel Archer realizes that her world has been reduced to one high, mean window, as her house of fiction becomes 'the house of darkness, the house of dumbness, the house of suffocation'.[6] If you hear it thus at the Palazzo Roccanera in the late 1870s, then a little earlier in 1873 on the outskirts of Cincinnati, in mumbling houses like 124 Bluestone Road, you hear the undecipherable language of the black and angry dead; the voice of Toni Morrison's *Beloved*, 'the thoughts of the women of 124, unspeakable thoughts, unspoken'.[7]

[...]

A half-paragraph giving other examples of the 'unhomely' in literature follows here.

[...]

[T]he 'unhomely' does provide a 'non-continuist' problematic that dramatizes – in the figure of woman – the ambivalent structure of the civil State as it draws its rather paradoxical boundary between the private and the public spheres. If, for Freud, the *unheimlich* is 'the name for everything that ought to have remained ... secret and hidden but has come to light,' then Hannah Arendt's description of the public and private realms is a profoundly unhomely one: 'it is the distinction between things that should be hidden and things that should be shown,' she writes, which through their inversion in the modern age 'discovers how rich and manifold the hidden can be under conditions of intimacy'.[8]

This logic of reversal, that turns on a disavowal, informs the profound revelations and reinscriptions of the unhomely moment. For what was 'hidden from sight' for Arendt, becomes in Carole Pateman's *The Disorder of Women* the 'ascriptive domestic sphere' that is *forgotten* in the theoretical distinctions of the private and public spheres of civil society. Such a forgetting – or disavowal – creates an uncertainty at the heart of the generalizing subject of civil society, compromising the 'individual' that is the support for its universalist aspiration. By making visible the forgetting of the 'unhomely' moment in civil society, feminism specifies the patriarchal, gendered nature of civil society and disturbs the symmetry of private and public which is now shadowed, or uncannily doubled, by the difference of genders which does not neatly map on to the private and the public, but becomes disturbingly supplementary to them. This results in redrawing the domestic space as the space of the normalizing, pastoralizing, and individuating techniques of modern power and police: the personal-*is*-the political; the world-*in*-the-home.

The unhomely moment relates the traumatic ambivalences of a personal, psychic history to the wider disjunctions of political existence. Beloved, the child murdered by her own mother, Sethe, is a daemonic, belated repetition of the violent history of black infant deaths, during slavery, in many parts of the South, less than a decade after the haunting of 124 Bluestone Road. (Between 1882 and 1895 from one-third to a half of the annual black mortality rate was accounted for by children under five years of age.) But the memory of Sethe's act of infanticide emerges through 'the holes – the things the fugitives did not say; the questions they did not ask ... the unnamed, the unmentioned.'[9] As we reconstruct the narrative of child murder through Sethe, the slave mother, who is herself the victim of social death, the very historical basis of our ethical judgement undergoes a radical revision.

Such forms of social and psychic existence can best be represented in that tenuous survival of literary language itself, which allows memory to speak.

[...]

Two short paragraphs offering examples of this in Auden and Goethe are cut here.

[...]

What of the more complex cultural situation where 'previously unrecognized spiritual and intellectual needs' emerge from the imposition of 'foreign' ideas, cultural representations, and structures of power? Goethe suggests that the 'inner nature of the whole nation as well as the individual man works all unconsciously.'[10] When this is placed alongside his idea that the cultural life of the nation is 'unconsciously' lived, then there may be a sense in which world literature could be an emergent, prefigurative category that is concerned with a form of cultural dissensus and alterity, where non-consensual terms of affiliation may be established on the grounds of historical trauma. The study of world literature might be the study of the way in which cultures recognize themselves through their projections of 'otherness'. Where, once, the transmission of national traditions was the major theme of a world literature, perhaps we can now suggest that transnational histories of migrants, the colonized, or political refugees – these border and frontier conditions – may be the terrains of world literature. The centre of such a study would neither be the 'sovereignty' of national cultures, nor the universalism of human culture, but a focus on those 'freak social and cultural displacements' that Morrison and Gordimer represent in their 'unhomely' fictions. Which leads us to ask: can the perplexity of the unhomely, intrapersonal world lead to an international theme?

If we are seeking a 'worlding' of literature, then perhaps it lies in a critical act that attempts to grasp the sleight of hand with which literature conjures with historical specificity, using the medium of psychic uncertainty, aesthetic distancing, or the obscure signs of the spirit-world, the sublime and the subliminal. As literary creatures and political animals we ought to concern ourselves with the understanding of human action and the social world as a moment when *something is beyond control, but it is not beyond accommodation*. This act of writing the world, of taking the measure of its dwelling, is magically caught in Morrison's description of her house of fiction – art as 'the fully realized presence of a haunting'[11] of history. Read as an image that describes the relation of art to social reality, my translation of Morrison's phrase becomes a statement on the political responsibility of the critic. For the critic must attempt to fully realize, and take responsibility for, the unspoken, unrepresented pasts that haunt the historical present.

Our task remains, however, to show how historical agency is transformed through the signifying process; how the historical event is represented in a discourse that is *somehow beyond control*. This is in keeping with Hannah Arendt's suggestion that the author of social action may be the initiator of its unique meaning, but as agent he or she cannot control its outcome. It is not simply what the house of fiction contains or 'controls' *as content*. What is just as important is the metaphoricity of the houses of racial memory that both Morrison and Gordimer construct – those subjects of the narrative that mutter or mumble like 124 Bluestone Road, or keep a still silence in a 'grey' Cape Town suburb.

[...]

Two pages follow dealing mainly with Aila, the female protagonist in Gordimer's *My Son's Story* (cf. Headnote).

[...]

In Aila's stillness, its obscure necessity, we glimpse what Emmanuel Levinas has magically described as the twilight existence of the aesthetic image – art's image as 'the very event of obscuring, a descent into night, an invasion of the shadow'.[12] The 'completion' of the aesthetic, the distancing of the world in the image, is precisely not a transcendental activity. The image – or the metaphoric, 'fictional' activity of discourse – makes visible 'an interruption of time by a movement going on on the hither side of time, in its interstices'.[13] The complexity of this statement will become clearer when I remind you of the stillness of time through which Aila surreptitiously and subversively interrupts the ongoing presence of political activity, using her interstitial role, her domestic world to both 'obscure' her political role and to articulate it the better. Or, as *Beloved*, the continual eruption of 'undecipherable languages' of slave memory obscures the historical narrative of infanticide only to articulate the unspoken: that ghostly discourse that enters the world of 124 'from the outside' in order to reveal the transitional world of the aftermath of slavery in the 1870s, its private and public faces, its historical past and its narrative present.

The aesthetic image discloses an ethical time of narration because, Levinas writes, 'the real world appears in the image as it were between parentheses.'[14] Like the outer edges of Aila's hands holding her enigmatic testimony, like 124 Bluestone Road which is a fully realized presence haunted by undecipherable languages, Levinas's parenthetical perspective is also an ethical view. It effects an 'externality of the inward' as the very enunciative position of the historical and narrative subject, 'introducing into the heart of subjectivity a radical and anarchical reference to the other which in fact constitutes the inwardness of the subject.'[15] Is it not uncanny that Levinas's metaphors for this unique 'obscurity' of the image should come from those Dickensian unhomely places – those dusty boarding schools, the pale light of London offices, the dark, dank second-hand clothes shops?

For Levinas the 'art-magic' of the contemporary novel lies in its way of 'seeing inwardness from the outside', and it is this ethical–aesthetic positioning that returns us, finally, to the community of the unhomely, to the famous opening lines of *Beloved*: '124 was spiteful. The women in the house knew it and so did the children.'

It is Toni Morrison who takes this ethical and aesthetic project of 'seeing inwardness from the outside' furthest or deepest – right into Beloved's naming of her desire for identity: 'I want you to touch me on my inside part and call me my name.'[16] There is an obvious reason why a ghost should want to be so realized. What is more obscure – and to the point – is how such an inward and intimate desire would provide an 'inscape' of the memory of slavery. For Morrison, it is precisely the signification of the historical and discursive boundaries of slavery that are the issue.

Racial violence is invoked by historical dates – 1876, for instance – but Morrison is just a little hasty with the events 'in-themselves', as she rushes past 'the true meaning of the Fugitive Bill, the Settlement Fee, God's Ways, antislavery, manumission, skin voting'.[17] What has to be endured is the knowledge of doubt that comes from Sethe's eighteen years of disapproval and a solitary life, her banishment in the unhomely world of 124 Bluestone Road, as the pariah of her postslavery community. What finally causes the thoughts of the women of 124 'unspeakable thoughts to be unspoken' is the understanding that the victims of violence are themselves 'signified upon': they are the victims of projected fears, anxieties and dominations that do not originate within the oppressed and will not fix them in the circle of pain. The stirring of emancipation comes with the knowledge that the racially supremacist belief 'that under every dark skin there was a jungle' was a belief that grew, spread, touched every perpetrator of the racist myth, turned them mad from their own untruths, and was then expelled from 124 Bluestone Road.

But before such an emancipation from the ideologies of the master, Morrison insists on the harrowing ethical repositioning of the slave mother, who must be the enunciatory site for seeing the inwardness of the slave world from the outside – when the 'outside' is the ghostly return of the child she murdered; the double of herself, for 'she is the laugh I am the laugher I see her face which is mine.'[18] What could be the ethics of child murder? What historical knowledge returns to Sethe, through the aesthetic distance or 'obscuring' of the event, in the phantom shape of her dead daughter Beloved?

In her fine account of forms of slave resistance in *Within the Plantation Household*, Elizabeth Fox-Genovese considers murder, self-mutilation and infanticide to be the core psychological dynamic of all resistance. It is her view that 'these extreme forms captured the essence of the slave woman's self-definition'.[19] Again we see how this most tragic and intimate act of violence is performed in a struggle to push back the boundaries of the slave world. Unlike acts of confrontation against the master or the overseer which were resolved within the household context, infanticide was recognized as an act against the system and at least acknowledged the slavewoman's legal standing in the public sphere. Infanticide was seen to be an act against the master's property – against his surplus profits – and perhaps that, Fox-Genovese concludes, 'led some of the more desperate to feel that, by killing an infant they loved, they would be in some way reclaiming it as their own'.[20]

Through the death and the return of Beloved, precisely such a reclamation takes place: the slave mother regaining through the presence of the child, the property of her own person. This knowledge comes as a kind of self-love that is also the love of the 'other': Eros and Agape together. It is an ethical love in the Levinasian sense in which the 'inwardness' of the subject is inhabited by the 'radical and anarchical reference to the other'. This knowledge is visible in those intriguing chapters[21] which lay over each other, where Sethe, Beloved and Denver perform a fugue-like ceremony of claiming and naming through intersecting and interstitial subjectivities: 'Beloved, she my daughter'; 'Beloved is my sister'; 'I am Beloved and she is mine.' The women speak in tongues, from a space 'in-between each other' which is a communal space. They explore an 'interpersonal' reality: a social reality that appears within the poetic image as if it were in parentheses – aesthetically distanced, held back, and yet historically framed. It is difficult to convey the rhythm and the improvization of those chapters, but it is impossible not to see in them the healing of history, a community reclaimed in the making of a name. We can finally ask ourselves:

Who is Beloved?

Now we understand: she is the daughter that returns to Sethe so that her mind will be homeless no more.

Who is Beloved?

Now we may say: she is the sister that returns to Denver, and brings hope of her father's return, the fugitive who died in his escape.

Who is Beloved?

Now we know: she is the daughter made of murderous love who returns to love and hate and free herself. Her words are broken, like the lynched people with broken necks; disembodied, like the dead children who lost their ribbons. But there is no mistaking what her live words say as they rise from the dead despite their lost syntax and their fragmented presence.

> My face is coming   I have to have it   I am looking for the join   I am loving my face so much   I want to join   I am loving my face so much   my dark face is close to me   I want to join.[22]

Looking for the Join

To end, as I have done, with the nest of the phoenix, not its pyre is, in another way, to return to my beginning in the *beyond*. If Gordimer and Morrison describe the historical world, forcibly entering the house of art and fiction in order to invade, alarm, divide and dispossess, they also demonstrate the contemporary compulsion to move beyond; to turn the present into the 'post'; or, as I said earlier, to touch the future on its hither side. Aila's in-between identity and Beloved's double lives both affirm the borders of culture's insurgent and interstitial existence. In that sense, they take their stand with Renee Green's pathway between racial polarities; or Rushdie's migrant history of the English written in the margins of satanic verses; or Osorio's bed – *La Cama* – a place of dwelling, located between the unhomeliness of migrancy and the baroque belonging of the metropolitan, New York/Puerto-Rican artist.

When the public nature of the social event encounters the silence of the word it may lose its historical composure and closure. At this point we would do well to recall Walter Benjamin's insight on the disrupted dialectic of modernity: 'Ambiguity is the figurative appearance of the dialectic, the law of the dialectic at a standstill.'[23] For Benjamin that stillness is Utopia; for those who live, as I described it, 'otherwise' than modernity but not outside it, the Utopian moment is not the necessary horizon of hope. I have ended this argument with the woman framed – Gordimer's Aila – and the woman renamed – Morrison's Beloved – because in both their houses great world events erupted – slavery and apartheid – and their happening was turned, through that peculiar obscurity of art, into a second coming.

Although Morrison insistently repeats at the close of *Beloved*, 'This is not a story to pass on,' she does this only in order to engrave the event in the deepest resources of our amnesia, of our unconsciousness. When historical visibility has faded, when the present tense of testimony loses its power to arrest, then the displacements of memory and the indirections of art offer us the image of our psychic survival. To live in the unhomely world, to find its ambivalencies and ambiguities enacted in the house of fiction, or its sundering and splitting performed in the work of art, is also to affirm a profound desire for social solidarity: 'I am looking for the join ... I want to join ... I want to join.'

Notes (cut and renumbered)

1. For an interesting discussion of gender boundaries in the *fin de siècle*, see E. Showalter, *Sexual Anarchy: Gender and Culture in the Fin de Siècle* (London: Bloomsbury, 1990), especially 'Borderlines', pp. 1–18.
2. W. Benjamin, 'Theses on the philosophy of history', in his *Illuminations* (London: Jonathan Cape, 1970), p. 265.
3. M. Heidegger, 'Building, dwelling, thinking', in *Poetry, Language, Thought* (New York: Harper & Row, 1971), pp. 152–3.
4. S. Rushdie, *The Satanic Verses* (London: Viking, 1988), p. 343.
5. H. James, *The Portrait of a Lady* (New York: Norton, 1975), p. 360.
6. ibid., p. 361.
7. T. Morrison, *Beloved* (London: Chatto & Windus, 1987), pp. 198–9.
8. S. Freud, 'The uncanny', Standard Edition XVII, p. 225; H. Arendt, *The Human Condition* (Chicago: Chicago University Press, 1958), p. 72.
9. Morrison, *Beloved*, p. 170.
10. Goethe, 'Note on world literature', p. 96.
11. T. Morrison, *Honey and Rue* programme notes, Carnegie Hall Concert, January 1991.
12. E. Levinas, 'Reality and its shadow', in *Collected Philosophical Papers* (Dordrecht: Martinus Nijhoff, 1987), pp. 1–13.
13. ibid.
14. ibid., pp. 6–7.
15. Robert Bernasconi quoted in 'Levinas's ethical discourse, between individuation and universality', in *Re-Reading Levinas*, R. Bernasconi and S. Critchley (eds) (Bloomington: Indiana University Press, 1991), p. 90.
16. Morrison, *Beloved*, p. 116.
17. ibid., p. 173.
18. ibid., p. 213.
19. E. Fox-Genovese, *Within the Plantation Household* (Chapel Hill, NC: University of North Carolina Press, 1988), p. 329.
20. ibid., p. 324.
21. Morrison, *Beloved*, Pt II, pp. 200–17.
22. ibid., p. 213.
23. W. Benjamin, *Charles Baudelaire: A Lyric Poet in the Era of High Capitalism* (London: NLB, 1973), p. 171.

9.4   LYNNE PEARCE: 'GENDERING THE CHRONOTOPE: *BELOVED*' (1994)

Lynne Pearce is lecturer in English and women's studies at the University of Lancaster. She has written a number of essays on Bakhtin and on women's writing, and is a prominent exponent of Bakhtinian theory in the UK. Her other works include: *Women/Image/Text: Readings in Pre-Raphaelite Art and Literature* (1991); 'Dialogic Theory and Women's Writing' in H. Hinds, A. Phoenix and J. Stacey, eds, *Working Out: New Directions for Women's Studies* (1992); '"Written on Tablets of Stone?": Roland Barthes, Jeanette Winterson and the Discourse of Romantic Love', in S. Raitt, ed., *Volcanoes and Pearl Divers: Essays in Lesbian Feminist Studies* (Onlywomen Press, 1995); and '"I the Reader": Text, Context and the Balance of Power', in P. Florence and D. Reynolds, eds, *Feminine Subjects: Multi-Media: New Approaches to Criticism and Creativity* (Manchester University Press, 1995).

Mikhail Bakhtin, the most significant of the Russian intellectuals of the 1920s and 1930s, has been profoundly influential on contemporary literary theory and criticism (for a brief introduction to his work, see *A Reader's Guide* 3/e, pp. 38–42, and Simon Dentith, *Bakhtinian Thought: An Introductory Reader* (Routledge, 1995), but his own writing on literature focused principally on Rabelais and Dostoevsky. However, his theories of 'carnival' and carnivalized writing (especially in the novel), which disrupt authority and liberate (multiple) alternative voices, have proved a fertile partner for many of the recent outgrowths from poststructuralism, especially psychoanalytic criticism, feminism, 'queer theory' and postcolonialism. Bakhtin's central concepts of dialogics, polyphony, heteroglossia, double-voiced discourse, carnival and chronotope are all aspects of this view of literary textuality as potentially subversive and libertarian. Pearce's book is an extended account of Bakhtin's work and of the way 'dialogics' have been appropriated (and redefined) by many other, very different, contemporary theorists and critics. In particular, she points to dialogism's significance for those seeking to formulate new models of subjectivity and for feminists attempting to define the specificity of women's writing. The concept of 'chronotope' is one of the hitherto less mobilized of Bakhtin's concepts, and is defined by Pearce in her section on his *The Dialogic Imagination* (Pearce, Ch. 1, VI, pp. 67–72). Derived from Einstein's theory of relativity and literally meaning 'time-space', chronotope is, in Bakhtin's words, 'the intrinsic connectedness of temporal and spatial relations that are artistically expressed in literature'; 'Time, as it were, thickens, takes on flesh, becomes artistically visible; likewise, space becomes charged and responsive to the movements of time, plot and history'. In the event, Bakhtin sees time as the dominant element in literary chronotopes – their specific nature varying from genre to genre – where, instead of the passing of real time, we have metaphorically realized conceptions of time and space, formed historically but transmitted through history as literature, which synthesize 'moments' in the historical process of the characters' lives the novel purports to represent. A single text can contain 'multiple' co-existent chronotopes – perceived dialogically by author and reader but, of course, invisible to the characters locked in their individual chronotope. It is this which Pearce finds especially helpful in considering ('polychronotopic') modernist and postmodernist texts, where a dominant chronotope is challenged by others and characters are allowed to invade each other's chronotopes.

In light of the above, analyse how Pearce puts the chronotope concept to work in *Beloved*. Do you think the novel itself *invites* the deployment of this theoretical device? Does it help in analysing the way 'history' works in the novel in a way that the previous three critics would have found useful? Trace the influence of psychoanalysis and feminism in this extract: how *does* Pearce 'gender the chronotope'? And why? How, also, would you characterize the *textual* analysis in this piece; does it seem to 'translate' the text, or to enable its 'not-said' (see, e.g., Ch. 3 on *Jane Eyre*) to emerge as a disruptive discourse? More generally, given the snapshot of Bakhtin's work above, consider whether you can perceive his influence in other essays, in this exercise and elsewhere, in which a 'transgressive aesthetics' (sexual, postcolonial, cultural-political) is at work.

The following essay forms the second part of Ch. 5 ('Dialogism and Gender: Gendering the Chronotope: Readings of Jeanette Winterson's *Sexing the Cherry* and Toni Morrison's *Beloved*') in Pearce's *Reading Dialogics*, Arnold, 1994, pp. 186–95. The first part is on *Sexing the Cherry*. Parenthetical references in the text are to the Picador edition of *Beloved* (1988).

Gendering the Chronotope: *Beloved*

In a conversation with Denver at the beginning of *Beloved*, Sethe makes clear just how 'thick' the chronotopes of the 'rememoried' past can be:

> 'Some things go. Pass on. Some things just stay. I used to think it was my rememory. You know. Some things you forget. Other things you never do. But it's not. Places, places are still there. If a house burns down, it's gone, but the place – the picture of it – stays, and not just in my rememory, but out there in the world. What I remember is a picture floating around out there outside my head. I mean, even if I don't think it, even if I die, the picture of what I did, or knew, or saw is still out there. Right in the place where it happened.'
>
> 'Can other people see it?' asked Denver.
>
> 'Oh, yes, yes, yes. Someday you will be walking down that road and you hear something or see something going on. So clear. And you think it's you thinking it up. A thought picture. But no. It's when you bump into a rememory that belongs to somebody else. Where I was before I came here, that place is real. It's never going away. Even if the whole farm – every tree and blade of grass of it dies. The picture is still there and what's more, if you go there – you who never was there – if you go there and stand in the place where it was, it will happen again; it will be there for you, waiting for you. So, Denver, you can't never go there. Never. Because even though it's all over – over and done with – it's going to be there always waiting for you. That's how come I had to get all my children out. No matter what.'
>
> Denver picked at her finger nails. 'If it's still there, waiting, that must mean that nothing ever dies'.
>
> Sethe looked right in Denver's face. 'Nothing ever does,' she said (pp. 35–36).

The palpability of time past, the way it can, at any moment, reach out and grab you – seize hold of you with the tenacity of a baby's clutch – is presented by Sethe not as a wonder to be embraced but as a hazard to be avoided. It is, in particular, the inextricability of time and space that make the chronotopes of the past so potentially dangerous; the way in which time *converts* to space ('Places, places are still there'), the way it 'takes on flesh' and 'thickens'. For the chronotopes that Sethe moves in and out of are not [...] the 'rich imaginings' of romance and fairy-tale but the dark, blood-stained annals of her own personal past and of her race. The multiple chronotopes that comprise this past are, moreoever, for the most part 'unspeakable' (p. 58), and much of her recent life has been spent in protecting Denver from their influence ('As for Denver, the job Sethe had of keeping her from the past that was still waiting for her was all that mattered', p. 42). For the protagonists of *Beloved*, the fact that past, present and future may be seen to coexist is not a liberatory delight but a threat.

The desire to shut a permanent door on the chronotopes of the past is something shared by both Sethe and Paul D. In the very first pages of the novel, Sethe recalls a conversation with Baby Suggs in which she explains the latter's inability to remember her eight children with the statement: 'that's all you let yourself remember' (p. 5). Paul D., similarly, has managed to contain the dark memories of his own past in the 'tobacco tin' lodged in his chest: 'By the time he got to 124 nothing in this world would pry it open' (p. 113). But 'prying open' the lid to the past and re-entering its chronotopes is what Morrison's novel is all about, and especially fascinating, in Bakhtinian terms, is the fact that it is a past reconstituted *through dialogue*. Things that have been 'unspeakable' for eighteen years are exposed and rematerialized through Sethe's dialogic encounters with Paul D. and Beloved. Both, in turn, though in significantly different (and differently gendered) ways, perform the role of the Bakhtinian interlocutor: they become the 'listening other' whose presence is necessary for 'the word' to be spoken, for the past to be narrativized and hence *realized*.

At first Sethe and Paul D. are frightened by the prospect of what unknown horrors their conversation might bring to light. The encounter serves not only to reactivate the 'rememory' of their personal pasts but also to lead them into previously hidden corners of their shared chronotope; to make visible events (such as Halle with 'butter all over his face', p. 8) which one or the other had not actually witnessed. After their first, involuntary 'rememory' the interlocutors are guilty and apologetic with one another ('I didn't plan on telling you that'/'I didn't plan on hearing it' (p. 71)), and Sethe is desperate to return to a present in which she can continue the 'serious work of beating back the past' (p. 73).

All the work Sethe puts into 'keeping the lid on' the Pandora's Box of the past is, however, undone by the appearance of Beloved who, from the start, compels her to speak the 'unspeakable':

> 'Tell me,' said Beloved, smiling a wide happy smile. 'Tell me your diamonds.'
>
> It became a way to feed her. Just as Denver discovered and relied on the delightful effect sweet things had on Beloved, Sethe learned the profound satisfaction Beloved got from storytelling. It amazed Sethe (as much as it pleased Beloved) because every mention of her past life hurt. Everything in it was painful or lost. She and Baby Suggs had agreed without saying so that it was unspeakable; to Denver's enquiries Sethe gave short replies or rambling, incomplete reveries. Even with Paul D., who had shared some of it and to whom she could talk with at least a measure of calm, the hurt was always there – like a tender place in the corner of the mouth that the bit left.
>
> But as she began telling about the earrings, she found herself wanting to, liking it. Perhaps it was Beloved's distance from the events itself; or her thirst for hearing it – in any case, it was an unexpected pleasure (p. 58).

At this stage, Sethe has no idea at all why Beloved's interlocutory presence should elicit this rememory, and attempts to explain it (ironically) by the latter's 'distance from the events' (ibid.). The story of the diamonds is, however, just one of several discrete chronotopes that are revisited in the course of the novel, with Beloved's clamour for stories of the past ('Denver noticed how greedy she was to hear Sethe talk', p. 63) opening up the floodgates of dialogue.[1] For although, as I shall discuss below, the dialogue between Sethe and Beloved is the most psychologically complex of all the interlocutory relationships represented in the text, her arrival is the catalyst for change between *all* the protagonists. Number 124, for years a silent house, becomes suddenly noisy, as Sethe and Beloved, Denver and Beloved, and Sethe and Paul D. reconstruct the 'unspeakable' past in the dialogic space between them.

The dialogue between Beloved and Denver (pp. 78–85) is a testament to Sethe's pronouncement (quoted at the beginning of this reading) that the chronotopes of the past can be 'accessed' even by those who have no original part in them. The chronotope, for Morrison as for Winterson, is not the property of the individual – her memory or her imagination – but is profoundly *intersubjective*, which would also seem to account for why it is most effectively reconstructed through dialogic exchange. Through an act of intense interlocutory concentration, Beloved and Denver access and enter the chronotope of Denver's birth. Although the reader has already had glimpses into this particular time/space through Denver's own rememory of it, it is significant that the climax of this story is realized only through the dialogic interconnection of the two girls, with Denver the speaker and Beloved the 'active' listener:

> Denver was seeing it now and feeling it – through Beloved. Feeling how it must have felt to her mother. Seeing how it must have looked. And the more fine points she made, the more detail she provided, the more Beloved liked it. So she anticipated the questions by giving blood to the scraps her mother and grandmother had told her – and a heartbeat. The monologue became, in fact, a duet as they lay down together, Denver nursing Beloved's interest like a lover whose pleasure was to overfeed the loved ... Denver spoke, Beloved listened, and the two did the best they could to create what really happened, how it really was, something only Sethe knew because she alone had the mind for it and the time afterward to shape it: the quality of Amy's voice, her breath like burning wood (p. 78).

But between them, Denver and Beloved *do* succeed in raising the spirit of that past (reproduced verbatim in the text which follows, pp. 78–85) in all its multisentient palpability. Correspondent with Bakhtin's theory of the dynamics of spoken dialogue (and, indeed, of 'hidden dialogue' and 'hidden polemic'), it is the pressure exerted by the 'future answer word' of the interlocutor (in this case, Beloved's 'questions') that prompts and shapes the discourse of the speaker, forcing her (Denver) to supply the 'detail' that was lacking in the earlier 'rememories' of the story. Chronotope here is thus made a causal expression of dialogicality, giving rise to a significant configuration between two discrete strands of dialogic theory.[2]

The interlocutory power that Beloved exerts over Denver and Sethe in order to make them feed her stories is very different from that of Paul D., and the difference is partly a difference of gender. Where Beloved elicits the rememories of her 'mother' and 'sister' through the affected intimacy of the 'beloved' child, Paul D. claims his patriarchal right to 'the truth' (p. 163). The conversation between them, in which Sethe circles 'dizzyingly' around the room and confesses, obliquely, to the murder of her child, is a 'court-room' dialogue in which Sethe is the guilty defendant and Paul D. the silent judge. The story of the horror gets told – but stammeringly, defensively. Explanation and self-justification subsume and veil the details of the act. These are not the words of a woman speaking to her lover but to the patriarchal authorities that would judge child murder, under any circumstances, a crime. Although she appeals to him as a friend ('You know what I mean?' p. 162) her voice is at all times thick with fear and shame. She has told her story, but she has not revisited its chronotope. The time-space which she re-enters in her confession to Paul D. is not the context of the baby's death but of her trial and imprisonment. These are not the dialogic conditions necessary to take her back to where she needs to be.

It is Beloved, alone, who can provide Sethe with the interlocutory support necessary for her to open the door on this, the most repressed of all her rememories. The strained and objectified account of her escape from Sweet Home as it is told to Paul D. is transformed, in Beloved's hearing, into a minute-by-minute reconstruction. It is a narration that is not only subjective but also intersubjective; as with Denver's experience, cited above, it is Beloved's interlocutory presence that allows Sethe to re-enter the time-space buried for the past eighteen years – and this, precisely because Beloved *shares* the chronotope, knows what she is about to say:

> Thank God I don't have to rememory or say a thing because you know it. All. You know I would never a left you. Never. It was all I could think of to do (p. 191).

> This is the first time I'm telling it and I'm telling it to you because it might help explain something to you although I know you don't need me to do it. To tell it or even to think over it. You don't have to listen either, if you don't want to (p. 193).

Having 'clicked' (p. 175) that Beloved is the reincarnation of her murdered baby, Sethe has at least found the interlocutory presence she needs to rememory and 'exorcise' her action: the only person close enough to the event to understand her motive and not pass judgement.[3]

The fact that Beloved later does become the most tyrannical of adjudicators, converting Sethe's candid vindication into a cringing self-flagellating plea for forgiveness, does not lessen the initial catharsis her presence affords the female occupants of Number 124. Although within the ideological denouement of the text, the 'incestuous' dialogic circuit Beloved forges between herself, Sethe and Denver has, at last, to be broken by the reinsertion of the masculine principle (Paul D.), the woman-only auditorium she creates is a temporary necessity.[4] Sethe and Denver can only gain access to the buried chronotopes of the past through her presence, and the total exclusion of men.

After Paul D.'s departure, 124 becomes a 'safe' all-female environment in which the three women give voice to the most 'unspeakable' thoughts and resurrect, through their dark dialogues, the most distressing of past chronotopes. For Sethe, 'locking the door' (p. 199) means that she is able to wander even further into the dark spatiotemporal corridors of her time at Sweet Home, and of her escape, and of the few precious days at 124 before the baby's death; a catalogue of sweet and painful rememories, given 'flesh' through Beloved's own introjected memory of them. It is significant that in the monologue beginning 'Beloved, she my daughter' (p. 200), Sethe slides back and forth, unselfconsciously, between the second- and third-person pronoun. Sometimes she is speaking about Beloved; sometimes she is speaking to her. But were it not for Beloved's presence we know that she would not be speaking at all.

For Denver, isolation at 124 with her mother and Beloved enables her finally to confront the extent of her fear of the one and her love of the other, and then her love of both, and her fear of both. The chronotopes she 're-enters' are the repressed rememories of her childhood: her time at Lady Jones's school, her days with Grandma Suggs, and – even more importantly – the time she never spent with the 'angel daddy' she never knew. None of Denver's monologue is actually addressed to Beloved, but she is its facilitation all the same: 'She played with me and always came to be with me when I needed her. She's mine, Beloved, she's mine' (p. 209).

For Beloved herself, meanwhile, Sethe is the vital interlocutory presence that enables her to put into sequence the dark, fragmented chronotopes of her own past: her own history and her own prehistory. The space/place that Beloved returns to is the ambiguous 'black hole' that Denver has identified earlier in the text as 'the time before' (p. 75). Whether this place is womb, tomb, limbo – or, putting aside metaphysical explanations – the 'brothel' of Paul D.'s suggestion (p. 52) is never clear. Nor is a proper temporal distinction drawn between the nasty place inhabited by the men 'without skin' (pp. 210–11), and the dark and pleasant waters ('the space under the bridge') where she is 'reunited' with her mother and effectively reborn (see pp. 210–13). The sequence in which these rememories are given suggests that the early happy union with mother simply dissolves into the period of masculine possession ('storms rock us and mix the men into the women and the women into the men that is when I begin to be on the back of the man', p. 210). But equally indistinct is the moment when Beloved flows back into the body of the mother and herself.

If the boundaries between the chronotopes are themselves indistinct, however, the dialogic conditions which activate this remembering are not. It is by addressing Sethe in the present that Beloved is able to realize the nature of the relationship between their two 'faces' in the past. By speaking the first person plural ('we') she glimpses the 'chora' of the mother–child dyad that she and Sethe have formed.[5]

Through Beloved's presence at 124, and through the temporary exclusion of the masculine principle (Paul D./Lacan's 'law of the father') Sethe's family are able to explore – through dialogue with one another – the preoedipal space (Kristeva's 'semiotic') that had previously been denied them. They are able to experiment with relationships that 'free' people take for granted: what it is to be a mother, a child, a sister. But once this exploration has been achieved, once the repressed 'infant babble' (the noises Stamp Paid hears emitting from the house, p. 172) is given voice, the incestuous female bond has once again to be broken; and this is effected, predictably, through Paul D.'s return.[6]

What is significant about Paul D.'s return in dialogic terms is that his displacement of Beloved's 'ghost' is complete only when he has finally replaced her as Sethe's interlocutor. His 'manly presence' which, at the start of the novel, seems enough to 'whoosh away' (p. 37) all the ghosts, is clearly not enough. His permanent union with Sethe, dependent upon their joint commitment to 'rememorying' the past together, is also dependent upon dialogic trust. Sethe has to accept that Paul D. can be an intimate interlocutory presence in the same way (though never, of course, in *quite* the same way) as Beloved was: she needs to and, indeed, does, trust her 'future answer word to him':

> She looks at him. The peachstone skin, the crease between his ready, waiting eyes and sees it – the thing in him, the blessedness, that has made him the kind of man that can walk into a house and make women cry. Because with him, in his presence, they could. Cry and tell him things they only told each other (p. 272).

In the latter part of this reading I want to move on from the dialogic conditions which facilitate the rememorying of the chronotopes in *Beloved* and focus, in some more detail, on how they are gendered.

In the last section we saw how 124, after Paul D.'s departure, becomes a woman-only space. This period of time, I would suggest (the time from his departure to when Denver breaks rank by seeking employment in the outside world), forms a discrete chronotope within the temporal management of the text, but is only one among several others which are also 'gendered female'. The eighteen years between the baby's death and Paul D.'s arrival, for example, are what first establish 124 as a 'separatist' zone, with the death marking a chronotopic watershed between the time when 124 was 'a cheerful, buzzing house' (p. 86) full of 'laughing children, dancing men, crying women' (i.e., a place of mixed gender) and when the men left and the neighbours no longer visited. The gendered identity of the house is so intense during this period (Denver observes that it is 'a person rather than a structure. A person [female?] that wept, sighed, trembled and fell into fits', p. 29) that the intrusion of Paul D. is registered by its bricks and mortar as an outrageous violation (see p. 18). Although Sethe and Denver interpret the quaking as the protest of the ghost rather than the house itself, it is clear from what follows that 124 has a gendered will of its own above and beyond any supernatural forces that might inhabit it. Thus when Paul D. exorcises the 'baby's venom' (p. 3) (or believes he does so), he fails to account to the chronotopic hold of eighteen years of woman-only occupation, and the house, in the end (and with the assistance of the rematerialized Beloved) expels him from its time-space.

Paul D.'s retreat from 124 may, indeed, be seen as a fascinating enactment of Bakhtin's 'chronotope of the threshold'. Although Bakhtin fails to describe how such chronotopes have been represented in literature in any detail, Paul D.'s movement from bedroom, to kitchen, to Baby Suggs's room, to storeroom, to coldhouse and, finally, to the shed may be read as a discrete chronotopic event within the textual time of the novel. Within a matter of days, Paul D. is sucked through an increasingly dark, increasingly cold, spatiotemporal corridor into a new chronotopic limbo. Because of the 'unfinished business' between Sethe and Beloved, 124 can no longer contain him.

Paul D.'s return to 124 demands that he pass through the same series of thresholds in the opposite direction: 'His coming is the reverse of his going. First the cold house, the store room, then the kitchen before he reaches the beds' (p. 263). Although Beloved has now left the house, Paul D. is still aware of it as a gendered space which he must enter with caution and respect. And it is only possible for him to stay, as I observed earlier, when Sethe decides to make him her partner in dialogue.

The various thresholds, then, that Paul D. must pass through before he arrives at the chronotopic core of 124 may be seen to represent the cultural and linguistic barriers separating women from men in the historical period covered by the novel. Men and women, in this nineteenth-century slave community, cannot easily pass into one another's worlds.[7] Indeed, the text makes it clear that in the same way that Paul D. will never fully understand the 'thickness' of the mother love that caused Sethe to murder her baby, nor will *she* ever properly understand his humiliation – his emasculation – during his last days at Sweet Home and his imprisonment in Alfred. The ideological 'hope' of the text rests, however, in the possibility of negotiating a new time-space which the men and women freed from slavery will eventually come to share, while the 'thresholds' of 124 Bluestone Road may be seen as emblematic of the transitional period that must precede such integration.

Although the majority of the chronotopes which comprise the fragmented temporal continuum of the text are gendered female, Paul D.'s rememories allow us glimpses into others which are emphatically masculine. These include life at Sweet Home after Mr Garner's death and following the arrival of 'Schoolteacher'. In the early days, Sweet Home, like 124 before the baby's death, was a place in which the sexes were equally represented; a time in which they were, in Sethe's words, 'all together' (p. 14). After Garner's death, however, the question of who really has power – men or women, masters or slaves – becomes newly visible. What had been hidden beneath Garner's paternalistic benevolence is now out in the open ('without his life each of theirs fell to pieces', p. 221). Suddenly all the men, including Paul D., are made aware both of the extent of their physical power as men, and the curbs upon it. In retrospect, Paul D. begins to perceive how his masculinity has been defined within the walls of slavery (symbolized, of course, by the walls of Sweet Home itself). He sees how it differs from the masculinity of 'free men' like Garner and the schoolteacher; how it is, in effect, a pseudo-masculinity because it has no purchase outside the chronotopic economy of Sweet Home itself. In terms of the gendering of the Sweet Home chronotope, Schoolteacher's arrival may be likened to the 'sin' of Adam and Eve in the Garden of Eden. Before he came, the male and female slaves appear to have lived together *relatively* unconscious of either their gender or their slavery. After Garner's death, and with Schoolteacher's teachings, they become painfully aware of both things and have to run away – both from their slavery and from one another. Paul D. attempts to escape for the sake of his self-respect (his 'manhood'), Sethe for the sake of her children.

After his attempted escape from Sweet Home, however, Paul D.'s punishment is to be plunged into a chronotope even more barbarously masculine. In Alfred, Georgia, Paul D. enters a time-space stripped bare of all 'feminine' love and tenderness: 'Listening to the doves in Alfred, Georgia, and having neither the right nor the permission to enjoy it because in that place mist, doves, sunlight, copper dirt, moon – everything belonged to the men who had the guns' (p. 162). It is in this world, far removed from the 'thick', maternal love that causes Sethe to twist a knife into her own daughter, that Paul D. comes face to face with the forces inscribing and denying his masculinity (brute strength; the gun) and perceives, in retrospect, how its ideology has ostracized him from the world of women. Thus when Sethe confesses her crime of love to him, he is unable to make the leap back into the space/time where people 'love big': 'Meanwhile the forest was locking the distance between them, giving it shape and heft' (p. 165).

In comparison to *Sexing the Cherry*, then, movement between chronotopes in Morrison's novel is a fraught, dangerous and frequently painful affair which finds symbolic parallel in the 'escape narratives' of Seth and Paul D. There is the difference, too, that chronotopic travel in *Beloved* is unidirectional: from present to past. Although the structure of the text is, like *Sexing the Cherry*, suggestive of a world in which past, present and future time are, in some manner, coextensive, most of the characters are even more wary of the future than they are of the past, and would never trust that a leap into the unknown would bring them happiness. It is a contrast that can be explained most pointedly by suggesting that where *Beloved* rewrites nineteenth-century American history from the perspective of the slave, Winterson writes seventeenth-century British history from the perspective of the colonizer. Although the latter designates its male characters 'explorers' whose sole quest is the discovery of exotic fruits, we know that the most rapidly expanding trade at that time was not in pineapples or bananas but in slavery. Viewed in this way, one can begin to recognize that it is only when chronotopes are seen in the full (social, ethnic, national *and* gendered) materiality that the 'thickness' which Bakhtin assigns them can be properly understood.

Morrison's text contrasts with Winterson's, too, in that we rarely see characters exploring a time-space outside their own, past subjective experience. Their travel across time is nearly always a rememorying of a chronotope they once occupied, although, as we saw in the dialogue between Beloved and Denver, the 'palpability' of time past (the way in which, in Sethe's words, 'places are still there', pp. 35–36) indicates that, for Morrison as for Winterson, we do have access to 'worlds' outside our own.

In *Beloved*, gender, like the ethnic consciousness with which it is so profoundly implicated, is presented as a significant obstacle to chronotopic migration. While Denver and Beloved have access to the chronotope of Sethe's escape and Denver's birth, for example, Sethe and Paul D. are unable to travel the distance between their gender-specific sufferings. Paul D. never visits the emotional time/space in which Sethe murdered her baby, and she is similarly oblivious of his time in Alfred.

The fact, however, that this is a text in which the female chronotope dominates means that the narrative is more focused on the 'exclusions' of women-only worlds than vice versa. Along with Paul D., we see Stamp Paid unable to cross the threshold of 124. Burdened with the guilt of telling Paul D. 'the truth' about Sethe, he stands outside her door and is confronted with a nonsensical 'babble': the 'undecipherable language' of women (pp. 198–99). It is, moreover, the women and not the men of Bluestone who take it upon themselves to 'exorcize' Beloved's ghost (p. 257) since they, alone, have the 'thickness' of love necessary to enter the chronotope of a child's murder.

In the years which follow, in which it is disputed whether there really *was* a ghost at 124, it is significant that – apart from Paul D., Edward Bodwin and the 'little boy' (p. 267) – it is only the women of the town who claim to have seen 'it' (p. 265). And this is clearly because 'Beloved' came from a time/space that, deep in their 'unspoken' hearts (p. 199), all slave mothers have visited.

Notes (cut and renumbered)

1. Although, as with *Sexing the Cherry*, the number of chronotopes to be found in *Beloved* will be dependent upon the different classificatory frameworks that may be imposed on the text, the following would seem to constitute discrete tempospatial horizons: (1) the narratological present (beginning with Paul D.'s arrival at 124 Bluestone Road); (2) early life at Sweet Home; (3) escape from Sweet Home (including Denver's birth); (4) the baby's death; (5) Sethe's trial and imprisonment; (6) Baby Suggs's life at 124 *before* the arrival of Sethe and the baby; (7) Paul D.'s imprisonment in Alfred and his escape; (8) Denver's childhood; (9) Sethe, Denver and Beloved's life at 124 after Paul D.'s departure; and (10) Beloved's 'time before'.

2. It is significant that Bakhtin himself never drew any specific parallels between chronotopes and his model of the dialogic/polyphonic text despite the fact (as was noted in the reading of *Sexing the Cherry* above) they belong to the same conceptual grid. What we are witnessing in this chapter are two texts whose multivocality is commensurate with their polychronotopic status; and, in the case of *Beloved*, a text whose chronotopes are (re)activated/made visible through dialogic exchange.

3. The fact that Sethe is dependent on this intimacy ('knowing') to speak out would seem to make her earlier observation that she could tell Beloved things because of 'her distance from the events themselves' (p. 58) deeply ironic.

4. This is a text whose sexual politics may be read as an appeal for the integration of male and female through a 're-education' of relations between the sexes. Certainly the separatist all-female family at 124 is not designed to survive permanently, but exists as a temporary chronotopic necessity. In *Sisters and Strangers* (Oxford: Basil Blackwell, 1992), Patricia Dunker observes that, throughout her work, Morrison has subscribed to 'the balance of women and men in "nurturing relationships"' (p. 254).

5. Kristeva's notion of the reciprocal 'holding' of mother and child.

6. Morrison's text is one in which the invitation to a psychoanalytic (specifically Lacanian) reading is explicit throughout, especially as Lorraine Liscio has pointed out, in its focus on the female characters' problems of 'crossing over' the 'threshold of language' and taking up their place in the Symbolic Order. Liscio also notes how this association between femaleness/speechlessness may be seen as problematic: 'Her use of this trope ... risks reinstating essentialist beliefs about maternal discourse: association with the mother means to be denied the status of a speaking subject and therefore to be always objectified in others' narratives' (p. 35). See L. Liscio, '*Beloved's* Narrative: Writing Mother's Milk', *Tulsa Studies in Women's Literature*, **11**, 1, 1992, pp. 31–46. Similarly problematic, it seems to me, is the way in which a Lacanian reading will posit Paul D. as the masculine agent necessary to restore Sethe and Denver to a (nonpsychotic) subject position within the symbolic realm. The advantage of my own dialogic reading of the text is that it makes the relationship between male and female characters (and masculine and feminine principles) much less

unidirectional. Even at the end of the novel, Sethe and Paul D. are actively negotiating their gendered identities via their interaction with one another.

7. This 'separate spheres' existence of men and women in the community is illustrated by Paul D.'s reference to 'house fits': 'the glassy anger men sometimes feel when a woman's house begins to bind them, when they want to yell and break something or at least run off' (p. 115).

9.5 PETER NICHOLLS: FROM 'THE BELATED POSTMODERN: HISTORY, PHANTOMS AND TONI MORRISON' (1995)

Peter Nicholls is Professor of English and American Literature, and Chair of the American Studies Graduate Division, at the University of Sussex. He is the author of *Ezra Pound. Politics, Economics, Writing* (1984); *Modernisms: A Literary Guide* (1995); and of a number of articles on modernism and postmodernism, including 'Divergences: Modernism, Postmodernism, Jameson and Lyotard', *Critical Quarterly*, 33, 3 (Autumn 1991), pp. 1–18. He is also reviews editor of *Textual Practice*.

Nicholls offers an explicitly psychoanalytical reading of *Beloved*, but one which uses ideas drawn from psychoanalytic theory to problematize and redefine notions of 'history'. He also proposes a conception of postmodernism, by way of *Beloved*, which then validates describing the novel as 'postmodern'. Try to work through the theoretical process by which Nicholls finds a psychoanalytic 'frame' in which he can legitimately read the 'historical imagination' at work in the novel. Compare his reading with Henderson's above and analyse the differences. Compare it also with other 'psychoanalytic' approaches in other exercises (e.g. on *Hamlet*). What does the essay *explain* about the text? Is there a 'politics of reading' perceptible here? Consider also Nicholls' redefinition of 'postmodernism' in relation to *Beloved*; what does he mean by it signalling 'the invasion of a cultural centre from its margins' (p. 443, below), and how is this exemplified in his reading? In this same context, compare the essay to the 'postcolonial' readings in Gilroy and Bhabha. Is the issue of 'marginality' treated similarly in these essays? Nicholls clearly values *Beloved* very highly (he speaks of Morrison's 'passionate historical imagination'; the novel's 'dramatic tension'; the 'distinctive rhythms of [her] prose': pp. 443, 445, 449, below). Are the terms of judgement here aesthetic, as they appear to be, or ideological? Does the essay assume these criteria are shared, or seek to persuade its readers of them? Are they consistent with the theoretical apparatus the essay otherwise calls upon?

The following extract comprises the first four sections (a fifth is largely on Morrison's later novel, *Jazz*) of Nicholls' essay with the above title, in Sue Vice, ed., *Psychoanalytic Criticism: A Reader*, Polity Press, 1995, pp. 50–63.

The Belated Postmodern: History, Phantoms and Toni Morrison

I

'The narrative into which life seems to cast itself surfaces most forcefully in certain kinds of psychoanalysis': so writes Toni Morrison in the introduction to her volume of essays, *Playing in the Dark*.[1] Morrison's preoccupation with themes of time, memory and mourning – especially in *Beloved* (1987) – makes it tempting to frame a reading of her work with concepts drawn from psychoanalysis (Freud's notion of 'working through', for example).[2] Morrison herself has so far said little about the relevance of psychoanalysis to her fiction, but the remark quoted above occurs in an account of Marie Cardinal's *The Words to Say It*: 'More than the enthusiasm of the person who suggested the book,' Morrison writes, 'I was persuaded by the title: five words taken from Boileau that spoke the full agenda and unequivocal goal of a novelist' (*PD*, p. v). A celebration of the talking cure, Cardinal's 'autobiographical novel' offers a striking model of therapeutic narration which may well have affected Morrison's attempts to present Sethe's process of 'remembering something she had forgotten she knew'.[3]

In the context of the lectures which make up *Playing in the Dark*, Cardinal's story of her illness has, too, a particular relevance to Morrison's archeology of the black presence in white American culture. Cardinal's account of her first anxiety attack records her feeling of panic at a concert given by Louis Armstrong. For Morrison, this first moment of *possession* by the illness which Cardinal would later come to call 'the Thing' provides a powerful figure for the intermittent invasion of white culture by 'the associative language of dread and love that accompanies blackness' (*PD*, p. x). Morrison reports her growing fascination with 'the way black people ignite critical moments of discovery or change of emphasis in literature not written by them' (*PD*, p. viii), and much of *Playing in the Dark* is an attempt to outline the multiple ways in which a mythological Africanism was constructed as an ideological and psychic defense against such disruptive incursions into white American culture:

> What became transparent were the self-evident ways that Americans choose to talk about themselves through and within a sometimes allegorical, sometimes metaphorical, but always choked representation of an Africanist presence. (*PD*, p. 17)

This metaphysical Africanism is 'choked', as Morrison puts it, by 'unspeakable thoughts, unspoken',[4] and the implication is that the counter-narrative of black fiction may have the capacity to recall what the historical record has 'forgotten', much as in psychoanalysis (in Ned Lukacher's words) 'The patient's speech "remembers", while the patient himself remains oblivious and utterly resists all the analyst's efforts to bring the "memory" to consciousness.'[5] To imagine Morrison's project in this way is to emphasize her sense of American history as irredeemably compromised by its metaphysical imperative to construct a white self (Africanism, she argues, has become 'a metaphysical necessity' [*PD*, p. 64]). 'History' has functioned like Lacan's Imaginary to provide 'an ego-reinforcing presence' (*PD*, p. 45), its fictions of wholeness and self-presence dependent on the 'duties of exorcism and reification and mirroring' that have fallen to the 'Africanist persona' (*PD*, p. 39) whose tabooed blackness has allowed 'the projection of the not-me', a veritable 'playground for the imagination' (*PD*, p. 38) in white American culture. Morrison's recent work might thus be read as a reversal of this 'exorcism', a shattering of the mirror through which the spectre of difference may suddenly emerge into the light.

When Marie Cardinal's narrator flees from the jazz concert it is with the feeling of being 'svelte in appearance but torn apart inside',[6] and while Morrison reads this internal violence as a figure for the relation of 'the cultural associations of jazz ... to Cardinal's "possession"' (*PD*, p. viii) it is tempting to connect it also to a particular sense of the postmodern. The term is not one that Morrison tends to use in her critical writings, although her comments in one interview suggest that she understands it primarily in relation to a dissolution of stable patterns of social and psychic identity.[7] There may seem little to be gained in designating Morrison's fiction as 'postmodern', especially as in its weaker forms the term frequently connotes exercises in aimless self-reflexivity which are worlds apart from the passionate historical imagination at work in a novel like *Beloved*. Perhaps for that reason, however, our sense of the postmodern might be productively sharpened by thinking it along the lines of Morrison's argument in *Playing in the Dark*. We might, in fact, discover an alternative postmodernism, one which is fully historical and obsessively cognizant of that fact, by reading Morrison's fiction as its outer limit, as the point at which the postmodern signals the invasion of a cultural centre from its margins.[8] As in the case of Marie Cardinal's 'possession', a forgotten history has the power to shake the social and metaphysical forms against which it breaks,[9] and this idea of history as a violent intrusion from somewhere else is clearly very different from the familiar forms of stylistic appropriation and unmotivated pastiche which have given us the more comfortable worlds of 'faction' and nostalgia movies. More specifically, the nature of that intrusion is one which refigures 'History' along the lines of a psychic temporality for which memory is less a matter of cultural allusion than of shock and trauma.[10]

From this point of view, the most productive formulation of the postmodern is surely that which regards it not as some new epoch succeeding the modern, but rather (following Lyotard) as a disruptive mode *within* the modern.[11] The postmodern and the modern thus coexist, inhabiting the same conceptual and historical space, and producing a tension which rends History from within. As Gianni Vattimo puts it, 'the post-modern displays, as its most common and most imposing trait, an effort to free itself from the logic of overcoming, development and innovation'.[12] Aesthetic forms have the capacity to release us from that particular logic of History, because they allow, in Heidegger's sense, 'the ungrounding of historicity, which is announced as a suspension of the hermeneutic continuity of the subject with itself and with history' (p. 125). And if, in Foucault's words, 'Continuous history is the indispensable correlative of the founding function of the subject',[13] any 'strong' concept of the postmodern will have less to do with forms of indeterminacy than with those of unresolvable *contradiction*. The dismantling of a racial metaphysics by causing it to be invaded by its other will thus amount to a violent 'possession' of its thematics of time and memory, leaving them also, we might say, 'torn apart inside'.

II

'The narrative into which life seems to cast itself surfaces most forcefully in certain kinds of psychoanalysis.' How, though, might the intimacies of the analyst's couch provide us with a way of talking about a history no longer grounded in metaphysics? One tempting answer to that question is to invoke Freud's concept of the 'return of the repressed', as Mae G. Henderson has done in one of the best discussions of *Beloved*.[14] The danger here, though, is that we begin to think of the 'repressed' as simply a lost fact or datum, a link which once restored will return us to a form of historical continuity. Yet psychoanalysis is concerned not so much with the discovery of a hidden content as with, in the words of Laplanche and Leclaire, 'an interpretive elaboration or working-through whose role is to weave around a rememorated element an entire network of meaningful relations that integrate it into the subject's explicit apprehension of himself'. From this point of view, then, 'the Freudian experience of "memory" has less to do with the recollection of an "event" than with the repetition of a structure'.[15] And for psychoanalysis, of course, memory leads a double life since it is (in David Krell's words) both 'the source of the *malady* with which it is concerned and the *therapy* it proffers'.[16] To remember is thus not simply to restore a forgotten link or moment of experience, nor is it unproblematically to 'repossess' or re-enact what has been lost.[17] That idea of recovering an occluded or 'buried' past derives from a traditional association of knowledge with recollection and depends on a thoroughly metaphysical 'presencing' of what is absent. The development of Freud's theory of memory is actually away from this phantasmatic form of recollection, and while his use of 'acting out' (*Agieren*) in therapy might seem tied to a form of 'presence', this is complicated, as Dominick LaCapra has argued, by a concept of memory which 'allowed for the distinction between mnemic trace and phantasm'.[18]

The distinction is a momentous one, connecting a major strand of Freud's thought to subsequent poststructuralism and to a certain theory of the postmodern for which concepts of time and memory are of central importance.[19] In the wake of Lacan, attention has recently been focussed on a related concept of deferral in Freud's theory which is codified in the word *Nachträglichkeit*, 'belatedness', or, in its usual technical translations, 'deferred action' and 'retroaction'. The concept is best known from the case history of the Wolf Man, though it is foreshadowed in the *Studies on Hysteria* and in some of Freud's early letters to Wilhelm Fliess. The Wolf Man, we recall, witnesses at the age of one and a half an act of sexual intercourse between his parents but the shock of this impression is deferred until some sexual understanding of its import is possible. As Freud puts it:

> At the age of one and a half the child receives an impression to which he is unable to react adequately; he is only able to understand it and to be moved by it when the impression is revived in him at the age of four; and only twenty years later, during the analysis, is he able to grasp with his conscious mental processes what was then going on in him.[20]

As Lacan observes, 'the event remains latent in the subject',[21] thereby giving rise to a complex temporality in which the subject is always in more than one place at any time. Deferred action is, then, a product of the excessive character of the first event which requires a second event to release its traumatic force ('only the occurrence of the second scene can endow the first one with pathogenic force').[22] John Forrester neatly defines this movement as 'the articulation of two *moments* with a time of delay'.[23] It is not simply a matter of recovering a lost memory, but rather of the restructuring which forms the past in retrospect as 'the original site [...] comes to be reworked'.[24]

What is involved, then, is not just a time-lapse between stimuli and response, but, as Laplanche and Pontalis are careful to point out, a particular kind of 'working over', a 'work of recollection'.[25] So too *Nachträglichkeit* must be distinguished from Jung's theory of 'retrospection' (*Zurückfantasieren*), for, as Laplanche explains, while the latter

> simply means the fact of creating a past to meet current needs, perhaps in an attempt to avoid present difficulties and to conceal them from oneself [...] Freud insists upon the tension between the old scene and the recent scenario.[26]

It is this 'tension' which implies a radical unsettling of that 'philosophy of representation – of the original, the first time, resemblance, imitation, faithfulness'[27] which postmodernism will also seek to disrupt. *Nachträglichkeit* calls into question traditional notions of causality – the second event is presented now as the 'cause' of the first[28] – and its retroactive logic refuses to accord ontological primacy to any originary moment. Since the shock of the first scene is not felt directly by the subject but only through its later representation in memory we are dealing with, in Derrida's words, 'a past that has never been present'.[29] Belatedness, in this sense, creates a complex temporality which inhibits any nostalgia for origin and continuity – the 'origin' is now secondary, a construction always contained in its own repetition (as Andrew Benjamin puts it, 'The original event is thus no longer the same as itself. The effect of the present on the past is to cause a repetition of the "event" within which something new is taking place').[30]

III

The abstractness of these ideas may seem a far cry from the dramatic tension of Morrison's writing, but her search for an alternative, 'ungrounded' historicity has some affinity with the critique of metaphysics outlined here. Let us return for a moment to Derrida's notion of 'a past which has never been present': in a later passage of *Memoires for Paul de Man*, he calls this particular past 'historicity itself – an historicity which cannot be historical, an "ancientness" without history, without anteriority, but which produces history'.[31] In contrast to the 'unfolding of presence'[32] which is 'history', 'historicity' is the movement of temporal difference, or, as Derrida puts it in *Dissemination*, 'a series of temporal differences without any central present, without a present of which the past and the future would be but modifications'.[33] This historicity shares with the temporality of the subject the qualities of self-division and disunity, but it must not be construed in terms of the empirical time of consciousness. For historicity, like the time of the unconscious, is a construction (Freud observes in his study of the Wolf Man that 'these scenes from infancy are not reproduced during the treatment as recollection, they are the products of construction'[34]). This is not necessarily to suggest that the traumatic event never took place, but rather that it has never been *present* and hence that it exists only as a repetition.[35] It is in this sense that what is 'remembered' can come to seem something *foreign* to the subject's lived experience, a fragment from another time when the subject was different, but a fragment which has the power drastically to restructure the self in its present moment (Lyotard speaks figuratively of 'this stranger in the house ... his clandestine entry and unnoticed stay' (*H*, p. 17)).

Historicity, then, in the sense used here, does not constitute itself as a unified object (or 'moment') which can be repossessed by a contemplative subject. In fact, it is precisely that particular present of contemplation which is torn by the intrusion of a different time. It is not fortuitous that Althusser, in defining his own conception of a 'differential temporality' which breaks decisively with the 'ontological category of the present'[36] should find a helpful model in Freud's theory:

> We have known, since Freud, that the time of the unconscious cannot be confused with the time of biography. On the contrary, *the concept of the time of the unconscious must be constructed* in order to obtain an understanding of certain biographical traits. In exactly the same way, it is essential to construct the concepts of the different historical times which are never given in the ideological obviousness of the continuity of time (which need only be suitably divided into a good periodization to obtain the time of history), but must be constructed out of the differential nature and differential articulation of their objects in the structure of the whole.[37]

Of particular interest here is Althusser's conception of historicity as a disruption of the subject's continuous, lived temporality (mired in 'ideological obviousness'). The contrast between empirical and historical time might in fact allow us to draw a broad distinction between modernist and postmodernist conceptions of temporality. As Lyotard has observed, a characteristically 'modern' approach to the past is to scrutinize it for its 'errors' and 'crimes', and thus to master it through interpretation.[38] To this we can add a related tendency to conceive the past as a phantasmatic space to be reinhabited and repossessed (historical events become the object of a desire which promises to draw them into some sort of symbiotic union with the present).[39] Both modes frequently depend upon a reformulation of the nineteenth-century poetic of epiphanies and arrested moments, and both stalk the past in search of 'ego-reinforcing' models of authority and insight. By way of contrast, a postmodern historicity – Morrison's *Beloved* is an almost overwhelming example – conceives the subject as shaken out of its secure metaphysical time and exposed to the shock of a temporality which is always self-divided. For the postmodern text, this is the subject's 'real' time, though it would be more accurate to say that the subject is possessed by it than that she or he possesses it.

Now we can begin to see why Freud's concept of *Nachträglichkeit* and traumatic memory might provide a way of thinking about this postmodern historicity. For, as Laplanche puts it, 'the recall of the first scene [...] sets off the upsurge of sexual excitation, *catching the ego in reverse*, and leaving it disarmed, incapable of using the normally outward-directed defenses, and thus falling back on a pathological defense, and "posthumous primary process".'[40] The ego is caught 'in reverse' partly because, in Lacan's words, 'the past [...] reveals itself reversed in repetition',[41] but also because the degree of excitation felt is disproportionate to the (second) event which appears to have occasioned it. It is precisely this effect of deferred action which Lyotard has developed to define a postmodern historicity. In *Heidegger and 'the Jews'*, for example, he proposes memory as anamnesis in contrast to a memorializing history which 'forgets' through discursive ordering ('one forgets as soon as one believes, draws conclusions, and holds for certain' (*H*, p. 10). 'Memorial history' functions as 'a protective shield' (*H*, p. 8), providing a series of psychic defenses which guarantee 'the diachrony of the self-assured spirit' (*H*, p. 26)

Belatedness as the constitutive element of the unconscious will therefore present a contrasting temporality in which anachronism is the principal feature. 'History' here is no longer a sort of container in which events are serially disposed, but a collision of two temporalities – following Freud's model of traumatic memory, Lyotard speaks of a first moment of shock without affect and a second moment of affect without shock (*H*, p. 12). This first moment, which Lyotard compares to the sublime, marks the irruption of the 'figural' which is always 'beyond' representation.[42] But can we remember without memorializing? As Lyotard observes, 'One *must*, certainly, inscribe in words, in images. One cannot escape the necessity of representing' (*H*, p. 26). None the less, the avant-garde will always pursue the 'sublime feeling' (*H*, p. 32) which lies beyond representation, and Lyotard characterizes such artistic projects as

> an aesthetics of shock, an anaesthetics. It is a shock that, in the Kantian *Gemüth* and in the Freudian apparatus, defies the power that is nevertheless constitutive of the mind according to Kant (i.e., that which synthesizes the manifold, its elementary memory). Not only does the imagination, required to present sensibly something that would re-present the Absolute, fail in its task but it falls into an 'abyss'. ... (*H*, p. 31)

This is 'shock' conceived not in its weaker sense (the modernist 'shock of the new') but as equivalent to 'trauma', and Lyotard alludes to Freud's early account of Emma to indicate the kind of excess of affect involved:

> Something, however, *will make* itself understood, 'later' [...] It will be represented as something that has never been presented. Renewed absurdity. For instance, as a symptom, a phobia (Emma in the store). This will be understood as feeling, fear, anxiety, feeling of a threatening excess whose motive is obviously not in the present context. A feeling, it seems, born of nothing that can be verified in the 'present' situation in a perceptible, verifiable, or falsifiable way, and which therefore necessarily points to an elsewhere that will have to be located outside this situation, outside the present contextual situation, imputed to a different site than this one. (*H*, p. 13)[43]

Emma's phobic reaction ('a trauma *after the event*', in Freud's words)[44] provides a sort of figure for a postmodern 'history': excessive affect cannot be properly integrated into a present context of meanings, and the past which seems now not to have been directly experienced (it is not remembered as 'present')[45] suddenly surges back into the self, causing pain and anxiety. Much of what Lyotard has written about Auschwitz has sought to present this sense of history as trauma, as the opening of a wound within the subject. The problem is always to acknowledge the 'protective shield' which our culture invokes against this resurgent past while at the same time recognizing (without 'memorializing') the alien and unassimilable nature of what is remembered. In contrast to the modernist desire to inhabit the past, in Lyotard's account of the postmodern it is the past which inhabits us, invading 'an apparatus constitutively unprepared to receive it' (*H*, p. 17). Perhaps it is not simply, then, that the ego is caught 'in reverse', but that it is opened to a vertigo in which defenses fall and something foreign lodges in what was formerly the 'centre' of the self.

IV

This trope of a return cannot but remind us of Morrison's *Beloved*, the text in which Morrison has explored most vividly what we might call the insistence of historicity in the self. There is a ghost here and a persistent haunting, as Morrison uncovers the intricate relations between love and possession, using the resources of fiction to free us from a metaphysical History.

The theme of possession, of a force invading the self, has itself haunted postmodern American writing, being first definitively broached in William Burroughs' *The Naked Lunch* (1959) and operating as a persistent metaphor of social control in experimental fiction of the last three decades.[46] Yet while *Beloved* also explores ways in which the body can be possessed by something external to it, Morrison tends to see the workings of power as inseparable from the disjunctive operations of a 'belated' temporality. This is the full force of 'unspeakable thoughts, unspoken', for feeling, understanding and speaking never seem to occur in the same moment. The fluid shifts between different times in this novel and in *Jazz* thus do not work to enforce some deterministic reading of the past's effects upon the present, but rather to evoke the traumatic force of a historicity which splits the subject, compelling it to live in different times rather than in a secure, metaphysical present.

Who is Beloved? A revenant, someone who comes back, she seems to offer precisely what we have always yearned for, the past made good, an origin restored, 'my girl come home' (*B*, p. 201), with 'new skin' (*B*, p. 50) to match her 'new shoes' (*B*, p. 66). But she is not that; or at least she is always more than that, at once Sethe's daughter and an African lost in the Middle Passage (and even as Sethe's daughter, she is not what she was, but grown to the age she would have been, her neck bearing 'the little curved shadow' left by the handsaw (*B*, p. 239)). This play of contradiction seems now the very mark of the postmodern, issuing in an insistence that something (someone) can be two things at once, that two things can occupy the same space, that the origin is irreducibly doubled.

And there is more: for this haunting is but one of many (as Baby Suggs points out, '"Not a house in the country ain't packed to its rafters with some dead Negro's grief. We lucky this ghost is a baby"' [*B*, p. 5]), and the voices heard in 124 are quickly understood by Stamp Paid: 'although he couldn't cipher but one word, he believed he knew who spoke them. The people of the broken necks, of fire-cooked blood and black girls who had lost their ribbons. What a roaring' (*B*, p. 181). So Beloved is also a figure of thwarted love, of the body literally possessed by others, of the entire tragedy of slavery which cannot adequately be spoken. Her belated appearance is traumatic in Freud's sense precisely because it embodies an over-whelming desire, a now unrepresentable excess of the emotional need suppressed under slavery ('to love anything that much was dangerous' [*B*, p. 45], and 'not to need permission for desire – well now, *that* was freedom' [*B*, p. 162]).[47]

Beloved returns, then, *nachträglich*, but she will be forever 'unaccounted for' (*B*, p. 275), impossible to memorialize in some metaphysical History. In her figure, historicity comes back with all the force of bewildering, unfulfilled desire, playing havoc with temporal and symbolic schemes. That force permeates the texture of Morrison's writing which, as in the later *Jazz*, makes powerful use of retroactive effects, embedding signs and images which will only become clear at a later stage. In some cases these are darkly proleptic of a story to be filled in later; in others Morrison constructs a complex sequence of displaced affect – early on we hear, for example, that Sethe's hurt 'was always there – like a tender place in the corner of her mouth that the bit left' (*B*, p. 9), but it is not until we have penetrated further into the narrative that we associate this portentous but unlocated image with the suffering of both Sethe's mother and Paul D. The distinctive rhythms of Morrison's prose create an intricate cross-weaving of times in which each moment comes to signify only in relation to at least one other. To re-read *Beloved* forewarned of this is to become increasingly attuned to the flickering trail of such emotional intensities, one illuminating another in a time which can never constitute a full present. This brief exchange between Denver and Beloved, for example:

'What is it?' asks Denver.
'Look,' she points to the sunlit cracks.
'What? I don't see nothing.' Denver follows the pointing finger. (*B*, p. 125)

But Beloved does, as we later know: 'at night I cannot see the dead man on my face daylight comes through the cracks and I can see his locked eyes' (*B*, p. 210). This is not some facile trick of composition, one time 'rhyming' with or passively echoing another;[48] rather, Morrison evokes the texture of a temporality which makes anachronism the condition of the psychic life, embedding its effects in the very detail of narration ('Sethe feels her eyes burn and it may have been to keep them clear that she looks up' (*B*, p. 261)).

If belatedness is a condition recognized in the local detail of the writing, it also frames the larger movement of the narrative. Beloved first exists in 124 as a troublesome ghost, 'not evil, just sad' (*B*, p. 8). Whereas the community tends to assume that 'the haunting was done by an evil thing looking for more', 'None of them knew the downright pleasure of enchantment, of not suspecting but *knowing* the things behind things' (*B*, p. 37). It is Paul D who 'beat[s] the spirit away', but 'in its place he brought another kind of haunting' which seems to conjure up the full horror of slavery (*B*, p. 96). 'Paul D ran her off so she had no choice but to come back to me in the flesh' (*B*, p. 200), and it is in this new embodiment that Beloved begins to play her ambiguous role in the narrative. At first she is a 'sweet, if peculiar guest' (*B*, p. 57) but as the very incarnation of a boundless desire (*B*, p. 58) she soon imposes intolerable demands upon Sethe.

The partial demonizing of Beloved runs parallel to a shifting conception of memory in the novel. In the opening stages, Sethe is troubled by frozen images of the past – 'I was talking about time. It's so hard for me to believe in it. Some things go. Pass on. Some things just stay' (B, pp. 35–6) – and the 'glittering' headstone which is her memorial to Beloved seems a way of 'keeping the past at bay' (B, p. 42). With the 'miraculous resurrection' (B, p. 105) of her lost daughter, however, Sethe begins to remember 'something she had forgotten she knew' (B, p. 61). Yet the process of remembering is at once a release and a bondage, snaring the mind in a deadly repetition even as it brings a part of the psyche back to life ('Anything dead coming back to life hurts' (B, p. 35)). The danger becomes clearer as the novel proceeds and the narcissistic identification with Beloved becomes stronger: 'But her brain was not interested in the future, loaded with the past and hungry for more, it left her no room to imagine, let alone plan for the next day' (B, p. 70). With her recognition of Beloved, Sethe is finally freed from the need to remember and left 'smiling at the things she would not have to remember now' (B, p. 182). But this release from 'rememory' is another kind of prison, bringing a claustrophobic introversion ('The world is in this room' (B, p. 183)) and leaving Sethe 'wrapped in a timeless present' (B, p. 184).[49]

Now we begin to see the darker effects of the 'miraculous resurrection' (B, p. 105), for having dropped her defences on the departure of the 'chastising ghost' (B, p. 86),[50] Sethe is, as it were, invaded by the spirit of her murdered daughter. It is the violence of this intrusion of one world into another which will later appall the pragmatic Ella:

> As long as the ghost showed out from its ghostly place – shaking stuff, crying, smashing and such – Ella respected it. But if it took flesh and came in her world, well, the shoe was on the other foot. She didn't mind a little communication between the two worlds, but this was an invasion. (B, p. 257)

The force of Beloved's desire, strongly marked by a language of orality and ingestion (chewing and swallowing), threatens to consume Sethe from within. 'Beloved ate up her life, took it, swelled up with it, grew taller on it' (B, p. 250), and the momentum of this desire, excessive and unspeakable because so long pent up by slavery, begins to carry us back into the past. If the novel opens with a grim rewriting of the primal scene (here a *dead* child witnesses the sexual act), now an equally macabre reversal takes place as 'Beloved bending over Sethe looked the mother, Sethe the teething child' (B, p. 250). To complete this traumatic looping back of the narrative we have the final sight of Beloved facing the singing women:

> The devil-child was clever, they thought. And beautiful. It had taken the shape of a pregnant woman, naked and smiling in the heat of the afternoon sun. Thunderblack and glistening, she stood on long straight legs, her belly big and tight. (B, p. 261)

Pregnant with Paul D's child? Or – the suggestion is ludicrous – with Sethe herself?

Perhaps one way of understanding this peculiar moment in the novel is to consider more closely the work of mourning which frames the story. Sethe's initial attempt to 'keep the past at bay' (B, p. 42) is in one sense a refusal to mourn which we might understand with the help of a distinction drawn by Nicolas Abraham and

Maria Torok between 'incorporation' and 'introjection'.[51] Whereas introjection assimilates to the self what is lost, incorporation perpetuates the existence of the lost object as something alive and foreign within the self. As Derrida explains in his introduction to Abraham and Torok's study of the Wolf Man:

> Sealing the loss of the object, but also marking the refusal to mourn, such a maneuver [incorporation] is foreign to and actually opposed to the process of introjection. I pretend to keep the dead alive, intact, *safe (save) inside me*, but it is only in order to refuse, in a necessarily equivocal way, to love the dead as a living part of me, dead *save in me*, through the process of introjection, as happens in so-called normal mourning.[52]

The dead person is thus not an object of identification but a phantasmatic presence within the self which gives rise to a topography which Abraham and Torok call the 'crypt':

> Grief that cannot be expressed builds a *secret vault* within the subject. In this crypt reposes – alive, reconstituted from the memories of words, images, and feelings – the objective counterpart of the loss, as a complete person with his own topography, as well as the traumatic incidents – real or imagined – that had made introjection impossible.[53]

This 'crypt' is equivalent to 'a split in the Ego',[54] a rift from which emerges 'a false unconscious filled with phantoms – to wit, fossilized words, live corpses, and foreign bodies'.[55] The lost object is thus incorporated as something live and present, 'fantasmatic, unmediated, instantaneous, magical, sometimes hallucinatory'.[56] The terms Derrida uses here are certainly suggestive in the context of *Beloved*, and indeed Morrison herself has spoken of her novel in a way which further confirms the relevance of this idea of incorporation as some sort of fragmentation of the self. In an interview with Gloria Naylor given when she was at work on *Beloved*, Morrison spoke of her interest in a theme connecting two stories (one was that of Margaret Garner, model for Sethe, the other would form the basis of Dorcas's story in *Jazz*):

> Now what made those stories connect, I can't explain, but I do know that, in both instances, something seemed clear to me. A woman loved something other than herself so much. *She had placed all of the value of her life in something outside herself.* That the woman who killed her children loved her children so much; they were the best part of her and she would not see them sullied.[57]

Is this, then, the major theme of *Beloved* and the one which ties it to *Jazz* (apparently the second novel of a projected trilogy)? If the crypt is a split in the ego, then Morrison's account suggests that in the case of *Beloved* the central problem for Sethe is to come to terms with 'what it is that really compels a good woman to displace the self, her self' (p. 584). Morrison explains to Naylor:

> So what I started doing and thinking about for a year was to project the self not into the way we say 'yourself', but to put a space between those words, as though the self were really a *twin* or a thirst or a friend or something that sits right next to you and watches you, which is what I was talking about when I said 'the dead girl'. (p. 585)

So for Morrison, it seems, the genesis of *Beloved* lay partly in that sense that 'the best thing that is in us is also the thing that makes us sabotage ourselves, sabotage in the sense that our life is not as worthy of our perception of the best part of ourselves' (p. 585). Beloved has striven to destroy the boundaries of her mother's self ('I want to join' (*B*, p. 213)), seeking now to possess – to incorporate – Sethe.[58] If Sethe's only hope lies in 'claiming ownership of [her] freed self' (*B*, p. 95) it is ultimately by managing, as Derrida puts it, to 'love the dead as a living part of me, dead *save in me*' that she will do so (Morrison has described the main problem in *Beloved* as 'how to own your own body and love somebody else').[59] The crucial recognition then will be Paul D's, that 'you your best thing, Sethe. You are' (*B*, p. 273).

But as Morrison emphasized in a recent talk,[60] something remains after the end of this particular story ('There is a loneliness that can be rocked ...' (p. 274)). In the gap between Sethe's final words ('Me? Me?') and the name which closes the narrative ('Beloved') the contradictions reappear. Beloved is exorcized, but in the last two pages of the novel she returns (again). This particular haunting is not over:

> Down by the stream in back of 124 her footprints come and go. They are so familiar. Should a child, an adult place his feet in them, they will fit. Take them out and they disappear again as though nobody ever walked there. (*B*, p. 275)

'Familiar', familial: this ghost seems the product of what Abraham and Torok term 'transgenerational haunting' in which something repressed is transmitted across several generations.[61] This phantom, writes Abraham, 'is not related to the loss of a loved one, it cannot be considered the effect of unsuccessful mourning, as is the case of melancholics or all those who carry a tomb within themselves' (p. 76). In line with his theory of 'transgenerational haunting', Abraham concludes instead that

> It is the children's or descendants' lot to objectify these buried tombs through diverse species of ghosts. What comes back to haunt are the tombs of others. The phantoms of folklore merely objectify a metaphor active within the unconscious: the burial of an unspeakable fact *within the loved one*. (p. 76)

The desire to forget is strong, but while 'This is not a story to pass on' (*B*, p. 275) the memory of 'Sixty Million and more' is somehow encrypted within us, in our time and in our bodies:

> So they forgot her. Like an unpleasant dream during a troubling sleep. Occasionally, however, the rustle of a skirt hushes when they wake, and the knuckles brushing a cheek in sleep seem to belong to the sleeper. Sometimes the photograph of a close friend or relative – looked at too long – shifts, and something more familiar than the dear face itself moves there. They can touch it if they like, but don't, because they know things will never be the same if they do. (*B*, p. 275)[62]

[...]

The essay concludes with a four-page section on Morrison's *Jazz*.

Notes (renumbered)

1. *Playing in the Dark: Whiteness and the Literary Imagination* (Cambridge, Mass. and London: Harvard University Press, 1992), p.v. (hereafter cited in the text as *PD*).
2. See Mae G. Henderson, 'Toni Morrison's *Beloved*: Re-Membering the Body as Historical Text', in Hortense J. Spillers (ed.), *Comparative American Identities* (London: Routledge, 1991), p. 74.
3. *Beloved* (London: Pan Books, 1988), p. 61 (hereafter cited in the text as *B*). Bruno Bettelheim calls the work an 'autobiographical novel' in his Introduction. Morrison apparently discovered Cardinal's account in 1983. Without enforcing the connection too rigorously, there are several other aspects of *The Words to Say It* which may have resonated with Morrison's work on *Beloved*, not least, perhaps, the account of Marie's mother's illness which is closely tied to the early death of a daughter: 'She no longer needed to come as often because, little by little, her dead baby had again begun to grow inside her and would live there for ever.' See below, pp. 451–2.
4. *Beloved*, p. 199. See also 'Unspeakable Things Unspoken: The Afro-American Presence in American Literature', *Michigan Quarterly Review*, 28 (1) Winter 1989, pp. 1–34.
5. Ned Lukacher, *Primal Scenes: Literature, Philosophy, Psychoanalysis* (Ithaca and London: Cornell University Press, 1986), p. 12.
6. Marie Cardinal, *The Words to Say It*, trans. Pat Goodheart (London: Pan Books, 1983), p. 36: 'The beauty of those thick, glossy flowers! I was running, they were already far behind, and yet the heart of one of them that I had glimpsed for a fraction of a second stayed with me, keeping me company in my race, as calm as I was agitated, svelte in appearance but torn apart inside.' Morrison (p. ix) quotes the last phrase in her account.
7. 'Living Memory' (Interview with Toni Morrison by Paul Gilroy), *City Limits* (31 March/7 April, 1988), p. 11: 'From a woman's point of view, in terms of confronting the problems of where the world is now, black women had to deal with "post-modern" problems in the nineteenth century and earlier. These things had to be addressed by black people a long time ago. Certain kinds of dissolution, the loss of and the need to reconstruct certain kinds of stability.'
8. Cf. Robert Young, *White Mythologies: Writing History and the West* (London: Routledge, 1990), pp. 19–20 for the view that postmodernism designates 'not just the cultural effects of a new stage of "late" capitalism', but 'European culture's awareness that it is no longer the unquestioned and dominant centre of the world'. See also Thomas Docherty, *After Theory: Postmodernism/ postmarxism* (London: Routledge, 1990).
9. Cf. *The Words to Say It*, p. 15: 'The Thing, which on the inside was made of a monstrous crawling of images, sounds, and odours, projected in every way by a devastating pulse making all reasoning incoherent, all explanation absurd, all efforts to order tentative and useless ...'
10. See also the discussion of 'time-lag' and its relation to *Beloved* in Homi K. Bhabha, '"Race", Time and the Revision of Modernity', *Oxford Literary Review*, 13 (1–2), 1991, pp. 193–219, especially pp. 215–16.
11. Jean-François Lyotard, 'Answering the Question: What Is Postmodernism?', in *The Postmodern Condition: A Report on Knowledge*, trans. Geoff Bennington and Brian Massumi (Manchester: Manchester University Press, 1984), pp. 71–82.
12. Gianni Vattimo, *The End of Modernity: Nihilism and Hermeneutics in Postmodern Culture*, trans. Jon R. Snyder (Cambridge: Polity Press, 1988), p. 105.
13. Michel Foucault, *The Archeology of Knowledge*, trans. A. M. Sheridan Smith (London: Tavistock Publications Ltd, 1982), p. 12.
14. Mae G. Henderson, 'Toni Morrison's *Beloved*', p. 63.
15. Jean Laplanche and Serge Leclaire, 'The Unconscious: A Psychoanalytic Study', *Yale French Studies*, 48 (1972), p. 128. Cf. John Forrester, *The Seductions of Psychoanalysis: Freud, Lacan, and Derrida* (Cambridge: Cambridge University Press, 1990), p. 199 on 'Freud's theory that it was a *way* of remembering that was traumatic, rather than *what* was remembered'.
16. David F. Krell, *Of Memory, Reminiscence, and Writing: On the Verge* (Bloomington and Indianapolis: Indiana University Press, 1990), p. 106.

17. Cf. Mae G. Henderson, 'Toni Morrison's *Beloved*', p. 64: 'Morrison seeks to repossess the African and slave ancestors after their historic violation.' And ibid., pp. 80–1 on Sethe's ability to '"relive" or re-enact the past'.

18. Dominick LaCapra, 'History and Psychoanalysis', in Françoise Meltzer (ed.), *The Trial(s) of Psychoanalysis* (Chicago and London: University of Chicago Press, 1988), p. 18.

19. This particular view of the postmodern is to be distinguished from that of Fredric Jameson who has argued consistently that postmodernity is characterized by a 'waning' of a thematics of time and memory ('memory has been weakened in our time', as he puts it in *Postmodernism, or the Cultural Logic of Late Capitalism*, Verso, 1991 [London and New York: p. 364]). For a critique, see my 'Divergences: Modernism, Postmodernism, Jameson and Lyotard', *Critical Quarterly*, 33(3), Autumn 1991, pp. 1–18.

20. *Pelican Freud Library*, 9 (Harmondsworth: Penguin Books, 1981), p. 278 n. 2. Cf. the letter to Fliess of 15 October 1895, in *The Origins of Psycho-Analysis: Letters to Wilhelm Fliess, Drafts and Notes: 1887–1902* (London: Imago, 1954), p. 127: 'Have I revealed the great clinical secret to you ...? Hysteria is the consequence of presexual *sexual shock*. Obsessional neurosis is the consequence of presexual *sexual pleasure* later transformed into guilt.' Freud goes on to observe that 'the relevant events become effective only as *memories*'.

21. *Ecrits: A Selection*, trans. Alan Sheridan (London: Tavistock, 1977), p. 48.

22. Jean Laplanche and J. B. Pontalis, *The Language of Psychoanalysis*, trans. Donald Nicholson-Smith, with an introduction by Daniel Lagache, (London: Karnac Books, 1988), p. 113. Cf. Laplanche, *New Foundations for Psychoanalysis*, trans. David Macey (Oxford: Blackwell, 1989), p. 112: 'This theory postulates that nothing can be inscribed in the human unconscious except in relation to at least two events which are separated from one another in time by a moment of maturation that allows the subject to react in two ways to an initial experience or to the memory of that experience.'

23. Forrester, *The Seductions of Psychoanalysis*, p. 206.

24. Andrew Benjamin, *Art, Mimesis and the Avant-Garde* (London: Routledge, 1991), p. 197. Cf. Lacan, *Ecrits*, p. 48: '... the effect of full speech is to reorder past contingencies by conferring on them the sense of necessities to come, such as they are constituted by the little freedom through which the subject makes them present.'

25. Laplanche and Pontalis, *The Language of Psychoanalysis*, p. 114.

26. Laplanche, *New Foundations for Psychoanalysis*. p. 118.

27. Michel Foucault, *Language, Counter-Memory, Practice: Selected Essays and Interviews*, ed. Donald F. Bouchard (Ithaca: Cornell University Press, 1977), p. 172.

28. See Lukacher, *Primal Scenes*, p. 35: 'Deferred action demands that one recognize that while the earlier event is still to some extent the cause of the later event, the earlier event is nevertheless also the effect of the later event. One is forced to admit a double or "metaleptic" logic in which causes are both causes of effects and the effect of effects.'

29. *Memories for Paul de Man*, rev. ed., trans. Cecile Lindsay et al., (New York: Columbia University Press, 1989), p. 58: 'Memory stays with traces, in order to "preserve" them, but traces of a past that has never been present, traces which themselves never occupy the form of presence and always remain, as it were, to come.' Cf. *Margins of Philosophy*, trans. Alan Bass (Brighton: Harvester Press, 1986), p. 21. The same point is stressed by Lyotard in *Heidegger and 'the Jews'*, trans. Andreas Michel and Mark Roberts (Minneapolis: University of Minnesota Press, 1990), p. 13 (hereafter cited in the text as *H*): 'It will be represented as something that has never been presented.' David Krell, *Of Memory, Reminiscence, and Writing*, p. 6 observes of Merleau-Ponty's elaboration of a similar idea in *The Phenomenology of Perception* that it 'heralds the passing of an epoch of mnemic metaphysics. It marks the inception of a memory beneath the traditional ontotheological uses of recollection, a memory no longer in thrall to presence.'

30. Andrew Benjamin, 'Translating Origins: Psychoanalysis and Philosophy', in L. Venuti (ed.), *Rethinking Translation: Discourse, Subjectivity, Ideology* (London: Routledge, 1992), p. 30. This logic is perhaps inscribed in the etymology of the verb 'to remember', from the Latin *rememorari*,

'call to mind again, remember *again*'; Morrison's 'rememory' is not, as is sometimes thought, a coinage, but an archaism which the *OED* defines as 'remembrance'.

31. *Mémoires*, p. 95.
32. Jacques Derrida, *Of Grammatology*, trans. Gayatri Chakravorty Spivak (Baltimore and London: Johns Hopkins University Press, 1976), p. 85: 'the word history has no doubt always been associated with a linear scheme of the unfolding of presence, where the line relates the final presence to the originary presence according to the straight line or the circle.'
33. Jacques Derrida, *Dissemination*, trans. Barbara Johnson (Chicago: University of Chicago Press, 1981), p. 210. See also *Writing and Difference*, trans. Alan Bass (London: Routledge, 1978), p. 212 for the connection of this central theme with Freud's *Nachträglichkeit*: 'That the present in general is not primal but, rather, reconstituted, that it is not the absolute, wholly living form which constitutes experience, that there is no purity of the living present – such is the theme, formidable for metaphysics, which Freud, in a conceptual scheme unequal to the thing itself, would have us pursue.'
34. *Pelican Freud Library*, 9, p. 284.
35. See Philippe Lacoue-Labarthe and Jean-Luc Nancy, 'Le peuple juif ne rêve pas', in *La Psychanalyse est-elle une histoire juive?* (Seuil, Paris, 1981), pp. 86–7.
36. Louis Althusser and Etienne Balibar, *Reading Capital*, trans. Ben Brewster (London: Verso, 1979), pp. 100, 95. Althusser's argument is underpinned by his critique of Hegel's 'historical present': 'the structure of historical existence is such that all the elements of the whole always co-exist in one and the same time, one and the same present, and are therefore contemporaneous with one another in one and the same present' (p. 94).
37. Ibid., p. 103 (Althusser's emphases).
38. See *L'inhumain: Causeries sur le temps* (Paris: Editions Galilée, 1988), pp. 35–8. The main question here is 'the insinuation of will into reason' – see Lyotard, *Tombeau de l'intellectuel et autres papiers* (Paris: Editions Galilée, 1984), p. 81.
39. For a discussion of these aspects of Modernism, see my 'Apes and Familiars: Modernism, Mimesis, and the Work of Wyndham Lewis', *Textual Practice* (forthcoming).
40. Jean Laplanche and J. B. Pontalis, 'Fantasy and the Origins of Sexuality', *International Journal of Psycho-Analysis*, 49, (1)1968, p. 4 (my italics).
41. *Ecrits*, p. 103.
42. Cf. *Heidegger and 'the Jews'*, p. 15: 'the force of the excitation cannot be "bound", composed, neutralized, fixed in accordance with other forces "within" the apparatus, and to that extent it does not give rise to a *mise-en-scène*'.
43. For the case of Emma, see *Project for a Scientific Psychology*, in *The Origins of Psychoanalysis*, pp. 410–14.
44. Ibid., p. 413 (Freud's italics).
45. Compare Lyotard's account (*Heidegger and 'the Jews'*, p. 11) of a past 'which is not an object of memory like something that might have been forgotten and must be remembered (with a view to a "good end", to correct knowledge'.
46. See *The Naked Lunch* (London: Corgi, 1974), p. 247: '"Possession" they call it [...] Sometimes an entity jumps in the body [...] As if I was usually there but subject to goof now and again [...] *Wrong! I am never here* [...] Never that is *fully* in possession ...' Thomas Pynchon's *Gravity's Rainbow* (1973; Harmondsworth: Penguin, 1987) provides one definitive exploration of the 'interiorization' of control: 'All these things arise from one difficulty: control. For the first time it was *inside*, do you see. The control is put inside. No more need to suffer passively under "outside forces"'. (p. 30).
47. For Beloved as the force of desire, see p. 58: 'A touch no heavier than a feather but loaded with desire. Sethe stirred and looked around. First at Beloved's soft new hand on her shoulder, then into her eyes. The longing she saw there was bottomless. Some plea barely in control.' The implications of the last phrase become clear as Beloved becomes increasingly demanding (p. 240): 'when Sethe ran out of things to give her, Beloved invented desire'.

48. For the temporal relation trivialized as 'echo', see, for example, Peter Ackroyd, *Hawksmoor* (1985) and *Chatterton* (1987).

49. Cf. *Beloved*, p. 244: 'like Sweet Home where time didn't pass'.

50. *Beloved*, p. 86: 'Her heavy knives of defense against misery, regret, gall and hurt, she placed one by one on a bank where clear water rushed on below.' But we have already had a forewarning (p. 57) of the conflict to come between Sethe and Beloved: 'In lamplight, and over the flames of the cooking stove, their two shadows clashed and crossed on the ceiling like black swords.'

51. As Laplanche and Pontalis explain (*The Language of Psychoanalysis*, p. 211), Freud uses 'incorporation' to define the 'Process whereby the subject, more or less on the level of phantasy, has an object penetrate his body and keeps it "inside" his body. Incorporation constitutes an instinctual aim and a mode of object-relationship which are characteristic of the oral stage ...' 'Introjection' (a term which Freud borrowed from Ferenczi) is 'closely akin to identification' and while 'close in meaning to incorporation [...] does not necessarily imply any reference to the body's real boundaries (introjection into the ego, into the ego-ideal, etc.)' (ibid., p. 229).

52. '*Fors*: The Anglish Words of Nicolas Abraham and Maria Torok', trans. Barbara Johnson, in Abraham and Torok, *The Wolf Man's Magic Word: A Cryptonymy*, trans. Nicholas Rand (Minneapolis: University of Minnesota Press, 1986), pp. xvi–xvii. Cf. ibid, pp. xxi–ii: 'By resisting introjection, it prevents the loving, appropriating assimilation of the other, and thus seems to preserve the other as other (foreign), but it also does the opposite. It is not the *other* that the process of incorporation preserves, but a certain topography it keeps safe, intact, untouched by the very relationship with the other to which, paradoxically, introjection is more open.'

53. Nicolas Abraham and Maria Torok, 'Introjection – Incorporation: *Mourning* or *Melancholia*', in S. Lebovici and D. Widlocher (eds), *Psychoanalysis in France* (New York: International University Press, 1980), p. 8. See also Maria Torok, 'Maladie du deuil et fantasme du cadavre exquis', in Abraham and Torok, *L'Ecorce et le noyau* (Paris: Flammarion, 1987), pp. 229–51.

54. *The Wolf Man's Cryptonomy*, p. 81: 'For the crypt is *already* constructed, and the Ego cannot quit the place where it had once been; it can only withdraw into seclusion and construct a barrier separating it from the other half of the Ego.'

55. Elisabeth Roudinesco, *Jacques Lacan & Co.: A History of Psychoanalysis in France, 1925–1985* (London: Free Association Books, 1990), p. 599.

56. Derrida, '*Fors*', p. xvii.

57. Gloria Naylor and Toni Morrison, 'A Conversation', *Southern Review*, 21 Summer 1985, p. 584 (my emphases). Further references will be given in the text.

58. Note how the struggle between them is permeated with images of orality and ingestion. The image of Beloved as pregnant reverses the phantasmal moment earlier in the novel when Sethe's water seems to break for the *second* time when she first sees Beloved (p. 51).

59. Interview with Salman Rushdie, *The Late Show* (BBC2), June 1992.

60. Bloomsbury Theatre, London, 6 June 1992.

61. Nicolas Abraham, 'Notes on the Phantom: A Complement to Freud's Metapsychology', trans. Nicholas Rand, in Meltzer (ed.), *The Trial(s) of Psychoanalysis*, pp. 75–80; further references will be given in the text. See also the use made of this idea in Jacqueline Rose, *The Haunting of Sylvia Plath* (London: Virago, 1991).

62. Cf. Abraham, 'Notes on the Phantom', pp. 77–8: 'The phantom's periodic and compulsive return lies beyond the scope of symptom-formation in the sense of a return of the repressed; it works like a ventriloquist, like a stranger within the subject's own mental topography.'

Chapter 10

Salman Rushdie:
Midnight's Children, Shame, The Satanic Verses

GENERAL INTRODUCTION

Salman Rushdie was born in Bombay and educated in England at Rugby and the University of Cambridge. He lived and worked in London as an advertising copy-writer before becoming a full-time writer. His novels are *Grimus* (1977), *Midnight's Children* (1981, winner of the Booker Prize), *Shame* (1983), *Satanic Verses* (1988) and *Haroun and the Sea of Stories* (1990); and he has produced a collection of four short stories *East, West* (1994). Most recently, he has published the novel *The Moor's Last Sigh* (1995). He is the author also of *The Jaguar Smile: A Nicaraguan Journey* (1987) and two documentary films, *The Riddle of Midnight* and *The Painter and the Pest*. His critical and other essays have been collected as *Imaginary Homelands* (1981).

Rushdie has been described as a postmodernist, a fabulist and a magic realist: all terms to describe the self-conscious hybridity of literary forms characterizing his novels and their working through of questions of contemporary national and cultural identity. The most shocking implications of this were revealed in the book-burning, demonstrations, murders and, of course, the issue of the *fatwa* following the publication of *The Satanic Verses*. This unprecedented and protracted episode has made Rushdie and this novel, especially, more symbols – or victims – of disparities between the values of Western societies and Islamic fundamentalism than, in any simple or straightforward sense, an individual author and literary text. These cultural and political complications have also only exacerbated the problems of reading. This issue is addressed below by Gayatri Spivak in relation specifically to *The Satanic Verses*. The two further essays discuss Rushdie's earlier fiction. These are included because they remind us that he is author of more than *The Satanic Verses*, because they point to some of the literary and ideological issues raised also by this earlier work, and for the more pragmatic reason that students are likely to encounter different moments of Rushdie's writing at different stages in their own undergraduate and postgraduate careers.

Further Reading
Lisa Appignanesi and Sarah Maitland, eds, *The Rushdie File* (ICA, Fourth Estate Ltd, 1989).
Timothy Brennan, *Salman Rushdie and the Third World: Myths of the Nation* (St Martin's Press, 1989).

Srinivas Aravamundan, 'Being God's Postman is No Fun', *Diacritics*, ii 19 (Summer, 1989), pp. 3–21.

Malise Ruthven, *A Satanic Affair. Salman Rushdie and the Rage of Islam* (Chatto & Windus, 1990).

Zianddin Sardar and Meryl Wyn Davies, *Distorted Imagination. Lessons from the Rushdie Affair* (Grey Seal, 1990).

Third Text, 11 (Summer, 1990). Special issue: 'Beyond the Rushdie Affair'.

10.1   LINDA HUTCHEON: FROM 'RE-PRESENTING THE PAST' (1989)

Linda Hutcheon is Professor of English and Comparative Literature at the University of Toronto. She is known chiefly for her studies of postmodernist fiction in the three volumes *Narcissistic Narrative* (1984), *A Poetics of Postmodernism* (1989) and *The Politics of Postmodernism* (1989). Her most recent work is *Irony's Edge. The Theory and Politics of Irony* (1994).

Postmodernism is commonly viewed as 'double-coded', as a mode which at once inscribes, as it undermines, literary and other norms through irony or parody. This suggests affinities between postmodernism and deconstruction, though for many this serves only to confirm postmodernism's ambiguous and at best latent, rather than actual, aesthetic or ideological effects. Some, indeed, view postmodernism as plainly complicitous with received ideas and the prevailing social and economic order. Hutcheon, on the contrary, views it in positive terms. Her special concern has been the treatment and changing conception of history in the developing form of what she calls 'historiographic metafiction'. Works of this kind make the constructedness of both fiction and history (or 'facts') overt, and Hutcheon views their use of irony and paradox as troubling the totalizing ambitions and set boundaries, the positivisms, certainties and unexamined literary and ideological assumptions of contemporary Western cultures. In her account, therefore, postmodernism problematizes and intervenes in the world of representations to real ideological effect.

For some further discussion and suggested reading on postmodernism, see *A Reader's Guide* 3/e, Ch. 7, pp. 174–88.

Hutcheon's reading of Rushdie's two novels, *Midnight's Children* (Picador, 1981) and *Shame* (Picador, 1983) – given in her text as Rushdie 1981 and 1983, respectively – occurs in the course of her more general arguments about postmodern fiction's representation of history in *The Politics of Postmodernism*. As well as Rushdie's novels, she considers a number of others relevant to this theme – amongst them Thomas Pynchon's *V*, John Berger's *G*, E. L. Doctorow's *The Book of Daniel* and Graham Swift's *Waterland*. She also briefly considers here the arguments of Lyotard's *The Postmodern Condition* and of Hayden White on narrative. Students are therefore referred to the original chapter for the details of her argument.

In assessing her discussion of Rushdie, below, students should give close attention to the passages she cites from the novels and her comments on these, but think also whether the novels as a whole confirm or contradict her argument. Clearly, Ahmad's reading of Rushdie's *Shame* understands both this novel and Rushdie's project differently, and students should have both essays in mind in considering the novel *Shame* in particular. These differences extend beyond different interpretations of a given text or author, however, and lead to some of the major issues in the debate on postmodernism. Conceptions of history are central to this and present an important point of contention between the two critics. Consider, in this respect, Hutcheon's remarks on Marxism and Ahmad's adoption of Marxist categories and appeal to a grounded community of left political activity and aspirations – a 'community of actual praxis' in his phrase in *In Theory* (1992, *op. cit.*, below), p. 158.

The following extract is from the chapter 'Re-presenting the Past', *The Politics of Postmodernism* (Routledge, 1989), pp. 65–78.

Re-presenting the Past

[...]

The totalizing impulse that postmodern art both inscribes and challenges should probably not be regarded either, on the one hand, as a naive kind of deliberately imperialistic desire for total control or, on the other, as utterly unavoidable and humanly inevitable, even necessary. The motivation and even existence of such totalization may certainly remain unconscious and repressed (or at least unspoken) or they may be completely overt, as in Fredric Jameson's deliberate totalizing in the name of Marxism as the only 'philosophically coherent and ideologically compelling resolution' to the dilemmas of historicism (1981: 18). But Jameson's 'History' as 'uninterrupted narrative,' however repressed, is exactly what is contested by the plural, interrupted, unrepressed histories (in the plural) of novels like Rushdie's *Midnight's Children*.

That novel's postmodern narrating historian might be seen as indirectly suggesting that not even Marxism can fully subsume all other interpretive modes. In his postmodern storytelling there is no mediation that can act as a dialectical term for establishing relationships between narrative form and social ground. They both remain and they remain separate. The resulting contradictions are not dialectically resolved, but coexist in a heterogeneous way: Rushdie's novel, in fact, works to prevent any interpretation of its contradictions as simply the outer discontinuous signs of some repressed unity – such as Marxist 'History' or 'the Real.' In fact, a novel like *Midnight's Children* works to foreground the totalizing impulse of western – imperialistic – modes of history-writing by confronting it with indigenous Indian models of history. Though Saleem Sinai narrates in English, in 'Anglepoised-lit writing,' his intertexts for both writing history and writing fiction are doubled: they are, on the one hand, from Indian legends, films, and literature and, on the other, from the west – *The Tin Drum*, *Tristram Shandy*, *One Hundred Years of Solitude*, and so on.

Rushdie's paradoxically anti-totalizing totalized image for his historiographic metafictive process is the 'chutnification of history' (Rushdie 1981: 459). Each chapter of the novel, we are told, is like a pickle jar that shapes its contents by its very form. The cliché with which Saleem is clearly playing is that to understand him and his nation, we 'have to swallow a world' and swallow too his literally preposterous story. But chutnification is also an image of preserving: 'my chutneys and kasaundies are, after all, connected to my nocturnal scribblings. ... Memory, as well as fruit, is being saved from the corruption of the clocks' (38). In both processes, however, he acknowledges inevitable distortions: raw materials are transformed, given 'shape and form – that is to say, meaning' (461). This is as true of history-writing as it is of novel-writing. As Saleem himself acknowledges:

> Sometimes in the pickles' version of history, Saleem appears to have known too little; at other times, too much ... yes, I should revise and revise, improve and improve; but there is neither the time nor the energy. I am obliged to offer no more than this stubborn sentence: It happened that way because that's how it happened.
>
> (Rushdie 1981: 560–1)

But does that opening 'It' of the last statement refer to the events of the past or to the writing and preserving of them? In a novel about a man writing his own and his country's history, a man 'desperate' for meaning, as he insists he is from the first paragraph, the answer cannot be clear.

To challenge the impulse to totalize is to contest the entire notion of *continuity* in history and its writing. In Foucault's terms discontinuity, once the 'stigma of temporal dislocation' that it was the historian's professional job to remove from history, has become a new instrument of historical analysis and simultaneously a result of that analysis. Instead of seeking common denominators and homogeneous networks of causality and analogy, historians have been freed, Foucault argues, to note the dispersing interplay of different, heterogeneous discourses that acknowledge the undecidable in both the past and our knowledge of the past. What has surfaced is something different from the unitary, closed, evolutionary narratives of historiography as we have traditionally known it: as we have been seeing in historiographic metafiction as well, we now get the histories (in the plural) of the losers as well as the winners, of the regional (and colonial) as well as the centrist, of the unsung many as well as the much sung few, and I might add, of women as well as men.

These are among the issues raised by postmodern fiction in its paradoxical confrontation of self-consciously fictive and resolutely historical representation. The narrativization of past events is not hidden; the events no longer seem to speak for themselves, but are shown to be consciously composed into a narrative, whose constructed – not found – order is imposed upon them, often overtly by the narrating figure. The process of making stories out of chronicles, of constructing plots out of sequences, is what postmodern fiction underlines. This does not in any way deny the existence of the past real, but it focuses attention on the act of imposing order on that past, of encoding strategies of meaning-making through representation.

Among the lessons taught by this didactic postmodern fiction is that of the importance of context, of discursive situation, in the narrativizing acts of both fiction and historiography: novels like Timothy Findley's *Famous Last Words* or Salman Rushdie's *Shame* teach us that both forms of narrative representation are, in fact, particularized uses of language (i.e. discourses) that inscribe social and ideological contexts. While both historians and novelists (not to mention literary critics) have a long tradition of trying to erase textual elements which would 'situate' them in their texts, postmodernism refuses such an obfuscation of the context of its enunciation. The particularizing and contextualizing that characterize the postmodern focus are, of course, direct responses to those strong (and very common) totalizing and universalizing impulses. But the resulting postmodern relativity and provisionality are not causes for despair; they are to be acknowledged as perhaps the very conditions of historical knowledge. Historical meaning may thus be seen today as unstable, contextual, relational, and provisional, but postmodernism argues that, in fact, it has always been so. And it uses novelistic representations to underline the narrative nature of much of that knowledge.

[...]

In writing about historical events, both the emplotting historian and the novelist are usually considered as working within certain constraints – those of chronology, for instance. But what happens when postmodern fiction 'de-doxifies' even such obvious and 'natural' constraints, when *Midnight's Children*'s narrator notices an error in chronology in his narrative, but then decides, 'in my India, Gandhi will continue to die at the wrong time'? Later he also inverts the order of his own tenth birthday and the 1957 election, and keeps that order because his memory stubbornly refuses to alter the sequence of events. Rushdie offers no real answer to the questions Saleem poses, but the issues are raised in such an overt manner that we too are asked to confront them. Worried about that error in the date of Gandhi's death, Saleem asks us:

> Does one error invalidate the entire fabric? Am I so far gone, in my desperate need for meaning, that I'm prepared to distort everything – to re-write the whole history of my times purely in order to place myself in a central role? Today, in my confusion, I can't judge. I'll have to leave it to others.
>
> (Rushdie 1981: 166)

Well, others (like us) are indeed left to ask – but not only of this particular error within this particular novel – if one error would invalidate the entire fabric of representation in history or fiction?

[...]

Which 'facts' make it into history? And *whose* facts? The narrating 'historian' of Rushdie's *Shame* finds that he has trouble keeping his present knowledge of events from contaminating his representation of the past. This is the condition of all writing about the past, be it fictional ('it seems that the future cannot be restrained, and insists on seeping back into the past' (Rushdie 1983: 24)) or factual ('It is possible to see the subsequent history of Pakistan as a duel between two layers of time, the obscured world forcing its way back through what-had-been-imposed' (87)). The narrator knows that it 'is the true desire of every artist to impose his or her vision on the world' (87). He goes on to ponder this similarity of impulse between historical and fictional writing: 'I, too, face the problem of history: what to retain, what to dump, how to hold on to what memory insists on relinquishing, how to deal with change' (87–8). What he knows complicates his narrative task in that he is dealing with a past 'that refuses to be suppressed, that is daily doing battle with the present' (88), both in his novel and in the actual, present-day history of Pakistan. He even admits that the inspiration for his fictive investigation of the notion of shame came from a real newspaper account of a murder in London of a Pakistani girl by her own father (116) – or so he says. The present and the past, the fictive and the factual: the boundaries may frequently be transgressed in postmodern fiction, but there is never any resolution of the ensuing contradictions. In other words, the boundaries remain, even if they are challenged.

It is at this level that these epistemological questions of postmodern narrative representation are posed. How can the present know the past it tells? We constantly narrate the past, but what are the conditions of the knowledge implied by that totalizing act of narration? Must a historical account acknowledge where it does not know for sure or is it allowed to guess? Do we know the past only through the present? Or is it a matter of only being able to understand the present through the past?

[...]

The issue of representation and its epistemological claims leads directly to the problem [...] regarding the nature and status of the 'fact' in both history-writing and fiction-writing. All past 'events' are potential historical 'facts,' but the ones that become facts are those that are chosen to be narrated. We have seen that this distinction between brute event and meaning-granted fact is one with which postmodern fiction seems obsessed. At a certain moment in his relating of the contemporary history of India and Pakistan in *Midnight's Children*, Saleem Sinai addresses his reader: 'I am trying hard to stop being mystifying. Important to concentrate on good hard facts. But which facts?' (Rushdie 1981: 338). This is a serious problem because at one point he cannot tell, from 'accurate' accounts in documents (newspapers), whether Pakistani troops really did enter Kashmir or not. The 'Voice of Pakistan' and 'All-India Radio' give totally opposing reports. And if they did (or did not) enter, what were the motives? 'Again, a rash of possible explanations,' we are told (339). Saleem parodies the historiographical drive toward causality and motivation through his reductive, megalomaniacal exaggeration: 'This reason or that or the other? To simplify matters, I present two of my own: the war happened because I dreamed Kashmir into the fantasies of our rulers; furthermore, I remained impure, and the war was to separate me from my sins' (339).

Such a perspective may be the only possible response left to a world where '[n]othing was real; nothing certain' (Rushdie 1981: 340). Certainly the text's grammar here alters – from assertive sentences to a long list of interrogatives that ends with what might be the ultimate example of contradictory postmodern discourse: 'Aircraft, real or fictional, dropped actual or mythical bombs' (341). Compared to what the sources and documents of history offer him, Saleem himself is 'only the humblest of jugglers-with-facts' in a country 'where truth is what it is instructed to be' (326). The ideological as well as historiographic implications here are overt. The text's self-reflexivity points in two directions at once, toward the events being represented in the narrative and toward the act of narration itself. This is precisely the same doubleness that characterizes all historical narrative. Neither form of representation can separate 'facts' from the acts of interpretation and narration that constitute them, for facts (though not events) are created in and by those acts. And what actually becomes fact depends as much as anything else on the social and cultural context of the historian, as feminist theorists have shown with regard to women writers of history over the centuries.

[...]

It is interesting that, in his influential discussion of the historical novel, Georg Lukács did not demand correctness of individual facts as a condition of defining the historical faithfulness of situation. Historical data traditionally enter nineteenth-century historical fiction in order to reinforce the text's claim to verifiability or at least to a persuasive rendering into fact of its events. Of course, all realist fiction has always used historical events, duly transformed into facts, in order to grant to its fictive universe a sense of circumstantiality and specificity of detail, as well as verifiability. What postmodern fiction does is make overt the fact-making and meaning-granting processes. The narrator of Rushdie's *Shame* announces:

> The country in this story is not Pakistan, or not quite. There are two countries, real and fictional, occupying the same space. My story, my fictional country exist, like myself, at a slight angle to reality. I have found this off-centring to be necessary; but its value is, of course, open to debate. My view is that I am not writing only about Pakistan.
>
> (Rushdie 1983: 29)

The open mixing of the fictive with the historical in the narrator's story-telling is made into part of the very narrative:

> In Delhi, in the days before partition, the authorities rounded up any Muslims ... and locked them up in the red fortress ... including members of my own family. It's easy to imagine that as my relatives moved through the Red Fort in the parallel universe of history, they might have felt some hint of the fictional presence or Bilquìs Kemal.
>
> (Rushdie 1983: 64)

A few pages later, however, we are reminded: 'If this were a realistic novel about Pakistan, I would not be writing about Bilquìs and the wind; I would be talking about my youngest sister' (68) – about whom he then does indeed talk. The seeming *non sequitur* here points both to the arbitrariness of the process of deciding which events become facts and to the relationship between realist fiction and the writing of history. Although the narrator writes from England, he chooses to write about Pakistan, acknowledging that 'I am forced to reflect that world in fragments of broken mirrors. ... I must reconcile myself to the inevitability of the missing bits' (69) – a warning meant for the reader of both fiction and history.

Historiographic metafiction like this is self-conscious about the paradox of the totalizing yet inevitably partial act of narrative representation. It overtly 'de-doxifies' received notions about the process of representing the actual in narrative – be it fictional or historical. It traces the processing of events into facts exploiting and then undermining the conventions of both novelistic realism and historiographic reference. It implies that, like fiction, history constructs its object, that events named become facts and thus both do and do not retain their status outside language. This is the paradox of postmodernism. The past really did exist, but we can only know it today through its textual traces, its often complex and indirect representations in the present: documents, archives, but also photographs, paintings, architecture, films, and literature.

10.2   AIJAZ AHMAD: FROM 'SALMAN RUSHDIE'S *SHAME*: POSTMODERN MIGRANCY AND THE REPRESENTATION OF WOMEN' (1992)

Aijaz Ahmad is professorial fellow at the Centre of Contemporary Studies, Nehru Memorial Museum and Library, New Delhi.

Linda Hutcheon writes in the extract above that postmodernism (or 'historiographic metafiction') present us with plural rather than single histories – 'of the losers as well as the winners, of the regional (and colonial) as well as the centrist, of the unsung many as well as the much sung few, and, I might add, of women as well as men' (p. 461, above). Ahmad's critique of homogenizing Western-based ideas of the 'Third World' in the essays in his volume *In Theory* (1992) would suggest that he shares or would sympathize with this strategy. If so, he strongly contests whether Rushdie, and *Shame* in particular, deliver this political challenge. The extracts below present the two central sections of his chapter on the novel. This opens with an account of Rushdie's double position, as Ahmad sees it, as inheritor of a metropolitan (modernist) canon and elected exponent of a 'Third-World' counter-canon. Essentially, in spite of his use of 'Third-World' narrative forms and postmodernist and poststructuralist predilections, Rushdie belongs ideologically, says Ahmad, to the 'High Culture of the modern metropolitan bourgeoisie' (*In Theory*, p. 127).

Ahmad's interest is in the perspectives and issues this hegemonic and 'centrist' canonizing gesture excludes. In the sections of the chapter included below, his principal question is what position this ideology ascribes to or allows women, an argument which leads him to charge Rushdie with misogyny. His conclusion is decisively at odds with Hutcheon's. For if *Shame* is a postmodernist novel, its treatment of women, in Ahmad's view, betrays at least one set of received notions which Rushdie does not, in Hutcheon's word, 'de-doxify'.

What is your view of the rightness of this judgement and of the textual evidence Ahmad adduces? From what position does he judge Rushdie and in whose interests? Consider, for example, his view of Rushdie's class position, his reference to 'our' society' (pp. 469, 473 below), his own representation of women and his closing remarks on human solidarity and historical action. What political position and beliefs emerge from these statements and are they an appropriate measure of Rushdie and Rushdie's novel? Ahmad says that he is attempting a 'symptomatic' reading of the book. What does he mean by this, and does he achieve his aim?

These questions and the relation particularly between works of fiction and social or historical fact and political action are also clearly relevant to Hutcheon's argument and position. They are taken up once more in Spivak's essay below. A *locus classicus* of the debates raised here on what it means to read a work of fiction historically and politically is Joseph Conrad's story, *Heart of Darkness*. Students are therefore advised to consider this example and the earlier set of essays on Conrad's text. Edward Said, it will be seen, refers directly to Salman Rushdie in his discussion of Conrad's story.

The following extract is from 'Salman Rushdie's *Shame*: Postmodern Migrancy and the Representation of Women', in *After Theory: Classes, Nations, Literatures* (Verso, 1992), pp. 139–52.

Salman Rushdie's *Shame*: Postmodern Migrancy and the Representation of Women

[…]

III

Virtually everyone has noted, as Rushdie himself has, that *Shame* – which is almost exclusively about Pakistan, although a couple of episodes do take place in India – is a much more severe and despairing book, more bleak and claustrophobic, than *Midnight's Children*. The sense that Pakistan is a cage is already there, in the opening episodes, where the Shakil sisters – the three mothers of the 'peripheral hero', Omar Khayyam – are cloistered twice over: first by their father, the patriarch of the macabre mansion, with whose death the book begins, and then by themselves, after their one hedonistic night in which their son is conceived. And this sense of being trapped permeates the whole book, right up to the final dénouement where we find that even dictators cannot cross the 'frontier' and escape their cage. In between, Bilquis is trapped in her 'elite actressy manner', her sentimentality, her 'horror of movement', her desire for sons and yet her lack of sons, as well as the crassness of her husband's ambitions, pieties and cruelties; Rani is trapped, likewise, in her own husband's infidelities and the rise and fall of his political career; Sufiya Zinobia – the heroine of the book, 'Shame' embodied – is trapped in her brain fever, her humiliation, and her volcanic urge to violence; her younger sister, Good News Hyder, is a much less substantial being, but she too is trapped, first in her superficiality and then, despite the marriage of her choice, in the constant demand on her fertility. The younger sister kills herself, the older kills her tormentors, but the cage never quite becomes anything other than itself.

We shall return to some of these characters presently, but first we should note the contrast with *Midnight's Children*, which had been about India, the country of Rushdie's own cherished childhood. What had given that earlier novel its narrative amplitude was the connection with autobiography – the baggage of memories that even a migrant – particularly a migrant – must carry. Pakistan, by contrast, is a society Rushdie never knew in those golden years before the uprooting. It is not 'teeming' (Rushdie's word for India, borrowed, significantly, from Kipling) for him with stories, and with the plenitude of life, because, as he himself puts it, he has learned it only in little slices, and because his own life's connection with that land – 'the new, moth-nibbled land of God', as he calls it – is so very tenuous. It is a country which he knows, beyond very personal affections, only as a polity, and primarily in the grotesqueries of its ruling class. Within the limits of that knowledge, the rage the book conveys is entirely well founded. The problem is that the experience of a certain class – rather, a ruling elite – is presented, in the rhetorical stance of the book, as the experience of a 'country'. Far from being about 'the East' or even about 'Pakistan', the book is actually about a rather narrow social stratum – so narrow, in fact, that Rushdie himself is able to portray all the major characters as belonging to a single *family*. This plot device of turning all the antagonists into relatives is a wonderful technical resolution for reflecting the monopolistic structure of dictatorial power and the very narrow social spectrum within which this power in Pakistan circulates. It also helps him to bypass the easy liberal dichotomy between military villains and civilian innocents; they are all of the same stripe. The main difficulty does not arise in his portrayal of this structure of power and cruelty at the apex; this he accomplishes, on the whole, superbly. The difficulty arises when this ferocious fable of the state is elided, again and again, in his own recurrent rhetoric throughout the book, with a society which is declared to be coterminous with this state structure, equally deformed and irretrievably marked by its purported civilization (Islam) and its genetic origin (the Partition), more catastrophically wounded even than Naipaul makes out India to be in A *Wounded Civilization*. The rulers and the ruled seem to be joined together, each mirroring the other, in a Satanic compact.

Thus the bulk of the narrative is focused on the careers, corruptions, ribaldries and rivalries of the two main protagonists in the political arena: Raza Hyder, an army officer whose origins and early career are quite different from Zia's but who comes increasingly to resemble him, and Iskander ('Isky') Harappa, who is modelled on the personality of Bhutto, the former Prime Minister. The problem, even here, is that those parts of the book which attempt to create fictional equivalents of the literal facts of recent Pakistani history tend too much towards parody, while many of the other parts tend too much towards burlesque. Both the parody and the burlesque are at times delicious, inventive, hilarious, but in re-creating the major strands of contemporary history in the form of a spoof, and then mixing up this spoof with all kinds of spooky anecdotes whose symbolic value is sometimes unclear and often excessive, Rushdie has given us a Laughter which laughs, unfortunately, much too often. The fictional equivalents of Bhutto and Zia are such perfect, buffoon-like caricatures, and the many narrative lines of the political parable are woven so much around their ineptitude, their vacuity, their personal insecurities and oneupmanships, their sexual obsessions, the absurdities of their ambitions and their ends, that one is in danger of forgetting that Bhutto and Zia were in reality no buffoons, but highly capable and calculating men whose cruelties were entirely methodical. It is this tendency either to individualize completely the moral failures of a ruling class (Bhutto, or Zia, or whoever, is a bad character) or to spread them far too widely through society at large (the country was *made* wrong; what else do you expect?) which gives to Rushdie's Laughter, so salutary in some respects, the ambience, finally, of the modern cartoon.

It is on this narrative line, and on the thematics gathered around it, that most readings of *Shame* have concentrated – and with reason. If the book is to be located in the counter-canon of 'Third World Literature', if it is to be read essentially as a document of post-coloniality, a myth of the 'Nation', a critique of dictatorship, a fictionalized biography of the Pakistani state, a dissent from the politics of Partition and of Islamicism, then surely *that* narrative, and all other narrative lines converging on that main one, should rightly be the point of focus. Who on the Left – and not only on the Left – could dissent from the abuse heaped on the likes of Zia, etc.? We can take infinite pleasure in the inventiveness and eloquence of the denunciations which are, because of their justness, our own; because we are already preoccupied with the twin problematics of the 'Third World' and the 'Nation', far too many of us are willing to set aside all sorts of things that the book says about women, minorities, servants, and others who are not of the ruling class. It is this very pleasure of those wide-ranging denunciations which makes it possible for the *New York Times*, let us say, to lift the book out of its immediate location and compare Rushdie's achievement in *Shame* – in one breath, as it were – with Sterne, Swift, Kafka, García Márquez, Günter Grass. What this particular angle on the book – the primary emphasis on the representation of the 'Third World' and the condition of post-coloniality on the one hand; the tradition of the Grotesque on the other – does, however, is to read the book back from the author's own declarations and fore-groundings, according to etiquettes stipulated by critics and theorists of 'Third World Literature'. Thus there is, a certain complicity of a shared starting point between the author and his critics, generated largely by the very conditions in which the idea of a 'Third World Literature' has arisen, which I have tried to specify elsewhere in this book. This complicity inhibits, then, other possible starting points for our readings: the issue, in the midst of all the political claims that go back and forth between authors and critics, of Rushdie's own politics and affiliations, for example; or his representation of women and the related issue of a possible misogyny; or the aesthetic of despair that issues both from his overvalorization of unbelonging ('floating upwards') and his own location within the modernist trajectories, both early and late, which are more than merely formal.

These other issues are the ones I want, briefly, to address, but I am concerned here mainly with Rushdie's representation of women, for four reasons: women occupy so large a portion of all the narratives in the book; Rushdie himself has drawn attention to this fact directly, through the narrator, within the book and then in numerous interviews, congratulating himself for these representations; the issue of misogyny is a central issue in any sort of oppositional politics; and the absence of any substantial male figures from among the oppressed and oppositional strata in this book – the absence, for example, of the male sections of workers and peasants, political militants, the patriotic intelligentsia – is so complete that it is only by analysing the author's representation of women that we can obtain any clue as to what his imaginative relation with *all* such strata might in fact be. In other words, Rushdie has so often declared himself a socialist of sorts that it is both legitimate and necessary to see what this book might look like if we were to read it from the standpoint of – no, not socialism, simply some determinate energies of an emancipatory project: not only in its representation of rulers, but also in its representations of the oppressed.[1]

This is by no means an uncomplicated undertaking, for Rushdie is not, in the way Orwell always was, a misogynist plain and simple. Living in the contemporary milieu of the British Left, he has not remained untouched by certain kinds of feminism; and he is clearly aware, and quite capable of effective narrativization, of many kinds of women's oppression in our societies. The complication is of a different order, and politically far more devastating than mere lack of sympathy. It is only after taking into account that structure of sympathy and the kind of politics in which it is embedded that one can proceed to examine the more central issues in his representation of women, and then to relate those issues back to the generality of his political positions.

Thus, alongside the stories of Isky and Raza, which together constitute the main narrative frame, are the tribulations of their wives, Bilquis and Rani. These portraits are drawn far more sympathetically than the portraits of their husbands, and some of the most moving episodes in the book are associated with these women: the episode, for example, of the fire at the time of Partition which burns away 'the brocades of continuity and the eyebrows of belonging' from Bilquis's vulnerable female body, while she is left with nothing save the 'dopatta of honor' in which she wraps herself as an only refuge; and the other episode, towards the end, when Rani, sequestered once more on her rural estate, takes stock of her life and embroiders eighteen shawls on which she traces, in intricate representational design, the debaucheries and cruelties of her husband's full career. Equally powerful are those last images of Bilquis, whose adult life started with forced, fire-propelled nakedness, shrouding herself at the end, an aged woman with defeated dreams, in black veils, so as to make permanent the distance between herself and the male-dominated world in which she has been caged all her life. Similarly, the episode in which Good News Hyder hangs herself in order to escape the constant, mad demand upon her procreativity is a moving episode, and it corresponds to very real horrors in our society. Even the initial conception of Sufiya Zinobia as one who is struggling to let the Beast out of the Sleeping Beauty is itself in the best tradition of Grotesque Realism. These are all powerful images.

Both Bilquis and Rani are, however – when all is said and done, and quite apart from the insult and neglect they suffer at the hands of their husbands – paltry, shallow creatures themselves, capable of nothing but chirpy gossip (in 'the elite actressy manner'), inertia or, at best, a tawdry affair with the owner of the local movie-house. They are not even remotely as evil as their husbands, and while Bilquis goes increasingly to pieces, Rani at least, in embroidering her shawls, manages to maintain a sort of dignity. Even hers, however, is the dignity of resignation. In general, moreover, what we find is a gallery of women who are frigid and desexualized (Arjumand, the 'Virgin Ironpants'), demented and moronic (the twenty-odd years of Zinobia's childhood), dulled into nullity (Farah), driven to despair (Rani, Bilquis) or suicide (Good News Hyder), or embody sheer surreal incoherence and loss of individual identity (the Shakil sisters). Throughout, every woman, without exception, is represented through a system of imageries which is sexually overdetermined; the frustration of erotic need, which drives some to frenzy and others to nullity, appears in every case to be the central fact of a woman's existence. What we have, then, is a real disjuncture between particular *episodes* which can delineate quite vivid sympathies for the respective female characters on the one hand, and, on the other, a generalized *structure* of representation in which each of those same characters turns out to be at least dislikable and frequently repugnant.

IV

The crux of the matter, however, is the characterization of Sufiya Zinobia, the girl who was supposed to have been a boy, the 'miracle which went wrong', the demented child who was born blushing, and is Shame personified. She is the one who provides the link between the stark title of the book and its many disjointed, sprawling narratives, and is at the centre of that marriage between shame and shamelessness which, the author tells us over and over again, breeds the all-enveloping violence; she blushes, we are told, not merely for herself but also, more consistently, for the world at large. In a world of utter evil, where everything that happens should evoke shame but everyone is entirely shameless, Sufiya Zinobia, this Shame personified, is no mere character; she is presented from the outset as the very embodiment of the principle of redemption—if redemption, in this altogether unheroic, unscrupulous world, is even possible.

Initially, of course, her blushes begin at birth, for the simple reason that she, like all babies, was expected to be a boy. This unending shame which begins at birth and hounds all her days on earth might well, in a different sort of trajectory, have been an appropriate metaphor for the way the generation of a sense of fundamental female inadequacy, and shame as a specifically female attribute, may be sought in the very social processes of gendering. But then two things happen. One is that she becomes ill, contracting brain fever, and thus permanently retarded, developing the brain of a six-year-old at the age of nineteen. Now, the problem with this metaphor of mental illness is that the pressures and processes of gendering – which are social and historical in character, and impose upon a great many women the possibility of deformation and incapacity, but are open to resistance and reversal by women's own actions – are given to us in the form of a *physiological* insufficiency on *her* part. The novel therefore becomes incapable of communicating to us, in whatever grotesque forms, the *process* whereby a woman's intellectual and emotional abilities may be sapped, or regained. We may be charitable and not recount here all the ways in which the fiction of women's physiological insufficiency has been mobilized in the past and present histories of gender politics. At the very least, however, this shift from the social to the physiological forecloses the possibility that the person in question can regain control of her body, let alone her brain, through her own initiative; reversals of such conditions are rare, and they require the agency not so much of the patient as of doctors and hospitals. That Bilquis, her mother, would henceforth be ashamed of the child because the child is a moron, or that Sufiya herself would become an object of medical interventions, or even that her marriage would remain sexually unconsummated, begins to make a certain sort of sense within the available social arrangements; we may now preach greater liberality of attitude towards such hapless creatures, but the essential social situation remains intractable and the novel simply fails to recover from this eliding of the social into the physiological.

In the course of the novel, moreover, Sufiya's shame comes to refer less and less to herself (her femaleness; her mental retardation) or to her family (which is ashamed of her on both counts, femaleness and retardation) and becomes increasingly focused on the world as Sufiya finds it; she becomes, almost literally, the conscience of a shameless world – a principle of honour, so to speak. This too is somewhat problematic, in the sense that when the complex moral obligations of a social conscience are reduced to the limiting emotiveness of mere shame, and when this shamed conscience is deposited in one who is physiologically incapable of intellection and sustained responsible conduct, the author precludes, by virtue of the very terms he has established, the possibility that this conscience would be capable of grappling with needs of social regeneration, or even with the sort of decency and daily heroism of which countless ordinary people are quite capable. Rushdie says over and over again, within the novel as well as in the interviews which have followed, that the encounter of shamelessness with shame can only produce violence. Precisely! But violence is not in itself capable of regeneration, and it is doubtful, Fanon notwithstanding, that violence is intrinsically even a cleansing virtue. In other words, the very dialectic – of shamelessness and shame, and their condensation in eruptions of violence – which governs the conceptual framework of the novel is fundamentally flawed; symbolic values which Rushdie assigns to Sufiya Zinobia simply exceed the terms within which he has fashioned her own existence. The double punning in her name – on the word 'Sufi' and on the name of Zainub, the granddaughter of the Prophet of Islam who is quite central to several of the popular strands derived from Sufic Islam – is, in context, excessive and merely prankish.

This becomes clear as soon as one recalls the stages in the escalation of her violences. The governing metaphor for these escalations – the Beast emerging from inside the Beauty, while the Beauty herself is anything but beautiful in any conventional sense – is again superbly within the tradition of the Grotesque, and the political idea which is inscribed within this metaphor – a woman's inherent right to be not a doll but a fighter – is equally powerful. One's sense of unease comes, however, from the irrational and spurious manner in which Sufiya's violences accumulate and from what she herself *becomes* (a destroyer of men, fields, animals; a four-legged beast herself) before she reaches her object: the murder of her husband, the 'peripheral hero', Omar Khayyam Shakil. The first such eruption comes at the age of twelve when she goes out and kills two hundred and eighteen turkeys with a certain orgiastic relish: 'Sufiya Zinobia had torn off their heads and then reached down into their bodies to draw their guts up their necks' (p. 150). The explanation for this, of course, is simple enough: 'twelve years of unloved humiliation take their toll, even on an idiot' (p. 149). The next eruption is, from the authorial standpoint, equally innocent: on the day of her sister's marriage she tries to do to her brother-in-law what she had previously done to the turkeys, but she manages only to twist his neck permanently out of shape, thus putting an end to his polo-playing career. The explanation is again quite simple: 'a pouring into her too-sensitive spirit of the great abundance of shame' at the circumstances, presumably, in which the marriage was taking place (p. 186). An instance of desolation in one case, a sense of honour in the other! But then comes something far more monumental. By then, more years have passed and she has married Shakil, who is forbidden to sleep with her and sleeps with Shahbanou, her servant, instead. She rightfully begins to wonder about sex, children, the meaning of marriage itself, and Shakil's treachery; she has, at this point, the brain of a six-year-old! One day – out of frustration and anger, it seems – she walks out of the house, picks up four men, has sexual intercourse with them, kills them, and comes home with semen and blood on her veils. The central passage in this whole episode is worth quoting:

> Shame walks the streets of night. In the slums four youths are transfixed by those appalling eyes, whose deadly yellow fire blows like a wind through the latticework of the veil. They follow her to the rubbish-dump of doom, rats to her piper, automata dancing in the all-consuming light from the black-veiled eyes. Down she lies; and what Shahbanou took upon herself is finally done to Sufiya. Four husbands come and go. Four of them in and out, and then her hands reach for the first boy's neck. The others stand still and wait their turn. And heads hurled high, sinking into the scattered clouds; nobody saw them fall. She rises, goes home. And sleeps; the Beast subsides. (p. 242)

In this passage, Sufiya becomes the oldest of the misogynist myths: the virgin who is really a vampire, the irresistible temptress who seduces men in order to kill them, not an object of male manipulation but a devourer of hapless men. And in thus discovering her 'true' self, she becomes the opposite not only of that other daughter in the book, Arjumand, the sexless 'Virgin Ironpants' (Rushdie's caricature of Benazir Bhutto), but also the opposite of the Muslim male who, in some interpretations of the Islamic *shari'a*, is allowed four wives: what she does to her 'four husbands' is, of course, much more extreme, perhaps because the backwardness of her mind is more than matched by the enormity of her sexual appetite as well as her malevolence.

She comes home and sleeps, but it is only a matter of time, obviously, before she escapes again, this time for good, 'because once a carnivore has tasted blood you can't fool it with vegetables any more', and because 'the violence which had been born of shame ... now lived its own life beneath her skin' (p. 268). And she does escape, but 'what now roamed free in the unsuspecting air was not Sufiya Zinobia Shakil at all, but something more like a principle ... a human guillotine ... ripping off men's heads' (pp. 268–70). Soon enough, she ceases to be human even in a literal sense and becomes, of all things, 'a white panther' with a 'black head, pale hairless body, awkward gait'; 'stories about her ... had begun to come from all over the country' (p. 280). And her achievements:

> Murders of animals and men, villages raided in the dark, dead children, slaughtered flocks, blood-curdling howls (p. 280). ... The killings continued: farmers, pie-dogs, goats. The murders formed a death-ring round the house; they had reached the outskirts of the two cities, new capital and old town. Murders without rhyme or reason, done, it seemed, for the love of killing, or to satisfy some hideous need. (p. 287)

What the author takes to be the meaning of all this dawns, improbably enough, upon Omar Khayyam Shakil, her husband who was also her doctor, who had until then been nothing but shamelessness personified:

> For the first time in her life ... that girl is free. He imagined her proud; proud of her strength, proud of the violence that was making her a legend, that prohibited anyone from telling her what to do, or whom to be, or what she should have been and was not; yes, she had risen above everything. (p. 281)

This is, of course, Rushdie himself speaking; there is nothing in Shakil's character to suggest that he is capable of such an act of imaginative understanding. Yet there is something profoundly unsettling about this idea of a 'freedom' which resides in rising 'above everything' (earlier in the book, we have already encountered the idea of 'floating upwards'), hence being able to commit limitless, senseless violence. And if this is indeed what Sufiya Zinobia has become, then it is very difficult, because of this moral perplexity, for a reader to sympathize with her in that last episode where she finally manages to kill Omar Khayyam Shakil himself. By then, it is no longer a confrontation between shamelessness and shame but, rather, between a man who is of course clearly a moral cripple, and a woman who has become – not in the metaphorical but in the most literal sense – a beast.

This portrayal of Sufiya Zinobia – combined with that of Bilquis and Rani, which we discussed above and that of Arjumand ('Virgin Ironpants'), which we have not had the opportunity to discuss at any length – raises a fundamental question about Rushdie's view of the world in general and women in particular. Considering that Rushdie himself has stressed the importance of women in *Shame*,[2] as well as his own conception of Sufiya as a principle of honour and redemption, he seems to have fashioned a macabre caricature of what female resistance to cruelties might be; the woman herself becomes, in this version, a rapist. For so wedded is Rushdie's imagination to imageries of wholesale degradation and unrelieved social wreckage, so little is he able to conceive of a real possibility of regenerative projects on the part of the people who actually exist within our contemporary social reality, that even when he attempts, towards the end of the novel, to open up a regenerative possibility, in the form of Sufiya's flight – and also her return, as Nemesis and all-devouring Fury – the powers which he, as author, bestows upon her in the moment of her triumph are powers only of destruction. It is indicative of the temper of the whole novel that even her innocence, up to the point where she remains innocent of the social corruptions of Rushdie's imagined world, is the innocence merely of the mad and the mentally retarded; she is doubtless the only one who finally obtains the energy to oppose and win, but this energy is itself rooted – literally, the novel tells us – in brain fever. Moreover, her power is not only purely destructive but also *blind*; even before she takes her revenge upon her tormenters, she has been on the prowl, we are told, through all the nooks and crannies of the country, eating up animals and men, destroying fields, creating terror. This kind of image, which romanticizes violence as self-redemption, has, of course, no potential for portraying regenerative processes; further, it is linked up, in a most disagreeable manner, with imperialist and misogynistic myths: the image of freedom-fighter as idiot-terrorist; the image of a free – or freedom-seeking – woman as vampire, Amazon, man-eating shrew.

What the characterization of Sufiya Zinobia illustrates once again is the limiting, even misogynistic nature of the typologies within which Rushdie encloses the whole range of women's experience. As I pointed out above, there are several episodes in *Shame* where a sense of the oppression of women is obvious enough; in one kind of response one may now pity the victims of this oppression, much in the manner of the liberal bourgeoisie which always pities the poor. It is also possible to concede within some limits, as regards the general structure of Rushdie's representation of women, that in real life many women have doubtless been driven to madness, violence, phobia, dementia. But women are not, in any fundamental sense, mere victims of history; much more centrally, women have *survived* against very heavy odds, and they have *produced* history. Madness, sexual frenzy, nullity of being, fevers of the brain, have been, by and large, very uncommon; the vast majority of women have consistently performed productive (and not only *re*productive) labour; and, like those men who also do productive work, they have retained with society and history a relation that is essentially imaginative, visionary, communal and regenerative. Erotic need has been, for women as for men, often important, but only in rare cases is it the lone desire, outside loves and solidarities of other kinds; work, in any case, has been for the great majority far more central; women are not, any more than men are, mere eroticized bodies. So there is something fundamentally awry in a system of imageries which overvalorizes, when it comes to describing women, the zones of the erotic, the irrational, the demented and the demonic. That is to say, there is something fatally wrong with a novel in which virtually every woman is to be pitied, most are to be laughed at, some are to be feared, at least some of the time, but none may be understood in relation to those fundamental projects of survival and overcoming which are none other than the production of history itself. Satirizing the masters is one thing, but it is a different matter altogether to give such chilling portraits – *only* chilling portraits – of women, in terms so very close to the dominant stereotypes.

Rushdie's inability to include integral regenerative possibilities within the Grotesque world of his imaginative creation represents, I believe, a conceptual flaw of a fundamental kind. In the book he speaks, again and again, of a 'country'; but what he gives us is a portrait, by and large, of the cruel and claustrophobic world of its ruling class. *That* world he seems to know very well, but to think of the portrait of rulers as a portrait of the 'country' itself is an error, I think, not only of politics, narrowly conceived, but also of the social imagination. Hence the remarkable fact that while Rushdie talks constantly of politics, *all* the political acts represented within the matrix of the novel are demagogic, opportunistic, self-serving, cruel, or at best petty. Politics is mostly farce, sometimes tragedy, but it is never capable of producing resistance to oppression, solidarity and integrity in human conduct, or any sort of human community; for all its marvellous humour, Rushdie's imagined world is, in its lovelessness, almost Orwellian. And that, too, fits. If the political vision of your imagined world does not include those who resist, or love, or act with any degree of integrity or courage, then you *will* conclude – as Rushdie does, in the 'worst tale in history' which comes in the final pages of the book – that it is a country in which brother has been betraying brother for generations! Now, Pakistan's history is, of course, replete with betrayals, as is India's, but it is this idea of the permanence and pervasiveness of betrayal – the Orwellian idea, in other words, that human beings *always* betray one another – which gives this book its quite extraordinary quality of lovelessness. For an equally bleak vision of human potentiality one would have to go, I think, to *Nineteen Eighty-Four* or to Naipaul's *A Bend in the River*.

There is, I believe, a connection between this view of the world and Rushdie's way of representing women. This question of the representation of women, I have argued, is important both because the issue of misogyny is always central to any kind of oppositional project and also because, in the absence of other kinds of representations of any other oppressed strata, the representation of women who *are* there in the book gives us crucial clues to the general structure of Rushdie's imaginative sympathies. Two points are, I think, worth making here. First, any representation of women, whether in fiction or in life, has to do, surely, with gender relations, but also with *more* than gender relations; it is almost always indicative of a much larger structure of feeling and a much more complex political grid. What I have attempted, in other words, is not a sufficient reading of the book but a *symptomatic* reading: the concentration on a symptom which is itself vividly central but one which may also, in the same sweep, give us some understanding of the structure as a whole. Second, politics appears to me to be a matter not so much of opposition as of solidarity; it is always much less problematic to denounce dictators and to affirm, instead, a generality of values – 'liberty, equality, fraternity', let us say, as Rushdie does indeed affirm towards the very end (p. 278) – but always much harder to affiliate oneself with specific kinds of praxis, conceived not in terms of values which serve as a *judgement* on history but as a solidarity with communities of individuals, simultaneously flawed and heroic, who act within that history, from determinate social and political positions.

[...]

Ahmad believes that Rushie's postmodern perspective, and its political implications, are decided by the valorizing attitude he adopts towards the experience of 'migrancy' and unbelonging. In Section V he examines Rushdie's essays on Günter Grass and 'Outside the Whale', where he feels this is even more evident. In the closing Section VI, he suggests certain similarities between Rushdie and George Orwell, and quotes Raymond Williams on Orwell to the effect that 'Exile, in the true sense, ... prevents one from "floating upward" (Rushdie's phrase) and denying the pain' (p. 158).

Notes (cut and renumbered)
1. Rushdie says in his interview with *Gentleman*: 'I am one of those writers who believes that a writer has a public function. ... It becomes almost an obligation of writers who know what is going on.' But then he resolves the relationship (or lack of it) between his 'socialism' and his 'writing' in a curious way. In his interview with *Third World Book Review*, for example, he comments: 'I would describe myself as a socialist, but I do nor write *as* a socialist any more than I write *as* a member of the group which is 5'9" tall, or any other group. I write as a writer.' The difficulty with that kind of formulation

is that physical height does not normally indicate the nature of one's social commitments, whereas terms like 'socialist' are meant to indicate those very sorts of things. Nor is membership of a group, *any* group, the issue; the ways of being a socialist in our time are actually far too diverse. The questions are rather different. What relationship might there be between these two practices, being a socialist and the assembling of political narratives? Does one contradict, or exclude, the other? Does a writer leave behind the one when she or he undertakes the other? And what history of discourse generates simple statements like 'I write as a writer'?

2. Thus, towards the end of the book, Rushdie declares:

> I had thought, before I began, that what I had on my hands was an almost excessively masculine tale. … But the women seem to have taken over; they marched in from the peripheries of the story to demand inclusion of their own tragedies, histories and comedies, obliging me to couch my narrative in all manner of sinuous complexities, to see my 'male' plot refracted, so to speak, through the prisms of its reverse and 'female' side. It occurs to me that the women knew precisely what they were up to – that their stories explain, and even subsume, the men's. (p. 189)

10.3   GAYATRI CHAKRAVORTY SPIVAK: FROM 'READING *THE SATANIC VERSES*' (1993)

For further details on Gayatri Spivak, see Ch. 3.

Spivak's essay, 'Reading *The Satanic Verses*', occurs in a series of deliberations in other accompanying essays in the volume *Outside in the Teaching Machine* (1993) on questions of postcolonialism, feminism, migrancy and nationhood – on questions, in short, of identity and position, including that of the reading critic. The following selection comprises two main sections of the essay in which Spivak offers to read the novel, in the first section, 'as if nothing had happened since 1988'; 'almost', as she adds later, 'as an act of disciplinary piety towards what is, after all, a novel' (pp. 219, 241); and, in the second section, to reflect on the questions of cultural politics it has raised after that date by way of a dossier of responses on the Rushdie case.

The 'Introduction' to her chapter and two short closing sections are omitted here. In the first, Spivak considers the question of authorship; the implications for the Rushdie affair of Barthes' 'metropolitan' idea of the death of the author, and Derrida's idea of 'the "staging" of the author *as* author by the author' (p. 219). In the closing sections she questions the assumption that the concept of 'reason', historically consonant with Christianity and monopoly capitalism, is '*necessarily* Eurocentric' (p. 241) and exhorts us finally to remember the woman, Shahbano, who, divorced from her husband but 'censored by the script of religion and gendering' (p. 487 below), refused the award of maintenance from him. Her case, Spivak argues, has been obscured by the public attention given to the dual male 'authors', the Ayatollah and Rushdie.

The role of women – Shahbano, the 'tall thin Bengali woman with cropped hair', and the female prophets in Rushdie's novel – is one of the marginalized topics Spivak discusses and is a point of comparison between her essay and Ahmad's. Above all, however, Spivak's essay is about what it means to read *The Satanic Verses* – about what textual and intertextual reference, cultural priorities and perspective its 'magic realism' brings into play, including the aim to displace metropolitan and androcentric Western values. These are complex issues but they return us to a quite basic underlying question. Is it possible to make or to preserve a distinction between 'the text' and 'the text in the world'? Is the Rushdie case *about* preserving such distinctions: about the autonomy of art and creative or critical freedom, and defending these? Or, to put this question in a broader context, is the 'Rushdie affair' about *types* of commitment and belief: the opposite schemes of belief associated, in this episode, with a Western, metropolitan and Enlightenment tradition, on the one hand; and an Islamic fundamentalist and anti-Enlightenment tradition, on the other?

Spivak directs us to these issues, but her own essay divides explicitly in its two sections between a reading of the novel and a discussion of its cultural politics. At the same time, she says the first is 'impossible' (p. 219). Is her essay therefore contradictory, or is this a strategic, self-conscious distinction? Consider the statement quoted above on reading the novel as an act of 'disciplinary piety' and her opening and later remarks (p. 217 and p. 484 below) on the relation in postcoloniality of art and political life. The second 'intercepts' the first, she says, deflecting its purpose and altering the ways it can be read. How does she respond to this 'interception' in her reading? Is this a deconstructive reading? Does it imply an alternative idea of the relation of art and political life?

For some discussion and further reading on postcolonialism, including Spivak's work, see *A Reader's Guide* 3/e, pp. 188–97, especially pp. 193–7. See also the commentary and essays in

Ch. 9 and, on deconstruction, Ch. 7 above. Nigel Wheale's *Postmodern Arts* (Routledge, 1995) contains some useful discussion of Rushdie's novel and Spivak's essay (pp. 189–206).

The following extract is from 'Reading *The Satanic Verses*', in *Outside in the Teaching Machine* (Routledge, 1993), pp. 219–38.

Reading *The Satanic Verses*

[...]

I

First, then, the reading:

The Satanic Verses, in spite of all its plurality, has rather an aggressive central theme: the postcolonial divided between two identities: migrant and national.

As migrant, the postcolonial may attempt to become the metropolitan: this is Saladin Chamcha (ass-kisser) in his first British phase: 'I am a man to whom certain things are of importance: rigour, self-discipline, reason, the pursuit of what is noble without recourse to that old crutch, God. The ideal of beauty, the possibility of exaltation, the mind'.[1] This self-definition of the migrant *as* metropolitan is obviously not the book's preferred definition.

The postcolonial way, also, to keep himself completely separated *from* the metropolis *in* the metropolis as the fanatic exile. This is represented in the least conclusive section of the book, the place of dark foreboding, the subcontinental Imam ('desh' is a north Indian word which signifies his country), who must destroy the woman touched by the West. This is also not preferred: 'Exile is a soulless country' (*SV*, 208).

What we see in process in the greater part of *The Satanic Verses* is the many fragmented national representations coming together in serious and comic – serious *when* comic and vice versa – figures of resistance. In the hospital, a highly paid male model based in Bombay,

> now changed into a 'manticore' ... [with] an entirely human body, but [the] head of a ferocious tiger, with three rows of teeth ... whisper[s] solemnly ... [while] break[ing] wind continually ... 'They describe us. ... They have the power of description, and we succumb to the pictures they construct' (*SV*, 167–168).

These monsters organize a 'great escape,' and 'take ... the low roads to London town ... going their separate ways, without hope, but also without shame' (*SV*, 170–171).

On another register, and two-hundred odd pages later, 'a minute woman in her middle seventies' gives us a related but more upbeat message:

> We are here to change things. ... African, Caribbean, Indian, Pakistani, Bangladeshi, Cypriot, Chinese, we are other than what we would have been if we had not crossed the oceans. ... We have been made again: but I say we shall also be the ones to remake this society, to shape it from the bottom to the top (*SV*, 413–414).

There is framing and dramatic irony everywhere, but never all the way. For example, it is at this meeting that Saladin encounters

a young woman [who gives] his [conservative British] attire an amused once-over. ... She was wearing a lenticular badge. ... At some angles it read, *Uhuru for the Simba*; at others, *Freedom for the Lion*, 'It's on account of the meaning of his chosen name,' she explained redundantly. In African, 'Which language?' ... she shrugged. ... It was African: born, by the sound of her in Lewisham, or Deptford, or New Cross, that was all she needed to know. ... As if all causes were the same, all histories interchangeable (*SV*, 413, 415).

Most strongly in the hospital section of the book, aptly called 'Ellowen Deeowen,' the effect of fragmentation, citation, fast-shifting perspectives is sustained through echoes from British literature. This embedding in the history of the literature of England and Ireland – the echoes from *The Portrait of the Artist As a Young Man* are a text for interpretation in themselves – may prove the most seductive for metropolitan readers.

But the book will not let us forget that the metropolitan reader is among 'the describers.' The postcolonial is not only a migrant but also the citizen of a 'new' nation for which the colonial experience is firmly in the past, a past somewhat theatrically symbolized in Gibreel Farishta's dream of Mirza Sayeed Akhtar's house *Peristan*, 'built seven generations ago,' perhaps 'a mere contraction of *Perown-estan*,' after 'an English architect much favoured by the colonial authorities, whose only style was that of the neo-classical English country house' (*SV*, 230).

Mirza Akhtar is a *zamindar* – member of a landowning class, collecting land-revenue for the British, transmogrified at the end of the eighteenth century. He and his wife thus mark modern Indian elite postcolonial public culture in rather an obvious way:

In the city [they] were known as one of the most 'modern' and 'go-go' couples on the scene; they collected contemporary art and threw wild parties and invited friends round for fumbles in the dark on sofas while watching soft-porno VCRs (*SV*, 227).

Because the migrant as paradigm is a dominant theme in theorizations of postcoloniality, it is easy to overlook Rushdie's resolute effort to represent contemporary India. Whereas the topical caricature of the Bombay urban worlds of the popular film industry, of rhapsodic 'left' politics, of Muslim high society, of the general atmosphere of communalism, carries an idiomatic conviction, it is at least this reader's sense that so-called 'magical realism' becomes an alibi in the fabrication of Titlipur-Chatnapatna, the village and the country town. But then, these might be the constitutive asymmetries of the imagination – itself a fabricated word – that is given the name 'migrant.'

(And perhaps it is only in this sense that the drifting migrant imagination is paradigmatic, of the 'imagination' as such, not only of the historical case of postcoloniality. Here migrancy is the name of the institution that in-habits the indifferent anonymity of space and dockets climate and soil-type and the inscription of the earth's body. In this general sense, 'migrancy' is not derived.)

But since this general sense is never not imbricated with the narrow sense – our contemporary predicament – the trick or turn is not to assume either the metropolitan or the national as the standard and *judge* some bit of this plural landscape in terms of it. In learning to practice the turn if only to sense it slip away, we can guess that the deliberate oppositional stance of the European avant-garde is itself part of an instituted metropolitan reversal, among the 'describers' – again.

Thus every canvas will have a spot that is less 'real' than others. Excusing it away as an entailment of migrancy in general is no less dubious a gesture than accusing it as a historical or sociological transgression. I do therefore note that, within the protocols of *The Satanic Verses*, it is contemporary rural India that clings to magical realism as an alibi and thus provides a clue to the politics of the writing subject, the scribe. This would lead us to a deconstructive gesture toward the claim of magical realism as a privileged taxonomic description, of decolonization, a gesture already made in Chapter Three, and a consideration of alternative styles and systems of the representation of rural India.[2]

Within the labyrinth of such gestures, we must acknowledge that, writing as a migrant, Rushdie still militates against privileging the migrant or the exilic voice narrowly conceived, even as he fails in that very effort. A *mise-en-abyme*, perhaps, the eternal site of the migrant's desire, but also a persistent critique of metropolitan migrancy, his own slot in the scheme of things. The message and the medium of his book are marked by this conflict.

In other words, I do not think the 'cosmopolitan *challenge* to national culture' is perceived by Rushdie as only a challenge.[3] Perhaps it is even an aporia for him, an impossible decision between two opposed decidables with two mutually canceling sets of consequences, a decision which gets made, nonetheless, for one set, since life must operate as a passive or active *différance* of death, as we know from our most familiar experiences: 'I wanted to write about a thing I find difficult to admit even to myself, which is the fact that I left home.'[4]

The Indian world of the book is Muslim-based. India's Islamic culture, high and low, is too easily ignored by contemporary hegemonic constructions of national identity as well as international benevolence. (These words have become derisive in the context of the genocide of Indian Muslims undertaken by Hindu fundamentalists since 1992.) Islamic India is another theme of migrancy, unconnected with the recent colonial past. For Islam as such has its head turned away from the subcontinent, across the Arabian Sea, perpetually emigrant toward Mecca. Within this turned-away-ness, Rushdie plants the migrant's other desire, the search for roots as far down as they'll go. The name of this radical rootedness is, most often, religion. Thus in the section called Mahound, Rushdie re-opens the institution of Revelation, the origin of the Koran. It is paradoxical that the protection against desacralization, writing in the name of the false prophet, Mahound rather than Mohammed, has been read, quite legitimately, by the Law where Religion is the 'real' (there can be no other Law), as blasphemy.

The question is not if the book is blasphemous. The question is not even the profound belief of heretics and blasphemers. The question is rather: how is blasphemy to be punished? Can it be punished? What is the distinction between punishment and nourishment? And further, in the name of what do we judge the punishers? We will look at these questions in the two following sections.

The story of Mahound in *The Satanic Verses* is a story of negotiation in the name of woman. As so often, woman becomes the touchstone of blasphemy.

One of the most interesting features about much of Rushdie's work is his anxiety to write woman into the narrative of history. Here again we have to record an honorable failure.[5] (But I am more interested in failed texts. What is the use of a 'successful' text? What happens to the recorder of failed texts? As a postcolonial migrant, 'a tall, thin Bengali woman with cropped hair' [*SV*, 536], like Swatilekha – the 'real' name of the woman playing the lead character in Ray's film version of Tagore's *The Home and the World* – an 'actress' acting out the script of female Anglicization – read emancipation – by male planning in the colonial dispensation, I am part of Rushdie's text, after all.) In *Shame*, the women seem powerful only as monsters, of one sort or another. *The Satanic Verses* must end with Salahuddin Chamchawalla's reconciliation with *father* and nationality, even if the last sentence records sexual difference in the idiom of casual urban fucking: '"My place," Zeeny offered. "Let's get the hell out of here." "I'm coming," he answered her, and turned away from the view' (*SV*, 547).

All through, the text is written on the register of male bonding and unbonding, the most important being, of course, the double subject of migrancy, Gibreel Farishta and Saladin Chamcha. The two are tortured by obsession with women, go through them, even destroy them, within a gender code that is never opened up, never questioned, in this book where so much is called into question, so much is reinscribed.

Gibreel is named after the archangel Gabriel by his mother. But his patronymic, Ismail Najmuddin, is 'Ismail after the child involved in the sacrifice of Ibrahim, and Najmuddin, *star of the faith*; he'd given up quite a name when he took the angel's' (*SV*, 17). And that name, Ismail, comes in handy in an echo of *Moby Dick*, to orchestrate the greatest act of male bonding in the book as an inversion of the angel of death, when Gibreel saves Saladin's life in the glazing Shaandaar Cafe: 'The adversary: there he blows! Silhouetted against the backdrop of the ignited Shaandaar Cafe, see, that's the very fellow! Azraeel leaps unbidden into Farishta's hand' (*SV*, 463). The allusion in the otherwise puzzling 'there he blows' is the white whale, of course.

Yet it must be acknowledged that in Mahound, we hear the satanic verses inspired by possible *female* gods. Gibreel's dream of Mahound's wrestling with himself, acting out an old script, restores the proper version, without the female angels, man to man. By the rules of fiction in the narrow sense, you cannot assign burden of responsibility here; although by the law of Religion, in the strict sense, the harm was already done. Rushdie invoked those rules against these Laws, and it was an unequal contest. We will not enter the lists, but quietly mark the *text's* assignment of value. The 'reality' of the wrestling, the feel of the voice speaking through one, is high on the register of validity, if not verifiability. By contrast, in 'Return to Jahilia,' prostitution is mere play. Ayesha, the female prophet, ('historically' one of his wives) lacks the existential depth of 'the businessman' prophet. To her the archangel sings in popular Hindi film songs. Her traffic with him is reported speech.

If postcolonial plurality is one aggressive central theme of *The Satanic Verses*, the artist's identity is another. Rushdie's tactic is boldly old-fashioned here, and the tone reminds one of, say, George Meredith's 'Authorial voice' in *The Egoist*. Everything is taken care of by this overt comic self-undermining miming manipulation of 'dramatic irony' on so many levels. The multiple dreams, carried to absurdity, support as they take away the power of this planning genius. Here is the entire shift from Religions' God to Art's Imagination – a high European theme – played out in the staging of author. Ostentatiously appearing as God or Devil (*upparwala* or *nichaywala* – the one above or the one below), he clearly produces error in Gibreel, who has a delusion of angelic grandeur and nearly gets run over by a motorcar as a result. Almost a hundred pages later, the authorial voice reveals that it had been the authorial voice posing as the Almighty, capable of 'mobiliz[ing] the traditional apparatus of divine rage ... [making] wind and thunder [shake] the room' (*SV*, 319), and looking like photographs of Salman Rushdie 'medium height, fairly heavily built, with salt-and-pepper beard cropped close to the line of the jaw ... balding ... suffer[ing] from dandruff and [wearing] glasses.' Does this make the author less reliable or more? Does this make the voice less real or more? Does this make the dream more true than truth? Is this a serious use of Romantic Irony in a contemporary comic format or a caricature of Romantic Irony? In an era of industriously decentered subjects and radicalized citationality, these questions are disarmingly cozy. Are we obliged to repeat the argument that, as metropolitan writing is trying to get rid of a subject that has too long been the dominant, the postcolonial writer must still foreground his traffic with the subject-position?[6] Too easy, I think. Not because the migrant must still consider the question of identity, plurality, roots. But because fabricating decentered subjects as the sign of the times is not necessarily these times decentering the subject. There in the wake of the European avant-garde is also a confusion of the narrow and general senses of the relationship between subject and center. The trick or turn is not to assume the representation of decentering to *be* decentering, and/or judge styles by conjunctures.

All precautions taken, there is no risk in admitting that Rushdie's book reads more like a self-ironic yet self-based modernism ('a myopic scrivener' setting two gentlemen a-dreaming) than an object-coded or subject-decentered avant-garde. Although he does broaden out to other empires – notably Argentina through the Rosa Diamond sequence which also stages the Norman Conquest as immigration – once you have finished the phantasmagoric book, the global slowly settles into the peculiar locale of migrancy.

What are these dreams, these phantasmagoria, these shape-changes that convince not only the shape-changers themselves but the inhabitants of the world of the book as well? Like the taxonomy of migrancy, Rushdie provides what may be called an oneiric multiplicity, the dream as legitimizing matrix. The story begins in a miracle, a series of supernatural events tamely accommodated into the reasonableness of the everyday. Vintage 'magical realism' – Asturias or Márquez – has taught us to expect a more intricate mosaic. Alleluia Cone's 'visions' can be validated by her personality and experience. Gibreel's fantasies have a firm diagnostic label: paranoid schizophrenia. But what about the peculiar authority of the many times repeated 'Gibreel dreamed' ... and then a noun of event or space? What is the relationship between this and the claim of 'and then ...' 'and then ...' that Deleuze and Guattari assure us is the mode of narrativization of the schizo?[7]

And what about the metamorphosis of the migrants in the hospital where Saladin is brought after the embarrassment of the discovery that he is a British citizen? What about his physical transformation into the Devil, setting a trend in the fashion world of 'Black Britain,' only to be canceled when he learns to hate Farishta? Saladin is never 'diagnosed'; he is the sidekick that negotiates the book from beginning to end. And isn't that story about eating kippers at public school supposed to be a bit from Rushdie's own life-story? Is this a clue? Is Rushdie graphing his bio here as President Schreber, British-citizen-escaping-the-angel-of-god-by-demonic-meta-morphosis-and-returning-home-for-a-wished-for-entry-into-the-real.?[8]

In *Capitalism and Schizophrenia*, Deleuze and Guattari have suggested that the schizo as a general psychic description entailed by capitalism stands as a critique of the Oedipal recuperation of the great branching-out of social – and desiring – production inscribing the unproduced. I should like to think that *The Satanic Verses* presents a portrait of the author as schizo under the desiring/social production of migrancy and postcoloniality, a displacement of the Oedipal project of imperialism as bringing into Law of the 'favorite son.'

[...]

Good and Evil, set up with such pomp and circumstance, have therefore no moral substance in the persons of the protagonists. They are no more than visual markers, inscribed on the body like special effects – a halo, a pair of horns. I am uncomfortable with this of course, but then ask myself if this is not the peculiar felicity of postcoloniality, good and evil as reactive simulation, overturning the assurance in the prediction that 'a performative utterance will be *in a peculiar way* hollow or void if said by an actor on the stage, or if introduced in a poem.'[9] Postcolonial women and men, in many different ways, utter metropolitan performatives on the stage of migrancy as they utter 'cultural-origin' performatives in a simultaneous shadow play; thus perhaps revealing the constitutive theatricality of all performatives.

I can anticipate critics suggesting that I give resistance no speaking part here. But the point is that a book such as this might at least be inviting us to consider the following question: who am I, or my critics, or indeed Salman Rushdie, to *give* resistance a speaking part? To 'state the problem' is not bad politics. In fact, it might be poor judgment to consider academy or novel as straight blueprint for action on the street. Chamcha gives himself the assurance that if a '"chimeran graft' ... were possible," as shown on TV, 'then so was he; he, too, could cohere, send down roots, survive. Amid all the televisual images of hybrid tragedies ... he was given this one gift' (*SV*, 406). In that very section, Rushdie's 'authorial voice' puts it in the first person singular in the classic tones of the psychotic as savant:

> But, it had to be conceded, and this was his [Chamcha's] original point, that the circumstances of the age required no diabolic explanation. I[authorial voice]'m saying nothing. Don't ask me to clear things up one way or the other; the time of revelations is long gone (*SV*, 408).

It is after this that we come to the only real act of intended, gratuitous, cunning cruelty and persecution represented in the book: the destruction of Farishta and Alleluia through the anonymous telephoned messages, in the pluralized ventriloquil-ism of the radio-waves, of sexual innuendo couched in childish doggerel. No conceivable high allegorical connection with the great narrative of postcoloniality can be found in this important nexus of the book's narrative energy: this is rather the absurd discontinuity of the hyper-real. *Etre-pour-la-mort* is *être-au-telephone*.

A final word about the 'tall, thin Bengali woman with cropped hair,' whom I cannot really leave behind. Rukmini Bhaya Nair gives her some importance:

> Narration in Rushdie's novels is shaped as gossip, an undervalued form of everyday talk that is now creatively empowered to reclaim the metaphors of an elite history. In *S[atanic]V[erses]*, Rushdie, tongue very much in cheek, presents the following case through one of his minor characters, an intellectual Bengali woman. ['] Society was orchestrated by what she called grand narratives; history, economics, ethics. In India, the development of a corrupt and closed state apparatus had "excluded the masses of people from the ethical project." As a result, they sought ethical satisfactions in the oldest of the grand narratives, that is, religious faith.['][10]

Ms. Nair goes on to make a persuasive case for *The Satanic Verses* as 'satirical gossip.'[11]

The case that I have made for religious faith as a counternarrative with a generalized subject focused on the moment when, *within the colonial rather than postcolonial context*, religious discursivity changed to militancy, gossip changed to rumor as vehicle of subaltern insurgency.[12] In the present essay, my opening point is that, in *post*coloniality, the praxis and politics of life (the *Lebenswelt*) intercept aesthetic objects away from their destined ends. Thus, if the project of the *novel* is gossip, the postcolonial *Lebenswelt* wrenched it into rumor, criticism by hearsay, a text taken as evidence, talked about rather than read.[13] Upon the wings of that rumor, the metropolitan migrant heterogeneity (rather different from the colonial subaltern in the colony, though we tend to forget this) forged a collectivity which they could stage as a strike *for* the Imam *against* the West. The narrative of the State and the narrative of religion overdetermined the rumored book into a general mobilizing signifier for crisis.

II

I come now to the cultural politics of the specific (mis)reading of the book as disposable container of blasphemy, signifier of cultural difference, rather than the field of the migrant's desiring/social production. As Aziz Al-Azmeh comments:

> The enracinations, deracinations, alienations, comforts, discomforts and mutations which constitute the novel are kept entirely out of view by Rushdie's islamist critics, and his putative treatment of Muhammed and Abraham brought into view.[14]

Literature is transactional. The point is not necessarily and exclusively the correct description of a book, but the construction of readerships. 'The birth of the reader must be at the cost of the death of the Author.'

A great deal has been written and said about the Rushdie affair in the last half-year. I will concentrate on a spectrum of historically constructed readerships here and assemble a highly selective dossier.[15] My main argument attempts to lay out the full implications of the statement made by Gita Sahgal, a member of the Southall Black Sisters, based in Britain. 'It is in this crisis where our own orthodoxies have collapsed that the doubters and transgressors must once more create a space for themselves.'[16]

India banned the book first: on October 5, 1988. Of the twenty-one deaths associated with *The Satanic Verses* to date, nineteen took place on the subcontinent. Of these, twelve were Muslim anti-Rushdie demonstrators, shot in Rushdie's hometown, Bombay, on February 24, 1989. Ayatollah Khomeini called for Rushdie's death on February 14.

Why did India ban the book? In the name of the rights of a religious minority in a secular state, Syed Shahabuddin, an opposition Muslim MP, launched a campaign against the book. 'Doubters and transgressors must create a space for themselves' by taking a distance from mere rational abstraction, and here is the first one: 'rights of a religious minority in a secular democratic-socialist state.' Rational abstractions can be staunch allies, but *they can always also be used as alibis*. Gita Sahgal's '*this* crisis' is *always* implicit in the principle of reason. Her 'once more' is the activist's shorthand for what must be persistent.

I have insisted throughout this book upon the catachrestic relationship between Enlightenment rational abstractions and postcolonial practice: theatrical performatives. In India thus, it was not an islamist decision, but a decision related to the functioning of the rational abstractions claimed catachrestically by the postcolonial state that banned the book. Artists and intellectuals were immediately vociferous against the decision, but, from personal accounts that I have heard, the logic of the protests was extremely hard to manipulate, still in the realm of rational abstractions.

In addition, perhaps precisely because the rational abstractions of democracy are claimed catachrestically and therefore critically by the secularist in the postcolonial state, there was a voice raised in India against the West's right to claim freedom of expression. The best succinct statement of this may be found in a letter to the *Economic and Political Weekly* signed by, among others, Asghar Ali Engineer, one of the strongest analysts and critics of 'communalism' (religious sectarianism) in India: 'We do not for a moment belittle [the] Ayatollah's threat. ... But we also see the danger of "freedom of expression" being fetishized and the embattled context in which a writer finds her/himself oversimplified.'[17]

Wole Soyinka, traveling in India in December wrote, as a native of Nigeria:

> a nation which is, in the estimation of many, roughly equally divided amongst Muslims and Christians and animists, with the former two constituting a floating adherent population of the 'animist' in addition to being what they publicly proclaim. ... I caught some flak from sections of the artistic and intellectual community for commenting that I quite understood the action of the Indian government in banning Salman Rushdie's book. ... I stated that, given India's harrowing situation of religious unrest, I probably would have done the same if I were the Prime Minister. I did not condone the ban; I merely tried to understand the horrible dilemma in which the government of India was placed.[18]

A dilemma, a crisis, an aporia, peculiar to democracy as checks and balances, rights and duties computed on the normative grid of rational abstractions inherited from the culture of imperialism. Bhikhu Parekh, a British-Indian political theorist has asked: 'Is there a release from this highly claustrophobic post-Enlightenment world-view?'[19]

Rushdie's own reaction was straightforward:

> The right to freedom of expression is at the foundation of any democratic society. ... My view is that of a secular man for whom Islamic culture has been of central importance all his life. ... You know, as I know that [the Muslim parliamentarians] and their allies don't really care about my novel. The real issue is the Muslim vote.[20]

Still within 'the claustrophobic post-Enlightenment world-view,' let us step back and ask, what exacerbated the situation of the Muslim vote so dramatically? It is of course idle to assign a single efficient cause to such trends but, for strategic reasons that I hope will he evident to at least a section of my readership, I choose the successful censoring of a woman, contained within national boundaries, a national *cause célèbre* for a time but nothing about which it can be said 'Islam today has displayed its enormous mobilizing power.' I refer, of course, to the Shahbano case. I quote a few passages from 'Shahbano' by Rajeswari Sunder Rajan and Zakla Pathak:

> In April 1985, the Supreme Court of India ... passed a judgment in favor of Shahbano in the case of Mohammed Ahmed Khan, appellant, versus Shahbano and others, respondents. The judgment created a furor unequalled, according to one journal, since 'the great upheaval of 1857 [the so-called Indian Mutiny]' ... awarding Shahbano, a divorced Muslim woman, maintenance of Rs. 179.20 (approximately $14) per month from her husband ... and dismissed the husband's appeal against the award of maintenance under section 125 of the 1973 Code of Criminal Procedure. ... When some by-elections fell due in December 1985, the sizeable Muslim vote turned against the ruling party (the Congress-I) partly because it supported the judgment. ... When Hindu fundamentalists offered to 'protect' her from Muslim men, her religious identity won. ... In an open letter, she denounced the Supreme Court Judgment 'which is apparently in my favour; but since this judgment is contrary to the Quran and the *hadith* and is an open interference in Muslim personal law, I, Shahbano, being a Muslim, reject it and dissociate myself from every judgment which is contrary to the Islamic Shariat.' ... When the battle was carried to Parliament and the government of India passed the bill that threw her on the mercy of the

male relatives of her natal family, her gender status was again activated. She became a Muslim woman pursuing the case for the return of her *mehr* (dower) under the provisions of the new act.[21]

Sunder Rajan and Pathak are quite right in saying that what is at issue here is not 'whether this spacing, temporalizing self is a deferral of the unified freely choosing *subject* or whether the latter is itself only a metaphysic.'[22] What we are concerned with here is the question of *agency*, even *national* agency within the effect of the nation in the real – just as Rushdie's novel is concerned with the *migrant* agency represented in a magical but none the less serious layout. 'Agent' and 'subject' are different codings of something we call 'being.' Shahbano, as citizen of the same postcolonial nation invoked by Rushdie in his letter to Rajiv Gandhi, has her *agency* censored by the script of religion and gendering. In this context, to bring up the question of the staging of free will in the *subject* has a hidden ethicopolitical agenda that may give support to the very forces that recode her as gendered and therefore make her dependent upon the institution of heterosexual difference. This has something like a relationship with what militants in the Rushdie case have pointed out: that arguments from cultural relativism are profoundly complicit, when invoked at certain moments, with racist absolutism. It is quite correct to point out the immense mobilization of national resistance – the provisional fabrication of a collective agency on the occasion of Shahbano. But woman *as* woman (unavailable to class agency in the particular context) is still only an occasion here. The question of free will should not be inscribed within arguments from subject-production; it is rather to be seen in connection with the presupposition of individual agency in collectivities. It is here that Shahbano stands censored. Within this frame, there is no real polarization between self-censoring and other-censoring (conversion and coercion); that is the opposition we must learn to undo. The definition of 'choice' as 'internalized constraint' is invaluable here. In the sphere of the production of political value, the mute as articulate in the service of 'orthodoxy' (to borrow Gita Sahgal's word) – a discontinuous naming of collective agency in the name of the 'sacred' rather than the 'profane' (in the other coding called 'secular,' 'national') – is more spectacularly muted because so abundantly audible. And, in the context of the international collectivization brought about by way of Rushdie's book, of which she is among the first efficient causes, she has dropped out, become invisible. How can she *become* one of 'the doubters and transgressors' before she can participate in their 'clearing a space for themselves'? By counter-coercion through the orthodoxy of reason? Paradoxically, it is the rationalist who can think reason as internalized constraint. *This* is the genuine dilemma, the aporia, the double-bind of the question of agency. The condition of (im)possibility of rational collectivities must be seen, not as instrument, but as last instance.

By being categorized as a vagrant – the destitute woman – widow, divorcée, or abandoned wife … fulfills her (anti-)social role. The psychological damage of potential vagrant status is partially minimized by the depersonalizing effects of legal action. Section 125 offers women 'negative' subjectivity: the new act responds by reinserting the divorcée within the family, this time as dependent on her natal family and sons.[23]

As impersonal instrument, rational abstractions can operate as *pharmakon*, a poison that can be a healing drug.[24] It is thus that one must turn to the extraordinary and (ex)orbitant category of 'legal vagrant.' In the subordinate, gendered, decolonized *national* space, the category of *female* 'vagrant' as 'access to public space' (section 125 of the Uniform Civil Code) must be recognized beside the category of 'migrant' within ex-colonial metropolitan space, where, as the migrant feminist group 'Women Against Fundamentalism' have pointed out, 'women's voices have been largely silent' – and, I repeat, audible as muted ventriloquists – 'in the debate where battle lines have been drawn between liberalism and fundamentalism.'[25] Paradoxically, categorization as vagrant is 'psychologically damaging' only if the religious coding of gendered heterosexuality is implicitly accepted by way of a foundational concept of subject-formation. The freeing pain of a violent rejection from a system of self-representation (a mode of value-coding) is not confined to the franchised or disenfranchised.

This would take me into the arena where the reversal empire-nation is displaced, about which I have written in Chapter Four [of *Outside in the Teaching Machine*]. Here we are obliged to go forward to the most visible agent, the late Ayatollah Khomeini.

Who punishes? How was the Ayatollah produced?

Although we cannot afford to forget, as Albert Memmi writes in the context of the Rushdie case, that 'monotheism, philosophically and pragmatically speaking, is totalitarian,' we must of course also see that the stake in Khomeini's agency (in every sense) is not Islam, but islamism.[26] And, at first glance, islamism is the regulation of diaspora/migrancy. In the words of Farzaneh Asari, a pseudonymous and exiled Iranian writer, 'it is the Muslims of America, Britain, India, Lebanon and so on whom the Islamic Republic wants to persuade of its continued hold on the Iranian people.'[27] It is important to underline that 'virtually all the pronouncements from Teheran on *The Satanic Verses* begin and end with the denunciations of *imperialism* and *colonialism*, accusing Rushdie of complicity in a crusade aimed at Islam,' writes Mehmet Ali Dikerdem.[28]

But who punishes? How was the Ayatollah produced? These are still merely the question of stakes. In answer to this question, Asari offers an account of Khomeini's bio-graphy, that concept-metaphor whose importance I have learned from Derrida:

> He ... chose his 'transcendent' self, the one that had been made into an almost Gandhian leader, over his 'real' theocratic self – what by temperament and belief he was and has remained. Khomeini's [political appointments] ... following the victory of the revolution to testify to the primacy of this 'transcendent' self in the crucial pre-revolutionary period.

Asari relates 'his gradual loss of popular support' as due to the overcoming by the 'real' of the 'transcendent.'

> This loss has been more than made up for by the reconstruction and vast extension of the Shah's repressive apparatus ... (though the social base of the present Iranian regime is still ... much broader and deeper than that of the Shah ...)

Here is a rather convincingly proposed doubling, then, of the man playing the monolith.[29] To sacrifice the heretic in a defense of the faith is a ruse to 'recover lost territory,' to cover over the political and military defeat in the war with Iraq. (This political text has new patterns now; the present piece records the initial phases of 'the Rushdie case.')

This monolithic face, defending an unchanging word, this 'construct' – with the piercing eyes under the iconic turban – 'at the center of attention, [desperately attempting to] mak[e] … reading, writing, and meaning seem to be very close to the same thing' is a product of complicity between Khomeini's 'direct interest in presenting Iran as a static monolith defined by the steadfast devotion of its people to a "fundamentalist" brand of Islam' and a sanctioned ignorance, 'the accepted wisdom which makes … ignorant lines eminently reasonable' (Asari).[30] 'Reason' and 'religion' are thus clandestine cooperators. Asari describes the conflation of 'the estimated five million that celebrated Khomeini's return in the streets of Teheran in February, to the fewer than three thousand that greeted his call for Rushdie's murder … in the same city in February 1989.' It is not certain that the corporeal textuality of Khomeini's body, levitated by helicopter, will do anything to rip apart this conflation. For this conflation of collectivities in fact projects a 'central image' of the 'omnipresent if often physically absent Ayatollah … when a crowd is large enough to fill the small screen, how is the viewer to know the number of people involved or the significance of such a number?'

Once again I emphasize the implausible connection-by-reversal – the simulated Khomeini as Author and the dissimulated Shahbano marking the place of the effaced trace at the origin: an invocation of collective support projecting a singular agent filled with divine intention; an invocation of collective resistance displacing a censored patient as cross-hatched by discursivities. If we yield ground and grounding by deliberately 'writing otherwise,' analyzing a Shahbano by subject-formation rather than agency-deformation, the forces of the Author claiming as Author to write 'the same' come forward to occupy the space cleared. The case of *The Satanic Verses*, a realist reading of magical realism, makes visible the violent consequences.

Deliberate cultural relativism is a seemingly benevolent rational abstraction that shows its insidious credential here. Al-Azmeh calls it 'apartheid – expressed in culturalist and religious tones.' Mehmet Ali Dikerdem calls it 'infecting … into … ethnic pathology'; Gita Sahgal insists that

> fundamentalism has been the main beneficiary of the adoption of relativist multi-cultural norms by large sections of the political establishment. … Anti-racist rhetoric … sees only that a black religion feels powerless in a racist society. Any debate within the community – among Muslims, between believers and non-believers, men and women – is irrelevant from this viewpoint.

Asari again:

> Clearly the explanation for [BBC's documentary *Inside the Ayatollah's Iran* (14 February 1989)] *Panorama's* account lies in the basic assumption of the radical otherness of 'the Ayatollah's Iran.' But Iran does not consist entirely of Ayatollahs.

The radically other is a warning to the power of reason, not a featured face blocking out accessible heterogeneity. Those of us who have been troubled by the fetishization of Levinas into a prophet of marginality feel comforted by Asari's enviably sober tones.[31]

> Cultural relativism and the recognition of the limitations of Eurocentrism have been important achievements in the radical consciousness and cultural anthropology that have developed in this century and whose wisdom must be preserved. But in the current climate these insights are being used or abused in unexpected ways.

I must, of course, insist that the 'use *and* abuse' are both entailed by institutionalized relativism, even as use and abuse are entailed by 'the principle of reason' that generates 'the post-Enlightenment claustrophobia' that such a relativism would contest. The answer is not the 'preservation' of the positive and perennial and the 'elimination' of the negative and contextual. It is not even to attempt to sublate – preserve and destroy. My peculiar theme is always *persistent* critique – and, I must emphasize, an *asymmetrical* persistent critique, focusing on different elements in the incessant process of recoding that shifts the balance of the *pharmakon's* effect from medicine to poison; while insisting on the necessity of the broad grounding position. Admittedly this brings practice to a breaking point in its acknowledgment of the everyday, but what else is new? I cannot develop this here, for, in this brief compass, I think it is more urgent to dramatize a diversity within the dossier that I have been presenting, in order to close this section by reminding ourselves first of an often unacknowledged desire and, second, of the United States, for we migrants in the U.S. are parked in a spot claimed by some to be united by democratic reason.

Gita Sahgal speaks as a migrant fighting for racial equality in a metropolitan space and sexual justice within the migrant community. Soyinka speaks as a national in a space where speaking of a *minority* religion would involve recasting dominance in the inaccurate language of numbers. Asghar Ali Engineer speaks as a national of a *religious* minority in a *secular* state. And Farzaneh Asari, speaking necessarily in a false name, speaks as an exile from Iran, *one* nation united under God. Standing in the United States, and accepting the responsibility for that highly dangerous positioning we must ask the question that Homi Bhabha has recently brought to our attention: 'what do these people want?' These people: migrant, national in an equally-divided-religion state, national in a majority-religion state, exile from a theocratic state.

Seen as collectivities (and that is not the only way to see them) they all want an access to generality *and* difference through the mediation of access to national agency. The migrant wants to redefine the nation, the postcolonial wants to identify the nation, the exile wants to explain and restore the nation and be an agent in terms of its normative and privative discourse. Rushdie's novel is not only a novel of migrancy, but also a novel of return. Thus Al Azmeh hears religion as the cry of the oppressed heart living in ghettos in a land of false dreams, 'impervious to the logic of cultural relativism and multi-culturalism but not to the logic of capitalism.' Soyinka wants to ban 'everything which is Iran ... as long as Ayatollah Khomeini remains accepted as a leader in Iran, everything except the voices of Iran's political and cultural dissidents and the protests of her repressed womanhood.' But to the Muslims in Bradford, where it all began, who wanted to conserve and establish Islamic education in Britain, the Ayatollah showed the fantasmatic vision of a nation, not a religion but a theocratic state. And Sahgal puts it this way:

> When [we] went to Bradford to make a documentary on *The Satanic Verses* ... it emerged that their main problem was to maintain faith in a secular society. What would future generations of Muslim children believe in, one asked rhetorically, if the book remained in circulation and was seen to be sanctified by society?

Yet the desire of these British Muslims is not to abdicate from the nation, but to insert Islamic education into the state. To participate in the nation in general, and yet to remain an enclave. And in the statement of the collective to which Sahgal belongs, it is the word 'nationality' that carries this contradiction: 'We will take up the right to determine our own destinies, not limited by religion, culture or nationality.'[32]

It is only if we acknowledge the heterogeneous desire for that great rational abstraction, agency in a nation, that we postcolonials will be able to take a distance from it. It is here that the transgressor must persistently critique that transgressed space, which she cannot not want to inhabit, even if coded another way. We can sometimes be released from the claustrophobia of the post-Enlightenment bunker if we acknowledge that we also want to be snug in it. What is punishment is also nourishment. It is only then that we can sense that the spectacular promise of democracy – those rational abstractions coded as Human Rights – is desirable precisely because those abstractions can be used as alibis to deflect critique. In fact, it is only then that we can begin to suspect that the ethical, without which any hope for civil society or social justice must crumble, and which must therefore remain eminently desirable, bases itself upon what might be the lowest common denominator of being-human, objectivity, and the universal, and yet *must* code itself as the highest.[33] *Neither* radical alterity *nor* universal ipseity is an unquestionable value.

The United States is the dream of post-Enlightenment Europe. It is here that the bunker is a *trompe-l'oeil* of the wide-open spaces. It is here that the rational abstractions of formal democracy are most resolutely trotted out on behalf of cultural relativism, sanctioned ignorance, idiot goodwill, as well as racism and classism. As Rushdie himself said in a less harried time, American liberals just can't shake the habit of wanting to take care of the world. By the logic of this coding, Communism and Capitalism have of course already been recoded as State Censorship versus Free Choice.[34] And the Rushdie affair has been coded as Freedom of Speech versus Terrorism and even as 'a triumph of the written word.' It has been domesticated into a possible 'Western' (why?) 'martyrship' for literature, or rather for the book trade! – 'to the cause that we [as an industry] supposedly espouse!'[35]

It is only if we recognize that we cannot not want freedom of expression as well as those other normative and privative rational abstractions that we on the other side can see how they work as alibis. It is only then that we can recode the conflict as Racism versus Fundamentalism, demonizing versus disavowal.[36]

In the name of what do we judge the punisher? In the name of right reason, of course, but from what does it detract our attention? It hides, and I quote Mehmet Ali Dikerdem again:

> one of the most elemental fears and phobias of European cultural consciousness which regarded this new faith as the incarnation of the 'anti-Christ' ... Islam and Christianity confronted one another for a millennium in possibly the longest and bitterest 'superpower struggle' of all time. ... Islam is thus the opposite of the accumulated values and institutions of the evolution from Renaissance and Reformation to the Industrial Revolution via the American and French Revolution.[37]

Dikerdem relates this adroitly to the political history of the Middle East since the Second World War. This therefore is the appropriate moment to record a response particularly to my dossier, from Alia Arasooghly, a diasporic Palestinian. Earlier in this piece, I remarked that, at first glance, it seemed that the stake in Khomeini's agency was islamism in the regulation of migrancy. Arasooghly points out persuasively how the production of the Ayatollah Khomeini as the punisher was also a *mise-en-scène* of the claiming of proper agency in Islam's own house, 'as though God's death were but a play.'[38] This is, paradoxically, not a realist reading of magical realism, but the reverse move: here scripture, the ground of the real, is performed as representation, a script. Arasooghly cites a counter-claim by the Iraqi film *al-Qadissiya* ...

> which recreates the early Arab/Muslim battle and defeat of the Persian/Zoroastrians at Qadissiyah which opened Persia to Islam and to the Arab Empire (at the time of the Ummayad dynasty the defeaters of the Shiites!), a most significant and crucial battle for the Arabs, against claims to leave the Persians alone.

By her reading,

> the main audience the Iranian Islamic Republic has addressed itself to since its inception, after its own people has been the 'real Muslims' – the Arabs, *Khomeini could not speak in the name of Islam if he did not also speak for the Arabs.* The Quran [and the Prophet] were sent to the Arabs in Arabic, other Muslims either have to learn Arabic, or have access to a second hand interpretation via a translation ... the largest ... Islamic Empire/State was during Arab rule. Ottoman rule brought stagnation and decay. Islam's three Holy cities, Mecca, Medina, and Jerusalem are in Arab lands.

The *mise-en-scène*, 'the main audience,' and now the substance of the performance: 'the Ayatollah declared/showed Muslims how to be powerful against the Great Satan, the U.S.A. and denounced its client satan, Israel.'

An interesting conclusion arises from Arasooghly's reading. Khomeini's 'anti-democratic, anti-Enlightenment' behavior was not only not direct and unmediated evidence of the immutable essence of Islam, but it was a deliberate cultural-political self-representation as an unmediated testifier for the immutable essence of Islam.

Thus Arasooghly suggests that 'Khomeini as Salahdin,' the countercrusader, 'baffled the "international" sensibility [by] not playing by the rules put out by Europe': the hostage syndrome, the death threat against Salman Rushdie.

[...]

Notes (cut and renumbered)

1. Salman Rushdie, *The Satanic Verses* (New York: Viking, 1989), pp. 135–136; subsequent page references have been included in the text after the initial letters *SV*.
2. For a somewhat tendentious but intriguing genealogy of 'magical realism,' see Jeffrey Hart, *Reactionary Modernism: Technology, Culture, and Politics in Weimar and the Third Reich* (Cambridge: Cambridge University Press, 1984).
3. Timothy Bennan, *Salman Rushdie and the Third World: Myths of the Nation* (London: Macmillan, 1989). Perhaps because of his clear-cut position on the nation, Mr. Brennan is weak in the representation of the place of the novel in the Indian literary traditions (pp. 18, 79–80). [...] Mr. Brennan's sense that *Midnight's Children* put 'the Indo-English imagination on the map' (p. 80) is a step ahead of Alan Yentob's inspired polarization of India/Pakistan and the West as 'oral tradition' and the 'modern novel'! (Lisa Appignanesi and Sara Maitland, eds., *The Rushdie File* [London: Fourth Estate, 1989], p. 197.) In Macaulay's day, Arabic and Sanskrit writing at least filled a school library shelf. With friends like these!
4. Rushdie, 'Interview with Sean French,' *File*, p. 9.
5. I feel solidarity with men who let women in. But I cannot see this gesture as the performance of feminism. On this particular point, I must take exception even from my friend Srinivas Aravamudan's outstanding essay, a full-dress scholarly treatment of the novel. To create women as 'strong characters' is not necessarily to 'pursue ... [t]he issue of *feminism* and Islam' ('"Being God's Postman Is No Fun, Yaar": Salman Rushdie's *The Satanic Verses*,' *Diacritics*, 19:ii [Summer 1989]: p. 13; emphasis mine). And it is here that I must also split from Rukmini Bhaya Nair's impressive 'Text and Pre-Text: History as Gossip in Rushdie's Novels': 'The Prophet's own intellectual, moral, and practical dilemmas are brought closer to us through his wives, Khadijah and Ayesha, who implicitly believed in him, and the (un)common whores of Jahilia who imitated every move of the women proximate to the Prophet. Through the gossip of women, we come to a truer understanding of the "sinuous complexities of history." Public facts alone are insufficient and unconvincing' (*Economic and Political Weekly*, 24:13 [May 6, 1989]: p. 997). That private-public divide is old gender-coding. We must set these things on the move. [...]
6. This is the productive unease in Fredric Jameson, 'Third World Literature in the Era of Multinational Capitalism,' *Social Text* 15 (1986).
7. Deleuze and Guattari, *Anti-Oedipus*, pp. 5, 36. See also p. 12.
8. For the notion of biography – the staging of the author is part of this – see Derrida, 'Otobiographies,' cited at the opening of this chapter. For Schreber, see Sigmund Freud, 'Psychoanalytic Notes on an Autobiographical Account of a Case of Paranoia (*Dementia Paranoides*),' *Standard Edition*, vol. 12.
9. J. L. Austin, *How to Do Things With Words* (Oxford: Oxford University Press, 1965), pp. 22–22; quoted in Derrida, 'Signature Event Context,' in *Limited, Inc.*, p. 16.
10. Nair, 'Text and Pre-Text,' p. 995.
11. *Ibid.*, p. 1000.
12. Spivak, 'Subaltern Studies: Deconstructing Historiography,' in *In Other Worlds*.
13. The phrase 'criticism by hearsay,' used in an academic context, comes from Paul de Man, 'The Resistance to Theory,' in *The Resistance to Theory* (Minneapolis: University of Minnesota Press, 1986), p. 15.
14. Aziz Al-Azmeh, 'More on *The Satanic Verses*,' *Frontier*, 21:25 (February 4, 1989): p. 6.
15. Appignanesi, *File*, is, of course, now a much more extensive source.

16. Gita Sahgal, 'Transgression Comes of Age,' *Interlink*, 12 (May–June 1989): p. 19. I am grateful to Peter Osborne and John Kraniauskas for help in assembling this dossier.

17. 'Dubious Defenders,' *Economic and Political Weekly*, 24:17 (April 29, 1989): p. 894. Ali A. Mazrui strikes a similar chord in 'The Moral Dilemma of Salman Rushdie's *Satanic Verses*,' in Appignanesi, ed., *File*.

18. Wole Soyinka, 'Jihad for Freedom,' *Index on Censorships*, 18:5 (May–June, 1989): p. 20. All references to *Index* are to this issue.

19. 'Identities on Parade: A Conversation,' *Marxism Today* (June 1989): p. 27.

20. 'Open Letter to Rajiv Gandhi,' *New York Times* (October 19, 1988). Since then, Rushdie's relationship to declarations of faith have taken many situational turns.

21. Rajewari Sunder Rajan and Zakia Pathak, '"Shahbano,"' *Signs*, 14:3 (Spring 1989): pp. 558–559, 572.

22. Sunder Rajan and Pathak, '"Shahbano,"' p. 573. Emphasis mine.

23. Sunder Rajan and Pathak, '"Shahbano,"' pp. 576–577.

24. For *pharmakon*, see Jacques Derrida, 'Plato's Pharmacy,' in *Dissemination*.

25. Sahgal, 'Transgression,' p. 19.

26. Albert Memmi, 'For Secularism,' *Index*, p. 18.

27. Farzaneh Asari, 'Iran in the British Media,' *Index*, p. 11.

28. Mehmet Ali Dikerdem, 'Rushdie, Islam and "Islam,"' *End*, 37 (June 1989): p. 4.

29. For another view see Afsaneh Najmabadi, 'Interview with Gayatri Spivak,' *Social Text*, 9:3 (1991): p. 122–134.

30. The first quotation is from Donna Haraway, 'The Biopolitics of Postmodern Bodies: Determination of the Self in Immune System Discourse,' *differences*, 1:1 (Winter 1989): p. 10. All quotations from Asari are from 'Iran in the British Media.'

31. The most astute discussion of the inaccessibility of the absolutely other is still Jacques Derrida, 'Violence and Metaphysics.' For a powerful feminist reading, see Luce Irigaray, 'The Fecundity of the Caress,' (discussed in Chapter Seven of *Outside in the Teaching Machine*).

32. Sahgal, 'Transgression,' p. 19.

33. For an extended discussion of this, see my forthcoming study of Peter Dickinson's *The Poison Oracle*.

34. For an astute practical account of this coding, see Barbara Epstein, 'The Reagan Doctrine and Right-Wing Democracy,' *Socialist Review*, 19:1 (January–March 1989). The dynamics of this coding has gone into many global moves since this writing.

35. Emily Prayer, 'Rushdie Judgment,' *Village Voice*, 34:10 (March 7, 1987): p. 23. The conduct of the Anglo-U.S. publishing world is undoubtedly an important matter. But to reduce the Rushdie affair to nothing but an assessment of that conduct is typically ethnocentric.

36. As I have argued in Najmabadi, 'Interview,' the British dossier shows that in Britain, as opposed to the U.S., this critical recoding is strongly present. [...]

37. The classic analysis of the representation of Islam is, of course, Edward W. Said, *Covering Islam: How the Media and the Experts Determine How We See the Rest of the World* (New York: Pantheon, 1981).

38. W. B. Yeats, 'Two Songs from a Play.' Arasooghly [...] is a filmmaker and teacher of Film Studies at Northeastern University. [...] 'The Fatwa' section of Appignanesi, ed., *File*, supports her point of view. See especially pp. 95, 106.

Acknowledgements

Grateful acknowledgement is made to the following sources for permission to reproduce material in this book previously published elsewhere. Every effort has been made to trace copyright holders, but if any have been inadvertently overlooked, the publisher will be pleased to make the necessary arrangement at the first opportunity.

CHAPTER I: *HAMLET*

1.1 'Hamlet and His Problems' from *Selected Essays* by T. S. Eliot, pp. 104–10, reproduced with kind permission of Faber and Faber Ltd (1953), the Eliot Estate, and © 1950 Harcourt Brace & Company and renewed 1978 by Esme Valerie Eliot.

1.2 Jacques Lacan, from 'Desire and the Interpretation of Desire in *Hamlet*', in Shoshana Felman, ed., *Literature and Psychoanalysis: The Question of Reading: Otherwise*. © Johns Hopkins University Press, 1982, pp. 11–54. Reprinted by permission of the Johns Hopkins University Press.

1.3 Elaine Showalter, from 'Representing Ophelia: Women, Madness and the Responsibilities of Feminist Criticism', in Patricia Parker and G. H. Hartman, eds, *Shakespeare and the Question of Theory* (Routledge, 1985), pp. 77–94. Reprinted by permission of the publisher.

1.4 Jacqueline Rose, from 'Hamlet – the Mona Lisa of Literature', in *Sexuality in the Field of Vision* (Verso, 1986), pp. 123–40. Reprinted by permission of the publisher.

1.5 Lisa Jardine, from '"No Offence i' th' World": *Hamlet* and Unlawful Marriage', in Francis Barker, Peter Hulme and Margaret Iverson, eds, *Uses of History. Marxism, Postmodernism and the Renaissance* (Manchester University Press, 1991), pp. 123–39. Reprinted by permission of the publisher.

CHAPTER 2: 'ODE'

2.1 Cleanth Brooks, from 'Wordsworth and the Paradox of the Imagination', Ch. 7 of *The Well-Wrought Urn: Studies in the Structure of Poetry* (1947) (Methuen, 1968), pp. 101–23, *passim*. Reprinted by permission of Routledge.

2.2   Geoffrey H. Hartman, ' "Timely Utterance" Once More', Ch. 10 of *The Unremarkable Wordsworth* (Methuen, 1987), pp. 152–62. Reprinted by permission of the University of Minnesota Press.

2.3   Marjorie Levinson, 'The Intimations Ode: A Timely Utterance', Ch. 3 of *Wordsworth's Great Period Poems: Four Essays* (Cambridge University Press, 1986), pp. 80–104, *passim*. Reprinted by permission of Cambridge University Press and Marjorie Levinson.

CHAPTER 3: *JANE EYRE*

3.1   Excerpt from *A Room of One's Own* by Virginia Woolf, Ch. 4, pp. 68–75, *passim*, © 1929 by Harcourt Brace and Company and renewed 1957 by Leonard Woolf and Random House Ltd UK, reprinted by permission of the publishers.

3.2   The Marxist-Feminist Literature Collective, from 'Women's Writing: *Jane Eyre, Shirley, Villette, Aurora Leigh*', in *Ideology and Consciousness*, 3, Spring 1978, pp. 27–34. Reprinted by permission of Helen Taylor.

3.3   Sandra M. Gilbert and Susan Gubar, from 'A Dialogue of Self and Soul: Plain Jane's Progress', Ch. 10 of *The Madwoman in the Attic: The Woman Writer and the Nineteenth-Century Literary Imagination* (Yale University Press, 1979), pp. 336–71, *passim*. Reprinted by permission of the publisher.

3.4   Gayatri Chakravorty Spivak, from 'Three Women's Texts and a Critique of Imperialism', in H. L. Gates, ed., '*Race*', *Writing and Difference* (Chicago University Press, 1985), pp. 262–78. Reprinted by permission of Gayatri Chakravorty Spivak.

CHAPTER 4: *MIDDLEMARCH*

4.1   F. R. Leavis, from Ch. 2 of *The Great Tradition* (1948) (Penguin, 1962), pp. 74, 86–93. Reprinted by permission of Random House and New York University Press.

4.2   Raymond Williams, from 'George Eliot', Ch. 3 of *The English Novel from Dickens to Lawrence* (1970) (Paladin, 1974), pp. 63–79, *passim*. Reprinted by permission of Random House UK Ltd.

4.3   Terry Eagleton, from Ch. 4 of *Criticism and Ideology* (1976) (Verso, 1978), pp. 110–25, *passim*. Reprinted by permission of the publisher.

4.4   J. Hillis Miller, from 'Optic and Semiotic in *Middlemarch*', in Jerome H. Buckley, ed., *The World of Victorian Fiction* (Harvard University Press, 1975), pp. 125–45, *passim*. Reprinted by permission of the publisher.

4.5   Colin MacCabe, from 'Introduction' to *James Joyce and the Revolution of the Word* (Macmillan, 1979), pp. 13–25, *passim*. Reprinted by permission of Macmillan Ltd.

CHAPTER 5: *DORIAN GRAY AND EARNEST*

5.1   Eve Kosofsky Sedgwick, from 'Some Binarisms (II), Wilde, Nietzsche, and the Sentimental Relations of the Male Body', Ch. 3 of *Epistemology of the Closet* (1990) (Harvester, 1991), pp. 131–81, *passim*. Reprinted by permission of Harvester Wheatsheaf, University of California Press and Eve Kosofsky Sedgwick.

5.2   Jonathan Dollimore, from Chs 1, 4 and 20 of *Sexual Dissidence* (Oxford University Press, 1991), pp. 10–11, 14–17, 64–73, 308–10. Reprinted by permission of the publisher.

5.3   Joseph Bristow, from 'Introduction' and 'Critical Commentary', in *The Importance of Being Earnest and Related Writings* (Routledge, 1992), pp. 17–20, 202–17, *passim*. Reprinted by permission of the publisher.

5.4   Alan Sinfield, from 'Aestheticism and Decadence', Ch. 4 of *The Wilde Century* (Cassell, 1994), pp. 98–105. Reprinted by permission of the publisher.

5.5   Terry Eagleton, from 'Oscar and George', Ch. 8 of *Heathcliff and the Great Hunger* (Verso, 1995), pp. 326, 331–41. Reprinted by permission of the publisher.

CHAPTER 6: *HEART OF DARKNESS*

6.1   F. R. Leavis, from *The Great Tradition* (Chatto & Windus, 1948), pp. 193–202. Reprinted by permission of New York University Press and Random House UK Ltd.

6.2   Tzvetan Todorov, '*Heart of Darkness*', from *Genres in Discourse*, trans. Catherine Porter (Cambridge University Press, 1990), pp. 103–12. Reprinted by permission of Cambridge University Press and Editions du Seuil, Paris.

6.3   Chinua Achebe, 'An Image of Africa: Racism in Conrad's *Heart of Darkness*', in *Hopes and Impediments: Selected Essays 1965–1987* (Cambridge University Press, 1988), pp. 1–13. Reprinted by permission from Chinua Achebe.

6.4   Edward Said, 'Two Visions in *Heart of Darkness*', from *Culture and Imperialism* (Chatto & Windus, 1994), pp. 20–35. Reprinted by permission of Random House UK Ltd and Aitken, Stone & Wylie Ltd.

CHAPTER 7: *ULYSSES*

7.1   Hélène Cixous, from 'Joyce: The (R)use of Writing', in D. Attridge and M. Ferrer, eds, *Post-Structuralist Joyce. Essays from the French* (Cambridge University Press, 1984), pp. 15–30. Reprinted by permission of Cambridge University Press, Editions du Seuil, D. Attridge, M. Ferer and Hélène Cixous.

7.2   Raymond Williams, from *The Country and the City* (Chatto & Windus, 1973), pp. 242–7. Reprinted by permission of Random House UK Ltd.

7.3   Wolfgang Iser, 'Doing Things in Style: An Interpretation of "The Oxen of the Sun" in James Joyce's *Ulysses*', Ch. 7 of *The Implied Reader* (Johns Hopkins University Press, 1974), pp. 179–95. Reprinted by permission of the Johns Hopkins University Press.

7.4   Fredric Jameson, '*Ulysses* in History', Ch. 9 of W. J. McCormack and Alistair Stead, eds, *James Joyce and Modern Literature* (Routledge, 1982), pp. 126–41. Reprinted by permission of Routledge.

7.5   Jacques Derrida, from 'Ulysses Gramophone: Hear Say Yes in Joyce', in Peggy Kamuf, ed., *A Derrida Reader: Between the Blinds* (Prentice Hall/Harvester, 1991), pp. 569–98. Reprinted by permission of the publisher.

CHAPTER 8: BRECHT: THEORY AND LATE PLAYS

8.1   Walter Benjamin, from *Understanding Brecht*, trans. Anna Bostock (New Left Books/ Verso, 1973), pp. 23–5, 37–41. Reprinted by permission of Verso.

8.2 George Lukács, from *The Meaning of Contemporary Realism* (Merlin, 1963), pp. 87–9. Reprinted by permission of Merlin Press Ltd.

8.3 Theodor Adorno, from 'Commitment', trans. Francis McDonagh, in *Aesthetics and Politics* (New Left Books/Verso, 1977), pp. 177–95. Reprinted by permission of Verso.

8.4 Roland Barthes, 'The Tasks of Brechtian Criticism' and 'Literature and Signification', trans. Richard Howard, in *Critical Essays* (Northwestern University Press, 1972), pp. 71–6, 261–4. Reprinted by permission of Northwestern University Press.

8.5 Louis Althusser, from 'The "Piccolo Teatro": Bertolazzi and Brecht. Notes on a Materialist Theatre', in *For Marx*, trans. Ben Brewster (New Left Books/Verso, 1977), pp. 142–51. Reprinted by permission of Verso.

8.6 Herbert Marcuse, from *The Aesthetic Dimension. Towards a Critique of Marxist Aesthetics* (Beacon Press, 1977), pp. 30–5. © English trans. by Herbert Marcuse and Erica Sherover. Reprinted by permission of Beacon Press, Editions du Seuil (Paris), Macmillan Press Ltd and Carl Hanser Verlag (Munich).

8.7 John Fuegi, from *The Life and Lies of Bertolt Brecht* (HarperCollins, 1994), pp. 261–4, 267–73, 369–70, 380–1. Reprinted by permission of HarperCollins Publishers Ltd and Grove Press Inc.

CHAPTER 9: *BELOVED*

9.1 Mae G. Henderson, from 'Toni Morrison's *Beloved*: Re-membering the Body as Historical Text', in Ch. 4 of Hortense J. Spillers, ed., *Comparative American Identities: Race, Sex and Nationality in the Modern Text* (Routledge, 1991), pp. 63–86, *passim.* Reprinted by permission of Routledge, Chapman and Hall Inc.

9.2 Paul Gilroy, from '"Not a Story to Pass On": Living Memory and the Slave Sublime', Ch. 6 of *The Black Atlantic* (Verso, 1993), pp. 218–23. Reprinted by permission of Verso.

9.3 Homi K. Bhabha, from 'Introduction', *The Location of Culture* (Routledge, 1994), pp. 1–18, *passim.* Reprinted by permission of Routledge.

9.4 Lynne Pearce, from 'Dialogism and Gender: Gendering the Chronotope: Readings of Jeanette Winterson's *Sexing the Cherry* and Toni Morrison's *Beloved*', Ch. 5 of *Reading Dialogics* (Arnold, 1994), pp. 186–95. Reprinted by permission of Edward Arnold Publishers.

9.5 Peter Nicholls, from 'The Belated Postmodern: History, Phantoms and Toni Morrison', in Sue Vice, ed., *Psychoanalytic Criticism: A Reader* (Polity Press, 1995), pp. 50–63. Reprinted by permission of Polity Press, Blackwell Publishers and Peter Nicholls.

CHAPTER 10: *MIDNIGHT'S CHILDREN, SHAME, THE SATANIC VERSES*

10.1 Linda Hutcheon, from 'Re-presenting the Past', in *The Politics of Postmodernism* (Routledge, 1989), pp. 65–78. Reprinted by permission of the publisher.

10.2 Aijaz Ahmad, from 'Salman Rushdie's *Shame*: Postmodern Migrancy and the Representation of Women', in *After Theory: Classes, Nations, Literatures* (Verso, 1992), pp. 139–52. Reprinted by permission of the publisher.

10.3 Gayatri Chakravorty Spivak, from 'Reading *The Satanic Verses*', in *Outside in the Teaching Machine* (Routledge, 1993), pp. 217–41. Reprinted by permission of the publisher.